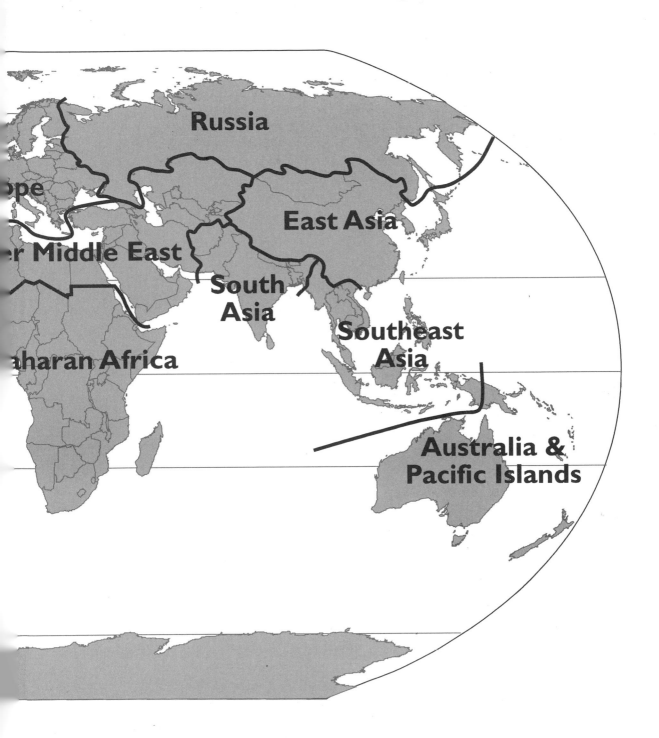

Russia

ope

East Asia

r Middle East

South
Asia

Southeast
Asia

aharan Africa

Australia &
Pacific Islands

Cities of the World

Cities of the World

World Regional Urban Development

FOURTH EDITION

EDITED BY
**STANLEY D. BRUNN, MAUREEN HAYS-MITCHELL,
AND DONALD J. ZIEGLER**

CARTOGRAPHY BY
ELLEN R. WHITE

ROWMAN & LITTLEFIELD PUBLISHERS, INC.
Lanham • Boulder • New York • Toronto • Plymouth, UK

ROWMAN & LITTLEFIELD PUBLISHERS, INC.

Published in the United States of America
by Rowman & Littlefield Publishers, Inc.
A wholly owned subsidiary of The Rowman & Littlefield Publishing Group, Inc.
4501 Forbes Boulevard, Suite 200, Lanham, Maryland 20706
www.rowmanlittlefield.com

Estover Road, Plymouth PL6 7PY, United Kingdom

British Library Cataloguing in Publication Information Available

Library of Congress Cataloging-in-Publication Data
Cities of the world : world regional urban development / edited by Stanley D. Brunn, Maureen Hays-Mitchell,
and Donald J. Zeigler ; cartography by Ellen R. White.
    p. cm.
 Includes bibliographical references and index.
 ISBN-13: 978-0-7425-5597-6 (cloth : alk. paper)
 ISBN-10: 0-7425-5597-6 (cloth : alk. paper)
 1. Cities and towns. 2. City planning. 3. Urbanization. 4. Urban policy. I. Brunn, Stanley D. II. Hays-
Mitchell, Maureen. III. Zeigler, Donald J., 1951- IV. White, Ellen R.
 HT151.C569 2008
 307.76—dc22
                              2008013566

Printed in the United States of America

♾™ The paper used in this publication meets the minimum requirements of American National Standard for
Information Sciences—Permanence of Paper for Printed Library Materials, ANSI/NISO Z39.48-1992.

Contents

List of Illustrations

Figures

Boxes

Tables

Preface

In the middle of 2007 a watershed event occurred in human history. For the first time, half of the planet's citizens were living in cities. This significant event happened because of the recent and rapid growth of cities in the Global South. The world's population has been edging toward this event as a result of rapid urban growth—especially in Africa, Asia, and to a lesser extent Latin America—during the past three decades.

This watershed event in itself should call for scholars of different disciplines, not only geographers but also anthropologists, economists, sociologists, political scientists, and biologists, to look critically and carefully at urban processes and patterns in all regions of the world. Undergraduate interdisciplinary programs focusing on area or regional studies, environmental studies, globalization, international affairs, and strategic studies, as well as on race and gender, need to ensure that their programs include some focus, or renewed focus, on the impacts of these changes in humankind's cities and urban systems.

Cities remain the major focus of the world's attention, whether we read about international, regional, or national crises in magazines, in newspapers, or on-line, or we see reports second-hand about where those crises are occurring. More often than not, cities, not states or countries, are the headline and dateline for major reports. Headline news is really urban world news. Reporters regularly submit images (photos and satellite images) and make commentaries about social, political, economic, and environmental events from major world capitals. Late 2007 and early 2008 examples include anomalous weather events, attributed to global warming, that affect coastline cities in South Asia and Western Europe; the disputed elections in Kenya; massive street protests by political and religious groups in Beirut; immigrant unrest in Paris; organizing and planning for the forthcoming 2008 Olympics in Beijing; the globalization of Chinese products appearing in discount stores (Wal-Mart, Home Depot, etc.) in Europe and North America and bazaars in Central Asia; discussions in Brussels about an expanded EU; political unrest in parts of Palestine as well as Karachi and Islamabad; environmental refugees moving to large cities in east and west Africa; protracted conflicts in Kabul; U.S. efforts to secure neighborhoods in Baghdad; potential nuclear threats from Pyongyang and Tehran; Moscow reasserting its position in a Eurasian world; and the uncertainties of global stock markets in Tokyo, London, and New York.

In this edition of *Cities of the World*, we have retained from previous editions much of what our colleagues reported to us as being most useful. Each regional chapter begins with a map of major cities in that region, a box of key urban facts, and a list of key chapter themes. These sections are followed by historical perspectives on the formation of cities and urbanization in each region; major contemporary economic, political, and social processes at work; discussions of the nature of daily life for urban residents; descriptions of representative and distinctive cities within the region; and analyses of urban trends, challenges, planning, and prospects. Seventy-eight cities are described in the text; these include 27 of the world's largest 35 cities in population.

Four new topics are given greater attention and coverage in this edition:

- Urban environmental issues
- Globalization and its national, regional, and international impacts on urban processes
- Human security issues (e.g., terrorism, violence, crime; food security, health care, personal safety)
- E-commerce, digital cities, virtual places, and impacts of the Internet

The first and last chapters have undergone substantial revision. Chapter 1 begins with a human-interest story about the local and global linkages of hypothetical residents. To introduce students to current intellectual debates within urban geography, we include focused boxes on approaches to the study of cities and urbanism in the first chapter; these include cultural historical, critical geographies, and political ecology approaches. In the final chapter we turn to discussions of globalization and urban linkages, digital technologies and the city, and urban environmental problems at the global scale. New maps and graphics of major cities and environmental topics appear in the first and concluding chapters. Many of the individual chapters address one or more of these new themes. Many

of the chapters contain new photos and boxes that touch on important urban themes and issues. New bibliographies accompany each chapter; they include books, journal articles, reports, films, and websites that will be particularly useful to students and instructors. Finally, new appendices provide data on the historical and projected populations of major urban agglomerations. These United Nations data are useful in gaining a perspective of the current global urban scene.

All chapters retain important sections from previous editions, and they are also infused with fresh material, updated information, and new perspectives, especially on environment, human security, and urban planning. This edition introduces 12 new authors. There are new author teams for chapters on the United States and Canada, Middle America and the Caribbean, Sub-Saharan Africa, and Australia and the Pacific Islands. All chapters include useful maps, tables, and graphics. Ten of the authors are women, and roughly half have received their PhD within the past 15 years.

In our view, the book can, might, and could be used in lower-division or upper-division undergraduate classes in urban geography, urban studies, area studies, urban and regional planning, and globalization. It also might be used in colleges, universities, and departments revamping their geography and social science curricula to provide students more exposure to topics of globalization, and especially the urban world. We see potential uses in classes with titles such as Cities of the World, World Urbanization, Global Cities, Our Urban World, Cities and Environments, and the World's Urban Systems. Individual chapters might be used in upper-division undergraduate or even graduate classes focusing on major world regions, the Global South, urban planning, regional planning and analysis, digital worlds, urban environments, or human security.

We wish to thank a number of individuals who played important roles in this edition's being published. Especially we thank Ellen White of Michigan State University for meeting tight deadlines, but always providing excellent maps and graphics for individual chapters. Second, we want to thank our good friend and coeditor of the first three editions, Jack Williams, also of Michigan State University, for his active role in working with Ellen and providing useful advice to all other editors throughout the publication process. And we also acknowledge the contributions of the individuals who wrote boxes in the chapters about a given city or specific process or problem; these additions illustrate again that any single individual or author team writing about the urban history, geography, or future in any region is a difficult task. We deeply appreciate the insights provided by these junior and senior scholars. We also thank the Rowman & Littlefield team that worked with us to ensure a higher quality and more useful final product: Susan McEachern, who has supported us enthusiastically in this and the previous three editions, Alden Perkins, and Jessica Gribble, who persuaded us of the importance of quality photographs. At Publication Services, we thank Al Davis, who cheerfully and diligently copyedited the manuscript, and Lisa Connery, who prepared PDF files for final production that included our last minute corrections. We are in debt to this fine team for their devoted commitments from start to finish. We also thank Donna Gilbreath for preparing the indexes and making them a vital ingredient for teaching and student learning. Finally, we thank our families, whose enthusiastic and selfless support made this project enjoyable and possible.

We welcome instructors' suggestions about how to make future editions more useful for teaching purposes, including innovative maps and insightful photographs for a website we are developing on cities of the world (and solicit contributions) that will make studying global and regional urbanization studies more interesting, appealing, challenging, and rewarding.

Stanley D. Brunn
Donald J. Zeigler
Maureen Hays-Mitchell

Cities of the World

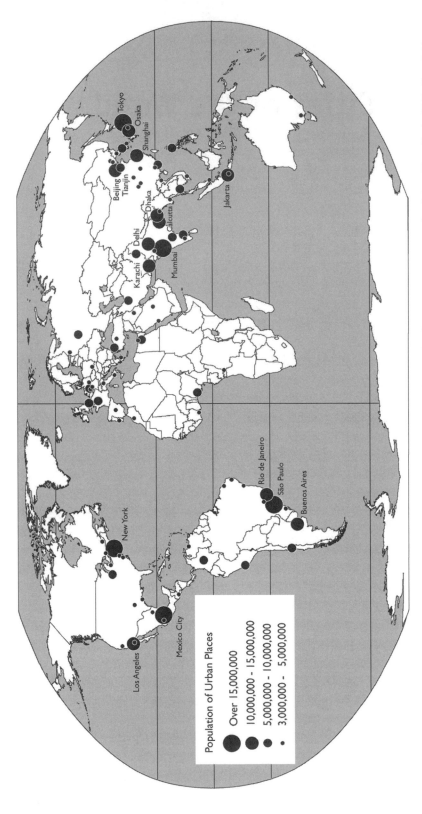

Figure 1.1 Major Cities of the World, 2005. *Source:* Data from UN, *World Urbanization Prospects: 2005 Revision* (New York: U.N. Population Division, 2006, http://esa.un.org/unup/).

1

World Urban Development

DONALD J. ZEIGLER, MAUREEN HAYS-MITCHELL, AND STANLEY D. BRUNN

KEY URBAN FACTS

Total World Population (2005)	6.5 billion
Percent Urban Population (2005)	48.5%
Total Urban Population (2005)	3.15 billion
Most Urbanized Countries (100%)	Nauru
	Singapore
Least Urbanized Countries	Burundi (10% urban)
	Bhutan (11.1%)
	Trinidad & Tobago (12.2%)
	Uganda (12.6%)
	Papua New Guinea (13.4%)
	Sri Lanka (15.1%)
	Nepal (15.8%)
	Ethiopia (16.0%)
Annual Urban Growth Rate	
2000–2005	2.04%
2005–2010	1.96%
Number of Megacities	20
Number of Cities of More than 1 Million	414
Largest Urban Agglomerations	Tokyo (35.2 million inhabitants)
	Mexico City (19.4 million)
	New York (18.7 million)
	São Paulo (18.3 million)
	Mumbai (18.2 million)
World Cities	~50
Global Cities	3 (New York, London, Tokyo)

KEY CHAPTER THEMES

1. In 2007 Earth became a majority-urban planet, yet the proportion of people living in cities varies widely, from 10% in Burundi to 100% in Singapore.
2. The world's population is growing rapidly, but the world's urban population is growing four times as fast.
3. Megacities, defined as cities with over 10 million population, are increasing in number but only in the developing world, which now accounts for 13 of the 20 largest urban agglomerations.
4. Geography—and its subfields of environmental, economic, political, and cultural geography—provides a holistic framework for understanding cities.
5. The scale of urbanization is increasing, as evidenced by the emergence of conurbations and megalopolises around the world.
6. Some countries' patterns of urbanization follow the rank-size rule, whereas other countries are characterized by urban primacy or dual primacy.
7. The evolution of cities is best understood as a three-stage process: preindustrial, industrial, and postindustrial.
8. Cities are usually classified by function: as market centers, transportation centers, or specialized service centers.
9. Four classic models have been proposed to explain the spatial organization of land use within cities: concentric zone model, sector model, multiple nuclei model, and inverse concentric zone model.
10. Urban management revolves around such issues as population size, growth rate, and geographic distribution; governance and the provision of services; accommodating globalization; and the natural environment.

If one were to compare a map of the world as it was around the year 1900 with one of the world in 2000, two changes would be strikingly apparent: (1) the proliferation of independent nations and (2) the mushrooming number and sizes of cities. The basically simple division of the world of 1900 between the independent industrialized countries of Europe, North America, and Russia and the vast colonial empires controlled by them in Latin America, Africa, and Asia has been transformed into a far more complex mosaic of more than 190 independent countries of all sizes and levels of economic and political development. Likewise, in 1900 a relatively small number of major cities were concentrated in the industrialized countries, whereas today the greatest numbers of cities, and the largest cities, are increasingly found in former colonial regions of the developing world (fig. 1.1). Around the year 1800, perhaps 3% of the world's population lived in urban places of 5,000 people or more. The proportion had risen to more than 13% by 1900 and had skyrocketed to more than 47% by 2000. By 2007, the "blue marble" on which we live had become an "urban marble." For the first time in human history, more than half of Earth's people made their homes in urban areas. With urbanization has come globalization, the result of technological advances in transportation and communication. Our urban marble pulsates with connections among its human inhabitants, especially those who live in cities (box 1.1). Our urban marble also pulsates with problems at the human-nature interface. These range from local problems of air quality, to regional problems of water shortages, to global problems materializing as the result of climate change. Yet, increasingly, we have come to realize that problems need to be approached from multiple levels. Global warming may be taking place worldwide (albeit differentially), but consequences are going to be felt at the local level, especially in coastal cities confronted by a rising sea level.

The present phenomenon of worldwide urbanization is as dramatic in its revolutionary implications for the history of civilization as were the earlier agricultural and industrial revolutions. In the industrial countries of Europe, North America, some of Asia, and Australia—the more developed countries (MDCs) as the UN calls them—urbanization accompanied and was the consequence of industrialization. Although far from utopias, cities in those regions brought previously undreamed-of prosperity and longevity to millions. Industrial and economic growth combined with rapid urbanization to produce a demographic transformation that brought declining population growth and enabled cities to expand apace with economic development. In the developing countries of Latin America, Africa, and most of Asia—the less developed countries (LDCs)—urbanization has occurred only partly as the result of industrial and economic growth, and in many countries it has occurred primarily as the result of rising expectations of rural people

who have flocked to the cities seeking escape from misery (and often not finding it). This march to the cities, unaccompanied until very recently by significant declines in natural population growth, has resulted in the explosion of urban places in the LDCs.

Urban nations tend to be more economically developed and more politically powerful. The relationship lags in a few regions, notably South America, where levels of urbanization approach those of North America and Europe but where indicators of social well-being do not indicate commensurate levels of development. Yet most nations that are highly urbanized experience high standards of living, whether measured in per capita income or by other indexes of well-being. For those still climbing the urbanization ladder, the challenge will be to bring rates of urbanization in line with rates of economic growth.

However, even in the MDCs, where life for the vast majority of urban residents is incomparably better than for those living in the cities of the LDCs, there are serious concerns about the future of the city. What, for example, is the optimum size of a city? Are cities in general getting too large to permit effective administration and to ensure an adequate, let alone ideal and humane, urban environment to live in? Is the megalopolis, or superconurbation, to be the norm for the 21st century? What will be the impact of ever-expanding urban agglomerations on human society, on life-sustaining environmental systems, on resource development, and on governments facing increased social disparities, cultural pluralism, and diversity of political expression? Can urbanization and sustainable development work hand-in-hand to improve life for all of earth's inhabitants? Are cities compatible with nature (box 1.2)?

Box 1.1 Our Global Lives: A Fictional Vignette

Stanley D. Brunn

José is a day laborer in Bogotá, Colombia. He works for a construction company with regional South American headquarters in Caracas, but the main international office is in Miami. During the past six months he and two of his brothers have worked laying cement and drywall for a new international bank and hotel that are being constructed in Bogotá's downtown. The bank's headquarters are in Amsterdam and the hotel's in Madrid. José's previous construction job was landscaping a new international zoo in suburban Bogotá. The zoo will include animals from tropical Africa and Southeast Asia; it is the city's latest effort to attract tourists from northern South America, Central America, the United States, and Europe. José's wife, Bonita, operates a dress shop near the main bus station in Bogotá; most of her goods originate with Catholic relief charities in Los Angeles and Houston. His sister, Sophia, works as an au pair for the deputy consul from Nigeria. José is proud of the international connections his wife and sister have. He is also quick to note that his cousins, who live three hours from Bogotá, raise orchids and ship them by truck to his city every morning. The best orchids are selected for markets in London, Paris, and Madrid; the others are sold by sidewalk vendors right there in Bogotá. José has other cousins, sorry to say, whose livelihoods include processing cocaine, which they sell to drug traffickers, who market their contraband in southern Texas, using cell phones and secret Internet codes. José's worldview is quite distinct from that of his parents, who were laborers on a plantation in the mountains of western Colombia, where coffee was produced for export. The company that owned

---

THE WORLD URBAN SYSTEM

On the eve of 2008, world population stood at 6,641,156,931, according to the Census Bureau's inhabitants clock in Washington, D.C. It was as recently as 1800 that world population stood on the brink of reaching its first billion. It took 130 years to reach its second billion, but only 11 years to add its most recent billion. Between 1950 and 2008, the world's population increased more than 2.5 times, but the world's urban population increased almost 4.5 times (fig. 1.2). Increases in urban populations have been felt worldwide, but the pace of urban change has been most dramatic in the world's developing regions, the "Global South" (fig. 1.3).

The UN's *World Urbanization Prospects: 2005 Revision* provides the most complete synopsis of urbanization trends. Among its major findings are the following:

1. In 2005, there were 3.2 billion urban residents in the world, nearly four times as many as in 1950. They represented 49% of the global population.
2. The urban population passed the 1 billion mark in 1961. It took 25 years to add another billion urban dwellers and just 17 years more to add a third billion. Thus,

the land traced its origins to a Spanish land grant in the 17th century. Like most Colombians, José's parents were mestizos, and José is proud of this mixed heritage.

On the other side of the world we find Gilda. She lives in Amsterdam and works for a major international banking conglomerate. Her job is to oversee the bank's accounts in Central and South America. The most recent loan this Dutch bank provided to private developers in South America was for a major zoo in Bogotá. Gilda is unmarried and has a number of close friends who regularly travel to other countries with their work. Two of these friends are Herman and Sigrid. Herman has spent the past several years working as a UN peacekeeper in the Middle East. While on assignment along the Syria-Israel border, he met his wife, Sophia, who was a translator for his peacekeeping team. Sigrid is Gilda's best friend; they studied together at an international high school in The Hague. Last summer, Sigrid and Gilda traveled on holiday to Venezuela and Colombia. They stayed in a recently completed international hotel next to the Colombian branch of the Amsterdam bank for which Gilda works. They enjoyed the city's zoo, even though it was not complete. And every day they began the morning with fresh Colombian coffee (fair trade?—they wondered), bought a few fresh-cut orchids from a street vendor, and planned their night on the town. One night they met some Nigerians who worked at the embassy. Before her holiday was over, Gilda sent postcards to her brother Klaus, who was in India recruiting for a call center, and to her brother Isaac, who is a day laborer in Amsterdam. Isaac's real love is painting, however. His specialty is coastal landscapes, many of which he sells at Amsterdam's Sunday market. Last Sunday he was approached by a visitor who invited him to enter a juried exhibition in Sydney, Australia. The exhibit's theme was The Impact of Global Warming on Coastal Cities.

the urban population reached 3 billion in 2003 and is projected to increase to nearly 5 billion by 2030.

3. With an annual urban growth rate of 1.8%, nearly double that projected for the total population (1%), the world's urban population is expected to increase from 3.2 billion in 2005 to 4.9 billion in 2030, when 60% of the global population is expected to live in urban areas.

4. Although the world is urbanizing rapidly, the number of rural dwellers is high and still growing. However, as of 2019 the rural population is projected to decline slowly. Consequently, the number of rural-dwellers in 2030 is expected to be slightly lower than that in 2005 (3.3 billion). In 2005, 71% of all rural dwellers lived in Asia, primarily in India, China, Indonesia, and Bangladesh.

5. Population growth is projected to be particularly rapid in the urban areas of the less developed regions, averaging 2.2% annually during 2005–2030. As a consequence, the urban population in the less developed regions will increase from 2.3 billion to 3.9 billion over the next 25 years.

6. Migration from rural to urban areas and the transformation of rural settlements

Box 1.2 Urban Political Ecology

Jessica K. Graybill

Urban regions can be understood as networks of connected environmental components that are (1) both human and physical, (2) patterned in geographical space, and (3) arrayed from local to global in scale. Cities depend on a myriad of connections to support and maintain urban life, such as the delivery of water and food, the removal and treatment of urban waste, urban drainage and stormwater treatment, and the sociopolitical actions of human communities.

In a world that is increasingly urban, understanding the connections of the city to internal and external human and physical landscapes is particularly important. As increasing numbers of people live in cities and suburbs, ecosystems in and outside of the city are also increasingly pressured. Nature, already a valued entity outside the city, is becoming increasingly valued within the city. But what is nature in the city? How do urban dwellers interact with their natural environment? How are these interactions structured by social and political considerations? Three theoretical orientations to providing answers are outlined below.

Urban ecology is based on the premise that cities (and humans) are not separate from nature and must therefore be considered in the study of ecosystems. This is an ecosystems approach to studying the city. An urban ecosystem includes both nature and humans. Spatially, it is the community of plants, animals, and humans that inhabit regions dominated by urban infrastructure (buildings, roads, sewers, etc.) but also containing green spaces (parks, yards, urban streams, vacant lots, etc.). Understanding how an urban ecosystem operates requires studying biogeophysical and human processes together. An example of such a study might be to look at how the behavior of nonhuman species (e.g., crows, wolves) changes in relation to dense urban, suburban, and exurban settlement patterns.

Urban political ecology differs from urban ecology in that the focus lies in understanding how political institutions mediate the interaction between humans and the environment in city settings. Drawing on knowledge created in urban ecological studies, urban political ecology is concerned with management and conservation of nature in cities. Two types of inquiries broadly define this field: urban sustainability studies and urban

into urban places are important determinants of the high urban population growth anticipated in the less developed regions. Assuming that migration and reclassification account for 40% to 50% of urban population growth in the less developed regions, a total of 250 million to 310 million people in developing countries are expected to become urban-dwellers between 2005 and 2015 either because they will migrate from rural to urban areas or because their rural settlements will become urban.

greening approaches. They are both political in the sense that human actions (in this case, management and planning) are always mediated by political processes that benefit and disrupt different communities unevenly and unequally.

First, **urban sustainability studies** recognize the need for economic, social, and environmental sustainability in human-dominated urban environments. Often, recognition is only a starting point, and academics, activists, and professionals work toward urban environmental management and nature conservation strategies in the city. For example, many cities worldwide have created local sustainability policies (e.g., the UN's Agenda 21) or have used footprint analyses (e.g., carbon footprinting) and the "urban metabolism" metaphor (charting the material flows in and out of the city) to increase awareness of consumption among citizens and to provide potential ways to consume less.

Second, **urban greening** is an approach targeting the (re)development of green spaces and corridors for multiple species (wildlife, humans) within the city, largely in recognition of their benefit to human communities. Imbued with conservation ideals, the urban greening approach highly values biodiversity and the conservation of native species. This approach is often interdisciplinary, as natural and social scientists work alongside urban planners, urban forest managers, and policymakers to create workable, green management and implementation plans.

Marxian urban political ecology makes a strong commitment to understanding inequality and how power and injustice are created around urban nature in sites of capitalist urbanization. One focus has been the exploration of the spatial inequalities associated with uneven green spaces (parks, forest cover) in neighborhoods of differing racial and ethnic compositions. Another focus has been the political ecology of lawnscapes and urban swimming pools.

The connection among these three approaches is understanding that cities are more than centers of commerce, industry, education, and culture. They are living entities connected in myriad ways: biogeophysically, socially, and technologically. As cities become increasingly populous and complex, understanding human interactions with nature in the city becomes crucial to leading a productive urban life. A necessary part of addressing urban ecosystems is acknowledging the social and political aspects of where, how, and for whom urban nature is produced and consumed—both materially (through actual use) and symbolically (through politics and culture).

7. The urban population of the more developed regions is projected to increase very slowly, rising from 0.9 billion in 2005 to 1 billion in 2030. Between 2005 and 2030, its average annual growth rate is projected to be 0.5%, about one-third of the 1.4% per year estimated for the period 1950–2005.

8. Urbanization is very far advanced in the more developed regions, where in 2005 almost three-quarters (74%) of the population lived in urban settlements. The proportion urban in the more developed

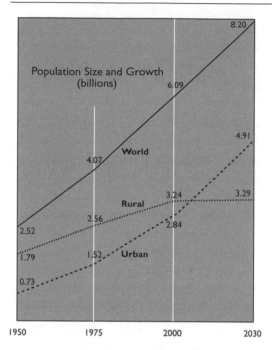

Figure 1.2   Growth of World and Urban Population, 1950–2030. *Source:* UN, *World Urbanization Prospects: 2005 Revision* (New York: U.N. Population Division, 2006, http://esa.un.org/unup/).

regions is projected to increase to 81% by 2030. In the less developed regions, the equivalent proportion was 43% in 2005 and is projected to rise to 56% by 2030.

9. Africa and Asia were the least urbanized areas in the world in 2005 (38% and 40%, respectively). A combination of a large starting population and a projected rate of urban population growth that remains relatively high over the next 25 years will result in a marked increase of the urban populations of both continents. By 2030, Asia will rank first and Africa second in terms of the number of urban dwellers. Indeed, in 2030, almost 70% of urban residents in the world will be living in Africa or Asia. The proportion urban is projected to reach 54% in Asia and 51% in Africa by 2030.

10. The region of Latin America and the Caribbean is already highly urbanized, with 77% of its population living in cities in 2005. By 2030, that proportion is projected to reach 84%.

11. In Europe the proportion of the population residing in urban areas is expected to rise from 72% in 2005 to 78% in 2030. In Northern America, the increase in the proportion urban is projected to be from 81% in 2005 to 87% in 2030. In Oceania, the equivalent rise is from 71% in 2005 to 74% in 2030.

12. The 20th century witnessed the emergence of megacities (i.e., cities with 10 million inhabitants or more). Never before had such large populations been concentrated in cities. From 1950 to 2005, the number of megacities rose from 2 to 20. Two additional megacities are projected to emerge by 2015, bringing the total to 22, 17 of which are located in developing countries. In 2005, megacities accounted for 9% of the world's urban populations.

13. The populations of megacities, being large, tend to grow less rapidly than those of other urban centers. Among the 20 megacities in existence in 2005, 13 had populations that grew by less than the average annual growth rate of the world's urban population during 1975–2005 (2.4%). Only 7 of the 20 megacities grew faster: Dhaka in Bangladesh and Lagos in Nigeria each grew by 5.8% annually; Delhi in India by 4.1%; Karachi in Pakistan by 3.6%; Jakarta in Indonesia by 3.4%; Mumbai (Bombay) in India by 3.1%; and Manila in the Philippines by 2.5%. For the future, 6 of the 22 megacities projected to exist in 2015 are projected to grow by

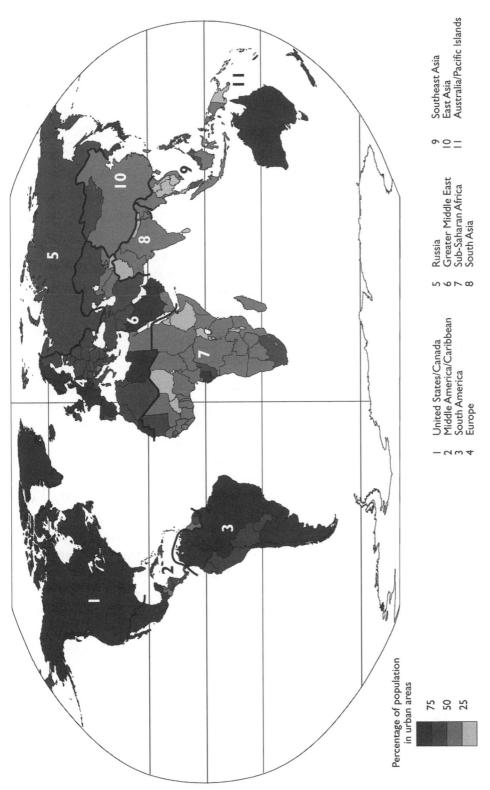

Figure 1.3   World Urbanization by Country, 2005. *Source:* Data from UN, *World Urbanization Prospects: 2005 Revision* (New York: U.N. Population Division, 2006, http://esa.un.org/unup/).

Percentage of population
in urban areas

75
50
25

1	United States/Canada	5	Russia	9	Southeast Asia
2	Middle America/Caribbean	6	Greater Middle East	10	East Asia
3	South America	7	Sub-Saharan Africa	11	Australia/Pacific Islands
4	Europe	8	South Asia		

more than 1.9% per year, the average annual growth rate projected for the global urban population during 2005–2015. These cities are, in order of their annual growth rates, Lagos in Nigeria, Dhaka in Bangladesh, Karachi in Pakistan, Jakarta in Indonesia, Guangzhou in China, and Delhi in India.

14. With 35 million residents in 2005, the metropolitan area of Tokyo was by far the most populous urban agglomeration in the world. Tokyo had slightly more residents than the entire country of Kenya in 2005 (34 million). Tokyo was also the most populous capital in the world. After Tokyo, the next largest urban agglomerations are Ciudad de México (Mexico City) and the urban agglomeration of New York–Newark, with 19 million inhabitants each, followed by São Paulo and Mumbai (Bombay) with 18 million people each.

15. In 2015 Tokyo will still be the largest urban agglomeration, with 35 million inhabitants, followed by Mumbai (Bombay) and Ciudad de México (Mexico City), with 22 million people each, and São Paulo with 21 million inhabitants.

16. Some cities dominate the urban system of their countries. The population of Kuwait City, for instance, accounted for 69% of all urban residents in Kuwait in 2005. In the same year, 68% of all urban residents in Puerto Rico lived in San Juan, and 64% of the urban population of Haiti resided in Port-au-Prince.

17. Small cities, defined as those with a population of less than 500,000, were the place of residence of about 51% of all urban dwellers in the world in 2005. Thus, the majority of urban dwellers lived in fairly small urban settlements.

18. The spatial distribution of population has always figured prominently on the policy agenda of governments, which have often expressed concern about being unable to provide basic services (e.g., water, sanitation, housing, transportation) for rapidly growing urban populations, especially in LDCs. Measures used to shape the spatial distribution of the population have included policies to reduce migration to urban agglomerations; among these are imposition of internal migration controls; the creation of new centers of economic growth by, for instance, moving the national capital to a new location; incentives for businesses and industry to locate in medium-sized cities; and the development of infrastructure and services in smaller or medium-sized cities to attract businesses and migrants alike.

19. In 2005, almost half of humanity lived in cities. By 2030, three out of every five people on earth will likely reside in urban centers, and nearly half of the world's population will live in the cities of developing countries. Urbanization brings with it both opportunities and challenges. The more developed regions are highly urbanized, indicating that urbanization is a natural concomitant of development. In the developing world, urbanization has been rapid, but major areas, such as Africa and Asia, still lag far behind the rest of the world in their levels of urbanization. Countries in those regions, in particular, face the double challenge of rising urbanization and continued rural population growth. If the 21st century is to respond creatively to the many opportunities that the growth of urban areas brings, then the economic dynamics of cities have to be nurtured.

The more developed regions of the world had a higher percentage of their population living in urban areas in both 1950 and 2005. In absolute numbers, there were also more urban dwellers in the more developed regions in 1950, but the tables had turned by 2000 (tab. 1.1). Unfortunately, throughout Central and South America, Africa and the Middle East, and much of Asia, urban development has not kept up with urban growth. Latin America and the Caribbean, for instance, have caught up to the world's MDCs in level of urbanization (now 75% urban), but economic development, health care, and education continue to lag. Sub-Saharan Africa remains the least urbanized region in the world—and the least developed. Latin America's urban explosion may be over, but in Africa, India, and China (among others), with only about one-third of their populations now living in cities, the urban population explosion continues.

The greatest number of cities and the greatest number of large cities (3 million and above) are now found in LDCs (fig. 1.4). This prevalence can also be seen in a list of the world's largest urban areas: those in the LDCs now outnumber those in the MDCs (tab. 1.2). Of the 20 largest urban agglomerations in 1950, 13 were in the MDCs and 7 in the LDCs. The 20 largest urban agglomerations in 2000 included only 5 in the MDCs, and those 5 were located in only three countries: Japan (Tokyo and Osaka), the United States (New York and Los Angeles), and France (Paris). Ciudad de México, now number two on the list with almost 20 million people, is larger than three-quarters of the world's independent states. Less developed regions are urbanizing at much more rapid rates since 1975, compared to more developed regions,

in terms of population size of urban settlements for the two periods 1975–2000 and 2000–2015 (fig. 1.5).

APPROACHES, CONCEPTS, AND DEFINITIONS

The geographer's approach to understanding the city is spatial, ecological, and holistic. Yet geographers employ alternative theoretical models for unraveling the truth about cities. The models range from "historical and cultural,"

Table 1.1 Urban Patterns in More Developed Regions (MDRs) and Less Developed Regions (LDRs): 1950, 2000, and 2005

	1950		
	Total Population (billions)	*Urban Population*	*% Urban*
World	2.5	0.73	29
MDRs	0.8	0.42	52
LDRs	1.7	0.31	18
	2000		
	Total Population (billions)	*Urban Population*	*% Urban*
World	6.1	2.84	47
MDRs	1.2	0.87	73
LDRs	4.9	1.97	40
	2005		
	Total Population (billions)	*Urban Population*	*% Urban*
World	6.5	3.15	49
MDRs	1.2	0.90	74
LDRs	5.3	2.25	43

Source: United Nations, *World Urbanization Prospects: 2005 Revision* (New York: United Nations Population Division, 2006), http://www.un.org/esa/population/unpop.htm.

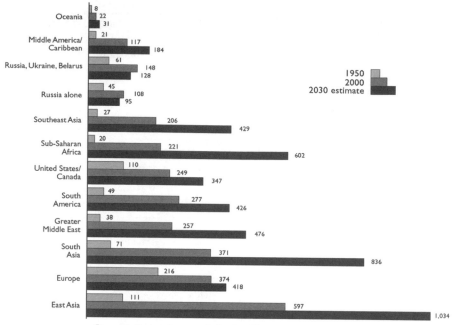

Figure 1.4   Urban Population of World Regions: 1950, 2000, 2030. *Source:* UN, *World Urbanization Prospects: 2005 Revision* (New York: U.N. Population Division, 2006, http://esa.un.org/unup/).

through "urban ecological," to "critical geographies." An essay on each of these theoretical frameworks can be found in this chapter (boxes 1.2, 1.3, 1.4). In one way or another, however, all approaches take advantage of the structure of the discipline and its major subfields: environmental geography, economic geography, political geography, and cultural geography (fig. 1.6). All require an understanding of concepts and definitions used in urban geography.

Urbanism

Urbanism is a broad concept that generally refers to all aspects—political, economic, social—of the urban way of life. Urbanism is not a process of urban growth, but rather the end result of urbanization. It suggests that the

urban way of life is dramatically different in all respects from the rural way of life; as people leave the country and move to the city, their lifestyles and livelihoods change.

Urbanization

Urbanization is a process involving two phases: (1) the movement of people from rural to urban places, where they engage in primarily nonrural occupations, and (2) the change in lifestyle that results from leaving the countryside. The important variables in the first phase are population density and economic functions. A place does not become urban in fact until its workforce is divorced from the soil; trade, manufacturing, and service provision dominate the economies of urban places. The important

Table 1.2   The 30 Largest Urban Agglomerations, Ranked by Population Size, 1950–2015

	1950			*1975*	
Rank	*Agglomeration and Country*	*Population (millions)*	*Rank*	*Agglomeration and Country*	*Population (millions)*
1	New York–Newark, USA	12.338	1	Tokyo, Japan	26.615
2	Tokyo, Japan	11.275	2	New York–Newark, USA	15.880
3	London, United Kingdom	8.361	3	Ciudad de México (Mexico City), Mexico	10.690
4	Shanghai, China	6.066	4	Osaka–Kobe, Japan	9.844
5	Paris, France	5.424	5	São Paulo, Brazil	9.614
6	Moskva (Moscow), Russian Fed.	5.356	6	Los Angeles–Long Beach–Santa Ana, USA	9.926
7	Buenos Aires, Argentina	5.098	7	Buenos Aires, Argentina	8.745
8	Chicago, USA	4.999	8	Paris, France	8.630
9	Kolkata (Calcutta), India	4.513	9	Kolkata (Calcutta), India	7.888
10	Beijing, China	4.331	10	Moskva (Moscow), Russian Fed.	7.622
11	Osaka–Kobe, Japan	4.247	11	Rio de Janeiro, Brazil	7.557
12	Los Angeles–Long Beach–Santa Ana, USA	4.046	12	London, United Kingdom	7.546
13	Berlin, Germany	3.338	13	Shanghai, China	7.326
14	Philadelphia, USA	3.128	14	Chicago, USA	7.160
15	Rio de Janeiro, Brazil	2.950	15	Mumbai (Bombay), India	7.082
16	Saint Petersburg, Russian Fed	2.903	16	Soul (Seoul), Republic of Korea	6.808
17	Ciudad de México (Mexico City), Mexico	2.883	17	Al-Qahirah (Cairo), Egypt	6.450
18	Mumbai (Bombay), India	2.857	18	Beijing, China	6.034
19	Detroit, USA	2.769	19	Manila, Philippines	4.999
20	Boston, USA	2.551	20	Tianjin, China	4.870
21	Al-Qahirah (Cairo), Egypt	2.494	21	Jakarta, Indonesia	4.813
22	Manchester, United Kingdom	2.422	22	Philadelphia, USA	4.467
23	Tianjin, China	2.374	23	Delhi, India	4.426
24	São Paulo, Brazil	2.334	24	Saint Petersburg, Russian Fed.	4.325
25	Birmingham, United Kingdom	2.229	25	Tehran, Iran (Islamic Republic of)	4.273
26	Shenyang, China	2.091	26	Karachi, Pakistan	3.989
27	Roma (Rome), Italy	1.884	27	Hong Kong, China, Hong Kong SAR	3.943
28	Milano (Milan), Italy	1.883	28	Madrid, Spain	3.890
29	San Francisco–Oakland, USA	1.855	29	Detroit, USA	3.885
30	Barcelona, Spain	1.809	30	Krung Thep (Bangkok), Thailand	3.842

(continued on next page)

Source: United Nations Department of Economic and Social Affairs/Population Division, *World Urbanization Prospects: 2005 Revision* (New York: United Nations Population Division, 2006), http://www.un.org/esa/population/.

variables in the second phase are social, psychological, and behavioral. As a population becomes increasingly urban, for instance, family size becomes smaller because the value placed upon children changes.

Urban Place

As a place increases in population, it eventually becomes large enough to assume that its economy is no longer tied strictly to agriculture

Table 1.2 (*continued*)

	2000			2015	
Rank	Agglomeration and Country	Population (millions)	Rank	Agglomeration and Country	Population (millions)
1	Tokyo, Japan	34.450	1	Tokyo, Japan	35.494
2	Ciudad de México (Mexico City), Mexico	18.066	2	Mumbai (Bombay), India	21.869
3	New York–Newark, USA	17.846	3	Ciudad de México (Mexico City), Mexico	21.568
4	São Paulo, Brazil	17.099	4	São Paulo, Brazil	20.535
5	Mumbai (Bombay), India	16.086	5	New York–Newark, USA	19.876
6	Shanghai, China	13.243	6	Delhi, India	18.604
7	Kolkata (Calcutta), India	13.058	7	Shanghai, China	17.225
8	Delhi, India	12.441	8	Kolkata (Calcutta), India	16.980
9	Buenos Aires, Argentina	11.847	9	Dhaka, Bangladesh	16.842
10	Los Angeles–Long Beach–Santa Ana, USA	11.814	10	Jakarta, Indonesia	16.822
11	Osaka–Kobe, Japan	11.165	11	Lagos, Nigeria	16.141
12	Jakarta, Indonesia	11.065	12	Karachi, Pakistan	15.155
13	Rio de Janeiro, Brazil	10.803	13	Buenos Aires, Argentina	13.396
14	Al-Qahirah (Cairo), Egypt	10.391	14	Al-Qahirah (Cairo), Egypt	13.138
15	Dhaka, Bangladesh	10.159	15	Los Angeles–Long Beach–Santa Ana, USA	13.095
16	Moskva (Moscow), Russian Fed.	10.103	16	Manila, Philippines	12.917
17	Karachi, Pakistan	10.020	17	Beijing, China	12.850
18	Manila, Philippines	9.950	18	Rio de Janeiro, Brazil	12.770
19	Soul (Seoul), Republic of Korea	9.917	19	Osaka–Kobe, Japan	11.309
20	Beijing, China	9.782	20	Istanbul, Turkey	11.211
21	Paris, France	9.692	21	Moskva (Moscow), Russian Fed.	11.022
22	Istanbul, Turkey	8.744	22	Guangzhou, China	10.420
23	Lagos, Nigeria	8.422	23	Paris, France	9.858
24	Chicago, USA	8.333	24	Soul (Seoul), Republic of Korea	9.545
25	London, United Kingdom	8.225	25	Chicago, USA	9.469
26	Guangzhou, China	7.388	26	Kinshasa, Dem. Republic of the Congo	9.304
27	Tehran, Iran (Islamic Republic of)	6.979	27	Shenzhen, China	8.958
28	Santa Fé de Bogotá, Colombia	6.964	28	Santa Fé de Bogotá, Colombia	8.932
29	Lima, Peru	6.811	29	London, United Kingdom	8.618
30	Tianjin, China	6.722	30	Tehran, Iran (Islamic Republic of)	8.432

or other primary activities. At that point, a rural place becomes an *urban place*. Translating the dividing line between rural and urban into a minimum population size varies significantly from country to country. In Denmark and Sweden, only 200 people are required for a place to be classified as urban; in New Zealand the figure is 1,000; in Argentina 2,000; in Ghana 5,000; and in Greece 10,000. In the United States, places are defined as urban by the Bureau of the Census if they have at least 2,500 people. Smaller places are defined as rural.

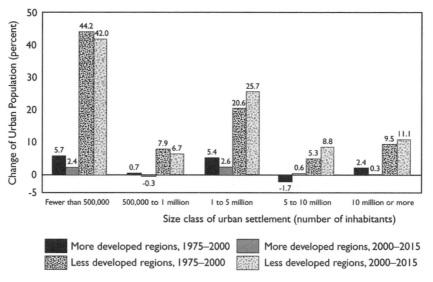

Figure 1.5   Urban Population in MDCs vs. LDCs by Size Class of Urban Settlement, 1975–2015. *Source:* UN, *World Urbanization Prospects: 2005 Revision* (New York: U.N. Population Division, 2006, http://esa.un.org/unup/).

City

The term *city* is essentially a political designation referring to a large, densely populated place that is legally incorporated as a municipality. However, a settlement of any size may call itself a city, whether it is large or small. Towns are generally smaller than cities. Megacity, a colloquial rather than legal term, is a designation for the largest urban places. A city with more than 10 million inhabitants may be called a megacity. In 1950, only New York City exceeded 10 million. Today, 20 cities worldwide fit that category.

Urbanized Area

As cities have expanded, the boundary between urban and rural has become increasingly blurred, especially in industrialized countries, such as the United States, where automobile transportation has fostered urban sprawl. Thus, an *urbanized area* (sometimes used interchangeably with urban area) is defined as a built-up area where buildings, roads, and essentially urban land uses predominate, even beyond the political boundaries of cities and towns. The urbanized area can basically be considered as a city and its suburbs.

Conurbation

When urbanized areas merge, the larger urban regions are called *conurbations*. The word is of 20th-century, European origin. Hence it is common to speak of the Randstad conurbation in the Netherlands or the Rhine-Ruhr conurbation in Germany. In the United States, although the word is infrequently used, the Dallas–Fort Worth urban area is a good example of a conurbation. As urban areas expand, they engulf smaller cities in the urban expansion zone, build nearby towns into full-fledged cities, sometimes stimulate the development of new cities, and bump into other expanding urban areas, thus forming urban megaregions.

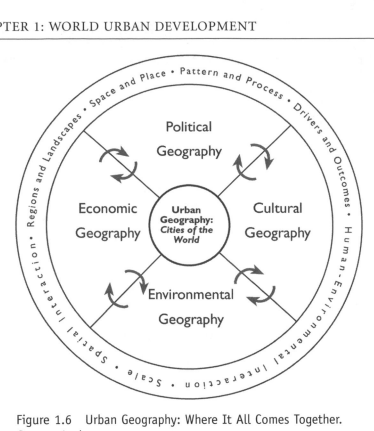

Figure 1.6   Urban Geography: Where It All Comes Together.
Source: Authors.

World Cities

World cities function as the command-and-control centers of the world economy. They offer advanced, knowledge-based producer services (businesses serving businesses), particularly in the fields of accounting, insurance, advertising, law, technical expertise, and the creative arts. The top-tier cities, defined by their financial centrality, are called *global cities*, of which there are three: New York, London, and Tokyo. One rung lower are the second-tier world cities: Paris, Frankfurt, Los Angeles, Chicago, Hong Kong, and Singapore, among others (figs. 1.7 and 1.8). Beyond that are several dozen more cities—Amsterdam, Moscow, Sydney, Toronto, San Francisco, and others—that draw their strength from particular megaregions or particular cultural and economic niches. Even cities such as Mecca and Jerusalem may be termed world cities because their influence is felt worldwide within particular religious niches.

Metropolis and Metropolitan Area

As cities have grown in size, territorially and demographically, a variety of terms have been coined to refer to ever-larger cities and city regions. One is *metropolis*—originally, the "mother city" of a country, state, or empire. Today, this term is used loosely to refer to any large city. A metropolitan area is anchored by a city large enough to be considered a metropolis. It includes a central city (or cities) plus all surrounding territory—urban or rural—that is integrated with the urban core (usually measured by commuting patterns). In the United States, they are officially termed *Metropolitan Areas* (MAs), of which there are three types: Metropolitan Statistical Areas (MSAs), Primary Metropolitan Statistical Areas (PMSAs), and Consolidated Metropolitan Statistical Areas (CMSAs). The U.S. Bureau of the Census has been designating metropolitan areas since 1950. While terminology and criteria have changed since that time, the core definition has remained the same in that metropolitan areas (1) have an urban core of at least 50,000 people, (2) include surrounding urban and rural territory that is socially and economically integrated with the core, and (3) are built from county (or county-equivalent) units. In Canada, their counterparts are officially termed Census Metropolitan Areas (CMAs), which must have an urban core of at least 100,000 people.

Megalopolis

Megalopolis is a 20th-century word of North American origin. It was first applied in 1961 by geographer Jean Gottmann to the urbanized northeastern seaboard of the United States from Boston to Washington. Its coinage focused attention on a new scale of urbanization. Today, megalopolis is used as a generic term referring to urban coalescence of metropolitan areas at the regional scale. That coalescence is channeled along transportation corridors connecting one city with another. It is evident in the magnitude of vehicle traffic, telephone calls, e-mail exchanges, and air transport among cities strung along a megalopolitan corridor. Metropolis and megalopolis are both derived from the ancient Greek word for city, *polis*.

Site and Situation

Why are cities located where they are? How and why do they grow? Concepts used by urban geographers to answer these and related questions are *site* and *situation*. Site refers to the physical characteristics of the place where the city originated and evolved. Surface landforms, underlying geology, elevation, water features, coastline configuration, and other aspects of physical geography are considered site characteristics. Montreal's site, for instance, is defined by the Lachine Rapids, historically the upstream limit of ocean-going commerce. Paris's site is defined by an island in the Seine River, known as Île de la Cité, which gave the city defensive advantages and offered an easy bridging point. New York City's site is defined by a deepwater harbor. A city's origin is often closely connected to its site.

Situation, by contrast, refers to the relative location of a city (fig. 1.9). It connotes a city's connectedness with other places and the surrounding region. Some cities are centrally located at the junction of trade routes, whereas others are isolated. A city's growth and decline are more dependent on situation than on site characteristics. In fact, a good relative location can compensate for a poor site. Venice, for instance, triumphed as a center of the Renaissance not because of its site (so water-saturated it is sinking), but because of its relative location at the head of the Adriatic Sea and its access to good passes through the Alps. New York City emerged as the United States' most populous city in the early 19th century, not because of a superior site, but because of a superior situation. After the opening of the Erie Canal in 1825, New York had easy access to the resource-rich interior of the United States via the Great Lakes.

Figure 1.7 and 1.8   Hong Kong is an excellent example of an economy that has evolved from industry to increasingly high-end services, and these two photos dramatically show the consequences of success. Both were shot on almost the same spot on the Peak on Hong Kong Island, the first in the mid-1970s, the second in the mid-1990s. (Photos by Jack Williams)

Urban Landscapes

Urban landscapes, visible and invisible, are the manifestations of the thoughts, deeds, and actions of human beings. They are charged with clues to the economic, cultural, and political values of the people who built them (fig. 1.10). At the macroscale, geographers may look at the vertical and horizontal dimensions of the landscape—at city skylines and urban sprawl. At the microscale, they may look at architectural styles, signage, or activity patterns near busy intersections. Interpreting, analyzing, and critiquing the landscape is one of the traditional themes of urban geography (box 1.3).

Capital City

"Capital" comes from the Latin word for "head," *caput. Capital cities*, as the headquarters of government functions, are "head cities." Every country has one (South Africa has three). Although not always the largest cities, their voices are often the loudest. Each is the seat of political power, the center of legislative decision making, and the locus of national sovereignty. Their landscapes are charged with the symbols of solidarity, real or imagined; their museums are the attics of the nation; their locations are symbolic of the central role they play in the national urban system. In some countries, national capitals share power with provincial

Figure 1.8

capitals. As a class of cities, they are among the best known in the world.

Preindustrial City

The term *preindustrial city*—sometimes referred to as the *traditional city*—identifies a city that was founded and grew before the arrival of industrialization in the 19th and 20th centuries and thus typically had quite different characteristics from industrial cities. Elements of the traditional city are still part of urban landscapes, particularly in the developing world, even though there is no longer a purely preindustrial city in existence. Remnants of the traditional city include central markets (hearty survivors in Europe and making a comeback in the United States), pedestrian quarters where the streets are too narrow for cars, walls and gates now serving as visual reminders of the past, and intimidating architecture (palaces and cathedrals) that preceded industrialization.

Industrial City

An *industrial city* has an economy based on the production of manufactured goods, sometimes light industrial products (e.g., food, textiles, footwear) and sometimes heavy industrial items (e.g., motor vehicles, appliances, ships, machinery). Factories and foundries anchor their urban landscapes. Although small-scale manufacturing characterized even preindustrial cities, the invention of the steam engine begat ever larger factories and the cities that provided them with workers and services.

Figure 1.9   Seattle grew initially on the basis of its site (superb harbor) and situation (jumping-off point to Alaska and Asia), but its phenomenal growth after World War II was primarily due to businesses that had little directly to do with site and situation: Boeing Aircraft Company and Microsoft. (Photo by Larry Ford)

Postindustrial City

A relatively new type of city is emerging, particularly in the world's wealthiest countries: the *postindustrial city*. Its economy is not tied to a manufacturing base but instead to high employment in the service sector. Cities that are mainly the headquarters for corporations or for governmental and intergovernmental organizations are examples, as are those specializing in research and development (R&D), health and medicine, and tourism/recreation, which are categories in the quaternary sector. With an increase in the number of people employed in tertiary and quaternary occupations, especially in fields such as finance, health, leisure, R&D, education, and telecommunications and in various levels of government, the cities with concentrations of these activities have an economic base that contrasts sharply with cities that originated in industrial economies.

Primate City

A type of city defined by size and function is the *primate city* (fig. 1.11). The term was coined by geographer Mark Jefferson in the late 1930s to refer to the tendency for countries to have one city that is exceptionally large, economically dominant, and culturally expressive of national identity. A true primate city is at least twice as large as the second-

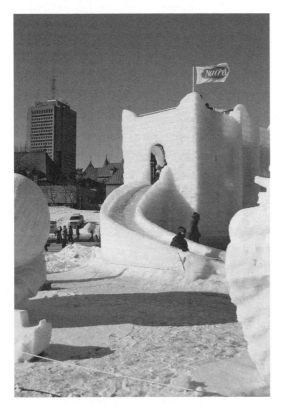

Figure 1.10   The annual Winter Carnival brings the world to Quebec City and bolsters the winter tourism industry. Here on the Plains of Abraham, the built environment is built of ice. (Photo by Donald Zeigler)

largest city, but the gap is often much larger. Paris, for instance, is seven times larger than France's second-largest city, Lyon. In general, however, primacy is more typical of the developing world. In a few instances, countries may be characterized by dual primacy, where two large cities share the dominant role, such as Rio de Janeiro and São Paulo in Brazil. The presence of a primate city in a country usually suggests an imbalance in development: a progressive core, defined by the primate city and its environs, and a lagging periphery on which the primate city may depend for resources and migrant labor. Some see the relationship between core and periphery as a parasitic one.

Rank-Size Rule

One concept that represents an alternative to primacy is the *rank-size rule*. This concept evolved out of empirical research on the relationships between cities of different population size in a given region. Simply put, the rule states that the population of a particular city within a country should be equal to the population of the largest city divided by its rank. In other words, the fifth-largest city in a country should be one-fifth the size of the largest city. A deviation from this ranking may mean that the urban system is unbalanced.

Colonial City

Although virtually gone from the face of the earth now, the *colonial city* had a profound impact on urban patterns throughout much of the world, starting around 1500 A.D. and culminating, with the global dominance of European imperial powers, in the 19th and early 20th centuries. The colonial city was unique because of its special focus on commercial functions, its peculiar situation requirements, and its odd blend of Western urban forms with traditional indigenous values and practices.

There were two distinct types of colonial city, depending on the age of the European or colonial enclave in relation to the age of the native or indigenous settlement. In one type, the European city was created virtually from scratch on a site where no other significant urban place had existed. This would then lead to in-migration of local peoples drawn by the economic opportunity created under colonial rule. Examples include Mumbai (Bombay), Hong Kong, and Nairobi. In the other type, the European city was grafted onto an existing indigenous urban place and then became the dominant growth pole for that city, typically

---

Box 1.3 Historical and Cultural Geographies of the City

Brian J. Godfrey

The oldest and most enduring traditions of urban geographical scholarship are historical and cultural in emphasis. By studying urban evolution in space and time, these approaches stress continuity as well as change in cities. Instead of relying on abstract models, they highlight the importance of particular peoples, places, and city forms and functions. Eclectic in their topics and methods, historical and cultural geographies underscore the role of long-term processes in shaping the contemporary spatial patterns of cities. Although these approaches originated primarily among academic geographers, they have become increasingly influential among scholars in architecture, history, and planning as well.

Early historical-geographical studies stressed locational and environmental prerequisites of urban growth, especially influences of the site (physical geography) and the situation (regional trade). On the other hand, Carl Sauer's seminal article of 1925, "Morphology of Landscape," argued against environmental determinants and in favor of human agency: "The cultural landscape is fashioned from a natural landscape by a culture group. Culture is the agent, the natural area is the medium, the cultural landscape the result." Contemporary critics have attacked Sauer's approach to culture as overly static and homogeneous, but his emphasis on the cultural landscape led to an ongoing and evolving geographical tradition. Intellectual successors such as J. B. Jackson, Peirce Lewis, Donald Meinig, and Wilbur Zelinsky broadened cultural-historical geography to include "vernacular" or "ordinary landscapes" in urban and suburban as well as rural settings. Thus, everyday landscapes came to be seen as providing clues to culture—"texts" to be "read" in terms of a society's priorities.

A related but distinct scholarly tradition focuses on the history of urban form, or morphology—the ground plan, spatial syntax, built environment, and architectural design.

---

swallowing up or overwhelming in size and importance the original indigenous center. Examples include Shanghai, Delhi, and Tunis. Either type of colonial city would eventually give rise to a *dual city* consisting of one modern, Western part and another more traditional, indigenous part.

Socialist City

Cities that evolved under communist/socialist regimes in the former Soviet Union, China, Eastern Europe, North Korea, Vietnam, and Cuba have given us the concept of the *socialist city*. Communism was characterized by massive government involvement in the economy, coupled with the absence of private landownership and free markets. Communism produced cities that were distinctive in form, function, and internal spatial structure (fig. 1.12). Although most communist regimes collapsed in the late 20th century, central planning and the command economy have left a lasting, visible impression on urban landscapes. Now, however, most of the socialist cities of the world are experiencing rapid

This morphological tradition grew out of detailed studies of particular cities by M. R. G. Conzen and J. W. R. Whitehand in Britain, Saverio Muratori in Italy, the "Versailles School" in France, and Michael Conzen, James Vance, Deryck Holdsworth, Larry Ford, John Reps, and Spiro Kostof, among others, in the United States. Morphological analysis employs various scales of resolution: plots, streets, and blocks; urban building fabrics; and larger morphological regions. Furthermore, scholars have argued that urban form must be understood historically in terms of morphological frames and morphogenetic periods, given the continual creation and transformation of city form. As Vance has noted, "physical traits of the city tend to persist, once established, and no city ever absolutely denies its past." Particular attention has also been given to cartographic representation of city-building processes in different periods of growth.

Although critics sometimes discount studies of urban morphology and cultural landscape as descriptive and light on theory, defenders point to the need to ground urban theory in historical process and geographical context. In addition, the contemporary rise of critical humanistic perspectives on the city has highlighted a convergence of social theory and post-structural approaches to urban form. For example, James Duncan, Paul Groth, Kevin Lynch, Edward Relph, John Stilgoe, and Yi-Fu Tuan have emphasized issues of perception, representation, and memory in cultural landscapes. Others such as Mona Domosh, Peter Jackson, Don Mitchell, Karen M. Morin, and Allan Pred have stressed the importance of cultural politics and conflicts over nationalism, race, class, and gender embedded in space and place. Work by Daniel Arreola, Lawrence Herzog, and Joseph Nevins has examined the conflicts and complexities of cultural landscapes in U.S.–Mexico borderlands. Such continuing contributions indicate that cultural-historical geographies, though contested, remain alive and well. Altogether, historical and cultural approaches to urban geography have sensitized us to the particularities of space and time in the city.

change. Although China is still the province of Communist Party rule, competitive enterprise is transforming its urban landscapes. Only North Korea, and to some extent Cuba, continue to maintain cities under the principles of communism.

New Town

The *new town*, narrowly interpreted, is a phenomenon of the 20th century; the term refers to a comprehensively planned urban community built from scratch with the intent of becoming as self-contained as possible by encouraging the development of an economic base and a full range of urban services and facilities. New towns have come into existence for any number of reasons: relieving overcrowding in large cities; helping to control urban sprawl; providing an optimum living environment for residents; serving as growth poles for the development of peripheral regions; and creating or relocating a national or provincial capital. The modern new-town movement began in Britain and later diffused to other European countries, the United

Figure 1.11   Mexico City, overwhelmingly the primate city of Mexico and one of the world's largest cities, seems to sprawl forever. With giant size comes giant problems, too. (Photo by Robert Smith)

States, the Soviet Union, and, in the post–World War II era, to many other newly independent countries. The idealized form of the new town, in the West at least, tends to follow the Garden City concept of the British, with its emphasis on manageable population size, pod-like housing tracts, neighborhood service centers, mixed land uses, much green space, pedestrian walkways, and a self-contained employment base (akin to that of premodern villages). After a century of experimentation, however, most countries have found new towns to be extremely difficult to establish and sustain. Nevertheless, they have served as laboratories for urban planners, symbols of national aspirations, and stimulators of economic growth in frontier areas.

Three types of new towns have been developed with some degree of success: (1) suburban-ring cities such as Reston, Virginia, in the United States; (2) new capitals such as Brasilia, Brazil; and (3) economic growth poles such as Ciudad Guyana, Venezuela.

WORLD URBANIZATION: PAST TRENDS

Early Urbanization (Antiquity to 5th Century A.D.)

The first cities in human history were located in Mesopotamia, along the Tigris and Euphrates Rivers, probably about 4000 B.C.

Figure 1.12   These heroic statues in front of the opera house in Novosibirsk, Russia, are typical of former socialist cities. Statues, paintings, and posters were designed to inspire the populace to sacrifice lives of personal comfort for the sake of national welfare. (Photo by Donald Zeigler)

Cities were founded in the Nile Valley about 3000 B.C., in the Indus Valley (present-day Pakistan) by 2500 B.C., in the Yellow River Valley of China by 2000 B.C., and in Mexico and Peru by 500 A.D. Estimates of the size of these early cities suggest they were relatively small. Ur in lower Mesopotamia, for instance, was the largest city in the world 6,000 years ago but probably had a population of only 200,000. In fact, most cities of antiquity remained in the range of 2,000 to 20,000 inhabitants, and the number of cities did not increase significantly. The largest ancient city was Rome, which Peter Hall has called "the first great city in world history." In the 2nd century A.D., Rome may have had 1 million inhabitants, making it the first city of that size in history. Between the 2nd and 9th centuries, however, Rome's population declined to less than 200,000. In fact, the world's largest cities in 100 A.D. were completely different from the largest cities in 1000 A.D. (fig. 1.13 and tab. 1.3).

Ancient cities appeared where nature and the state of technology enabled cultivators to produce more than they needed for themselves and their families. That surplus set the stage for a division of labor among specialized occupations and the beginning of commercial exchanges. Cities were the settlement form adopted by those members of society whose direct presence at the places of agricultural production was not necessary. They were religious, administrative, and political centers. These ancient cities represented a new social order, but one that was dynamically linked to rural society.

In these ancient cities were specialists working full-time, such as priests and service workers, as well as a population that appreciated the arts and the use of symbols for counting and writing. Other attributes of these early cities included taxation, external trade, social classes, and gender differences in the assignment of work. Each city was surrounded by a countryside of farms, villages, and even towns. Ancient cities demonstrated the emergence of specialization. Rural life limited the exchange of goods, ideas, and people, as well as the complexity of technology and the division of labor. Thus, trade was a basic function of ancient cities, which were linked to the surrounding rural areas and to other cities by a relatively complex system of production and distribution, as well as by religious, military, and economic institutions (fig. 1.14).

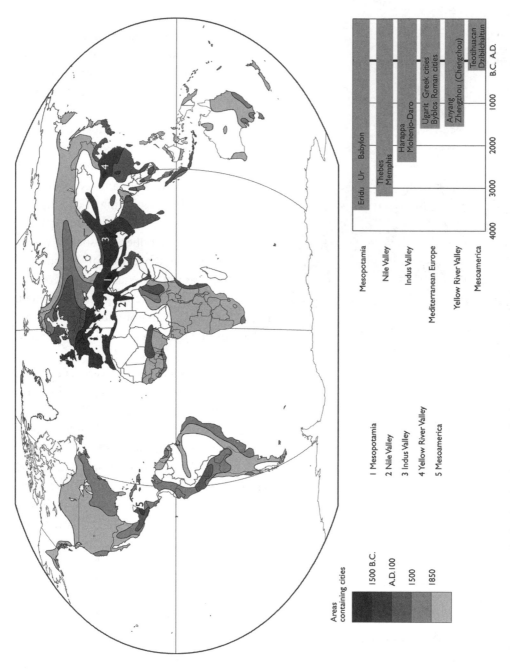

Figure 1.13 Spread of Urbanization, Antiquity to Modern Times. *Source:* Adapted from A. J. Rose, *Patterns of Cities* (Sydney: Thomas Nelson, 1967), 21. Used by permission.

Table 1.3   The Largest Cities in History

	Largest Cities in the Year 100			*Largest Cities in the Year 1000*	
1	Rome	450,000	1	Cordova, Spain	450,000
2	Luoyang, China	420,000	2	Kaifeng, China	400,000
3	Seleucia (on the Tigris), Iraq	250,000	3	Constantinople (Istanbul), Turkey	300,000
4	Alexandria, Egypt	250,000	4	Angkor, Cambodia	200,000
5	Antioch, Turkey	150,000	5	Kyoto, Japan	175,000
6	Anuradhapura, Sri Lanka	130,000	6	Cairo, Egypt	125,000
7	Peshawar, Pakistan	120,000	7	Baghdad, Iraq	125,000
8	Carthage, Tunisia	100,000	8	Nishapur (Neyshabur), Iran	125,000
9	Suzhou, China	n/a	9	Al-Hasa, Saudi Arabia	110,000
10	Smyrna, Turkey	90,000	10	Pata (Anhilwara), India	100,000

	Largest cities in the year 1500			*Largest cities in the year 2000*	
1	Beijing, China	672,000	1	Tokyo, Japan	34,450,000
2	Vijayanagar, India	500,000	2	Ciudad de México (Mexico City), Mexico	18,066,000
3	Cairo, Egypt	400,000	3	New York–Newark, New York	17,846,000
4	Hangzhou, China	250,000	4	São Paulo, Brazil	17,099,000
5	Tabriz, Iran	250,000	5	Mumbai (Bombay), India	16,086,000
6	Constantinople (Istanbul), Turkey	200,000	6	Shanghai, China	13,243,000
7	Guar, India	200,000	7	Kolkata (Calcutta), India	13,058,000
8	Paris, France	185,000	8	Delhi, India	12,441,000
9	Guangzhou, China	150,000	9	Buenos Aires, Argentina	11,847,000
10	Nanjing, China	147,000	10	Los Angeles–Long Beach–Santa Ana, USA	11,814,000

Sources: Historical cities: Tertius Chandler, *Four Thousand Years of Urban Growth: An Historical Census* (St. David's University Press, 1987); http://geography.about.com/library/weekly/aa01201a.htm; Year 2000 data: United Nations, *World Urbanization Prospects: 2005 Revision* (New York: United Nations Population Division, 2006, http://esa.un.org/unup).

The Middle Period (5th–17th Century A.D.*)*

From the fall of the Roman Empire to the 17th century, cities in Europe grew slowly or not at all. The few large cities declined in size and function. Thus, the Western Roman Empire's fall in the 5th century A.D. marked the effective end of urbanization in western Europe for over 600 years.

The major reason for the decline of cities was a decrease in spatial interaction. After the collapse of Rome and the empire it commanded, urban localities became isolated from one another and had to become self-sufficient in order to survive. From their very beginnings, cities have survived and increased in size because of trade with their rural hinterland and with other cities, near and far. The disruption of the Roman transportation system, the spread of Islam in the 7th and 8th centuries, and the pillaging raids of the Norse in the 9th century almost completely eliminated trade between cities. These events, plus periodic attacks by Germanic and other groups from the north, resulted in an almost complete disruption of urban and rural

Figure 1.14   Countless ancient cities have ended up like these ruins of a former city in China's Xinjiang province. The city was once a thriving commercial center along the famous Silk Road, but once that economic base disappeared, the city withered and died also. (Photo by Stanley Brunn)

interaction. Rural and urban populations both declined, transportation networks deteriorated, entire regions became isolated, and people became preoccupied with defense and survival.

Although urban revival did occur 600 years after the fall of the Roman Empire via fortified settlements and ecclesiastical centers, growth in population and production remained quite small. The reason is simply that exchange was limited largely to people within an immediate surrounding region. Most urban residents spent their lives within the walls of their cities. Thus, urban communities developed very close-knit social structures. Power was shared between feudal lords and religious leaders. The economically active population was organized into guilds—for craftspersons, artisans, merchants, and others. One's social status was determined by one's position in guild, family, church, and feudal administration. Gender roles were also well defined. Merchants and the guilds saw innovative possibilities in "free cities," where a person could reach his or her full potential within a community setting.

Over time, commerce expanded and linked the city to expanding state power, resulting in a system called *mercantilism*. The purpose of mercantilism was the use of the power of the state to help the nation develop its economic potential and population. Mercantile policies protected merchant interests through the control of trade subsidies, the creation of trade monopolies, and the maintenance of a strong armed force to defend commercial interests. Cities were mercantilism's growth centers, and specialization and trade kept the system alive.

Mercantilism, though based on new economic practices, had one important element in common with the system of the previous period: it restrained and controlled individual merchants in favor of the needs of society. However, the merchants and industrial capitalists of the rising new middle class were against any restrictions on their profits. They opposed economic regulation and used their growing power to demand freedom from state control. They desired an end to mercantilism. As the power of the capitalists increased, the goal of the economy became expansion, with economic profit the function of city growth. Although the new market economy did provide means to social recognition, the social costs were high. The greatest hardship fell on those receiving the fewest benefits—women, poor farmers, and members of the rising industrial working class. The new force of capitalism pushed aside the last vestiges of feudal life and created a new central function for the city—industrialization. It was capitalism that ushered in the Industrial Revolution and led to the emergence of the industrial city.

While Europe was going through this process of decline and then rebirth in its cities, areas of the non-Western world experienced quite different patterns. In East Asia, for example, the city did not suffer the decline it went through in medieval Europe. In China, numerous cities founded before the Christian era remained continuously occupied and economically viable through the centuries. Moreover, long before any city in Europe again grew to a size to rival ancient Rome, very large cities were thriving in East Asia. Changan (present-day Xi'an), for example, reputedly had more than 1 million people when it was the capital of Tang China in the 7th century. Kyoto, the capital of Japan for over a thousand years (and modeled after ancient Changan), had a population exceeding 1 million by the middle of the

18th century. Although most of the ancient cities of Asia had populations of less than 1 million, they were still far larger than cities in Europe until the commercial/industrial revolutions there. The principal explanation for this historical pattern of urban growth lies in the very different cultures and geographical environments of the great Asian civilizations. Although empires waxed and waned in Asia, just as in Europe, premodern cities in Asia continued to serve as vital centers of political administration, cultural and religious authority, and markets for agricultural surplus.

It was not until the arrival of Western colonialism that those societies and their cities began to be threatened. The several centuries of Western colonialism in Asia added a new kind of city to the region, a Western commercial city sometimes grafted onto a traditional city, sometimes created anew from virgin land. In either case, these new cities came eventually to dominate eastern Asia's urban landscape. That dominance has continued into the contemporary period.

In the Greater Middle East, the traditional city also existed and thrived through the centuries, long before Europeans began to claim pieces of the region as colonial territory. But once colonialism was fully asserted in the region, the same process of grafting and creating new Western commercial cities occurred, with consequences similar to those in eastern Asia.

In Sub-Saharan Africa and Latin America, the urban experience varied somewhat from that of much of Asia and the Middle East. In the case of Latin America, the traditional city—along with the societies that created that city, such as the Mayan, Incan, and Aztec—was obliterated by Spanish conquest and colonization. The Spanish, as well as the Portuguese, thus created new cities in the vast realm of Latin America, cities that reflected the cultures of Europe. In Sub-Saharan Africa, the indigenous cities of various African kingdoms, such as Mali, Songhay, Axum, and Zimbabwe, had existed for centuries, but they also felt the impact of European colonialism. By the 19th century, they had been largely destroyed, and Europeans had created new commercial cities, usually coastal, that quickly grew to dominate the region.

Hence, as it materialized in Europe and was exported with the creation of colonial empires after 1500 A.D., the European-created city became the model for urban growth and development worldwide. In some regions, it was imposed on indigenous societies that were exterminated or shoved aside (as in North and South America, Australia, and the Pacific). In regions with long histories of indigenous cultures and urban life, it existed alongside indigenous cities and transformed them (as in most of Asia, the Middle East, and Africa).

Industrial and Postindustrial Urbanization (18th Century to the Present)

Only after the Industrial Revolution, which began around 1750, did significant urbanization occur. It was not until the 19th century that cities emerged as important places of population concentration. By 1900 only one nation, Great Britain, could be regarded as an urbanized society in the sense that more than half of its inhabitants resided in urban places. During the 20th century, however, the number of urbanized nations increased dramatically. In the United States, the census of 1920 was the first to reveal that a majority of Americans lived in cities. Only Africa and parts of Asia continue to lag behind the rest of the world in urbanization.

The city is not a static entity, but a system in flux. Within the city, some sectors may decline and die as investment is withheld, while others may grow and prosper as investments increase. Every change in urban function has both positive and negative multiplier effects. Adjustment to the changed situation may occur slowly. If the change is a reduction in functions, poverty levels will usually rise as unemployment spreads through the city in a cumulative manner, producing greater effects in some neighborhoods than in others. Whether the city is growing or declining, spatial change within it will occur as a result of the decline of older neighborhoods, an influx of poor rural families or of immigrants from foreign areas, labor shedding as a result of automation, the development of new suburbs or satellite towns, and the migration of businesses and industries to the suburbs. Those without access to opportunities, skills, or transportation will be left out by the operation of the market system. Whenever and wherever the market system operates, it serves the affluent rather than the poor. Thus, the problems of urbanization are in a sense the problems of marginalized peoples and unheard voices.

CITY FUNCTIONS AND URBAN ECONOMIES

City Functions

Some cites come into being because a strategic location needs to be defended; others serve the demands of trade and commerce; others the needs of governmental administration or religious pilgrimage; and still others the need to turn primary commodities into manufactured goods. Geographers have traditionally classified cities into three categories based on their dominant functions: (1) market centers (trade and commerce); (2) transportation centers (transport services); and (3) specialized service centers (such as government, recreation, or religious pilgrimage). Some cities may serve a single function—the "textile cities" of the southeastern United States, for instance—but functional diversity is more often the case.

Cities categorized as market centers are also known as *central places*, because they perform retail functions for the surrounding area. Central places offer a variety of goods and services (from grocery stores and gas stations to schools and corporate headquarters). Small central places, or *market centers*, depend less on the characteristics of a particular site and more on being centrally located with respect to their market areas. These centers tend to be located within the trade areas of larger cities: people living in small cities must go to larger cities to make certain purchases for which there is not a sufficient market locally. There is thus a spatial order to the settlements and their functional organization. *Central place theory*, as developed by Walter Christaller in the 1930s, is concerned with explaining the regular size, spacing, and functions of urban settlements as they might be distributed across a fertile agricultural region, for instance. In central place theory, the largest cities, or highest-order centers, are surrounded by medium-sized cities that are in turn surrounded by small cities, each category forming an integrated part of a spatially organized, nested hierarchy. The locational orientation of market centers is quite different from the locational orientation of transportation and specialized-function cities.

Transportation cities perform break-of-bulk or break-in-transport functions along waterways, railroads, or highways. Where raw materials or semifinished products are transferred from one mode of transport to another—for example, from water to rail or rail to highway—cities emerge either as processing centers or as transshipment centers. Unlike central places, whose regularity in location is accounted for by marketing principles, transportation cities are located in linear patterns along rail lines, coastlines, or major rivers. Frequently, major transport cities are the focus of two or more modes of transportation—for example, the coastal city that is the hub of railways, highways, and shipping networks. Today, of course, almost all cities have multiple transportation linkages. Exceptions tend to be isolated towns, such as mining centers in Siberia that may have only air connections or primitive seasonal roads to the outside.

Cities that perform a single function, such as recreation, mining, administration, or manufacturing, are labeled *specialized-function cities*. A very high percentage of the population participating in one or two related activities is evidence of specialization (fig. 1.15); Oxford, England, is a university town; Rochester, Minnesota, is a health care town; Norfolk, Virginia, a military town; Lincoln, a state capital; Canberra, Australia, a national government town; and Cancún, Mexico, a tourist town. Specialization is also evident in cities where the extraction or processing of a resource is the major activity. Cities labeled as mining and manufacturing cities have much more specialization than those with diversified economic bases.

Sectors of the Economy

The economic functions of a city are reflected in the composition of its labor force. Preindustrial societies are associated with rural

Figure 1.15   Lincoln, Nebraska, is a university town, but, as in cities everywhere, the pole banner is being used to inspire pride and enhance the "spirit of place." (Photo by Donald Zeigler)

economies; these economies have the largest percentages of their labor force engaged in the *primary sector*. Primary economic activities are agriculture, fishing, forestry, and mining. Preindustrial cities have historically been commercial islands in seas of rural-oriented populations. The Industrial Revolution triggered the emergence of cities oriented to manufacturing. The *secondary sector* of the economy, another name for manufacturing, expanded, and so did the demand for labor to work in the factories. As larger percentages of the population began living in cities, retail trade, transportation, and all kinds of services began to flourish. The service sector, or *tertiary* economic activities, grew at the expense of the primary and secondary sectors, which declined in their proportions of the total labor force. The *quaternary sector*, a more advanced stage of the service sector, consists of information services, which are playing an increasingly important role in the world economy. The mix of primary, secondary, tertiary, and quaternary activities within urban regions, as it has changed over time, helps to identify specific stages in humanity's economic evolution (fig. 1.16).

The association between urbanization and industrialization has been characteristic of Europe, North America, Japan, Australia, and New Zealand. That is, cities and industries grew in synchronization with each other. In many parts of Africa, Asia, and Latin America, countries that have recently become increasingly urban have not experienced a corresponding increase in the manufacturing sector of the economy. Rather, their service sectors have provided jobs for growing urban populations. Included in service-sector employment are small retailers, government servants, teachers, professionals, and bankers. Also included are many service workers in the

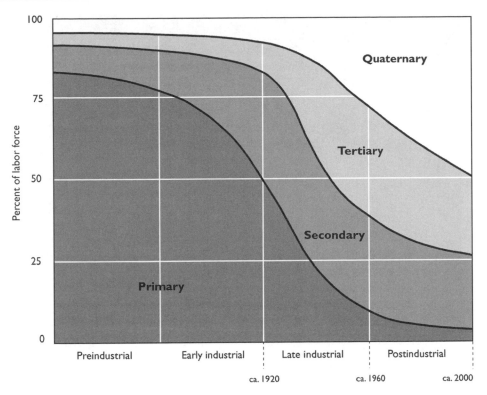

Figure 1.16   Labor Force Composition at Various Stages in Human History. *Source:* Adapted from Ronald Abler et al., *Human Geography in a Shrinking World* (Belmont, CA: Wadsworth, 1975), 49.

informal economy, including those willing to perform odd jobs (watching parked cars or cleaning houses) and those working in unskilled service occupations, such as street vending, scavenging, and laboring at construction sites. In the informal sector, barter and the exchange of services often take the place of monetary exchanges, thus bypassing government accounting and taxation.

Basic and Nonbasic Economic Activities

Economic functions are keys to the growth of cities. The *economic base concept* states that two types of activities or functions exist: those that are necessary for urban growth and those that exist primarily to supplement the necessary functions. The former are called *basic functions* or city-forming activities. They involve the manufacturing, processing, or trading of goods or the providing of services for markets located outside the city's boundaries. Economic functions of a city-servicing nature are called nonbasic functions. Grocery stores, restaurants, beauty salons, and so forth are nonbasic economic activities because they cater primarily to residents within the city itself (fig. 1.17).

Of the two, the basic functions are the key to economic growth and prosperity. A city with a high percentage of its labor force in the production of such items as automobiles,

Figure 1.17   This textile retailer in Kashgar, China, caters primarily to local residents, but tourist business helps, too. The cell phone, an increasingly visible sign of globalization around the world, helps the owner keep in touch and stay competitive. (Photo by Stanley Brunn)

furniture, and electronic equipment depends on sales beyond the city's boundaries to bring money into the community. Income generated by the sales of those industrial goods is channeled into the city's nonbasic sector, where employees in those industries purchase groceries, gasoline, insurance, entertainment, and other everyday needs and wants.

The economic base of some cities is grounded in manufacturing industries, the secondary sector of the economy. Manchester, England, and Pittsburgh, Pennsylvania, are prime examples of older industrial cities whose growth and prosperity depended upon world markets, for cotton textiles and steel, respectively. Since World War II, both cities have lost their manufacturing base and have been challenged to find service industries for which there is a larger market. The economic base of postindustrial cities, in fact, is to be found in the tertiary and quaternary sectors of the economy (fig. 1.18). *Silicon valleys* developed around the world in the late 20th century to service the needs of the computer industry. In the early 21st century, *biotech valleys* are becoming the economic base of choice. Cities such as Geneva, Singapore, San Francisco, and Boston are competing to have biotechnology firms move into their regions. Money from biomedical and pharmaceutical research provides an economic base tied to high-level applications of technology and brainpower. Banking, accounting, architecture, and advertising are other service industries that some cities depend upon for their economic bases.

As a city's economic base increases, it has a multiplier effect throughout the community. Growth (and conversely, decline) becomes a cumulative process in which growth begets

Figure 1.18   The Renaissance Center in downtown Detroit was an initiative to help Detroit make the transition from its original auto industry focus to a more service-based economy, a transition that has been fraught with all kinds of difficulties. (Photo by Larry Ford)

growth. This is known as the *principle of circular and cumulative causation*. For instance, one of the major ways cities grew in the past was by attracting more manufacturing enterprises. Each new factory in an urban area stimulated general economic development and population growth. Business output increased because of a greater demand for products. Rising profits increased savings, causing investments to rise. Increased productivity resulted in greater wealth. The growing population then reached a new level, or threshold, resulting in a new round of demands. Larger cities are able to offer a greater number and variety of services than smaller cities. Conversely, cities stagnate because they lose industries and population, conditions that create a negative circular and cumulative causation—a downward spiral. Thus, it is easy to understand why city mayors and chambers of commerce work so hard to promote their respective cities

as favorable sites for investment and new business locations.

THEORIES ON THE INTERNAL SPATIAL STRUCTURE OF CITIES

In addition to the origin and growth of cities, geographers have long been intrigued by cities' internal spatial structure (box 1.4). Components of that structure include industrial zones, commercial districts, warehouse rows, residential areas, parks and open space, and transportation routes, among others. A variety of theories have been developed to describe and explain the pattern of land use and the distribution of population groups within cities. The four most widely accepted theories, or models, of city structure are the concentric zone model, the sector model, the multiple nuclei model, and the inverse concentric zone

---

Box 1.4 Critical Urban Geographies

Natalia Oswin

In the mid-1940s, when sociological theories of cities were already well-established, geographers began to enter the field of urban studies. Urban geography gathered steam in the 1950s, and its direction was strongly influenced by a dominant trend within the discipline that sought to turn geography into "spatial science." Adopting the principles and practices of the "hard" sciences (particularly influenced by economics and physics), most geographers' main aim during this period was to search for underlying laws of location, interaction, and movement. Urban geographers were accordingly preoccupied with mapping and modeling such things as patterns of urban land use and interactions between cities. With the aid of rigorous statistical techniques, they systematically studied urban centers to come up with theories of urban space that might help policymakers run cities with maximal efficiency.

By the 1970s, some geographers had begun to question the value of this body of work on the ground that it failed to address the inequalities prevalent in urban contexts. In particular, David Harvey's *Social Justice and the City* (Edward Arnold, 1973) challenged urban geographers to rethink their theoretical and political stances. Insisting that "it is the emerging objective social conditions and our patent inability to cope with them which essentially explain the necessity for a revolution in geographic thought" (129), Harvey's text inaugurated what has since come to be called *critical urban geographies*. Much early work followed Harvey's lead in utilizing a Marxist framework to understand the ways in which cities are structured by capitalist processes of production and class division. Instead of the previous preoccupation with determining whether relations within urban space were maximally efficient, Harvey and others began to consider urban spatial processes as capitalist processes and to examine their effects on the distribution of income.

In the decades since the publication of Harvey's pivotal text, many critical urban geographers have argued that geographic work based solely on an analysis of capitalism

---

model (fig. 1.19). All evolved from observations of urban landscapes that suggested that different land uses were predictably, not randomly, distributed across the city.

The Concentric Zone Model

The concentric zone theory was first conceptualized by Friedrich Engels (coauthor of the *Communist Manifesto*) in the mid-19th century. Engels observed that the population of Manchester, England, in 1844 was residentially segregated on the basis of class. He noted that the commercial district (offices plus retail and wholesale trade) was located in the center of Manchester and extended about half a mile in all directions. Besides the commercial district, Manchester consisted of unmixed working people's quarters, which extended a mile and a half (2.3 km) around

is inadequate because of the range of axes of social differentiation involved in urbanization processes. Feminist geographies have pointed out that a primary emphasis on class oppression ignores the realities of sexism and unequal gender relations. For instance, capitalist processes are also gendered processes insofar as women participate in the workforce in different ways than do men and disproportionately shoulder the burden of the social reproduction of the workforce (in terms of child rearing and household management). Likewise, queer geographies emphasize the sexual aspects of city life. They seek to challenge the presumed naturalness of the heterosexual character of urban space. Further, work influenced by postcolonial theory has highlighted the importance of exploring the ways in which the politics of race, ethnicity, and nationality are crucial to understanding former colonial cities as well as former imperial cities. This work has also problematized the practice of extending concepts developed in the context of the study of Western cities to cities beyond the West and thus challenged urban theory's "Eurocentric" bias.

Critical urban geographies is an umbrella term that encompasses a range of theoretical approaches to the study of the city. Recognizing the diversity of human experiences and rejecting an assumption of widely shared class interests (while still acknowledging the importance of capitalist inequalities), critical urban geographies bridge various approaches to analyzing the ways that economy *and* culture contribute to oppression and inequality. As defined by the editors of a prominent critical geographies journal, critical geographies are "for example, anarchist, anti-racist, environmentalist, feminist, Marxist, postcolonial, poststructuralist, queer, situationist, and socialist. By critical thinking and radical analysis we mean that the work is part of the praxis of social and political change aimed at challenging, dismantling, and transforming prevalent relations, systems, and structures of capitalist exploitation, oppression, imperialism, neo-liberalism, national aggression, and environmental destruction" (Pamela Moss, Lawrence D. Berg, and Caroline Desbiens, "The Political Economy of Publishing in Geography," *Acme: An International E-Journal for Critical Geographies* 1, no. 1, 2001: 3).

the commercial district. Next, extending outward from the city, were the comfortable country homes of the upper bourgeoisie. Engels believed this general pattern to be more or less common to all industrial cities.

Engels may have described the pattern first, but most social scientists consider E. W. Burgess, a University of Chicago sociologist, to be the father of the *concentric zone model.* According to Burgess, the growth of any city

occurs through a radial expansion from the center so as to form a series of concentric rings—in essence, a set of nested circles that represent successive zones of specialized urban land use. The five zones Burgess described during the 1920s, before the automobile transformed Chicago, were (1) the central business district (CBD), with its retail and wholesale areas; (2) the zone of transition, characterized by stagnation and social

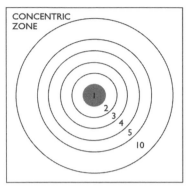

I   Central business district   5 High-class residential   8 Residential suburb
2   Wholesale light manufacturing   6 Heavy manufacturing   9 Industrial suburb
3   Low-class residential   7 Outlying business district   10 Commuter zone
4   Medium-class residential

Figure 1.19   Generalized Patterns of Internal Urban Structure. *Source:* Adapted from various sources.

deterioration; (3) the zone of factory workers' homes; (4) the zone of better residential units, including single-family dwellings and apartments; and (5) the commuter zone, extending beyond the city limits and consisting of suburbs and satellite communities. The process Burgess used to explain these concentric rings was called *invasion and succession.* Each type of land use and each socioeconomic group in the inner zone tends to extend its zone by invasion of the next outer zone. As the city grows or expands, there is a spatial redistribution of population groups by residence and occupation. Burgess further demonstrated that many social characteristics are spatially distributed in a series of gradients away from the central business district. Such characteristics include the percentage of foreign-born groups, poverty rates, and delinquency rates. Each tends to decrease outward from the city center.

The Sector Model

The *sector model* was developed in the 1930s by Homer Hoyt, an economist. Hoyt examined spatial variations in household rent in 142 American cities. He concluded that general patterns of housing values apply to all cities and that those patterns tend to appear as sectors, not concentric rings. According to Hoyt, residential land use seems to arrange itself along selected highways leading into the CBD, thus giving land-use patterns a directional bias. High-rent residences were the most important group in explaining city growth, because they tended to pull the entire city in the same direction. New residential areas did not encircle the city at its outer limits, but extended farther and farther outward along a few select transportation axes, giving the land-use map the appearance of a pie cut into many pieces. The sectoral pattern of city growth can be explained in part by a filtering process. When new housing is constructed, it is located primarily on the outer edges of the high-rent sector. The homes of community leaders, new offices, and stores are attracted to the same areas. As inner, middle-class areas are abandoned, lower-income groups filter into them. By this process, the city grows over time in the direction of the expanding high-rent residential sector.

The Multiple Nuclei Model

In 1945 two geographers, Chauncy Harris and Edward Ullman, developed a third model to explain urban land-use patterns: the *multiple nuclei model*. According to their theory, cities tend to grow around not one but several distinct nodes, thus forming a polynuclear (many-centered) pattern. The multiple nuclei pattern is explained by the following factors:

1. Certain activities are limited to particular sites because they have highly specialized needs. For example, the retail district needs accessibility, which can best be found in a central location, whereas the manufacturing district needs transportation facilities.
2. Certain related activities or economic functions tend to cluster in the same district because they can carry on their activities more efficiently as a cohesive unit. Automobile dealers, auto repair shops, tire shops, and auto glass shops are examples.
3. Certain related activities, by their very nature, repel each other. A high-class residential district will normally locate in a separate area from a heavy manufacturing district.
4. Certain activities, unable to generate enough income to pay the high rents of certain sites, may be relegated to more inaccessible locations. Examples include some specialty shops.

The number of distinct nuclei occurring within a city is likely to be a function of city size and recentness of development. Auto-oriented cities, which often have a distinct horizontal as opposed to a vertical appearance, include industrial parks, regional shopping centers, and suburbs layered by age of residents, income, and housing value. Rampant urban sprawl is likely to be reflected in a mixed pattern of industrial, commercial, and residential areas in peripheral locations. Geographer Peirce Lewis describes this sprawling urban landscape as the *galactic metropolis* because the nucleations resemble a galaxy of stars and planets. Some of those nucleations become cities in the suburbs, what some have called *edge cities*. These edge cities are, in effect, the CBDs of newly emerging urban centers scattered through the suburban ring surrounding older central cities. This pattern reinforces what has been described as the typical urban spatial model for most U.S. urban areas: the *doughnut model*. In this model, the hole in the doughnut is the central city (with poor, mostly non-white, blue-collar/working-class residents, large numbers of whom are on welfare, and with a declining tax base and economy), and the ring of the doughnut is formed by the suburbs (rich, mostly white middle and upper class, white-collar employment, and an expanding tax base and economy). Old, often declining manufacturing tends to be found in the hole; new, often high-tech manufacturing tends to be located in the suburbs, in the edge cities.

The Inverse Concentric Zone Theory

The preceding three theories of urban spatial structure apply primarily to cities of the MDCs and to American cities in particular. Many cities in the LDCs follow somewhat different patterns. A frequent one is the *inverse concentric zone pattern*, which is a reversal of the concentric zone model. Cities where this pattern exists have been called preindustrial; that is, they are primarily administrative or religious centers (or were at the time of their founding). In such cities, the central area is the place of residence for the elite class. The poor live on the periphery. Unlike most cities in the MDCs, social class in these places is inversely related to distance from the center of the city.

The reasons for this pattern are twofold: (1) the lack of an adequate and dependable transportation system, which thus restricts the elites to the center of the city so they can be close to their places of work; and (2) the functions of the city, which are primarily administrative and religious/cultural, are controlled by the elite and concentrated in the center of the city (with its government buildings, cultural institutions, places of worship, etc.).

As many developing countries have begun to industrialize, newer growth industries have tended to locate not in city centers but on the periphery, often in industrial parks or enterprise zones established by the government for the purpose of attracting domestic and foreign investors. The city centers tend to be far too congested to accommodate industrial plants of any considerable size. Moreover, the elites in the city centers often do not want large industrial plants near their place of work and residence. Hence, emerging gradually in many of the larger cities of the LDCs is the pattern of the multiple nuclei model, with new industrial parks serving as the nuclei. In other words, the inverse concentric zone pattern, while still valid in many LDCs, is merging with the multiple nuclei pattern.

As useful as these four models are, they must be viewed with caution as generalizations of the extremely complex mix of factors that influence the use of land within cities. One can commonly find elements of more than one model present in a given city. Moreover, each of the models must be viewed as

dynamic. There are changes going on all the time in economic functions, social and administrative services, transportation, and population groups that will alter the size and shape of specific sectors or zones (fig. 1.20). Furthermore, the complexities of applying these theories multiply severalfold when working with non-Western cultures and economic systems. Nowhere is this more apparent than in China and the former communist countries, where various forms of the so-called socialist city were being created and where internal spatial structures were quite unlike those described by any of the four theories mentioned. The legacy of those socialist patterns lingers on, even as free-market forces transform those cities.

URBAN CHALLENGES

Managing Population Size and Growth

Excessive size of urban regions, both in population and in geographical area, might more properly be described as a cause of problems than a problem in itself. It presents a particularly severe challenge in less developed regions, where the economic base of cities is inadequate to cope with the stresses created by more and more people. A concomitant of excessive size is overcrowding, meaning too many people occupying too little space, but excessive population does not always equate to population density. Some cultures are more adapted to high densities than others. For Americans or Europeans, though, it is sometimes difficult to fully comprehend the magnitude and effects of very severe urban overcrowding. Seeing or being caught up in the tidal wave of humanity that one can find in the larger cities such as Manila, Shanghai,

Figure 1.20   The Frontenac Hotel was built by the Canadian Pacific Railway. As the most well-known signature landscape in Quebec City, it still functions as a tourist magnet even though most visitors no longer come by train. (Photo by Donald Zeigler)

or Cairo is a vivid lesson in the consequences of excessive size that one never forgets.

The rate of population growth—or decline—may present cities with challenges as well. Some cities, especially in the developing world, are growing so fast that economic development cannot keep up. *Hyperurbanization* is sometimes used to describe what is happening in the world's most rapidly growing cities. Conversely, some cities in the developed world may be stagnating or declining in population. Whether in Russia, Germany, or the United States, the problems of no-growth cities are very similar. They are often home to companies that have outdated technology, high production costs, expensive labor, an aging workforce, and products with declining demand. In the developing world, these cities are generally victims of deindustrialization. They have not kept up with the transition from a manufacturing to a service-based economy.

Managing Urban Services

With so many people in urban settings, city governments are hard-pressed to provide all the human services that residents need—education, health care, pharmacies, clean water, sewage disposal, garbage pick-up, police and fire protection, disaster relief, public parks, mass transit, and numerous others. How can a city in the developing world that is doubling in population every 10 years or so maintain the economic growth needed to provide for so many new arrivals, particularly when those new residents are poor? Although these problems exist around the world, cities in the developed world are more likely to have the resources to deal with them. Yet even in the world's most developed countries, providing services to sprawling, energy-inefficient suburban and exurban regions can strain municipal budgets.

Managing Slums and Squatter Settlements

Most cities of the world have slums or squatter settlements, poorer communities that are not fully integrated, socially or economically, into the development process (fig. 1.21). Slums tend to be found in old, run-down areas of inner cities (sometimes, paradoxically, on very valuable land) throughout the world. Squatter settlements, typically new, are made up of makeshift dwellings erected without official permission on land that the squatters do not own. These settlements are usually located on the outskirts of cities in the developing world. They may be constructed of cardboard, tin, adobe bricks, mats, sacks, or any other available materials. They tend to lack essential services, sometimes even electricity. Squatter settlements go by various names in different countries: barriadas in Peru, favelas in Brazil, geçekondu in Turkey, bustees in India, and bidonvilles in former French colonies.

Managing Social Problems

Perhaps one of the most insidious effects of hyperurbanization throughout the world is a reduction in people's sense of social responsibility. As more and more people compete for space and services, the competition tends to breed antisocial, even sociopathic, attitudes. City life can bring out the worst in human behavior. People exhibit social pathologies when they resist waiting in line for services; think nothing of despoiling public property; disregard traffic regulations; or show a disregard for the rights of fellow citizens. To the extent that large cities provide neither a sense of community nor a respected police presence, crime soars. Social norms that hold people in check in rural areas may be absent in cities.

Managing Unemployment

Virtually everything else connected with the city is related in one way or another to the economic health of its population, and economic well-being is dependent on people having jobs. In capitalist economies, however, employment is not guaranteed. The result is often unemployment and underemployment. In the developing world, too many people may be competing for too few jobs, driving down the cost of labor. In the developed world, large segments of city populations may lack the skills necessary to find jobs in the high-end service sector of the economy. Sometimes the result is underemployment: people take jobs that are not commensurate with their skills. These jobs pay less than a living wage, meaning that some have to take more than one job to survive and others have to supplement their income with employment in the informal sector of the economy with long hours and no fringe benefits. In cities of the developing world, unemployment rates of 30% to 40% or more are not uncommon. Women and children, recent migrants, and the elderly are often the most victimized by problems of employment and underemployment.

Figure 1.21   Scavengers push their carts past squatter shacks in Smokey Mountain, a once-notorious slum of Manila that got its name from the continuously burning garbage. It has been the target of redevelopment in recent years (see chapter 10). (Photo by James Tyner)

Managing Ethnic Issues

Unemployment, underemployment, and other factors breed a variety of subsidiary problems related to ethnicity and class status. For example, relative economic prosperity in the United States has produced a tidal wave of illegal immigrants, primarily from Mexico and other Latin American countries, who come seeking a better life. These people, along with large numbers of legal immigrants and refugees, commonly settle in the cities, as did Cuban refugees in Miami, Florida. Refugees and new migrants may come into conflict with (1) community elites who find their power diluted, (2) groups, often other minorities, with whom they compete for jobs, and (3) majorities who have completely different languages, religions, and worldviews. Throughout the world, many cities must manage severe centrifugal forces generated by cultural diversity (fig. 1.22).

Managing Modernization and Globalization

One phenomenon that is sweeping the world's cities, especially the larger ones, is the dilemma of Westernization versus modernization. The problem facing the LDCs is how to raise standards of living without completely abandoning traditional cultural values and ways of life. Some might argue that tradition and modernization are incompatible, that modernization automatically entails change, and that change is likely to take the form of Westernization. To be sure, there are ample signs of this Westernization (some might wish to call it homogenization or globalization) of the world's major cities in the forms of skyscrapers, modern architecture, the automobile society, advertising, the focus on high mass consumption, and so forth. Nonetheless, as anyone who has lived in cities of the LDCs for any length of time can attest, traditional cultural values and lifestyles do

Figure 1.22   The square in Rotorua, a city famous for its geothermal pools, has been brought to life with a modern rendition of Maori art. To the Western world, Rotorua is in New Zealand; to the indigenous Maoris, it is in Aotearoa. (Photo by Donald Zeigler)

somehow manage to persist even in the most modern metropolis.

Almost the entire world—rural and urban—is adjusting to changes in global economies. Globalization means the movement of products, money, information, and human talent around the world in ever larger quantities at ever lower costs and in ever less time. Mayors and governing councils must now think globally as well as locally. Companies produce items for world, not local or regional, markets. Money is transferred electronically from major financial centers in Europe to Asia and from North to South America. Trade barriers are being reduced between countries. Transnational corporations

and nongovernmental organizations (NGOs) promote a "world without borders." The net result is an easier flow of people, money (including credit), and products across boundaries that once separated those with different ideologies and economies. In all of this, there are winners, losers, and adjustments demanded of society. And there are also potential problems, because change does not come easily.

Managing the Environment

Pollution of air and water, excessive noise levels, visual blight, and hillside clearance for urban expansion are among the many serious environmental problems in cities around the world (box 1.5). Moreover, global climate change adds a new dimension to the environmental problems experienced by cities as water becomes scarcer, heat waves more frequent, and sea levels higher. Cities in the richer parts of the world at least have the means to do something about these problems, but cities in the poorer countries often regard such concerns as less important in the face of more immediate life-and-death issues. For instance, the cities with the greatest air pollution are no longer London (formerly nicknamed "the Big Smoke") and Los Angeles (once dubbed "Smog Central"), but cities such as Shanghai, Mexico City, and São Paulo. An additional environmental problem arises from the expansion of urban areas into agriculturally productive land close to the city. China has been estimated to be losing 2 million acres of farmland to urban expansion each year, and the United States almost 1 million acres.

Managing Traffic

Another obvious effect of urbanization, produced in large part by the growing number of

Box 1.5 Tackling Urban Environmental Problems with GIS

Joseph J. Kerski

People have always been fascinated with investigating their home—the Earth. For centuries, maps have stirred imaginations and inspired explorations of the unknown. Navigating one's way through expanding cities and expanding commerce have made city maps a natural application of cartography in the centuries since the Babylonians first mapped the city of Nippur about 3,500 years ago. However, by the latter part of the 20th century, the complex and interconnected nature of urban areas brought an end to the old "city street map" as an effective planning tool. Geographic Information Systems (GIS) and associated geotechnologies, especially Global Positioning Systems (GPS) and Remote Sensing, transformed the ways in which cities managed environmental, transportation, zoning, and other planning issues. The organizational transformation brought about by the use of GIS also meant that all city departments could work from a common mapping framework, eliminating duplication and increasing efficiency within city government departments and across multi-government metropolitan areas. As GIS became embedded in the internal information technology infrastructure of these organizations, it was increasingly relied upon for daily decision making.

Although the advent of GIS has certainly not eliminated urban environmental problems, technicians and managers can now visualize relationships among population growth, demographic characteristics, climate, vegetation, landforms, river systems, underground cables, land use, soils, natural hazards, crime, security, and other components of the urban infrastructure. They can also model how that infrastructure is changing. With the advent of web-based GIS tools at the dawn of the 21st century, coupled with the beginnings of a worldwide set of high-resolution vector and raster data sets, geotechnologies began to be applied to identify and address urban environmental problems. People began to realize the efficiencies that could be achieved if data and models of spatial analytical procedures were shared to address problems of mutual concern. These problems operated at scales of region, hemisphere, and even the planet. For example, air pollution from one megalopolis could have impacts on human health thousands of kilometers away, while urban sprawl in one country could affect deforestation rates in a faraway country if trees are cut to support construction of the new homes in sprawling subdivisions.

Researchers use GIS in many ways: (1) collecting data, (2) analyzing data, and (3) communicating data. Data collection can range from air quality to vehicle counts, but all data must be geocoded, either by street address, latitude-longitude locations, mile or kilometer markers, or by other means so that they can be mapped and understood. Data analysis can range from querying the number of houses that would be submerged in a 100-year flood to the amount of additional energy use required to keep homes cool if global temperatures rise by 1°C over the next 40 years. Analysis depends upon accurate spatial data sets and the ability to apply different models to study the changes that are continually occurring within cities and across the global network of cities. For example, consider a

(continued on next page)

map produced within a GIS environment showing which cities in the southwest part of the North Atlantic Ocean could be submerged if sea levels rose by 50 meters (fig. 1.23). It was produced by one specific model of climate change, and based on digital elevation information and coastline information collected under spatial data standards. If and when the model and the data change, the GIS must be able to reflect those changes.

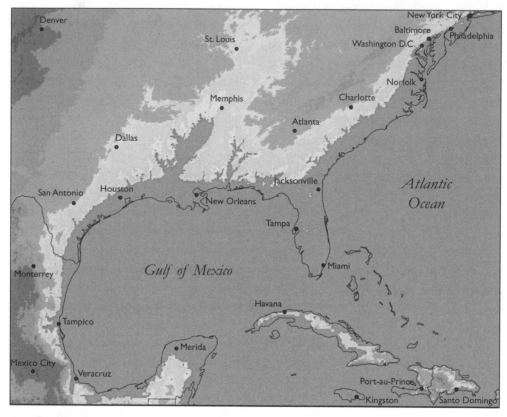

Figure 1.23   The Impact of a Hypothetical 50-Meter Sea Level Rise on the Caribbean and Atlantic Coasts of North America. *Source:* Joseph Kerski.

Data communication is still conducted via paper maps plotted from a GIS and via public presentations. Increasingly it is also conducted over the Internet—beginning with posting static maps for viewing only, and later, serving spatial data that others can use and modify. These developments may herald the beginnings of a global urban spatial information infrastructure.

Thus, GIS is encouraging an information infrastructure both within cities and between cities. Because urban environmental issues are interdisciplinary by their very nature, and because GIS was created as an interdisciplinary, problem-solving tool, GIS found a natural home in urban environmental analysis. GIS data in urban analysis are increasingly tied to ground monitoring stations, which collectively form a kind of "nervous system" for the city and, increasingly, for the planet. The goal in using GIS is better and more coordinated decision making to build a sustainable urban future.

Figure 1.24   Portland, Oregon, offers a lesson in many aspects of successful urban development, including its trolley system to reduce reliance on private automobiles. (Photo by Judy Walton)

motor vehicles, is traffic congestion. Superficially, this might be viewed as a mere nuisance, an aggravation of much less consequence than survival-level problems such as employment, housing, and social services. Nonetheless, traffic congestion is a serious dilemma that is choking many cities to a standstill in terms of the movement of people and goods. Consequences include economic inefficiency (loss of time and waste of resources), social stress, and pollution, all of which diminish a city's development potential (fig. 1.24).

Managing Urban Governance

Urban governments around the world face challenges related to the balance between revenues and expenditures. Few governments have the funds to meet every need, so priorities must be established. Those priorities may be set by higher levels of government (sometimes authoritarian) or by the democratic process locally. In any case, the task of governing or administering services to a mushrooming city is daunting, whether the city is New York or Mumbai (Bombay). In some countries, such as the United States, problems arise because urban areas are fragmented among so many jurisdictions, some overlapping. In other countries, many in the developing world, government bureaucracies are bloated with excess employees, are suspected of serving elites alone, and have a generally hard time combating pressing urban problems.

Problems or management challenges? At least some countries in the developing world and a great many in the developed world are successfully attacking the problems of urban life and urban growth. The solutions tried or planned are far too numerous and complex even to summarize here. There are undoubtedly pessimists who contend it is too late to solve the urban ills of humankind. Optimists hope this is not so. In the following chapters, we will observe both the problems and promises of urbanism in major world regions.

SUGGESTED READINGS

Amin, Ash, and Nigel Thrift. 2002. *Cities: Reimagining the Urban.* Cambridge, UK: Polity. Challenges the notion that the contemporary city is separate from the country and offers a model of the New Urbanism.

Caves, Roger W. 2005. *Encyclopedia of the City.* London, New York: Routledge. Experts from many disciplines define and interpret the city.

Davis, Mike. 2007. *Planet of Slums.* New York: Verso. A documentation of poverty in cities of the developing world.

Hall, Peter. 1998. *Cities in Civilization.* New York: Pantheon. Looks at the world's great cities during their golden ages, with an emphasis on culture, innovation, and the arts.

Knox, Paul L., and Linda M. McCarthy. 2005. *An Introduction to Urban Geography.* Upper Saddle River, NJ: Prentice Hall. A basic textbook on the city that captures the dynamism of both urbanization and urban geography.

Lynch, Kevin. 1960. *The Image of the City.* Cambridge, Mass.: M.I.T. Press, 1960. Seminal work on the "visual quality" of cities and how to read the urban landscape.

Sassen, Saskia. 2001. *The Global City: New York, London, Tokyo,* 2d ed. Princeton, N.J.: Princeton University Press. An exploration of the world's three leading centers for international transactions and their impact on the global urban hierarchy.

Soderstrom, Mary. 2006. *Green City: People, Nature and Urban Places.* Montreal: Véhicule. An examination of 11 cities and their interactions with the natural environment.

United Nations Human Settlements Programme. 2003. *The Challenge of Slums: Global Report on Human Settlements.* London: Earthscan Publications. First global assessment of slums, emphasizing problems and prospects, supported by statistics, graphics, and case studies.

Vance, James E. Jr. 1990. *The Continuing City: Urban Morphology in Western Civilization.* Baltimore: Johns Hopkins University Press. Explores the role of the city in Western society and its changing form through time.

Whitfield, Peter. 2005. *Cities of the World: A History in Maps.* Berkeley: University of California Press. Through their maps, we see how cities have perceived themselves over time.

Worldwatch Institute. 2007. *State of the World: Our Urban Future.* New York: W.W. Norton. Examines changes in the ways cities are built, managed, and occupied with particular focus on urban sustainability.

WEBSITES

Center for International Earth Science Information Network (CIESIN)
http://www.ciesin.columbia.edu
Data and research on population and the environment, especially climate change.

Cities.com
http://www.cities.com
The latest news from cities all over the world.

City Population
http://www.citypopulation.de
Presents population statistics and maps for cities around the world.

Cyburbia
http://www.cyburbia.org
A large directory of Internet resources relevant to planning, architecture, urbanism, growth, sprawl, and other topics related to the built environment.

Demographia
http://www.demographia.com/
Data and full-text reports on cities and urban processes.

ESRI Community Showcase
http://resources.esri.com/showcase/
Has resources from Environmental Systems Research Institute (ESRI) and web-based geographic information system (GIS) portals built and hosted by city and regional governments.

GaWC—Globalization and World Cities
http://www.lboro.ac.uk/gawc/
Includes an inventory of world cities, data presentations, commentaries on specific cities, and articles of scholarly interest.

NASA "Search the Cities from Space" Collection
http://city.jsc.nasa.gov/cities/
Color photographs of the world's cities taken by National Aeronautics and Space Administration (NASA) astronauts during spaceflights.

United Nations Population Division
http://www.un.org/esa/population/unpop.htm
Voluminous information on population, including the annual report on world urbanization prospects.

U.S. Bureau of the Census
http://www.census.gov/
Copious data on towns and cities in the United States.

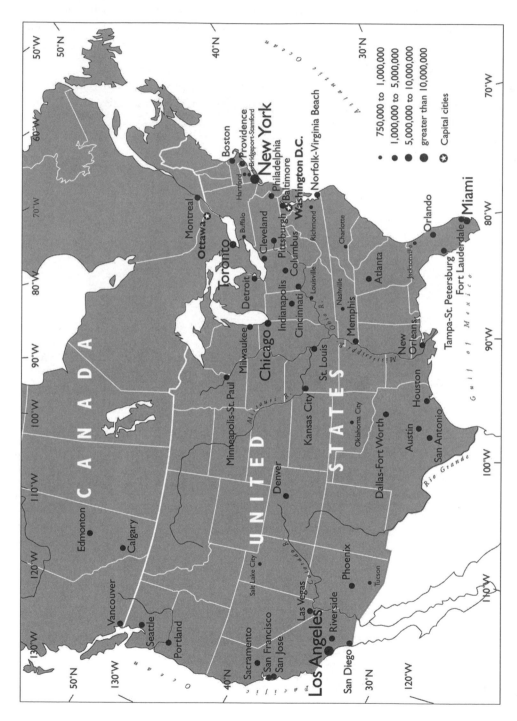

Figure 2.1 Major Cities of the United States and Canada. *Source:* Data from UN, *World Urbanization Prospects: 2005 Revision,* http://esa.un.org/unup/.

2

Cities of the United States and Canada
LISA BENTON-SHORT
JOHN RENNIE SHORT

KEY URBAN FACTS

Total Population	330 million
Percent Urban Population	81%
Total Urban Population	267 million
Most Urbanized Country	United States (80.8%)
Least Urbanized Country	Canada (80.1%)
Annual Urban Growth Rate	1.26%
Number of Megacities	2
Number of Cities of More Than 1 Million	45
Three Largest Cities	New York, Los Angeles, Chicago
World Cities	New York, Los Angeles, Chicago, Washington, San Francisco, Atlanta, Miami, Toronto, Montreal, Vancouver
Global Cities	New York

KEY CHAPTER THEMES

1. After 1950 the United States and Canada became metropolitan societies, as a majority of their populations came to live in metropolitan areas.
2. The United States and Canada compose one of the most urbanized regions of the world, with a developed urban hierarchy composed of a multitude of small, medium, large, cities; cities of multi-millions; and even several megacities.
3. Although there are variations in urban land-use patterns, the most pronounced pattern is of a declining core and an expanding suburban area; however, in some cities, the core has seen some resurgence.

4. Cities in the United States and Canada have been recently shaped by the intensification of economic globalization and heightened competition in the global urban hierarchy.

5. The reliance on the automobile and weak investment in public transportation has resulted in low population densities and increased sprawl.

6. Both U.S. and Canadian cities have responded to dramatic economic changes since the 1980s by employing a variety of redevelopment schemes designed to increase investment through tourism related to waterfront redevelopment, sports, historical districts, and cultural events.

7. A long history of industrialization has left cities dealing with numerous environmental issues, including air, land, and water pollution, all of which threaten to erode quality of life for many urban residents.

8. Immigration is transforming numerous cities as immigrants gravitate toward long established immigrant magnets such as New York, Chicago, and Toronto as well as to newly emerging cities such as Las Vegas, Washington, D.C., and Calgary.

9. The composition of immigrants in U.S. and Canadian cities has become more diverse as recent immigrants arrive from countries in Africa, Latin America, Asia, and the Middle East.

10. In a post-9/11 world, heightened concerns about security have begun to transform urban space through the installation of security cameras and the fortressing of selected spaces with security features such as bollards, barriers, and bunkers.

Many urban scholars suggest the world is in the midst of the Third Urban Revolution, a complex phenomenon that began in the middle of the 20th century and that is marked by a massive increase, in both absolute and relative terms, in urban populations, the development of megacities, the growth of giant metropolitan regions, and the global redistribution of economic activities, as former manufacturing cities decline and new industrial cities emerge elsewhere. The cities of the United States and Canada embody the dynamic and challenging trends of this Third Urban Revolution (fig. 2.1). In both countries, a rising percentage of the population resides in cities. In 2000 79% of the U.S. population lived in urban areas. In Canada, 65% of the population lived in metropolitan areas, with half of this population residing in the three largest urban areas:

Toronto, Montreal, and Vancouver. Nearly three out of four Americans and Canadians live in cities, and experts predict that by 2030 this percentage could be as high as 85%. Without a doubt, urbanism is the norm in the United States and Canada (hereafter, "North America" in this chapter).[1]

North American cities are being transformed by this third revolution. Central cities have characteristically become sites of new urban spectacles: inner cities are pockmarked with sites touched by the gentrification renaissance but also feature rampant poverty and criminality; inner suburbs are showing the

[1]Although Honolulu is a U.S. city, it is included in chapter 12, "Australia and the Pacific Islands," where it is profiled as a distinctive city in that region.

first inklings of decline; and exurban development continues apace as gated communities and mixed-use developments sprawl into the former countryside. The new lexicon that has emerged to describe many North American cities—"postmodern," "global," "networked," "hybrid," "splintered"—offers some hint of the rich complexity and deep contradictions of the Third Urban Revolution. Yet much remains to be said and done before we can make sense of the new forms of urbanism that characterize the 21st century North American city.

One important trend in the Third Urban Revolution is the emergence of giant urban regions and megacities. A number of recent studies suggest that large urban regions are the new building blocks of both national and global economies. Scholars have identified globalizing city regions in which urban and industrial growth is concentrated.

The largest city region in the United States is the urbanized northeastern seaboard, a region first designated by Jean Gottmann as a megalopolis. This megalopolis stretches from just south of Washington, D.C., north through Baltimore, Philadelphia, and New York to Boston. It is responsible for 20% of the nation's gross domestic product. In 1950 this megalopolis had a population of almost 32 million people. By 2000 the population had increased to almost 49 million. It continues to remain a significant center for the nation's population with almost one in six U.S. residents living in this giant urban region.

Another term used to describe new urban transformations is *megalopolitan*. Megalopolitan regions are defined as clustered networks of metropolitan regions that either have populations of more than 10 million or will exceed that number, on current growth projections, by 2010. They derive from at least

Table 2.1 Megalopolitan Areas in the United States

Area	Anchor Cities
Cascadia	Seattle, Portland, Eugene
NorCal	San Francisco, San Jose, Oakland, Sacramento
Southland	Los Angeles, San Diego, Las Vegas
Valley of the Sun	Phoenix, Tucson
I-35 Corridor	Kansas City, Oklahoma City, Dallas, San Antonio
Gulf Coast	Houston, New Orleans, Mobile
Piedmont	Birmingham, Atlanta, Charlotte, Raleigh
Peninsula	Tampa, Miami, Orlando
Midwest	Chicago, Madison, Detroit, Indianapolis, Cincinnati
Northeast	Richmond, Washington, D.C., Philadelphia, New York, Boston

Source: Adapted from the Metropolitan Institute at Virginia Tech University.

two or more contiguous metropolitan areas. A megalopolitan area is created when big cities bump up against small towns, gobble up farmlands, and ultimately merge into expansive urban forms. In the United States there are 10 megalopolitan regions that include New York, Chicago, Los Angeles, Atlanta, Dallas, Miami, San Francisco, Houston, Seattle, and Phoenix (tab. 2.1). Collectively, these 10 large city regions constitute only 19.8% of the nation's land surface, yet they comprise 67.4% of the population and approximately three-quarters of all predicted growth in population and construction from 2010 to 2040.

Yet another term to describe the ways that global investment, sophisticated communications, and widespread corporate and personal mobility are transforming cities in North America into a new type of urban form is the *global city-region*. In an era of globalization, cities increasingly function as the nodes of the global economy, so it is more appropriate to see the city, or networks of cities, in its regional context. The term global city-region attempts to capture the reorganization of metropolitan areas as a result of globalization. Metropolitan areas such as Toronto are expanding the scope of services and influences beyond their greater metropolitan zones. Los Angeles is also touted as a global city-region, as are San Diego, Seattle, and New York. These cities are making a transition from national or regional economic capitals to more integrated cities of the world. Toronto, which has traditionally been the focus of an economic and cultural East–West Canadian economy, is increasingly turning its attention to the North–South opportunities created by the North American Free Trade Agreement. Distinguishing features of global city-regions are elite, globally oriented corridors that contrast sharply with disadvantaged, insular residual cities.

There are numerous transformations occurring in contemporary North American cities that contrast with long held myths about them. One myth is that cities in the United States and Canada lack historic character. This is simply not true in history-rich cities such as Savannah, Charleston, Boston, Montreal, and Quebec City, where historic preservation has retained some portion of the historic built environment. This myth is also at odds with cities that are increasingly restoring or reconstructing historic areas and districts. Another myth generalizes about the form and function of North American cities—the ubiquitous skyscrapers, freeways, shopping malls, office parks, and bland suburban "boxes"—are often cited as "distinct" to North American cities. However, in the age of globalization, these features can be found in cities throughout the world. The study of

cities in Canada and the United States is not only interesting but also critical to a more complete understanding of contemporary urbanization, and geographic information systems (GIS) are becoming more important in creating that understanding (box 2.1).

URBAN PATTERNS AT THE REGIONAL SCALE

U.S. and Canadian cities vary tremendously in size, form, and fortune. Regionally, there has been a concentration of population into certain metropolitan regions. In the United States, for example, recent urban growth has been robust in cities located in the West and Southwest, whereas some cities in the East and Northeast have seen economic decline and population exodus. In Canada, the fastest growing metropolitan areas are in Calgary and Edmonton. In the United States, Philadelphia and Buffalo have recorded population loss. At the local level (within urban regions), there has been a deconcentration of population from the central city coupled with suburban growth and exurban development.

One of the distinguishing features of urban North America is the tremendous range of diversity in both population and physical size: from the megacities of New York (at 21 million residents), Los Angeles (at 16 million), and Chicago (at nearly 10 million), to large cities of 5 million or more such as Miami, Atlanta, Toronto, Houston, Washington, D.C., and Philadelphia, to cities of 2 million such as Denver, Portland, Baltimore, Vancouver, and Ottawa, to smaller cities under 1 million such as Tulsa, Nashville, Calgary, Winnipeg, and Edmonton. And there are hundreds of small cities of less than 1 million people (fig. 2.1).

Box 2.1   Using GIS to Solve Urban Problems

Urban geography has been revolutionized by Geographic Information Systems (GIS). Computerized spatial analysis and GIS techniques allow geographers to interpret spatial patterns and trends within and across urban areas. GIS is used to analyze segregation (including housing, immigration, gentrification), flows and linkages (e.g., commuter flows, migration), politics (e.g., gerrymandering), locating economic activities (such as retail, manufacturing, and services), and to define the urban spatial structure such as rural–urban boundaries, suburbanization, and land-use change.

Using GIS, geographers can explore the internal structure of cities. For example, GIS can be used to study the location of hazardous waste facilities in relation to low-income or minority neighborhoods to understand the patterns and processes of the natural environment and how contaminants influence quality of life. This field, known as environmental justice, seeks to understand the inequities of environmental hazards and call attention to the fact that not all groups in the city are affected by pollution to the same degree. Another example involves the use of census data to show various demographic changes over time. These could include changes in income, ethnicity, home ownership, and rates of poverty.

GIS can also be used to explore the changing structure of urban areas and particularly the urban periphery. Land-use change maps, which show the change from open space and farmland to developed areas, are useful in determining patterns of suburbanization. And GIS can be used to compare and contrast cities. For example, using historical data, geographers can determine how housing density over time reveals patterns in exurban development. These patterns might reveal development and job growth along major highways and transportation corridors. GIS is increasingly becoming a critical tool for urban scholars and urban planners.

Historical Geography of Urban Development in the United States and Canada

Cities of North America are rather recent developments in terms of world urban history. Most cities are less than 300 years old; many developed only in the last 100 years. The contemporary North American city is primarily the product of economic forces, notably those that pertain to industrial development in the 19th and 20th centuries.

Colonial Mercantilism (1700–1840)

In the late 16th century, the British, French, Spanish, and Dutch began to colonize eastern North America. Colonial mercantilism was the result of European expansion into the Americas based on a collection of economic and political policies designed to keep the European state prosperous. Each European power in North America exercised various controls over commerce and industry and intervened in the markets. These economic regulations resulted in an export-based market. For example, the production of commodities in North America such as sugar, timber, and other staples were exported to Europe to satisfy changing patterns of consumption. In the colonial era, cities were very small in both population and physical size. They served as trading hubs that were essentially export centers for raw materials including fish, furs, timber, and agricultural products destined for Europe. The largest cities during this era were found along the Atlantic coast, such as Boston and Philadelphia, and along rivers and the Great Lakes. Quebec City and Montreal, located along the St. Lawrence River, controlled the northern route into the region, whereas New Orleans later became the gateway of the Mississippi.

The growth of cities during the colonial era was greatly influenced by the types of exports from the region. Quebec City was founded in 1608 by Samuel de Champlain. The French settlement was at first sparsely inhabited, serving mainly fur traders and missionaries. The French settlers established relations with the Algonquins, who traded beaver pelts in return for metal knives, axes, cloth, and other goods. Beaver pelts became highly prized and very expensive in European markets, thus fueling the continued export of beavers until they were overhunted. The physical layout of Quebec was typified by narrow, winding streets and a city wall, complete with watchtowers, built by the conquering British.

The city of New Orleans owes its origins and economic rationale to the Mississippi River. French traders, Jesuit priests, and functionaries traveled along the Mississippi in search of pelts, converts, and allies. The city of New Orleans was founded by a French merchant company in 1718. The attempt to build a trading city close to the mouth of the river encountered the watery geography of a giant delta, half marsh, half mud—a floating, spongy raft of shifting vegetation. The city was located 120 miles (193 km) from where the river flows into the Gulf of Mexico, at a bend in the river close to Lake Pontchartrain, a site that enabled the portage of goods from the lake to the city. It was easier to ship goods to the lake and transport them to the city than to sail up the ever-shifting Mississippi River. The city was an outpost of the French empire, part of a global network of colonial possessions that stretched from the Americas to Africa and Asia. And yet the city grew slowly. A 1764 map shows that one-third of the blocks were empty. Yet one distinguishing feature was the imposition of the French tradition of "long lots" fronting on the river, rather than irregular or square parcels of land.

In contrast to the French influence in New Orleans and Quebec City, Philadelphia was initially designed on a grid system, with a series of four major squares or markets. Philadelphia was founded in 1681 as an English Quaker settlement at the confluence of the Delaware and Schuylkill rivers. The city's founder William Penn designed the plan in reaction to the disorder of his hometown, London. His symmetrical, orderly plan became the template for Philadelphia's later growth. The city became a busy shipping port, for both external goods (feed, food, and tobacco destined for England) and internal products (rifles and Conestoga wagons). It was also a major banking center and was home to the first U.S. stock exchange (1790). Yet for nearly two centuries Philadelphia, like many colonial cities, would remain small.

For much of the colonial era, cities were "walking cities" that rarely covered more than a few square miles or had more than 100,000 people. The outward expansion of many North American cities was limited by several "site" factors including topography and transportation. In some cities the high ground was avoided because it was difficult to pump water or to get horse-drawn fire services uphill. Early forms of public transport, primarily carts and carriages, also found steep hills hard going. Economic growth would later bring new forms of transportation, and cities would begin to grow outwards and upwards.

Early Industrial Capitalism (1840–1870)

The era of industrial capitalism marks the transformation of the U.S. economy from one that was based primarily on trade in natural resources to one that processed resources and manufactured products. (Canada's transformation would come later.) An industrial economy is one dominated by industry and machine manufacture. In 1800 approximately 7% of the U.S. population was urban. By 1900, it was more than 40% urban. Urban growth went hand-in-hand with the industrialization of the economy. The economic foundations of the industrial city were the exploitation of the coal mine, the vastly increased production of iron, and a source of steady, reliable mechanical power—the steam engine. All of this was accompanied by an unprecedented population increase and the subsequent enlargement of urban areas. By 1830 New York, Philadelphia, and Baltimore were the main industrial coastal cities in the United States, and Toronto and Montreal dominated in what would become Canada. Interior urban development was also fueled by industrial expansion. Cities located along rivers and lakes took advantage of advances in transportation technology, such as canals and

railroads, to become important hubs in the distribution of goods. Buffalo, Pittsburgh, St. Louis, Chicago, and Cincinnati emerged as key gateways. In Canada, Winnipeg became the hub of rail service for the west, and Edmonton and Calgary emerged as major regional service centers by the 1870s.

National Industrial Capitalism (1870–1935)

As industrial capitalism progressed, the emergence of powerful national corporations and large-scale assembly-line manufacturing prompted robust economic growth. Growth was also stimulated by the enormous influx of more than 25 million immigrants from Europe between 1885 and 1911. Although many of the biggest cities were still located in the Northeast, Midwest cities such as Chicago, Detroit, and Cleveland gained in importance (fig. 2.2).

From 1885 to 1935, the U.S. economy completed its transformation from an agricultural and mercantile base to an industrial-capitalist one. Cities around the Great Lakes area grew into vital industrial centers by the 1920s. Also during this time, Canada's economy experienced major transformation and urban growth in the West, spurred by manufacturing in central Canada and by the rapid growth of the petroleum and natural gas industry in the urban centers of Calgary and Edmonton.

Industrialization was more than just a proliferation of factories. Many key inventions changed the look of cities and transformed spatial patterns. The use of iron, and then steel, in construction launched the era of skyscrapers. In the 1880s the electric street-trolley helped to make mass transit possible and laid the foundations for 20th century suburbanization by allowing people to live

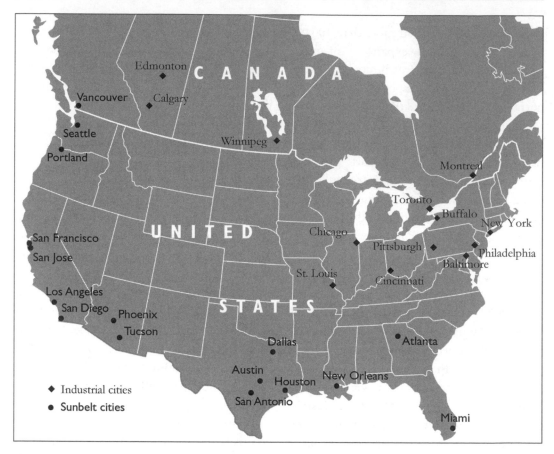

Figure 2.2   Industrial and Sunbelt Cities. *Source:* Compiled by authors.

farther away from the city center. As a result, most industrial cities grew outwards at the edges as well as upwards in the center.

The industrial city, however, had become saturated with air, water, and refuse problems. Few cities had paved roads, sanitary systems, or garbage collection. Pollution was no longer just a nuisance—it was an unwanted and sometimes dangerous by-product of industrialization. Cities in which disease was common began to lose business to those that were healthier. New Orleans, which suffered ongoing outbreaks of cholera, lost out to Chicago; in Memphis, outbreaks of typhoid and dysentery almost destroyed the economy. An increased concern for public health launched

the sanitary revolution that ushered in widespread construction of clean water systems, sewer systems, and waste-water treatment plants, thereby dramatically decreasing the outbreak of diseases.

Although most cities had open land within city limits (vegetable gardens, squares, commons), these were not often formalized as public spaces or recreational areas. The urban public park movement began with a recognition of the importance of open spaces to the health and vitality of the urban population. Landscape architects such as Frederick Law Olmsted designed parks including Central Park (New York City), the Boston Common and Emerald

Necklace (Boston), Golden Gate Park (San Francisco), Mont Royal Park (Montreal), and the Lakeshore area of Chicago. In Vancouver, Stanley Park was completed in 1888. Toronto's High Park, today considered the "crown jewel" in a very large urban park system, was ceded to the city in 1873. The legacy of the public park movement of the 19th century continues to provide 21st century urban residents with vital spaces for recreation and contemplation.

Mature Industrial Capitalism (1935–1975)

During this economic era, many U.S. and Canadian national corporations merged or expanded into large multinational corporations and achieved dominance with respect to the North American market. The end of World War II marked a significant turning point for cities in North America. It was the beginning of a new era in which the United States would emerge as the largest, richest economy and by the end of the 20th century as the world's single superpower. It was also the era of the automobile and suburbanization. Reliance on the automobile and weak investment in public transportation resulted in low population densities and increased sprawl, particularly for cities in the West. Cities such as Los Angeles, San Diego, Houston, Phoenix, Dallas, and Denver grew horizontally as much as vertically. The vast geographical expanse of these cities was propelled by the automobile, which had permeated society by the 1940s and 1950s. From 1950 onward, the United States simultaneously became more urban and more suburban. While urban regions continued to grow, there was an exodus of people from the core to the surrounding regions. To lure suburbanites back to the city, municipalities undertook immense urban renewal projects that included public works, highways, bridges, and civic centers. By the late 1960s, however, significant changes materialized that would have profound impacts on cities throughout North America: globalization and deindustrialization.

Postindustrial Capitalism (1975 to the Present)

We have entered into a new era of global capitalism. Four impacts of globalization on urban development include deindustrialization, decentralization, the expansion of Sunbelt cities, and the rise of service-sector economies.

By the 1970s and 1980s many corporations were moving out of North America to developing countries where lower labor costs and tax breaks promised higher profit margins and/or larger market shares. In cities such as Pittsburgh, Syracuse, Buffalo, Akron, Cleveland, and Detroit companies fired or relocated workers, closed factories, and moved out of the region or country. These cities transformed from "industrial" to "Rustbelt," from vibrant manufacturing centers to ghost towns of despair. Even growth cities such as Los Angeles and San Francisco struggled to cope with a decline in manufacturing employment that had both economic and social consequences. The loss of manufacturing employment marked a critical shift in the North American economy. Michael Moore's 1989 documentary "Roger and Me" chronicled the massive job losses and factory closings in Flint, Michigan, home to General Motors. Between 1980 and 1989 General Motors laid off 40,000 people in Flint—some 50% of Flint's GM workforce—an event of unprecedented proportion in American history. Jobs fell from 76,000 in 1978, to 62,000 in 1986, to 19,000 in 2002. Flint continues to face hard times. In 2004, Flint's unemployment rate was about 16%, three times the national average. For many industrial cities, high unemployment rates continue to impact local economies. We should keep in mind that U.S. and Canadian cities are always evolving. In traditional industrial cities, political and economic leaders have generated strategies to replace lost jobs and investment by attracting other economic sectors such as services or tourism.

At the same time that many cities in the Northeast saw economic decline, others experienced rapid growth. Cities such as Seattle, Orlando, Miami, Phoenix, and San Diego successfully blended an existing industrial base with an expanding service sector. Newer cities, such as Atlanta, Charlotte, Fort Worth, and Silicon Valley (an urban region located between San Francisco and San Jose in proximity to several area universities in the foothills along the San Andreas Fault), came into their own at this time. Silicon Valley is home to Apple and Hewlett-Packard, leaders in the high-technology sector that emerged after the 1980s.

The process of decentralization also characterizes this era. Decentralization occurs when city centers lose either population or jobs. A serious result is a decline in the tax base for the city, which limits city funding of social services, education, and infrastructure (box 2.2). Residents and jobs leave the center of the city for the suburbs or other metropolitan and even nonmetropolitan areas. 1970 marks the first time there was an actual decline in central-city populations, and by 1980 the trend was intensifying. Most people were relocating to the suburbs.

The rise of the service sector has also played a critical role in urban development. The service sector (wholesale and retail trade, finance, insurance, real estate, information and communication technologies, and services including education and hospitals) has replaced manufacturing employment as a key component of the urban economy. The service sector is highly diverse. Some jobs are low-level and pay at or slightly above minimum wage; these jobs include data entry, cleaning services, and retail (salesclerks at the Gap, or waiters at a restaurant). Other jobs—often referred to as quaternary activities—generate far higher wages. These include research and development, brokerage services, banking, medicine, law, advertising, computer engineering, and software development.

The Sunbelt, a region that stretches from Florida to California and south of the 37th parallel, has seen the most dramatic growth in the past 20 years. The term "Sunbelt" refers less to an absolute geographic area and is used as shorthand to describe cities in the South, West, and Pacific Northwest that have seen increased economic growth, increased population, and increased prestige within the urban hierarchy (fig. 2.2). Sunbelt cities have been successful primarily because their economies were more diverse and did not rely on industrialization. In addition, the Sunbelt grew primarily as a result of the expansion of the service sector. Sunbelt cities benefited from significant government investment in aerospace (Houston, Seattle, Los Angeles), petrochemicals (Houston, Dallas), and the emergence of information technology corridors such as Silicon Valley (San Jose, San Francisco). Some cities have become global transaction centers, linking local, regional, and national economies to the network of international capital markets. As a result,

Box 2.2   Homeless in Los Angeles

Los Angeles became the homeless capital of the United States in the 1980s. In alarming numbers, Angelenos were cast away from traditional anchors of family, job, and community as waves of economic and social polarization resulted in spreading homelessness. Many thousands were precariously housed, living in fear of eviction or foreclosure, doubled up with family or friends, or constantly on the move as livelihoods and life-sustaining relationships eroded and personal vulnerabilities came to outweigh strengths.

There are many pathways to homelessness in Los Angeles, and as many poignant and disturbing variations on those pathways as there are homeless people. Without detracting from the authority of those homeless voices, it is clear that Angelenos became homeless in record numbers because of powerful systemic forces that shaped their lives in profound ways. These forces, operating at spatial scales ranging from global to local, led to a restructuring of the regional economy, loss of critical welfare state supports, and a shrinking supply of low-cost housing. Combined, they created a swelling population of economically marginalized and precariously housed people. Some of these people became homeless, outcasts from the city's riches and entitlements. . . .

The shift to post-Fordism meant the elimination of thousands of jobs from traditional manufacturing industries. Additional jobs were lost as the public sector retrenched, and defense downsizing led to massive loss of aerospace jobs in the region. . . . The poor and homeless faced ever-dwindling federal and state health and welfare supports and increasingly hostile and penurious local welfare systems. . . .

With notable exceptions, local government officials remained spectators at the unfolding homelessness crisis. . . . Their (in)actions ranged from suing one another over perceived dereliction of duties to simply transporting homeless people to neighboring cities. Most cities spent little or nothing on the homeless and did little in the way of adjusting their plans and policies to encourage the delivery of homeless services or prevent people from becoming homeless in the first place. . . .

Thus have hundreds of thousands of people been impoverished by the complex interaction of global, national and local economic forces; becoming marginally housed in crowded, unaffordable dwellings; and found the social welfare safety net swept out from beneath them without much local assistance in sight. They now teeter on the edge of homelessness with little except chance to hold them back. For those that lose this high-stakes game of chance, a new mendicancy awaits on street corners throughout Los Angeles, where homeless people cluster to beg coins from passersby.

Source: Jennifer Wolch, "From Global to Local: The Rise of Homelessness in Los Angeles during the 1980s," in Allen J. Scott and Edward J. Soja, eds., *The City: Los Angeles and Urban Theory at the End of the Twentieth Century.* (Berkeley: University of California Press, 1996), 201–202, 210.

Dallas, San Francisco, Los Angeles, Vancouver, Seattle, and Miami have become significant players in a global urban hierarchy.

THE CHANGING CHARACTER OF U.S. AND CANADIAN CITIES

Globalization and the Urban Hierarchy

A major factor underlying urban change today is the tie of cities to global trends. The past two decades have seen intensified competition among cities at the global scale. At the apex of the global urban hierarchy are *global cities*. Global cities have been defined as major sites for the accumulation of capital, command points in the world economy, headquarters for corporations, important hubs for global transportation and communication, intensified areas of social polarization, and points of destination for domestic and international migrants. London, New York, and Tokyo sit atop the global urban network.

Globalization has spatially restructured cities. In the most competitive and successful world cities, new financial districts, luxurious residential areas, and unprecedented property booms are indicators of the benefits of globalization and a competitive position in the urban hierarchy. Almost all cities are impacted by globalization, but not all cities become "global cities." For example, many urban boosters no longer focus solely on recruiting or attracting domestic firms, but attempt to secure investment internationally. The presence of international banks, department stores, and other retail establishments provide a visual cue that cities bear the imprint of globalization. However, the term global city is reserved for those cities that are among the most influential within the global economy.

Consider the changing urban location of *Fortune 500* company headquarters. In the 1950s and 1960s the largest cities in the Northeast and Midwest, including Chicago, Boston, Philadelphia, Pittsburgh, and Toronto, were home to the world's largest industrial companies. In 1960 New York was home to 6 of the top 10 *Fortune 500* headquarters including Standard Oil, General Electric, U.S. Steel, Mobil Oil, Texaco, and Western Electric. Today the number of *Fortune 500* corporate headquarters in New York has fallen by half. Some firms such as General Electric and Xerox have moved to the suburbs or the Sunbelt. Just recently, Seattle-based Boeing decided to move its headquarters to Chicago, and Volkswagen announced it would leave Detroit and move to Washington, D.C. The biggest growth in corporate headquarters is occurring in Orlando, West Palm Beach, Greensboro, Atlanta, Dallas, and Houston. The changing geographic distribution is the result of many factors: the relocation of a company, the rise and fall of local firms, or the merger of two companies. The lower costs of office space and housing in medium-sized cities such as Houston or Greensboro provide another reason for a company to relocate. Although many global firms have relocated, most have chosen metropolitan areas of at least 1 million.

Because the key globalization arenas have been concentrated in Europe and North America, and more recently East Asia, cities in these regions tend to dominate the global urban hierarchy. Cities such as Miami, Phoenix, San Diego, Los Angeles, San Francisco, Washington, D.C., Toronto, and Vancouver have become key urban centers in the global economy and North American urban hierarchy. Some cities have benefited from globalization and have eclipsed their rivals. For example, many corporate headquarters have moved from Montreal to Toronto, which has become the major conduit between the rest of the country and the international capital markets, whereas Calgary and Edmonton serve as crucial links to the more specialized international petroleum industry. Quebec City has also transitioned to a more diverse, postindustrial economy. The North American Free Trade Agreement of 1993 has resulted in an increase of exports from Quebec City to the United States. In addition to a fairly robust aerospace industry, tourism, information technology, and biotechnology compose some of the economic growth sectors for Quebec City.

Other cities have fallen down the hierarchy. Detroit, Cleveland, Buffalo, and Pittsburgh have experienced a decline, as manufacturing has left the region. These cities struggle to compete for coveted global linkages and networks that promise to reinvigorate their economies. In Canada, Thunder Bay, St. Johns, and Halifax contend with the challenges of an urban economy based on natural resources. Halifax, historically a major port for maritime trade in fish and forest staples, has seen economic decline as those products have ceased to be as central to eastern Canada's economy. The city has also declined in population as many young people leave the region for other Canadian cities in search of better job opportunities. However, the potential for offshore oil and natural gas may make Halifax more relevant in the future.

There are various articulations of the urban hierarchy. Some cities compete for financial command functions—stock markets, banks, multinational corporate headquarters, and other forms of capital exchange. New York is the most important city in this regard, followed by Chicago and Toronto. Other articulations include the multicultural command centers that make important linkages to other regions via their immigrant populations. These cities include Vancouver, Miami, and Los Angeles. Some cities have found a niche in the hierarchy by establishing important air route connections through the global airline network. These cities include Toronto, Los Angeles, Seattle, Memphis (home to Federal Express), Atlanta (home to UPS), and Anchorage (important for military air routes). There are also cities resurrecting their place in the urban hierarchy. For example, both Cleveland and Pittsburgh, which experienced economic decline and massive job losses associated with deindustrialization, have successfully realigned their economies. Although some of the old industrial companies remain, their revamped economies are currently growing based on health-care facilities that have gained national reputations. To some extent they have moved back up the hierarchy, albeit in a more specialized role.

The North American urban hierarchy reflects and embodies social, economic, and demographic changes associated with globalization. As competition within the urban hierarchy continues, a city's perceived position within the hierarchy can drive local urban development.

Cities and the Olympic Games

The creation of a more global city is one of the main goals and consequences of hosting the Games. In some cases the goal is explicit, as cities now use the Olympics as a way to open up the city region to the wider world. The Games provide an opportunity for a city to showcase itself to a global audience. The city becomes more physically connected to the rest of the world while its image is circulated through the mass media. Hosting the Games allows the city to achieve global recognition with the possibility of increased tourism and investment. The Summer Games in particular have a wider global television audience, more participants, and more spectators than the Winter Games. Hosting the Summer Games is a highly coveted opportunity.

Many North American cities have hosted both Winter and Summer Games (tab. 2.2). Recently, Toronto bid, unsuccessfully, to host the Summer Games in 1996 and 2008; New York City's bid for the 2012 games was also unsuccessful (they were awarded to London). Vancouver was awarded the 2010 Winter Games. The participation of North American cities is second only to Europe and indicates these cities' reputation and influence in the global urban hierarchy.

Hosting the Games involves not only a creative vision but also a physical restructuring of the city, an opportunity for urban renewal. The construction of the Olympic Village and projects such as the construction of new roads and sewer systems, and the creation or improvement of parks, plazas, and streets, links the Games with urban renewal. Often this involves upgrading the city's infrastructure and transportation networks, renovating of the seafront, and/or organizing the historic center. The cooperation between public and private agencies and the new use of metropolitan-wide governments necessitates better comprehensive planning. Hosting the Games leaves a physical legacy that has

Table 2.2   U.S. and Canadian Host Cities of Olympic Games, 1976–2012

Summer Games	Winter Games
1996 Atlanta	2010 Vancouver
1984 Los Angeles	2002 Salt Lake City
1976 Montreal	1988 Calgary
1932 Los Angeles	1980 Lake Placid, NY
	1932 Lake Placid, NY

Source: International Olympic Committee.

longer-term development potential. Perhaps the largest infrastructural legacy is the upgrade of airports, telecommunications, mass transit schemes, and road networks that quite literally better connect the city to global flows of people, ideas, and commerce.

The large and expensive nature of facility provision raises the issue of post-Games usage. In the case of Los Angeles and Atlanta, the facilities were turned over to various private and nongovernment public agencies. In Atlanta, for example, the specially built 85,000-seat Olympic Stadium was converted into the 52,000-seat home of the Atlanta Braves baseball team. The 15,000 resident Olympic Village became student housing for Georgia State University. There were some public legacies. The most notable is Centennial Olympic Park in the middle of downtown Atlanta. The Park was handed over to the state of Georgia after the Games and has become a popular public park, a centerpiece of downtown activities that hosts 160 events and receives 1 million visitors a year. It is a multipurpose space that contains a fountain, green space, and hardscape, and it is used as a children's playground and a concert site. It is a space tied into further downtown investment and development.

Figure 2.3   The Olympic venue in Montreal, built for the 1976 summer games, now stands neglected. (Photo by John Short)

However, not all cities have been successful at converting Olympic venues into vibrant urban centers. In Montreal, the main Olympic Stadium is deteriorating and is widely seen as a monument to a costly experience (fig. 2.3). Sadly this deterioration is not unique; the city was unable to retain its National League Baseball Team, the Expos, which has now relocated to Washington, D.C., with the promise of a new state-of-the-art stadium.

The Games are a catalyst for urban renewal, environmental remediation, and improvements to a city's infrastructure that can make the city more competitive on the world stage. The Games can also reposition the city in the global imaginary. A successful Games can promote a positive global image of the city and stimulate tourism and investment. Hosting the Olympics has become an important goal for many urban political regimes around the world because they provide a huge development opportunity with the possibility of changing how their city is perceived. An interesting question is whether the Games move cities up the hierarchy, or whether they are the result of cities that have moved up the hierarchy.

Greening the City

Before the 1970s, ecology had little role in urban planning and landscape design. By the 1980s, however, urban planners noted the importance of nature in the city and recognized that it has powerful implications for how the city is designed, built, and maintained (box 2.3). There are numerous examples of ways that cities have begun to reconnect to the natural world within the urban landscape. Greening the city can involve tree-planting programs, heritage preservation, smart buildings, urban farms, urban forests, ecosystem restoration, bicycle-friendly programs, improved recycling programs, restricted use of cars, and expansion of open spaces. Whether called green

Box 2.3   Cities and Nature: Toronto's Don River

Toronto was first settled in 1787 when surveyors laid out a city plan for the future capital of Upper Canada, and in 1793 John Graves Simcoe became its first lieutenant Governor. The settlers harnessed the river's energy, built mills for lumber, flour, wool and paper, and mined the valley's clay and shale for brick-making, from which much of the early city was built. In less than 150 years, they cleared the lower valley of merchantable trees. The Don River was also perceived as a threat and an obstacle. Floods swept away mills and bridges, the river was an obstacle to the eastward expansion of the city and the great wetland, its mouth reviled as unhealthy swamp, lent credibility to the argument that straightening out the river and filling in the marshes would "secure the sanitary condition . . . to the said river." By the end of the century, engineers had turned the last 5 kilometers of the river's meanders, where it dropped its sediments, into a canal. The railways were built in the valley, and the Ashbridges Bay marshes were filled in to create the port lands, the most massive engineering project on the continent in its time, forcing the Don into a right-angle turn into the harbour. By the mid-20th century, the city had turned its back on the river, a gap between places rather than a place in itself. As a sensory experience it has become a forgotten place; unloved and unused. The roads and expressway, a legacy of the 1950s, have made the valley a transportation corridor, inhibiting access for walkers and cyclists. . . .

Moves to restore the river became an act of faith by the citizens of Toronto that grew out of the concerns of many people for the natural heritage of their city. Beginning as an informal citizen's organization, the "Task Force to Bring Back the Don" was formalized and supported by Toronto City Council in 1990. Its purpose was to begin the process of renewal of the most degraded part of the river that flows through the city of Toronto, and ultimately to imitate the restoration of the entire watershed. . . .

As an ongoing process of renewal and healing, the Don strategy involves key principles, including a fundamental understanding of process as a biological idea that is also integrated with social, economic and political agendas, economy of means where the most benefits are available for minimum input in energy and effort, and environmental education, where the understanding of nature in cities becomes part of a learning experience that begins with community empowerment and action.

Source: Michael Hough, *Cities and Natural Processes: A Basis for Sustainability*, 2nd ed. (New York: Routledge, 1995), 39, 42, 54.

cities, sustainable cities, or sustainable urban development, planning in U.S. and Canadian cities today more fully embraces urban ecology.

For many years cutting-edge architecture and sustainable design have, to a large extent, existed in separate camps. More recently, however, green builders, architects, and interior designers have created avant-garde designs for green buildings and, at smaller scale, green houses. Because buildings consume enormous quantities of the earth's resources in both their construction and daily operation, they are tremendous opportunities to showcase innovative, eco-friendly design. The conceptual framework behind green buildings is the incorporation of features that support the conservation of the environment. Green buildings are often designed and oriented to minimize summer afternoon solar heat gain and optimize winter solar heat gain. Some may use solar energy as an alternative to fossil fuels and green materials, which are produced without harming the environment, can be recycled, and may help reduce energy use. Many green builders select materials that do not have formaldehyde and that have nontoxic proprieties to improve indoor air quality. Another example is installing landscaping rather than paved surfaces, which impede storm-water infiltration. In large buildings, coverings called green roofs reduce energy costs and soak up rainwater. Even interiors incorporate materials and products that have high levels of renewability or reusability, such as bamboo flooring or cork tiles. Seattle, Portland, and Vancouver have been lauded as leaders in green design and green buildings (fig. 2.4); there are some 30 in Seattle alone. Chicago and Toronto have won numerous awards for advancing green roofs. Toronto initiated a "Green Roofs for Healthy Cities" program and has proposed a series of "green walls" where vegetation will grow on the sides of buildings. In addition to the cities mentioned above, others that are included as among the "greenest" by National Geographic's *Green Guide* are Austin, Boulder, Madison, Minneapolis, Oakland, and San Francisco.

Beginning in the 1960s and accelerating in the 1980s, many U.S. and Canadian cities have

Figure 2.4   Freeway Park in Seattle bridges over I-5 and other city roads. The 5.2-acre park, designed by Lawrence Halprin and opened on July 4, 1976, is a precedent-setting park that single-handedly defined a new land-use typology for American cities. (Photo by John Short)

sought to "reclaim" the waterfront for their urban populations by pursuing waterfront redevelopment. Deindustrialization resulted in abandoned warehouses and buildings and unused port facilities on city waterfronts. The advent of port containerization meant many older port facilities were inadequate for the new technology and became obsolete. Cities were forced to adapt to changed circumstances, to adjust to new economic impacts, and to create new spaces out of old industrial sites. Vacant lands were now opportunities. Today, waterfront redevelopment is widespread. Many

Figure 2.5   Baltimore's Inner Harbor is a success story showcasing the multi-use development strategy of restaurants, retail, office space, hotels, and residences. (Photo by John Short)

cities have transformed their waterfronts into vibrant public spaces that attract locals and tourists. Baltimore's Inner Harbor is often cited as a model U.S. waterfront redevelopment project. It has become the city's gathering place: home to the national aquarium, two sports stadiums, hotels, restaurants, museums, high-rise condominiums, and hotels. Similarly, in New York City, Battery Park was transformed into a vast complex of multi-use spaces that include office buildings, shops, restaurants, public space, and residences. In Boston, Pittsburgh, Toronto, and Vancouver, waterfronts have become the new festival spaces filled with sports stadiums, restaurants, and hotels. Even smaller cities such as Syracuse, Buffalo, Savannah, Victoria, Charleston, Austin, and Cleveland have transformed their harbors, lakes, or riverfronts.

Redevelopment is not without contestation: how and for what purposes these waterfronts are redeveloped can generate fierce debate and is not without a high price tag. The reconstruction of Baltimore's Inner Harbor cost $2.9 billion (fig. 2.5). Some criticize the social costs as well. The diversion of funds to Baltimore's Inner Harbor contrasts with the city's poor public school system and the perceived decline in many public services. In some cases, waterfront development is part of a valorization of selected parts of the urban landscape that can allow for the further enrichment of real estate interests at the expense of social welfare programs. While Baltimore's Inner Harbor flourishes, many inner-city neighborhoods continue to experience high crime rates, population loss, and housing abandonment.

Figure 2.6   The license plate on this bicycle in New York's Battery Park attests to the environmental, social, and political culture of this trendy public space. (Photo by Donald Zeigler)

Despite the substantial costs, waterfront transformations represent a dramatic story of urban rebirth—economically and environmentally (fig. 2.6). Waterfront redevelopment has restored the centers of cities to economic, social, and ecological health. It is one way cities have become "green."

MODELS OF URBAN STRUCTURE

Although there exits no single model that explains why things are located where they are within cities, we can generalize about the structure of North American cities. There are two general features that characterize most North American cities. The first is "sprawl," or the horizontal spread out from the central city. This is different from many other world regions where cities have remained densely developed. A second feature is that most North American cities are built on the grid system.

The average city in the United States and Canada has a land-use pattern that breaks down as follows: residential (30%); industrial/manufacturing (9%); commercial (4%); roads and highways (20%); public land, government buildings, and parks (15%); and vacant or undeveloped land (20%). The layout of these various land-use categories will differ according to the age of the city. For example, cities established prior to 1840 tend to have very dense or compact cores. For cities that developed later, during the 20th century, industrial activities might be located outside the core area, to take advantage of advances in transportation facilities such as railroads. Still other cities that saw development occur after 1950 have less concentrated cores with expansive residential zones because of the rise of the automobile and the emergence of suburbs. Typically however, North American cities have both high-rent and low-rent residential areas in the inner core, and moving outward into the suburbs, the price (and size) of single family homes tends to increase. Patterns of expansion and land-use often follow the concentric zone model.

The emergence of *edge cities* provides another contrasting model of urban structure. Edge cities consist of predominately large-square-footage office space located beyond the central city. The journalist Joel Garreau coined the term "edge cities" and defined them as:

- Having more than 5 million square feet of office space. This is enough to house between 20,000 and 50,000 office workers (as many as some traditional downtowns).
- Having more than 600,000 square feet of retail space, the size of a medium shopping mall.
- Having more jobs than bedrooms.
- Having nothing like a city before 1960.

These newer urban forms attract large numbers of service-sector workers during the day, but empty at night as residential areas are scarce. Garreau identified 123 places as being true edge cities, including two dozen in greater Los Angeles, 23 in metropolitan Washington, D.C., and 21 in greater New York City. Tyson's Corner, Virginia, west of Washington, is an example of an edge city. Other examples are found in Dallas–Forth Worth, Orlando, and Atlanta.

Edge cities may be a phenomenon of the 20th century, however. Because edge cities are built in and around major highway intersections, traffic congestion has become a problem. Pedestrian access is poor, and public transportation is nearly absent. Ironically, edge cities may stimulate redevelopment of the downtown core as people seek to leave their cars and commute by public transportation. Additionally, as development continues in and around edge cities, they may "merge" into megalopolitan areas with nodes of residential areas and nodes of commercial/business activity.

The grid plan, which imposes a rectangular street grid on urban space, dates from antiquity. Some of the earliest planned cities were built using grids; it is by far the most common pattern found in a variety of political societies from absolutionist powers to monarchies to democratic societies. The grid is a simple, rational order of packing the land, setting streets at right angles to one another. However, despite a multitude of geographies and topographies, of altitudes and latitudes, many North American cities on the grid share common design features: a lack of sensitivity to the physical environment, the imposition of the grid regardless of topography, a focus on the geometric (geometry over geography), and an underlying sense of the ability to control urban space. The 1734 Map of Savannah shows the rigid adoption of the grid (fig. 2.7). Similarly, San Francisco, which bears the Spanish imprint, nevertheless imposed a grid on what must be considered among the most dramatic topographies of North American cities.

In many U.S. and Canadian cities, the grid plan was nearly universal in the construction of new towns and cities. In part, this was the result of the influence of the European system. But another advantage of adopting the grid plan was that it allowed rapid subdivision of large parcels of land. As U.S. cities have grown outward, particularly after the mid-20th century, the grid has become less prevalent. The suburbs, designed with cul-de-sacs, winding lanes,

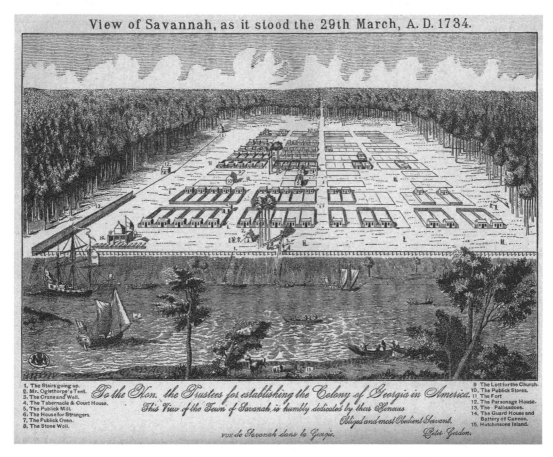

Figure 2.7 "View of Savannah, as it stood the 29th March, A.D. 1734." *Source:* Report on the Social Statistics of Cities, Compiled by George E. Waring Jr., U.S. Census Office, Part II, 1886. Courtesy of the University of Texas Libraries, University of Texas at Austin (http://www.lib. utexas.edu/maps/historical/savannah_1734.jpg).

and more organic forms, provide a purposeful contrast to the gridironed city. When cities and suburbs merge, as many have, the grid merges into a series of loops, curves, and open spaces, and its rigidity begins to disappear.

REPRESENTATIVE CITIES

New York City: Global Metropolis

The premier city in the United States and, in fact, all of North America, measured in terms of population, economic assets, corporate offices, and cultural attractions is New York City. In the city live 8.2 million people. In the tri-state metropolitan area live almost 19 million, making it larger than three-quarters of the world's independent nations. To many Americans, New York is the "pulse" of the nation and the world, and much of what occurs there reverberates through time and space. The economic preeminence of the "Big Apple" is one of its major trademarks: it is the nation's leading financial, shipping, transportation, communications, and convention center. The world's cultures, trends, and languages meet and mix on the streets of

New York and, more formally, in the headquarters of the United Nations.

New York City occupies a flat to very gently rolling landscape at the junction of two rivers, the Hudson and the East. The interpenetration of land and deep water makes the city one of the world's premier natural harbors: protected, yet within easy reach of the open ocean. The basement complex on Manhattan consists of hard metamorphic rocks that permit the construction of skyscrapers. The 102-story Empire State Building, built during the Great Depression, was for decades the tallest building in the world; only in 1973 was that role usurped by the twin towers of the 110-story World Trade Center. The collapse of the towers on September 11, 2001, left a gaping hole in the financial center of the city—both literally and figuratively. In 2006, however, construction began on Freedom Tower (a symbolic 1776 feet in height), which is destined to anchor the new World Trade Center complex. The extreme height of Manhattan's skyscrapers and the filling-in around the island's shoreline for warehouses and docks betray intense competition for land and its ultra-high cost. Central Park, a product of the urban parks movement of the Progressive Era, is the only extensive open space on the island of Manhattan.

Manhattan itself is one of five boroughs that comprise New York City. Although united since 1895, they all have distinct characters, ethnic identities, land uses, and problems. Manhattan represents the greatest concentration of wealth and vertical development in the country. Brooklyn (2.5 million) is noted for its beaches, parks, historic residential areas, cemeteries, and shipyards. The Bronx (1.3 million) is mainly a residential borough of extremes: the rich live along the Hudson River in Riverdale, and the poor in an area south of Bronx Park. Queens (2.2 million) is a residential suburb that experienced a growth surge after each of the world wars; it is also the site of LaGuardia and John F. Kennedy international airports. Staten Island is a more suburban residential area of New York, famous for the free passenger ferry that is its only direct link to Manhattan.

The earliest residents of what is presently New York City were the Algonquins, who called the island Man-a hat-ta, which meant "island of hills." The first European to enter New York harbor was the Italian explorer Giovanni da Verrazano, in 1524. Henry Hudson is credited with reaching Manhattan in 1609 and sailing up the river that bears his name. The Dutch West India Company, interested in establishing a trading base in North America, sent a group of settlers to Manhattan in 1624. Two years later a settlement was laid out and named New Amsterdam. That same year Governor Peter Minuit reputedly bought the entire island for goods worth about $24 from the Native Americans, an economic transaction heralded as one of the most prudent purchases of all time, at least from the settlers' viewpoint. The new settlement grew slowly and was initially confined to the southern tip of the island. Along the settlement's northern edge, a wall was built for protection; it was eventually torn down and later became Wall Street, the heart of today's financial district.

Since its beginning, New York was destined to become a major regional, national, and international city. Initially, the city vied with Philadelphia and Boston for commercial leadership. As the American population pushed westward, however, New York found itself to have an advantage over any other Atlantic coastal city; it occupied the terminus of a natural corridor through the

Figure 2.8   The Erie Canal, running through downtown Syracuse, New York, was critical in helping to establish New York City as the leading port and city in the United States.

Appalachians (via the Hudson Valley and Mohawk lowlands) and into the very heart of the continent, a region around the Great Lakes that was to become the nation's breadbasket and a preeminent foundry. By 1800, New York City, with its 60,000 residents, had become the largest in the country. With the completion of the Erie Canal in 1825 from the Hudson River to Lake Erie, New York was destined to become the unchallenged economic capital of the nation, and the focal point of what geographer Jean Gottmann was later to call Megalopolis (fig. 2.8). Stoking the growth of Megalopolis and the nation were the 12 million immigrants who arrived in New York City during the late 1800s and early 1900s. Past the Statue of Liberty (a gift from the French in 1886) they glided, destined for "processing" at nearby Ellis Island. The recent refurbishment of both landmarks was

planned to call attention to the role immigrant nationalities played in building the United States, the role New York City played as a gateway to a land of opportunity. Today metropolitan New York is one of the nation's most ethnically diverse areas. That characteristic, as much as anything, has made the "Big Apple" one of the world's premier cities, a position it seems destined to maintain.

Los Angeles: The World's Media Mogul

Los Angeles developed differently from urban places "out east." The form of its growth—horizontal and sprawling—reflected the popularity of a new transportation technology, the space-consuming automobile. The city itself shares Los Angeles County with 80 other municipalities, including Beverly Hills, Santa Monica, Pasadena, and Burbank. The sprawl of Greater Los Angeles makes the multicounty area one of the best examples of the multiple nuclei theory. That gargantuan sprawl, typified by the massive use of concrete for almost every structure, has leaped across the Santa Monica Mountains to the north, where it has completely transformed the landscape of the San Fernando Valley—"the Valley." It has also pushed eastward for 80 miles (129 km) into San Bernardino and Riverside counties on the edge of the desert, creating "the inland empire." Greater Los Angeles is home to almost 18 million people, 4 million of whom live in the city of Los Angeles. More than a third of the city's population is foreign-born, with the most recent waves of immigrants originating in Latin America, particularly Mexico, and Asia.

Los Angeles is truly a world city, not simply because of its size and metropolitan amenities, but also because of the people there assembled. In the Los Angeles Unified School District, with its 680,000 students (only about 15 cities in the United States are larger in total student population) at least 80 different languages are spoken, and a major topic of debate is whether to encourage such linguistic diversity or to make English the official language. Also controversial is the conflict that has evolved between long-time minority groups, notably African Americans, and newcomers—Hispanics and Asians— particularly as it relates to jobs and housing.

Images of Los Angeles that readily come to mind include (1) the worship of the automobile, evident in the city's 650 miles (1,050 km) of freeway, ubiquitous parking ramps and lots, drive-in establishments of every kind, wide streets, and numerous shopping centers; (2) the neatly arranged, but "placeless," subdivisions with single-family ranch houses equipped with outdoor patios, barbecue grills, and swimming pools; (3) the prevalence and seeming acceptance of widely held differences in political philosophy (extremes on the right are more acceptable here than in San Francisco), lifestyles, and religious practices; (4) the apparent disregard for many potentially serious environmental hazards, including earthquakes (treated on the evening news in the same manner as baseball scores), brush fires, and mud slides; (5) the affinity for glamour, glitter, and Porsches that is attributed to movie and television stars and recreational amenities of Southern California; and (6) a more relaxed and open atmosphere than is evident in either New York City or Chicago.

The site of Los Angeles was originally occupied by a small branch of Shoshone Indians, who lived along a perennially flowing section of the Los Angeles River. They were there when the explorer Juan Cabrillo, supported by the Spanish crown, discovered the village of Yangna in 1542. The next Spanish contact was in 1769, when a captain and Franciscan priest led an expedition north from San Diego. The party visited Yangna, liked the site, and called it El Pueblo de Nuestra Señora la Reina de Los Angeles de Porcíuncula ("The Town of Our Lady the Queen of the Angels of Porcíunula") after an Italian chapel associated with St. Francis of Assisi. The Spanish settlement became a center for farming and ranching. The first Anglo settlers arrived by land in 1841, but Mexicans and Spaniards remained the dominant populations. When Mexico lost the Mexican War in 1848, the United States obtained control of both the city and the territory. In 1850, the village had only 1,600 inhabitants. Growth continued at a slow pace until railroads came in 1876 and 1885, linking the city to the rest of the United States. Competition between the Southern Pacific and Santa Fe lines drove down the price of transportation, increasing Los Angeles's attractiveness for industry and fueling its population growth. Once rail routes were open to northern California and the Middle West, the population leaped to 50,000 by 1890 and to 100,000 by 1900.

The city's growth started in earnest with the completion of the artificial harbor at San Pedro in 1914. (Los Angeles cannot boast the inviting natural harbors that San Francisco or San Diego can.) San Pedro has matured into the combined ports of Los Angeles and Long Beach, which together comprise the largest port on North America's west coast, handling bulk and container cargo, plus cruise ships and a ship construction and repair industry. Tourism and the entertainment business brought in additional jobs and investment dollars as did the oil industry, which had begun somewhat earlier. Thousands of unemployed workers moved into Los Angeles and Southern California during the Great Depression of the 1930s. While the city was not as hard hit as others, it did benefit by having a large talent pool for manufacturing a variety of industrial and military goods needed for World War II. Petroleum, chemicals, aircraft, tires, and motor vehicles were all in great demand. The companies and industries attracted new migrants from all over the United States, but particularly from the South and the Middle West. By 1945 the city had mushroomed and was still growing because of the area's situation vis-à-vis expanding West Coast markets; its physical amenities, which attracted tourists and retirees; and huge outlays of federal monies supporting military and aerospace industries. Today, Los Angeles is the West Coast's leading wholesale distribution center and financial center, and Los Angeles International Airport is the world's fifth busiest in passenger traffic.

Despite its vibrant economy, Los Angeles also has problems. A major one is the extremely high cost of living. Others include high transportation costs, traffic congestion, the lack of an effective mass transit system, and extremes of wealth and poverty that remain in spite of riots by Black Americans during 1965 and 1992 and by Mexican Americans in 1970 and 1971. Large numbers of both groups feel the brunt of discrimination in housing, employment, and education; they are not part of the publicized Southern California lifestyle. Automobile- and industrial-based smog is only one of several environmental problems the city faces, and lack of water is calling into question the ability of this semiarid region to support any further growth of population, industry, or agriculture (fig. 2.9). The only alternatives seem to be conservation and a turn toward the sea. Until very recently, the city was without a downtown skyline of significance because most tall buildings were declared vulnerable to earthquakes in the 1930s and thus prohibited. In the 1980s, however, the policy changed, and the decade saw a downtown boom in high-rise office buildings, three-quarters of which are now foreign owned or controlled.

Cleveland and Detroit: Shrinking Cities

Overall the U.S. national economy has seen growth and prosperity; however, some cities confront a still declining or stagnant economy and a shrinking population. In 1950, the population of municipal Cleveland was 900,000, but by 2005 it had fallen to less than half of that. In 1950, Detroit, once home to both GM and Ford and dubbed "Motor City" and "Motown," was home to 1.8 million residents. By 2005 its population had also fallen by half. These two former industrial giants have experienced a reversal of fortune.

Figure 2.9   Los Angeles, long plagued by smog problems, has also led the way in automobile emissions reductions. Cars are required to pass yearly emissions testing at smog stations such as this. (Photo by John Short)

Cleveland has struggled with the legacy of deindustrialization to reinvent itself in the more competitive global economy. Initiatives to rebuild Cleveland have replicated the "formula" that many cities have employed: new museums, sports stadiums, convention centers, the renovation of old industrial warehouse districts for housing and retail, and waterfront development. Cleveland has tried them all. One of the most successful projects is the "Rock and Roll Hall of Fame and Museum," which opened to the public in 1995. The building, located on the shore of Lake Erie, was crucial in the redevelopment of Cleveland's waterfront area. In addition, new downtown sports stadiums for the professional teams have revitalized the area. The Gateway Sports Complex cost $360 million and features an open-air stadium for baseball and an indoor arena for basketball. Currently, the city is redeveloping the waterfront along both Lake Erie and the Cuyahoga

River as a destination for tourists and locals alike. Despite the redevelopment of its downtown, many of Cleveland's inner suburbs continue to decline, and overall urban growth remains negligible.

In Detroit, when high-paying manufacturing jobs became scarce and unemployment high, many residents lost their homes or apartments to foreclosure or eviction. Record rates of suicide, spousal abuse, and alcoholism became prevalent. At the same time that unemployment plagued the city, the crack cocaine epidemic of the 1980s and 1990s led to drug-related violence and property crimes, which gave Detroit the notorious distinction of being one of the most crime-ridden cities in North America.

Redevelopment has been a buzzword since the 1990s, but the process has had mixed results. The Renaissance Center was originally walled off from the city and looked more like an imposing   fortress   than   a   welcoming redevelopment project. In the mid-1990s, three casinos opened up in the downtown. In 2000, Comerica Park replaced historic Tiger Stadium as the home of the Detroit Tigers, and in 2002 the NFL Detroit Lions returned to a new downtown stadium, Ford Field. The 2004 opening of "The Compuware" gave downtown Detroit its first significant new office building in a decade. The city hosted the 2005 Major League Baseball All-Star Game and Super Bowl XL in 2006, both of which prompted more improvements to the downtown area. Currently, Detroit is constructing a riverfront promenade park similar to the one directly across the river in Windsor, Ontario, replacing acres of train tracks and some abandoned buildings with several miles of uninterrupted parkland.

Yet in 2006, metropolitan Detroit's unemployment rate of 8.6% was topped only by communities devastated by Hurricane Katrina. Detroit remains one of the nation's poorest cities, with more than one-third of residents below the poverty line; the city is also highly segregated. As of 2001, the city of Detroit was 81% African American, 12% White, and 5% Hispanic. The city's foreign-born population stood at 4.8%, one of the lowest percentages in the 50 largest cities in the country. Abandoned housing ranks as one of the city's most persistent problems. According to the U.S. Census, more than 38,000 housing units, or 10% of the city's housing, are vacant or abandoned, creating obstacles to urban revitalization. Both Detroit and Cleveland continue to experience mixed results in efforts to realign and reinvigorate their economies.

Calgary and "The Research Triangle": Boom Cities

In contrast to shrinking cities, North America is also home to cities experiencing tremendous growth, including Calgary, Alberta, and the Research Triangle of North Carolina, which is anchored by Raleigh, Durham, and Chapel Hill. Other boom cities include Phoenix, Tucson, San Diego, and Las Vegas, some of the fastest growing metropolitan areas in the West.

Calgary is home to the majority of Canada's oil and gas production companies, major pipeline operators, oilfield service and drilling companies, and energy-related engineering and consulting firms. Since 2005, oil prices have been at an all-time high, and Alberta's prosperity has created an economic boom unrivalled since the first heady oil days of the 1970s and early 1980s. The city has seen job growth and a rising housing market. In 2006, 22,000 new jobs were generated. Even the city's vacancy of office space is at an all time low of 9.7%. Its current economic prosperity has drawn numerous young people to the city. As a result, Calgary is one of the "youngest" cities in Canada.

Although it might appear that Calgary is a one-industry town, urban economic and political leaders are working hard to diversify the city's economic base in an effort to protect it from the volatility of the petroleum and energy sector. More than 4,300 petroleum engineers and 77,600 workers (nearly 9% of the city's population) are employed in natural and applied sciences–related careers in Calgary. And while some wonder if the city will repeat the more traditional boom-to-bust cycle, others contend that western cities will be more powerful in the Canadian context over the next several decades.

North Carolina's Research Triangle Area is one of the nation's premier growth regions, led by research and development, education, government, and a close relationship with major national universities: Duke University in Durham, North Carolina State University in Raleigh, and University of North Carolina in Chapel Hill. In 1959, a committee of government, university, and business leaders established the Research Triangle Park (RTP) as a joint effort to attract research. It was fashioned after a similar industrial research complex outside of Boston that capitalized on the already existing research facilities at the neighboring universities. The vision for the RTP was to harness the physical infrastructure and brain power of the three area universities for research-oriented companies, which could also employ the highly educated local workforce. Since RTP's founding, many of the nation's largest firms have located their research headquarters in the Park, including GlaxoSmithKline, IBM, Nortel, and Cisco Systems. By 2007, the Park employed almost 50,000 people in 20 million square feet of facilities.

A recent study suggested that biotechnology research may bring as much as $5.5 billion to the Research Triangle cities. Other growth areas include computer software, pharmaceuticals, and telecommunications. The diverse regional economy is not dependent on a single industry and has had consistently low unemployment rates accompanied by high rates of job growth (fig. 2.10). In 2006 *Forbes Magazine* named Raleigh the number two "Best Place for Business and Careers" in the United States. The Research Triangle cities have experienced economic growth, an influx in population, and a $2 billion boom in building in their downtowns, which added hotels, new bank headquarters, condominiums, parking decks and more—all evidence of good economic times.

Not everyone wins in a supercharged economy, however. In Calgary, for example, the average home price jumped 49% from 2005 to

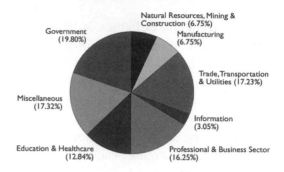

Figure 2.10   Raleigh-Durham-Chapel Hill Employment by Industry, 2005. *Source:* Adapted by authors from the 2006–07 Research Triangle Regional Data Book (http://www.raleigh-wake.org/index.cfm?fuseaction=page&filename=data-databook.html).

2006. There have been reports of rents increasing from $650 a month to $2,000 per month. Boom cities can be hard-pressed to keep pace with rapid expansion and the accompanying need for new roads, schools, hospitals, utilities, and housing. Moreover, traffic congestion and local air pollution increases as roads become more crowded. There are winners and losers in any economic boom.

Washington, D.C., and Las Vegas: New Immigrant Gateways

No longer are the world's immigrants going to the older, established destinations of the 19th and early 20th centuries. In the 21st century, many immigrants choose to settle in cities where immigration is a relatively new phenomenon, but where economic growth demands both high-skilled and low-skilled workers. Two cities, Washington, D.C., and Las Vegas, have become home to hundreds of thousands of new immigrants in the past 15 years (fig. 2.11). Washington, D.C., has seen

Figure 2.11   Pollo Campero, a Guatemalan chain, markets itself to a significant Central American immigrant presence in the metro Washington, D.C., region. In this case, globalization is the movement of products from the periphery (Guatemala) to the core (United States). (Photo by Lisa Benton-Short)

economic growth as a result of federal jobs and contract work (government externalities) as well as the information technology sector. Military-funded aerospace firms such as Northrup-Grumman and Lockheed Martin have established East Coast headquarters in D.C. to be close to the Department of Defense. More recently, the emergence of the Dulles "High Tech Corridor," which reaches from northern Virginia westward toward Dulles International Airport, has attracted high-skilled software engineers and other high-technology workers. AOL (a unit of Time

Warner), for example, employs 5,000 in its headquarters there. A shortage of high-skilled workers in the 1990s resulted in the creation of an H1 Visa specifically designed to target foreigners with college degrees in computer-related fields. As a result, many skilled immigrants from India, South Korea, and Hong Kong and mainland China moved to the Washington region during this time. Prosperity in the region has led simultaneously to an increased demand for domestic labor. Many immigrants from El Salvador, Bolivia, Peru, Brazil, Mexico, and Guatemala have arrived in D.C. to work as nannies, landscapers, construction workers, and service providers in the hotel/hospitality sector.

Similarly, Las Vegas has become a major tourist destination for gambling and entertainment. Some 37 million people visit the city each year. In 2004, nearly 20% of the jobs in Las Vegas were gaming related. Las Vegas has consistently maintained the highest job growth in the country. The 1990s saw major developments in the casino/resort area, with 18 new venues alone built in the last two years of the century, many themed after famous cities throughout the world (fig. 2.12). The construction industry continues to be a major employer as the demand for luxury hotels and casinos, and residential, resort, office, and industrial space, continues to soar. In 2000 more than 21,000 new homes and 26,000 resale homes were purchased. In early 2005 there were 20 residential development projects of more than 300 acres each currently under way. Many emigrants from Central America, Mexico, and the Philippines are going to Las Vegas; many immigrants already in cities like Los Angeles and San Diego are relocating to Las Vegas where low-skilled construction jobs are plentiful. Others find

Figure 2.12   Las Vegas, a city of play, represents one way cities "sell" themselves in a tourist economy. Here a recreated New York City within the Vegas Strip attracts millions of visitors each year, one reason why this is one of the fastest growing cities in the United States. (Photo by Joe Dymond)

work in the casinos or hotels and other service sectors that support a rapidly growing population.

While the recent economic prosperity of Washington, D.C., and Las Vegas has made these cities magnets for a range of immigrants from diverse countries, the immigrants themselves are impacting these cities in ways that challenge conventional thinking about immigrant settlement patterns. In 1970, only 4.5% of the population of Washington, D.C., was foreign-born; in Las Vegas, only 4% was. By 2005, Washington, D.C., was home to 1 million foreign-born individuals, who accounted for nearly 20% of the urban population. Las Vegas, a rapidly growing metropolitan area of 1.6 million, was home to more

than 300,000 foreign-born residents, also approximately 20% of the population. Indeed, most of the newcomers have arrived since 1990. Because immigration is relatively new, Washington, D.C., and Las Vegas, together with Charlotte (NC), Orlando, and Atlanta, are considered newly emerging gateways for immigrants.

These new gateways, however, do not appear to follow the same sort of settlement patterns and processes seen in more established gateways such as New York or Chicago. Contrary to the conventional model of spatial assimilation that assumes that immigrants first cluster with their co-ethnics in center-city enclaves such as Chinatowns and Little Italys and, as they

Figure 2.13 Migrants make their presence felt in numerous ways. In this case, there are sufficient Brazilian immigrants to form a Brazilian service at this Baptist Church outside Washington, D.C. (Photo by Lisa Benton-Short)

gain higher levels of education and income, leave the enclaves to reside in suburban areas with higher social status and larger homes, in Washington, D.C., and Las Vegas many immigrants have located first in the suburbs, not the central-city. Immigrants in these new gateways are thus becoming a vital force shaping the suburban future. In addition, many immigrants to Washington, D.C., live in moderate- to high-income neighborhoods, not in the poorest ones. In fact, many are settling in places that only 30 years ago were mostly White and had very few foreign-born residents. The implications are interesting. For Washington, D.C., the historic image of the city polarized into "Black and White" no longer holds true, and city leaders and residents are grappling with how an increase in diversity has impacted their communities (fig. 2.13).

New Orleans: Vulnerable City

Cities like New Orleans that have experienced disasters remind us that many cities are vulnerable to the environment. Hurricanes and floods are not new to New Orleans. The city was originally located near the junction where the Mississippi River flows into the Gulf of Mexico, at a bend in the river close to Lake Pontchartrain. The original city was sited on a relatively high piece of land where French traders had already been encamped close to a Native American trail. This became known as the French Quarter. The low water table created difficulties in construction, and the river threatened the city with regular flooding. The city grew first along the river and then north toward the lake. Initially, development was restricted to the higher ground above sea level because of the fear of flooding, but improvements in pumping technology in the early 20th century encouraged more development in the lower-lying areas of the city, which tended to be settled by working class, poor, and minority populations. The river that gave the city economic prominence also threatens its destruction from flooding. The history of New Orleans is one of floods, responses to floods, and measures to avoid floods.

In 2005, New Orleans was devastated by Hurricane Katrina. Damage resulted from three main agents: rain, wind, and flood. Hurricanes can produce downpours of up to 25 inches in 30 hours. The high winds tear buildings and other structures away from their moorings. Everything, whether tied down or not, becomes subject to the vagaries of the wind and the waves it generates. Storm surges associated with the high winds can reach over 20 feet above normal sea level, causing massive flooding. For most coastal cities flooding is a serious problem; for a city below sea level it is potentially catastrophic. Much of New Orleans is below sea level.

It was not the ferocious winds of Katrina that most damaged the city but the storm surge that breached its levees. The city was flooded when parts of levees at 17th Street and Industrial Canal collapsed. Almost 80% of the city was flooded, in some cases by water over 20 feet in depth. An estimated 1,000 people were killed, most of them drowned by the rapidly rising floodwaters. Much of the city was destroyed in the flooding that followed the hurricane.

At first glance Hurricane Katrina seemed like a natural disaster. A hurricane is a force of nature. But Katrina was a force of nature whose impacts and effects were mediated through the prism of socioeconomic arrangements. The flooding of the city was caused by poorly designed levees that could not withstand a predictable storm surge. The levees were poorly constructed with pilings set in unstable soils. Pilings that should have been 15 feet high had settled in many places to only 12 to 13 feet above sea level. It was not Katrina that caused the flooding, but shoddy engineering, poor design, and inadequate funding of vital public works.

As Katrina approached New Orleans, federal officials issued first a voluntary and then a mandatory evacuation order. Those with cars were able to exit the city, but there was little provision for the most vulnerable. Those without access to private transport were abandoned; the very poorest, the most disabled, the Black, the elderly, and the infirmed were trapped. Between 50,000 and 100,000 people were left in the city when the hurricane struck and the levees failed. Some made their way to the Superdome and the Convention Center, which over the course of the following several days housed between 30,000 and 50,000 people. They remained for days, a stunning indictment of social and racial inequality in its starkest and bleakest form.

Even the effects of Hurricane Katrina on the city were socially and racially determined. Flooding disproportionately affected the poorest neighborhoods of the city. The more affluent, predominantly White sections, such as the French Quarter, Audubon Park, and the Garden District, were at a higher elevation and escaped flood damage. The flooded areas were 80% non-White, and most of the high poverty tracts were flooded (fig. 2.14). The racial and income disparities in the city were cruelly reflected in the pattern of flood damage. In closer detail, the "natural" disaster appears as a social disaster. As a Congressional bipartisan report noted, "Katrina was a national failure, an abdication of the most

Figure 2.14   After Hurricane Katrina in 2005, many houses in New Orleans stood waiting for clean-up. (Photo by Jesse Goldman)

solemn obligation to provide for the common welfare." The case of Katrina supports the proposition that there is no such thing as a "natural" disaster. Environmental disasters and calamities are social in the sense that the ways they are handled and their effects reflect social differences. It is not the simple case that a hazard causes a disaster. It is the vulnerability to an environmental hazard that causes a disaster—and vulnerability is related to wealth and power.

Hurricanes are not unusual events. Coastal properties and beach locations attract development and growth as populations and investments congregate close to the shoreline. We have transformed mangrove stands into beach resorts, swamps into cities, and strandlines into suburbia. Cities along the Gulf and southeast Atlantic coasts will continue to be vulnerable to hurricanes and other environmental events. In addition, the long term consequences of global climate change may

exacerbate the impact of hurricanes, storms, and floods as sea level rises, thus increasing the reach of storm surges. Ironically, as Americans flock to the arid west, desert cities such as Las Vegas, Phoenix, Tucson, Albuquerque, and numerous others also become vulnerable to water-related disasters. How elected officials, planners, and emergency personnel coordinate with those at the state and federal levels may determine how vulnerable urban residents ultimately are.

CHALLENGES FACING CITIES IN THE UNITED STATES AND CANADA

Nature and the City

In 1995 a heat wave struck the city of Chicago. By its end more than 700 people, mostly elderly living on their own, had died in what was considered the unfortunate outcome of freak meteorological circumstances. The tragedy was not simply a natural disaster but the outcome of the social isolation of seniors, retrenchment of public assistance, and declining neighborhoods. Most elderly victims lived alone in neighborhoods that lacked a sense of community and where there was perception of danger in the streets. Trapped inside their homes and with few visits from public health officials, many poor, isolated seniors died. The disaster was not the result of high temperatures alone; the excessive heat was mediated through a complex set of social and political relationships. The disaster reminds us that the city is part of the natural ecosystem, in this case part of the rising temperatures of summer warming.

Urban studies have tended to ignore the physical nature of cities; the emphasis has been on social, political, and economic issues rather than ecological ones (box 2.4). And yet cities are ecological systems, and these systems impact the social, political, and economic realms of the city. The city itself can be seen as an ecosystem with inputs of energy and water and outputs of noise, climate change, sewerage, garbage, and air pollutants. Water, for example, is an essential ingredient of life, especially in the city. One of the largest urban differences between the First and Third worlds is the clean, easily accessible water in First World cities compared with the expensive, inaccessible, and polluted water of Third World cities. In many North American cities, immense engineering projects have been undertaken in order to provide cheap, clean water. As cities have grown, water catchments have extended outwards, and the engineering sophistication of piping in water has grown and deepened. The availability of fresh water is a determinant of the limits of urban growth. In the arid western United States, for

example, urban growth has been predicated upon massive federal subsidies and expensive engineering projects that have provided fresh water at low cost to urban consumers. Cities that have benefited include Las Vegas, Tucson, Phoenix, and Los Angeles. The ecological limits are always more flexible than the environmental determinists suggest, but they are not infinitely extendable. We may be reaching the "water limits" of urban growth in the arid areas of the United States.

Cities also modify the environment. Human activity in the city produces pollutants. Industrial processes and auto engines emit substances that include carbon and sulfur oxides, hydrocarbons, dust, soot, and lead. In the Canadian province of Ontario, for example, which has a population of 11.9 million, air pollution costs citizens at least $1 billion annually in hospital admissions, emergency room visits, and worker absenteeism. In 2005 Toronto had 48 "smog days" of unhealthy air, the highest since 1993. The pollutants of cities are not only injurious to the health of individuals, they also cause more general damage; cities are in part a major cause of global warming and ozone depletion.

Cities also reference nature, and since the 19th century there has been an explicit urban parks movement (fig. 2.15). Landscape architects such as Frederick Law Olmstead have left a permanent legacy on cities. It is difficult to imagine New York without Central Park, San Francisco without the Golden Gate, Vancouver without Stanley Park, or Washington without the National Mall. Today city parks are developed as much for their recreational opportunities as their aesthetic appeal. Urban planners realize that the successful referencing of nature is an important element in creating the right atmosphere, and it is often linked with the promise of economic redevelopment.

Box 2.4 Pale Male and Lola

Nature is present in cities in often unforeseen and unplanned ways. Wildlife in a variety of forms continues to find ecological niches in the city. Urban tensions can be written through the narration of the relationship between cities and wildlife. Urban animal geographies can tell us much about the city–nature dialectic whether it is in the stories of rats or of hawks in the city.

Consider the case of Pale Male and Lola, two red-tailed hawks that made their nest in the facade of an exclusive high-rise apartment block in New York City's Fifth Avenue. Hawks have been noticed in the area since 1998, and every year the birds would return to nest, breed, and feed their young. Birdwatchers followed their progress through binoculars, cameras, and websites. There is something heroic about the capacity of hawks to thrive in the city.

Some residents of the apartment block thought otherwise. The president of the co-op board, wealthy real estate developer Richard Cohen, unilaterally ordered the nest removed in 2004. Residents had complained that the hawks caused a mess on the sidewalk. Red-tailed hawks are rare enough to have been protected by a treaty signed in 1918 between several nations, including the United States, Canada, and Russia. An earlier attempt to evict the birds was blocked when their defenders invoked this international agreement. Under a provision a red hawk nest could be removed if it contained no eggs or chicks. The co-op board used this loophole.

Their decision sparked a major protest. Protesters dressed as birds mounted a vigil across the street from the building. The media publicized the story. One subtext was resistance to the power of the wealthy to write the ecology of the city. Apartments at 927 Fifth Avenue can sell for as much as $18 million, and residents include the wealthy and the famous. The image of very rich residents evicting hawks from their perch was too delicious to ignore. The extremely negative publicity for the apartment building and its residents eventually led to a reversal of the eviction. Pale Male and Lola still nest on the building. You can even follow the urban saga of Pale Male and Lola at their own website, www.palemale.com.

Increasingly, urban residents are recognizing the various scales of nature, from vest-pocket parks, urban gardens, greenways, and rooftop gardens to large expansive megaparks. Whether it is on the beaches of southern California, along the lakeside shore of Chicago, in the parks of Vancouver, or in the community garden in Montreal, a commonly accepted attractive feature of urban life is the successful (re)incorporation of nature into the urban lifestyle, the city's image, and the metropolitan experience (box 2.5).

Migration and Increasing Diversity

Immigration is a window through which to view the reconfiguring of urban and global networks as millions of economic migrants

Figure 2.15   The beaches of Los Angeles are an important cultural and ecological feature of the city. (Photo by Lisa Benton-Short)

settle in select cities around the world. Although we tend to think of immigrants as coming from and going to countries, most immigrants go to cities, as our earlier discussion of Washington, D.C., and Las Vegas attests. Although these localities or "immigrant gateways" take on different forms, many are hyperdiverse and are globally linked through transnational networks. Hyperdiverse immigrant cities are those places where the percentage of foreign-born residents exceeds the national level and where immigrants come from many regions of the world with no single country of origin dominating. Immigrant cities are growing in number because of globalization and the acceleration of migration driven by income differentials, social networks, and various state policies to recruit skilled and unskilled laborers as both

temporary workers and permanent residents. As large numbers of foreign-born and ethnically distinct people are thrown into the mix, cities become the places where global differences are both celebrated and contested. Immigrants can add to a city's global competitiveness by enhancing a city's diversity and talent, thus making such places better able to compete in a global age. With birth rates declining in both Canada and the United States, migration has become a more important determinant of differential urban growth (or decline).

Although it is true that that immigration is a global phenomenon, it is also true that some regions of the world receive significantly more immigrants than others. North America, long an established region of immigrant settlement, is among the highest. Of the top 20

Box 2.5   Landfills: Monuments to a Consuming Lifestyle

Landfills can be considered silent "monuments" to our consuming lifestyle. Americans discard more garbage per capita than citizens of other prosperous nations, and far more than those in the developing world. The production of garbage reveals much about levels of affluence, household formation, commercial activity, and values. In North America, we have favored convenience over conservation, short-term needs over long-range resourcefulness. The fast food of McDonald's is both indicative of a cultural value that embraces convenience and accepts the short-term duration of packaging. Food arrives within minutes. The food wrappers and drink cups have a life span of less than one hour, yet they survive in landfills for years. The quintessential fast-food society has become a disposable society. This extends beyond the fast food restaurants into many aspects of our culture. It is often less expensive to purchase a new radio or DVD player rather than repair a broken one. We now purchase purposely "disposable" products such as razors, toothbrushes, paper plates and cups, and writing pens.

One of the more infamous landfills is Fresh Kills. Fresh Kills (originally from the Dutch *kill*, meaning water) covers some 3,000 acres and is located on the western shore of Staten Island in New Jersey. Beginning in 1948, Fresh Kills served the city of New York as its sole landfill until 2001. At its height, Fresh Kills received some 17,000 tons of trash per day! It was a putrid mountain of waste and the largest human-made structure in the history of the world. It, along with the Great Wall of China and the Egyptian Pyramids, was, at one point, one of three human-made structures visible from space.

In 1996, officials announced that Fresh Kills would close. They began phasing out the use of the landfill and announced that the city would expand its recycling program and search for alternative landfill destinations. Today, trash from the Bronx, Brooklyn, and Manhattan is exported out of New York State. However, exporting trash cost the city some $622 million between 1998 and 2002, not counting unpredicted costs. For those who live along city truck corridors, there has been a "remapping" of the flow of garbage. At one time, trash was hauled to Fresh Kills via trash barges, but trucks and transfer stations have now taken their places. Floors and windows of homes and apartments vibrate when the trucks roll by; the smell of rotting garbage and truck exhaust fills the air outside. Proposed solutions to the refuse problem include transporting the trash by rail or barge to landfills in New Jersey, Virginia, and states in the Midwest and South. Since its closure, the mounds at Fresh Kills have been covered with a foot of dirt, topped with a foot of sand, followed by a plastic liner and two more feet of soil. The plan is to "reclaim" the landfill as a "postmodern forest." Landscape architects envision Fresh Kills as a thriving park and bird sanctuary, where in another 30 years or so people might walk on natural trails or picnic among the re-made wilderness.

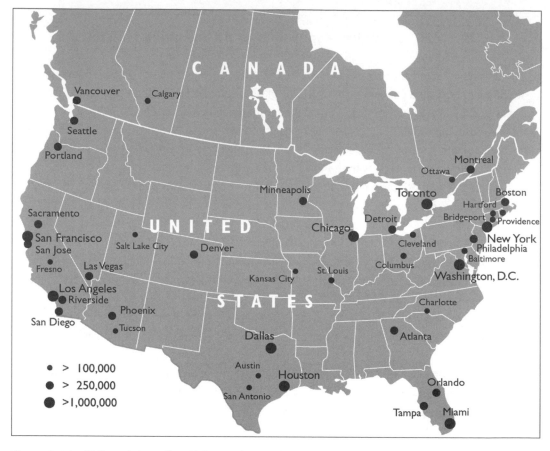

Figure 2.16   U.S. and Canadian Cities with Significant Foreign-Born Residents. *Source:* M. Price and L. Benton-Short, Globalization, Urbanization and Migration dataset, 2007 (http://gstudynet.org/gum/).

immigrant destinations in the world, 9 are U.S. and Canadian cities (fig. 2.16).

Although the three largest immigrant destinations in the region are New York City, Toronto, and Los Angeles, there are 60 other metropolitan regions with more than 100,000 foreign-born residents (table 2.3). In Canada immigrants primarily go to one of three cities: Vancouver, Montreal, and Toronto. But smaller Canadian cities such as Ottawa and Calgary are places where 20% of the population is foreign-born. Similarly in the United States, immigrants are targeting newer gateways such as Las Vegas, Phoenix, Charlotte, and Atlanta, where the relative increase in the foreign-born population is much higher than in traditional gateways.

Yet crude measurements of the foreign-born populations in urban North America tell us little about the composition or distribution of the foreign-born within cities. There are cities that are home to a "hyperdiverse" foreign-born population and cities that are home to a large, but not particularly diverse, number of foreign-born residents (box 2.6). Two of the most hyperdiverse cities in the

Table 2.3   Major Immigrant Cities of the World

City	Country	Census Year	Metropolitan Population	Foreign-Born	% Foreign-Born
Dubai	United Arab Emirates	2005	1,272,000	1,056,000	83.02%
Toronto	Canada	2001	4,647,960	2,091,100	44.99%
Muscat	Oman	2000	661,000	294,881	44.61%
Hong Kong	China	2005	7,039,169	2,998,686	42.60%
Vancouver	Canada	2001	1,967,475	767,715	39.02%
Mecca	Saudi Arabia	1996	4,467,670	1,686,595	37.75%
Miami	USA	2005	5,334,685	1,949,629	36.55%
Tel Aviv–Yafo	Israel	2002	2,075,500	747,400	36.01%
San Jose	USA	2005	1,726,057	614,304	35.59%
Medina	Saudi Arabia	2000	5,448,773	1,893,213	34.75%
Los Angeles	USA	2005	12,703,423	4,407,353	34.69%
Singapore	Singapore	2000	4,017,733	1,350,632	33.62%
Auckland	New Zealand	2001	1,103,466	354,126	32.09%
Perth	Australia	2001	1,336,239	422,547	31.62%
Riyadh	Saudi Arabia	2000	4,730,330	1,477,601	31.24%
Sydney	Australia	2001	3,961,451	1,235,908	31.20%
Jerusalem	Israel	2002	678,300	208,700	30.77%
San Francisco	USA	2005	4,071,751	1,201,209	29.50%
Melbourne	Australia	2001	3,367,169	960,145	28.51%
Amsterdam	Netherlands	2005	742,951	211,260	28.44%
New York	USA	2005	18,351,099	5,117,290	27.89%
Frankfurt	Germany	2000	650,705	181,184	27.84%
Tbilisi	Georgia	1999	1,339,105	370,932	27.70%
London	United Kingdom	2001	7,172,091	1,940,390	27.05%
Rotterdam	Netherlands	2005	596,597	157,395	26.38%

world are New York and Toronto, home to millions of foreign-born individuals who come from every region of the world.

At the dawn of the 20th century, when New York City was the premier immigrant gateway in the United States, nearly all the immigrants were European. The city was linguistically and ethnically diverse, but not racially. At the dawn of the 21st century New York City is one of the most racially and ethnically diverse places on the planet. Of the top 10 sending countries to metropolitan New York, only 1 is European. The top 10 sending countries represent half of the city's foreign-born and include immigrants from the Dominican Republic, China, Jamaica, Mexico, Guyana, Ecuador, Haiti, Colombia, and Italy (fig. 2.17).

A similar pattern holds for Toronto. In 2001, 45% of the city's population was foreign-born, one of the highest percentages for any major metropolitan area. Some 70,000 immigrants from approximately 170 countries arrive in the city annually. No one group dominates Toronto's immigrant stock. Nine countries account for half of the foreign-born population, led by China, and then India, the United Kingdom, Italy, the Philippines, Jamaica, Portugal, Poland, and Sri Lanka (fig. 2.18). Other hyperdiverse

Box 2.6   Anchorage, Alaska

With a 2006 population of 278,000, Anchorage is the largest city in Alaska. It is also home to almost 40% of the state's population. The loss of native-born citizens through out-migration since 2000 has been offset by increased international immigration. Currently there are some 21,000 foreign-born residents in Anchorage. This represents 8.2% of the population, a number that is lower than the U.S. average but higher than that of the state of Alaska at 5.9%. Similar to cities such as Las Vegas and Washington, D.C., nearly 40% of the foreign-born in Anchorage have arrived since 1990. The major countries of origin for Anchorage immigrants include the Philippines, Korea, Mexico, the former Soviet Union, and Canada.

As with many U.S. cities, the history of economic development in Anchorage is a history of boom–bust cycles. Located at the head of Cook Inlet, this relatively new city was founded in 1915 as a construction port for the Alaska Railroad. Anchorage remained a relatively small frontier town until the beginning of World War II. During World War II, Anchorage became a key aviation and defense center. The influx of federal defense spending during the 1950s increased Anchorage's population and business community. During the 1950s, Anchorage became a "boom town," led primarily by federal government investment. In 1964 a major earthquake caused a number of deaths and extensive property damage. This earthquake, the largest ever recorded in North America, measured 8.6 on the Richter scale. Because Anchorage lies only 80 miles (129 km) from the epicenter, damage to structures ran into the hundreds of millions of dollars. The latter half of the 1960s was devoted to recovery and regrowth.

The 1970s brought yet another "boom" to Anchorage: the development of the Prudhoe Bay oil fields in northern Alaska. In 1972, Congress authorized the trans-Alaska pipeline system. Oil discovery and pipeline construction fueled a modern-day boom when oil and construction companies set up headquarters in Anchorage. Construction began in 1974, with oil flowing from the North Slope to the ice-free port of Valdez in 1977. The petroleum industry also provided skilled employment opportunities for thousands. Population, office space, and housing tripled by the 1980s. Anchorage International Airport boomed as well, and Anchorage marketed itself as the "Air Crossroads of the World," because of its unique geographical position. Oil revenue to the Alaskan state treasury was used to develop the city's infrastructure: between 1980 and 1987 nearly a billion dollars worth of capital projects were constructed in the city including a new library, civic center, sports arena, and performing arts center. However, by the late 1980s the price of oil had dropped dramatically, and a recession hit Anchorage.

Since 2000 the increase in the price of oil has, once again, made Anchorage a "boom town." Seeking to avoid the boom–bust cycles, Anchorage is gradually broadening its economic base with more retail trade and a larger service sector to serve tourists. Although the U.S. government and the oil industry have been integral to the Anchorage economy, new economic opportunities include construction, light manufacturing, high technology, software development, commercial fishing, and seafood processing.

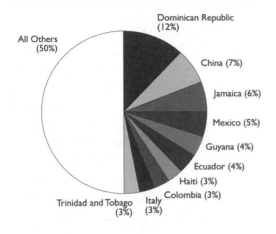

Figure 2.17   New York's Foreign-Born Population. *Source:* M. Price and L. Benton-Short, Globalization, Urbanization and Migration dataset, 2007 (http://gstudynet.org/gum/).

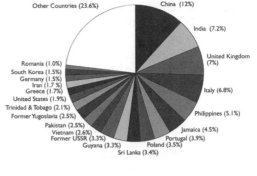

Figure 2.18   The Diversity of Toronto's Foreign-Born Population. *Source:* M. Price and L. Benton-Short, Globalization, Urbanization and Migration dataset, 2007 (http://gstudynet.org/gum/).

metropolitan areas in North America include Washington, D.C., San Francisco, and Seattle. The globalization of migration has led to a tendency for immigrants to come from a broader range of sending counties and, in the process, has created cities that are more racially and ethnically diverse.

Not all immigrant gateways are hyperdiverse. Mexicans account for about half of foreign-born residents in cities such as Los Angeles, Chicago, Houston, and Dallas. These millions of Mexicans impact their cities often in unexpected ways. For example, 4 of the top 10 television shows in the Los Angeles market are Spanish-language broadcasts (tab. 2.4). Similarly foreign-born Cubans dominate in Miami. Immigrants from mainland China and Hong Kong are over 25% of the foreign-born in Vancouver. It is fair to say that North American cities will continue to be home to many of the world's immigrants well into the 21st century.

Security and Urban Fortification

Responses to the potential of terrorism, whether domestic or international, have had a profound impact on many North American cities. Intense surveillance and security have changed both the physical and symbolic landscapes of many cities.

It is not unusual in times of war and conflict for visible forms of fortification to appear on the urban landscape. Fortification of urban space is not merely a recent phenomenon. However, since September 11, 2001, security has become much more visible in most North American cities. Given that many of our barricaded urban spaces are valued public places with important symbolic and spatial connections to local, regional, or national identity, this trend is of significant concern to many citizens.

The rise of security policing, new forms of surveillance, and control of urban spaces is not a new subject. Mike Davis's 1990 *City of Quartz* diagnosed what he calls "fortress

Table 2.4   Top 10 Television Shows in Los Angeles, March 2005

1. *American Idol* (Tuesday), KTTV
2. *American Idol* (Wednesday), KTTV
3. *CSI*, KCBS
4. *American Idol* (Monday), KTTV
5. *Rubi*, KMEX
6. *Without a Trace*, KCBS
7. *Amor Real* (Thursday), KMEX
8. *Amor Real* (Friday), KMEX
9. *Amor Real* (Tuesday), KMEX
10. *CSI: Miami*, KCBS

Source: Los Angeles Times, March 2005.

cities" as a response to perceived urban disorder and decay, primarily from domestic sources. He noted that the car bomb could well become the ultimate weapon of crime and terror, and predicted that the urban authorities might create fortress style rings of steel as a counter response. The fortress metaphor describes a landscape that is demarcated by physical borders such as gates and walls as well as by often invisible surveillance devices such as closed-circuit television cameras that watch city streets, parks, and gated communities. This is a vision of a city that can be controlled. For some, security and surveillance offer reassurance in an uncertain age; for others these measures are the architecture of paranoia.

Although cities have long had police forces and emergency plans, prior to the early 1990s many did not have a comprehensive security and defensive strategy. Attempts to design out terrorism occurred often after an event or a direct threat raised the issue of vulnerability. Today terrorists target high profile cities to attract global media publicity. And since 9/11, it is clear that symbolic targets—such as monuments, memorials, landmark buildings, and other important urban public spaces—are increasingly at risk. The responses have been highly intense and visible counter-terrorist measures. In New York, Toronto, Los Angeles, and Philadelphia, for example, bollards, bunkers, and other barriers have been placed around selected "high-risk" targets and buildings. Some fortifications such as barriers and fences have impacted people's access to public spaces such as museums, monuments, memorials, and parks. Many see heightened fortification as a threat to public space. When security measures are particularly visible in capital cities, such as Washington, D.C., the symbolic impact of fortress architecture is elevated to represent a national discourse of war, fear, and entrenchment.

Washington, D.C., is one of the most visibly fortified cities in North America. Miles of fences, jersey barriers, and bollards surround federal buildings, monuments, and memorials throughout the city. In addition, closed-circuit television cameras keep an eye on the streets, sidewalks, and public spaces and are mounted on roofs and the sides of libraries, shopping malls, and banks. Security cameras are even on some of the most public of spaces: the monuments and memorials on the National Mall (fig. 2.19). The prevalence of security cameras in many cities has become commodified in popular culture as those "caught in the act" provide hours of video entertainment for television shows and YouTube. Regardless of whether security cameras actually deter crime or not, more and more urban residents are photographed, videotaped, and otherwise placed under surveillance. This raises troubling questions about what happens to old video footage, whether police use videos to create criminal profiles, and whether law-abiding residents should be concerned that they are often under surveillance, knowingly or not.

Figure 2.19   Here, framed by a black box, a security camera has been positioned atop the Jefferson Memorial in Washington, D.C. What messages do surveillance cameras convey in a public space that memorializes freedom, liberty, and independence? (Photo by Lisa Benton-Short)

Memorials and monuments, like Philadelphia's Liberty Bell (fig. 2.20), are not merely ornamental features in the urban landscape; they are highly symbolic signifiers that confer meaning on urban space and thus represent the politics of power. Changes or alterations to these memorials via CCTV, fences, bollards, or other barriers also provide a glimpse of competing agendas on security and terrorism, as well as the power relationships that can ultimately determine its realization. Perhaps more contentiously, by physically impeding public space, security cameras do more than inconvenience public access to memorials and other spaces: they inhibit the types of radical political protest such as civil rights protests, anti-war marches, and protests from marginalized voices that occur in public spaces in cities around North America. Although the stakes have changed, it is unclear how the need for improving security translates into acceptable levels of fortification, the loss of

civil liberties, inhibited public access to public space, and the implied messages of new hypersecurity. The ambiguous nature of security remains unresolved.

Preserving and Re-creating Urban Historical Landscapes

In North America, there has always been some appreciation of our cultural and architectural heritage, but only in the last few decades have we become increasingly aware of the significance of our urban historic structures and sites. The unprecedented urban changes of the 20th century, particularly under urban renewal; the growth of the interstate highway system and other massive public works; and the skyscraper building boom provided momentum for the emergence of a preservation movement.

In the United States the preservation movement evolved from two distinct paths.

Figure 2.20   As a result of post–September 11 security measures, the Liberty Bell in Philadelphia is now behind bars, security check points, and other fences. (Photo by Lisa Benton-Short)

The private-sector path focused on important historical figures and landmark structures. One of the first major historic preservation undertakings from the private sector, for instance, was that of George Washington's plantation estate, Mount Vernon, along the Potomac River not far from Washington, D.C.

The public-sector path was involved with establishing national parks, but its area of concern also included historic buildings. The public sector was successful at establishing some historic districts, such as Charleston, South Carolina (1931); the Vieux Carré (French Quarter) section of New Orleans (1936); and Alexandria, Virginia (1946). In 1949, several organizations evolved into the British-inspired National Trust for Historic Preservation. The purpose was to link the preservation efforts of the private sector with federal government/National Park Service activities. The most important piece of historic preservation legislation was the National Historic Preservation Act of 1966. Preservation no longer focused on saving single landmarks; instead, entire areas were delineated as historic districts and became important tools of urban revitalization during the 1970s and 1980s. Historic Districts are defined as areas of cultural and physical distinction that contribute to a local identity. Cities can have multiple historic districts. For example, there are more than 20 historic districts in Chicago, including the Pullman district (the first planned industrial town) and the Black Metropolis district (a series of nine buildings that were home to numerous nationally prominent, African American– owned and—operated businesses and cultural institutions). Many historic districts cover a wide geography. The Freedom Trail in Boston is a 2.5-mile (4-km) red-brick walking trail that winds through the city and leads the visitor to 16 historic sites: a collection of museums, churches, meeting houses, burying grounds, parks, and a ship—all with historic markers that tell the story of the American Revolution. Today there are thousands of local preservation associations and thousands of designated historic sites, buildings, and other structures in cities in the United States.

Canadian preservation history follows a similar trajectory. The primary conservation tool is Canada's Historic Places Initiative. This was the result of a major collaborative effort among federal, provincial, territorial, and municipal governments; heritage conservation professionals; heritage developers; and many individual Canadians. As a pan-Canadian collaboration, it is intended to reinforce the development of a culture of conservation in Canada. So far, over 1,500 places, persons, and events have been commemorated.

Today, historic preservation is composed of a variety of strategies: preservation, restoration, reconstruction, and rehabilitation. Preservation refers to the maintenance of a property without significant alteration to its current condition. When preservation is the guiding strategy, the only intervention is normal maintenance or special work needed to protect the structure against further damage. An example of innovation in preservation is Pike Place Market in Seattle. The old city market was threatened with demolition to make way for an urban renewal project. In a city-wide vote, however, residents voted to save the market as an important part of their city's life and culture. In order to prevent the loss of its original character as an everyday working market run by local farmers, fishermen, and small entrepreneurs, the city developed an ordinance that protected not only the structure, but also the activities within.

Restoration refers to the process of returning a building to its condition at a specific time period. It can involve cleaning, minor repair, major repair, and the replacement of part of the building that is damaged or missing. For example, nearly all of the 21 missions on the California mission trail (located along the urban corridor that begins in the south with San Diego, proceeds north to Los Angeles and along the coast to San Francisco, and ends in Sonoma) have been restored to varying degrees. The missions, a legacy from the Spanish era of the 18th century, needed to be reconstructed after the ravages of time, weather, earthquakes, and neglect took their toll. In some cases restoration may mean the removal of features from other periods in a structure's history and the reconstruction of missing features from the restoration period. This form of restoration is more common in historic homes, farms, and churches. This strategy, however, is not without criticism, as it casts doubt on the authenticity of restored structures; critics believe that it can lead to a more contrived picture of a structure's "original condition."

The term reconstruction refers to the use of replicated designs and/or materials on a historic structure. This approach is taken when the historic structure no longer exists. In some cases reconstruction goes hand-in-hand with restoration. The earliest and best example is Williamsburg, Virginia (fig. 2.21). In 1926 John D. Rockefeller was persuaded to fund the restoration of the entire colonial town of Williamsburg. The primary problem was that much of the original town had been lost over the centuries; although many of the historic buildings remained, a few central buildings from the town's original layout were missing. Planners decided to reconstruct the Governor's Palace (which had been destroyed by a fire in 1781). The efforts to reconstruct Williamsburg were not without controversy,

Figure 2.21   Virginia's Colonial Williamsburg presents a good example of both historic restoration and reconstruction. Actors portray townspeople from the 18th century in this "living history" theme park. (Photo by Lisa Benton-Short)

as some buildings were removed to make way for reconstructed ones. Yet it remains one of the most visited historic districts in the United States. In addition to both restoration and reconstruction, Colonial Williamsburg presents live recreations of historic events by actors in period costumes. This way of presenting historical places and artifacts, often referred to as the "living history museum" concept, has become increasingly popular.

Lastly, many buildings no longer perform their original function or use but retain their architectural integrity. For these structures, a common strategy is rehabilitation, sometimes referred to as adaptive use. The purpose is to modify or update portions of the structure and adapt the building for a new purpose. Numerous examples abound such as abandoned factories that are adapted into a variety of reincarnations—as microbrewery pubs,

museums, or residential lofts. Increasingly, rehabilitation is a strategy employed by those seeking to revitalize old areas of the city.

Historic preservation and recreation is increasingly at the center of urban redevelopment efforts as cities search for a way to celebrate their past while looking to the future. In some cases, the financial investment in preservation and recreation efforts can provide economic returns in increased tourism and the (re)attraction of commercial and residential interests. Cities are learning that preservation and recreation can make good economic sense.

Smog Cities

Residents in many North American cities confront air pollution. Since the 1970s the U.S. and Canadian governments have taken steps to control pollution emissions from automobiles and factory stacks. Catalytic converters capture much of the automobile exhaust, and vapor traps on gas pumps help prevent the evaporation of carbon dioxide into the air. Recent efforts to develop hybrid and zero-emission vehicles (such as electric cars) are other ways both private and public interests are using technology to alleviate air pollution. However, new sources of pollution, combined with increased use of fossil fuels for myriad needs, has meant that air pollution for many U.S. and Canadian cities has continued to increase despite regulatory efforts.

Smog represents the single most challenging air pollution problem in most North America cities. Smog is produced by the combination of pollutants from many sources including smokestacks, cars, paints, and solvents that interact with ground-level ozone. Smog is often worse in the summer months when heat and sunshine are more plentiful. Short-term exposure can cause eye irritation, wheezing, coughing, headaches, chest pain, and shortness of breath. Long term exposure scars the lungs, making them less elastic and efficient, often worsening asthma and increasing respiratory tract infections. Because ozone penetrates deeply into the respiratory system, many urban residents are at risk, including the weak and elderly, but also those who engage in strenuous activity. In the United States more than 81 million people, or approximately 27% of Americans, live in urban areas that exceed air quality concentrations for ozone. According to the American Lung Association, the worst U.S. cities for smog in 2005 were Los Angeles, Bakersfield, Fresno, Houston, Sacramento, Dallas, New York, Philadelphia, and Washington, D.C. In Canada, Windsor, Toronto, Montreal, and

Vancouver are cities where acceptable ozone levels are exceeded on an average of 10 or more days in the summer.

Smog is one pollutant that is often exacerbated by geography. Cities located in basins and valleys—such as Los Angeles—are particularly susceptible to the production of smog. Denver, the Mile High City, suffers from smog and other air pollutants that are made worse by its elevation in the Rocky Mountains. Because of Denver's high altitude, the city experiences frequent temperature inversions when warm air is trapped under cold air and cannot rise to disperse the pollutants to a wider area. As a result, smog may hover in place for days at a time, generating a "smog soup" that envelopes the city. Having once been a city that regularly failed to meet federal standards, Denver has worked to turn its air pollution problem around. In 2007 the EPA noted that Denver was ahead of schedule in the effort to reduce smog. Still, Denver exceeds federal standards for several days each year (down from dozens). Another issue of "smog geography" occurs in Montreal and Toronto. These cities are upwind of major industrial cities in the Midwest, and some of the air pollutants that generate smog in Toronto and Montreal originate across the border.

Much air pollution improvement has been offset by increased populations that demand more energy as well as by increased automobile use. Between 1970 and 2000, the U.S. population increased 36%, while energy consumption increased 45%, and vehicle miles traveled increased 143%. Despite decades of regulation and good intentions, cities in North America remain far from eliminating the threat of air pollution to both public health and environmental quality.

CONCLUSIONS

Cities in the United States and Canada have entered the 21st century facing numerous and complex challenges. For one, there is the challenge of dealing with continued rapid economic, social, and environmental change. Economic restructuring, which has included deindustrialization and the rise of a diverse service-sector economy, has resulted in uneven development. Some cities are experiencing economic growth and increased prosperity. Those unable to tap into the global circuits of capital struggle to realign and expand their economies in the wake of deindustrialization. Cities are in greater competition with each other in the urban hierarchy to retain center-city populations, attract domestic and international businesses and investment, and develop a diverse economy. Urban boosters have responded to the underlying economic restructuring with a number of redevelopment and growth strategies that include raising their visibility by hosting Olympic Games, redeveloping waterfronts, and preserving and re-creating historic landscapes for both local and tourist consumption. Yet economic diversification is no guarantee of success. It remains to be seen what the driving engine of the next boom–bust cycle to impact the urban economy will be.

Change is occurring socially as well. Suburban sprawl continues. And issues of immigration (both legal and undocumented) have become part of a wider public debate around citizenship, race, gender, and ethnicity. Traditional immigrant cities such as New York and Toronto continue to see the influx of immigrants, but cities without a long history of immigration have begun to attract large numbers of foreign-born individuals. These new immigrant gateways often lack the institutional mechanisms to cope with increased cultural diversity and are challenged to provide a range of social services (such as English language instruction in schools and translation services in hospitals). The events of September 11th and the war on terror have resulted in physical changes to the urban landscape as cities attempt to deal with safety, security, and the vulnerability of urban populations. Cities now grapple with protecting "national security" and building fortifications, yet true public debate about the trade-offs of security versus public access and free speech has yet to occur.

Finally, environmental factors are transforming the urban landscape in many ways. The impact of Hurricane Katrina on New Orleans and many cities and towns in the Gulf is a forceful reminder that many cities are vulnerable to environmental events and disasters. Any geographic location has risk, as the many challenges of preparing for and recovering from disasters such as hurricanes, earthquakes, floods, and droughts have revealed. Urban growth patterns illustrate that the environment can be a constraining element, but in the 21st century we often fail to recognize this and instead continue to develop along coasts, river valleys, deltas, and earthquake fault lines, and in arid areas such as Phoenix where fresh water is disappearing. As much as cities are subject to environmental influences, they are also agents of environmental change. Cities emit tremendous amounts of pollutants into the air, land, and water. In some cities air pollution has significant health impacts on urban residents, despite efforts to reduce and control pollution since the 1970s. In recognizing the inter-related human–environment nexus, many cities have developed plans to green the city through the development of parks and waterfronts, often reclaiming once polluted land and waterways.

North American cities are in constant motion; social, economic, political, and environmental changes ensure that as current challenges continue, new ones will arise. Many cities have taken positive and often creative steps to address these challenges. Cities in the United States and Canada remain some of the most interesting and dynamic in the world, and they often lead the way in dealing with issues that cities in other regions are just beginning to confront.

SUGGESTED READINGS

Anisef, Paul, and Michael Lanphier, eds. 2003. *The World in a City*. Toronto: University of Toronto Press. Analyzes the challenges of immigrants in Toronto and the value of municipal policies that provide resources to aid in settlement and integration.

Breen, Ann, and Dick Rigby. 1997. *Waterfronts: Cities Reclaim Their Edge*. Washington, DC: Waterfront Press. Details three decades of urban waterfront development in North America using contextual analysis and 75 case studies.

Fogelson, Robert M. 2003. *Downtown: Its Rise and Fall*. New Haven, CT: Yale University Press. Describes the evolution of urban centers in America from 1880 to 1950 including the influence of construction, business, and transport.

Fyfe, Nicholas, ed. 1998. *Images of the Street: Planning, Identity and Control in Public Space*. London: Routledge. A collection of essays that critically examine the interaction of society and urban design in city streets.

Florida, Richard. 2005. *The Flight of the Creative Class: The New Global Competition for Talent*. New York: Harper Business. Details the pool of skilled workers crucial for urban growth and the forces of globalization that pull these workers away from the United States.

Hartman, Chester, and Gregory D. Squires, eds. 2006. *There Is No Such Thing as a Natural Disaster: Race, Class and Hurricane Katrina*. New York: Routledge. Scholarly essays on the impact and implications of Hurricane Katrina for urban planning and social policy in the United States.

Price, Marie, and Lisa Benton-Short, eds. 2007. *Migrants to the Metropolis: The Rise of Immigrant Gateway Cities*. Syracuse, NY: Syracuse University Press. Examines immigration to 13 cities around the world and investigates the ways in which immigrants are transforming urban space.

Short, John R. 2006. *Alabaster Cities: Urban U.S. since 1950*. Syracuse, NY: Syracuse University Press. A comprehensive historical analysis of U.S. cities that explores urban development patterns and their relationship to community life.

Vale, Lawrence J., and Thomas J. Campanella, eds. 2005. *The Resilient City: How Modern Cities Recover from Disasters*. New York: Oxford University Press. A collection of case-based and theoretical essays analyzing the response and ultimate recovery of cities to natural and non-natural disasters throughout history.

Wheeler, Stephen. 2004. *Planning for Sustainability: Creating Livable, Equitable and Ecological Communities*. London: Routledge. A comprehensive framework for sustainable planning at every scale.

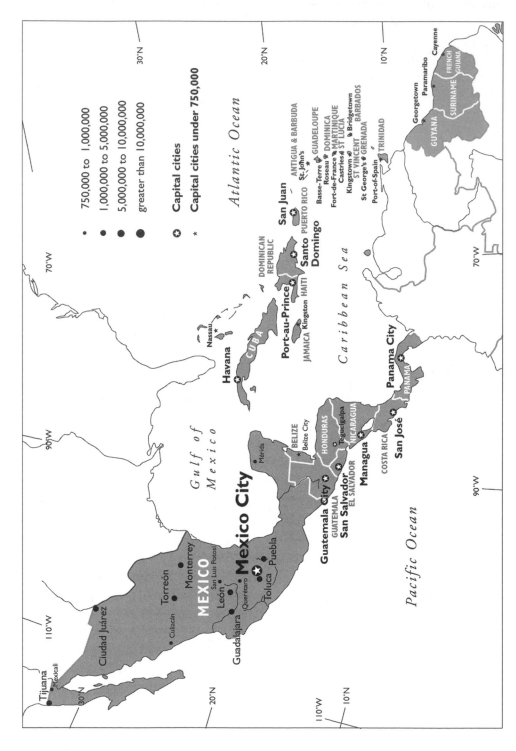

Figure 3.1 Major Cities of Middle America and the Caribbean. *Source:* Data from UN, *World Urbanization Prospects: 2005 Revision,* http://esa.un.org/unup/.

3

Cities of Middle America and the Caribbean

IRMA ESCAMILLA, JOSEPH L. SCARPACI, AND
ADRIÁN GUILLERMO AGUILAR

KEY URBAN FACTS

Total Population	186 million
Percent Urban Population	69%
Total Urban Population	128 million
Most Urbanized Countries	Guadeloupe (99.8%)
	Martinique (97.9%)
	Puerto Rico (97.6%)
Least Urbanized Countries	Trinidad and Tobago (12.2%)
	Montserrat (13.5%)
	St. Lucia (27.6%)
Annual Urban Growth Rate	1.7%
Number of Megacities	1
Number of Cities of More Than 1 Million	17
Three Largest Cities	Mexico City, Guadalajara, Monterrey
World Cities	Mexico City

KEY CHAPTER THEMES

1. The Mexican urban system was forged in large measure by the Aztec pattern of urbanization. It was subjugated militarily by the Spanish to facilitate the colonizers' dual mission of proselytizing and mining.
2. It was not until the second half of the 19th century that new important regional centers emerged, stimulated by foreign investment and the development of railways and highways.
3. Between 1900 and 1940, the urban population of Mexico grew at a rate far greater than that of the Mexican population in general; most urban growth was concentrated in the larger cities of Mexico.

4. Today, urban growth in Mexico is occurring in intermediate cities located close to large cities, in cities along the U.S.–Mexican border, and in independent cities in remote regions far from the large agglomerations.

5. The urban systems of Central America and the Caribbean developed under various European powers and followed an agricultural-driven model of colonial and post-colonial growth.

6. Today, Central America is nearly 70% urban, ranging from approximately 45% in Honduras and Guatemala to 59% and 66% in Costa Rica and Panama, respectively. National poverty rates parallel urbanization rates in that the poorest countries are the least urbanized countries.

7. Social and geographic segregation has deepened in Central America's cities; crime and violence are serious problems.

8. Four patterns highlight contemporary urbanization in the Caribbean: urban primacy characterizes every island; the number of cities with 1 to 5 million residents has more than doubled; mid-sized cities (500,000 to 1,000,000 residents) have held the same relative proportion of urban residents while smaller cities have declined; and insularity is a key constraint on many islands.

9. Since the mid-20th century, Cuba has taken the most divergent path to urban and national development in the past half-century with its variant form of socialist cities.

10. Natural disasters in the Caribbean, Central America, and Mexico compound the challenges of urban poverty.

The European settlement of the western hemisphere imposed the most dramatic landscape modification in the history of the human race, while unleashing a tragic chapter of intercontinental slavery and the annihilation of millions of Native Americans. The human drama that unfolded over the ensuing five centuries built upon and significantly transformed preexisting patterns and processes of urbanization throughout the region (fig. 3.1).

The Mexican urban system was forged in large measure by the Aztec pattern of urbanization, which was subjugated militarily by the Spanish so the colonizers' dual mission of proselytizing and mining could proceed. Mexico, both in the 15th and 21st centuries, became the economic and urban anchor to mainland production. Mexico's pre-Columbian mining and agricultural system allowed this nation, in both its colonial and independent phases, to enter the Industrial Revolution before the rest of the region. The urban geographies of Mexico City and Monterrey, explored later in this chapter, highlight the relationship between these resource endowments and industrial-led urbanization.

Meanwhile, the urban corridors of Central America and the Caribbean followed an agricultural-driven model of colonial and postcolonial growth. Caribbean urbanization developed slowly and was confined in large measure by limited flatlands in the Caribbean and tied to the fortunes of monocultural exports such as sugar, bananas, and spices. The urban geographies of St. Thomas, U.S. Virgin Islands, and Havana, Cuba, highlight this region's external dependency on trade, sugar, and slavery that, in turn, shaped the process of urbanization.

HISTORICAL GEOGRAPHY OF MIDDLE AMERICAN AND CARIBBEAN URBAN DEVELOPMENT

Mexico

The historical antecedents of the urban system in Mexico date back to the precolonial era when the cities were first established. Many pre-Columbian cities remain to this day, and Tenochtitlan (now Mexico City) is the most renowned. At the time of the Spanish conquest in the 16th century, Tenochtitlan, located in the Valley of Mexico, had a population of approximately 300,000. It was the most important urban settlement of the Aztec Empire (also known as Culhua-Mexica) and the largest pre-Columbian settlement in the Western Hemisphere. Theirs was an empire that stretched across a large part of Mesoamerica. Important settlements co-existed, including the Mayan population in the Yucatan Peninsula; the Tarascos in the present-day states of Michoacán, Jalisco, Colima, and Guanajuato; and the Zapotecas and Mixes in the state of Oaxaca.

Two particular aspects of these patterns of population settlement stand out. First, these large population agglomerations adopted a "city-state" model of organization, whereby a large commercial and religious settlement dominated rural communities and other smaller political-religious localities within their hinterland. Second, the major urban cultures were particularly prominent in the central region of Mexico. Estimates place this dispersed population in 1521, the time of contact, at 2.5 million. This region played a

historically significant role in the formation of the subsequent urban agglomerations of the Spanish. Tenochtitlan, refounded as Mexico City, became the capital of the Spanish Empire (Nueva España).

During the 300 years of the colonial era, urban development expanded northwards and toward the Gulf of Mexico. The Spanish developed new cities to carry out administrative and political functions and to serve as economic centers to facilitate commerce with Spain. Developments to the north exploited natural resources, especially minerals, while expansion east of Mexico City connected colonial Mexican exports with the Spanish port of Seville. Colonial Mexico inherited and upheld the central region (the highlands) as its historic and geographic core. In many regions, colonial cities coincided almost exactly with pre-existing indigenous settlements. In other regions, especially in the central part of the country and the lowlands of Yucatan where Mayan groups had developed, old indigenous towns co-existed with the new Spanish settlements.

Mining and agricultural centers constituted the first phase in the colonization of the northern region of the country. Spanish mining towns were founded close to important silver mines, whose indigenous settlements included Taxco, Pachuca, Zacatecas, and Guanajuato. These centers and company towns functioned as enclave economies. Bajio, in western central Mexico, was (re)constructed during the colonial period as a key base of the agriculture and livestock sector. Abundant natural resources in this region—its fertile plains supported food and fiber for the colonial government—were key factors in its colonization and in the establishment of conditions favorable to future urban growth.

It was not until the second half of the 19th century, following Mexico's independence in 1821 and during the presidency of Porfirio Díaz that new important regional centers emerged. During this period, moderate regional growth was stimulated through foreign investment and the development of railways and highways. Until the 1910 Mexican Revolution, foreign investment was concentrated in railways (33%) and mining (24%). Port development linked the railway network to maritime trade. Together, these technological and commercial links led to a proliferation of mining centers in northern Mexico, which, in turn, triggered regional markets and urban growth.

Railroad expansion played a crucial role in stimulating urban growth in various cities in the central and northern regions of the country. Mérida (the hub of commercial sisal plantations) and Guadalajara, Veracruz, Monterrey, and San Luís Potosí (all with direct transport links to Tampico on the Gulf of Mexico) grew rapidly. Old mining towns in the north gave way to new cities. Monterrey, at one time known as the "Pittsburgh of Mexico," became a major center of heavy industry (e.g., steel, foundries, manufacturing). Veracruz, a principal transport node, handled nearly all import and export shipping cargo.

The economic, geographic, and political changes that took place during the Porfirio Díaz presidencies (1876–1880 and 1884–1911) had long-term implications for Mexico's urban system. A communication network facilitated interaction between the central and northern regions of the country. High dependency on exports to the United States largely inhibited the formation of a balanced urban system, and those cities that were the largest agglomerations at the start of the 20th century retained their economic and political dominance in subsequent years.

Particular national and international events slowed urban growth in the first decades of the 20th century. The revolutionary movement within Mexico of 1910–1921 and the global economic depression of the 1930s curtailed exports and urban growth. Nevertheless, between 1900 and 1940, the urban population grew at a rate far greater than the total population, increasing from 1.4 to 3.9 million inhabitants. Although the number of cities increased from 33 in 1900 to 55 in 1940, most urban growth was concentrated in the larger cities of Mexico. In 1900, there were only two cities with populations greater than 100,000. Yet, these made up one-third of urban Mexico and represented 10.5% of the national population. By 1940, there were six cities of this size, accounting for 12% of the urban population and 20% of the total population. By this time, the population of Mexico City had reached 1.5 million, and its primacy index had increased; it was nearly seven times larger than the second largest city, Guadalajara.

In the 1950s, the population of Mexico City reached 3 million, whereas Guadalajara and Monterrey, the two next largest cities, had populations of a little over 250,000. Industrialization policies received wide support, and manufacturing activity, financed by both the private and public sectors, took advantage of economies of scale in Mexico City. This led to further demographic concentration in Mexico City.

At the beginning of the 1970s, a shift towards metropolitan expansion emerged as a new form of urban growth in Mexico City and some secondary cities. There was a massive rural–urban migration flow, with approximately 3 million migrants moving to Mexico City in the 1960s. This gave the capital an annual growth rate of 5.7, which was a historic high at that time. Eleven secondary cities experienced notable metropolitan expansion: Monterrey, Guadalajara, Puebla, Orizaba-Córdoba, Veracruz, Chihuahua, Tampico, León, Torreón, Mérida, and San Luís Potosí. Of these, the first three had populations of over half a million. Three border cities—Tijuana and Mexicali in Baja California, and Ciudad Juárez in Chihuahua—expanded significantly and strengthened their relationships with twin cities across the border (tab. 3.1).

Mexico's border cities grew in importance when the demand for contractual migrant labor during World War II cast these cities as "staging areas" for border crossings of laborers into the United States. Between the 1940s and the early 1960s, the Bracero workers' program (named for the day-laborers who were contracted) brought specified numbers of Mexican laborers into U.S. corporate farm operations. When the program was discontinued in the 1960s, concern grew for the service industries that had developed on the Mexican side of the "twin cities" and for potential unemployment problems. In response, *maquiladora* factories were established as part of the Border Industrialization Program. This arrangement allowed American companies to import manufacturing parts to Mexican cities, have them assembled in maquiladora (e.g., piecemeal assembly) plants, and re-import the finished products into the United States while paying only value-added tax. However, with the creation of the North American Free Trade Act in 1992, the relative locational advantage of being close to the United States dissipated, as trade barriers excluding the rest of Mexico fell for trade with the United States and Canada. Today, the border cities identified in Table 3.1 retain high levels of manufacturing and service workers

Table 3.1   The U.S.–Mexican Border Twin Cities Phenomenon: Population and Employment Data

City	Population	Formal Employment
El Paso, Texas	732,613	255,700
Ciudad Juárez, Chihuahua	1,420,262	331,623
Laredo, Texas	219,760	75,700
Nuevo Laredo, Tamaulipas	363,919	118,561
McAllen, Texas	642,776	179,200
Reynosa, Tamaulipas	504,748	175,495
Brownsville, Texas	370,268	114,700
Matamoros, Tamaulipas	486,941	167,362

Source: Federal Reserve Bank of Dallas, *Crossroads*, Issue 2, 2005. Accessed November 11, 2007 at http://www.dallasfed.org/research/crossroads/2005/cross0502.html, Table 1.

and, except for the Mexican twin city of Reynosa-Tamaupilas, have even larger labor markets than their U.S. counterparts. Accordingly, it is more appropriate to think of these twin cities as a single conurbation, working in similar manufacturing and service sectors, rather than as discrete cities divided by an international boundary.

Between 1950 and 1970, Mexico's urban population grew at a rate of almost 5% per annum, while the rural population (in settlements of fewer than 2,500 inhabitants) grew only at an average rate of 1.5% per year; 8 out of every 10 new inhabitants were urban dwellers. From 1950 to 1970, most demographic factors signaled improvements in the quality of life. Life expectancy increased from 51.9 to 63.1 years, and infant mortality fell from 116 deaths per 1,000 live births to 73. Despite this progress, there were significant gaps between urban and rural areas. Millions left the countryside in search of work in cities, but there were very few destinations for gainful employment. Almost half of the rural migrants ended up in Mexico City, and one-fifth went to Guadalajara and Monterrey. Although Mexico became predominantly urban, it revealed substantial disparities between urban and rural living conditions, as well as regional inequality.

By the start of the 1980s, a process of urban growth deconcentration was under way, as intermediate cities in various regions began to experience greater growth rates than larger cities. This process took advantage of the opportunities offered by medium-sized cities located close to large cities. Such amenities included lower costs of land and housing, newer infrastructure, more parks and open space, and less congestion.

By 1970, Mexico's urban, industrial, and demographic transitions were well under way, as overall growth rates had fallen. By 2006, 70% of Mexico's 103 million people lived in cities. Although a persistent trend nationwide is the concentration of population in an increasing number of large cities, it is important to note that growth rates have dropped for cities of all sizes. Since the 1970s, growth rates of cities in excess of 1 million residents have been consistent with overall national population growth rates. However, wide social differences remain; these exist not only between central and peripheral regions of the country, but also between economic sectors and between different ethnic groups. Southern, more indigenously populated areas of Mexico around the states of Chiapas and Oaxaca, for example, remain some of the poorest regions of the country. They are also a principal source of out-migration to the United States because job opportunities are so limited there.

The new millennium signals emerging trends in Mexico's urban system. Currently, urban growth is occurring not only in intermediate cities located close to large cities, but also in independent cities in remote regions far from the large agglomerations. That manufacturing in Mexico City has decreased in recent years due to Asian competitors is likely related to this phenomenon.

From a socioeconomic perspective, it is interesting to evaluate national and subnational levels of human development in an international context. In 2000, the United Nations Human Development Index (HDI) ranked Mexico 54th out of 173 countries. This ranking revealed an HDI approaching a medium-high to high level. Within Latin America and the Caribbean, Mexico ranks seventh, below Argentina, Chile, Costa Rica, Uruguay, the Bahamas, and Cuba. There are significant geographic differences in the HDI at a sub-national level. The Federal District (containing Mexico City) and Nuevo León (which contains the city of Monterrey) carry a significant human development advantage over other states such as rural and indigenous Chiapas and Oaxaca in the south. The Federal District has an HDI comparable to that of European countries such as Portugal and Greece, whereas Oaxaca and Chiapas have HDIs similar to those found in the Palestinian Territories, Uzbekistan, and Algeria. Key differences are even more pronounced at the municipal level. In Mexico City for example, the wealthy residential area of Delegación Benito Juárez registers an HDI comparable to the national index of Germany. At the other extreme are municipalities equal to levels found in African countries, as is the case in various municipalities of the states of Guerrero and Oaxaca.

Strongly associated with the HDI is the Marginalization Index. This demonstrates the exclusion of certain social groups from the development process and its benefits. Five variables make up the index: access to health care, access to education, access to housing and basic services, perception of adequate income, and gender inequality. It is calculated at the level of the smallest urban census units, the Basic Urban Geostatistical Area (BGAs). Results show that 31.7% of these units have a "very high" level of marginalization, and 20.6% reveal a "high" level of marginalization. Together, they account for 52% of all BGAs. Put another way, 29.1 million urban dwellers— nearly one-third of the country—live in conditions of "high" or "very high" poverty.

BGAs with the highest urban marginalization concentrate in small cities with populations under 100,000 inhabitants. Yet, given the higher total populations found in larger cities, these urban centers absorb greater total numbers of inhabitants living in conditions of high or very high marginalization. Thus, marginalization afflicts almost half the national urban population (48%) that resides in cities with populations exceeding 1 million.

Mexican urbanization and industrialization have created environmental problems, particularly air pollution. Monitoring data show that the most important pollutants are ozone (O_3) and particulates smaller than 10 micrometers (PM_{10}). In Mexico City, ozone is the main problem. In 2004, levels were high for 170 days, a considerable decrease from previous years. Ozone levels in Guadalajara have also decreased over recent years, with only 47 days passing normal levels in 2004. Most other cities maintain rates of less than 40 days per year.

There has been an overall improvement in air quality in the main cities because of the use of low-lead and -sulfur gasoline and the imposition of strict limits on emissions for new vehicles. In the case of PM_{10}, rates in Mexico City dropped from 135 days above the normal level in 1996, to just 5 days in 2004. Accordingly, the capital is no longer the zone with highest rates of contamination, as Toluca and Monterrey have shown increased levels of pollution since 2000. The overall trend has been towards reduced levels of PM_{10}, carbon monoxide (CO) and sulfur dioxide (SO_2). Nevertheless, more investment is required to reduce air pollution. Public sector spending on pollution reduction in 2002 totaled 91.6 million pesos (US $8,193,000), a mere 0.3% of total environmental expenditures. These contemporary problems are a manifestation of Mexico's complex history of conquest, settlement, and urbanization.

Central America

If the conquest of the Aztec population in the Valley of Mexico was facilitated by a large city whose leadership was quickly subjugated by Spanish rule, the smaller, more dispersed towns of the lands south of Mexico delayed conquest. The growth of significant cities in Central America dates to the colonial era when Spain was responsible for the politico-administrative division of the region. The Captaincy General of New Spain (Spanish Empire) first used the city of Antigua, Guatemala, as its base, but after a series of earthquakes devastated Antigua, it moved the capital to present-day Guatemala City. Each captaincy (colonial jurisdiction) had a provincial capital: San Salvador in El Salvador, Comayagua in Honduras, Granada in Nicaragua, Cártago in Costa Rica, and Panama La Vieja in Panama. Shortly after 1821, the year in which independence from Spain was achieved, most of these provincial capitals became national capitals. Guatemala, initially part of the post-independence Mexican Empire, seceded from it in 1823 when the Federal Republic of Central America was established. At that time, Guatemala City played dual roles as both state capital and federal capital.

The urbanization process in Central America can largely be divided into two main phases. The first period, from 1821 to 1930, includes the first century of independence from Spain and the foundation and subsequent peak of agricultural export economies. The second period dates from the 1930s until the present day and marks a transition in both the economic model in the region and a phase of accelerated urbanization.

The era of independence shifted hegemonic control of the region from Spain to Great Britain and opened new external markets for the region's agricultural produce, which significantly influenced the nature of urbanization in the region. The early decades of independence marked a transition for some countries from the export of various agricultural products to the nearly exclusive export of coffee. In 1835, San José became the capital of Costa Rica, first because of tobacco production and later because of coffee, as it became home to the country's coffee oligarchy. The colonial export base of Guatemala shifted from grain production and pig farming to coffee in the second half of the 19th century. By the end of the 19th century, practically all countries in the region depended largely on income from coffee exports. The coffee boom consolidated the Central American capitals. This was apparent in Guatemala City (Guatemala), San Salvador (El Salvador), and San José (Costa Rica), where national governments expanded to fill this new political and economic role, and city populations and physical expanse grew accordingly.

Meanwhile, North American investment in banana plantations, first in Costa Rica, then in Guatemala, and finally in Honduras,

accelerated urbanization in these regions. Together with the coffee economy, it actively produced social differentiation through the need for agricultural, transport, and dock laborers in cities, ports, and hinterlands, and for salaried employees in the emerging urban centers of Puerto Barrios (Guatemala), Bluefields (Nicaragua), Limón (Costa Rica), and Colón (Panama). International capital co-opted and monopolized the communication, transportation, and commercial infrastructures of much of the region and its cities. For example, between 1875 and 1885, the banana enclave appropriated more than 300 miles (480 km) of railroad in Guatemala; this infrastructure had been built with national funds. Multinational companies also controlled the docks and port installations of Puerto Barrios in Guatemala and San José in Costa Rica. Foreign railroad tycoons, such as the American Minor Keith, wielded considerable economic and political influence in expanding the railroads and developing international trade throughout Central America.

Panama City developed in a markedly distinct way as a capital city, as it traded its links with Spain for the geopolitical project of Gran Colombia (Great Colombia). Its subsequent growth was based on the development of inter-ocean communication, initially via railroad and later via the canal projects driven first by France and later by the United States (figs. 3.3, 3.4).

Yet the Central American urbanization process was most prolific around the middle of the 20th century as rural dwellers came to cities in search of work and improved quality of life in terms of education, health care, personal security, housing, transportation, and communications. In some cases, their expectations have been met; in other cases, they have encountered disappointment.

Today, Central America is nearly 70% urban (tab. 3.2), ranging from approximately

Figure 3.2   The Panama Canal is a great engineering feat, which allows deep-draft ships to transport merchandise of every type between the Atlantic and Pacific Oceans. It is also one of the main tourist attractions of the city. (Photo by Jorge González)

45% in Honduras and Guatemala to 59% and 66% in Costa Rica and Panama, respectively. National poverty rates seem to mirror urbanization rates. Poverty is lowest in Costa Rica (20%) and Panama (35%) and highest in Honduras (75%) and Guatemala (65%). Concomitantly, Guatemala has the highest indigenous population of any country in the region, standing at approximately 5 million, or 80% of the total indigenous population of Central America (fig. 3.4). Although levels of urbanization in Central American cities have increased over the past 30 years, they still lag behind the Latin American average (tab. 3.2).

The largest and most important urban centers in Central America essentially correspond to the capital cities of the seven countries, together with other cities important for their economic integration and population levels, such as Antigua in Guatemala or León in Nicaragua. Next are a series of medium-sized and small cities, such as Cártago and Puntarenas in Costa Rica, Acajutla and New San Salvador in El Salvador, Chichicastenango and Esquipulas in Guatemala, San Pedro Sula and Copán in Honduras, Chinandega in Nicaragua, and Portobelo in Panama.

City and population distribution relates to Central America's physical geography, which criss-crosses the region with extensive mountain ranges and volcanoes, as well as innumerable rivers, waterfalls, and lakes. Central

Figure 3.3   Modern Panama City, with its many ultra-modern skyscrapers, is a vision of economic growth. (Photo by Jorge González)

America is also influenced by geological faults and continental plates. Together with the confluence of weather phenomena, these environmental conditions combine to make most of the human settlements of the region vulnerable to natural disasters, including earthquakes, volcanic eruptions, landslides, floods, and hurricanes. Unfortunately, most countries lack the resources to prevent, prepare for, or manage these hazards. Yet it was precisely the availability of water and land resources that induced the growth of settlements on volcanic soil and flood plains, and which in turn allowed the development of agriculture as the basic economic activity.

Except for El Salvador, which has only a Pacific coastline, and Belize, which borders the Caribbean (Atlantic section), the remaining Central American countries all have coastlines on both the Pacific and Atlantic Oceans. This allowed seaports to be established which were of vital economic importance to the individual countries and the region as a whole. Construction of the Pan-American Highway, dating back to the 1930s, has also promoted urban development throughout Central America. The Pan-American Highway winds along the western edge of Central America and connects all the capital cities. Serving as a vertical axis, the highway has allowed roads linking yet other urban centers and smaller settlements to be developed.

Urbanization has played a crucial role in providing the necessary infrastructure to allow

Table 3.2   Levels of Urbanization in Central America

| | 1970–2000 | | |
| | *Level of Urbanization (%)* | | |
Country	1970	1980	2000
Panama	47.6	50.4	65.8
Costa Rica	38.8	43.1	59.0
Belize	51.0	49.4	47.7
El Salvador	39.4	44.1	58.4
Nicaragua	47.0	50.3	57.2
Guatemala	35.5	37.4	45.1
Honduras	28.9	34.9	44.4
*Total:			
Latin America & Caribbean	57.2	65.1	75.4
Central America	53.8	60.2	68.8
Caribbean	45.4	52.3	62.1

Note: Countries are ordered by level of urbanization in 2000.
*Urban population as a percentage of the total population.
Source: Population Division of the Department of Economic and Social Affairs of the United Nations
Secretariat, World Population Prospects: *The 2004 Revision and World Urbanization Prospects: The 2005*
Revision, http://esa.un.org/unup, Monday, December 03, 2007; 12:58:42 PM.

ease of movement between a range of traditional tourist and newer eco-tourist sites. The rise of adventure tourism in recent years generates multipliers in the economies of local communities, especially those of indigenous peoples who are able to organize the control and development of tourist activity. Tourism in all its variations attracts both regional and international tourists, and thus provides an important source of income for the region.

Despite the economic, cultural, and political development that has occurred within and around many cities, the urban panorama in Central America is not promising. Priority is often given to property development serving the high-earning population, including gated residential communities, business and commercial centers, corporate offices, and franchises. Economic liberalization at the global scale has led to pronounced social polarization and economic insecurity in cities throughout Central America. Child and adolescent labor is rampant as families

press their children into petty commerce, service provision, and begging. Regardless, their contributions to family income are often not enough for the family to subsist. Many families face the difficult decision of pushing one or more family members to migrate to larger cities or even to the United States. It is common among Central American women, particularly from El Salvador, to make the long trip to Europe, where they characteristically labor in domestic or care-giving work in an effort to support their families economically.

In recent decades, the widespread poverty and exclusion that affects large sections of the population in Central American cities has led to a proliferation of gangs. Gang members are typically young and tend to live in peripheral zones of large cities such as Guatemala City (Guatemala), Tegucigalpa (Honduras), and San Salvador (El Salvador). In 2005, gangs were allegedly responsible for 5,200 deaths in Guatemala, 2,349 in Honduras, and more

Figure 3.4   Most Guatemalan indigenous women still wear a traditional blouse called the *huipil*. This ornate garment is woven on traditional looms and then hand-embroidered. Villages and towns have their own unique design, which is particularly useful at periodic and regional markets, so both vendors and buyers can readily identify the community of the seller, which in turn means that certain goods and produce might be available there. (Photo by Matthew Taylor)

than 3,000 in El Salvador. The principal gangs are the "Mara Salvatrucha" and the "Mara 18." They define themselves by extensive tattoos on the face and body. They are linked with criminal acts such as the trafficking of drugs and people, assassinations, rape, and assaults. It is estimated that more than 100,000 young people have joined these gangs—40,000 in Honduras, 60,000 in Guatemala, and 10,000 in El Salvador (box 3.1).

The influence of the *maras* has spread beyond Central America into Mexico, Spain, and the United States. The social and eco-nomic instability in Central America, evidenced in scarce educational and job opportunities, and family disintegration, leaves many young people to believe they have only two viable options: attempt to migrate to the United States or join a gang.

The Caribbean

In 1502 Nicolás de Ovando claimed what may well be the first permanent European settlement in the Americas, when he and 2,500 Spanish colonists settled in eastern Hispaniola. The fierce

Box 3.1 Gangs: A Violent Urban Social Development

The rise of gangs throughout the cities of Central America is associated with many factors. Some hold that gangs reflect the struggle of some young people to search for an identity. Others argue they are the outcome of widespread and persistent poverty and political disenfranchisement. Most concur that, in seeking to improve the quality of their lives and acquire what is otherwise unattainable, some youths resort to violence. Gangs are associated with such violent/criminal activities as organized crime, arms trafficking, forgery, gangsterism, rape, kidnapping, extortion, and the sale and consumption of drugs. Some gangs demand "taxes" from bus drivers in order to pass through their territory, whereas others extort protection money from small business owners who operate on their turf.

In Central America, the most notorious and violent type of gangs are known as *maras*, the most infamous of which is the *Mara Salvatrucha* or MS 13. It is made up primarily of young men between the ages of 12 and 25. Although the *Mara Salvatrucha* is dominant in El Salvador, where it represents approximately 70% of all youth gangs, it has spread throughout the Americas from Canada to Colombia. It has taken particular hold in impoverished border regions of Mexico and cities of Central America where alternative sources of fulfillment are conspicuously absent. These gangs are particularly distinctive in their highly visible use of tattoos, with many gang members having identifying gang tattoos on their faces, necks, chests, and hands.

The word *mara* has become the generic term for youth gangs in Central America. *Mara Salvatrucha* was founded on the streets of Los Angeles by immigrant Salvadoran youths fleeing the Salvadoran civil war. It is alleged that *Mara Salvatrucha* was formed in response to the discrimination and victimization Salvadoran youths experienced at the hands of ethnic gangs proliferating in Los Angeles in the 1970s. Later, other Central American immigrants were integrated into the gang. The word *Salvatrucha* refers to one who is a "shrewd Salvadoran". It is widely thought that the current proliferation of violent gangs in Central and parts of South America is related to large-scale repatriations from the United States because many gang members find fertile conditions in the poverty that is so prevalent in the cities of their home region. Gangs have come to represent (at least in the popular and political imagination) one of the most serious threats to security and democracy in the region. The formal political power vacuum created by many Central American governments enhances the power of gangs. In many cities, virulent attacks have become an issue of national security. The spread of the *maras* has undermined the authority of the police and weakened the ability of governments to protect communities.

Caribs thwarted European settlement in the eastern Caribbean until the 17th century and relented only in the 18th century. During this time, the Spanish focused their energies on the Greater Antilles. Accordingly, Spanish administrative control fanned out from Santo Domingo (the general term for eastern Hispaniola) into Jamaica (1509) and Trinidad (1510). By 1511, Florida marked the eastern expansion of Spanish territories. Caribbean ports were scoped for harbor protection, fresh water, and provisions, and for nexuses between what little mineral and agricultural wealth might be extracted from port hinterlands.

Hernán Cortez's conquest of Mexico in 1519, with its gold and silver, created some disinterest in the Caribbean. Spain would gradually relinquish its control over selected parts of the Antilles to the English, Dutch, and French, and sugar and tobacco would come to replace the pursuit of precious minerals. Accordingly, that required an elaborate trans-Atlantic slave trade. Greed, inhumanity, and arduous demands placed on plantation slave workers between 1518 and 1870 drove the trans-Atlantic slave trade. Of the nearly 10 million slaves brought to the Americas, the Caribbean would absorb nearly half. The majority arrived during the 18th century to toil in the sugar economies of Jamaica, Barbados, and the Leeward Islands. Antislavery societies from Britain and France enlisted rationalist arguments from the Enlightenment to challenge slavery, but the Spanish colonies were keen on expanding sugar production. Indeed, cycles of slave importation, sugar production and processing, and the exporting of semi-processed (brown sugar and molasses) sugar and refined sugar established a vast network of plantations and small ports throughout the Caribbean. This historical economic geography set the stage for the distribution of cities, towns, and villages in the region.

It took nearly two centuries for European powers to establish maritime control over the dispersed ports and islands that covered more than 1 million square miles (2.7 million sq km) of the Caribbean basin. Even that control was tenuous at best. For instance, the ports of Barbados and Nelson's Dockyard in Antigua attracted pirates who preyed on cargo ships traveling from Spain, England, and Holland. Bluebeard, Bartholomew Roberts, Stede Bonet, and Henry Morgan are the most notorious buccaneers and privateers who plied these waters in hope of snatching cargo shuttled between Europe and the Americas. In response, Caribbean ports developed fortresses to protect their fleets and provide succor to mariners and friendly merchants. Until the Treaty of Madrid in 1670—when Spain and England finally agreed on territorial claims—many privateers defended the interests of the European colonists. Henry Morgan defended Jamaica for the British and invaded Puerto Principe (now Camaguey), Cuba, and Puerto Bello, Panama. Caribbean colonial ports became key centers for island control, inter-island transfer points, and European enclaves of colonial resources (fig. 3.5).

Four striking patterns highlight the contemporary urbanization and settlement patterns of the Caribbean. First, no Caribbean island is without its primate city. And with the exception of Havana (Cuba) and San Juan (Puerto Rico), most primate cities are located on the leeward coast, immune from the brisk trade winds (*vientos alisios*), and are often nestled along a deep and protected bay. These historic ports were well suited for anchorage or for loading sugar and unloading cargo (e.g., rum, spices). Colonists built gun sites and forts on commanding hilltops and ridges to protect the locals from marauding pirates and rival European colonists. Second, Caribbean urbanization in the past half-

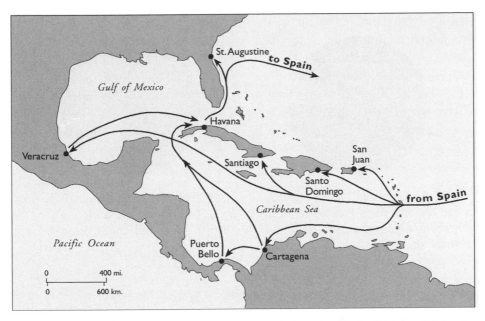

Figure 3.5   Spanish Ports and Convoy Routes in the Colonial Era. *Source:* Adapted from Robert C. West and John P. Augelli, *Middle America: Its Lands and Peoples,* 2d ed. (Englewood Cliffs, NJ: Prentice Hall, 1976), 64.

century shows that mid-sized cities (500,000 to 1,000,000 residents) have held the same relative proportion of urban residents, whereas those with fewer than half a million residents have declined (fig. 3.6). Third, places with 1 to 5 million residents have more than doubled (fig. 3.6). These trends are particularly striking given the limited amount of low-lying land along the bay fronts, coastal plains, and river valleys etched in the islands' landscapes that can accommodate city growth.

Fourth, beyond the Greater Antilles (Cuba, Hispaniola, Puerto Rico, Jamaica), insularity is a key constraint. With the exception of Barbados, most of the low-lying islands (roughly less than 1,500 feet in maximum elevation) are rather small and therefore pale to the scale of continental urbanization found elsewhere in Latin America. The highest points on these rugged islands include, but are not limited to, Anguilla (213 ft), St. Martine (1,360 ft), St. Bartélemy

(992 ft), Barbuda (992 ft), Antigua (1,330 ft), Désirade (912 ft), Marie Galante (672 ft), and Barbados (1,100 ft). Mountainous islands are more prevalent as St. Kitts (4,314 ft), Nevis (3,596 ft), Montserrat (3,002 ft), Guadeloupe (4,869 ft), Dominica (4,747 ft), St. Lucia (3,154 ft), St. Vincent (4,048 ft), and Grenada (2,749 ft) illustrate.

Spanish and English settlement patterns provide historical backdrops to contemporary urbanization. Spanish settlements needed to defend the windward approaches into the Caribbean and fortress towns. These locations marked early landfalls for those ships riding the trade winds. San Felipe del Morro castle in San Juan, Puerto Rico, characterizes this defensive posture, as do El Morro castle in Havana, Cuba, and the fortress guarding the entrance to Santiago de Cuba. In turn, these key ports relied on nearby forests for shipbuilding and repair. Spanish towns in the Caribbean followed the

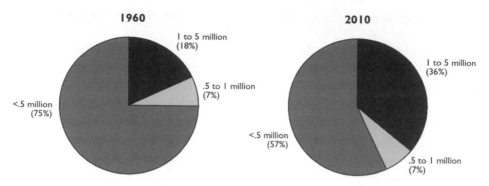

Figure 3.6   Caribbean Urbanization by City Sizes, 1960 and 2010. *Source:* Data from United Nations, *World Population Prospects: The 2004 Revision and World Urbanization Prospects, 2005 Revision* (2006, http://esa.un.org/unup), Sunday, February 18, 2007.

same grid-style settlement plan dictated by the Law of the Indies as towns in Mexico and Central America. Towns were centered upon the main plaza, usually anchored by a government building (*cabildo*) and church at each end. Block size and street width were predetermined; locally unwanted land uses such as garbage dumps, slaughterhouses, and cemeteries were sited at the periphery of the new towns. Early Spanish Caribbean ports depended mostly on adjacent hinterlands for food crops and stock-raising; salted beef was of particular appeal to mariners and town-dwellers. Because the function of these settlements was in large measure to facilitate extraction of mineral wealth from Mexico and other parts of the mainland, little urban growth took place in Caribbean ports of the 16th century.

Non-Spanish settlements were less orthodox and more haphazard in form. In Britain, for instance, royal favor was doled out to loyalists by the Proprietary System. Caribbean settlers from England had learned from Atlantic seaboard settlements in North America. Accordingly, their priorities entailed clearing land for wood and agriculture, constructing fortresses, and coming to terms with indige-

nous peoples. Although the British originally planted tobacco and cotton on their settlements, they would gradually turn to sugar monoculture. In both British and Spanish settlements, little colonial architecture other than military structures, a few churches, and fortified (brick and stone) sugar plantations have survived until today because of fire, tropical storms, and rebuilding. Subsequent discussion of Charlotte Amalie, U.S. Virgin Islands, and Havana, Cuba, will situate these historical settlement patterns.

REPRESENTATIVE CITIES

Mexico City: Ancient Aztec Capital, Contemporary Megacity

Mexico's Distrito Federal or capital city (Mexico City) was founded in the 14th century by the Aztecs. Called Tenochtitlan, it soon became the center of the largest empire in pre-Columbian Mesoamerica. As the current capital of the United States of Mexico, it is also the country's largest urban center and serves as the nation's economic, social, educational, and political hub. With a population of over 19 mil-

Figure 3.7   The Zócalo (Main Square) in Mexico City is surrounded by colonial buildings, most notably the Metropolitan Cathedral and the headquarters of the Federal and Capital Governments. (Photo by Irma Escamilla)

lion in 2005, it is the largest city in Latin America and among the largest cities in the world. Its growth in the 20th century burgeoned from 3.4 million in 1950 to about 9 million in 1970, and just shy of 15 million by 1990.

In local parlance, "Mexico City" refers to the entire metropolitan area, which not only covers the Federal District, but also includes parts of the states of Mexico and Hidalgo. At the beginning of the 21st century, its metropolitan area stretched over an area of more than 1,900 square miles (5,000 sq km), or four times the size of the state of Rhode Island, of which the Federal District accounted for nearly 30%. Mexico City is located in a closed drainage basin at an altitude of approximately 7,280 feet above sea level. It is surrounded by six mountain ranges. A plain extends from the east of the city, ending in the Sierra Nevada range with its two striking landmarks: Volcano Iztacíhuatl (17,323 ft) and Volcano Popocatépetl (17,887 ft). Toward the north of the city is the Sierra de

Guadalupe, around which new urban areas have developed. Although Mexico City lies within the tropics, its altitude affords it a more temperate climate.

The Zócalo or main square—now officially called the Plaza de la Constitución—is the traditional center of the city (fig. 3.7). On the northern side of the square, close to the ancient site of the main Aztec temple, is the Metropolitan Cathedral. Spanish conquistadores frequently subjugated the Native American population by rebuilding churches atop indigenous temples. To the east is the Palacio de Gobierno (main government building); built on the ruins of the ancient Aztec emperor's palace, it is another symbolic replacement of political power. The colonial city extended in an orderly fashion for various blocks around this square, as prescribed by guidelines specified in the Law of the Indies. These orders, first issued in Spain in 1494, became the military engineer's template and mandated the location

Figure 3.8   The colonial architecture of the streets and houses of the *colonia* Pedregal de San Ángel has been preserved to this day. The area is one of the most exclusive zones in the south of the city, and is also an important tourist attraction. (Photo by Irma Escamilla)

of many colonial- and independence-era buildings in this zone. Many of the original structures and buildings of the traditional urban core—known as the centro histórico, or historical center—remain intact.

In general, Mexico City typifies the urbanization patterns and processes of Middle America and the Caribbean. Unlike the Anglo American model of urbanization that is prone to use the bulldozer, build limited-access highways, and embark on massive urban redevelopment projects to restructure the traditional downtown, the historic quarters of most cities in Middle America and the Caribbean have been safeguarded. The more "modern" aspects of 20th century urbanization developed just beyond the centro histórico. Also in contrast with the Anglo American and European models of urbanization, the national

elite in Spanish America placed more social value on centrality. Therefore, many elite families and key government offices remained near the traditional colonial core until the 20th century when congestion, the automobile, and the need for new construction encouraged a slow process of middle- and upper-income suburbanization *a la norteamericana*. As a result, Mexico has dozens of World Heritage Sites that celebrate these colonial quarters. This leaves the urban poor in most Middle American and Caribbean cities to concentrate at the city edge where land values are cheaper, and self-help housing develops. In the case of Mexico City, the wealthy districts are concentrated in the west and various zones in the south, and in *colonias* such as Lomas de Chapultepec, Polanco, and Pedregal de San Ángel (fig. 3.8). These districts contrast sharply

Box 3.2 GIS and the Solution of Urban Problems

Mexico City has been expanding since the second half of the 20th century. Since 1995, a range of technological innovations has been used in determining irregular human settlement in former conservation lands in the southern part of the city. GIS and remote sensing aid in identifying biophysical, economic, and social features that cannot be observed with the naked eye.

One analysis identified 8,017 areas of squatter settlements (shantytowns) and examined a sample of 493 of these areas. It determined that shantytowns expanded into the eastern and western extremes of the conservation area at an annual rate of 13.2% between 1995 and 2000, and to the west-central and south-central zones at a rate of 4.6% between 2000 and 2005. The study found that expansion was taking place beyond settlement borders. It further detected fragmentation of the properties as well as differences in relief variation among the settlements under study because of road construction. In some traditional settlements there are areas of relatively continuous building, whereas in others there is notable dispersion. Squatter settlements account for as much as half the total area of all new expansion of traditional settlements (i.e., the total expansion including legally zoned and regulated development).

The use of GIS and remote sensing techniques may contribute to the design of policies appropriate both for these vulnerable populations and for ecologically fragile lands.

with the poverty in the northern zones and the illegal settlements in the eastern edges, beyond the Benito Juárez International Airport, where many communities lack basic services in zones such as Chalco and Ixtapaluca (box 3.2).

Given its metropolitan character, the city is a multinucleated place where every large sector of the city has developed its own commercial and service structure. The city center, at one time the preferred shopping district of the middle classes, has lost its prestige with the upsurge of shinier suburban shopping centers that offer glitzier retailing and new places for consumption. As in other corners of the world, suburban retailing challenges the traditional role of the city center as the main retailing district. Examples include the Plaza Satélite in the north of the city, Perisur in the South (fig. 3.9),

and Sante Fé in the west. The market La Merced, which had been the main food market for the city since colonial times, was replaced in the 1980s with a modern market in the east of the city (fig. 3.10).

What factors account for the changing social and economic geography of Mexican cities? One reason stems from the import-substitution industrialization strategy implemented in the 1940s, which created conditions of stability and prosperity that made Mexico City the most important industrial center in the country. Today, it is responsible for 30% of national industrial production. In the second half of the 20th century, encouraged by the Border Industrialization Program of 1964, heavy industry began moving from the capital to border cities of the north. Just as many U.S.

Figure 3.9   Perisur is one of the large shopping malls in the south of Mexico City, where the presence of globally recognized prestigious stores provides stark evidence of globalization. (Photo by Irma Escamilla)

manufacturing towns lost jobs to lower-wage labor in maquiladoras, so too did Mexico City. *stail herl*

Today, the most important industries in Mexico City are chemicals, plastics, cement, and textiles; light industry is becoming increasingly important. Due to the good quality of life enjoyed by a large proportion of its inhabitants, and because it is the most important supply center of the country, Mexico City accounts for around 45% of the country's commercial activity. Perhaps more than any other economic activity, financial services are particularly concentrated here. In addition to the headquarters of banks, the country's stock exchange and central bank are located in Mexico City.

Likewise, Mexico City is the hub of the national transport system. Five main highways link the capital to the different regions of the country, as well as to Guatemala and the United States through the now 70-year-old Pan-American Highway. Benito Juárez International Airport receives both national and international flights, in a proportion of 75% and 25% of total flights, respectively. In addition, there is an extensive intracity transport network, including the metro system that is used by over 2 million people daily, and a range of different types of buses.

Mexico City has always been one of the most important cultural centers in Latin America. It boasts a number of major cultural

Figure 3.10   The Central de Abasto in Mexico City is the city's main collection and distribution point for retailers and wholesalers, which means thousands of daily transactions in the buying and selling of goods as diverse as fruit and vegetables, cereals, seeds, cleaning products, pharmaceutical goods, sweets, and cigarettes. (Photo by Irma Escamilla)

sites, and its cinema, film, theatrical, and television industries rival those of Buenos Aires. The Palacio de Bellas Artes in the center of the city is an important opera and concert venue, and the Cultural Center of the National Autonomous University of Mexico in the south hosts the National Library, a large concert hall, and various theatres. The National Museum of Anthropology is considered one of the most important of its kind, and some monuments, such as the Chapultepec Castle and the Monument of Independence, are considered national symbols (fig. 3.12). Mexico City is a megacity of significant history, impressive scale, and striking contrasts (fig. 3.13).

Monterrey, Mexico: Mexico's "Second City"?

Monterrey is the capital of the state of Nuevo León and is situated approximately 125 miles (200 km) from the Texan border. It is the third largest city in Mexico, with a 2005 population of 3.6 million. Most Mexicans consider it the second most important city because of its crucial industrial and financial roles. Urbanization in Monterrey derives in large measure from its proximity to the U.S. border. Its relative location is also advantageous because it is located where the plains of the Gulf of Mexico and the eastern Sierra Madre meet. A pass through these two features gives Monterrey

Figure 3.11   The Metro is the backbone of Mexico City's public transport system, transporting over 2 million passengers a day via 11 lines. (Photo by Irma Escamilla)

direct access to the sea at the Tampico-Altamira port.

Monterrey was founded in 1579 as San Luís Rey de Francia. In 1596, it became known as the Metropolitan City of Monterrey. It was built on the west bank of the Santa Catarina River, according to the grid system dictated by the Law of the Indies, with streets crossing at right angles around a central plaza, which at the time was the Plaza de Zaragoza. Given its distance from the center of the country, Monterrey's population remained stationary until the 18th century, and it was not until the 19th century that the city began to grow significantly. In 1810, it had a population of only 7,000. After Mexico gained independence, the city established significant commercial links with the ports of Tampico and Matamoros. When Mexico ceded the territory of Texas to the United States in 1848, the new border region

around the Rio Bravo (called the Rio Grande in the United States) began to prosper. Contraband and the cotton trade during the American Civil War promoted the growth of Monterrey and that of many other border cities. Between 1882 and 1905, railroads linked Monterrey with Laredo in Texas and with Tampico, Matamoros, and Mexico City, establishing the base for Monterrey's industrial development.

Monterrey's greatest industrial development took place between 1890 and 1910, when local elites invested in industry. They took advantage of the domestic market and proximity to industrializing regions in the United States. Corporations established by the Monterrey business elite at this time were notably diverse, ranging from capital goods (e.g., cement, bricks, glass, machinery) to consumer products (e.g., beer, soft drinks, furniture, textiles, cigarettes, soap). This diversification pro-

Figure 3.12 Among the most distinctive monuments in Mexico City is the Angel of Independence, which located on the Paseo de la Reforma. It is here that the city's inhabitants congregate in collective celebration, for example, of sporting victories. (Photo by Irma Escamilla)

duced a multiplier effect among other sectors of the economy such as mining, agriculture, financial services, and transport. About 40 members of the original 10 powerful families have been linked to more than 260 corporations involved in diverse economic activities. After the Mexican Revolution of 1910, most of these family members formed part of the famous Monterrey Group.

The economic expansion of the 1940s spurred industrial integration for the Monterrey Group. This entailed investing in factories in other regions of the country, taking advantage of the internal protection measures granted by the Mexican government. Industrial investment fortified the banking and

financial sectors, and in 1943 the Monterrey Technological Institute of Advanced Study (Instituto Tecnológico de Estudios Superiores de Monterrey, ITESM) was founded to provide future generations of executives and administrators for Monterrey's industry with high-quality university educations. By 1960, the electronics industry was established, with pronounced growth in transport and car manufacturing. Factories spread along the edge of the city and transportation corridors. The automobile industry began supplying the growing Mexican automobile industry as well as the traditional core in Detroit, Michigan. In 1950, Monterrey generated 8% of Mexico's GDP; by 1970 this had increased to 10%. The oil boom of the late 1970s stimulated development of the petrochemical industry in Monterrey through petroleum-derived materials and fibers, marine exploration rigs, and submarine ducts.

Economic liberalization in the late 1980s ended advantages previously granted to Monterrey by the government. As a result, Monterrey looked to the export market. The arrival of foreign investment allowed various corporations to sell holdings, develop strategies of co-investment, and form strategic capital alliances with the United States, Europe, and Asia. Population grew at 2.3% per year in Monterrey from 1990 to 2005, which surpassed the growth rate in both Mexico City and Guadalajara.

In addition to hosting key educational, cultural, health-care, and business centers, Monterrey boasts entertainment attractions that are significant for both national and international tourism. One of the most famous landmarks of the city is the Cerro de la Silla, a hill that is famous for its likeness to a riding saddle (fig. 3.14). The Macroplaza, situated in the heart of Monterrey, is one of the largest plazas in the world. It stretches on for 100 acres

Figure 3.13   The demand of (primarily the young) population to "be connected" has meant a number of Internet cafes opening throughout the city, particularly in areas with schools nearby. (Photo by Irma Escamilla)

and contains a playful mix of green areas, monuments, and colonial buildings. Among the most important pieces are the bronze sculpture Fuente de Neptuno (Fountain of Neptune) by Spanish artist Luís Sanguino, the Homenaje al Sol (Homage to the Sun) by Mexican painter and sculptor Rufino Tamayo, and the Faro del Comercio (literally, the Lighthouse of Commerce) by renowned architect Luís Barragán. There are also art galleries, theaters, and a number of museums in the historic center, including the Museo Metropolitano de la Ciudad de Monterrey (Metropolitan Museum of Monterrey); the Museo de Historia Mexicana (Museum of Mexican History); the Museo de Arte Contemporáneo (Museum of Contemporary Art); the Museo de Ciencia, Arte y Tecnología (Museum of Science, Art, and Technology); and the Museo El Blanqueo. The Blanqueo Museum is a national heritage site; it has

had its original façade restored and is home to the oldest manufacturing installation in Nuevo León. Commercial activity and services are evident in the large shopping malls such as Galerías Monterrey, Galerías Valle Oriente, Plaza Fiesta San Agustín, and Plaza San Pedro, which all host various "shopertainment" services including cinemas and restaurants, which attract shoppers from within and beyond the city limits.

San José, Costa Rica: Spanish America's Troubled Cultural Capital

San José is the political and economic capital of Costa Rica. Like most Latin American cities, San José is laid out in a grid pattern anchored by a series of town squares fronted by churches. In 2006, the Union of Spanish American City Capitals declared San José the

Figure 3.14   A panoramic view of Monterrey illustrates the process of metropolitanization and shows the distinctive physical feature of this Northern city: the *Cerro de la Silla*. (Photo by Google-Earth)

cultural capital of Spanish America. Costa Rica's relative economic prosperity and political stability has made San José the safest city in the region. In recent years, however, crime has risen and is a serious concern.

San José is the largest city in Costa Rica. It is more than twice the size of Limón, Costa Rica's second largest city, located on the Atlantic/Caribbean coast. In contrast to most primate cities in Latin America, San José is located in the geographic center of Costa Rica. The semi-humid and temperate climate and fertile soils of the region favor intensive agriculture, and high-quality export products such as specialty leaf tobacco grow well there.

The region has long benefited from its privileged absolute and relative location. Since the colonial era, settlement and development have been concentrated in this part of Costa Rica. Over time, settlement gradually spread outward toward the coastal plains, a pattern that runs counter to the patterns experienced in most Latin American countries, where settlements first took hold at navigable ports on the coasts and gradually moved inward.

A series of hills within the Central Valley has not curtailed San Jose's expansion, whose metropolitan zone today encompasses Alajuela, Cártago, and Heredia. This conurbanization constitutes the "Central Region" and spills into adjoining valleys and mountain regions. Although the Central Region includes just 15% of the country's land area, more than half of the national population lives there. Wealth generated from Costa Rica's mining and agricultural sectors has supported business investment in San José and the subsequent expansion of its metropolitan region. Relative improvements in health conditions and public services, in addition to natural increase and rural emigration, have contributed to the rapid growth of San José. The spread of metropolitan San José into once rural areas produces a steady reclassification of rural areas to urban zones. Urban sprawl has overtaken small towns and outlying villages to such an extent that some peripheral zones lack basic services such as housing, jobs, and schools.

Metropolitan San José, like most primate cities, contains the most important and largest industries, businesses, and residential areas of the country. This concentration implies changes in land use, private-sector investment, and the distribution of wealth. San José consists of 14 *cantones* (administrative units similar to counties in the United States). Most *cantones* are residential areas that function as bedroom communities and are distant from most places of work, retail commerce, and medical and educational facilities. There is a growing demand in the more distant *cantones* for jobs, housing, and infrastructure to accommodate the city's growth. As such agglomeration reinforces San José's primacy, it disadvantages other regions of Costa Rica which are less densely populated and suffer from poor public services, which in turn reinforces primacy. Urban sprawl imposes high economic costs, necessitates the consumption of fossil fuels, and exacts human costs in the form of long and stressful commutes. These problems are exacerbated by a

road network that cannot accommodate present usage. Moreover, San José's sprawl threatens rich agricultural and protected lands in the Central Valley. In general, rapid growth and congestion threaten the sustainability of this capital city.

An unanticipated consequence of metropolitan sprawl is the hollowing out of the city's core as residential and business development shifts to peripheral zones of the city. The historic center of San José is no longer the economic, political, and social nexus of the country. San José's uncontrolled growth has led to a loss of identity, especially in the historic core. As often occurs in the process of industrialization and urbanization, the social fabric of residents in the traditional center is frayed. Crime, juvenile delinquency, and the proliferation of gangs threaten overall security and the longstanding high quality of life in San José. These problems afflict both residents and tourists. To address problems associated with San José's rapid and unplanned growth, various public–private partnerships have been formed by public agencies, international associations, nonprofit organizations, and the municipality. Efforts, not unlike those under way in some Anglo American cities, are now directed at revitalizing and bringing people and jobs back to the city center.

In recent years, Costa Rica has developed its tourism industry. It takes advantage of a variety of natural resources, including an excellent climate and such spectacular physical features as mountains, volcanoes, beaches, and rainforests. Tourism has energized the national economy because it has attracted hard currency expended by visitors from North America, Europe, and Asia. Most tourist ventures start in San José and fan out to the interior of the country. Although this creates economic multipliers for San José and its hinterland, it also creates economic and environmental stress. The tourism infrastructure (e.g., expansive networks of hotels, restaurants, and land and air transportation) must be maintained and upgraded continually to meet international expectations. Not only is this costly, but it threatens the sustainability of the very attractions that draw tourists. As the arrival point for international tourists and the embarkation point for most tours, San José experiences the financial, infrastructural, and environmental pressures that accompany Costa Rica's international notoriety as a safe, secure, and high-quality tourist destination.

Charlotte Amalie: A U.S. City in the Lesser Antilles

Charlotte Amalie on the island of St. Thomas is the port capital of the U.S. Virgin Islands (fig. 3.15). The mountainous island of St. Thomas has long been a deep-water port whose warehousing district includes structures that date to the 19th century. The bay affords vistas from lookout points as high as 1,500 feet, including the well-known Drake's Seat. In addition to a small airport and cruise ship port in Charlotte Amalie, visitors to St. Thomas take advantage of renowned beaches such as Magen's Bay. In recent years, Charlotte Amalie has benefited from proximity to Puerto Rico's Luís Muñoz Marín International Airport in San Juan, which brings in larger aircrafts filled with passengers who can transfer to smaller aircrafts for a 30-minute flight to Charlotte Amalie.

Christopher Columbus encountered a small number of natives in the present-day Virgin Islands during his second voyage to the Americas in 1493. Archaeological records indicate that Taino, Arawak, Carib, and Ciboney peoples occupied the islands and lived in small fishing communities. As was the case elsewhere in the Caribbean, the native populations died off relatively quickly after European contact. The Spanish focused their energies on Puerto Rico, and St. Thomas remained unprotected, leaving Charlotte Amalie's sheltered coves to be frequented by mariners and pirates, including Blackbeard and Bluebeard, as well as by European settlers.

The Danish West India Company chartered the islands in 1671 after King Christian V decided to secure them for plantations. The Danish government supplied male convicts to work the plantations, but soon opted to allow colonists from neighboring islands to settle there, as well as to permit the importation of African slaves. By 1680, there were more Black slaves (175) than European settlers (156). Adjacent islands Buck and Water served as pasture lands for St. Thomas, and Taphus (meaning "tap house" or beer hall) was renamed Charlotte Amalie in 1691 after King Christian V's wife. It was the main port and was connected to about 50 plantations by a single road, which remains a main highway today. By the early 18th century, more than 3,000 residents occupied St. Thomas, and sugar production and slave trading were the economic mainstay.

After the Danish Government took over the administration of the islands in 1754, the capital was moved from St. Thomas to Christiansted, St. Croix. St. Thomas's economy transitioned from agriculture and slave trading to general commerce. Charlotte Amalie prospered as a free port in 1815, and English, French, German, Italian, American, Spanish, Sephardic, and Danish importing houses operated there. A growing share of West Indian trade passed through the port. By the 1840s, the rise of steamships made Charlotte Amalie an ideal coaling station for ships sailing between

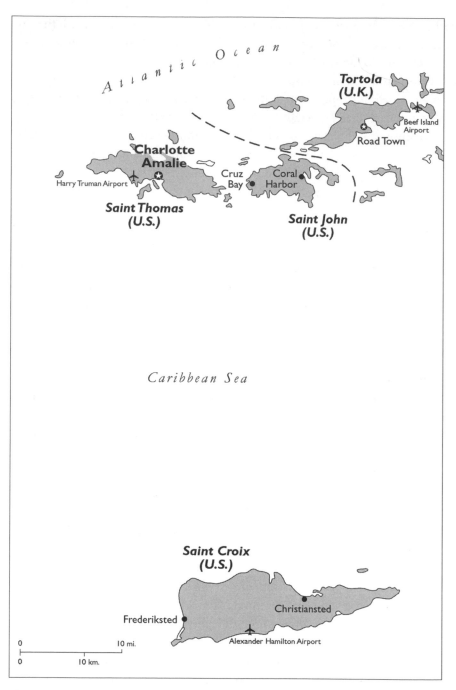

Figure 3.15   Charlotte Amalie, St. Thomas, U.S. Virgin Islands.

South and North America. However, Spanish and English islands gradually began importing coal directly from producers, and Charlotte Amalie was eventually sidestepped in this trade. The abolition of slavery in 1848 further diminished St. Thomas's commercial role in the region.

The United States purchased the Danish West Indies for $25 million in gold in 1917. St. Thomas fell under U.S. Navy Rule until

Figure 3.16   View of Charlotte Amalie, St. Thomas, from the tram station. (Photo courtesy of United States Virgin Islands Department of Tourism)

1931. When Cuba was barred to American tourists in 1960, St. Thomas's prominence rose. As a U.S. possession, it has proven to be a haven for mainland Americans seeking second homes. In 2000, Charlotte Amalie was home to 11,004 of the 51,181 residents populating St. Thomas Island. Today, the historic warehouses, halls, and downtown buildings of this small island, just 13 miles (21 km) long and 4 miles (6 km) wide (approximately 31 sq mi [126 sq km]) anchor a thriving tourist industry. Charlotte Amalie is a bustling, congested port with small, narrow cobblestone streets packed with duty-free shops that sell a variety of goods to tourists. Its checkered colonial history and shifting economic base afford tourists a variety of cultural attractions. The "99 steps" form part of a well-known stairway that dates to the mid-1700s. Built by the Danes of ship ballast from Denmark, the steps were planned by Danish engineers who visited St. Thomas. They symbolize the lack of bottomlands for easy urbanization, industrial production, and agriculture.

Tourism will continue to drive the Virgin Island economy, while a relatively small island with limited flatlands will constrain Charlotte Amalie's growth. The city is well endowed to accommodate the more than 1 million cruise ship passengers who saunter through its colonial streets. Only land-use controls and a carefully monitored master plan will safeguard the spread of hilltop homes that stake a claim overlooking blue Caribbean waters, yet indelibly alter the viewscape (fig. 3.16).

Havana: The Once and Future Hub of the Caribbean?

Diego de Velázquez de Cuéllar founded San Cristóbal de Habana in 1519 as one of seven military outposts (*villas*) around the island. Just two of these original settlements—Camaguey (then Puerto Principe) and Santiago—were founded on good harbors. Havana was first located in 1514 on the Broa Inlet, at the Gulf of Batabanó, on the island's southern (Caribbean) side (fig. 3.17). A shallow port and generally swampy (and unhealthy) site forced colonists to relocate directly north, on the Atlantic side of the

Box 3.3 Getting By in Kingston, Jamaica

Kingston—roughly 12 times the size of Montego Bay, Jamaica's second largest city—is a classic primate city. Efforts at urban planning have been thwarted by lack of administrative authority and funds, resulting in a highly mixed urban landscape.

Older, declining neighborhoods, built over the past century near the colonial center, are now densely occupied. They are said to have been "tenementized," as original one-family houses have been subdivided many times over and rented to very poor rural migrants who share cooking and bathing facilities. Life in these now lower-class neighborhoods tends to take place on the streets and in the yard because interior spaces are too crowded.

Kingston also houses squatters. The city is situated on uneven land crossed by many gullies that carry intermittent rainfall south to the sea. Rural migrants now occupy the gully interstices that separate more formal neighborhoods. These squatters fence their spaces and raise gardens and animals, much to the annoyance of their middle-class neighbors. Some manage to tap into electricity illegally and even gain access to piped water, but they rarely have sufficient sanitary plumbing facilities. As a result, urban groundwater pollution is a serious problem. In the Kingston periphery, squatter shantytowns are occupied by people who have gathered enough personal and material resources to flee inner-city slums. Shantytowns actually afford their residents greater potential for social and spatial mobility than does more formal inner-city housing. Their location near the sea or agricultural land makes fishing and small-scale gardening possible; thus, the cost of living is lower and saving,

narrow island. Although Santiago de Cuba reigned as the official island capital until the late 16th century, Havana's relative location was enhanced by the discovery of the Bahamian Channel which served as a key transshipment route for goods exchanged between the Americas (chiefly Mexico) and Europe. In fact, Havana's coat of arms includes its three principal fortresses (La Fuerza Real, El Morro, and La Punta) and a key that designates the city's strategic location as the "key" to the Gulf of Mexico and the Americas. Lacking mineral wealth and a large native population to enslave or evangelize, Havana served as a strategic refurbishing port and a temporary holding place for precious metals coming from Mexico and Andean South America.

Military engineers enhanced this colonial port by building a network of fortresses over the next two-and-a-half centuries. Flotillas carrying wealth out of the ports of Cartagena and Santa Marta in Colombia, Nombre de Díos in Panama, and Veracruz in Mexico would dock in the safe waters of Havana before crossing the Atlantic for Seville, Spain (see fig. 3.5). Accordingly, Havana's role as a major supply port meant that ranching, timber, shipping, and allied services would define the colonial city's economy. It lacked the wealth of Lima, Peru, and Mexico City but served as a vital link in the Spanish colonial empire. The completion of a major aqueduct in 1592 that brought fresh water from the Almendares River west of the city sealed Havana's fate as an official city in the Spanish

rendering investment in self-improvement possible for those who have steady jobs. Community relations can be strong and supportive. Shanty housing stock is upgraded fairly rapidly, with old structures built out of scrap being soon replaced with more substantial concrete block and wood structures.

Inflation, recession, and job loss have forced approximately half of Kingston's labor force to create its own forms of employment. The Caribbean urban informal economy got its start during slavery, when slaves, legally blocked from working for wages, devised ways to supply high-demand products and services for cash. The range of informal jobs is now vast, including the provision of transport; the procurement and delivery of home-grown produce to urban households; the preservation of food for sale in market stalls; the provision of sewing services; and the production crafts for tourists. Although the flourishing Jamaican informal economy serves a host of positive social functions, these small-scale enterprises retain inefficiencies that inhibit overall economic growth. Few informal businesses grow into larger firms that create jobs and pay taxes. There is rarely money left over for reinvestment, and entrepreneurial innovation can be stifled by cronyism and reciprocal obligations.

Life for most people in Kingston is circumscribed by low income, poor housing, high crime rates, and lack of adequate transportation to jobs, schools, and shopping. Yet most who have studied urban life there seem to concur that the sense of community is strong. People survive by constantly exchanging favors: surveillance of each other's property, shared care of children and elderly, shared food, the lending of small amounts of money, and personal support during times of triumph or sadness.

empire. It surpassed Santiago de Cuba in political and economic significance and has not ceded that position in over four centuries.

Havana's location on a pocket-shaped bay, one of several geological formations dotting the island, made it an ideal warehouse and transshipment point. So narrow is the entrance to the harbor from the Florida Straits that military officers often drew chains across it at night to entrap intruders. Located on a plain with mild marine terrace escarpments that yield to a gently undulating topography, the city is unconstrained by topographic barriers except for the bay (which curtailed growth to the east until a tunnel was completed in 1957). Rather, settlement was confined by a wall on the western flank, the rudimentary construction of which commenced in 1663. By

1740, when the last stone was laid, a polygon consisting of nine bastions, several parapets, and escarpments completed the city's defensive system. The walled city at the time included 179 blocks, 56 streets, 5 plazas, 14 churches and convents, 2 hospitals, 6 military barracks, and a jail. However, a wise British officer knew the city was unprotected on the eastern flank of the bay, and in 1761 disembarked a small squadron of men to the east of Havana. In just one month, the British bombarded the old city, disrupted its food supplies, and forced the flag of the British Empire to fly over Havana. The following year Cuba was traded for Spanish Florida, and Havana's urban geography would never be the same.

In 1740, slave laborers replaced the simple ramparts with an expensive wall made from

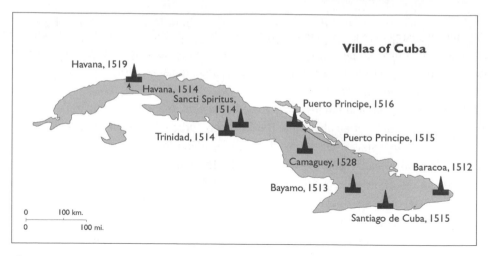

Figure 3.17   Map of Villas of Cuba. *Source:* Joseph Scarpaci, Roberto Segre, and Mario Coyula, *Havana: Two Faces of the Antillean Metropolis* (Chapel Hill: University of North Carolina Press, 2002), 13.

crushed limestone and crudely pressed rock that was cemented by a mixture of oxen blood, eggs, and sand. However, with just two main gates, traffic inside the old quarters became congested, and the tons of manure and urine that accumulated in the tropical heat made life unpleasant. A sugar boom following the British occupation of the 1760s brought commerce and residents to Havana, and crowding exacerbated problems within the walls. In response, new neighborhoods sprung up outside the walled city, and the elite gradually left the walled quarters. In the early 1860s, Havana's walls were torn down, opening up a huge expanse of city blocks that were ideal for urban development. A series of civil wars between the Cuban colony and Spain, however, would delay new construction. Between 1868 and 1898, war aggravated the quality of life, deteriorated the city's infrastructure, and—except for the Albear water system completed in 1893—few public works enhanced Havana.

When the Americans occupied Cuba after the 1898 Spanish–American War under the terms of the Platt Amendment (1889–1902), they found Havana to be a lackluster place. It had few paved roads and modern amenities such as telegraph wires, public lighting, sidewalks, and regular refuse pick-up and disposal. Ripe for investment, U.S. business speculators poured into the city. Road construction, railroad expansion, banks, custom's houses, sugar and cigar-factory construction, telephone services, and the newly arrived automobile offered opportunities for American capitalists. The U.S. Army Corps of Engineers lent a hand, particularly in expanding, raising, and extending the seaside promenade El Malecón—a striking boulevard that graces Havana's scenic waterfront (fig. 3.18).

Over the course of the 20th century, Havana would become a horizontal city in the mode of Los Angeles and less a high-density, New York–like city. Unlike Charlotte Amalie and other Caribbean ports, Havana could expand across a wide coastal plain. It developed a series of suburban enclaves west and south of the bay. Automobile commuting for a middle class of white-collar workers drove this suburbanization model, and led to a scattered and deeply segregated pattern of urban growth. While a streetcar network operated until the early 1950s, the automobile and bus would link Havana's new suburban and exurban developments. When the revolution of 1959 triumphed, about 1 in 20 residents were living in shantytowns of some sort. The socialist government imported models of high-rise prefabricated buildings like those used in Eastern Europe and the former Soviet Union. Planners and politicians curtailed population movement to Havana because the city was considered a sort of parasite that for centuries had drawn disproportionate wealth at the expense of the rest of the nation. Only 1 million residents claimed Havana as their home in 1959, and the population had barely surpassed the 2 million mark 50 years later. Over the same period, Mexico City and Lima, Peru, had increased six- and three-fold respectively.

This checkered pattern of urban history, warfare, and revolutions has given 21st century Havana a unique urban morphology. It is a polycentric city that has preserved distinctive architectural designs and land uses. Colonial, Republican, and new government centers, as well as social and cultural districts, characterize this panoply of urban nodes (fig. 3.19). Although the capital is, like Washington, D.C., largely devoted to services, it is one of the few Latin American cities where rather benign light industry (i.e., cigar making) surrounds the colonial and Republican government centers. This economic activity ranks among the top hard currency generators for the government, but remains relatively unnoticeable to the casual pedestrian.

In the first three decades of the revolution, Havana was largely a "closed" destination; few tourists came, and those who did hailed primarily from the former Soviet Union trading-bloc member states. Moreover,

migration to Havana from elsewhere is strictly controlled by a food-ration book (*la libreta*) and other government controls. However, the demise of the USSR in 1991 led to a major crisis called the "Special Period in a Time of Peace." The government tightened gasoline rations as Cuba's ability to exchange sugar for Soviet oil disappeared. Thousands of un- and underemployed Cubans continue to migrate illegally to Havana, mainly from the eastern provinces where the dwindling sugar economy has been devastated. In typical Cuban humor, these immigrants are called *palestinos* because they hail from the east.

Other changes are also visible in Havana. As fuel subsidies from the USSR ended, and the relative cost of gasoline soared, bus routes were scaled back to half their number, and bicycling boomed (from some 70,000 bicycles in 1989 to 1 million in 1999). Tourism was seen as a "necessary evil" to sustain the island's economy, and the city's Old Havana district (Habana Vieja), a UNESCO World Heritage Site since 1982, became a prime destination for newfound cultural tourism. In 1993, the City Historian of Havana created a moneymaking corporation to address housing, hotel construction, road paving, plaza reconstruction, and urban revitalization. This firm, Habaguanex, has become one of the most powerful state enterprises in post-Soviet Havana. The firm has embarked on an ambitious project to rehabilitate buildings and spaces in Habana Vieja. International tourism has grown from about 25,000 annual visitors to Cuba in the late 1970s to just over 2 million visitors in 2006, equivalent to tourism to nearby Cancún, Mexico. Tourism is the new engine of economic growth in both Havana and in Cuba more generally.

Unlike Charlotte Amalie and many other Caribbean port capitals, Havana is home to a world-class biotechnology industry and boasts the third busiest airport in the region.

Figure 3.18   El Malecón as seen from atop the Focsa Building in Vedado, looking east, running along the Florida Straits past Centro Havana to Habana Vieja. (Photo by Joseph Scarpaci)

It possesses the open space for more growth, either in the form of vacation homes for North Americans or returning Cuban-Americans or to accommodate a U.S. tourist market. Such growth, however, depends on how Washington and Havana negotiate the terms of the long-standing trade embargo that the United States has imposed on Cuba since 1962. In contrast to Charlotte Amalie, Havana attracts only a few thousand cruise ship passengers annually, largely because shipping companies face legal problems from the United States if they conduct business in Cuba. Nevertheless, the Caribbean manages some of the busiest maritime traffic in the world; approximately 50,000 ships navigate there and carry 14.5 million tourists annually. Havana will be on the radar of urbanists who are interested in issues of smart growth, sus-

tainable development, and sustainable tourism as the 21st century unfolds.

URBAN CHALLENGES

Some of Middle America's and the Caribbean's largest metropolises, particularly those in Mexico, reveal slowing urban rates of growth that can be attributed to a demographic transition and a decline in rural-to-urban migration. Nevertheless, these metropolitan expanses are increasingly spreading out well beyond their original limits. As a result, the pattern of urban settlements has become more dispersed than in the past as cities increasingly encroach on the adjacent countryside. Urbanization has spatially, economically, and socially incorpo-

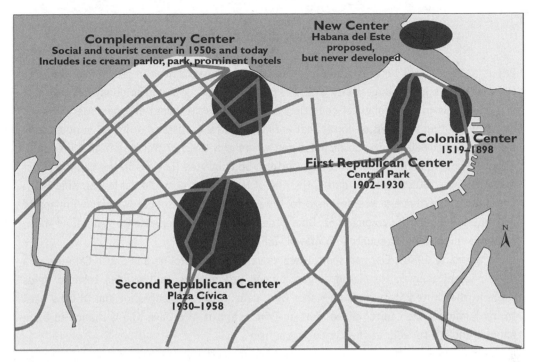

Figure 3.19   The polycentric city of Havana. *Source:* Based on Joseph Scarpaci, Roberto Segre, and Mario Coyula, *Havana: Two Faces of the Antillean Metropolis* (Chapel Hill: University of North Carolina Press, 2002), 87.

rated many smaller towns and cities in this process. Guadalajara, Puebla, and Mexico City in Mexico; San José in Costa Rica; and Guatemala City in Guatemala reflect this process. Tools of urban and regional planning are needed to manage this level of urbanization (see box 3.2). Despite a population loss or "hollowing out" of the city center in these metropolises, the capital city continues to dominate in most countries.

Mid-sized cities, on the one hand, have maintained an impressive rate of population growth. Most mid-sized cities in the region have increased their relative contribution to the national urban population. Intermediate-sized cities, more than very large cities, now offer new promise for job creation and enhanced quality of life. Nevertheless, urban planners and administrators in these cities will be challenged to avoid replicating the problems that have plagued larger metropolitan areas. The viability of intermediate-sized cities will depend mainly on their economies, including the degree of integration at the global scale, the type of articulation they maintain at the national and regional level, and the extent to which they can tap into their comparative advantages.

Traditional rural–urban patterns of migration have been replaced in the last 15 years by a more diverse process characterized by movement from city to city. For instance, inter-urban migration is the principal form of population movement in Mexico, where almost half of all migrants leave one city for another. Given that this migration pattern will continue to be important, planning guidelines and policies need to pay attention to this dynamic. It is important to recognize that cities in the region, despite the many

Box 3.4 Race, Status, and Remittances in Haiti

Edy is a 52-year-old horseman and assistant tour guide who lives in the outskirts of Cap Haitien, Haiti's fourth largest city with 113,000 residents. He is a trim ebony-skinned man who clearly is in good physical condition despite his white beard and hair. He earns his living by holding the reins of horses that are mounted by tourists who ride 90 minutes from the Sans Souci palaces to the mountaintop where the UNESCO World Heritage Site of La Citadel is located. The Citadel is a huge fortress built by free Haitians in the country's first army between 1805 and 1813, during the rule of Haiti's first postcolonial leader, King Henri Christophe. The fortress was designed to thwart an invasion should Napoleon Bonaparte attempt to reclaim the colony of St. Domingue, which after independence was called Haiti, meaning "mountainous country" in Arawak-Taino languages.

In the early 1980s, Edy had spent three years in North Carolina and South Carolina as a legal migrant laborer. He picked apples, pruned peach trees, and weeded tobacco fields while in the United States. His day-labor work generated remittances for him to send back to his family in the capital city of Port-au-Prince, and it also gave him a chance to learn enough English to work at the Citadel in tourism.

The lives of Edy's two children have also been impacted by transoceanic travel, but with an added layer of kinship and paternity. In the late 1970s, Edy fathered a young boy, Claude, but refused to recognize the child. Claude's mother toiled as a domestic servant in the upper-income neighborhood of Petionville in Port-au-Prince and raised the boy as a working single mother. When Claude was five years old, Edy fathered a daughter, Loraine, in a brief relationship with a light-skinned, high-school educated civil servant. Shortly after Loraine's birth, her mother left Edy (taking Loraine) and married a similarly light-skinned man.

Two notable differences surface between siblings Claude and Loraine. Being born out of wedlock and having darker skin than his sister has made life challenging for Claude. He

---

challenges outlined in this chapter, are still attractive to those in search of gainful employment. Moreover, the countryside seems little able to retain rural residents because of the structural problems that are entrenched there.

Social and geographic segregation in the region's cities has deepened and is a serious problem. Demand for exclusive high-income communities often leads to the displacement of poor groups from targeted urban neighborhoods. Public housing projects concentrate at the city's edge because of lower land values. In turn, this exacerbates social and spatial segregation. High-income groups increasingly isolate themselves defensively in limited-access or gated communities that are adorned with costly houses and attractive retail, entertainment, and recreational facilities, and which feature close proximity to occupational sites, schools, and other amenities. At the same time, poor households continue to occupy precarious houses on remote and marginal lands that lack infrastructure and are adjacent to high-risk and undesirable land uses (e.g., landfills, utility plants, factories, water-treatment plants, flood plains, steep terrain). City legisla-

never received financial support from his father, and it is only in recent years that Edy has made contact with his son. Loraine, on the other hand, is a lighter-skinned mulata whose stepfather gave her a good education at a private, English-speaking school. She was able to earn a fellowship to a midwestern state university in the United States through the United Methodist Church.

Claude has felt the swings of the Haitian economy's expansions and contractions. With only a formal education to the eighth grade, he had been working in menial jobs with little security and no benefits. Recently though, he has been working as a crew leader for a jobs and training program founded by the international reggae, hip hop, and folk singer, Haitian-born Wyclef Jean. This NGO, Yelé Haiti (a U.S. 501c (3) nonprofit organization) funded Claude's trip to Miami for a meeting with different functionaries in the NGO. The capital city is replete with Yelé Haiti workers in green t-shirts who sweep the streets and sidewalks and try to keep garbage in the city's dumpsters from overflowing. As the Haitian state retreats in the delivery of public services, nonprofit organizations such as Wyclef Jean's are increasingly providing essential services.

Claude and Loraine were not able to meet in Miami during Claude's recent visit because Loraine was in the middle of final examinations. Still, the trip provided Claude with a new opportunity to prove himself as a leader, and it has brought new attention to the man who for so long was shunned by his family for being born out of wedlock and for having dark skin. Yet Claude is leery of his father's new attention because he knows that he will be expected to provide support as Edy ages and can no longer climb the arduous trails up to the Citadel.

Wyclef Jean, himself an immigrant to Brooklyn, New York, at the age of nine, is providing gainful employment for thousands of Haiti's youth, especially those in Port-au-Prince's vast shantytowns (*bidonvilles*). However, neither the state nor NGOs will be able to provide Edy with any form of social security. Extended kinship ties will be the only resource he will have in his golden years.

tion should attenuate this kind of urban segregation by influencing the powerful forces of the real estate market.

About 40% of the region's population was living below the poverty line in 2005, while 15% of the population lived in extreme poverty. Data further reveal an increase in the concentration of the poor in urban areas. Two of every three poor persons resided in cities in that same year, a greater portion than in the previous decade. Considerable disparity is also evident within the region. While the poor in Costa Rica amount to about one-fifth of the national population, Mexico and Panama reveal a 35% poverty rate, and Guatemala, Honduras, and Nicaragua exceed the 60% mark. These latter three countries have levels of extreme poverty in excess of 30%. Haiti not only has the highest poverty rate in the region, but in the entire western hemisphere (box 3.4). Part of the indigence is mired in political instability, rampant corruption, and centuries of inept rule and colonialism. However, Haiti is not the only country in the region struggling to break through these structural and historical constraints. Rapid

Figure 3.20   Two aerial views of shantytowns (*bidonvilles*) in low-lying areas just north of the Port au Prince, Haiti city center. Flooding occurred in these areas after Hurricane Noel struck the island of Hispaniola on October 29–31, 2007. The storm claimed at least 30 lives in the Dominican Republic and 20 in Haiti. (Photos by Joseph Scarpaci)

urbanization has led millions of Haitians to precarious shanties (fig. 3.20). Poverty should be a priority on urban development agendas throughout the region.

Natural disasters in the Caribbean, Central America, and Mexico compound the challenges of regional poverty. A combination of physical factors and socioeconomic difficulties increase environmental risk and make preventing or mitigating natural disaster one of the main challenges of urban and regional planning. Most of the poor already live adjacent to hazardous conditions. Some of these are seemingly benign but are actually hazardous, such as low-lying areas near water

(e.g., flood and coastal plains, creek beds) that may be prone to flooding, or deforested steep slopes that could be prone to mudslides. These settlements exist because of negligence in the enforcement of laws that would otherwise control where housing can be built. At times, however, turning a blind eye to informal settlements affords the state a less expensive option to providing healthy neighborhoods. Many settlements in the Caribbean, both shanties and planned developments, are fragile economically, socially, and environmentally. Natural disasters such as hurricanes merely exacerbate these conditions.

The severity of human, material, and environmental risk posed by different events does not always have a direct bearing on outcomes. This is especially true with fragile urban and productive infrastructure, the quality of housing, and the existence of regional planning. Early warning systems, capable management, and institutional and political development are fundamental steps in dealing with emergency preparedness and rebuilding in cities throughout Middle America and the Caribbean. Strong political will is needed to tackle the problems affecting the daily lives of people living in cities throughout the region, in keeping with 21st century goals of economic development through environmental sustainability.

SUGGESTED READINGS

Aguilar, Adrián G., and Boris Graizbord. 2002. "Evolution and Maturing of the Mexican Urban System." In Hermanus S. Geyer, ed., *International Handbook of Urban Systems: Studies of Urbanization and Migration in Advanced and Developing Countries.* Northampton, MA: Edward Elgar Publishing, 419–454. Presents studies of urbanization and migration in advanced and developing countries.

Blouet, Brian W., and Olwyn M. Blouet. 2006. *Latin America and the Caribbean.* New York: John Wiley. A survey of the physical and human geography of the region with a chapter on cities and a special section on housing.

Bolay, Jean-Claude, and Adriana Rabinovich. "Intermediate Cities in Latin America: Risk and Opportunities of Coherent Urban Development," *Cities,* 21, no. 5 (2004), 407–421. Examines how medium-sized cities relate to other cities in their national urban systems and to the wider world.

Edge, Kay, Heather Woofard, and Joseph L. Scarpaci. 2006. "Mapping and Designing Havana: Republican, Socialist, and Global Spaces," *Cities,* 23, no. 2, 85–98. Examines how aspects of Havana's built environment can be read as a window to past influences from the United States, the Soviet Union, and Spain, as well as to Cuba's own creative styles.

Lattes, Alfredo E., Jorge Rodríguez, and Miguel Villa. 2004. "Population Dynamics and Urbanization in Latin America: Concepts and Data Limitations." In Tony Champion and Graeme Hugo, eds., *New Forms of Urbanization: Beyond the Urban-Rural Dichotomy,* London: Ashgate, 89–111.

Potter, Robert, and Dennis Conway. 1997. *Self-Help Housing, the Poor, and the State in the Caribbean.* Knoxville: University of Tennessee Press. A case study of the ongoing tensions between state commitment to basic social services and the pressure that the urban poor exert to extract concessions from the state.

Rajewski, Brian, ed. 2002. *Cities of the World, Vol. 2: The Western Hemisphere,* 6th ed. Farmington Hills, MI: Thomson Gale. Presents profiles of large and medium-sized cities.

Richardson, Bonham. 1994. *Igniting the Caribbean's Past: Fire in British West Indian History.* Chapel Hill: University of North Carolina Press. Historical review of the use of fire throughout the Caribbean; slave rebellions, urban arson, and field clearing carry important implications for landscape modification and for pressuring elites into concessions.

Scarpaci, Joseph L., Roberto Segre, and Mario Coyula. 2002. *Havana: Two Faces of the Antillean Metropolis.* Chapel Hill and London: University of North Carolina Press. Reviews 500 years of urbanization and Havana's spatial configuration as a mirror to periods of economic development, political control, and architectural imprint.

Scarpaci, Joseph. 2005 *Plazas and Barrios: Heritage Tourism and Globalization in the Latin American Centro Histórico.* Tucson: University of Arizona Press. Referencing nine historical districts, this study covers, in the context of globalization, the rise of heritage tourism as an alternative to mass, Cancún-like, venues.

Figure 4.1   Major Cities of South America. *Source:* Data from UN, *World Urbanization Prospects: 2005 Revision* (New York: United Nations Population Division, 2006, http://esa.un.org/unup).

4

Cities of South America

MAUREEN HAYS-MITCHELL AND
BRIAN J. GODFREY

KEY URBAN FACTS

Total Population	374 million
Percent Urban Population	81.6%
Total Urban Population	306 million
Most Urbanized Countries	Venezuela (93.4%)
	Uruguay (92.0%)
	Argentina (90.1%)
Least Urbanized Countries	Paraguay (58.5%)
	Ecuador (62.8%)
	Bolivia (64.2%)
Annual Urban Growth Rate	1.75%
Number of Megacities	3
Number of Cities of More than 1 Million	38
Three Largest Cities	São Paulo, Buenos Aires, Rio de Janeiro
World Cities	São Paulo, Buenos Aires, Rio de Janeiro

KEY CHAPTER THEMES

1. South America is highly urbanized, but its rate of urban growth has declined in recent years.
2. The region contains four of the world's largest megacities and a large number of cities of more than 1 million.
3. Cities of Andean America reveal large indigenous and mestizo populations sharing urban space with small elite groups of European heritage.

4. Southern Cone cities are generally heavily European in ethnic composition as well as in urban planning traditions.

5. Brazil's cities have a Portuguese colonial heritage and urban forms distinct from their Hispanic counterparts.

6. Most countries in South America are dominated by a primate city, which is in each case the national capital.

7. The cities (and countries) of South America exhibit extreme disparities in wealth, which is directly reflected in the land-use patterns and quality of life within cities.

8. Economic globalization is benefiting only a small segment of the urban population, and intensifying socioeconomic polarization and spatial injustice within cities.

9. Rapid urbanization has caused serious environmental problems, especially air and water pollution, in many South American cities.

10. In recent decades, self-help movements have proliferated to try to overcome the severe imbalances and other problems within the cities, and so too have urban protest and calls for social justice.

South America's cities (fig. 4.1) evoke dramatic, if conflicting, mental images. The mere mention of Rio de Janeiro, Buenos Aires, Bogotá, Caracas, Lima, Quito, or Santiago conjures up scenes of spectacular natural settings, breathtaking vistas, cosmopolitan populations, exquisite colonial architecture, charming market streets, and modern amenities. By contrast, their mention also evokes images of decaying urban centers, sprawling squatter settlements, overwhelming poverty, random violence, hapless street children, congested motorways, filthy air, and polluted waterways. To be sure, both images accurately portray different aspects of contemporary urban life in South America. Just as the continent is a land of great extremes, so are its cities. Despite many outward similarities, South American cities are quite diverse in urban form, physical setting, culture, economic function, political governance, and quality of life.

South America's urban centers have long been part of a worldwide economic system. Since the colonial era, urban societies throughout the region have served as important producers and consumers within a global economy. Today, the region's major cities openly compete for the opportunity to serve as world centers for financial, manufacturing, and service-oriented multinational enterprises. Cultural currents from around the world— art, architecture, music, fashion, cuisine, athletic events, and digital technology— flow across South America's urban landscapes. Both advocates and critics of globalization agree that societies are being propelled in broadly similar socioeconomic, political, and cultural directions. Is it inevitable, then, that the particular places caught up in this process are destined to look and feel alike? South America's cities suggest otherwise.

Collectively, the region's cities contrast with cities of other world regions in many ways. Various factors account for their shared characteristics: a common colonial experience with Iberian urban planning; similar paths of historical development; recent globalization of tastes, production, and technology; and growing socioeconomic polarization, spatial segregation, and informal economies. Nonetheless, while similar processes have shaped urban development throughout the South American continent in many analogous ways, the diversity of national and local experiences also stands out. South America features some cities that originate with the Spanish conquest and others that derive their identity from the Portuguese. Many in both categories are infused with the presence of indigenous cultures, European cultures such as German and Italian, and African cultures that date from the slavery era. These cities exhibit widely disparate urban forms, contrasting levels of economic development, and varying forms of political governance, all spread across some of the most diverse natural environments on earth.

SOUTH AMERICAN URBAN PATTERNS

South America's cities may be grouped into three major cultural-ecological regions: (1) Andean America (Colombia, Venezuela, Ecuador, Peru, and Bolivia), (2) the Southern Cone (Chile, Argentina, Uruguay, and Paraguay), and (3) Portuguese America (Brazil). The cities of Guyana, Suriname, and French Guiana are more appropriately understood in the context of the Caribbean region. Despite a general adherence to many broad continental trends, there are also significant regional differences.

The cities of Andean America reveal a greater indigenous presence than do those of the Southern Cone and Brazil. Andean cities are divided by ethnicity, as large indigenous and mestizo populations share urban space with small elite groups of European heritage.

The rapidly growing Andean cities also are dominated by an "alternative economy" of the informal sector and popular markets.

Southern Cone cities, with the exception of Paraguay, are heavily European in ethnic composition as well as in urban planning traditions. Although most human development indicators suggest relative prosperity, these cities contend with long-standing problems of economic stagnation and a restive middle class. Despite its geographic location in the Southern Cone, Paraguay is similar to Andean countries in its strong indigenous presence, along with its generally low socioeconomic indicators and high rate of urbanization.

Brazil's cities have a Portuguese colonial heritage and language, a unique popular culture, and various urban forms entirely distinct from their Hispanic counterparts. The Roman name for Portugal was Lusitania; hence we speak of the Luso-American cities of Brazil, which have displayed distinctive spatial patterns in their siting and internal organization of space since colonial times. In sociocultural terms, the important African admixture makes patterns of black-white stratification a key urban issue in many Brazilian cities.

Contemporary Urban Trends

A century ago, fewer than 10% of South Americans resided in urban centers. By the middle of the 20th century, only the national populations of Argentina, Chile, and Uruguay were predominantly urban (tab. 4.1). Today, all but one country is more than 60% urbanized, and that outlier—Paraguay—is at 59%. Five countries are more than 80% urbanized, with Argentina, Uruguay, and Venezuela surpassing 90% (tab. 4.1). It is expected that by 2030 the portion of national populations residing in

Table 4.1   Urbanization in South American Countries, 1850–2005

| Country | *Percentage of National Population in Urban Areas* | | | | |
	1850	1910	1950	1970	2005
Argentina	12.0	28.4	65.3	78.9	90.1
Bolivia	4.0	9.2	33.8	39.8	64.2
Brazil	7.0	9.8	36.2	55.8	84.2
Chile	5.9	24.2	58.4	75.2	87.6
Colombia	3.0	7.3	42.1	56.6	72.7
Ecuador	6.0	12.0	28.3	39.3	62.8
Paraguay	4.0	17.7	34.6	37.1	58.5
Peru	5.9	5.4	41.0	57.4	72.6
Uruguay	13.0	26.0	77.9	82.4	92.0
Venezuela	7.0	9.0	46.8	71.6	93.4

Sources: Clawson, David L., *Latin America and the Caribbean: Lands and Peoples,* McGraw-Hill, 2006, p. 350; Population Division of the Department of Economic and Social Affairs of the United Nations Secretariat, *World Urbanization Prospects: The 2005 Revision,* http://esa.un.org/unup, June 25, 2006.

urban areas will be approach 90% across the entire continent. With more than four-fifths of the region's population residing in urban areas, cityward migration and natural increase have declined in recent years, thus slowing urban growth rates. Still, South America continues to face problems associated with what arguably has been the world's most rapid and large-scale urban transformation.

The urban transformation of Latin America is characterized by urban primacy. At present, roughly 40 South American urban centers contain at least 1 million people. South America contains four of the world's 35 largest cities: São Paulo, Buenos Aires, Rio de Janeiro, and Lima. Much of the region's urban population resides in metropolitan megacities. Yet, South America's largest cities are unevenly distributed, suggesting significant spatial differences in the urban experience. Of the continent's 20 largest cities, 10 are located in Brazil, eight are located in Andean America, and 2 are located in the Southern Cone (fig. 4.2). These data reflect notable variations in regional urbanization:

- The Southern Cone (except for Paraguay) underwent its urban and demographic transitions by the mid-20th century. Urbanization rates in these relatively high-income countries peaked long ago. The large cities—such as Buenos Aires and Montevideo—are growing slowly vis-à-vis the cities of Brazil and Andean America.

- Brazil is now just emerging from an exceedingly rapid and recent urban transition. The growth of Brazil's largest cities—São Paulo and Rio de Janeiro—is currently slowing, as the focus of urban growth shifts to smaller and peripheral cities.

- Andean America is at present the most rapidly urbanizing region of South America. Its cities are operating in an environment of fiscal constraint and hence are experiencing social, political, environmental, and logistical crises.

Due primarily to urban-based industrial development, South American countries

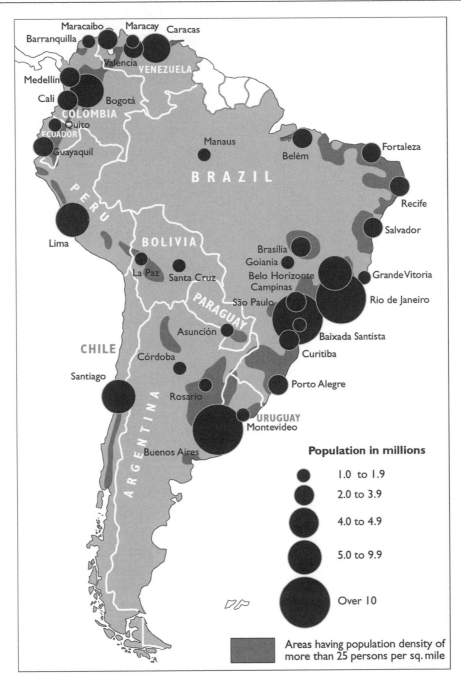

Figure 4.2   Largest Metropolitan Areas of South America. *Source:* Data from UN, *World Urbanization Prospects: 2005 Revision* (New York: United Nations Population Division, 2006, http://esa.un.org/unup).

began their urban transition earlier than other regions of the developing world. Its cities today appear poised on the global semiperiphery, exhibiting characteristics of cities in the more developed "core" and the less developed "periphery." Although the developing countries of Africa and Asia are urbanizing rapidly, South America's current urban levels already approximate those of North America and Europe. Yet, South American cities are less affluent and less open socially and politically than their northern counterparts. Sadly, urbanization and economic growth have not necessarily been synonymous in South America. In contrast to North American and European cities, South American cities have grown more rapidly and within a highly competitive and constraining global context, as well as a regional context of poorly distributed wealth and endemic poverty.

Critical Issues

South America's cities are confronted with pressing social, economic, political, and environmental issues, many of which reflect the continent's distinctive regional and local experiences. The following issues set the stage for subsequent discussion of the region's distinctive cities.

Urban Primacy and the Growth of Large Cities

Nearly every country in South America is dominated by a primate city, almost invariably the national capital (tab. 4.2). Bolivia, Ecuador, and Venezuela are dominated by two primate cities. Brazil is dominated by a huge megalopolis anchored by two large cities, São Paulo, and Rio de Janeiro. The disproportionate growth of primate and other large cities emerged historically, as early colonial centers became modern gateway cities, attracting foreign investments, immigrants and internal in-migrants, transportation innovations, and infrastructural subsidies from governments. The concentration of population, economic activity, and political influence generates far-ranging problems, including the stagnation of smaller cities as resources concentrate in the primate city. Although decentralization plans are underway in several countries, they are yet to yield an impact.

Economic Polarization and Spatial Segregation

Although South America's megacities are centers of great wealth, this wealth is poorly distributed, a lingering impact of the hierarchical governance system that was implanted during the Spanish and Portuguese colonial period. Economic liberalization at the global scale has led to pronounced socioeconomic polarization at national and local scales. The region's growing social divide can be read on its urban landscape. It is estimated that as many as 4 out of every 10 urban dwellers in South America live in conditions of absolute poverty. Although many South Americans are participating in—and benefiting from—economic globalization, regular employment remains elusive for a large proportion of urban dwellers. Many are forced to cobble together meager livelihoods in the urban informal economy, laboring in such low-paying and insecure occupations as street trading, inhome manufacturing, domestic service, spot construction, itinerant transportation, and money-changing. Similarly, elite and professional districts are luxurious

Table 4.2 Urban Primacy in South America, 2005

Country, Ranked by Urban Primacy	Largest Urban Agglomeration (LUA)	LUA Population, in Thousands, 2005	LUA as Percentage of National Urban Population	LUA as Percentage of Total National Population
Paraguay	Asunción	1,858	51.6	30.2
Chile	Santiago	5,683	39.8	34.9
Uruguay	Montevideo	1,264	39.7	36.5
Argentina	Buenos Aires	12,550	36.0	32.4
Peru	Lima	7,186	35.4	25.7
Ecuador	Guayaquil	2,387	28.7	18.0
Colombia	Bogotá	7,747	23.4	17.0
Bolivia	La Paz	1,527	25.9	16.6
Brazil	São Paulo–Rio de Janeiro	29,802	19.0	16.0
Venezuela	Caracas	2,913	11.7	10.9

Source: Population Division of the Department of Economic and Social Affairs of the United Nations Secretariat, *World Urbanization Prospects: The 2005 Revision*, http://esa.un.org/unup, June 25, 2006.

and characterized by limited access residential units, business and commercial centers, and entertainment facilities. Yet, a large proportion of the urban population is housed in inadequate conditions and seeks shelter in dangerous structures with poor sanitation and limited, if any, rights to the land on which their homes are built. As the gap in wealth widens in South America's cities, violence and crime are rising; personal security and political unrest are growing concerns (box 4.1).

Declining Infrastructures and Environmental Degradation

According to the terms of ongoing programs of economic restructuring, municipal governments have been forced to curtail expenditures, payrolls, and services. Such fiscal constraint makes urban management more difficult. The gradual breakdown of urban infrastructure and service systems places enormous stress on an already strained metropolitan system. The lack of appropriate infrastructure contributes to water and air pollution, as household and industrial waste and traffic congestion degrade the urban environment. Unplanned and unregulated growth exposes vulnerable populations to environmental hazards and health risks. With basic services inaccessible for many and air pollution pervasive, the quality of urban life steadily erodes. Indeed, mortality rates in some parts of South America's largest cities are rising.

Social Movements and Protest

Although many scholars interpret the contemporary problems of South America's large cities as yet another expression of the intense social and economic divisions that have characterized the region since Spanish and Portuguese colonization, others consider them a manifestation of an unfair global economy. Meanwhile, many urban dwellers are taking matters into their own hands by participating in self-help social movements for housing, health care, and service provision. Self-help movements have proliferated in recent decades, serving to fill critical needs cast off as

Box 4.1   Community-Based Websites and GIS in Rio's *Favelas*

Arriving in Rio de Janeiro, visitors are struck immediately by the spectacular setting of mountains and seaside districts, the warm and humid air, and the exuberant tropical vegetation. This mesmerizing vision of paradise is quickly tempered by the unmistakable presence of extensive hillside slums known as *favelas*—impoverished shantytowns precariously perched over the city, above such affluent high-rise beach districts as Copacabana and Ipanema, or set in swampy, polluted, or otherwise undesirable terrain. Despite the geographic proximity, the obvious socioeconomic distance draws a powerful line between the two poles of society. Officially about 20% of Rio's total population (6.1 million in 2007) now lives in more than 500 *favelas*, but realistic estimates suggest that up to a third of the population resides in these irregular settlements.

A similar experience unfolds for visitors to other South American cities, although local topographies do not always make the social divisions so obvious. As the region has urbanized, cities have become increasingly segregated along socioeconomic, racial, and ethnic lines. The poorest districts consist of self-constructed housing, where residents often squat without legal title to the land. Here they struggle to obtain decent livelihoods, improve their residences, and obtain urban services like water, sewerage, and electricity. Official statistics tend to underestimate the presence of these informal settlements, but they form undeniable parts of the urban landscape. They are known by a variety of local names, such as *poblaciones callampas* (Chile's "mushroom populations"), *villas miserias* (Argentina's "towns of misery"), and *pueblos jóvenes* (Peru's "young towns").

While governmental agencies often ignore the slums, community groups have developed innovative websites featuring oral histories, photography, and GIS to document their existence. NGOs work to change the public's prejudices, while enhancing the residents' pride of place. For example, "Viva Rio" (www.vivario.org.br) was founded in 1993 to combat urban violence, promote community development, and facilitate the education of "at risk" youth. This NGO subsequently started the "Viva Favela" (www.vivafavela.com.br) program to focus exclusively on low-income neighborhoods. A related website, "Favelas Have Heritage" (*Favela Tem Memória*, www.favelatemmemoria.com.br), features social histories and ongoing struggles of the communities. GIS analysis of the evolving distribution of *favelas* from 1920 to 2000

municipal budgets have contracted. Yet as frustrations mount, so, too, do urban protest, social tension, and political violence. Increasing numbers of urban residents are joining broad-based calls for economic relief, human rights, and environmental justice. In a world of instantaneous communication, their causes are garnering attention far beyond the region.

HISTORICAL PERSPECTIVES ON SOUTH AMERICAN URBAN DEVELOPMENT

Pre-Columbian Urbanism

Urban settlements have long played an important role in South American societies. The

indicates a relative decline in the affluent central and southern locations, along with an overwhelming shift to outlying northern and western "suburbs." In addition, graphs contrast selected *favelas* with citywide standards to document glaring disparities in socioeconomic status (income, employment, literacy) and service provision (trash collection, sewage, water provision). Conservatively citing the 2000 census, the site notes that several *favelas* have reached populations of over 50,000 residents: Rocinha (56,313), Complexo do Alemão (56,903), and Maré (69,851). Community activists claim the census severely undercounted these populations.

Other NGOs take different approaches evident in their websites. "Favela Faces" (www.favelafaces.org) is a bilingual English/Portuguese site, which relies on photographs and video interviews to present "the problems facing *favela* residents, the ways in which they are working to overcome them, and how they have and continue to improve their communities with the limited resources available to them." Although mentioning violence and drugs, depictions emphasize the circumstances forcing residents into the *favelas,* including the government's forced removals from affluent southern districts, and current social struggles. Alternatively, the "Favela Painting" (www.favelapainting.com) program began in 2006 to improve the image of the *favelas* by enhancing and beautifying them: "In order for the lives of people living in the favelas to improve, the popular perception of their neighborhoods must improve. The core of our idea is to help this happen by painting an entire hillside favela." This project aims first to improve the structure of each house, and then to paint it in coordination with the surrounding homes. Finally, Catalytic Communities, or CatComm (www.comcat.org), is an internet network that showcases community-generated solutions to everyday problems in poor neighborhoods. Describing itself as a tool for community support, "Catalytic Communities uses technology to link grassroots community groups so they can learn from each other's successes, and support one another's work." Since its inception in 2000, CatComm has facilitated over 130 projects in nine countries. The program's founder, Theresa Williamson, traces her inspiration "to direct observation of positive things that were going on in our communities here in Rio de Janeiro." This work for positive social change at the community level, despite largely negative media representations of the urban poor, suggests the importance of NGO community groups currently struggling to improve life in the *favelas.*

spectacular settings and monumental beauty of the Inca cities of Cuzco and Machu Picchu spring readily to mind. The Inca, however, were only the final stage in a 4,000-year history of urban development in pre-Columbian Andean America. Even though the urban heritage of Andean America has garnered most attention, significant evidence indicates that large sedentary communities also flourished across a range of ecological settings in the Amazon region. Similarly, permanent settlements are known to have existed in the Southern Cone region, primarily in the Andes Mountains of present-day Chile and Argentina, at the southern limits of Inca imperial expansion. Two notable features unite settlements in these distinct cultural-ecological regions. First, their successful adaptation to and strategic use of the challenges and opportunities of a diverse habitat. Second, their near total destruction by invading Europeans through violence or disease and, in some cases, their reconstruction to reflect a new and unfamiliar value system.

Colonial Cities: Spanish versus Portuguese America

After their initial voyages of discovery and conquest in the early 16th century, both the Spanish and the Portuguese established settlements to exploit and administer their new territories in South America. In their urban expressions, the Spanish and Portuguese colonies differed in terms of site selection, general morphological characteristics, and geopolitical strategies. In both cases, however, the enduring importance of the early colonial cities has been perpetuated in the continuing patterns of urban primacy that persist to this day. The enduring importance of the Spanish and the Portuguese is also reflected in the religious and linguistic landscapes of South America's cities. Roman Catholic cathedrals and parish churches dominate central cities and residential neighborhoods, but the continent is split by language into a Spanish-speaking region and Brazil, where the population speaks Portuguese.

The main center of Spanish colonial power in South America lay in the Viceroyalty of Peru, centered on the extensive domain of the former Inca Empire in the Andean highlands. The dramatic fall of the Inca Empire provided a rich source of labor, silver, and gold. Spain proceeded to extend this initial conquest with expeditions into other areas of the continent. Spain founded towns both on the coast and in highland areas. Port cities such as Callao on the Pacific, Buenos Aires on the Atlantic, and Cartagena on the Caribbean linked the new colonies to the Spanish homeland. In highland areas, the Spanish subjugated dense indigenous populations, along with their minerals, complex agricultural systems, and other natural resources. They conquered and rebuilt important indigenous centers to serve as colonial cities in the new empire. They forcibly concentrated the indigenous populations into arbitrarily created villages known as *reducciones,* razed and rebuilt the Inca capital of Cuzco (although Inca construction was so solid, many walls could not be razed) (fig. 4.3), and established such enduring Andean centers as Bogotá, Medellín, Quito, La Paz, and Potosí (see fig. 4.1). Town founding served as a central instrument of colonization, dominating the countryside and imposing a profoundly urban civilization.

Spain did not centrally plan its earliest colonial settlements, but new towns generally adhered to a set of standards established during the late medieval Reconquista of southern Iberia and codified in the Discovery and Settlement Ordinances of 1573. The so-called Laws of the Indies decreed the distinctive physical form and location of Spanish settlements in the New World. The Spanish-American city adopted the distinctive feature of a right-angled gridiron of streets oriented around a central plaza. The imposed urban form of the Laws of the Indies towns essentially served as an effective instrument of social control: urban morphology and social geography were intertwined. Important institutions such as the Roman Catholic cathedral, the town hall (*cabildo*), the governor's palace, and the commercial arcade bordered the central plaza. Spanish residents clustered around the urban core, often in houses built with the defensive architecture of an external

Figure 4.3   Spanish conquistadores built Mediterranean-style structures atop Inca stone walls in pre-Columbian cities such as Cuzco in present-day Peru. (Photo by Maureen Hays-Mitchell)

wall and an enclosed inner courtyard. Indians and undesirable land uses were banished to the urban periphery, a pattern replicated in contemporary cities. These features continue to distinguish the Spanish-American city from cities founded by the Portuguese in Brazil and by the French and British in the Caribbean.

In Portuguese America, the eastern coast of the continent initially proved less alluring than Spain's Andean empire, with its rich silver and gold mines. Consequently, the early Luso-Brazilian settlements were somewhat smaller and less carefully planned. Early settlements in Brazil generally were located close to the coast, at convenient points of interchange between the rural areas of production and metropolitan Portugal. Except for São Paulo, all the towns established before 1600 were located directly on the coast and functioned essentially as administrative centers and military strongholds, ports and commercial entrepôts, residential and religious

centers. To reinforce strategic footholds, the Portuguese crown began to designate captaincies, or land grants, in 1532. The captaincy system divided Brazil's coastal strip. It allowed Portugal to combine elements of feudalism and capitalism and to employ relatively few of the crown's funds. Yet Brazil was constantly under attack from other European powers, so Portugal created a more centralized Spanish-style system in 1549, with Salvador da Bahia as capital. From about 1530 to 1650, sugarcane cultivation on coastal plantations became enormously profitable, powered by imported African slaves. With a population of 100,000 by 1700, Salvador grew to become the most important early Portuguese settlement and the second largest city in the entire Portuguese realm, after Lisbon itself (fig. 4.4).

The coastal location of most early settlements underscored the importance of a good port and a defensible site, so settlers often favored hilly and topographically irregular terrain in the extensive Serra do Mar, the

Figure 4.4   The Pelourinho historic district, named for the "pillory" formerly used to castigate slaves, reflects the strong Afro-Brazilian influence in Salvador da Bahia. The historic center of Salvador da Bahia became a UNESCO World Heritage Site in 1985. (Photo by Brian Godfrey)

rugged mountains that stretch along much of the central Brazilian seacoast. These towns took on polynuclear and linear forms. Irregular mazes of streets focused on a series of squares along the waterfront, as opposed to the more regular grid plans of the Spanish cities. Despite their apparently picturesque confusion of city streets adapted to the topography, Portuguese settlements adhered to coherent but flexible principles of spatial order. The colonial towns were set on defensible hilltop sites, where they prominently featured fortifications, important public buildings, churches and convents, and residential areas, all connected by a maze of winding streets and punctuated by ornate public squares. Class-segregated neighborhoods emerged, as elite mansions for rural

aristocracy and urban merchant classes were set apart from slave districts.

Neocolonial Urbanization: Political Independence, Economic Dependence

Between 1811 and 1830, independence came to each of the countries of South America (except for "the Guianas"). However, throughout South America, characteristically colonial urban forms persisted, even after political independence was achieved. Until the mid-19th century, when elites embarked on campaigns of economic expansion, cities remained relatively small. Thereafter, South America became increasingly integrated into the global economy through the export of primary commodities—beef, minerals, coffee,

Table 4.3   Population Estimates for South American Cities, 1810–1905

City	1810	1850	1880	1905
Buenos Aires, Argentina	50,000	91,000	290,000	1,200,000
Rio de Janeiro, Brazil	100,000	186,000	350,000	850,000
São Paulo, Brazil	24,000	26,000	40,000	400,000
Santiago, Chile	30,000	115,000	150,000	300,000
Montevideo, Uruguay	7,000	25,000	90,000	300,000
Salvador, Brazil	70,000	108,000	130,000	250,000
Lima, Peru	64,000	107,000	100,000	150,000
Recife, Brazil	25,000	86,000	115,000	120,000
Bogotá, Colombia	28,000	40,000	40,000	110,000
Caracas, Venezuela	38,000	44,000	55,000	100,000

Sources: Clawson, David L., *Latin America and the Caribbean: Lands and Peoples,* McGraw-Hill, 2006, p. 342; Charles S. Sargent, "The Latin American city," in Brian W. Blouet and Olwyn M. Blouet, *Latin America and the Caribbean: A Systematic and Regional Survey,* p. 188; Instituto Brasileiro de Geografia e Estatística (IBGE), various years.

rubber—and the import of manufactured goods. Focused on trade with North America and Europe, economic expansion fostered population growth, social change, and urban morphological adaptation. Urban growth proceeded with the creation of new transportation links, rural-urban migration, urban infrastructures, and general commercial development. First affected were mercantile cities, such as Rio de Janeiro, Montevideo, Buenos Aires, and Santiago (see fig. 4.1). These leading cities in turn diffused technological innovations and capital investments to the inland centers of primary-commodity production, that is, their interior hinterlands. New urban services gave the privileged cities images of modernity and attracted migrants from the interior.

Mounting internal migration and foreign immigration contributed to South America's increasing rates of urbanization. By 1905, Buenos Aires' population surpassed 1 million and Rio de Janeiro's exceeded 800,000. Eight other South American cities—São Paulo, Santiago, Montevideo, Salvador, Lima, Recife, Bogotá, and Caracas—had between 100,000

and half a million inhabitants (tab. 4.3). Correspondingly, the percentage of the national population living in the largest city rose in the late 19th and early 20th centuries. Commercial expansion and demographic growth led to widespread deficiencies in urban housing, transportation, sanitation, and health problems, often the subjects of reform movements. The modern city emerged as entrepreneurs invested in new building projects and planners mounted ambitious public works projects to rationalize urban form. Architects, engineers, and planners looked to London, Paris, and Vienna as the main sources of urban inspiration. For example, as the late-19th-century center of Paris was gentrified into an elegant residence for elites, Latin American architects and engineers, often schooled at the École des Beaux Arts in Paris, were inspired to apply similar styles of urban planning in their own cities. The two leading centers, Buenos Aires and Rio de Janeiro, subsequently underwent significant urban renewal programs as they competed for continental leadership. This Eurocentric focus to South American city

Box 4.2   Historic Preservation and Heritage Sites

Cities of South America, as elsewhere in the world, became enamored of historical preservation and cultural heritage during the late 20th century. Although historic monuments date originally from institutional recognition by nationalist regimes of the 1930s, such as Getúltio Vargas in Brazil, the contemporary boom in urban heritage began in 1972, when the United Nations Educational, Scientific, and Cultural Organization (UNESCO) began designating World Heritage Sites—known in Spanish as *Patrimonios de la Humanidad,* or in Portuguese as *Patrimônios da Humanidade.* By 2007, UNESCO had recognized 59 World Heritage Sites in Spanish and Portuguese South America, concentrated largely in Brazil (17 sites), Argentina (8 sites), Peru (8 sites), Bolivia (6 sites), and Colombia (6 sites). About two-thirds of these sites represent "Cultural Heritage" rather than "Natural Heritage," reflecting the importance of Latin America's historic towns and urban historic districts.

The distribution of UNESCO cultural heritage sites has emphasized the built heritage of colonial cities, often constructed over preexisting indigenous settlements, rather than 19th and 20th century sites. The first World Cultural Heritage Site in South America was the City of Quito, which gained UNESCO recognition in 1978, when the International Commission on Monuments and Sites (ICOMOS) called it "the best-preserved, least altered historic centre in Latin America." In 1980, the Historic Town of Ouro Preto, Brazil, became the continent's second UNESCO Cultural Heritage site, as ICOMOS commended "the focal point of the gold rush and Brazil's golden age in the 18th century" and the "many churches, bridges and fountains [that] remain as a testimony to its past prosperity and the exceptional talent of the

---

planning paralleled the continent's political-economic and cultural dependence on neocolonial powers abroad (box 4.2).

Twentieth Century: The Urbanizing Century

As South America moved into the 20th century, the pace of urbanization accelerated. The urban metropolis, not the rural countryside, would come to define the landscape of the region. The neocolonial trade status that marked South America's place in the world economy in the 19th century determined the course of early industrialization, and consequently urbanization, well into the 20th century. The region's cities were promoted as

poles of "modernization," defined in terms of an urban-industrial infrastructure and an expanding industrial labor force. In reality, cities became enclaves of modernization whose existence was premised on facilitating the extraction and basic processing of primary products, principally agricultural and mineral, for an export market. Their fate was dependent upon the transfer of technology and expertise from more technologically advanced trading partners. The benefits of this were confined to the metropolitan region and had little effect on the wider regional economies.

With the worldwide depression of the 1930s, demand for the region's primary products plummeted, unemployment soared, and

Baroque sculptor Aleijadinho." Other early UNESCO designations included the Historic Center of Olinda, Brazil (1982); the City of Cuzco, Peru (1983); the Port, Fortresses, and Monuments of Cartagena de Indias, Colombia (1984); the Historic Center of Salvador da Bahia, Brazil (1985); the City of Potosí, Bolivia (1987); and the Historic Center of Lima, Peru (1988). One notable exception to the colonial emphasis of UNESCO sites was Brasília, a planned city built from scratch and inaugurated only in 1960, which UNESCO recognized in 1987 as an international icon of modernist architecture and planning. Of course, legislation at national and local levels now recognizes thousands of additional historic landmarks and sites in the region.

Heritage tourism has gained favor as a contemporary mechanism for urban revitalization and economic development in deteriorating historic centers, which gradually lost their upper classes and high-end businesses during the late 20th century. As a sign of the times, the Inter-American Development Bank (IDB) began during the 1990s to fund development projects dedicated specially to "urban heritage" in the historic city-centers of Latin America and the Caribbean. South American countries now struggle to finance heritage conservation in their historic cities, where beleaguered localities and hard-pressed preservation NGOs struggle with problems of infrastructure deterioration, real-estate speculation, social services, and public security. Given fiscal constraints, local governments seldom invest in popular housing in the revitalizing *centros históricos,* but instead favor private commercial and tourist development. Historic preservation thus has created opportunities for physical conservation and economic revitalization in long-declining central cities, but it also has raised issues of socioeconomic diversity and equity.

poverty spread. By the early 1950s, a spirit of economic nationalism gripped most South American governments, as they intervened directly in the workings of their economies. The goal was to alter the pattern of producing primary products for export in favor of producing manufactured goods for domestic, and ultimately foreign, consumption. The development of domestic industry focused on major urban centers, because they offered broad access to the national market, a concentrated pool of labor, political influence, and the infrastructure of transport and communication facilities. Investment in the urban-industrial sector was generally favored over the rural-agricultural sector and life became increasingly untenable for small-scale agricultural producers. Thousands of rural dwellers were drawn to cities in the hope of finding jobs, housing, education, health care, and cultural opportunities for themselves and their families. Cities grew at an unprecedented rate, due to both in-migration and relatively high fertility rates (tab. 4.4).

Initially, most cities were able to accommodate their expanding populations. Rapid industrialization created manufacturing jobs as well as demand for commercial, financial, and public services. New building technologies, coupled with new forms of transportation, ensured that living conditions were at least adequate. Medical technology made cities relatively

Table 4.4   Metropolitan Populations of South America, 1930–2005

Metropolitan Area, Ranked by 2005 Estimates	Population (in thousands)				
	1930	1950	1970	1990	2005
1. São Paulo, Brazil	1,000	2,334	7,620	14,776	18,333
2. Buenos Aires, Argentina	2,000	5,098	8,105	10,513	12,550
3. Rio de Janeiro, Brazil	1,500	2,950	6,637	9,595	11,469
4. Bogotá, Colombia	235	676	2,391	4,905	7,747
5. Lima, Peru	250	973	2,927	5,825	7,186
6. Santiago, Chile	600	1,322	2,647	4,616	5,683
7. Belo Horizonte, Brazil	350	412	1,485	3,548	5,304
8. Porto Alegre, Brazil	220	488	1,398	2,934	3,795
9. Recife, Brazil	300	661	1,638	2,690	3,527
10. Salvador, Brazil	350	403	1,069	2,331	3,331

Sources: Charles S. Sargent, "The Latin American City," in Brian W. Blouet and Olwyn M. Blouet, *Latin America and the Caribbean: A Systematic and Regional Survey*, p. 188; Population Division of the Department of Economic and Social Affairs of the United Nations Secretariat, *World Urbanization Prospects: The 2005 Revision*, http://esa.un.org/unup, June 25, 2006.

healthy places in which to live. However, as conditions of urban primacy intensified throughout the region, smaller cities languished. Rapidly growing primate cities were as dependent as ever on imported technology, in the form of modern machinery and replacement parts, fostering external indebtedness and balance-of-payment deficits.

To address these shortcomings, national development shifted from an exclusive focus on nurturing domestic industries to a focus on establishing development growth poles. Growth-pole development precipitated elaborate national development plans with a range of outcomes. In the Southern Cone, it was embraced by Chile, where it served to reinforce preexisting patterns of industrialization and urban primacy. In Brazil, it was invoked in an effort to allay the extreme differences in living standards between the more prosperous and industrializing coastal south and the largely agrarian and impoverished northeast. Although growth-pole development can be credited with the expansion of industry in the northeast and large-scale mining and highway projects in Amazonia, it can also be blamed for environmental degradation in Amazonia and the enduring socioeconomic disparity in the northeast. The most successful example of growth-pole development exists in Andean America, where the new town of Ciudad Guayana was founded in 1961 along Venezuela's Orinoco River, in a region without cities. Ciudad Guayana, the beneficiary of hydroelectric power and nearby mineral resources, is a leading steel and heavy manufacturing center in South America.

By the mid-1970s, many growth poles were perceived to be mere enclaves of foreign capital, since investment favored export industries, which were more closely linked to northern firms than to regional or national economies. Hence, most surplus capital left the region, precluding any significant spin-off of related firms and services. Development failed to trickle down the urban hierarchy and, instead, elicited massive cityward migration and further growth of already dominant cities (tab. 4.4).

Figure 4.5   Carpenters in a Lima shantytown (*pueblo joven*) are typical of the informal economy that is so widespread in Lima and other South American cities. (Photo by Rob Crandall)

Few well-paying manufacturing jobs were available to the largely underskilled rural migrants who swarmed to the cities. Most were left to seek employment at low pay and low levels of productivity, further polarizing rich and poor throughout the region (fig. 4.5).

Despite this, national governments throughout South America continued to finance costly development—especially industrialization and infrastructure—through borrowing on foreign capital markets. Northern commercial banks aggressively courted both private and state interests in South America, as nearly every country in the region accumulated significant debt. Yet, each moved steadily along the economic and social development trajectory. Primate cities remained important. They served as national headquarters for local ruling groups and multinational enterprises and as centers for the accumulation of capital and diffusion of a globalizing consumer-based lifestyle. Moreover, they provided living space for increasing numbers of working-class and marginalized peoples.

The period between 1950 and 1980 saw consistent improvement in urban living standards. Most urban centers were characterized by an expanding middle class and active government promotion of home ownership. Mortgage systems became more accessible and urban infrastructure and services improved. Water, sanitation, education, medical care, and cultural opportunities were readily accessible. Although updated motorways and increased automobile ownership facilitated the growth of elite suburban communities, cars and mortgages were largely inaccessible to lower-income city-dwellers. Consequently, cities underwent explosive growth in self-help housing—primarily squatter settlements—and related programs to service them.

By the early 1980s, however, the global economy had experienced a series of unanticipated shocks that would devastate urban life within the heavily indebted countries of South America. The International Monetary Fund forced countries to exercise extreme fiscal restraint at every level of national life, in order to build up state revenue for debt service and eventual repayment. The debt crisis and related reforms precipitated a sustained period of deep recession and development reversal. Through the 1990s, extreme economic conditions debilitated the region and its cities and, early in the 21st century, Buenos Aires ground to a financial halt because of "debt fatigue." Nevertheless, urbanization continued, although at a slower rate. This gave rise to the phenomenon of urban growth without economic growth and to unprecedented urban poverty.

With the onset of the debt crisis in the early 1980s, the advantages of urban living declined dramatically. Factories closed, public-sector employees were laid off, and social programs critical to the poor were slashed. Throughout the region, access to adequate shelter and public services worsened, and physical and social infrastructures deteriorated. Underemployment (the underutilization of one's skills or the inability to secure full-time employment) came to characterize a large portion of the economically active population in many cities. At the close of the 20th century, over half of South America's poor resided in urban centers. Although countries are showing signs of potential recovery, life chances for the majority of the working class and urban poor remain grim.

DISTINCTIVE CITIES OF SOUTH AMERICA

Internal Structure of the Contemporary City: Urban Spatial Models

The spatial structure of South American cities has been an important topic for comparative urban research. The literature on Latin American city structure emphasizes the distinctive qualities of Latin American urbanization, but it downplays internal diversity within the vast region. The best-known model of urban spatial structure is that proposed by Ernst Griffin and Larry Ford in 1980 (fig. 4.6A). As originally formulated, the model notes the original dominance of a traditional colonial core in Latin American cities, which was transformed by the influx of modern high-rises and commercial activities in the 20th century.

Such generalized models of Latin American urban structure obscure the degree of local variation within the region. For example, one of the most sweeping, and questionable, assumptions is that Brazilian cities followed general Spanish-American patterns of historical development. Although they included no Brazilian case studies, Griffin and Ford argued that Portuguese settlements followed regular Spanish practices of the "Laws of the Indies." However, Luso-Brazilian settlements were notable for their informal, spontaneous, and essentially medieval patterns of organic (as opposed to planned) urbanization. Clearly, the early Portuguese colonial outposts in Brazil were somewhat less regular in form than the Spanish-American settlements, since they lacked the comprehensive Laws of the Indies orthogonal gridiron plan, though they contained coherent elements of spatial order. In addition, recent years have witnessed more complex and decentralized forms of urbanization than predicted by the Griffin-Ford model. As Latin American cities have grown, they have experienced greater socio-spatial differentiation: new areas have emerged through processes of inner-city gentrification, affluent suburbanization, and peripheral commercial development of "edge cities." In the larger metropolises, urban

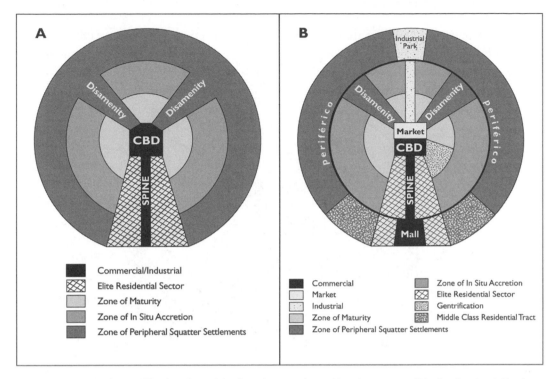

Figure 4.6   (A) The Griffin/Ford Model of Latin American City Structure; (B) the Revised Ford Model of Latin American City Structure. *Source:* (A) Earnst Griffin and Larry Ford, "A Model of Latin American Urban Land Use," *Geographical Review* 70 (1980): 397–422. (B) Larry Ford, "A New and Improved Model of Latin American City Structure," *Geographical Review* 86, no.3 (1996): 438. Reprinted with permission.

realms of varying socioeconomic levels have attained an unanticipated degree of autonomy and local variation.

In response to these and other shortcomings, Crowley proposed a highly differentiated model (fig. 4.7) and Ford offered a "new and improved" model (fig. 4.6B) that included greater peripheral development of mall and "edge city" sectors, separate industrial parks, and selective areas of historic preservation in the core (fig. 4.7). Today, a North American–style metropolis of decentralized urban realms, composed of a series of autonomous activity areas functionally divorced from the older CBD (central business district), is evident in larger and more affluent metropolises, such as São

Paulo. In the end, no abstract spatial model can fully describe the diversity and complexity of cities in South America, much less in all of Latin America. A better approach may be to start inductively with the historical and geographical record of various cities and then to deduce the general regional processes that stand out.

Although contemporary cities of South America look and feel modern and international, they are beset by problems unparalleled in the north. It is tempting to speak of these urban landscapes as "dual cities" in which a modern, affluent, and progressive element has little to do with a poor, obsolete, and unseemly element. In reality, however, the modern, globally linked city and

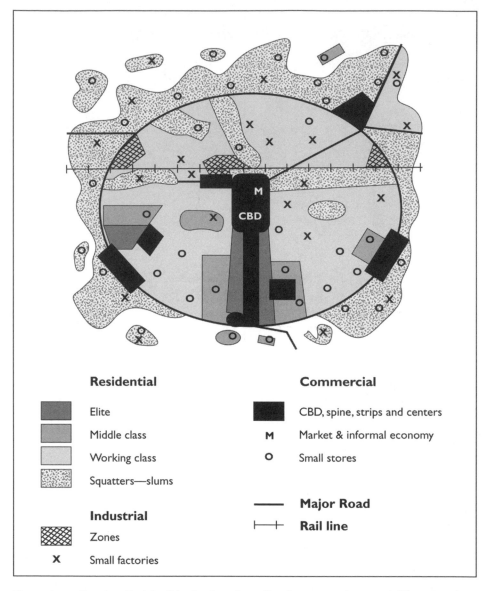

Figure 4.7 Crowley Model of Latin American City Structure. *Source:* William Crowley, "Order and Disorder—A Model of Latin American Urban Land Use," *Yearbook of the Association of Pacific Coast Geographers* 57 (1995): 28. Reprinted with permission.

the impoverished, pollution-plagued city are intertwined aspects of the same metropolitan landscape. This landscape of extreme wealth and poverty epitomizes the region's enduring legacy of underdevelopment, economic polarization, and social injustice. Yet each of South America's cities is unique. Rio de Janeiro and São Paulo, anchors of Brazil's megalopolis, epitomize Luso-American urbanization, and emerging cities in the Amazon Basin have a uniquely frontier character. The case of Brasília deserves study because it was the most famous new capital city of the 20th

Table 4.5   São Paulo–Rio De Janeiro Extended Metropolitan Region, 2005

Areas of the São Paulo-Rio de Janeiro Extended Metropolitan Region	Total Population (thousands)	Number of Municipalities	Area (km²)	Population Density (per km²)
São Paulo	28,856	177	53,771	537
São Paulo Metropolitan Region	19,130	39	8,051	2,376
Campinas Metropolitan Area	5,916	90	27,079	218
Santos/Baixada Santista Metropolitan Area	1,625	9	2,373	685
São José Dos Campos Metropolitan Area	2,185	39	16,268	134
Rio de Janeiro	14,286	70	28,708	498
Rio de Janeiro Metropolitan Region	11,331	17	4,686	2,418
Metropolitan Paraíba Valley/RJ	1,900	36	16,199	117
Cabo Frio/Costa Verde Metropolitan Areas	1,055	17	7,823	135
Total SP–RJ Extended Metropolitan Region	**43,142**	**247**	**82,479**	**523**

Sources: Brazilian Institute of Geography and Statistics (IBGE), http://www.ibge.gov.br/home/; State of São Paulo Data Analysis Foundation (SEADE/SP), www.seade.gov.br; State of Rio de Janeiro Information and Data Center (CIDE/RJ), http://200.156.34.70/cide/; and Hamilton Tolosa, "The Rio/São Paulo Extended Metropolitan Region: A Quest for Global Integration," *Annals of Regional Science* (2003), 37: 479–500.

century and a bold experiment in city planning. As Lima epitomizes Spanish-American urbanization for Andean America, Buenos Aires does so for the Southern Cone. Although each city is distinct, each is representative of the evolving urban experience in South America.

Rio de Janeiro and São Paulo: Anchors of South America's Megalopolis

In his classic book *Megalopolis*, first published in 1961, Jean Gottmann profiled the unprecedented size, complexity, and interdependence of the U.S. northeastern urbanized corridor. Gottmann noted the high population densities, blurring of rural-urban distinctions, economic integration and decentralization, relatively high levels of education and income, rise of the service-sector, and concentration of governmental and corporate managerial functions. Such characteristics now apply to the urban region of southeast Brazil, centered on São Paulo and Rio de Janeiro but also

encompassing several other metropolises. With a population of about 45 million people in 2005, 95% urbanized, the extended São Paulo–Rio de Janeiro (SP-RJ) metropolitan region has become one of the world's largest agglomerations (tab. 4.5). It represents a quarter of the national population and one-third of the GNP. Composed of about 250 municipalities, Brazil's megalopolis covers 32,400 square miles (84,000 km²)—the size of Austria. Two-thirds of the 2005 population (28.8 million) lay in São Paulo state, including the greater capital area (19.1 million) and the metropolitan areas of Campinas (5.9 million), Santos (1.6 million), and São José dos Campos (2.2 million). Rio de Janeiro state's portion (14.3 million in 2005) of this extended metropolitan region included the capital region (11.1 million), the central Paraíba Valley (1.9 million), and the adjacent coastal areas of the Costa Verde and Capo Frio/Búzios areas (1.1 million). The metropolis of Juiz de Fora in the neighboring state of Minas Gerais (0.5 million) also forms part of this integrated

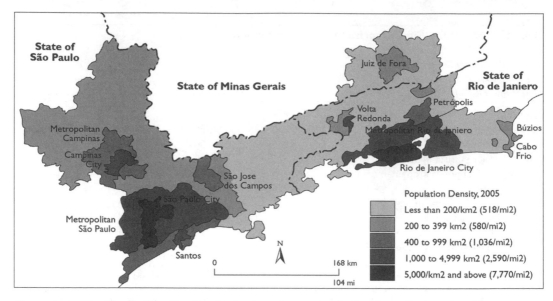

Figure 4.8   The Rio de Janeiro–São Paulo–Campinas extended metropolitan region. *Sources:* Instituto Brasileiro de Geografia e Estatistica (IBGE); Centro de Informações e Dados do Rio de Janeiro (CIDE); and the Fundação Sistema Estadual de Análise de Dados (SEADE), 2007. (Map by Brian Godfrey and Laurel Walker)

urban region. Overall, the SP–RJ extended metropolitan region had a population density of 523/km^2 (1,355/mile^2) in 2005, ranging from about 2,400/km^2 in the capital regions to lower densities in the exurban fringes of this expansive and multi-centered megalopolis (fig. 4.8).

Despite their increasing regional integration, São Paulo and Rio de Janeiro retain their own distinct identities. Residents of Rio (known as *Cariocas*) and those of São Paulo (known as *Paulistas* for the state or *Paulistanos* for the city) are famous for their dueling dispositions and intense competition. The hackneyed image of the fun-loving, easy-going *Carioca* and the intense, hard-working *Paulista* is exaggerated, but like many stereotypes it reflects a particular social history. Rio de Janeiro—famous for its spectacular seaside views and unique popular culture of the samba, bossa nova, and

carnival celebrations—has long been an international jet-set playground and beach resort. By the time that Rio lost the national capital to Brasília in 1960, rival São Paulo had taken the economic and demographic lead in this rapidly modernizing country. While Rio deindustrialized and grew increasingly dependent on tourism and other urban services, São Paulo grew through industrial, commercial, and financial dynamism to become the preferred location for multinational corporate headquarters in South America. Now considered the business capital of Mercosur—the emerging common market centered on Brazil and Argentina—São Paulo is known as a fast-paced, resourceful, temperate metropolis with distinctly urban charms and challenges. The presence of such striking differences between Brazil's two largest cities suggests a significant variation in city structure and underscores the

Figure 4.9 The classic postcard view of Rio de Janeiro includes scenic Sugarloaf Mountain (Pão de Açúcar), which guards the entrance to Guanabara Bay. (Photo by Brian Godfrey)

limitations of regional or continental models of urbanization.

Rio de Janeiro: A Luso-Brazilian Model of Coastal Urbanism

The Portuguese founded São Sebastião do Rio de Janeiro in 1565 at the entrance of Guanabara Bay, one of the world's great natural harbors. With prosperous local sugar plantations and steady trade, the settlement maintained a population of several thousand, composed largely of slaves, until the discovery of gold and diamonds in Minas Gerais led to a regional spurt of growth in the 18th century. As a result, the colonial capital was transferred from Salvador da Bahia to Rio de Janeiro in 1763. After the Napoleonic invasion of Portugal, the royal family fled to Rio de Janeiro and the city served as capital of the Kingdoms of Portugal and Brazil from 1808 to 1815. Royal sponsorship after the arrival of the Portuguese court stimulated building and new institutions were founded. Extending along Guanabara Bay and scaling the surrounding hills, Rio de Janeiro acquired a linear, polynuclear spatial pattern (fig. 4.9).

Rio de Janeiro's status as the main port and capital of independent Brazil (1822–1960) secured its national primacy for over a century. Political patronage and commercial interests encouraged Rio's growth, infrastructural development, and a continual modification of the settlement's physical site. As both the capital and the principal national metropolis, the city's port boomed, industry and commerce prospered, and cultural affairs flourished. By 1872 Rio de Janeiro had a population of

Figure 4.10   Copacabana Beach, Rio's world-famous tourist playground, is also home to a dense urban neighborhood in the city's affluent Southern Zone (Zona Sul). (Photo by Brian Godfrey)

274,972, compared with a mere 31,385 in São Paulo (see tab. 4.3).

Determined to compete with Buenos Aires as South America's most cosmopolitan city, Mayor Francisco Pereira Passos (1902–1906) promoted extensive urban renewal to transform Rio de Janeiro into a "tropical Paris." Using yellow fever as a rallying point, municipal authorities mounted an extensive sanitation campaign and demolished thousands of buildings to make way for new boulevards and high-rise structures. The port was transferred from the downtown core to modernized facilities to the north on Guanabara Bay. The new transportation arteries encouraged real estate development in socially sorted neighborhoods during the early 20th century. Gradually the northern zone became predominantly industrial and working-class in character, while affluent populations gravitated to fashionable

districts to the south (fig. 4.10). Even as Rio de Janeiro has spatially decentralized, social-class barriers have remained in place. The poor are primarily nonwhite and the middle and upper classes remain overwhelmingly white, and these racial disparities largely coincide with patterns of residential segregation.

The main exception to the sharp north-south split in social geography stems from the highly visible presence of hillside shantytowns, informal housing known locally as *favelas*, above the fashionable southern districts. By the late 1940s, as a result of the rapid rural-urban migration, the favelas overtook the run-down tenements of the central slums as the main form of housing for the urban poor. Today nearly one-fifth of the city population is housed in some 600 *favelas*, scattered in hillside shacks (fig. 4.11). Providing rent-free housing on government or disputed terrain

Figure 4.11 A narrow commercial street in the Rocinha district indicates the informal, improvised nature of one of Rio's largest favelas. (Photo by Brian Godfrey)

close to employment, the favelas have become a permanent feature on the landscape, despite recurrent efforts by authorities to remove them. Recent programs to ameliorate conditions in the favelas focus on infrastructure improvements and better social services, including street paving, hillside stairways, water provision, and recreational facilities.

Rio's environmental problems have mounted along with contemporary metropolitan growth. Torrential summer storms often devastate precariously perched *favelas* and flood low-lying streets below. Fifty years ago thick hillside vegetation absorbed most of the rainfall, but most of the rainfall now runs off urbanized surfaces, dislodging unstable structures and blocking major transportation arteries. Water pollution is another major problem. State and city agencies have made

notable progress in curbing pollution of Guanabara Bay and the popular Atlantic beaches, but much remains to be done to conserve Rio's spectacular natural site.

São Paulo: An Inland Model of Modern Urbanism

São Paulo's distinctive colonial origins began with its inland site, which contrasted with the coastal locations of most colonial centers of Brazil. Jesuits founded São Paulo de Piratininga in 1554 on the gently rolling hills of a vast inland plateau, strategically located at a critical transportation juncture between the coast and Brazil's plains. Lacking valuable resources or lucrative plantations nearby, the village remained small for three centuries. São Paulo's locational advantage only became apparent during the mid-19th century, when the city became the center of a prosperous coffee-growing region, favored by fertile soils and generally mild subtropical climate. With railroads financed by British capital, São Paulo became the chief point of transshipment for the lucrative new cash crop. As a result, turn-of-the-century São Paulo grew rapidly, especially through European immigration, largely from Italy, after the abolition of slavery in 1888 led to a shortage of labor in the coffee fields (see tab. 4.3).

Profits from the coffee trade were invested in urban commerce, industry, and real estate development. Enterprising immigrant families made fortunes in food processing, textiles, and other early industries. By the 1920s São Paulo overtook Rio de Janeiro as the principal industrial center of Brazil. Programs of import-substitution industrialization, initiated under President Getúlio Vargas in the 1930s, cemented São Paulo's national industrial dominance. After President Kubitschek designated São Paulo as the site of the nation's foreign-led automobile industry in the 1956 Development Plan (Plano de Metas), Volkswagen established the country's first automobile assembly plant in Sao Bernardo do Campo, some 13 miles from the core. Subsequent factory investments by other multinationals and large Brazilian firms created a vast industrial plant in the metropolitan area.

The dizzying growth of 20th century São Paulo created successive urban layers. The modern city began to take shape in the early 20th century with demolition of inner-city tenements (cortiços) to widen streets. In 1929, future mayor Prestes Maya (1938–1945) published his influential Boulevard Plan (Plano de Avenidas), which provided a blueprint for opening major avenues in central areas. Large-scale demolition, redevelopment, and new transportation lines facilitated the development of a burgeoning office and commercial district downtown; in outlying areas served by trains and streetcars, real estate speculation encouraged housing development in socially sorted districts. Working-class districts emerged in run-down central slums and near industry in the low-lying river basins and railroad corridors. Generally, the wealthy sought higher terrain in the city's southwestern districts. Along the Avenida Paulista, the townhouses of coffee-barons and business leaders created a fashionable residential district in the 1920s, but after World War II the mansions here gave way to the headquarters of banks and corporations. With the emergence of a business district on the Avenida Paulista, the inner "Jardim" neighborhoods witnessed widespread conversion from houses to affluent high-rise apartment living and the trajectory of affluent single-family residences extended into the southwestern districts (fig. 4.12).

Figure 4.12   The juxtaposition of a modern high-rise apartment tower and an older single-family detached home in central São Paulo illustrates the dramatic verticalization that has dominated the city in recent decades. (Photo by Brian Godfrey)

Construction of São Paulo's modern freeway and subway systems encouraged new areas of urban expansion in peripheral areas. In fact, contemporary problems of urban transportation crystallize the city's social inequalities. Since the 1950s, metropolitan transportation policy has favored individual automobile travel by the middle and upper classes through a massive investment in new arterial roads, while the poorer sectors of society are underserved by the city's inadequate public transportation system. Working-class areas and peripheral shantytowns often depend on tortuous, unreliable bus service.

Figure 4.13   The skyline of downtown São Paulo reflects the dynamic growth of Brazil's dominant commercial center and corporate headquarters city. (Photo by Brian Godfrey)

Greater São Paulo now assumes a complex morphology as a result of contemporary economic restructuring, deindustrialization, and decentralization (fig. 4.13). With the transition from an industrial to a commercial and administrative-service emphasis in the urban core, the once compact downtown has been split into two nodes: the traditional business center near the Praça da República and the financial district of the Avenida Paulista. Shopping malls now draw customers to the outlying areas, especially in the prosperous central-southwestern zone. The suburban industrial "ABC region"—Santo André, São Bernardo do Campo, and São Caetano do Sul—with its automobile sector and strong labor unions, faces cutbacks and job loss as industries move away to neighboring states, which have offered attractive tax breaks to lure automobile assembly plants. Meanwhile,

outlying satellites beyond the 39 municipalities of the official São Paulo Metropolitan Region, such as Campinas and São Jose dos Campos, are known for their universities and high-technology sectors. São Paulo now constitutes a vast and decentralized metropolis on the scale of New York, Los Angeles, or Tokyo (see fig. 4.8).

São Paulo also now faces the problems of environmental degradation and related health concerns accumulated during years of explosive growth. Given its inland location and concentration of heavy industry, automobiles and buses, and informal peripheral growth, Greater São Paulo endures heavy air and water pollution. Air pollution worsens particularly in the winter, when temperature inversions trap pollutants and prevent contaminants from blowing away. State agencies do monitor pollution and use fines with some success to force

Box 4.3   Urban Security and Human Rights

Increasing concerns with violent crime now plague South American cities. Widespread fears of urban violence have been fed by vivid accounts in the news media, tourist guides, governmental travel advisories, and popular films. For example, such acclaimed recent films as *City of God* (Brazil, 2002) or *Our Lady of the Assassins* (Colombia, 1999) feature racy stories full of sex, drugs, and armed conflict in urban slums. Such representations sensationalize violence and serve to stigmatize the urban poor, who happen disproportionately to be of indigenous or African racial origins. The preoccupation with urban insecurity has created a culture of fear, which Brazilian anthropologist Teresa Caldeira (see Suggested Readings) relates to "the increase in violence, the failure of institutions of order (especially the police and the justice system), the privatization of security and justice, and the continuous walling and segregation of cities."

Official statistics often underreport crime, since distrust of the police discourages many residents from reporting incidents. Even so, studies indicate steadily increasing rates of violent crime over the last three decades. Rates of homicide (murder and manslaughter) represent the most reliable data, given compulsory death registrations. In 1980 national homicide rates in Brazil and the United States were about the same (about 10 per 100,000 population), but by the late 1990s the Brazilian rates were twice as high, and now the difference has widened to nearly fourfold. In South America, the highest rates of homicide ranged from Colombia (84/100,000), followed by Brazil (32), Venezuela (25), and Ecuador (16) in 2003. Of course, violent crime tends to be worse in large cities. São Paulo, Rio de Janeiro, and Recife have been among the most violent Brazilian metropolitan regions with homicide rates persistently over 40/100,000 since the 1990s. Although several large U.S. cities had such high rates in the 1990s, subsequently violent crime tended to decline, often dramatically.

São Paulo's contemporary evolution points to widespread trends. A 2004 study by the U.S. Centers for Disease Control (www.cdc.gov/mmwr/preview/mmwrhtml/mm5308a1.htm) found

industries to install filters and to cut contamination. It has proved harder to regulate the more than 4 million cars and buses, now the main polluters, since automobile emissions are considered a concern of federal regulation. Despite governmental efforts, the construction of sewage and waste treatment systems remains inadequate, particularly in the peripheral informal settlements, where untreated waste often pollutes surrounding areas. Fiscal prob-lems have hindered ambitious clean-up programs in the befouled Tietê River, which snakes through the metropolitan area.

Future Prospects for the Brazilian Megalopolis

After decades of rapid growth, Brazil's two leading metropolitan areas now face the disadvantages of massive scale, such as inadequate

that in the city of São Paulo homicide rates more than tripled, from 17.5 in 1980 to 53.9 in 2002. (By comparison, 2002 homicide rates in U.S. large cities ranged 45.8 in Washington, D.C., 22.2 in Chicago, 17.5 in Los Angeles, and 7.3 in New York City). Of the 5,719 homicides reported in São Paulo during 2002, firearms were involved in the vast majority. Most victims were young males (15–29 years old). The risk of homicide varied enormously by district, ranging from 1.2 in wealthy Jardim Paulista to 115.8 in impoverished Guaianazes. Investigators found a strong negative correlation between the average monthly income of heads of households and homicide rates in the city.

Various causes have been hypothesized for the rise in urban violence. Factors cited include rapid urbanization, illegal drug and firearms trafficking, economic crises and high unemployment, and widening income inequality. The study above notes that "the strong negative correlation between monthly average income and homicide rates in São Paulo city described in this report is consistent with homicide research in other urban areas worldwide." Caldeira emphasizes the interrelationship of democratization, urban segregation, and socio-economic polarization, which together have created urban fortified enclaves surrounded by walls, security cameras, and private security. The widespread concern over crime has served to maintain class and racial boundaries, despite the expansion of formal democratic rights.

Put into a social context, the rise in urban violence becomes an important issue of human rights. Community development initiatives now feature programs to prevent violence, particularly among young people in poor communities. In Rio de Janeiro, the Viva Rio non-governmental organization (NGO) began in the 1990s to offer programs to reduce firearm injuries, promote social justice, and provide vocational training for young people in poor communities. Similarly, the Mangueira Social Project, located in one of the city's *favelas,* provides after-school programs for local youth who demonstrate regular school attendance. These and other NGOs have embarked on grassroots campaigns to change the perception of their communities through the internet, media outreach, and partnerships with the government, universities, and the private sector.

physical and social infrastructure, traffic congestion, pollution, fear of crime, housing scarcity, stagnant job markets and relatively high labor costs. Industries have shown an increasing tendency to relocate out of the two largest metropolitan areas to small cities in the interior. The fastest-growing Brazilian cities are now the intermediate centers scattered throughout the country's interior, as illustrated by Amazon frontier urbanization. Even as Rio de Janeiro and São Paulo face the challenges of metropolitan decentralization and economic restructuring, the two cities are not likely to lose either their prominence as national centers or their key distinguishing characteristics. As the nerve centers of a vast country, these two cities have sprawled to form the joint nuclei of an integrated megalopolis with the population of a medium-sized European country in southeastern Brazil (box 4.3).

Figure 4.14   The spectacular modern architecture of Brasília, designed by Brazilian architect Oscar Niemeyer, focuses on the government ministries and the Congress buildings located along the federal district's Monumental Axis (Eixo Monumental). The "Pilot Plan" (Plano Piloto) of Brasília was declared a UNESCO World Heritage site in 1987. (Photo by Brian Godfrey)

Brasília: Continental Geopolitics and Planned Cities

Urbanization has now spread to South America's long-forsaken interior, particularly the Brazilian central plateau (planalto), the Amazon Basin, and other inland areas. The founding of new inland cities has presented a prime opportunity for modern urban planning and industrial development, as in Ciudad Guyana of Venezuela and, in Brazil, Goiânia, Belo Horizonte and, most famous of all, Brasília. The transfer of the federal capital from Rio de Janeiro to Brasília in 1960 served dramatic notice of the determination to redistribute the population from the coast to preconceived cities of the interior. Under Juscelino Kubitschek, president of Brazil from January 1956 to January 1961, construction of the new capital constituted an important part of an ambitious program of national urban-industrial development. The new capital's spectacular modern design and rigorous land-use controls were meant to contrast with more spontaneous earlier cities, seen to be plagued by irregular urban growth (fig. 4.14).

Brasília's construction began in 1957 on a barren site in the state of Goiás, on the central plateau (planalto central), about 600 miles (970 km) from the coast. Brazilian architect Lúcio Costa designed the new capital's visionary plan, and his colleague Oscar Niemeyer designed the city's most impressive modernist buildings, such as the Cathedral, Senate and Chamber of Deputies complex, the Itamaraty Palace of the Foreign Relations Ministry, the Planalto Palace executive building, and the Alvorada Palace of the president. Costa's highly symbolic "Pilot Plan" of Brasília features two

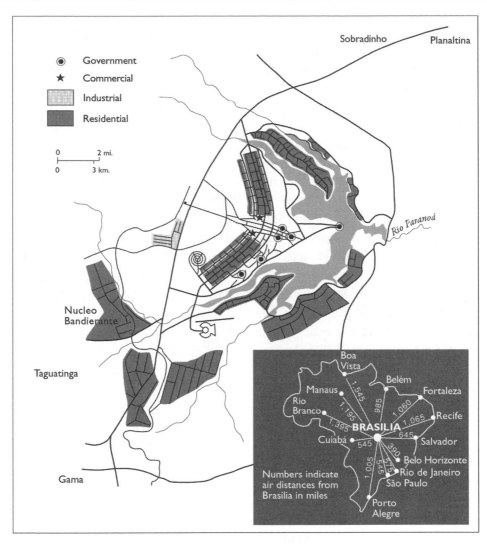

Figure 4.15   Brasília. *Source:* Complied by the authors.

great intersecting axes, one governmental and the other residential, together forming the rough outline of an airplane (fig. 4.15). Federal government buildings cluster at the eastern end of the plane's body or "fuselage," around the Plaza of the Three Powers. Near the central intersection of important boulevards lie the bus terminal, stores, hotels, and cultural institutions. Farther west are the governmental complex of the Federal District, along a sports arena and recreational facilities.

Residential areas, which extend north and south along the "wings" of the plane, comprise groups of six-story apartment buildings to house government functionaries and their families. Each "superblock" of apartments contains a school, playground, shops, theaters, and so on. On the eastern side of the Pilot Plan lies scenic Lake Paranoá, where the most expensive private residences have been built, especially in the exclusive Lago Sul ("South Lake") sector.

Early residents and architectural critics often found Brasília sterile and monotonous, lacking the vibrant street life of other Brazilian cities. Many government officials initially maintained homes in the former capital, Rio de Janeiro. In time, however, Brasília filled in with upscale businesses, diverse services, attractive residences, and along with the new amenities, the capital developed a certain character. Brasília has become an effective symbol of national integration and central planned area—the Pilot Plan—was designated a World Heritage Site by UNESCO in 1987. The organization's International Committee on Monuments and Sites (ICOMOS) concluded that "the creation of Brasília is unquestionably a major feat in the history of urbanism," although it also cautioned that the "new capital of Brazil encountered serious problems which, even today, have not been totally overcome." UNESCO's decision to recognize Brasília included a precautionary warning that "minimal guarantees of protection" must "ensure the preservation of the urban creation of Costa and Niemeyer." That the central Pilot Plan of the modernist capital of Brazil would be historically preserved, less than 30 years after its founding, reflects more than admiration of an architectural icon: it also speaks to widespread concerns over the rapid and largely unplanned urbanization of the rest of the Federal District.

Away from the central Pilot Plan of the new capital, informal settlements quickly emerged in what were called the "satellite cities"—out of sight but within commuting distance of the city center. Housing was not provided for the construction crews, other workers, and their families. So a series of spontaneous suburbs some distance from the attractive residential "superblocks" of the city center were built by and for the migrant laborers and their kin.

These unplanned communities were composed mainly of low-rise, self-constructed wooden homes and initially exhibiting a ramshackle frontier atmosphere. Several of the early settlements, such as Taguatinga, in time became established centers with public services, whereas other more recent areas are still in rudimentary conditions. The vast majority of the population—in 2005, 2.3 million in the Federal District and 3.3 million in the metropolitan region—lives outside the Pilot Plan in what are now preferably called "surrounding cities" (*cidades do entorno*). Despite the widespread early criticism of Brasília, the federal district's steady growth suggests a successful pole of in-migration. Yet, the inability to plan effectively the entire federal district, symbol of a modernizing regime, underscores the persistence of familiar social problems, such as widespread poverty, self-constructed housing, and the informal sector. The experience of Brasília speaks to the difficulty of implementing centralized planning in a developing country beset by high levels of income concentration and a dearth of basic public services.

The Amazon Basin: An Urban Frontier

In the Amazon Basin, inter-regional migration and rapid urbanization now transform one of the world's last great settlement frontiers. The Amazon River and its tributaries drain a watershed of approximately 2.7 million square miles (7 million square kilometers), or 40% of the South American land surface. Although the Amazon region occupies large parts of Bolivia, Peru, Ecuador, Colombia, and Venezuela, two-thirds lies in Brazil. In all six Amazonian countries, contemporary regional development programs have attempted to integrate scantily populated peripheral areas in the interests of national sovereignty. These projects have resulted in disorderly and often violent processes of frontier urbanization, which have pitted native peoples, agricultural colonists, gold miners, forestry interests, cattle ranchers, transnational corporations, governmental agencies, and others in land conflicts. Although tropical deforestation has received the most attention, urbanization has created serious deficiencies in service provision, health problems, and environmental degradation in the burgeoning towns and cities.

Urbanization has been most dramatic in Brazilian Amazônia, which became predominantly urbanized during the late 1970s. Considering the six primary states of the Brazilian North Region—Acre, Amapá, Amazonas, Pará, Rondônia, and Roraima—the urban population skyrocketed from 28% in 1940 to 52% in 1980, and reached 70% by 2000. Although the region remains somewhat less urbanized than Brazil as a whole (81.2% in 2000), Amazônia faces particular urban problems due to its relative isolation, precarious infrastructure, and dependence on resource extraction. Historically, boom-and-bust cycles in natural resources—rubber, gold and diamonds, and other natural resources—generated the two primary regional metropolises of Belém (2005 population 2.0 million) and Manaus (2005 population 1.6 million). Founded during colonial times as defensive and commercial nuclei, these and other urban centers burgeoned during the height of the trade in natural rubber (circa 1870–1910). Yet, these cities remained remote and inaccessible by land and air transportation until the late 20th century, when they became regional growth poles and tourist centers. As immigration has mounted, new housing has come partly from residential towers in central areas, but mainly from self-constructed housing in peripheral low-lying areas, often subject to flooding by tides and rains, and ill-served by urban services.

Belém do Pará: Metropolis of the Lower Amazon

As the main gateway to the lower Amazon Basin, Belém has long served as the region's most important city and port of call. Originally home to the Tupinambá Indians, in 1616 the Portuguese crown established a fortress here to claim the area and to protect against incursions by rival European powers. A settlement initially called Feliz Lusitânia, but soon rechristened Santa Maria de Belém do Grão Pará, arose around the colonial fort, located on a defensible peninsula at the confluence of Guamá River and Guajará Bay, near the mouth of the vast Amazon River system and about 60 miles (100 kilometers) from the Atlantic Ocean. Popularly known ever since as Belém do Pará, or simply Belém ("Bethlehem" in Portuguese), the city's population is predominantly racially mixed and descends from intermarriage of the indigenous peoples with smaller European and Afro-Brazilian groups. With its humid-equatorial climate, the city is famous for daily afternoon rains, graceful streets lined with mango trees, and unique Amazonian foods and native handicrafts.

Named capital of the colonial province of Maranhão and Grão Pará in 1751, Belém's strategic location made it the geopolitical, missionary, and commercial center for the lower Amazon Basin. In the late colonial period, trade mounted in the *drogas do sertão*—"drugs of the forest"—such as guaraná, cinnamon, and cacao. As part of independent Brazil, resource extraction climaxed in the "rubber boom" (approximately 1850–1915). Lucrative trade in latex from native *Hevea brasiliensis* trees permitted urban expansion, infrastructure improvements, and such monuments as the neoclassical Teatro da Paz (1878) and the Ver-o-Peso ("Watch-the-Weight") Market, an iron-framed structure imported from England (1899–1901). The boom had ended by World War I, and Belém thereafter stagnated for several decades. Despite continuing extraction of rubber, Brazil nuts, diamonds, mahogany, and other natural resources, profits could not approach those of the boom years. The opening of the Belém-Brasília Highway in 1960—the first major overland road connecting the Amazon to the rest of Brazil—encouraged in-migration and revived the city's fortunes. Belém became a federal and state-level administrative center for development programs in agriculture, cattle ranching, tropical forestry, iron-ore extraction, gold mining, and other activities.

As one of Brazil's 10 largest metropolitan regions, greater Belém now approaches a population of 2 million and juxtaposes an affluent sector of sleek skyscrapers and modern businesses with a burgeoning informal sector of peripheral shantytowns. Roughly half the population lives in low-lying baixadas—self-constructed housing equivalent to the favelas of other Brazilian cities—that suffer from recurrent flooding and offer only rudimentary piped water, sewerage, public transportation, and other services. Despite such infrastructural challenges, contemporary urban redevelopment programs have restored much of the historic waterfront and Old City, now renamed "Feliz Lusitânia." On the second Sunday of October, Belém hosts one of the country's largest religious festivals, known as the Círio of Nazaré, dedicated to the Virgin of Nazareth. The Amazonian native heritage remains evident in a distinctive popular culture, inimitable cuisine and regional fruits, and such native crafts as woven baskets, decorated gourds, and earthen ceramics of the pre-historic "Marajoara" style.

Manaus: Growth Pole of the Upper Amazon

As the capital and regional development pole of Brazil's vast Amazonas state, Manaus dates back to 1669, when the Portuguese crown established the Fort of São José da Barra do Rio Negro to protect its claims to the Upper Amazon. Popularly known as Lugar da Barra, this military outpost sat strategically near the confluence of the Rio Negro and Amazon Rivers, roughly 750 miles (1,200 km) from the Atlantic Ocean. The settlement grew initially as a colonial center of defense and missionary activity. Local native groups, most notably the Manaós people, for whom the city was later named, converted to Christianity and intermarried with the Portuguese colonizers, creating a racially mixed population.

After joining independent Brazil in 1823, Lugar da Barra was raised to the status of vila, or town, in 1832. As steamship transport made the town more accessible for trade and communication, Vila da Barra became the City of Barra do Rio Negro in 1848. Subsequently the city became an increasingly important commercial center for trade in natural resources, such as fish, minerals, and forest products. Brazil's upper Amazon region, long a subordinate administrative district of Pará with its capital at Belém in the lower Amazon, seceded to form the Province of Amazonas with its capital at Barra do Rio Negro in 1850. The city had only about 1,250 inhabitants when it was renamed Manaus in 1856, but thereafter it benefited from a boom in the trade of rubber latex, produced by Hevea Brasiliensis trees native to the region. The city's population increased from 29,334 residents in 1872 to 75,704 in 1920, while urban amenities included expanding trolley lines, streetlights, and the ornate Teatro Amazonas opera house, inaugurated in 1896. By World War I, the golden age of the rubber trade had ended with the increasing competition of Asian plantations in the international market, and Manaus fell into an economic depression that lasted for several decades.

In 1940, President Getúlio Vargas gave a famous "Speech of the Amazon River," promising new policies for the Amazon Region. Reelected president, Vargas created in 1952 the National Institute for Amazon Research to foster the "scientific study of the environment and living conditions of the region, taking into account human welfare and demands of culture, economy and national security." Nonetheless, the regional economy stagnated until the creation of the Manaus Free Trade Zone in 1967, which promoted an export-enclave model of industrialization through the development of multinational electronic and communications assembly plants. Associated infrastructural projects included a network of regional highways, a new container-shipping port, and a new international airport. In contrast, the burgeoning peripheral districts feature stilted huts or residential riverboats, often lacking in basic urban services, for many recent migrants to the city. With the relative decline of the Free Trade Zone in recent years, ecological tourism has received growing attention as an alternative form of regional development and Manaus has become Amazônia's main point of departure for riverboat expeditions and rainforest treks.

Frontier Urbanization: Boom Towns of the Interior

Even as the traditional metropolises of Belém and Manaus grow to unprecedented sizes, the most significant regional transformation now proceeds in the small towns and medium-sized cities of the interior, which now experience the highest rates of urban growth. In terms of urban primacy in the Brazilian Amazon, the two largest cities have gradually declined in relative terms from 68% of the urban population in 1950 to 30% in 2000. Conversely, other Brazilian Amazon cities have grown proportionally from 32% in 1950 to 70% in 2000. The rates of increase in the intermediate and small cities have often been staggering. For example, Rio Branco in the state of Acre officially grew from 17,154 in 1970 to 197,098 in 2000—a whopping 35% annual change. Double-digit rates of increase can be found in countless other regional cities, such as Porto Velho, Ronônia; Macapá, Amapá; Santarém, and Marabá, Pará. The transformation of small towns into booming cities has raised considerable problems of urban infrastructure, housing, and social services.

A prototypical case of boomtown evolution occurred in southern Pará, where the town of Xinguara spontaneously emerged in 1976 at the intersection of new roads linking the Xingu and Araguaia Rivers (fig. 4.16). The settlement metastasized into a thriving growth pole of roughly 8,000 people by 1978, fueled by reports of available agricultural lands, timber extraction, gold mining, and commercial opportunities. By 1991, Xinguara was the seat of an independent municipality with a population of 27,292. Although local lands had been largely

Figure 4.16   The fledgling boomtown of Xinguara is typical of the Amazon settlement frontier in recent decades. (Photo by Brian Godfrey)

occupied, and timber and mineral resources exhausted by this point, Xinguara's strategic location made it an enduring commercial center. Still field surveys in 1990 indicated that urban services and public health remained precarious: the vast majority of households lacked modern water and sewage systems; not surprisingly, about half the population had suffered from gastrointestinal disorders and a quarter had contracted malaria. By 2007, Xinguara's population had stabilized at about 30,000, though conditions reportedly remained rudimentary.

Although Brazil's Amazon expansionism attracts the most attention, the Andean countries also have vast, scantily populated, and historically remote eastern "oriente" regions. In the 1960s, Peruvian President Fernando Belaúnde Terry envisioned a Marginal Jungle Highway (Carretera Marginal de la Selva), which would encircle the upper Amazon Basin from Venezuela to Bolivia. The pan-Andean road network would have linked the various countries and provided a unifying basis for planned

urbanization of the upper Amazon settlement frontier. Although territorial suspicions among the Andean countries prevented the full implementation of the ambitious highway network and settlement program envisioned in the regional plan, the various governments subsequently all built new roads and launched colonization schemes in their own territories. Most schemes were intended to spur inland migration and thus alleviate crowding in coastal or highland cities. The discovery of oil, gold, diamonds, copper, and other minerals has fueled inland migrations into the Amazonian territories. Northeastern Ecuador, for example, has had an active pioneer zone as a result of the construction of an oil pipeline to the coast during the 1970s; environmental groups, indigenous peoples, highland migrants, and oil companies have battled over land claims here. Similarly, with improved road access to the Peruvian interior since the 1960s, Tingo Maria has become a crossroads town in the embattled Huallaga region, a rich agricultural and coca-

Box 4.4   Addressing Air Quality in Latin American Cities

Rising automobile use, expanding industrial production, and increased energy generation associated with rapid urbanization in Latin America's cities exposes more than 100 million people to air contaminant levels exceeding those set by the World Health Organization (WHO). The yearly cost, according to WHO, is thousands of premature deaths, billions of dollars in medical costs and lost productivity, and a hefty contribution to global climate change.

Air pollution in cities throughout the region affects the health and well being of hundreds of millions of people. Children, with their immature organs, are especially at risk of developing debilitating ailments. The very elderly are more susceptible to lung cancer and cardiovascular disease. And the poor, by virtue of where they live and work and how they make a living, are disproportionately exposed to dangers associated with prolonged exposure to polluting agents known to cause cancer, cardiovascular disease, and other ailments. Air pollution affects the natural and built environments of cities, causing deterioration to buildings and monuments, stifling the growth and air-cleansing benefits of trees and gardens, and affecting crop yields in downwind regions.

The predicted impacts of climate change in the Latin American region are severe. Temperature elevations will likely result in an increase in respiratory diseases linked to air pollution, as climate change could influence meteorological factors that impact the frequency and duration of "poor air quality episodes" in cities throughout the region. Urban water supplies, already in short supply, will likely diminish due to the loss of snowpack and glaciers in the Andes Mountains. The majority of primate cities in South America

(continued on next page)

growing area. The formerly sleepy town of Santa Cruz de la Sierra in eastern Bolivia—with a 2005 population of 1.5 million, now the country's largest—has become a dynamic regional metropolis as a result of agricultural colonization, exploitation of natural gas, and improved transportation connections with neighboring countries.

Lima: Hyperurbanization on South America's Pacific Rim

Historical and modern, cosmopolitan and deprived, luxurious and squalid, problem-plagued and splendid—this is Lima. Although the Lima of today bears slight resemblance to the settlement established nearly five centuries ago, its most intractable problems date to the historical processes of development and underdevelopment that have shaped the world economy since that time.

Since its founding by the Spanish in 1535, Lima's fate has been interwoven with that of the world capitalist system. Initially, the city served as a point of contact between Spain and its colonial empire in South America, the vast Viceroyalty of Peru, which encompassed most of Andean America and the Southern Cone. Lima quickly evolved into a transshipment point for the mineral, agricultural, and textile

are located in coastal zones and hence vulnerable to coastal flooding due to predicted sea-level rise.

As the impacts of air pollution and climate change on public health and the environment are better understood, the need to adopt strategies that recognize the importance of effectively integrating air quality and climate change considerations into social and economic development planning becomes more apparent. In September of 2007, the Clean Air Institute released the draft of "The Clean Air Initiative Strategy for Latin American and Caribbean Cities 2007–2012" (CAI-LAC). The Clean Air Institute, an independent non-profit organization, was founded in 2006. It is a multi-stakeholder effort dedicated to addressing the environmental and public health concerns associated with air pollution in large cities throughout the region, as well as the region's contribution to and impacts from global climate change.

The draft initiative understands that, despite many common sources, conventional air pollutants and greenhouse gas emissions are rarely considered jointly. Jointly focusing on these factors is particularly important in Latin American cities, where resources are scarce, significant institutional and technical barriers exist, and compelling evidence suggests the societal costs of air pollution will continue to present an enormous challenge to countries of the region. To begin, efforts will focus on increasing the supply of clean energy and the efficiency of energy across the transportation, industry, commerce, and residential sectors. Thousands of lives are at stake.

Source: Adapted from "The Clean Air Initiative Strategy for Latin American and Caribbean Cities 2007–2012," *The Clean Air Institute*, draft September 10, 2007.

wealth extracted from the Andean interior and ultimately it was a market for finished goods produced in more prosperous regions of the world. Lima, capital of Peru since independence, is centrally located on South America's Pacific coast. Along with its port, Callao, Lima is squeezed into a narrow coastal desert between the Pacific and the Andes.

The original site of Lima was located several kilometers inland, along the southern bank of the Río Rímac, from which the city takes its name. Bays on either side of the mouth of the Rímac formed a natural harbor. The natural advantages of the site supported complex civilizations for at least 4,000 years before the arrival of the Spanish conquistadors. The site, however, also had its perils: the region is prone to frequent earthquakes, flooding, drought, and other disturbances (box 4.4).

Although Lima was founded before the Laws of the Indies, its founding anticipated them. Hence, the city was laid out in a grid pattern, with streets radiating from a central plaza in a regular east-west and north-south pattern. Official buildings and residences of the principal conquistadors were erected around the central plaza. Lima's development was further influenced by its proximity to the Rímac River, which served as a resource for irrigation and waste disposal. Although archi-

Figure 4.17   Plaza Bolivar in downtown Lima is a world heritage site. (Photo by Rob Crandall)

tecture was Spanish in style and inspiration, the environmental features of coastal Peru influenced it. The dry, temperate climate allowed the use of flat roofs and light materials. The scarcity of local stone necessitated the use of wood and adobe. Frequent tremors limited buildings to two stories. Long vistas of bare adobe walls, interrupted by elegantly carved wooden doors, were the architectural norm of early Lima. In the late 17th century, a surge in the construction of monumental buildings added grandiose Baroque designs (fig. 4.17). Diagonals—some following pre-Columbian indigenous roads—eased the rigid grid of streets, while numerous small plazas enhanced public space.

Lima quickly emerged as the center of wealth, power, and royal justice for the entire Viceroyalty of Peru. In 1551, the first university in the Western Hemisphere, La Universidad de San Marcos, was founded there. By the close of the 17th century, Lima contained over 30,000 people and displayed all the essentials of a cosmopolitan center and primate city. Its intensely artistic lifestyle confirmed it as the unrivaled capital of Spanish-American high culture. Beyond the ostentation of colonial elites, however, there existed another Lima. Most Limeños subsisted in conditions of poverty and privation. The city was extremely unsanitary and epidemics were common.

Independence in 1821 did little to change the social system or regional hegemony of Lima. However, the demolition of the city's walls in the latter half of the century set in motion a process of significant alteration. A beltway was constructed along the path of the demolished walls, more bridges were built over the Rímac River, and broad avenues and rail lines were built to the coast, where upper-class suburbs took hold. By the end of the 19th century, Lima could be considered a fully modern city. Installation of a new sanitation system greatly diminished the incidence of waterborne disease. Electricity throughout the city brought light to homes and power to industry.

Trolleys, bicycles, and automobiles facilitated movement throughout the city. Medical facilities were improved, fire companies were established, and police protection was extended. For the first time, the death rate in Lima dropped below the birth rate. Meanwhile, population growth, agricultural stagnation, and economic injustice were making life in rural Peru increasingly untenable and set off an early process of rural-to-urban migration.

Demographic growth quickly pushed Lima beyond its old colonial perimeter. Urban development took hold along a set of axes, each of which had a distinctive character. The area northwestward to the port of Callao became the city's industrial corridor; the seacoast to the southwest developed into an elite residential zone; and small industry intermingled with working-class housing to the east. Small middle-class and upper-class communities sprang up in the open country between Lima and the coast. By 1960, the areas radiating from the old Lima center to the Pacific coast were fully urbanized. Shantytowns were commonplace in the desert regions to the north and south of the city, known today as the Cono Norte and Cono Sur (fig. 4.18).

Migration to Lima has occurred in a series of waves, each generating distinct changes within the city. Until World War II, mostly rural elites and people from nearby provinces migrated to Lima. Many had family contacts or skills to secure employment. In the two to three decades following the war, migration became a more generalized phenomenon, as people from all regions, lured by new industry, found their way to the city. Finally, the political and economic crisis of the 1980s and 1990s brought an influx of poorly prepared and highly traumatized displaced persons, primarily from the southern highlands, seeking safety and refuge. In relatively short order,

provincial migrants and their offspring transformed Lima from a bastion of elitist creole culture (European culture within America) into a microcosm of contemporary Peru. Today, food, music, dance, artisanry, accents, dress, and festivals from every region of Peru are found in Lima. Migrant families maintain close ties with their provincial communities. Indeed, many informal housing communities are named for particular provincial communities, and provincial clubs can be found in nearly all urban neighborhoods.

Demographic growth has reinforced the city's primacy. Lima dominates all aspects of national life. Peru's most recent census indicates that 73% of the national population currently resides in cities, with 40% of that population living in greater Lima. Today, upwards of 8 million people live in the metropolitan region, which is more than ten times larger than the next city, Arequipa. Ironically, Lima's primate status is the cause and effect of growth. Due to its location, Lima has long served as the gateway between the outside world and the rest of the country. The concentration of political influence, capital, industry, communications, workforce, consumers, and the most prestigious institutions of research, learning, and culture induces further concentration of all these activities. The concentration of these features reinforces Lima's primacy and works against efforts toward decentralization. Indeed, in times of economic expansion, the gap between Lima and the rest of the country grows more pronounced, with little synergy between Lima's economy and the provinces.

Today in downtown Lima, ornate colonial architecture contrasts sharply with the modern high-rise buildings that accommodate banks, law firms, businesses, and government services. Most of the remaining colonial mansions have been subdivided into slum housing that accommodates as many as 50 families per building. The enclosed wooden balconies that typified the colonial city have become a point of interest for preservation (fig. 4.19). In 1991, much of old Lima was designated a UNESCO (UN Educational, Scientific, and Cultural Organization) World Heritage Site (see box 4.2). There is little evidence of gentrification in Lima. Instead, many private-sector businesses and international agencies have moved their offices to the less congested and more secure suburbs. Indeed, the most defining feature of Lima is its expansive barriadas, which have been euphemistically renamed *pueblos jovenes* (young towns) and most recently *asentimientos humanos* (human settlements). Hundreds of thousands of shanties have been constructed on the barren, unoccupied slopes that rise above the red-tiled roofs of the inner suburbs and on the flat desert benches that encircle Lima (fig. 4.20). In four short decades, shantytown housing has become the norm. Approximately half of the city's population is estimated to reside in *asentimientos humanos,* with the Cono Norte and Cono Sur the most populous districts in the city. Many of these settlements have evolved into permanent communities, having been awarded titles to land and provided basic services. Still others languish in poverty and neglect.

The social fabric of present-day Lima is more complex than ever. Race, ethnicity, and class defy easy classification. The enduring difference is that between the rich and influential on the one hand and the poor and powerless on the other. This is visible on the urban landscape. As Lima's population shifts, Andean, and to a lesser extent Amazonian, culture infuses its streets and public spaces. Pressure to assimilate is less today as migrants

and their offspring assert their cultural heritage and their claim to Lima as a multicultural city. In response, wealthy Limeños pick up the process begun centuries ago of distancing themselves from the poor. Now they are moving not simply to the traditionally more elite western districts of the city, but also beyond to quasirural settings to the east as well as the more distant seaside communities to the north and south. Private security, gated communities, and chauffeurs are markers of their attempt to withdraw. Notwithstanding, luxury and squalor exist side by side. As family stores give way to chic boutiques and hygienic supermarkets in upscale neighborhoods, they in turn are encircled by ambulantes (street vendors) selling every conceivable item (box 4.5). Despite the municipality's determination to reclaim the city center for pedestrians and sightseers, bedraggled children join the infirm and elderly in begging. This has sparked discussion in academic and policy circles of the role that public spaces may play in enhancing the quality of urban life and creating a shared civic identity.

The economic context of Lima's rapid demographic and territorial growth has been one of constraint. National economic policies and international market forces have made life increasingly difficult within Lima. Early attempts to develop domestic industry were financed by hefty borrowing of foreign capital and focused primarily on Lima. However, most new manufacturing jobs were capital-intensive and provided employment for only modest numbers of skilled and semiskilled workers. They were inappropriate for the majority of rural migrants who flocked to the capital in the hope of finding jobs and better lives. Ironically, at a time when migration to Lima was increasing, the urban labor market was actually shrinking.

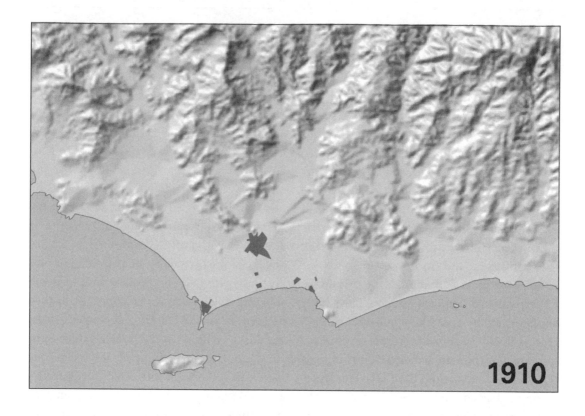

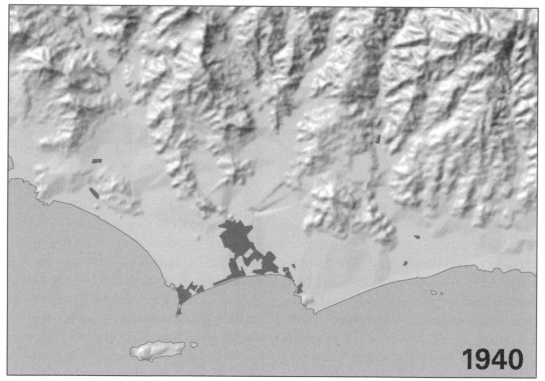

Figure 4.18 Growth of Lima, 1910–2000. *Source:* Centro de Promoción de la Cartografía en el Perú, Avda. Arequipa 2625, Lima 14, Peru.

1970

2000

Figure 4.19   Enclosed wooden balconies on colonial buildings typify the historic district in Lima, a UNESCO World Heritage Site. (Photo by Rob Crandall)

Today, Lima, and to a lesser extent Peru in general, is emerging from two decades of economic and political crisis. Improving economic conditions have allowed infrastructural improvements to be made in the capital. Roads are being paved, public spaces illuminated, parks restored, and walkways built. A small construction boom is benefiting the middle class. The economic situation of some *asentamientos humanos* appears to be improving slowly, as small businesses and industries take root there.

However, Lima confronts problems of unprecedented proportion and complexity. Opening Peru's economy to global markets has accentuated the importance of Lima as an economic center; the majority of international and national corporations operating in Peru are located in the capital. Yet, the decline of Lima's manufacturing sector and expansion of its service sector only accentuate longstanding polarization within its labor market and society in general. Most poor residents of Lima do not experience the positive effects of economic globalization, and the gap between the Limeños who do and those who do not is growing ever wider.

Lima's rapid and unplanned growth, within a context of fiscal constraint, has caused severe environmental degradation, especially of the city's air and water. Lima is a mega-city in a desert where the nearest rivers are polluted by runoff from mining and agriculture. As the Rímac, Chillón, and Lurín rivers—the very rivers that gave rise to human settlement here some 4,000 years ago—pass through the city, residential and industrial waste is dumped in their waters. Urban sprawl has eaten away at the green space in their valleys and has consumed wetlands, reducing biodiversity and affecting microclimates within the metropolitan region. Total potable water has decreased in the past decade, and nearly half a million people do not have water service,

Figure 4.20   A shantytown (*pueblo joven*) outside of Lima. (Photo by Rob Crandall)

while more than 15% of Lima's 8 million residents lack sewer service. The UNEP (United Nations Environmental Program) has identified water as the most critical environmental problem in the Lima-Callao conurbation.

Most Limeños, however, consider air pollution the most pressing environmental issue. The installation in August 2006 of an air-quality monitoring system by the National Environmental Council (CONAM) and the Ministry of Health would seem to confirm this. Limeños who frequent the city center and/or reside in certain districts breathe large quantities of airborne particulates and other pollutants. A recent study estimated that respiratory and heart problems related to airborne particulate matter are responsible for some 6,000 deaths per year—nearly double the number in 2000. The primary source of air pollution is poorly maintained vehicles. CONAM estimates that 8.5 million public transport and 2 million private transport trips are made each day in Lima.

However, automobiles and aging buses are not the sole source of air pollution. Industry contributes significantly to the problem, especially the countless unregulated factories, home industries, and restaurants that abound in Lima's shantytowns. In one *asentamiento humano* on the northern edge of the city, recyclers use homemade furnaces with oil-drum chimneys to melt lead from discarded car batteries into ingots for sale in the informal economy. In July 2005, lead levels exceeding the World Health Organization's recommended limit were found in the blood of all but 1 of 27 children tested in the community. Despite the health risks posed to children, shutting these informal businesses is contentious because such action would impact livelihoods within the community. Moreover, industries such as this one exist

Box 4.5   Women of the Streets

"Cómprame, Cómprame casera, Cómprame." "Buy me, buy me," they call to the potential customers who pass in the streets. These women are not selling themselves, but rather a vast array of foods and manufactured goods. They are the street vendors, or *ambulantes,* who fill the streets of South America's cities. Street vending, along with prostitution, is one of the few occupations by which women can earn a living on city streets. Whether or not it is considered "proper" is something few women street vendors can afford to consider. They are compelled to earn their livings on the streets by the endemic poverty and limited occupations open to poor women in most South American countries.

Throughout South America, the ranks of street vendors—as all components of the urban informal economy—have swelled as the region's economic crisis has intensified (fig. 4.21). Interviews with women *ambulantes* in cities throughout Peru indicate that, although most are from humble backgrounds, an increasing proportion are relatively well-educated women who cannot find employment in their professions. Those women who depend entirely on their income from street vending tend to be heads of households; they are elderly, widowed, abandoned, single mothers, or wives of imprisoned or "disappeared" men. These women encounter the most restricted range of employment opportunities. Within their set of options, street vending is the most viable. Increasingly, otherwise unemployed men are turning to street vending, heightening competition.

In Huancayo, a bustling commercial center in the Peruvian central highlands, nearly one-half of *ambulantes* are women. As to be expected, they are rational decision makers. More than half deal in volumes of products sufficiently large to gain access to wholesale prices. Those who do not deal in sufficient volume often band together to create the

Figure 4.21   A peddler (*ambulante*) selling fresh vegetables in Hauancayo, Peru. (Photo by Rob Crandall)

requisite demand. In keeping with the traditional image of women as providers of food and domestic service, they tend to specialize in sales of fresh produce, hot meals, clothing, and household items—the most poorly capitalized product lines, with the lowest profit margins. It is likely that those who sell household items and prepared foods, rather than filling a niche, are creating their own demand. In contrast, nearly the entire supply of fresh produce is commercialized by ambulantes. Although the majority of fresh produce vendors are women, they tend to deal in smaller volumes than their male counterparts, thus reaping less than men from this potentially lucrative market.

To assert their interests, many have turned to political activism. Street vendors are organized into trade unions, called *sindicatos,* for the purpose of protecting and furthering the interests of all *ambulantes.* In Huancayo, many of the leaders of these organizations are women. Women have proven effective in organizing their unions as well as guiding meetings away from rhetorical exhortations and toward important business matters. Despite this, they tend to be relegated to subservient roles within the organizations—an exercise that only adds to their already heavy workload.

Like women everywhere, women *ambulantes* hold worries and concerns as well as hopes and aspirations. Many, especially those who sell prohibited goods, such as raw meat, or who choose to operate without the requisite licenses, worry about harassment by the municipal police. They run the risk of losing their inventory and hence their investment. Many are bound to disadvantageous credit schemes—a cycle that ensures a lifetime of street vending. Bringing their young children to work, seen by some as an advantage offered by street vending, can be a worrisome burden for many women. Children distract their mothers, who must be alert in this competitive occupation. Children are exposed to the elements and many young ones contract respiratory illnesses and die. Once they become toddlers, they play in the streets, where they often sustain injuries. Those who are school age soon become street vendors themselves. Moreover, the streets of their cities are not particularly safe. Petty thieves work them at all hours. Not even the *huachimanes* (night watchmen hired by individual *sindicatos*) can be trusted. They routinely pilfer the stands that *ambulantes* meticulously wrap and leave behind.

throughout low-income communities. Not surprisingly, the very parts of Lima where life expectancy is estimated to be five to six years lower than the city's average, are low-income communities with high levels of contamination.

Due to its status as national capital and primate city, Lima has turned to the national government of Peru as well as international development agencies for assistance, arguing that Lima's problems—economic, political, social, environmental—are national problems.

Buenos Aires: World City of the Southern Cone

Long regarded as one of Latin America's greatest cities, Buenos Aires stands as the most visible symbol of Argentina's history and national identity. As the capital and economic pivot of a leading country, the city reflects a high degree of urban primacy common in South America. Once a minor colonial outpost of Spain, Buenos Aires grew rapidly as a center of immigration, urban design, and modernism from roughly 1880 to 1930. While the country emerged as an agricultural and industrial power, the Argentine capital became known as the "Paris of South America": an elegant city of broad boulevards, graceful public squares, and impressive public buildings. Monumental Buenos Aires has served as the stage for national political movements, as dramatized by the famous scenes of Juan and Eva Perón addressing the multitudes from the balcony of the Casa Rosada, the presidential palace. Despite a relative decline in regional importance vis-à-vis São Paulo and other continental mega-cities since the heyday of Peronism in 1950, greater Buenos Aires remains a vital metropolis with a 2005 population of 12.5 million. The city's residents, known as *porteños* (port-dwellers), continue to be trendsetters. On the other hand, the Argentine metropolis now faces growing problems of socioeconomic inequality, popular discontent and insecurity, and spatial segregation. Buenos Aires' urban history is one of continuity and change.

The founding of Buenos Aires reflected the territorial ambitions of an expansive 16th-century Spanish Empire. After conquests in Mexico and Peru, Castile turned its attention to the southern flank in the Americas. In 1536, Pedro de Mendoza led a Spanish expedition into the Río de la Plata (also known as the River Plate) and founded "Puerto de Santa María del Buen Aire" at the entrance to a small river, the Riachuelo. Although the southern shore of the Plata estuary generally is low and marshy, with wide mud flats, the Riachuelo inlet is deep enough for anchorage by shallow-draught ships. Subsequently known as La Boca ("The Mouth") this original port of Buenos Aires provided the best maritime landing available at the northeastern rim of the vast Argentine Pampas, where land expeditions could depart for the interior plains.

Lacking precious minerals and other natural resources, and subject to continual attacks by hostile native groups, the colonists abandoned this original settlement in 1541. But the location remained strategic, so Spanish forces under Juan de Garay refounded Buenos Aires in 1580. Garay designed the ground plan for the fledgling town, which followed the characteristic Spanish-American urban form. The central plaza (later named the Plaza de Mayo) served as the core of the colonial settlement, surrounded by the important governmental, religious, and commercial structures. The city council, or *Cabildo*, sat across from the Cathedral and a commercial arcade lined much of the plaza (fig. 4.22). Leading families claimed the desirable central properties in the gridiron pattern of streets radiating outward from the plaza.

The city and its port suffered from regional isolation and official neglect until the late colonial period. Andean trade routes long favored such inland cities as Tucumán, rather than the Rio de la Plata port. The Buenos Aires population grew to about 12,000 by 1750, largely due to participation in contraband trade. The Bourbon liberal reforms of the late 18th century enhanced the regional position of Buenos Aires, which became capital of the new Viceroyalty of La Plata in 1776. With relaxation of trade restrictions, the port flourished and the city's population grew to 50,000 by 1800. By this point the city became a regional center of agitation for independence, which aspiring local leaders proclaimed during the revolution of May 25, 1810.

Colonial Buenos Aires typified the Spanish-American "Laws of the Indies" town, but the post-colonial city's design increasingly reflected French and British influences. To

Figure 4.22   The colonial *cabildo*, or a town hall, now preserved in the historic core of Buenos Aires. (Photo by Brian Godfrey)

resolve prolonged centralist-federalist conflicts, Buenos Aires was federalized and removed from the dominant Buenos Aires Province in 1880, and thereafter the president appointed the city mayor. This federal district of 78 square miles (203 km²) developed rapidly. British-financed railroads fanned out into the pampas, opening up an agricultural breadbasket to world trade, and the development of refrigeration allowed export of Argentine beef to Europe. Despite the preferred Parisian aesthetic imagery, another appropriate comparison for emergent Buenos Aires would be the "Chicago of South America," given reliance on the plains for meat and grains, the urban slaughterhouses, the web of railroad connections, and the expansive residential subdivisions.

As Argentina became an outpost of fin-de-siècle order and prosperity, the country became a magnet for massive immigration from Europe. More than 6.4 million Europeans officially immigrated to Argentina between 1821 and 1932, a figure surpassed worldwide only by the United States. By 1914, 30% of the Argentine population was foreign-born, over twice the U.S. proportion. Nearly half of Argentina's immigrants were from Italy, and about a third from Spain. Late 19th century military campaigns, equipped with modern firearms, overwhelmed indigenous populations of the interior, which had resisted colonial assimilation. Large agro-pastoral estates known as *estacias* occupied the best lands, however, so immigrants tended to remain in the urban centers, primarily in the port of entry, Buenos Aires.

As the federal capital, transportation hub, commercial center, cultural mecca, and immigrant port of entry, Buenos Aires experienced a high degree of urban primacy in the national city-system. In 1881 the new federal district had 305,000 residents, roughly 12% of the Argentine population; and by 1914 the city leaped to more than 1.5 million inhabitants, fully 20% of the national total. The capital's population peaked at 2.9 million between 1947 and 1991, but dropped to 2.7 million in 2001. In relative terms, the city's share of the total Argentine population has declined since 1920. On the other hand, the metropolitan region of 12.5 million now represents roughly a third of the country's total population and more than 36% of the Argentine city-dwellers. The vast developmental disparities between the metropolis and the interior have long troubled Argentina, prompting national poet Ezequiel Martínez to call Buenos Aires "The Head of Goliath"—a big-headed giant with a weak body.

❿Rapid urbanization created a series of infrastructural problems during the late 19th century, including traffic circulation, sanitation, and housing provision. Traffic congestion overwhelmed the Spanish gridiron pattern of narrow streets. In addition, drainage, sewerage, and water provision had always been problems of the city's low-lying, marshy site. An emergent country needed a world-class capital city, graced by monuments and public buildings, worthy of Argentina's new wealth and aspirations. Not surprisingly, the urban landscape of modern Buenos Aires came to emphasize the European cultural influences. The 19th-century remodeling of Paris particularly impressed Argentine elites. Similarly, the Argentine capital's remodeling emphasized grand public buildings, fashionable boulevards, and elegant public spaces. The Avenida de Mayo, begun in the 1870s, was torn through downtown to connect the planned capitol building with the Plaza de Mayo and at the Casa Rosada. On completion in 1894, the new boulevard provided a striking visual corridor, reminiscent of the Champs-Élysées in Paris, linking the executive seat of government and the national capitol, built between 1887 and 1906. Admired by *porteño* elites, the Avenida de Mayo became the city's most fashionable address until development of the Palermo district. In the early 20th century, several additional boulevards opened in central Buenos Aires, culminating with the Avenida 9 de Julio in 1936, one of the world's widest avenues, centered on an Obelisk visible from various

vantage points downtown (fig. 4.23). These beautification campaigns inspired similar urban reforms in Rio de Janeiro and other South American capitals bent on appearing modern and sophisticated.

Largely unimpeded by physical barriers, districts called *barrios* covered the federal district by 1930. New immigrants first settled in central *barrios* near the port, such as San Telmo and La Boca: the local Italian-Spanish dialect known as "Lunfardo" emerged here, along with the Argentine "Tango" dance. The city's southeastern areas generally became industrial, working-class districts. In contrast, upper-class areas emerged on the northwestern side of Buenos Aires in such elegant neighborhoods as Recoleta, Palermo, and Belgrano. This affluent axis continued into such elite suburbs as Vicente López, Olivos, San Isidro, and San Fernando. The two socially sorted residential sectors—generally more affluent to the northwest of downtown, more working-class toward the southeast—continued their historic trajectories in contemporary metropolitan growth outside of the federal district. Although greater Buenos Aires grew from 3.0 million to 7.3 million between 1930 and 1960, the percentage living in the central city dropped from 74.1% to 46.4%. With suburbanization, the metropolitan region of Buenos Aires has grown to cover an area of 1,837 square miles (4,758 km^2). Only about a fifth of the metropolitan population (12.5 million in 2005) now resides in the city itself, which has enjoyed autonomous status and has elected its own mayors since 1994.

The 20th-century economic development of Buenos Aires reflected national programs of import-substitution industrialization, begun during the 1930s depression and continued after World War II. As Argentina's rural economy and provincial centers stagnated, the capital offered employment in industry, commerce, and services. In addition, the populist

Figure 4.23 The Diagonal Norte Northern Diagonal Boulevard, officially the Avenida Presidente Roque Saenz Pena, highlights the imposing Obelisk monument in downtown Buenos Aires. (Photo by Brian Godfrey)

politics of Peronist governments encouraged rural-urban migration as a way to win political power for the masses. This proletarianization process has continued in recent decades with the influx of impoverished migrants from the Argentine interior, Bolivia, and Paraguay. Such poverty-stricken migrants have created extensive shantytowns or *villas miserias* ("towns of misery") on the metropolitan outskirts, providing some aspects of a Third World city previously uncommon in Buenos Aires.

Argentine society has long been regarded as relatively homogenous—given widespread European ancestry, middle-class affluence, and high levels of education and public health—compared to the more stratified and racially

diverse countries of the Andes and Brazil. But economic restructuring, lowering of protective tariffs, and neoliberal reforms shattered illusions of Argentine exceptionalism during the 1990s. Under President Carlos Menem (1989–1999), the country grew economically but experienced a contraction of government services, privatization of state enterprises, and widespread deindustrialization. Although elites prospered, much of the population suffered from increasing unemployment and poverty. An economic recession began in 1998 and culminated in the crisis of 2001–2002, when Argentina defaulted on international debt obligations and devalued the peso. With growing public protests came new social movements, such as the *piqueteros*, unemployed workers who blocked roads, bridges, and buildings in greater Buenos Aires and elsewhere. "Unemployed Workers Movements" organized into cooperative markets and businesses during the crisis, and neighborhood-based assemblies (*asambleas populares*) arose. After the election of President Néster Kirchner in 2003, such grassroots activism declined with the return of political stability and economic growth.

As elsewhere, Buenos Aires has witnessed a proliferation of gated communities in recent decades, characterized by low-density residential complexes protected by defensive enclosure and private security. By 2001, more than 500 such gated communities had been developed in suburban Buenos Aires, occupying about 200 square miles (500 km^2)—two and a half times the size of the federal district—and representing a residential population of at least 100,000. These affluent enclaves cluster primarily in suburban areas with good highway access and, paradoxically, the highest rates of poverty. Although the wealthiest municipalities tightly control land use and discourage the development of gated communities, contemporary decentralization of planning regulations has allowed the less affluent municipalities to modify building codes and to attract real estate developers. The clustering of exclusive gated communities in low-income jurisdictions has deepened social polarization by juxtaposing wealthy and poor households. Although social differentiation of barrios is not new, contemporary trends have created more pronounced and finely grained forms of residential segregation.

Despite the emergence of suburban shopping centers, office parks, and gated communities, redevelopment projects suggest a continuing concern for the urban core. For example, the renovation of the abandoned downtown piers at Puerto Madero created a waterfront district of offices, restaurants, convention facilities, and apartments downtown during the 1990s. With such projects, Buenos Aires retains a cosmopolitan air, and given the high degree of Argentine urban primacy the city probably always will. Even with an affluent central city, however, the contemporary rise of socioeconomic inequality and spatial segregation temper metropolitan prospects. Long thought to be different from other South American mega-cities, greater Buenos Aires now converges with them in terms of growing urban problems.

URBAN CHALLENGES
AND PROSPECTS

The Urban Economy and Social Justice

Recent trends in economic globalization, although benefiting some, have amplified long-standing conditions of economic polarization and social injustice in South America's cities. Over the past 25 years, indicators of human development—including health, nutrition, education, housing, purchasing power, and social security—have declined in most countries. Issues of employment, housing, and environmental degradation affect the poor more severely than they do other sectors of urban society. They are creating an increasingly differentiated urban landscape and precipitating social turmoil in cities throughout the region.

It is not uncommon for many urban residents to spend more than half their cash income on food—only to barely meet nutritional needs. In the absence of unemployment insurance or an adequate social security system, most South Americans cannot afford to be unemployed. The majority of urban dwellers are forced to turn to their own resourcefulness. Research on urban labor markets in South America indicates that, although participation within the paid workforce has intensified, participation in the informal economic sector has increased far more rapidly. This is especially true among lower-income groups and the more vulnerable (e.g., poor women and children).

Despite indicators of stabilization at the macrolevel (e.g., growth in gross national income), socioeconomic polarization has worsened in South American cities. Increases in real wages have favored skilled workers only, and informal-sector employment now encompasses nearly half of the urban population throughout the region (fig. 4.24). When such conditions are concentrated among certain social groups or regions, they can generate restive conditions that challenge the cohesion of a society and the stability of a government. The rise of indigenous politics and social protest in Bolivian cities is a fascinating example. Although these conditions have placed the first indigenous president, who appears

Figure 4.24   This home-based workshop in a Lima shantytown is typical of the informal economy. (Photo by Rob Crandall)

determined to gain greater control of Bolivia's resources and to use them for social welfare and economic development, political polarization has widened. Activists on opposing sides of the political divide state their cases in the streets of La Paz, the national capital, and Santa Cruz, where a secession movement is underway.

Urban Housing

Today, one-third to two-thirds of the population of any given city resides in informal-sector housing. Similar to its employment counterpart, the informal housing sector exists outside the bounds of "officialdom" in

that it ignores building codes, zoning restrictions, property rights, and infrastructure standards. In South America, informal-sector housing is commonly known as "self-help" housing, a term that carries a double meaning. Most commonly, self-help refers to the characteristics of the homes and the process through which they are built. Self-help housing tends to be built by the inhabitants themselves, using simple—often hazardous—materials that the owner-builder-occupier has accumulated over time. Additionally, the term conjures up images of impoverished, yet well-intentioned urban dwellers "helping themselves" to unoccupied land—in the absence of a more viable option. Self-help housing communities are commonly considered shantytowns. Many settlements lack basic services, such as running water, sewerage, electricity, and garbage removal. They are constructed of scrap materials that often do not provide adequate protection from inclement weather, have limited access to services, are overcrowded, and lack the security of tenure (i.e., title to the land). Shantytowns—or self-help communities—are marginal in terms of both their location on the urban periphery and the quality of the land occupied, which tends to be undesirable and often unhealthy and dangerous. They may be constructed on toxic "brownfield" sites, alongside noxious landfills, on steep hillsides, or in gullies. Their overcrowded conditions are ideal for the transmission of disease. Shanties are the first structures to fall in mudslides and the first to be carried away in floods, and they easily go up in flames.

It is widely assumed that self-help communities strengthen and improve over time. Numerous social scientists have documented how, after the initial land invasion, settlements evolve into consolidated and well-organized communities. Structures are steadily improved

Box 4.6   Planning for Sustainable Development in Curitiba

The Brazilian city of Curitiba has been widely admired as a model of sustainable development in a context of rapid urbanization. Since the 1960s, civic leaders and planners have adopted innovative policies to encourage compact, livable, and environmentally friendly urban growth. The city avoided costly subways and instead opted for a public transit system of express buses along major corridors, which has proven so efficient and affordable that variations have been adopted in Mexico City, Bogotá, and other cities. Planners have emphasized pedestrian streets and preservation of the historic center, clustered commercial corridors, parks and open spaces, ecological design, recycling of materials, educational programs, and other progressive measures.

Located 250 miles (400 km) southwest of São Paulo and 65 miles (105 km) inland from the coast, Curitiba is the capital of the state of Paraná. With an official city population of 1,788,559 in 2007, and a metropolitan population of more than 3.2 million, Curitiba is a major political and economic center of southern Brazil. In the 19th century, as a center of coffee and tea plantations, farming and ranching, and timber extraction, Curitiba attracted European immigrants—mainly Germans, Italians, Poles and Ukrainians. In the late 20th century, as agribusiness displaced small farmers, rural-urban migrants poured into the city. Curitiba industrialized and became a pole of relative prosperity, encouraging migration from other regions. The city became one of Brazil's fastest growing urban centers: urban growth rates reached about 5% annually in the 1960s, and remained high at 2.5% annually in the 1990s.

Fears that rapid urban growth threatened the city's quality of life led to the development of a 1965 Preliminary Plan by a university team led by architect Jaime Lerner, who later served several terms as mayor as well as state governor. The Institute for Urban Research

and basic services are addressed in one way or another. With time, municipal governments officially recognize the communities and extend urban infrastructure, supplying water and electricity, paving roads, extending public transportation lines, providing garbage removal, building schools, and staffing clinics. In reality, living conditions have steadily deteriorated within the self-help housing sector since the onset of economic restructuring in the 1980s. The decline in real income, experienced by most shantytown residents, has slowed the self-help consolidation process. Shantytown dwellers have less income to spend on construction materials and less time to spend on

home improvements. Self-help communities are also receiving fewer services, as the privatization of utility companies has prompted rates to rise or services to be redirected to more profitable neighborhoods.

Despite the celebration of the self-help movement in many circles, it is nevertheless a substitute for regulated housing and urban services. Although many international donors are favorably disposed toward the self-help movement—and they display this by providing financial aid, technical advice, and construction materials—the vast majority of self-help housing in South American cities is spontaneously built without assistance of any sort.

and Planning of Curitiba (IPPUC, in Portuguese) developed a Master Plan *(Plano Diretor),* which was officially adopted in 1966. This plan proposed to minimize traffic congestion, control urban sprawl, preserve the historic city-center, provide parks and open space, and develop an efficient public transit system. The famous "Trinary" road system, consisting of five traffic arterials that converge downtown, separated automobile traffic in two outer lanes, going opposing directions, from central lanes reserved for express buses. "Tube stations," which feature raised bus shelters with attendants collecting fares, speed entry and exit to buses in the express lanes. Bus lines, operated by private companies granted concessions by public authorities, include a hierarchy of routes extending service in smaller vehicles. Beginning in the 1980s, the Integrated Transport Network (RIT in Portuguese) permitted transit between any points in the city with a unified fare.

Zoning regulations have concentrated development along the arterial corridors to reduce traffic away from the main roads, revitalize the commercial core, and maintain peripheral open space. One of the major downtown thoroughfares, Rua XV de Novembro, became a pedestrian street in 1972. Although angry motorists initially threatened to ignore the traffic ban, they were frustrated by a famous act of public theater, when authorities unfolded large sheets of paper and invited school children to paint on the street. (The pedestrian mall now features a weekly celebration of children painting.) Curitiba also has promoted design-with-nature principles of urban ecology: low-lying areas subject to floods were reserved for parks; altogether, public parks now provide about 50 m² of green space per resident. Despite continuing problems of poverty and service provision in peripheral shantytowns, the city's program of "Faróis de Saber" (Lighthouses of Knowledge) has offered free educational centers, including libraries, internet access, and other social and cultural resources.

Segregation, Land Use, and Environmental Injustices

Although South American cities have long been highly segregated, the pattern of segregation is more complex today. Population expansion and variegated topography are bringing distinct social groups into closer contact within many South American cities. As intervening land is occupied, self-help communities and elite developments often exist side-by-side. However, there is little indication that residential segregation is abating. Indeed, South American cities are characterized by greater polarization in lifestyle. The fear of crime has forced the urban elite to retreat into protected areas in luxury apartment buildings or into gated suburban communities where their security is enforced by walls and armed guards and where their children are chauffeured to private schools. Likewise, glass-fronted skyscrapers and shopping malls characterize business districts and elite neighborhoods, while peripheral shantytowns are built of scrap materials and lack basic services.

Metropolitan expansion and decentralization have eroded the relative dominance of the traditional city center. Employment in the center is decreasing as industrial activity shifts to peripheral or nearby rural locations, and government and professional offices move to affluent suburbs that are less plagued by traffic congestion and crime. There is little evidence of sustained gentrification or commercialization in most declining central cities. Notwithstanding, some major cities are exceptions to this trend. For example, the Brazilian and Southern Cone cities of Rio de Janeiro, São Paulo, Buenos Aires, and Santiago have experienced less central-city decline than have their Andean counterparts (e.g., Bogotá, Lima) and all now have witnessed the rehabilitation of selected central neighborhoods into vibrant commercial and residential districts. To stave off further decline, Lima has converted its historic district into a World Heritage Site.

A differentiated urban landscape is further noted in environmental terms. As elsewhere, urban elites are more likely to enjoy the advantages and to escape the disadvantages of urban living. Affluent business and residential districts tend to be better serviced with running water, sewerage, electricity, garbage service, public transportation, paved streets, sidewalks, and public parks. In contrast, low-income districts are characterized by inadequate urban services and infrastructure. Air pollution in some cities, such as Santiago, São Paulo, Caracas, and Lima, commonly surpasses safe levels as established by the World Health Organization. The wealthy can more readily escape these negative externalities as they listen to car stereos while waiting out traffic in air-conditioned cars. Meanwhile, the less affluent are crowded onto hot, noisy, diesel-spewing buses. The discharge of untreated urban sewage into rivers and streams occurs more regularly in low-income districts. Indeed, children who live in shantytowns are especially vulnerable to gastrointestinal and respiratory illnesses, due to the poor water, inadequate sanitation, contaminants, open garbage, and burning refuse that characterize their living space. In contrast, the better-off reside in less polluted areas, are more able to control some aspects of their living environment, and are more able to escape to country clubs and vacation homes. Indeed, evidence suggests that vulnerability to environmental hazards parallels income and status in South American cities (box 4.6, p. 196).

AN UNCERTAIN FUTURE

The cities of South America have long played a crucial role in a global urban network and capitalist economy. Economic, political, social, and cultural currents from around the world have flowed through the region's cities since the arrival of Iberian conquistadors. Today, as in the past, these global forces and the region's cities continue to shape and influence one another. Indeed, the escalating pace and reach of globalization is adding new urban dimensions to long-standing regional problems of underdevelopment, environmental degradation, social polarization, and spatial injustice. The region's intensifying social divide can be read on its urban landscape, which is at once magnificent and tragic. South America's cities contain a disproportionate concentration of regional wealth and power, as well as a disproportionate concentration of marginalized people who are undeterred in laying claim to their cities. Although the future remains uncertain, it is being debated, contested, and acted on now. Meanwhile, conflicting and compelling extremes will continue to define the urban scene of South America.

SUGGESTED READINGS

Browder, John, and Brian Godfrey. 1997. *Rainforest Cities: Urbanization, Development, and Globalization of the Brazilian Amazon.* New York: Columbia University Press. A comparative study of urbanization in the Brazilian Amazon, including a general regional review and in-depth case studies of boomtowns in the states of Pará and Rondônia.

Caldeira, Teresa. 2001. *City of Walls: Crime, Segregation, and Citizenship in São Paulo.* Berkeley: University of California Press. A provocative interpretation of contemporary trends in urban "fortress" design, gated communities, social polarization, and crime in South America's largest metropolis, emphasizing how widespread contemporary insecurities reinforce prejudices based on class and race.

Cifuentes, Luis, Alan Krupnick, Rául O'Ryan, and Michael Toman. 2005. *Urban Air Quality and Human Health in Latin America and the Caribbean.* Washington: Inter-American Development Bank. Detailed report on the impact of poor air quality on human health in Latin America's and the Caribbean's major cities, especially measured in hospital admissions, lost productivity, and shortened life spans.

Dangl, Benjamin. 2007. *Price of Fire: Resource Wars and Social Movements in Bolivia.* Oakland, CA: AK Press. An analysis of the rise of social movements in Bolivia over access to and control of natural resources such as water, natural gas, coca, and land, including clashes between social movements and corporate interests.

Gilbert, Alan. 1998. *The Latin American City.* London: Latin American Bureau. A study of urbanization in Latin America addressing rural to urban migration, the informal sector, slum growth, and urban politics.

Knapp, Gregory, ed. 2002. *Latin America in the Twenty-First Century: Challenges and Solutions.* Congress of Latin Americanist Geographers: Austin, TX. Showcases the achievements of geographers in helping understand and solve major problems facing Latin America. Chapters include case studies of recent problems or issues in Latin America and provide examples of geographic research that has helped illuminate or solve these problems.

Lejeune, Jean-François. 2005. *Cruelty and Utopia: Cities and Landscapes of Latin America.* New York: Princeton Architectural Press. A collection of illustrated essays on the region's cites, focusing on how they emerged as colonial, national, and global centers—contains useful materials on architectural, cultural, and social histories of urban Latin America.

NACLA (North American Congress on Latin America) Report on the Americas. 2007. *Space, Security and Struggle: Urban Latin America,* vol. 40, no 4. Washington: NACLA. Issue devoted to Latin American urban spaces occupied by the poor, paying attention to how local power is exerted and how the issue of security is addressed. Special attention paid to Honduras, Brazil, Peru, Bolivia, and El Salvador.

Rotker, Susana, ed. 2002. *Citizens of Fear: Urban Violence in Latin America.* New Brunswick, NJ: Rutgers University Press. An interdisciplinary analysis of urban violence in Brazil, Colombia, Mexico, and Venezuela.

Scarpaci, Joseph. 2005. *Plazas and Barrios: Heritage Tourism and Globalization in the Latin American Centro Histórico.* Tucson, AZ: University of Arizona Press. A study of the rise of globalization and heritage tourism in nine of Latin America's historical centers, including examples come from Mesoamerica (Puebla, Mexico); the Caribbean (Havana and Trinidad, Cuba; Cartagena, Colombia); the Andes (Santa Fe de Bogotá, Colombia; Quito and Cuena, Ecuador); and the Southern Cone (Buenos Aires, Argentina; Montevideo, Uruguay).

Figure 5.1 Major Cities of Europe. *Source:* UN, *World Urbanization Prospects: 2005 Revision* (New York: United Nations Population Division, 2006, http://esa.un.org/unup).

5

Cities of Europe
LINDA McCARTHY AND
BOIAN KOULOV

KEY URBAN FACTS

Total Population	529 million
Percent Urban Population	72.4%
Total Urban Population	383 million
Most Urbanized Countries	Belgium (97.2%)
(excluding microstates)	Iceland (92.8%)
	United Kingdom (89.7%)
Least Urbanized Countries	Albania (45.4%)
(excluding microstates)	Bosnia-Herzegovina (45.7%)
	Slovenia (51.0%)
Annual Urban Growth Rate	0.12%
Number of Megacities	0
Number of Cities of More Than 1 Million	31
Three Largest Cities	London, Paris, Madrid
World Cities	London, Paris, Brussels, Milan,
	Randstad, Vienna, Madrid, Zurich,
	Frankfurt, Berlin, Rome, Dublin
Global Cities	London

KEY CHAPTER THEMES

1. Europe is integral to the study of urban development because of its long history and the extraordinary impact of European urban forms worldwide.
2. Europe's urban system is dominated by the world cities of London and Paris, the result of their dominance within former vast empires.
3. Europe has a great number of cities with more than 1 million people, but in general these cities are growing more slowly than those in other world regions.

4. European cities exhibit great diversity in style and form, the result of the region's long history and complex mix of people and cultures.

5. The demand for low-wage labor in western Europe has meant that immigration has gradually produced new cultural mixes in the largest urban areas.

6. Complex land-use patterns within European cities share certain similarities but also important differences with U.S. cities.

7. The cities within the EU form part of an international trading bloc that contains nearly half a billion people with a combined gross national income greater than that of the U.S.

8. Since the end of the Cold War, communist-era cities have undergone radical transformations, bringing them closer to their western European counterparts.

9. Europe became the birthplace of modern city planning as it reacted to the drawbacks of uncontrolled growth during the industrial period.

10. Sustainable urban management (including environmental protection and urban transportation) is an increasing priority in European cities.

Europe is a vital focus in the study of urban geography for a number of reasons. First, cities here are interesting in their own right; indeed, the great ones, such as London, Paris, and Rome, generally come to mind when we think about Europe or plan a European trip. Second, because European cities are quite old, some with roots going back 3,000 years, they reveal the history of many different economic, political, social, and technological systems (feudalism, socialism, capitalism). Third, as a hearth area of urban design, European cities are essential to understanding the landscapes of urbanization elsewhere. Fourth, a study of European urbanization is made all the more exciting by the tumultuous changes that have gone on since the fall of Communism between 1989 and 1991.

History, even recent history, has strongly conditioned the character of European cities. During the period of Soviet-style totalitarian governments following World War II, for instance, cities in eastern Europe diverged in form and function from their western European counterparts. Late 20th century history witnessed the reconvergence of these socialist cities into the "new" Europe as modern democracies emerged and as cities of the formerly communist "East" made the transition back to capitalism. Today, cities within the expanding European Union (EU) fall under a single umbrella. They share markets and labor, are part of a single international trading bloc, and have all either adopted or are moving toward using the euro as their common currency. The predominantly urban EU contains nearly half a billion people with a combined gross national income greater than that of the United States. Yet although cities across Europe do share many characteristics, including bustling city centers, high density, and compact form, fundamental differences remain in terms of land-use patterns, quality of urban infrastructure, municipal governance, level of retail facilities, and city planning and architectural design.

Today, Europe is about 75% urban, but there is no standard definition for exactly what qualifies as a city. National definitions range from a minimum population of 200 in Norway and Sweden to 20,000 in Greece and Spain. Nevertheless, most Europeans live and work in urban areas, and Europe's urban population of 445 million represents 14% of the world's urban population (fig. 5.1). In fact, Europe contains more than 30 cities with populations of more than a million. Yet wide variation is found from country to country. Bosnia and Herzegovina, Albania, and Moldova have the lowest levels of urbanization, whereas the United Kingdom, Luxembourg, Iceland, Belgium, and Monaco have the highest. This variation reflects the close correspondence between the urbanization of a country and factors such as level of economic development, historical circumstances, relative location, and even terrain and climate. And, just as there is disagreement over what constitutes an urban population, there is also disagreement over what constitutes Europe (box 5.1).

HISTORICAL PERSPECTIVES ON URBAN DEVELOPMENT

One of the exciting aspects about studying cities is learning to decipher the historic landscapes of bygone eras—their streets, buildings, and monuments. History is necessary for understanding the evolution of the European urban system because the same forces that produce and modify the built environment of today's individual cities also determined where these cities were initially located and how they flourished or declined over time.

The Classical Period (800 B.C. to 450 A.D.)

In early Greek culture, independent city-states were located mainly along coastlines, reflecting their seafaring cultures, and on easily defendable hill sites, reflecting the need for security in turbulent times. As cities such as Athens, Sparta, Corinth, and Thebes grew in population, bands of colonists left to establish cities around and in the area between the Aegean and Black Seas, along the Adriatic Sea,

and as far west along the Mediterranean as present-day Spain.

The Thracian tribes, which inhabited the Balkan Peninsula during the Hellenistic period, located their cities inland along the larger rivers and mountain foothills. These cities—called "second in number only to the Hindus" by Herodotus in the 5th century B.C.—were built around royal palaces and surrounded by stone-brick log walls with quadrangle towers.

Greek towns shared some common traits. At the center was the *acropolis,* or high city, which contained temples, municipal buildings, and storehouses. Below the high city, in the "suburbs," were the *agora,* or market place, more government buildings, temples, military quarters, and residential neighborhoods. Urban facilities generally were available to all citizens equally. These cities were laid out in a north–south grid pattern and were surrounded by defensive walls. Greek cities, though, remained quite small by today's standards. Although Athens probably reached a population of about 150,000, most large places ranged from 10,000 to 15,000 inhabitants, and the majority of cities had only a few thousand people.

Greek civilization was displaced during the 2nd and 1st centuries B.C. by the expanding Roman Empire. Although the structure of Roman cities like Pompeii and Herculaneum was similar in some respects to that of their Greek predecessors—including the grid system, central market place (called a *forum* in Roman cities), defensive walls, and deliberate establishment in new territories—they had some important differences. Roman cities were established mainly inland and functioned as command-and-control centers. They functioned within a well-organized empire and were designed along hierarchical lines, reflecting the rigid class system of the Romans.

Box 5.1   Where Does Europe End and Asia Begin?

When people talk about Europe, they often refer to it as a continent. Take a look at a map of the world, however, and it is evident that Europe is, in fact, a western peninsula of Eurasia. The reason Europe is often referred to as a continent, separate from Asia, is because it is perceived, both internally and externally, as distinctive culturally from the rest of Eurasia.

This raises the question: where does Europe end and Asia begin? Based on one widely recognized physical geography boundary, which follows the ridge of the main Caucasus Mountain chain, Armenia, Azerbaijan, and Georgia would lie in the Greater Middle East. Historically, they have been part of Middle Eastern civilizations, often serving as a buffer zone between empires, and alternating between periods of independence and long occupation by Assyrians, Romans, Byzantines, Persians, Arabs, Mongols, Ottomans, and Russians.

Politically, however, Armenia, Azerbaijan, and Georgia were constituent republics of the Soviet Union until its demise in 1991. Moreover, the contemporary economic, political, and military relations with their large neighbor, the Russian Federation, prompt many experts to classify these countries as post-Soviet. Notably, some experts on post-Soviet Russia perceive Armenia, Azerbaijan, and Georgia as a southern tier of the Russian "Near Abroad," rather than among the "New East Europeans"—Belarus, Ukraine, and Moldova.

Culturally, different religious traditions draw a clearer line through the region, separating Armenia and Georgia as largely Christian, from Azerbaijan, which is predominantly Islamic. Many people in Armenia, which converted to Christianity in 301 A.D., take deep pride in their country being the first Christian state. Georgia has also been a traditional part of the predominantly Europe-oriented Christian world for about 17 centuries.

Since the collapse of the Soviet Union, the South Caucasus states have become more integrated with their European neighbors to the west. The Council of Europe—as well as other pan-European organizations, such the as Union of European Football Associations and the European Association for the Promotion of Science and Technology—officially recognized the South Caucasus as part of Europe by granting Armenia, Azerbaijan, and Georgia membership and helping to guide them through the difficult process of political and economic restructuring.

In Armenia and Georgia particularly, the sentiment surrounding integration with Europe is best summarized by the Armenian Foreign Minister, Vartan Oskanian, who stated recently that: "Armenia is Europe. This is a fact; it's not a response to a question." Most importantly, the general population in these two states identifies as European. All three states enjoy a special relationship with the European Union. Azerbaijan, however, has been more ambivalent. In the 1990s, the country sought closer relations with Turkey and, in 1992, joined the Islamic Economic Cooperation Organization.

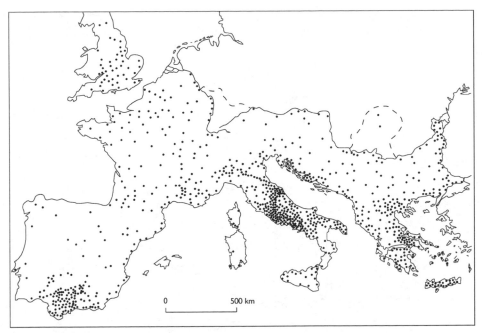

Figure 5.2   Roman Cities in Europe, 2nd century A.D. *Source:* Adapted from N. J. G. Pounds, *An Historical Geography of Europe* (Cambridge, UK: Cambridge University Press, 1990), 56. Reprinted with permission.

By the 2nd century A.D., the Roman Empire extended over the southern half of Europe (fig. 5.2). Roman cities, however, remained fairly small. Although Rome's population probably reached the 1 million mark by 100 A.D., large Roman towns contained only about 15,000 to 30,000 inhabitants, while most places had no more than 2,000 to 5,000.

The vacuum created by the collapse of the Roman Empire in the 5th century A.D. was filled by various tribes that greatly disrupted urban patterns. Most urban centers became depopulated, and their buildings crumbled. At the same time, the constant threat of attack spurred the construction of castles and other fortifications, even in some parts of eastern Europe that had previously been underrepresented by urban development.

The Medieval Period (450–1300 A.D.)

Feudalism curtailed the development of European cities during the early medieval period because its highly structured nature favored the self-sufficient country manor as the basic building block of settlement. The only urban places to thrive or even survive were religious, trade, or defensive centers. With the resumption of long distance trade after 1000 A.D., many medieval towns grew along the commercial routes that crisscrossed Europe (fig. 5.3).

At the center of the typical medieval city was an open square for holding markets. In the larger cities, it was surrounded by the main cathedral or church, the town hall, and the guildhalls, palaces, and houses of prominent citizens. Close to the center were streets

Figure 5.3   This elaborate church tower preserves the medieval flavor of central Prague. (Photo by Darrick Danta)

or districts that specialized in particular functions, such as banking or the production and sale of furniture or metal wares. The streets and alleys were quite narrow and unplanned. The enclosing walls, punctuated at intervals by gates that were sometimes very elaborate, often had water-filled moats outside to enhance their defensive capacity. Finally, medieval towns were decidedly unhygienic. Given their cramped quarters, lack of air circulation, poor sanitation, and absence of waste removal or treatment, it is little wonder that the Black Death (1347–1351) progressed so easily through the towns of Europe killing one-third of the population.

Most development during the medieval period was in the western and southern portions of Europe, which had a Roman heritage of city building. Urban development was impeded in the areas of southeastern Europe that were under the control of the Byzantine Empire, whereas much of eastern and northern Europe remained largely in a pre-urban state. Conversely, the Moors, who spread into Iberia beginning in the early 700s, founded or restored many cities and generally elevated urban culture in what would become Spain.

At the close of the medieval period, Europe had about 3,000 cities containing some 4.2 million people, or 15 to 20% of the total population. Nearly all of these urban areas had fewer than 2,000 people, and only Milan, Venice, Genoa, Florence, Paris, Córdoba, and Constantinople had more than 50,000.

The Renaissance and Baroque Periods (1300–1760 A.D.)

The Renaissance (1300–1550 A.D.) was marked by significant changes in the economic system (a transition from feudalism to

Box 5.2 The Hanseatic League

A precursor to today's European Union, the Hanseatic League marks the first organization that united a region of Europe into an economic association. With roots dating back to the 12th century, the League was an association of cities in and around the North and Baltic Seas that entered into agreements for mutual protection and to promote trade. Over time, more and more cities joined in pursuit of the increased opportunities that membership provided; conversely, embargoes were instituted against ports that were hostile to the organization.

By the 14th century, membership numbered some 200 towns along the coasts of the Baltic Sea (Riga, Königsberg, Rostock, and Stockholm) and the North Sea (Bergen, Hamburg, and several towns in what is now the Netherlands), along with important inland ports along rivers (Berlin, Magdeburg, Cologne, and Cracov, to name a few). Later, several English, Belgian, and even Russian cities joined the League.

By the early 16th century, however, the Hanseatic League had begun to unravel, a casualty of the turmoil brought on by the Reformation coupled with the desire of towns to exercise greater individual control. By 1648 the League was all but dead. A strong architectural legacy is still present in the old Hansa towns in the design of buildings.

merchant capitalism), in the political system (rise of the nation-state), and in art and philosophy. Beginning in Florence in the 1300s, these changes generally spread throughout western Europe; conversely, feudalism was still going strong in eastern Europe, southeastern Europe fell under the grip of the Ottoman Empire, and much of northern Europe remained outside the progressive influences of the Renaissance.

Spurred by heightened demand for such luxury goods as spices, silks, and cloth introduced into Europe during the time of the Crusades (1095–1291 A.D.), merchants greatly expanded the trade, wholesaling, and distribution functions of Mediterranean cities; later, the economic center of gravity shifted to the port cities along the North and Baltic Seas (box 5.2).

Changes in the political system, in particular the growth of countries with national capitals, had an impact on European urbanization. This process is best exemplified by France and Spain; the central location of their capitals (Paris and Madrid, respectively) aided the process of political consolidation; in turn, both cities were given further impetus for growth by their administrative functions, and they achieved enhanced status at the vortex of social, economic, and political change. Similarly, regional centers and seats of county government emerged to fill out expanding national urban networks.

The overall appearance and structure of cities changed because of the introduction of new forms of art, architecture, and urban planning. Especially in Europe's capital cities, flourishing artistic and architectural expression brought about the greater use of sculpture in public areas and of other forms of urban beautification, such as fountains and embellishments on monumental buildings, that reached a peak during the baroque period (1550–1760).

Figure 5.4   Schonbrunn Palace, Vienna, gives a glimpse of the prestige and opulence of Renaissance European nobility. (Photo by Darrick Danta)

The greatest change in the realm of urban design, though, was brought about by several factors. First, after the introduction of gunpowder, massive city walls became obsolete. In many cities, the walls were removed to make space for wide boulevards that were becoming fashionable. Second, the accumulation of great wealth by the nobility led to the building of opulent palaces in many cities, notably Vienna and Paris (fig. 5.4), and to the replanning of cities. Beginning in Paris, many districts containing narrow medieval streets were torn down to make way for wide boulevards that radiated outward from and connected the various palaces and formal gardens laid out for the nobility (fig. 5.5). The emphasis on the control of visual perspective and on the rediscovery of classical models of design marked a significant departure from medieval times.

The European urban network remained largely unchanged during the Renaissance period; however, individual cities got bigger (fig. 5.6). By around 1500, more than a dozen cities in northern Italy, west-central Europe, and Iberia had grown to more than 50,000 inhabitants. Cities such as Krakow, Prague, and Thessaloniki had grown to more than 25,000 people.

The Industrial Period (1760–1945 A.D.)

The large-scale manufacturing of the Industrial Revolution began in the English Midlands in the mid-1700s and spread to Belgium, France, and Germany, reaching Hungary by the 1870s. New factories, foundries, and mills changed the structure of cities and led to massive in-migration of rural workers.

In many cities, whole districts of factory buildings emerged, easily identified by their belching smokestacks, deafening machinery, and general hustle-bustle of industrial activity. Trains transported much of the industrial inputs and products, so new tracks, stations, and rail traffic began to play a significant role in urban development.

Figure 5.5   Beginning in the 1860s, old Paris was remade by Baron Haussmann who gave the city its boulevards, grand views, and monumentality that we know today. Thanks to Haussman's reforms, café society has flourished in Paris ever since. (Photo by Donald Zeigler)

Public transportation in the form of trolleys and subway systems also modified the look and functioning of cities. Large tracts of worker housing (often cramped) were constructed. The industrial period also heralded the development of the Central Business District (CBD) with its office buildings and corporate headquarters.

The growth of cities closely mirrored the diffusion of industrialization. By the early 1800s, industrial towns in the English Midlands and Scotland had grown to more than 100,000 inhabitants, and the proportion of the population living in cities greater than 10,000 had risen to 30%. The growth of industrial cities in France, Belgium, Germany, and countries further east reflected the same pattern. In contrast, expansion of the industrial sectors in Romania, Bulgaria, Albania, and Greece did not occur until the early- or mid-20th century.

URBAN PATTERNS AT THE REGIONAL SCALE

A glance at the map of Europe shows the impact of central place theory on the size and spacing of urban places. In France, for example, the seven largest metropolitan areas, Paris, Marseille, Lyon, Lille, Nice, Toulouse, and Bordeaux, are distributed throughout the country; in Hungary, centrally located Budapest is ringed by the regional centers of Debrecen, Miskolc, Szeged, and Pécs. Of course, political, economic, cultural, environmental, technological, and other changes can alter the role and rank of a place within an urban hierarchy. Still, the empirical observation of rank-size distribution holds for Belgium, Germany, Italy, Norway, and Switzerland. In other national urban systems, a deviation occurs at the upper end of the hierarchy to create primacy. Primate cities,

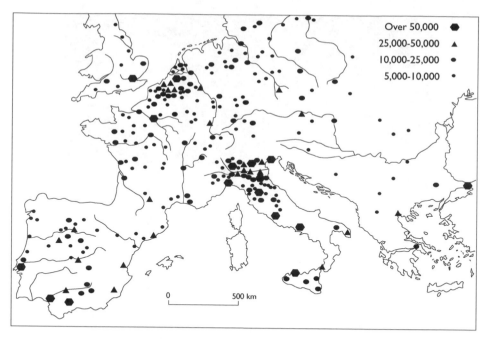

Figure 5.6   Distribution of European Cities around 1500. *Source:* Adapted from N. J. G. Pounds, *An Historical Geography of Europe* (Cambridge, UK: Cambridge University Press, 1990), 222. Reprinted with permission.

which are often national capitals, include Budapest, Vienna, Reykjavik, Dublin, Athens, and Sofia.

Historically, population movement into cities has been the most important component of urban growth, and this was especially the case during the industrial period. This form of internal migration within Europe, however, has largely ceased. And as birth rates in most countries have fallen considerably in recent decades, European cities are among the slowest growing in the world, averaging just 0.12% a year.

The cities of Europe, however, have begun to expand outward and to coalesce into conurbations because of advances in transportation and communications. Europe now contains about 40 conurbations with more than a million inhabitants. The Rhine–Ruhr conurbation in Germany has a

diameter of about 70 miles (115 km) and runs from Düsseldorf and Duisburg in the west, through Essen, Wuppertal, and Bochum, to Dortmund in the east (fig. 5.7). Of similar diameter is the Randstad, a densely populated horseshoe-shaped region in the Netherlands. This "ring city" runs from Utrecht, Amsterdam, and Haarlem in the north through The Hague, Delft, and Rotterdam in the west, to Dordrecht in the southeast (fig. 5.8). Only 60 miles (100 km) apart, these two conurbations may eventually coalesce along the E36 motorway to become a dominant European metropolitan core. Similarly, the London, Birmingham, Liverpool, Manchester, Leeds, and Newcastle metropolitan regions form an area of extensive urbanization in England.

The contemporary European urban system displays quite remarkable resilience and

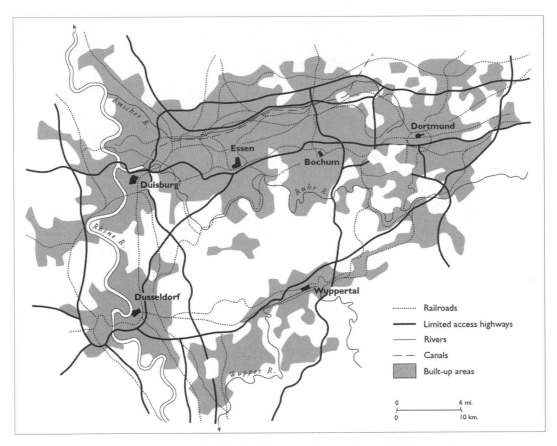

Figure 5.7   The Rhine–Ruhr Conurbation in Germany. *Source:* Compiled from various sources.

continuity—it has survived and adapted to the impacts of tremendous economic, political, social, technological, and other changes since the early days of the Greek city-states. More recently, the wars of the 20th century (especially World War II) unleashed appalling damage, with few cities coming through the conflict unscathed.

Western Europe

After World War II, separate urban systems developed on either side of the Iron Curtain—the boundary that divided Europe into a capitalist West and a communist East. Cities in western Europe cultivated connec-

tions with the capitalist world, especially with the United States, whose Marshall Plan funded clearance and rebuilding in cities that had suffered massive wartime destruction. The reconstruction effort was seen as an opportunity to replan bombed-out urban areas. Some of the most heavily damaged cities, such as Rotterdam, Dortmund, and Le Havre, completely redesigned their street systems for new commercial and industrial buildings. Most cities, including Cologne and Stuttgart, incorporated the surviving historic structures and medieval street patterns into their reconstructed city centers. Cities like Rouen and Nuremberg went so far as to recreate some of their destroyed historic buildings.

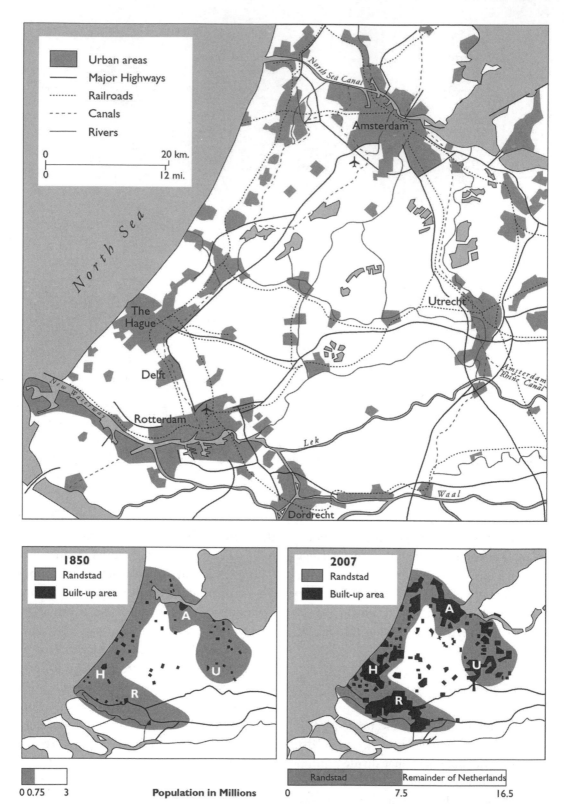

Figure 5.8   The Randstad Conurbation of the Netherlands. *Source:* Compiled from various sources.

Figure 5.9   Having been impacted adversely by metropolitan decentralization, this derelict inner-city area in Dublin contains vacant and deteriorating residential and industrial properties. (Photo by Linda McCarthy)

Beginning in the late 1960s, the process of counterurbanization or metropolitan decentralization led to rapid development in suburban areas and nearby towns, whereas growth slowed in the inner cities. Peripheral areas attracted residents and businesses looking for more space and less pollution and crime. Hardest hit were the national capitals and largest metropolitan regions in the most urbanized countries (fig. 5.9). Counterurbanization affected cities from the traditional manufacturing and port regions of northern Britain, northeastern France, and the Ruhr to the larger old industrial cities in southern Europe, like Milan, Genoa, and Turin.

Deindustrialization has contributed to metropolitan decentralization. In an effort to enhance profitability in traditional manufacturing activities like steel, chemicals, and shipbuilding, corporations have restructured by relocating labor-intensive production to lower-cost areas. This has led to massive job losses and urban decline in traditional centers of industry. The jobs created by the relocation of labor-intensive manufacturing have benefited some urban areas in Ireland, Spain, Portugal, and Greece. Branch plant operations, however, are vulnerable to decisions made outside the area and to company relocations when initial government tax incentives expire.

Some CBDs have benefited from the shift to a service economy and have gained shopping and office activities. Most city centers, however, have lost retail and office employment to outlying areas. Medium-sized cities have attracted employment in expanding sectors of the economy like information services, high-technology industries, and modern distribution activities. These smaller cities at the periphery of major metropolitan centers avoid the high rents and congestion at the core while enjoying nearby transportation routes, airports, universities, and skilled workers. Many of these cities escaped serious problems of crime, pollution, and social conflict because of their location, far from declining manufacturing centers. These cities are found in axial regions such as the Rhine between Frankfurt and Mulhouse, the Rhône-Saône valleys from Lyon to Geneva, and the Côte d'Azur east of Marseille. In addition, some cities on the periphery of southern Europe, such as Córdoba and Seville in Spain and Regio di Calabria in Italy, continue to experience growth, much of which has resulted from falling agricultural employment and resulting rural-to-urban migration.

Eastern Europe

Socialist Urbanization

Following World War II, cities in eastern Europe developed independently of their western counterparts, as a result of historical legacy and Soviet-imposed communist thinking, which lasted until the late 1980s. Totalitarian governments engaged in sweeping reforms that led to considerable changes in their national urban systems, which evolved in response to centralized planning rather than as a result of market forces.

Eastern European governments had to contend with the pressing need to repair and reconstruct cities left in ruins after World War II. The damage sustained by these cities, particularly Dresden, Berlin, and Warsaw, was generally far more severe than that suffered in western Europe, and subsidies were not available through such programs as the U.S.-sponsored Marshall Plan. The earliest stage of postwar economic development involved rapid expansion of heavy industry, particularly iron and steel, chemicals, and machinery. Coupled with collectivization and increased mechanization in agriculture, this *extensive* industrial development soon led to unprecedented rural-to-urban migration. As a result, the level of urbanization rose very quickly. The outcome was rising levels of primacy, severe housing shortages, insufficient social infra-

structure (schools, kindergartens, hospitals), lack of basic services, and environmental degradation.

By the late 1960s, for example, Budapest contained 44% of Hungary's urban population. However, the numbers masked a new reality: underurbanization. The number of industrial jobs during the early period of socialist industrialization grew faster than the number of housing units, forcing workers to commute to national capitals over long distances and often for up to a week at a time. Thus, beginning in the mid-1970s, eastern Europe entered a phase of *intensive* industrial and urban development. Communist governments set out to erase the difference between city and village life. They emphasized light industry and services, decentralized production from the capital and larger cities to smaller ones, developed their transportation networks, and increased the level of public infrastructure and housing in cities. Rural-to-urban migration slowed significantly. Despite these efforts, by 1990, after nearly 45 years of socialism, the urban network in eastern Europe was still less developed than that of the West. Only seven cities, all national capitals, contained more than a million people: Budapest (2.1), Bucharest (2.0), Warsaw (1.7), Belgrade (1.5), Prague (1.2), East Berlin (1.2), and Sofia (1.1).

Post-Socialist Changes

Since the fall of the Iron Curtain in the late 1980s, communist governments have been replaced; Germany has been reunited; and Czechoslovakia, Yugoslavia, and the USSR have divided into constituent parts. Central economic planning has been abandoned in favor of democratization and unprecedented transformation from socialist to market economies. The demise of the Soviet Union opened the way for western investment to move in and people to move out. Most countries—Bulgaria, the Czech Republic, Poland, Slovakia, Hungary, Romania, and Slovenia—have since joined western political, economic, and military alliances, including the North Atlantic Treaty Organization (NATO) and the European Union (EU).

These changes have impacted the cities and urban systems of eastern Europe in a number of ways. First, city names that were communist inspired, such as Leninváros (Lenin City) in Hungary (now Tiszaujvaros), Tolbukhin in Bulgaria (now Dobrič), and Karl-Marx-Stadt in Germany (now Chemnitz) were changed back to their prewar designations or were renamed to honor individuals or events associated with the revolutions of 1989. Statues of communist and Soviet leaders were removed and relocated to city peripheries; in the case of Budapest, a special museum of communism was erected. Second, foreign direct investment flooded in to Hungary, the Czech Republic, Poland, and Slovenia, targeted mainly at capital cities. This investment boosted the transition to capitalism, fueled construction booms, and led to the reemergence of a region-wide urban hierarchy. Third, countless border towns emerged as important trade gateways. Fourth, the disappearance of national planning gave more authority to city planners who had to work without state subsidies in a new market economy.

The transition to a market economy, however, did not come without hardship. In addition to the sudden loss of state subsidies, some cities lost revenues that had been generated by the Soviet military presence. Other towns lost economic status because of the reorientation of trade routes. The industrial towns, which were heavily subsidized during the socialist era, suffered severely as a result of the closure of outdated plants. Rapid, large-scale privati-

Figure 5.10   These high-rise buildings in central Sarajevo were badly damaged by the Serbs during Bosnia's struggle for independence. (Photo by Stanley Brunn)

zation brought skyrocketing unemployment, previously unknown under socialism. The number of industrial workers dropped sharply compared to the number of those engaged in services. These processes particularly affected large and industrial cities and resulted in dilapidated infrastructure, especially roads; leaking water mains; overconstruction in resort towns; loss of green areas; and problems with solid waste disposal and wastewater treatment. In much of the former Yugoslavia (Bosnia, Serbia, Kosovo), postcommunist hardship was accentuated by wars that debilitated much industrial, transportation, communication, and municipal infrastructure along with buildings, housing, and religious structures (fig. 5.10).

Less uniformity, more color, and neon lights now characterize the cities of eastern Europe. Advertisement billboards have replaced communist slogans on house facades. Shabby, old department stores have been closed or completely renovated. Boutiques now line the main streets, and shopping malls compete with "mom-and-pop" stands located in garages and basements. Beggars have appeared, as have casinos and many night clubs; crime has

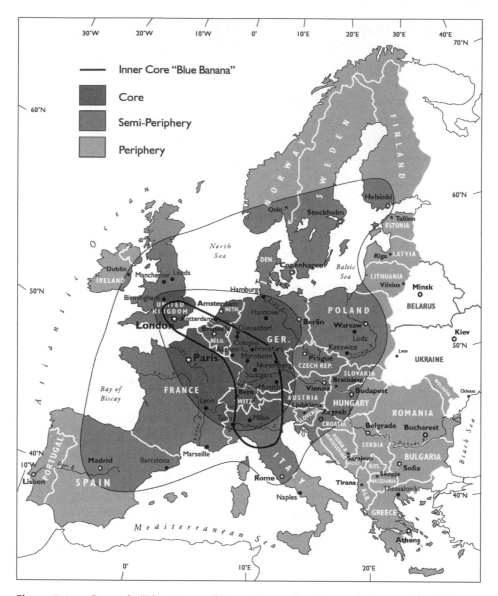

Figure 5.11   Europe's "Blue Banana" Superimposed on Europe's Core and Periphery.
Source: Linda McCarthy.

risen significantly, and congestion has become ubiquitous. Social differentiation in housing has increased tremendously, as closed, walled housing complexes emerge next to guarded houses and apartments. Today, democratization and the transition to a market economy are erasing the communist legacy in the cities of eastern Europe and bringing them closer to their western European counterparts.

Core–Periphery Model

A core–periphery model is often used to describe the urban patterns of Europe (fig. 5.11). The dominance of cities in the core is based on their superior endowment of factors influencing the location of economic activity, such as accessibility to markets. The largest cities are connected by the most advanced transportation and communications systems. Labor force quality and government policies make the core the most attractive area for modern companies, institutions, and industries. French geographer Roger Brunet identified what has become known as the "Blue Banana." It is a curving urban corridor of modern industry and services that includes core cities such as London, Brussels, Frankfurt, and Zurich.

Cities in the core and periphery are linked in a symbiotic if unequal relationship. Core cities prosper and maintain their economic dominance at the expense of the periphery by capturing flows of migrants, taxes, and investment in cutting-edge industries such as high-technology manufacturing and in command-and-control functions like the headquarters of transnational corporations. Peripheral cities have more limited potential for economic development, and attract tourists, innovations, and investment in branch plants from core locations. In between are the semi-peripheral cities that have economic links with both the core and the periphery.

The core has now shifted to the south and east, to areas of modern industrial growth. New core cities include Frankfurt, Stuttgart, and Munich in southern Germany; Zürich and Geneva in Switzerland; Milan and Turin in northern Italy; and Lyon in southern France. The southeastward shift of the core has intensified since the fall of the Iron Curtain; people and companies have been attracted to eastern European cities like Berlin because of the surge in economic activity, as well as to the region as a whole as a result of its relatively low production costs. London and Paris, however, have managed to retain their historic importance in the urban hierarchy because of their size and established positions as major national and international cities. The continued economic strength of the core is reinforced by the considerable political control that comes with the role of the largest core cities as major centers of international decision-making.

IMMIGRATION, GLOBALIZATION, AND PLANNING

Integrating Immigrants: A Problem of European Urbanization

The rebuilding of western Europe's infrastructure and industry after World War II generated strong demand for labor, especially in the cities of the more prosperous countries. In the 1950s and 1960s, rural-to-urban migration fueled growth, especially in the largest cities. Foreign-born guestworkers were brought in to fill low-wage assembly-line and service-sector jobs. Guestworkers came from the countries of Mediterranean Europe and from former colonies. West Germany attracted immigrants from Turkey and Yugoslavia, France brought in workers from northern and western Africa, and Britain drew on Commonwealth citizens from the Caribbean, India, and Pakistan.

The volume of incoming migrants paralleled the business cycle, with peaks in the mid-1960s and the early 1970s. By the mid-1970s, there were nearly 4 million foreign immigrants in West Germany, 3.5 million in France, 1.5 million in the United Kingdom, nearly 1 million in Switzerland, and about half a million each in Belgium, the Netherlands, and Sweden.

An estimated 20–25 million immigrants live in Europe today. More than one-third of the immigrants in France are concentrated in the Paris region where they represent more than 15% of the population. Foreign-born residents comprise 15 to 25% of the population in German cities like Frankfurt, Stuttgart,

Figure 5.12   Kurds, with flag unfurled, assemble in front on the Parliament building in Helsinki. Even though Finland has one of Europe's smallest immigrant communities, the numbers are growing. (Photo by Donald Zeigler)

and Munich. More than half the population of Amsterdam is non-Dutch, being composed primarily of individuals from Indonesia and Suriname. Even Finland's immigrant community is growing (fig. 5.12).

The immigrants have had a very localized impact within these cities. In continental Europe, they live in poor-quality suburban high-rise apartments or in inner city enclaves left vacant by the suburbanization of the upwardly mobile indigenous population. Each enclave is dominated by a particular ethnic group. For example, the enclaves in Frankfurt, Cologne, and Vienna contain mostly Yugoslavs or Turks, whereas in Paris and Marseille, the different enclaves house Italians, Algerians, or Tunisians. In large British cities, in contrast, there is significant mixing of different ethnic groups. Although there are large numbers of Asians, West Indians, and Irish, the foreign-born population represents only 15 to 20% of the population within most neighborhoods. Within each

neighborhood, however, ethnic groups are highly segregated from each other, and especially from the local community.

In addition to outright discrimination, the operation of the labor and housing markets is important in producing inner city enclaves. Low wages force immigrants to rent lodgings in deteriorating inner city locations. The internal cohesiveness of ethnic groups also contributes to residential segregation. Existing residents are more likely to share information about vacancies in their neighborhood with members of their own ethnic group.

The cities of Europe show stability in the size and age of their populations, whereas private consumption and the demand for consumer services workers have continued to grow. The demand for low-wage labor, however, can only be met from abroad. There has been a backlash by some people, often xenophobic and racist, against newcomers and even against some second- and third-generation residents. Most countries have immigration re-

Figure 5.13   The euro, Europe's new currency, has united the urban economies of Europe by making it easier to do business across national frontiers. Here, a flag in the Netherlands symbolizes Dutch membership in the Eurozone. (Photo by Donald Zeigler)

strictions. The contradiction between rising demand for low-wage labor and an unwillingness to accept non-nationals has proven quite costly and dangerous, as the weeks of rioting in the largely Muslim working-class suburbs of Paris amply demonstrated in 2005. The living and working conditions of immigrants are expected to continue influencing urban life in Europe, making national cohesion an issue that will be salient for years to come.

European and Global Linkages

European urban areas are part of networks of cities that operate at a number of spatial scales. Since 1989, cities on either side of the former Iron Curtain have become more interconnected. Cities like Berlin, Prague, Vienna, and Ljubljana, formerly at the edge of Western Europe, are well placed to take advantage of the reestablishment of trade between East and West and have emerged as vital links at the heart of the "new" Europe.

Many cities are located within the EU. The increasing economic and political integration of the more than two dozen countries in the EU influences the development of the European urban system. For example, the removal of national barriers to trade within the EU, with the internationalization of the European economy, has encouraged population increases along certain border regions. Urban growth zones straddle the boundaries between the Netherlands and Germany, Italy and Switzerland, and the southern Rhine regions of France, Germany, and Switzerland.

European cities are linked through trade and other mechanisms to major urban areas throughout the global economy. The cities within the EU form part of an international trading bloc—an evolving Eurozone as the euro has grown in strength as a currency—that contains nearly half a billion people, with a combined gross national income greater than that of the United States (fig. 5.13). The euro is managed by the European Central Bank in Frankfurt.

A select group of European cities contain the headquarters of major international agencies, many of which were founded after World War II to promote economic, political, or military cooperation. Geneva is the main European center for the United Nations. Paris is the headquarters for the Organization for Economic Cooperation and Development (OECD) and the European Space Agency. Vienna is the headquarters for the Organization of Petroleum Exporting Countries (OPEC).

Important decision-making functions are located in the EU's "capital cities." The offices of the major decision-making bodies of the EU are located in Brussels, Strasbourg, and Luxembourg. Brussels is also the headquarters of NATO. Strasbourg serves as the headquarters of the Council of Europe, an organization with more than 45 member countries that promotes European unity, human rights, and social and economic progress.

The major centers of international banking and finance in Europe historically have been London and Paris; they now include Frankfurt, Zürich, and Luxembourg. Frankfurt hosts the Bundesbank, Germany's respected and influential central bank, as well as the European Central Bank, making it the financial capital of the EU.

London and Paris rank among the small number of world cities that contain the headquarters of some of the most powerful transnational corporations in the world. London contains about 23 of the 500 largest global companies (59% of Great Britain's total), including BP, GlaxoSmithKline, and Lloyds. Paris has even more—27 of these companies (71% of France's total), including Total, Christian Dior, and Alcatel. In addition to housing 5 of the 500 largest global companies, Rome contains Vatican City, the seat of the Roman Catholic Church. Milan and Paris are major European centers of culture and design, while London is the premier insurance and reinsurance center.

Accessibility via the latest transportation and communications technologies allows some cities to strengthen their international positions. The high-speed train network rein-forces the dominance of cities like London, Paris, Brussels, Amsterdam, Cologne, Madrid, Barcelona, Zurich, and Milan. The cities with the busiest airports are London, Paris, Amsterdam, and Frankfurt.

Located at the mouth of the Rhine, Rotterdam is Europe's largest port. Its annual turnover of about 370 million metric tons of cargo is third only to the world's number one and two ports, Shanghai and Singapore. Rotterdam's water and pipeline connections with the Ruhr in Germany make it the main oil distribution and refining center in Europe. Antwerp, Marseille, and Hamburg are also major European ports.

Trucking is the most important mode of ground transportation. More than 1,200 billion tons of goods are transported by road each year compared to only about 237 billion by rail. There are more than 420 passenger cars for every 1,000 people in Europe; and the number in western Europe is nearly 500. With nearly 550 cars per 1,000 inhabitants, German and Italian levels already match those of Canada, but are still far below the U.S. level. The steady increase in automobile ownership, with the overall distance traveled by road vehicles tripling in the last 30 years, has overwhelmed existing and new highway capacity and led to traffic congestion within and between cities across Europe.

In eastern Europe, national urban systems evolved under socialism and were highly centralized in nature. Rail networks were of the "hub-and-spoke" variety, usually focusing on the national capital. The border changes associated with the partition of Germany into West and East after World War II severely dislocated the transportation routes and the development of the urban systems on either side of the Iron Curtain. Most rail and road links across the new border were either closed or greatly restricted. More significantly, the government of East Germany had to develop Rostock as a new port to replace Hamburg.

An ironic aspect of urban development in Eastern Europe under socialism concerned the lack of sufficient international connections. Despite calls for greater cooperation among the socialist countries, close intercity connections did not develop. Indeed, suspicion rather than cooperation generally prevailed; countries tended to site sensitive industries and other vital resources in interior rather than border regions. Likewise, the heightened level of internal security resulted in a decrease in border crossings not only across the Iron Curtain and into the Soviet Union, but also between the countries of eastern Europe.

Urban Policy and Planning

Europe became the birthplace of modern city planning as it reacted to the drawbacks of uncontrolled growth during the industrial period. Planning to address urban trends and problems now pervades European city life. In western Europe, postwar planning for redevelopment and growth ended in the early 1970s. Declining population growth rates and widespread economic recessions forced governments to reevaluate the efficacy of large-scale, publicly funded projects. In response to the general dissatisfaction with alienating highrise buildings and lack of open spaces, policy shifted to planning for conservation and restructuring and to combating urban decline.

This reappraisal of policy and planning has had two, often conflicting, components. On one hand, budgetary constraints force governments to actively seek private-sector participation and investment in urban revitalization projects. On the other hand, there is growing concern for issues of social equity, citizen participation, environmental protection, and aesthetic quality. These competing elements are pitted against each other at three levels of government: local, national, and international.

Local Policy-Making and Planning

Since the early 1970s, urban revitalization policies in older industrial cities of western Europe have promoted economic restructuring away from traditional manufacturing. Cities use local, national, and EU funds to attract private-sector investment in hightechnology and service industries. The transition toward knowledge economies (K-economies) has tended to favor metropolitan areas with diversified economies, highly educated and skilled workforces, major universities and research institutes, and good quality of life. Fueled by national government policies such as low corporate taxes and investment in higher education combined with EU funding that helped generate the "Celtic Tiger," the Dublin region has attracted global information technology companies including Dell, Google, Intel, and Microsoft.

Traditionally in southern Europe, cities in lower-cost production areas attracted laborintensive branch plant industries. More recently, cities such as Montpellier in southern France, Bari in southern Italy, and Valencia in southeastern Spain have focused on providing attractive environments for high-technology industries. Since the early 1990s, communistera cities like Rostock, Budapest, Prague, and Warsaw have actively worked to attract new commercial and industrial investment (box 5.3). In addition, urban revitalization policies include conservation efforts that reflect the economic importance of tourism in Europe.

In recent years, most countries in western Europe have decentralized power and responsibility for urban planning to local governments. In addition, small units of local

---

Box 5.3   City Break: The New Craze in European Tourism

A notable change in vacation behavior has marked European lifestyles over the past 10 years. Greater mobility, higher connectedness, relative affluence, and an emphasis on quality of life have transformed travel habits so that, instead of taking the traditional long summer vacation, an increasing number of people now take frequent short breaks of two to five days. Tourism industry experts point to the boom in low budget airlines, high level of Internet use, and the popularity of tourism websites as major factors facilitating changes in travel habits.

Most short-break travel has been to European cities. Since 2000, urban tourism has been the fastest growing segment of the leisure industry. This trend is globally significant—the European market currently accounts for 50% of worldwide tourist arrivals—and shows no signs of diminishing. Neither 9/11, nor the conflicts in the Middle East, nor the terror attacks of 3/11 in Madrid have seriously derailed tourism's dynamic development. City trips doubled between 2000 and 2004, and they currently account for about 40% of European outbound trips. Additionally, more is being spent on accommodation.

Traditional major destination cities—London, Paris, Rome, Madrid, and Vienna—remain important, but secondary city destinations such as Barcelona are developing even faster. Other growing tourist destinations include Bilbao, Dubrovnik, St. Etienne, Valencia, Potsdam, Split, Graz, Saragossa, and Tarragona. In most cases, these cities outperform their state capitals in terms of total hotel stays. The most rapidly growing market share in city tourism belongs to the new EU member states. The up-and-coming regional city destinations in eastern Europe reported an average annual growth of 3.6% in total hotel stays between 1997 and 2003, whereas tourism in the capitals and largest national city centers grew by only 2%.

Source: European Cities Tourism (www.tourmis.info).

---

government have been consolidated into larger regional ones in an attempt to achieve economies of scale. These policy and administrative changes have set the scene for more coordinated regional planning. The Dutch "compact city" policy in the Randstad endeavors to curb counterurbanization in this region by concentrating new development within existing major cities in an effort to maintain their economic competitiveness.

National Policy-Making and Planning

In western Europe, national policies promoted regional decentralization after World War II. Industry, commercial activity, and population were redirected from the large congested cities to new towns. Many new towns were built as satellite centers or dormitory communities to accommodate overspill population from larger cities, as in the case of Abercrombie's Plan for Greater London. In the 1970s, declining population growth and widespread economic recessions forced national governments in western Europe to reassess the need for new town planning.

By the 1980s, a national policy shift reflected the recognition of a number of factors—the difficulty of achieving the decentralization of economic activity, the severity of decline in the central parts of larger cities, and the importance of these larger cities as national engines of growth in a global economy. The U.K. government established Urban Development Corporations to attract businesses to declining industrial and port areas in cities like London and Liverpool. In the 1990s, government policy shifted yet again—away from expensive nationally devised strategies toward "community empowerment" initiatives in which local communities carry out revitalization programs and projects that are sensitive to local challenges and opportunities.

In eastern Europe after World War II, government planning was guided by the basic tenets of Marxist-Leninist ideology: to remove the "contradiction" between living standards in urban and rural areas and, ultimately, to create a classless society. Urban planners sought to avoid excessive population concentration in large cities and to achieve a balanced urban infrastructure. These social goals, however, often clashed with economic directives that called for the rapid development of heavy industry and the collectivization of agriculture.

In an attempt to increase overall industrial capacity, balance the urban system, and provide urban functions to underserved areas, governments implemented a program of new town construction. These cities were developed around a large industrial facility, typically an iron and steel mill or a chemical processing plant. The cities were consciously sited away from existing towns, either on a vacant piece of land or on the site of an existing village.

New towns in eastern Europe included Eisenhüttenstadt in the former East Germany, Nova-Huta in Poland, and Dimitrovgrad in Bulgaria. They grew rapidly during the period of extensive economic development between 1950 and 1970, eventually becoming important not only for their industrial products, but also for their role as urban centers for their hinter-

lands and in creating more balanced national urban systems.

By the 1970s and 1980s, planners in eastern Europe had turned their attention away from promoting large-scale industry and new towns to developing light industries and filling out the national urban systems. In many countries, central place theory became an explicit guide for development efforts as planners tried to create multitiered urban hierarchies that provided goods and services to particular regions according to their size and function.

Since the early 1990s, cities have experienced dramatic changes as eastern Europe's transition to a market economy has involved rapid, large-scale privatization of state-owned housing, industry, and services. National policies have evolved substantially to address urban problems that were previously unknown in the former socialist states, such as extremely high levels of unemployment, rampant crime, poverty, and homelessness. The provision of subsidized housing, unsegregated schools, and basic hospital care during the transition period has proved insurmountable in most eastern European cities that face a severe lack of resources. The Roma quarters in the larger cities have been disproportionally affected. The traditionally poor "Roma" prefer this designation instead of "Gypsies," which is considered derogatory. EU integration has helped alleviate some of the problems through a number of different projects, including "Beautiful Romania."

International Policy-Making and Planning

Europe is the scene of significant international urban planning and management initiatives (box 5.4). The Council of Europe promotes historic preservation and urban regeneration through initiatives such as European Architectural Heritage Year.

Box 5.4   GIS and European Cities

GIS has revolutionized the way city governments serve their constituents. Spatial Data Infrastructures (SDIs) are vital components of most major European cities. A common geographic information strategy, however, is still missing at the EU level. No legal entity has a mandate to maintain European geographic information. Researchers envision the creation of a European Reference Center for Geographic Information, which would assist the European Commission in the conception, creation, and harmonization of pan-European spatial databases and would support EU policies.

Projects such as PROPOLIS (Planning and Research of Policies for Land Use and Transport for Increasing Urban Sustainability) use GIS to develop and test integrated land-use and transportation policies, planning tools, and comprehensive assessment methodologies. Some objectives involve strategic monitoring of the impact of urban development on the environment, as well as policy packages to help enhance the environmental, social, and economic sustainability of European cities and urban regions. Cities as diverse as Geneva, Dublin, and Belgrade use GIS as an urban management tool for monitoring, scenario modeling, and forecasting, as well as for engaging citizens and stakeholders in planned social, economic, and environmental changes.

In 2006, the European Parliament created INSPIRE—Infrastructure for Spatial Information in Europe. This directive strengthened the knowledge base for environmental policy and made it more publicly accessible. A European geographic information portal and a policy discussion forum (EGIP) have been established to facilitate exchange of information. INSPIRE covers a very wide array of spatial data ranging from basic mapping information, such as geographic names and administrative units, to key environmental information, such as emissions, environmental quality, and the location of protected sites. ROMANSE, another GIS-based application—the ROad MANagement System for Europe—integrates traffic and travel information, and has become a model for transport management. Through visitor-created maps, the interactive ROMANSE website provides on-demand, real-time information on traffic volumes, accidents, and parking so that travelers can make informed choices. This GIS-based traffic control and travel information system can also be used by public agencies to improve transportation and promote the use of alternate methods of transit, such as buses and bicycles.

EU integration efforts have led to unprecedented achievements in international policy and planning. Since 1975, for example, EU regional policy has promoted urban development in economically weak peripheral regions and in areas suffering industrial decline. Increasing east–west economic and political integration in Europe as well as the globalization of the economy create opportunities and challenges for the cities of Europe.

MODELS OF URBAN STRUCTURE

"Our cities are like historical monuments to which every generation, every century, every

Figure 5.14   Skenderberg Square in Tirana, Albania, shows the premium placed by socialist planners on political showplaces in the heart of the city. (Photo by Darrick Danta)

civilization has contributed a stone" (Ildefons Cerdà, Spanish town planner, 1867). Surviving historic elements represent an incomplete catalog of urban development and redevelopment. Although no two cities are identical, history's strong legacy gives European cities a common character, which typically includes the following:

Town (Market) Squares

The town square, the heart of Greek, Roman, and medieval towns, has often survived as an important open space. Some medieval town squares in Europe boast a continuous tradition of regular open-air markets. In eastern Europe, the large open square, typical of socialist cities, was used for public gatherings and political rallies (fig. 5.14). Today, following the economic and social changes accompanying the transition to a market economy and EU integration, many central squares and

their historic buildings contain modern commercial functions, such as "haut couture" shops, office space, advertising, tourist offices, and fashionable restaurants and cafés.

Major Landmarks

Historic landmarks in western European city centers have become symbols of religious, political, military, educational, and cultural identity. Many cathedrals, churches, and statues serve their original purpose and often still dominate the urban skyline. Some town halls, royal palaces, and artisan guildhalls have been converted into libraries, art galleries, and museums. Medieval castles and city walls have become tourist attractions. Today, of course, the major landmarks are expressions of economic power—the offices of transnational corporations and sports stadiums, for instance.

In eastern Europe, the hallmarks of socialist cities were the massive buildings in "wedding

Figure 5.15   The House of Science in Bucharest is typical of the Soviet-inspired architecture found throughout eastern European cities. Note the pedestal in front of the building, which formerly supported a large statue of Lenin. (Photo by Darrick Danta)

cake" style (fig. 5.15), red stars, and "heroic" statues. Since the late 1980s, socialist political symbols have been replaced mainly by billboards advertising the trappings of consumer culture.

Complex Street Pattern

The unplanned narrow streets and alleys of the medieval core developed in the pre-automobile era (fig. 5.16). During the medieval period, suburban areas grew around long distance roads that radiated outward from the city gates. In the 19th century, cities like Munich, Marseille, and Madrid made radial or tangential boulevards the axes of their planned suburbs.

High Density and Compact Form

The constraints of city walls kept population density high during medieval times. A number of factors maintained this compact, densely built-up form that is now characteristic of large cities in western Europe. A long tradition of planning that restricts low-density urban sprawl dates back to the application of strict city building regulations in the earliest suburbs. Compact urban form also reflects the relatively late introduction of the automobile in Europe, as well as the high price of gasoline.

Bustling City Centers

The high density and compact nature of European cities create city centers that bustle with activity (fig. 5.17). Heavily used public transportation systems (trains, buses, subways) converge on the core, and one or more central train stations figure prominently in the urban landscape. In larger cities, distinct functions dominate particular districts. Institutional districts house government offices and universities. Financial and office districts contain banks and insurance companies. A

Figure 5.16   Here on Ludgate Hill in the City of London, a new immigrant from Bangladesh directs people to the nearest McDonalds. In medieval times, this landscape would have been a shadowy tangle of narrow alleys that passed for streets. (Photo by Donald Zeigler)

Figure 5.17   A busy pedestrianized shopping street in the heart of Dublin. (Photo by Linda McCarthy)

pedestrianized retail zone leads to the rail station. Cultural districts offer museums and art galleries. Entertainment areas include theater and "red light" districts.

Many buildings in the city center have multiple uses. Apartments are found above shops, offices, and restaurants. Large department stores, such as Harrods in London and Printemps in Paris, are prominent features in most European city centers. Modern city center malls include Les Halles in Paris and Eldon Square in Newcastle, England. Suburban malls are becoming prevalent. Many coastal or riverine cities have also refurbished old port and industrial buildings to house mixed-use

waterfront developments like the one at Liverpool's Albert Dock. Other cities have renovated obsolete historic structures, such as London's Covent Garden, as festival marketplaces with specialized shops, restaurants, and street performers.

In keeping with trends in the West, luxury hotels and restaurants, department and fashion stores, and fast food establishments began to appear in the downtowns of communist-era cities during the 1980s. Likewise, the equivalent of shopping malls cropped up, mainly at the intersections of major transportation lines. Pedestrian shopping streets, containing the most exclusive shops, are now an important part of the retail structure of eastern European cities.

Low-Rise Skylines

For North American visitors, the most striking aspect of the older parts of western European cities is the general absence of skyscraper offices and high-rise apartments. City centers were developed long before reinforced steel construction and the elevator made high-rises feasible. Master plans and building codes designed to minimize the spread of fire maintained building heights between three and five stories during the industrial period. Paris fixed the building height at 65 feet in 1795, whereas other large cities introduced height restrictions in the 19th century. Still regulated today, high rises are found only in redevelopment areas or on land at the periphery of the city. Skyscrapers have also been built in the central commercial and financial districts of some of the very largest cities, including London.

In socialist eastern Europe, there was no private ownership of land, and therefore no urban land market. With few transnational corporations doing business in these countries, socialist cities were usually devoid of tall commercial buildings to mark their CBDs. The tallest buildings in most communist-era cities were usually Communist Party and state administrative buildings, massive "Houses of the People," international hotels, or TV towers.

Neighborhood Stability

Western European cities enjoy remarkable neighborhood stability. Europeans relocate much less frequently than do North Americans. As a result, older neighborhoods at or near the center of large cities are maintained and enjoy remarkably long lives, despite suburbanization.

The districts of handsome mansions built by speculative developers for wealthy families in the 17th and 18th centuries remain stable, high-income neighborhoods; examples include Belgravia, Bloomsbury, and Mayfair in central London. High-income suburban neighborhoods developed typically in the western part of older industrial cities, upwind of smokestacks and residential chimneys.

Wealthy residents, in fact, have remained at or near the city center in western Europe since before the Industrial Revolution. Higher taxes on city land until the late 19th century kept the poorest residents and immigrants outside the city walls. Beginning with Paris in the second half of the 19th century, this tradition was strengthened by the replacement of areas of slums and former city walls with wide boulevards and imposing apartments.

Since the 18th century, however, urban growth has spread to suburban zones and has even enveloped freestanding villages and towns. Yet these separate urban centers became distinct quarters within the expanding city as they maintained their long-established social and economic characteristics, major landmarks, and shopping streets. During the second half of the 19th century, annexations of these suburban quarters produced distinctive city districts with their own shopping areas and government institutions.

In the past few decades, governments in older industrial cities have funded urban renewal projects designed to attract higher-income residents to the revitalized parts of central areas. The success of these large-scale redevelopments has given rise to gentrification in the surrounding area. Demand for housing that has the potential to be renovated for higher-income occupants, however, has raised property values in certain areas and pushed out lower-income residents.

Housing

Apartment living is common in Europe. Apartments are a good land use choice when space is at a premium and land values are high. Instead of growing outward, cities grew upward, to the limit of the height regulations.

The multistory apartment house originated in northern Italy to accommodate the wealthy during the Renaissance. By the early 18th century, the apartment house had spread to the larger cities in continental Europe and Scotland. Until the invention of the elevator, social stratification within individual buildings was vertical: wealthier families occupied the lower floors, while poorer residents lived in smaller units above. Horizontal social stratification also developed within apartment blocks. The large expensive units were located in the front of buildings, with small low-rent units facing the rear. By the late 18th century, as the Industrial Revolution spurred increasing urbanization, apartment blocks had spread to medium-sized cities. Speculators built large-scale, standardized tenements for middle-income occupants and barracks for low-income residents.

The two-story, single-family row house is distinctive to England, Wales, and Ireland. This tradition can be traced back to efforts to restrict congestion in London in the late 1500s that made it illegal for more than one family to rent a new building.

The serious housing shortage that started with the economic recession of the 1930s was exacerbated by the lack of construction and significant destruction that occurred during both world wars. The public housing programs that began in Vienna in the early 1920s were stepped up after World War II across western Europe. Modern architecture and urban design principles were combined with low-cost factory production methods. Many war-damaged historic houses and dilapidated 19th century tenements in the central parts of cities were replaced by monotonous high-rise apartments after World War II.

In the 1950s and 1960s, most governments adopted a policy of metropolitan decentralization. Modern high-rise apartment blocks were concentrated in large peripheral estates known by their French name—*grands ensembles.*

Historically, the severity of need and the political leanings of governments determined the amount of public housing provided within each city. The amount was highest in cities with serious housing shortages and liberal municipal governments such as Edinburgh and Glasgow in Scotland, where the number of public units grew to well over half the total housing stock. Traditionally, public housing comprised 25% of the total in England, France, and Germany, and 10% in Italy. Public housing represents only 5% or less of the housing in the more affluent and conservative Swiss cities. Since the 1970s, however, dependence on public housing has declined as a result of government cost-cutting and privatization programs.

In general, eastern European cities that developed under socialism were less spatially segregated than those that evolved under capitalism. Certainly, mansions, the prewar residences of the social elites, were used for political purposes to house party officials, foreign delegations, or institutes. But housing was viewed as a right, not a commodity, and each family was entitled to its own apartment at reasonable cost.

In the face of the tremendous housing shortfalls following World War II, as well as the need for rapid industrialization, communist governments began building massive housing estates and continued through the 1970s. Apartment blocks, typically multistory and prefabricated, were often constructed in groups to form a

Figure 5.18   This neighborhood unit in the new industrial town of Dunaujvaros, Hungary, was built during the socialist era. (Photo by Darrick Danta)

neighborhood unit, with shops, green space, and play areas for children in the center (fig. 5.18). The individual apartments were small (about 460 to 650 sq ft), poorly constructed, and almost universally disliked by residents. Often, housing estates were built in large clusters, sometimes forming massive concrete curtains, usually on land near the edge of cities. As a result, urban population densities could actually *increase* near the urban periphery.

MODELS OF THE EUROPEAN CITY

The concentric zone model, which describes concentric circles of increasing socioeconomic status as distance from the central city grows, is most applicable to British cities. In contrast, Mediterranean cities, as in Latin America, exhibit an inverse concentric zone pattern. There, the elite concentrate in central areas near major transportation arteries, whereas the poor live in inadequately serviced parts of the periphery. In Europe, the number of persons per household usually increases with distance from the city center.

The sector model explains best the pattern of socioeconomic status in which different income groups congregate in sectors radiating outward from the city center. The wealthy may prefer to locate along pleasant monumental boulevards or upwind of pollution sources. Poorer residents may be left with unattractive linear sectors along railway lines or strips of heavy industry. Finally, the multiple nuclei model describes best the pattern of ethnic differentiation. Different groups are concentrated in ethnic neighborhoods within the inner city or in high-rise public housing near the periphery.

Northwestern European City Structure

In northwestern Europe, the preindustrial city center contains the market square and historic structures such as a medieval cathedral and

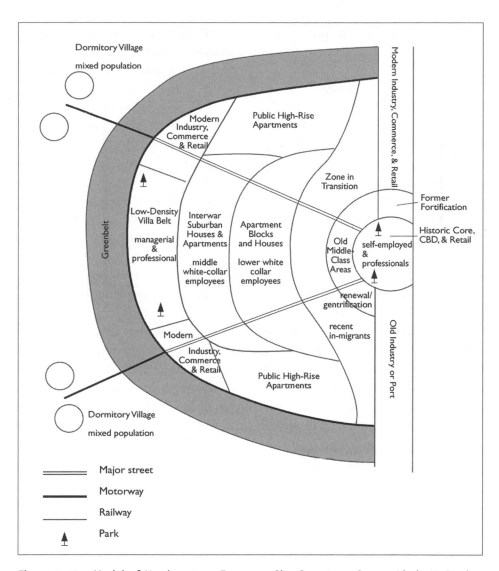

Figure 5.19   Model of Northwestern European City Structure. *Source:* Linda McCarthy.

town hall (fig. 5.19). Apartment buildings host upper- and middle-income residents above shops and offices. Narrow, winding streets extend out about a third of a mile. Some wider streets may radiate out from the square to form a pedestrianized corridor that runs to the train station and contains national and international department stores, restaurants, and hotels. Skyscrapers are concentrated in the commercial and financial district. There are new downtown shopping malls or festival marketplaces in refurbished historic buildings. Some old industrial and port areas may have been recycled into new retail, commercial, and residential waterfront developments.

Encircling the core are some zones in transition. The area of the former city wall is a circular zone of 19th century redevelopment. Some of the deteriorated middle-income housing has been gentrified by upper-income residents, whereas other sections provide low rent accommodation for students and poor immigrants.

Surrounding this area is another zone in transition—an old industrial zone with disused railway lines. In the 1950s and 1960s, new industrial plants (e.g., light engineering, food processing) replaced many of the derelict old factories and warehouses. Low-income renters and owners live in run-down 19th century housing. Some houses have been refurbished or replaced with new units. Certain neighborhoods are quite distinctive because they house foreign immigrants who often live above their exotically painted stores and restaurants.

Beyond this inner area is a zone of "workingmen's homes": a stable, lower-middle-income zone dating from the first half of the 20th century. These *streetcar suburbs* contain apartment blocks and houses without garages, and are typically anchored by a small shopping area, community center, library, and school. Outside this area are middle-income automobile suburbs containing apartments and single-family homes with garages that correspond with the zone of better residences in the concentric zone model. Further out are nucleations containing the most exclusive neighborhoods.

The multiple nuclei model also explains the estates of public high-rise apartments and new middle- and lower-middle-income "starter" homes at the urban periphery that lack basic amenities like shops and banks. The periphery also contains commercial and industrial activities, such as shopping malls, business and science parks, and high-technology manufacturing.

Beginning in the early 20th century, cities like London established a greenbelt at the edge of the built-up area, on which development was prohibited. The greenbelt was intended to prevent urban sprawl and to provide recreational

space. Commuters live outside the greenbelt in dormitory villages and small towns that correspond with the commuters' zone in the concentric zone model. Airport and related activities, such as hotels and modern factories, are located further out on major freeways.

Mediterranean City Structure

The structure of the preindustrial core reflects the distinct history of each Mediterranean city (fig. 5.20). In Greece and Italy, the historic core can exhibit traces of the grid pattern of streets from the first walled enclosure of Greek or Roman origin. In Iberia, remnants of narrow alleys of the Arab quarters date back to the period of Moorish control. The central marketplace is home to markets and festivals, and in Spain to bullfights. The area around the town square contains the cathedral, the town hall, and the narrow winding streets of the walled medieval city. Low-income and lower-middle-income residents live at high densities above street-level shops and offices. A retail corridor runs from this old commercial core to the train station. The high-rise offices of the modern CBD are nearby.

Labor-intensive traditional manufacturing and port activities survive in some cities. As in the multiple nuclei and sector models, new industries are found in former old industrial sites and in locations well served by the Mediterranean region's generally more limited transportation infrastructure.

Until the 19th century, urban growth was absorbed in increasing densities within the medieval city. Larger cities that removed their medieval walls in the 19th century drew up plans of expansion and laid out new monumental districts in the area of the former wall. A grand new thoroughfare lined with public works such as statues and foun-

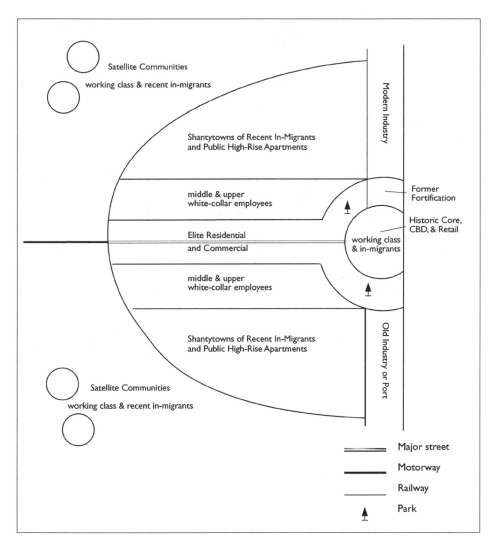

Figure 5.20   Model of Mediterranean City Structure. *Source:* Linda McCarthy.

tains extended out from the city. This area attracted commercial development and wealthy residents, as suggested by the sector model. These elite residential areas of parks and tree-lined boulevards were flanked by middle-income and upper-middle-income neighborhoods.

In the early 20th century, suburban sprawl became a problem, especially in cities experiencing rapid growth as a result of industrial-ization and rural-to-urban migration. Squatter settlements encircled the outskirts of cities. After World War II, they were replaced with low-cost high-rise public housing that today contains low-income and lower-middle-income households. Further out, near a natural resource or industrial operation, are the remote, poorly serviced satellite communities for low-income residents and recent immigrants.

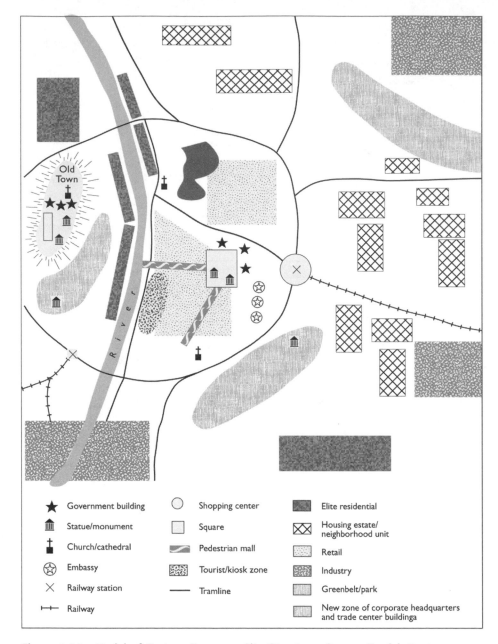

★	Government building	○	Shopping center	▨	Elite residential
🏛	Statue/monument	▢	Square	⊠	Housing estate/neighborhood unit
✝	Church/cathedral	▰	Pedestrian mall	▨	Retail
✪	Embassy	▨	Tourist/kiosk zone	▨	Industry
✕	Railway station	—	Tramline	▨	Greenbelt/park
⊢⊣	Railway			▨	New zone of corporate headquarters and trade center buildinga

Figure 5.21   Model of Eastern European City Structure. *Source:* Darrick Danta.

Eastern European City Structure

Prior to World War II, the internal structure of cities in eastern Europe was much the same that of as cities in western Europe. Beginning in the late 1940s, however, the imposition of socialist planning set "Eastern Bloc" cities on a different development trajectory, resulting in a set of features that typified communist-era cities (fig. 5.21).

A typical socialist city contained a central square for political gatherings, which was often created by razing existing buildings. Former mansions were converted to government use, public buildings came to dominate strategic locations in the city, and statues of revolutionary heroes dotted the cityscape. Clusters of housing estates and neighborhood units were interspersed with factories, transportation hubs, and retail establishments. Overall, these cities did not conform to Western models of urban structure because land use was based more on governmental decisions than economic forces.

Not all places exhibited these features to the same degree. Few socialist elements are evident in cities like Prague, which escaped major destruction during World War II. The socialist city model was most clearly achieved in cities such as Warsaw and East Berlin that had been severely damaged during the war, in the industrial new towns, and in countries where socialist ideology was especially strong. In Albania, for example, cities adopted the classic socialist form: religious establishments were used for other purposes, and private ownership of automobiles was forbidden. Large cities in Bulgaria also assumed rather sterile dimensions during the socialist period. In contrast, Polish industrial towns looked much the same as their western European counterparts.

One of the first changes to occur in the structure of communist-era cities after 1989 was an increase in tourist facilities—hotels, restaurants, and various forms of entertainment—to cater to foreign visitors. Another change, spurred by economic hardship during the transition to market economy, was the appearance of informal bazaars lining certain streets where people sold household goods, cheap (mostly fake) imported items, and regional craft products. In addition, *kiosks* (small buildings on the sidewalks of busy streets) offered printed material, tobacco, and alcoholic products, plus a variety of imported items.

The past few years have also witnessed a building boom, especially in the capitals, larger cities, and tourist centers. Foreign-owned or -financed office buildings, trade centers, retail outlets, and other establishments are now a common feature of cities like Berlin, Budapest, Warsaw, and Prague. Corporate logos, names, and billboards have become very visible signs of change. Giant letters placed atop buildings scream "Levis," "Sony," and "Coca-Cola." Domestic private construction, including luxurious houses, villas, and apartments, was often financed by funds from emigrants to western Europe and the United States.

REPRESENTATIVE CITIES

London: Europe's Dominant World City

London is the preeminent metropolitan area of Europe. Greater London has a population of more than 7.5 million. The metropolitan fringe brings London's population to 14.5 million. As hub of the British Empire, this city became the center of global economic and political power in the 19th century. Today, London enjoys a global city status shared only by New York and Tokyo. Sited at the head of navigation on the Thames River, London dominates the United Kingdom from its location in southeast England. It is the seat of national government, the core of the English legal system, the headquarters for major British and transnational corporations, and a leading center for banking, insurance, advertising, and publishing. London's newspapers and national television and radio stations reach all parts of the country and the world.

In 1665, a great plague killed 75,000 Londoners. The next year, a fire destroyed virtually the entire city. As a result, London experienced a building boom, and many of the historical structures from this period survived until they were bombed during

World War II. London's old nickname, "The Smoke," recalls the days when a haze of pollution from industrial and domestic chimneys hung over the city. London has since undergone deindustrialization and a shift to services and modern manufacturing. Despite these changes, London remains firmly rooted in its historic past and cultural traditions.

Central London grew around two core areas, both along the Thames River: the City of London (the old port and commercial hub) and the city of Westminster (the governmental and religious hub). The former developed from a Roman fort known as Londinium, which became the fifth-largest city north of the Alps and had trade networks extending as far as the Baltic and Mediterranean. In the medieval period, London's protected inland site and strategic location for North Sea and Baltic trade allowed port and commercial activities to thrive. The docks spread from the Tower of London into the East End. Specialized market areas developed to the north and east of St. Paul's Cathedral in the original square mile of the Roman city. The "City of London" is now the financial precinct. It is dominated by Tower 42 and the "Gherkin," the cone-shaped high-rise of insurance giant Swiss Re. The City also contains powerful institutions such as the Stock Exchange, the Bank of England, and the Royal Exchange. Pressure from the world's largest banks and insurance companies to locate in this prime financial area pushes up the density and height of office buildings.

About 2 miles (3 km) upriver, the "City of Westminster" developed around Westminster Abbey to become a second core during the medieval period. The present Houses of Parliament were built in the mid-19th century (fig. 5.22). Queen Victoria made Buckingham Palace the monarch's residence in 1837. This institutional core grew eastward toward the

Figure 5.22   The Houses of Parliament dominate the City of Westminster. The Clock Tower (often called Big Ben) and the London Underground (the subway) are landmarks that symbolize London to the world. (Photo by Donald Zeigler)

commercial core along Whitehall, where government offices include 10 Downing Street, the prime minister's residence. The royal hunting grounds in the west became St. James's, Green, Hyde, and Regent's Parks. The area between the parks and the City attracted mansions of the nobility, centers of culture such as the Royal Academy and the National Gallery, and exclusive shops. In the 17th and 18th centuries, large-scale developments of townhouses and squares were speculatively built for the aristocracy. Belgravia, the last of these West End residential developments, has survived as an affluent neighborhood.

In the 19th century, major retailing axes developed along east–west Oxford Street and north–south Regent Street. In addition to the West End and the City, the inner city (13 of London's 32 boroughs) comprises a ring of 19th- and early 20th-century suburban growth. From the early 1840s, the railways allowed upper-middle-income families to move further out. The higher density Victorian and Edwardian housing nearer the center included middle-income detached and row houses such as those in Islington and laborers' cottages in the East End. With increasing industrialization and the incredible growth of new docks and manufacturing facilities, the East End became home to the poorest immigrants.

Much of the original housing in the East End is gone—destroyed in World War II air raids or replaced by high-rise blocks of public housing, now deteriorating. Other housing, dispersed among old factories, warehouses, docks, and railway yards, is mostly in poor condition as well. Many of the decaying middle-income residences have been subdivided into low-rent apartments. Within the inner city, however, residents are differentiated into neighborhoods, each with its own high street, socioeconomic and ethnic mix, and political and sporting allegiances.

Since the early 1980s, an extensive area of London, known as the Docklands, has been revitalized through a combination of public and private investment. The British government established an Urban Development Corporation in 1981 that used public funds to stimulate private-sector development. The city's tallest building, a 50-story tower containing offices and specialty stores, was built at Canary Wharf. Dockland revitalization projects now extend as far west as the tiny and largely upscale Saint Katharine Dock (east of the Tower of London). These dockland developments have attracted higher-income occupants and promoted gentrification of older properties by wealthy residents in adjacent areas.

Outer London is a lower density belt of interwar housing with some shopping streets and industrial parks. These outer suburbs comprise the remaining 19 of London's 32 boroughs. The expansion of the London Underground (subway transit system) and the spread of private automobile use promoted suburbanization between 1918 and 1939. Middle-income residents live in well-maintained detached and semi-detached houses with gardens. Neighborhood stability is strong, despite a slight decline in the aging population of empty-nesters. Second-generation immigrants have moved into pockets of older housing. Private automobile use far in excess of road capacity causes severe traffic congestion. One innovative approach to Central London's severe traffic congestion problem has been the introduction of a daily congestion charge for motorists driving into the most heavily congested part of the city. The estimated benefits have been a 15% reduction in both traffic and journey times, and funds to reinvest in the city's system of buses and subways.

The outer suburbs end abruptly at a 5- to 10-mile (8–16 km) wide greenbelt within which development is restricted in an effort to prevent urban sprawl and provide recreational space. Villages and small market towns remain much as they were when the greenbelt was established in 1939. Growth pressures are evident only in the rural dwellings that have been gentrified by new wealthy residents. Prohibiting development within the greenbelt has forced growth into either the existing built-up area or the zone outside the greenbelt. Eight new towns were built beyond the greenbelt to house London's overspill population and the large number of migrants from the rest of the United Kingdom. This metropolitan fringe now extends up to 50 miles (80 km) from the city center and includes large towns like Guildford, Reading, and Luton. The relatively strong economy, the removal of trade barriers within the EU, and business brought by the Channel Tunnel after 1994 have put pressure on housing, government infrastructure, and transportation services in the Southeast.

Paris: France's Primate City Par Excellence

With a population of more than 11.6 million including its metropolitan fringe, Paris is Europe's second-largest metropolitan area. As France's primate city, Paris dominates the national urban system and the country's economy, politics, and culture. In the wake of widespread deindustrialization, Paris has become a major international center for modern industry and finance. The outer suburbs contain high-technology plants and research-and-development companies, as well as vehicle and airplane factories. Inner-city workshops produce exclusive items such as fashion clothing and jewelry.

Paris has survived wars and plagues; the Black Death alone reduced the population by one-third, to 200,000 in 1347. Since World War II, the city has grown almost continuously as a result of in-migration from the rest of France and the former French empire, and of the city's high proportion of young adults of childbearing age. Much of this growth has been concentrated in the outer suburbs. The city center and inner suburbs are losing population.

The original site of Paris was an island in the Seine, today called Île de la Cité. The Romans seized the island in 52 A.D. from the Parisii, a Gallic tribe, and named it Lutetia Parisiorum ("Midwater Dwelling of the Parisii"). There they built a temple and a palace for the city's governor. In addition to the seat of government, the island settlement attracted convents and churches. The magnificent Gothic cathedral of Notre Dame, for instance, was begun in the 12th century and took more than 170 years to complete.

As a royal center, the grandeur of its architecture and planning made Paris an intensely monumental city. The "Royal Axis" is the imposing entry to the city. It runs from the Louvre (a royal palace, now the national art gallery) and Tuileries Gardens across the Place de la Concorde, along the Champs-Élysées, to the Arc de Triomphe. The nearby Eiffel Tower was erected for the Paris exposition of 1889. The tallest structure in Paris, the Eiffel Tower is one of the most recognized monuments in the world. Paris still produces imposing architectural works today. Recent, initially controversial structures built in the historic core include the sleek glass pyramid in the 19th-century forecourt of the Louvre (fig. 5.23) and the Pompidou Center, the national museum of modern art, nicknamed the "arty oil refinery" for its multicolored exterior ventilation, visible ducts, and steel-and-glass escalators.

The Paris region, Île de France, comprises eight administrative units or *départements*, that date from the French Revolution. Most familiar to tourists, the innermost *département*, Paris, coincides with la Cité, the historic City of Paris. This high-density area developed within the confines of the medieval walls. Its distinct quarters include Île de la Cité. Facing downstream, the "right bank" of the Seine has become the economic heart of Paris. It contains offices, fashionable shops, hotels, restaurants, and high- and middle-income apartments. The "left bank," the seat of intellectual and cultural life, is dominated by its oldest part, the Latin Quarter, with the Sorbonne university, bookshops, theaters, and middle- and low-income apartments. Unlike London, Paris has few large parks. Instead, it gets its feeling of openness and greenery from its wide boulevards and tree-lined river walkways.

The outer parts of Paris include the "little ring" (*petite couronne*) of inner suburbs that extends out about 15 miles (25 km) from the center. It developed between the late 1800s and World War II. Interwar speculative develop-

Figure 5.23   The sleek glass pyramid, designed by I. M. Pei, is the new, famous entrance to the Louvre, the national art gallery established in a former royal palace, in Paris. (Photo by Linda McCarthy)

ments of single-family homes were built on the prime sites in this area. Public mid- and high-rise apartments were erected later on the less marketable land. The big ring (*grande couronne*) of outer suburbs spreads out another 10 to 15 miles (15–25 km) and contains the postwar public *grands ensembles* of poorly serviced low-cost high-rise apartments.

Beginning in the late 1940s and with the publication of Jean-François Gravier's book, *Paris and the French Desert,* planners began to focus on counteracting the extraordinary economic and demographic primacy of Paris. National decentralization policies attempted to limit growth and congestion problems within the Paris region, while promoting development in the eight *métropoles d'équilibre* (balancing metropolises) of Lille–Roubaix–Tourcoing, Metz–Nancy, Strasbourg, Lyon, Marseille, Toulouse, Bordeaux, and Nantes–St. Nazaire. Five new towns (St. Quentin-en-Yvelines, Evry, Melun-Senart, Cergy-Pontoise, and Marne-la-Vallée) were built along two east–west axes of

growth to the north and south of Paris. These new towns grew as extensions to the city, however, and became middle-income dormitory communities for some of the one million daily commuters to central Paris.

Complementing the new towns are four suburban employment centers. The largest and most successful is La Défense (fig. 5.24). It boasts high-rise office buildings containing the headquarters of major financial and other transnational corporations, shops, public buildings, and housing. Its modern Grand Arche is visible from the Arc de Triomphe along Avenue Charles-de-Gaulle—the modern extension of the "Royal Axis."

Brussels: Centrality and the EU

With over 2 million people, Brussels (Bruxelles in French) is Belgium's national capital and largest city. It is also an international administrative, financial, commercial, and modern manufacturing center. Both the EU and NATO

Figure 5.24   Looking northwest from the Eiffel Tower in Paris, one can see the Palais du Chaillot in the foreground. It was built for the International Exposition of 1937. In the distance, beyond the Bois de Boulogne, is La Défense, a planned suburban central business district. (Photo by Linda McCarthy)

have their administrative headquarters there. The Franks established a settlement on an island in the Senne River in the 7th century. It grew as a trading center at the crossroads of a major commercial corridor running between England and Germany that included ports on either side of the English Channel as well as cities in Flanders such as Bruges, Ghent, and Antwerp. Although it is predominantly French-speaking, Brussels spans the linguistic divide between Dutch and French and reflects the dual character of Belgium itself.

During the medieval period, the "Pentagon" was the high-density core inside the five-sided city fortifications. This lower city housed artisans, merchants, and laborers. Its centerpiece, La Grand Place, is a market square containing the Hôtel de Ville, the

14th-century town hall, and many ornate 17th-century guildhalls, which are now restaurants and shops. In the 18th and 19th centuries, public buildings, royal palaces, and mansions of the nobility were built nearby in the upper, or high, city along wide, tree-lined avenues and spacious squares. A series of boulevards replaced the city walls during the 19th century.

The EU's offices are concentrated in a massive executive district of more than 85 city blocks to the east of the medieval Pentagon and the federal administrative office complex. The demand for office space in the central administrative district has driven significant turnover of land from residential to commercial uses. This trend has reinforced the migration of young local professionals to the periphery of the city.

During the interwar years and after World War II, medium- and high-rise apartments were built instead of traditional row houses. Single-family townhouses have also been subdivided into two or more apartments. Despite this increase in the number of dwelling units, the population of the Brussels municipality has declined since the 1970s because of suburbanization and the lower fertility of the older long-time residents.

Since the 1960s, the number of foreign-born residents has risen to about 30% of the population. Immigrants from the United States and the richer EU countries such as France and the Netherlands live in the more affluent communes in the east and southeast of the city. Thousands of poorer migrants have come from countries around the Mediterranean and live in the deteriorated old housing in the Pentagon or in the declining traditional manufacturing areas to the north and west of the city. Suburban municipalities now attract the new services and high-technology employment.

Brussels is known for city planning that is laissez-faire at best and is dominated by private-sector development interests at worst. Several factors hinder effective urban planning: land use regulations are complicated and fragmented; there is a general aversion to national control of planning; and little coordination occurs between the central autonomous municipalities and the surrounding suburban municipalities.

Barcelona: Capital of Catalonia

With about 1.6 million people, Barcelona is Spain's second largest city after the capital, Madrid. Located on the northeastern coast of Spain, Barcelona is the country's largest port and leading industrial, commercial, and cultural center. Housing the seat of the Catalan government, this regional capital of Catalonia is a bilingual city: Spanish and Catalan are both official languages and are both spoken widely (fig. 5.25).

The Phoenicians founded Barcelona more than 2,000 years ago. The city's street plan reflects its three main phases of growth—its ancient and medieval origins, 19th-century additions, and late 20th-century suburbs. The old town is the symbolic and administrative center of the city. Remnants of the Roman wall and grid pattern of streets are overlain by the high-density, narrow, winding streets of the medieval core. Here, residents and tourists alike come to stroll along the famous Ramblas. Barcelona is the most popular tourist port in the Mediterranean with more than 5 million annual visits, including 24,000 from cruise ships (fig. 5.26).

In 1859, Ildefons Cerdà drew up a plan of expansion into the area of the former medieval wall. His pioneering design was based on a grid pattern with wide, straight

Figure 5.25   Throughout Catalonia, signs of Catalan nationalism—
and separatism—abound. This banner, in Girona, speaks to the
world in English. (Photo by Donald Zeigler)

boulevards and eight-sided blocks containing central parks and gardens surrounded by apartment houses. Largely ignored during the 19th- and early 20th-century era of speculative growth, Cerdà's plan was fully realized only in the Eixample district, a new core precinct that was built just north of the old city. This new development also contains the high-rise offices and apartments of the modern CBD.

At the end of the Spanish Civil War in 1939, Francisco Franco established one-party rule. Under his dictatorship, Barcelona's Catalan culture was suppressed, and the city experienced uncontrolled speculative development without adequate public infrastructure and services. Massive rural-to-urban migration fueled rapid population growth. Tens of thousands of illegal squatters ended up in the shantytowns at the sprawling edge of the city. In the 1960s and 1970s, several hundred thousand poorly designed and serviced peripheral high-rise public apart-

ments were built to address the acute housing shortage.

Since the mid-1970s and the establishment of Spain's new parliamentary democracy, the increased autonomy of Barcelona's elected local governments has contributed to a rebirth of planning as well as to growing prosperity. Barcelona's urban renewal program benefited from funding for infrastructure from the EU. The construction of the 1992 Olympic village helped rejuvenate an area of derelict docks into popular waterfront redevelopments. Tourists are attracted to its museums, live music, and theater offerings. Popular World Heritage sites in Barcelona include a park designed by Antoni Gaudí—Park Güell—and his still unfinished church—Sagrada Familia—which has been under construction since 1882 financed by private donations.

At the same time, continued in-migration of poor residents has put pressure on housing, infrastructure, and services. These poor migrants become socially, economically, and locationally

Figure 5.26   The Costa Brava is Barcelona's coastal playground.
Here in Platja d'Aro, the creativity of the Catalan region is
expressed in public art. (Photo by Donald Zeigler)

polarized in inner-city slums, peripheral public apartment blocks, or surviving extensive shantytowns. In contrast, higher-income residents live in nicer central districts or well-serviced lower-density parts of the suburbs.

Oslo: Low-Key Capital of Norway

Oslo is the largest urban center in Norway as measured by both the nearly 550,000 people who inhabit the city and its metropolitan area population of about 1.3 million. Located at the mouth of the Oslofjorden, this city is Norway's capital, main port, and leading commercial, communications, and manufacturing center.

The city was founded around 1000, became the national capital in 1299, and joined the Hanseatic League during the 14th century. Given the predominance of wood as a building material, fire was an early problem, particularly during the frequent sieges that befell Oslo. Following a particularly devastating fire in 1624, King Christian IV of Denmark designated another site for the town nearer Akershus Castle on the east side of the bay. The new town was named Christiania (later Kristiania). It was planned with a grid system of spacious streets, a square located between the town and castle, and ramparts protecting the northern flanks. Significantly, buildings in the town were required to be constructed of brick or stone; soon, however, extensive tracts of wooden houses were built on the outskirts of the built-up area. The town grew slowly: in 1661 only around 5,000 residents had made Christiana their home; by 1800 the population had risen to only 10,000.

During the mid-1800s, the administrative function of the city was augmented by industry, based mainly on textiles and wood processing. Many landmarks, such as the university, royal palace, parliament, national theatre, and stock exchange, were built during the 19th century. The city expanded in a largely unplanned manner as the population swelled to 28,000 by 1850 and 228,000 by 1900. In 1925, the city reverted to its original name, Oslo. After World War II, Oslo's outward expansion continued, largely as a result of public policies that heavily subsidized owner-occupied housing.

Oslo has 40 islands and 343 lakes; about two-thirds of the city comprises protected natural areas, which give it a picturesque appearance. While most of the surrounding forests and lakes are private, the public is strongly against developing them. As is common throughout northern Europe, Oslo city extends around the port, is flanked by the centrally located train station, has a royal palace overlooking the historic core, and has a center marked by pedestrian shopping areas.

Despite being Scandinavia's oldest capital, Oslo today is a modern, though low-key, city.

Berlin: Reinventing Germany's National Capital

Located on a flat, sandy plain on the Spree River, Berlin dates from the 13th century and assumed a prominent role in the Hanseatic League during the 14th century. In addition to its location in the heart of Europe, the city owes much of its growth to political factors. Berlin rose to prominence after its selection as the seat of power of the electors of Brandenburg (1486) and the kings of Prussia (1701). Some of the city's most representative structures along its famous boulevard, Unter den Linden—the Armory, the Palace of the Crown Prince, the State Opera House, and the Brandenburg Gate—date back to the 18th century. Berlin's growth continued during the early 1800s as it became the center of an expanding rail and canal network and an industrial and commercial center. Another boost to Berlin's international political and economic status came after 1871, when the city was made the capital of Germany. Berlin's population increased from 172,000 in 1800 to 3.8 million in 1920, by which point it was already Europe's largest city and cultural metropolis.

As the capital of Nazi Germany, Berlin was routinely bombed during World War II. At the end of the war, the United States, Great Britain, France, and the Soviet Union divided both Germany as a whole and the city of Berlin into four sectors. In 1949, the Soviets declared their sector of Berlin as the capital of that part of Germany which they administered: East Germany. The western part of Germany chose Bonn as its postwar capital city. The American, British, and French sectors of Berlin became West Berlin, an exclave of West Germany wholly within communist-run East Germany. Thus, Berlin came to be divided into a communist East and a democratic West. Travel between West Berlin and the remainder of West Germany was permitted only on specially designated transit routes and air corridors.

Not satisfied with the division of Berlin, the Soviets tried to gain complete control of the city by instituting a blockade in 1948. The 1.5 million residents of West Berlin suddenly found themselves cut-off from all forms of ground transportation and in desperate need of food and other supplies. Rather than allow the residents of West Berlin to submit to this pressure, the United States ordered airlifts of supplies. American and British pilots flew transport planes, fully loaded with food, coal, and other necessities, into the besieged city. Flights were made 24 hours a day, seven days a week, landing in three different airports approximately every 10 minutes until the blockade was lifted.

In 1961, in an effort to stem the tide of almost 200,000 East German refugees trying to escape from the poverty and harsh political conditions in East Berlin to the relative prosperity and freedom of West Berlin, the Soviets built a wall between East and West. The Berlin Wall, and "Checkpoint Charlie," the main crossing point, soon became poignant symbols of the Cold War. Until 1989, when mass demonstrations led to the removal of the Wall and the reunification of Germany in 1990, the two Berlins developed under very different political and economic regimes.

In 1952, under the communists, the "national building program for Berlin" turned Stalinallee (Karl-Marx-Allee as of 1961) into "Germany's first socialist street." The apartment houses in the "gingerbread style" of the

Soviet Stalinist era are today classified as historical monuments and are still very much in demand. The large central square, Alexander Platz, was dotted with socialist statues, flanked by a hotel, and punctuated by a highly visible TV tower featuring a restaurant and an observation platform. Leading west from the square, Unter den Linden (Berlin's most fashionable boulevard) winds past the Palast der Republik, Museum Island, and Humboldt University, through much sought-after residential districts, and through the Brandenburg Gate. From 1961 to 1989 the Berlin Wall cut through the city at this point. The Wall was heavily patrolled, monitored from strategically placed observation towers, and surrounded by open areas of "no man's land." Today, a section of the wall to the north of the Brandenburg Gate has been preserved, but for the most part little trace remains of this once ominous edifice.

In West Berlin, large peripheral housing estates were also built until the end of the 1970s. West Berlin, however, was a world away from its eastern twin. Its main boulevard, Kurfürstendamm, acted as the center of a typical western European city, complete with office buildings, department stores, restaurants, entertainment facilities, billboards, and other symbols of a strong corporate presence. Located here also was one of the few reminders of World War II, the remains of a bombed-out church, oddly juxtaposed with a modern church tower.

Since reunification in 1989, five types of building projects have been initiated. First has been the construction of a new government complex for Berlin as the capital city of a reunited Germany. Second has been massive reconstruction along Friedrichstrasse. This boulevard, stretching from the site of Checkpoint Charlie north to Unter den Linden, now contains upscale retail outlets, a mall, and office buildings, making it the "Fifth Avenue" of Berlin. Third have been the enormous construction projects at Potsdamer Platz, just south of the Brandenburg Gate. Ironically, the land that ran along the Wall—located at the boundaries of East and West Berlin and now at the center of the reunited city—is the most valuable building site in Europe. Following reunification, it was much sought after by corporations eager to take advantage of Berlin as a springboard to eastern Europe. This multibillion-dollar development area, involving such corporate giants as Sony and Daimler-Benz, has significantly changed the look of Berlin.

Fourth has been extensive improvement of public transportation systems. The most pressing need was to reconnect rail and subway lines that had been severed during the Cold War. New subway stations have been constructed, along with improved train stations and an auto tunnel. Finally, various structures commemorating World War II have been completed. The area containing Hitler's Bunker has been preserved, and the "Topography of Terror," an outdoor exhibit illustrating the horrors of the secret police, has been built nearby.

For political reasons, both the West and East German governments concentrated scientific and academic potential in Berlin. As a result, Berlin boasts the highest concentration of scientific, academic, and research facilities in Europe. Europe's most modern research-and-technology park, for instance, is emerging at Adlershof. Berlin's economy today revolves around information and communications technology, the media industry, environmental engineering, medical technology, biotechnology, and transportation technology.

The EU's recent enlargements have opened great economic opportunities for Berlin. The city conducts advertising campaigns aimed at attracting new businesses from eastern Europe. It is also an attractive international congress and trade fair location. Berlin's securities exchange has become a specialized market for eastern European stocks. Given all these changes, Berlin is moving to take its place among the world's premier urban places.

Bucharest: The Legacy of Soviet Domination

No city in Europe bears the personal imprint of an individual to the same extent as Bucharest came to at the hands of deposed leader Nicolae Ceauçescu. As such, Romania's capital allows fascinating insights into the impact that a megalomaniac personality can have on a city.

Bucharest is relatively young by European standards: the first references to the city date to 1459. During the 1800s, Bucharest became an important transportation hub, acquired a manufacturing base, and became Romania's capital when the country was formed in 1862. By the end of the century, Bucharest boasted a tram system and the world's first electric streetlights. The city enjoyed continued growth up to World War II. Its elegant architecture and high culture elite made it the "Paris of the East." Population totals for Bucharest rose from about 60,000 in 1830 to slightly more than 1 million at the end of World War II. Today, it has a population of almost 2 million.

Bucharest suffered heavy damage during World War II both from Allied and Nazi bombing. Following the war, socialist planning principles guided the city's development: industrial capacity was greatly expanded; new housing was constructed; and former villas were converted into government offices and foreign embassies. Population increased to 1.4 million by 1966, the year Ceauçescu came to power. The new leader's program for urban redevelopment, *systematization,* led to single family houses in some Bucharest suburbs being replaced with apartment blocks. Ceauçescu greatly expanded housing estate construction within existing districts and redesigned certain boulevards leading into the city as impressive entryways to represent the revolutionary aesthetics of socialism.

In the 1980s, Ceauçescu turned his attention to central Bucharest. By his overthrow in 1989, approximately 25% of the historic central area had been bulldozed to make room for a new civic center. At the heart of the scheme was The House of the Republic, a grandiose structure measuring almost 900 by 800 feet on the sides and about 330 feet high, making it one of the world's largest buildings. The structure cost over $300 million, required 10,000 workers on average during construction, and was to be the new seat of government. This building consumed virtually all the country's marble during construction and featured hand-carved wood paneling and crystal chandeliers. The second component of the scheme was the construction of the Victory of Socialism Boulevard. This finely appointed ceremonial route was intended to be longer and grander than the Champs-Élysées in Paris and eventually was adorned by a lavish fountain and lined by Bucharest's finest apartments. Another rather bizarre element of Ceauçescu's modifications involved churches. The leader simply did not like them; but rather than being accused of ordering their destruction, he had many of them moved to locations behind other buildings. Nevertheless, some historic neighborhoods did survive and are undergoing restoration.

Although damage from the 1989 Romanian Revolution has been largely repaired, Bucharest still suffers under the specter of Ceauçescu. The city is characterized by dust, potholes that make driving difficult, crumbling apartment blocks, construction that is still not complete, and hundreds of homeless children on the streets. Since 2000, though, it has also experienced a property and retail boom.

URBAN CHALLENGES

Compared with the problems faced by cities elsewhere, and particularly those in less developed countries, European cities are fairly well off. Nevertheless, cities in Europe suffer from problems similar to those in other more developed parts of the world, such as North America. Like cities all over the world, European cities have also had to contend with the terrorist threat (box 5.5).

As the earliest place to experience industrialization, western Europe was also the first to be hit by deindustrialization. Rising long-term unemployment among inner-city residents has concentrated poverty and a wide range of social problems in some inner-city neighborhoods of older industrial cities. These neighborhoods also contain the city's oldest and most deteriorated housing and urban infrastructure. Privatization of public housing by governments attempting to cut back on public expenditures has exacerbated the shortage of decent affordable housing. The enormous cost of upgrading the urban infrastructure, in conjunction with ongoing budgetary constraints, translates into inadequate municipal services in the inner city.

Box 5.5   Tackling Terrorism in London

Cities—especially world cities like London—have become a preferred location for large-scale terrorist attacks. A 2004 tally enumerates well over 500 international terrorist incidents in cities around the world.

There are several reasons for this. First, cities have considerable symbolic value. They are not only dense agglomerations of people and buildings but also symbols of national prestige and military, political, and financial power. A bomb in London's Underground (subway) arouses international alarm and will be communicated instantly to a world audience. Second, the assets of cities—densely packed as they are with a large mix of industrial and commercial infrastructure—make them rich targets for terrorists. Third, cities are nodes in vast international networks of communications—reflecting not only their power but also their vulnerability. A well-placed explosion can produce enormous reverberations by triggering fear and economic dislocation. Finally, word gets around quickly in high-density localities. These kinds of environments can facilitate recruitment for terrorist organizations.

Central London has sought to reduce the real and perceived threat of terrorist attacks. Physical and increasingly technological approaches to security have been adopted at increasingly expanding scales. In 1989, the Prime Minister installed iron security gates at

Figure 5.27   The iron security gates at the entrance to Downing Street in London prevent the public from getting close to the official residence of the Prime Minister. (Photo by Linda McCarthy)

the entrance to Downing Street in order to control public access (fig. 5.27). In 1993, a security cordon was put into place to secure all entrances to the central financial zone of the City of London (the "Square Mile"). The 30 entrances to the City were reduced to 7 and outfitted with road-checks manned by armed police. Over time the scale of this security cordon was increased to cover 75% of the "Square Mile" (fig. 5.28).

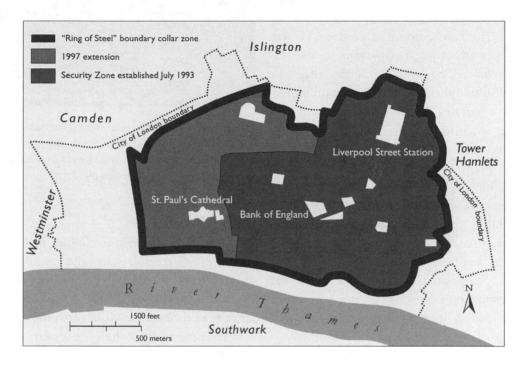

Figure 5.28   Since the 1990s, the threat of terrorism has increased and so has the security zone in London's financial district known as The City.

As a territorial approach to security, this cordon was augmented by retrofitting the closed circuit TV (CCTV) system. The police, through its "CameraWatch" partnership effort, encouraged private companies to install CCTV. At the seven entrances to the security cordon, 24-hour Automated Number Plate Recording (ANPR) cameras, linked to police databases, were installed. Within a decade the City of London had been transformed into the most surveilled space in the United Kingdom, and perhaps in the world, with more than 1,500 surveillance cameras operating within it.

Sources: Jon Coaffee, "Rings of Steel, Rings of Concrete and Rings of Confidence," *International Journal of Urban and Regional Research* 28 (2004), 201–211; Hank V. Savitch with Gregoryi Ardashev, "Does Terror Have an Urban Future?" *Urban Studies* 38 (2001), 2515–2533.

Beginning in the early 1990s, governments across eastern Europe faced the daunting problem of transforming their command economies into market-based systems. Under socialism, workers were publicly employed and all businesses—from large-scale industries to bread shops—were owned by the state. The vast majority of economic assets were privatized quickly. Governments sold the state-run facilities mostly to foreign investors but also to individuals or groups within their own countries. Many economic activities under socialism were run inefficiently, so privatization also resulted in reduced production, plant closures, and unemployment, something unheard of previously.

Privatization has also had a particularly troubling impact on the housing sector. People in eastern Europe were accustomed to paying very little for housing. With privatization, a burgeoning land market, and a general atmosphere of lawlessness, some investors have reaped huge profits; most individuals, though, have suffered economic hardship.

As private automobile ownership has risen continuously, traffic congestion and air pollution, especially in the medieval cores, have reached critical levels (fig. 5.29). Transportation policies in western Europe typically shifted from investment in freeways and central parking facilities to transportation demand management involving ride sharing and public transit. Since the late 1960s, many cities have built or extended subway and light-rail systems.

The inadequate road system throughout eastern Europe, particularly in view of the dramatic increase in car ownership rates there since 1990, has placed considerable strain on roads and parking facilities. Previously, most people could not afford a car, waiting periods for car orders were long, and

Figure 5.29   European mini-cars, such as this one parked along a canal in Amsterdam, are a practical response to narrow streets and high gas prices in Europe. (Photo by Donald Zeigler)

restrictions on ownership applied in some countries. Currently, state and municipal governments are busy constructing new roads and parking structures. A major challenge is to connect the cities of western and eastern Europe by a new European-wide transportation infrastructure.

The presence of significant numbers of foreign workers and their families has generated a series of problems in western Europe. Language differences create problems for the educational system in countries with large numbers of children born to foreign workers. These students represent more than 10% of the school population in some French, German, and Swiss cities. The general recession and rising unemployment of the early 1990s served to intensify existing prejudices among the indigenous population based on differences in language, culture, or race. Since that time, anti-foreigner sentiments have led to some governments such as France banning "conspicuous religious symbols" including headscarves worn by Muslim girls. Vicious attacks on migrants by violent elements within the indigenous population have occurred, especially in some German and French cities. Discrimination against African immigrants, along with high unemployment and lack of opportunities in France's poorest immigrant suburbs (*banlieue*), has sparked riots, the burning of cars and buildings, and violent clashes between groups of youths and the police.

More recently, the considerable economic and social changes in eastern Europe have increased the opportunities for criminal activity. The incidence of petty crime, such as pickpocketing, has increased. Organized crime has also grown enormously. Besides the more typical drugs, gambling, and prostitution, "Mafia"-type crime organizations have made their appearance in many cities. These groups have sought to control the expanding small-scale retail sector, especially kiosk operators. In scenes reminiscent of 1920s Chicago, small operators are offered "protection," and if they refuse to pay, their kiosks are vandalized. Other groups have corrupted public officials to gain unfair advantage in the privatization process.

Pollution is a problem in nearly every city of the world, though western European cities rate more favorably than most (box 5.6). Indeed, Swiss, Austrian, and Scandinavian cities are practically sanitized daily and citizens there are conscious not to litter. Many streets and squares in Italy and Spain are routinely washed down. Ironically, levels of pollution in most of the former heavy industrial regions have fallen. Indeed, air quality in the English Midlands has improved since polluting industries have closed or relocated, and even the Ruhr area boasts clear skies and clean lakes.

Eastern Europe, in contrast, is still attempting to tackle the legacy of weak Soviet-era environmental standards, use of higher risk industrial processes, and greater reliance on aging Soviet-type nuclear reactors. In the past, smoke belching plants, largely using outmoded technology, caused very high levels of pollution.

Since the early 1990s, improved air, rail, and road transportation linkages connecting the major urban centers in both the East and the West have been laying the foundation for the complete reintegration of the European urban system. Businesses and city governments in the eastern European countries that joined the EU in 2004 (Poland, the Czech Republic, Hungary, Slovenia, Estonia, Slovakia, Latvia, and Lithuania) have already developed stronger ties with their counterparts in the preexisting 15 member states in western Europe. Bulgaria and Romania joined the EU in 2007 and have been quick to follow.

Membership in the EU will enhance the opportunities for the former socialist cities to address their pressing social and economic problems. Certainly, the future and prosperity of the entire "new" Europe in the global economy depends on creating a more economically and socially equitable situation for all European urban residents.

When the common currency, the euro, is extended throughout eastern Europe, the European urban system will undergo even more profound changes as the governments, businesses, and people in cities across Europe and elsewhere reorient their activities to take advantage of the new economic environment.

At some point in the future, serious consideration will be given to moving some of the administrative functions of the EU to cities further east. While London, Paris, Frankfurt, Brussels, and Milan will continue to dominate as major financial, political, and cultural centers, Berlin, Vienna, Warsaw, Prague, and Budapest will surely shift the center of gravity of the core–periphery model further east as the 21st century progresses.

Box 5.6   Sustainable Cities in Europe

The continuously increasing road traffic in European urban areas has led to a wide range of problems, including congestion and accidents; enormous wastes of time, energy, and capital resources; environmental damage; and health issues associated with air pollution and noise. City governments have prioritized the development of cleaner, more sustainable transportation options in order to directly improve quality of life and protect the environment for current and future generations. Partly for this purpose, local governments from more than 130 large cities in over 30 countries founded the EUROCITIES network in 1986. They committed to more sustainable urban transportation systems, convenient and accessible public transit, and the safety of drivers, pedestrians, and cyclists. Many cities signed the European Road Safety Charter and are encouraging traffic reduction (including telecommuting and video conferencing), as well as non-motorized modes of transportation, such as walking and cycling.

Since publication of the European Commission's Green Paper on Urban Environment in 1990, city governments have called for greater attention to environmental challenges. Four years later, the First European Conference on Sustainable Cities and Towns took place in Denmark, and more than 2,000 local and regional governments signed the "Charter of European Cities and Towns Towards Sustainability." Subsequent achievements have been positive. After extensive consultation with stakeholders, the European Commission adopted the Thematic Strategy on the Urban Environment in 2006. This proposes that all cities with more than 100,000 inhabitants develop and implement integrated plans for sustainable urban management that cover all aspects of the environment and urban transportation.

Other sustainable development issues relevant to European urban areas include inadequate efforts to decouple transportation growth and GDP increase. Future EU investment in Trans-European Networks (TENs) will integrate an urban dimension because this program delivers increased volumes of traffic to cities that are already struggling to reduce traffic congestion and control the number of private motor vehicles entering their busiest zones. According to EUROCITIES, strengthening the EU Directive on public procurement of "green" vehicles (such as buses and waste collection trucks) will promote cleaner road transportation.

Urban governments in Europe play a decisive role in creating a new mobility culture by changing attitudes toward sustainable consumption and efficient transportation planning. Cities are becoming key players in preserving green areas, as well as in ensuring improved air quality and tackling climate change. Helsinki, Manchester, Glasgow, and Barcelona are among the cities with best practices for biodiversity protection.

Source: http://www.eurocities.com.

SUGGESTED READINGS

Hall, Peter. 2002. *Urban and Regional Planning,* 4th ed. London: Routledge. Provides an historical account of how British planning evolved.

Hamilton, F. E. Ian, K. Dimitrovska Andrews, and Nadasa Pichler-Milanovic, eds. 2005. *Transformation of Cities in Central and Eastern Europe: Towards Globalization.* Tokyo and New York: United Nations University Press. An excellent overview with rich examples of the experiences of major cities on the road to globalization and European integration.

Kazepov, Yuri, ed. 2005. *Cities of Europe: Changing Contexts, Local Arrangements, and the Challenge to Urban Cohesion.* Malden, MA: Blackwell. Chapters focus on important issues such as segregation, gentrification, and poverty.

Kresl, Peter K. 2007. *Planning Cities for the Future: The Successes and Failures of Urban Economic Strategies in Europe.* Cheltenham, UK: Edward Elgar. Examines the relationship between urban competitiveness and economic-strategic planning for 10 internationally networked cities.

Moulaert, Frank, Arantza Rodriguez, and Erik Swyngedouw, eds. 2003. *The Globalized City: Economic Restructuring and Social Polarization in European Cities.* Oxford: Oxford University Press. Case studies of large-scale redevelopment projects and their social implications, including the Olympic Village in Athens.

Müller, Bernhard, Maro' Finka, and Gerd Lintz, eds. 2005. *Rise and Decline of Industry in Central and Eastern Europe: A Comparative Study of Cities and Regions in Eleven Countries.* Berlin and New York: Springer. Reviews the challenges of structural change for industrial cities and regions in this part of Europe.

Murphy, Alexander B., Terry G. Joran-Bychkov and Bella Bychkova. 2008. *The European Culture Area.* Lanham, MD: Rowman and Littlefield. An updated version of a major text on European regions that contains chapters on cities, culture, population, the environment, and EU initiatives.

Ostergren, Robert C., and John G. Rice. 2004. *The Europeans: A Geography of People, Culture, and Environment,* New York: Guildford. A comprehensive view of Europe, which includes two chapters on European towns and cities.

Penninx, Rinus, Karen Kraal, Marco Martinello, and Steven Ventovec, eds. 2004. *Citizenship in European Cities: Immigrants, Local Politics, and Integration Policies.* Aldershot, UK: Ashgate. Examines citizenship in European cities with a focus on immigration policies and immigrant participation in local civil society.

van den Berg, Leo, Peter M. J. Pol, Willem von Winden, and Paulus Moets. 2005. *European Cities in the Knowledge Economy.* Aldershot, UK: Ashgate. Examines local dimensions of the knowledge economy and policy options using case studies of Amsterdam, Dortmund, Eindhoven, Helsinki, Manchester, Munich, Munster, Rotterdam, and Zaragoza.

Wagenaar, Michiel, Virginie Mamadouh, and Gertjan Dijkink, eds. 2000. *GeoJournal,* 51 (2000). Contains 12 essays on European capital cities, including one that examines how central Paris was transformed into an awe-inspiring national capital in the late 1800s.

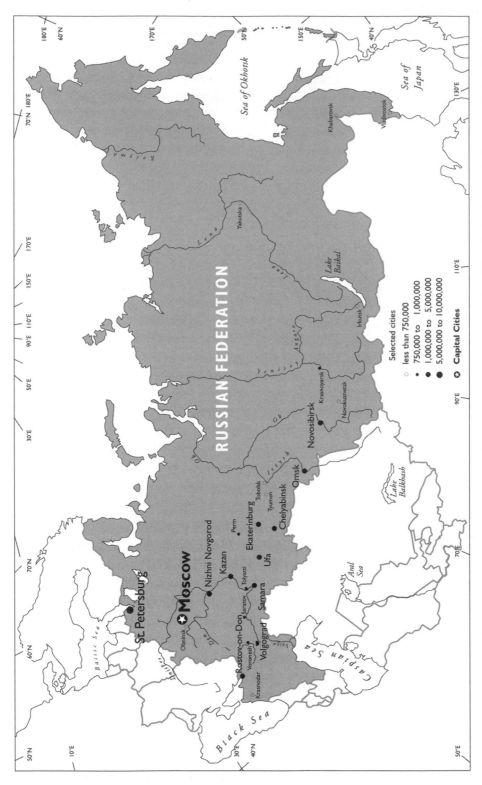

Figure 6.1 Major Cities of Russia. *Source:* UN, *World Urbanization Prospects: 2005 Revision* (New York: United Nations Population Division, 2006, http://esa.un.org/unup).

6

Cities of Russia

JESSICA K. GRAYBILL AND BETH A. MITCHNECK

KEY URBAN FACTS

Total Population	143 million
Percent Urban Population	73.4%
Total Urban Population	105 million
Annual Urban Growth Rate	−0.57%
Number of Megacities	1
Number of Cities of More Than 1 Million	17
Three Largest Cities	Moscow, St. Petersburg, Novosibirsk
World Cities	Moscow

KEY CHAPTER THEMES

1. Russia's urban development reflects the impact of three distinct eras in the country's history: tsarist, Soviet (communist), and post-Soviet.

2. Russia's cities experienced two reconstruction phases in the 20th century, one after the creation of the Soviet Union in 1917 and the other when the Soviet Union collapsed in 1991.

3. The main pattern of the urban system, with its strong reflections of European urban planning characteristics, was established in the tsarist era.

4. Despite experiencing one of the most rapid urbanization patterns in the early 20th century, Russia has historically experienced urban growth and contraction for the last thousand years.

5. As a result of the disintegration of the Soviet-era socialist support system, crime and corruption have hindered the emergence of a democratic post-Soviet government and civil society.

6. Environmental issues in Russia's urban centers are increasingly recognized as severe and have become an important issue to be addressed by post-Soviet city leaders.

7. The need for an overhaul and redesign of urban places and urban governance raises new questions about the roles of government and citizens in the post-Soviet era.

8. Changing demographics and shifting cultural and religious identities have reinvigorated questions about tolerance and acceptance of multiculturalism in the post-Soviet period.
9. In the post-Soviet period, cities are no longer subsidized by the central government; many have experienced economic recession, significant population loss, and at least seasonal deurbanization or ruralization.
10. Cities that are prospering are those with superior locations, strong historic roots, or attractive environments for foreign investment and economic growth.

The urban landscape of the Russian Federation, commonly known as Russia, is today characterized by ornate tsarist-era buildings and monuments (palaces, churches, museums) standing alongside utilitarian, concrete-and-steel structures of the Soviet era (office buildings, communal apartments, community centers) and the newly erected European-style elite apartments and shopping centers of the post-Soviet era. Although such a landscape at first seems incongruous, it reflects the impacts of three distinct periods in the country's history: tsarist, Soviet (communist), and post-Soviet.

Diverse ethnic groups have inhabited this region of Eurasia for at least a thousand years, continually contributing to the multicultural character of Russia's population. For centuries, the blending of diverse cultures and histories across the European and Asian realms of Russia has resulted in multicultural urban populations. That multiculturalism was simultaneously tempered and encouraged during most of the 20th century by one of the most audacious nation-building experiments of the 20th century. This experiment with communism ended on December 25, 1991, when the eighth—and last—Soviet leader, Mikhail Gorbachev, resigned. The Soviet hammer-and-sickle flag of the communist era was lowered, and the red, white, and blue of the Russian flag was raised, quietly and with no announcement.

What had been the Soviet Union (or USSR) had become 15 independent states, of which the Russia Federation was the largest.

Although it has been almost two decades since the end of the Soviet period, the imprint of Soviet-era cities remains scattered across the present-day Russian Federation (fig. 6.1) and the other post-Soviet states. Many elements of the Soviet-built cultural landscapes remain in the former Soviet Union, and Russia continues to undergo a deep series of economic, political, and social transformations. These transformations have both precipitated crises and encouraged their resolution, resulting in urban trends that seem illogical to those unfamiliar with the country (box 6.1). For example, at the beginning of the post-Soviet period, many factory workers, teachers, and other urban workers moved from cities back to rural areas to practice subsistence farming, a process known as *ruralization*. Many attribute this process to the severity of the economic collapse following the disintegration of the Soviet Union and the process of integrating Russia into the world economy. Not surprisingly, in a country nearly twice the size of the United States, the relatively recent emergence of capitalism as a social and economic system and the visual imprint of capitalism on the landscape are unevenly distributed across Russian cities (box 6.2). The harsh climate, a

Box 6.1   HIV/AIDS in Russian Cities

In 2002, the International Crisis Group declared Russia to be one of the five nations where AIDS would pose a threat to global security if rapid increases in HIV infections were not brought under control. The high prevalence of AIDS in the armed forces, a mobile demographic group with high exposure rates to HIV, is of special concern to security analysts. Some reports indicate that by 2020, AIDS will likely have affected Russia's growth severely, consuming 1–3% of GDP and reducing a workforce already undergoing demographic decline as a result of emigration and low birth rates. Infection rates are reportedly highest among young people and are becoming significant among women of childbearing age. The third most common means of transmission is now from mother to newborn child.

Almost unknown in the Soviet Union, the rate of HIV infection has climbed rapidly since the mid-1990s and is generally considered an urban phenomenon in Russia. Many reasons are cited to explain the urban nature of this disease in Russia, including economic and social dislocation, drug use, and illegal drug trade. Some recent research suggests, however, that populations living in more prosperous cities have higher infection rates. Unfortunately, no clear data exist explaining why the epidemic is located in particular urban centers.

Approximately three-quarters of HIV infection cases are linked to injecting drug users. Because of this, some observers have urged the implementation of "harm reduction" strategies, such as needle-exchange programs, across the country. Several such programs are run by private charities in port cities such as St. Petersburg—the Russian city worst hit by HIV—and Kaliningrad. Although the Russian government opposes these programs, some success has been noted in the regions employing them.

The prevalence of treatment and intervention programs differs regionally. High-priced medication and low levels of public commitment to outreach partially explain the less-aggressive-than-necessary treatment programs given relatively high infection rates. In 2002, the Russian government approved a $3 million budget for AIDS drug treatments, enough to treat 500 of its 201,000 registered HIV cases. In 2003, Russia received a $50 million loan from the World Bank for treatment and prevention campaigns.

Although the AIDS epidemic in Russia has primarily spread through intravenous drug use, the disease is moving into other populations. In Kaliningrad, where trends often presage events in the rest of Russia, sexual contact accounted for an estimated 30% of new cases in 2001. Growing awareness, increasing drug prices, and needle exchange programs have helped slow the disease's spread. Although some regions in Siberia now have higher infection rates than Kaliningrad, officials in western regions fear a new wave of HIV infections linked to increasing prostitution, particularly along borders with Lithuania and Poland.

Box 6.2   International Human Trafficking

Since the beginning of Russia's market reforms, the economic and social position of women has deteriorated markedly throughout the region. Privatization and the withdrawal of state subsidies forces women to pursue a wider range of income-generating activities and has induced some to migrate within or outside of their region. There has been a rise in households headed by single mothers, who generally receive lower levels of state support than pensioners. Women earn approximately 70% of what men earn and suffer from much higher unemployment rates. Domestic violence, although underreported, is also thought to have increased.

One result of increased poverty and vulnerability is an increase in sex work and trafficking, as well as the proliferation of marriage services for foreign men seeking Russian brides. Although now working in brothels and massage parlors worldwide, Russian sex workers are mostly concentrated in the nearby markets of the Balkans, Western Europe, Turkey, and Israel. Some observers link the rise in trafficking to the proliferation of war and the presence of NATO forces and NGOs in the Balkans. In other words, social and economic processes in Russian cities influence urban change in the surrounding region. Russian cities are also a destination for women trafficked or moving to escape poverty. One survey in Moscow found that 88.5% of prostitutes were not native Muscovites and less than half had lived in Moscow for over a year. This point underscores the idea that many of the women trafficked are not even native to Russia, but find Russia as their destination from other former Soviet countries.

Many women hope to migrate abroad, even if only for temporary employment. One survey in St. Petersburg found that around 70% of the women interviewed would leave Russia for work if the opportunity arose. With visas being difficult to acquire, women are vulnerable to promises of arranged jobs or marriages that would allow legal migration. Once abroad, these women find they have been sold to work as prostitutes in brothels or nightclubs from which escape is difficult if not impossible. For example, a woman from Moscow might answer an ad for employment as a teacher in Israel and face the same fate. Albanian criminal networks control much of the trade into the Balkans and Italy. Even when law enforcement officials are committed to stopping the trade, understaffed local authorities rarely have the resources needed to fight powerful trafficking organizations.

Beyond the human rights implications of trafficking, there are serious consequences related to health, including physical and emotional abuse. Urban problems such as unemployment, underemployment, and urban fiscal crises must be addressed before the trafficking problem can be tackled. Impoverishment is often cited as a contributing factor leading to trafficking, and many traffickers pose as employment agencies—especially in Russian cities with high unemployment. Government-funded social programs to help trafficking victims are sorely lacking in Russia, mostly because of a lack of funding for municipal social services. For example, as of 2005, no women's shelters existed in eastern Russia, and space in Moscow is so insufficient that women who manage to escape stay in locations where they can be and are often located by their traffickers.

Figure 6.2   Despite cold winter days, street peddlers are attracted to busy thoroughfares in cities throughout Russia. (Photo by Jessica Graybill)

Figure 6.3   St. Basil's Cathedral on Red Square, just outside the Kremlin, is one of the most colorful and oldest Russian Orthodox churches in Russia, and in many ways it is a symbol of Moscow. (Photo by Donald Ziegler)

poorly developed (and frequently impassable) network of roads, and immense distances exacerbate the fragmentation of the Russian urban system.

For some Russian cities, the built environment has changed so dramatically since 1991 that they are nearly unrecognizable to those accustomed to quiet, somber Soviet landscapes. The advent of commercial retailers, private transportation, and new housing construction is changing Russian urban landscapes (fig. 6.2). For example, Moscow's Red Square is no longer a nearly deserted public space awaiting military parades. Instead, it is a bustling retail and tourist space (fig. 6.3). Russian cities were originally constructed around modernist urban principles (for pedestrians and mass transit) and were neither built nor developed to accommodate the now increasing number of commercial and private vehicles. The concept of rush hour has great meaning now, and for many Russian cities, including Moscow, rush hour begins very early and extends through the evening (fig. 6.4). The typical Soviet rings of monolithic apartment complexes on city outskirts are increasingly mixed: new elite apartment buildings are constructed alongside Western-style suburban developments of "cottages" and even gated communities

Figure 6.4   Since the fall of communism, automobile ownership in Moscow has soared, and with it has come urban gridlock. (Photo by Jessica Graybill)

(fig. 6.5). For other cities, change is noted not so much in the built environment, but in the replacement of Communist Party billboards (formerly present in every city and town) with brilliant neon and banner-type commercial advertisements along major urban thoroughfares.

Post-Soviet Russia is grappling with changes in the location and nature of urban development and the legacy of the spatial structure of the urban system left behind by the Soviets. No longer do central planners choose a site for a new factory and then build a city around it, as was the case in the Soviet Union. The Soviet planning system resulted in the construction of cities in unexpected, potentially hazardous, and ultimately unsustainable sites, such as the remote reaches of Siberia and the Arctic. Cities were often sited

near natural resources, regardless of the location of those resources. To give but one example, Noril'sk, a nickel-smelting city with over 100,000 inhabitants, was built far above the Arctic Circle. But in the post-Soviet period, the introduction of capitalist notions of economic efficiency has made the location of cities like Noril'sk unsustainable, producing a population outflow from the city. The Soviet system created an urban spatial pattern of economic flows between quite distant cities because the locations of suppliers, intermediate producers, and markets were of little concern in a system where transportation and energy costs were state determined and subsidized and therefore perceived to be free. This has changed, and urban governments today are challenged to transform into post-Soviet, capitalist entities responsible for

Figure 6.5   New *microrayon* developments, with varied architectural styles, are rapidly changing the face of Russia's suburbs. This picture is from Yuzhno-Sakhalinsk. (Photo by Jessica Graybill)

self-sufficiency and promoting their own futures (rather than buying subsidized goods and services from the state).

Also deemphasized now is the focus on the military–industrial complex (MIC) in determining the location of urban investment and growth. In both tsarist and Soviet Russia, many cities owed their existence and location to questions of national security. By the Soviet period, many cities had become *closed cities* (cities requiring permission to visit) because of their role in the MIC. For example, the city of Zhukovsky (south of Moscow) was a closed city because an air base and airplane institutes and production facilities were located there, and the far eastern city of Yuzhno-Sakhalinsk was closed to foreigners and most Soviet citizens for border security reasons. Cities in the Urals, such as Perm and Magnitogorsk, grew in economic importance and population precisely because they were integral parts of the MIC.

Decades of defense-related investment in these cities' industrial bases, housing stocks, roads, schools, and other urban infrastructure influenced their urban geographies in ways impossible in capitalist economies, in which economic efficiency is the most important criterion for attracting new investment. Today, cities previously entrenched in the MIC are undergoing economic restructuring processes not dissimilar from the restructuring experienced by major North American and European cities during deindustrialization beginning in the 1970s. For example, cities such as Ekaterinberg are becoming transportation and corporate centers for European businesses, and other gateway cities near the Chinese border (such as Khabarovsk) are transforming Russian–Chinese business relations.

In response to economic collapse and restructuring, increasing poverty (especially urban poverty), and large inflows of refugees

Table 6.1   Percent Urban Population in Each Federal Okrug (2002 Census Data)

Federal Okrug	1926	1939	1959	1970	1979	1989	2002
Central	19.0	34.2	52.0	64.3	72.8	78.0	79.1
Northwest	29.2	48.0	64.6	73.3	79.3	82.2	81.9
Southern	19.2	31.0	44.4	52.1	57.4	60.0	57.3
Privolzhskaya	12.1	23.8	44.6	56.1	64.8	70.8	70.8
Ural	21.0	45.4	66.1	71.3	76.2	80.2	80.2
Siberia	13.3	32.6	52.9	62.5	68.8	72.9	70.5
Far East	23.4	46.5	67.5	71.5	74.5	75.8	76.0
Russian Federation Total	17.7	33.5	52.4	62.3	69.3	73.6	73.0

from more troubled parts of the former Soviet Union, the 1990s marked the beginning of rapid and widespread changes in the location of urban development both within cities and between them. Changes to Russian urban economic and demographic systems and structures will continue as dynamic processes well into the 21st century and beyond.

EVOLUTION OF THE RUSSIAN URBAN SYSTEM

Russia began the 20th century with less than one-fifth of its population living in urban places and ended it almost three-quarters urban. Since the mid-20th century, the majority of the Russian population has lived in cities, many of which are large metropolitan centers. The percentage steadily increased throughout the Soviet period: by 1989, 74% of Russia's population lived in urban places. The percentage declined slightly until the late 1990s, when it leveled off at about 73%, a figure that remains stable today.

The regional distribution of the urban population (tab. 6.1) highlights two important characteristics of urban demographic change in Russia during the Soviet period: (1) rapid urbanization as a result of industrializa-

tion and (2) the growth of cities in harsh, inhospitable regions such as Siberia, the far east, and the far north. Russia rapidly urbanized after the communist era began in 1917; however, significant levels of urbanization continued in every region of Russia throughout the Soviet period. For ideological and security reasons, Soviet central planners promoted both rapid urbanization and urban settlement in Siberia, the far east, and the far north. High rates of urbanization in the Arctic and Siberian regions existed as early as 1959. Even in agricultural regions, such as the Central Chernozem and the North Caucasus (which correspond to the Central and Southern Federal Okrugs), more than half of the population lived in urban places by 1979.

Prior to the Soviet period, small villages and settlements were scattered across the vast territory of the Russian far north and east. Modernization of these settlements and ways of life in the early Soviet period was achieved by pushing people off their native lands and into regional towns and *collective farms* (*kolkhozi*). Ostensibly undertaken to ease central management and regional planning for cities and towns, the Soviet era greatly altered both settlement patterns and traditional ways of life in these regions. By the late 1990s, the population of the far north (the Arctic region) was nearly 80% urban, well above the Russian average of 73%. In the post-Soviet period, the urban population in the Far Eastern and Siberian Federal Okrugs has decreased along with government investment in the region. Out-migration occurs to European Russia, but others who either cannot or do not want to leave (often the elderly, the poor, and the very young), return to older villages, at least for part of the year, to survive—an example of ruralization. Although Siberia and the far east are used as examples here, this is a phenomenon happening across Russia.

Soviet doctrine envisioned urban life bringing people closer to communist ideals. Urban development became synonymous with the notion of civilized society and the construction of communism. But significant population losses nationwide and depopulation of many urbanized regions in the post-Soviet period (tab. 6.1) are clear signs of the failure of communism. These nationwide data also illustrate the post-Soviet phenomenon of ruralization. The small decline in the percentage of urban population in the Southern Federal Okrug, an agricultural area along the southern border, is most likely the result of an influx of in-migrants and refugees from former Soviet Republics who were assigned housing in rural areas of the Russian Federation. This demographic change exemplifies the complex relationship between Russia and its newly independent neighbors, countries that were formerly part of the Soviet Union.

During the 20th century, Russia underwent one of the most dramatic urbanization processes anywhere in the world, and it is now experiencing further dramatic change associated with urban centers in the 21st century. In the final years of the century, Russia's cities lost population and experienced a significant urban crisis. They began the 21st century well into a new phase characterized by a dramatic reversal of long-established Soviet practices, and a new urban settlement pattern resulted. For centuries, the population moved out from the European core of Russia primarily to cities in the south (often to capital cities in Soviet Central Asia) and to Siberian and Arctic cities. As a direct result of the change from Soviet central planning to market-driven locational choices in the post-Soviet period, there has been significant movement out of Siberian and Arctic cities (as well as from cities in the newly independent countries in Central Asia and the Caucasus) back to European Russia. Without central planning, the introduction of market forces in cities in harsh and inaccessible places, such as Noril'sk and Surgut, caused rapid increases in once heavily subsidized energy and transportation costs. As subsidies dwindled, food, housing, and industrial production costs soared. Faced with ever-increasing costs and the need to transport frequently poor quality goods thousands of miles to distant markets, urban industrial complexes closed, and unemployment surged. Those who could simply pulled up stakes and moved. Other people, largely the elderly, the poor, and those without relatives in other parts of the former Soviet Union, remained behind. Existing communities in cities and towns operate as social safety nets for those who have migrated to establish new lives. Irrespective of the period, however, Russia has experienced a significant mismatch between the location of labor resources, markets, and urban-industrial power in the western portion of the country, and the location of natural resources, including energy, in the eastern portion of the country.

Reversal of the long time west-to-east trend of urban population movement is accompanied

Figure 6.6   New construction has now extended well beyond the traditional suburban boundaries of Moscow. Mitino, a new suburb, has upscale apartments, townhomes, and retail outlets; it relies heavily on private transportation. (Photo by Beth Mitchneck)

by a new trend: suburbanization and new housing development outside the city limits (fig. 6.6). This may be viewed as a market adjustment given the extreme housing shortage, a legacy of Soviet planners' focus on the construction of housing located close to public transit. Many new housing developments require residents to use private transportation—contributing to increased traffic woes. While there are no systematic data on suburbanization processes across Russia, it is clear that this trend is especially prevalent in the European portion of the country. Yet like past urban processes, it is spreading eastward.

The Pre-Soviet Period: Birth of the Urban System

The century-old pattern of the eastward spread of urban population may be traced to the first Slavic cities that appeared on the Russian plain at the end of the 9th century. From that time, historical settlement patterns have been largely related to access to water, transportation, and the location of military and economic outposts. The Russian plain served as a vital trade route between Scandinavia and the eastern Mediterranean. A vast river network provided connectivity between regions. The Vikings established a set of city-principalities, at once both military outposts and long-distance trading centers, where they collected tolls from merchants who traveled through the region. Kiev (or Kyiv, now the capital of independent Ukraine), Novgorod, and Smolensk were among the earliest urban settlements of this type.

The region gradually began to function independently from the Viking settlers, and one city, Kiev, became the focal point for Slavic political and economic development because of its favorable location on the navigable Dnieper River with access to the Black Sea and

Constantinople. Most cities in Kievan Rus were located along the vast network of rivers in Russia and were originally established as forts, known as *kremlins,* because of constant conflict among the settlements and for protection against raids by the Tatars. Many of these cities have survived today with their kremlins still intact. The famous Golden Ring of cities outside of Moscow (e.g., Yaroslavl, Suzdal, Vladimir) have Kievan Rus origins and continue to thrive as historic centers of Russian culture.

After the formal downfall of the Tatars in 1480, a new phase of urban settlement began with emphasis on eastern urban development. By the late 14th century, and once again for security reasons, a new type of urban network had developed called Muscovy Rus. Moscow dominated this new region of settlement from its location at the center of a river system, permitting trade and communication by water and allowing for economic growth in several directions. Access to the Volga and its tributaries gave a route to the east; the Western Dvina led to the Baltic; and the Don and Dnieper rivers led to the Black Sea.

As in other medieval walled cities, the importance of hills for defense and rivers as communication main lines during this period explains common features of many old Russian city centers. Kremlins were always located on high riverbanks. The layout of streets was usually radial, reflecting the concern about rapid dispatching of troops from the Kremlin. Cities developed mostly in imperfect circles away from rivers, and often not on the other side of the river until the belated construction of bridges (only in the 1960s and 1970s) occurred. This historic imprint characterizes the spatial structure of many contemporary Russian cities.

Russian settlements expanded eastward across the Ural Mountains into Siberia, en-

countering little resistance once Tsar Ivan the Terrible defeated the Tatars at Kazan in the middle of the 16th century. New settlements, such as Tobolsk (1587) and Yakutsk (1632), began as military outposts. Trappers plundered Siberia for furs, but little else of value came from this vast wilderness until 1647, when Russia settled Okhotsk on the Pacific Ocean. As the 17th century drew to a close, Russia remained essentially landlocked, controlling a vast territory with about 300 cities, the same number as had existed three centuries earlier.

Tsar Peter the Great founded St. Petersburg in 1703, touching off a spectacular transformation of urban Russia as he sought to catch up to western Europe. Consistent with Russian urban history, St. Petersburg was built for economic reasons, to be a showcase naval and commercial port city. New to Russian urban development, however, was the cultural purpose of becoming the country's "window on the West." As the new national capital, St. Petersburg quickly supplanted Moscow, and the urban focus moved westward physically as well as culturally. Reforms undertaken by Tsar Peter revitalized both local and long-distance trade, encouraging growth in new market centers as well as in more established ones. The creation of this new, Western-oriented city fueled social tension between those who believed in westernizing the country and those who emphasized Russia's Slavic origins. Current debates about Russia's direction of development mirror these earlier ones. The development of St. Petersburg was also a great precursor of the Soviet belief that humans can conquer nature in the name of economic development. St. Petersburg's location in originally inhospitable swampy land caused thousands of Russians to lose their lives while building the city and today continues to cause parts of the city to be threatened with flooding.

By the end of the 19th century, about 16% of Russia's population lived in urban places. Two main industrial regions fueled economic and urban development. In Moscow and surrounding centers (Tver, Vladimir, Ivanovo, Kostroma), textile manufacturing predominated. Beyond Moscow, most new manufacturing centers were located outside Russia proper. The second area of industrialization and urbanization was the Donbass, in Ukraine, where there were abundant coal supplies.

The Soviet Period: New Urban Patterns

The Russian Revolution (1917) and ensuing civil war ended with the establishment of a political-economic and urban system unlike any other worldwide. The Communist Party took control and used its clout to establish an economic system guided by communist and socialist principles instead of market forces. This new economic system was called the *command economy* because a group of central planners located in Moscow determined not only what was produced, but where, who could acquire products, and at what price. With the force of law, central planners allocated all investment resources, made location decisions, and set national standards for urban development. Central planning meant national needs superseded local ones, including those related to urban development. Central planning meant that city governments and residents had relatively little influence over local economic development, urban growth, and internal city structure.

Soviet planners used mathematical algorithms based on models of European and North American urbanization to choose so-called optimal locations for economic investment and industrial activity. This led to the construction of new cities with predetermined sizes (e.g., less than 50,000 people, more than 100,000 people) in previously less developed regions like Siberia. Planners considered natural resource proximity and the impact of defense when locating new economic activity. They often chose sites that dispersed production to reduce national economic vulnerability in the case of military attack. For example, at the beginning of World War II, Soviet central planners dismantled factories in western Russia and reassembled them in the Urals and Siberia. Because many cities related to industry were new, workers with specific skills were often sent to these cities to aid with industrialization and modernization. In this model of controlled urban development, previously underpopulated—and often undeveloped—regions were urbanized.

After acquiring political control over the country, the Communist Party took steps to consolidate its political power and reshape the economy. In 1918, the leadership moved the capital from St. Petersburg (subsequently renamed Leningrad) back to Moscow. The move was both symbolic and strategic: the relatively recent capital built by the tsars as a window on the West was replaced by a far older capital in the country's heartland, which would be easier to defend. It also made a statement that the country's gaze was no longer to the West but to the East and within the former Russian Empire. The communist leadership established a hierarchical urban administrative system to assist in carrying out political and economic agendas, as well as to reflect the new ideology. By setting up a system of administrative centers in the *oblasts* (political units comparable to states or provinces), central planners controlled resource allocation and use in each region. Not surprisingly, administrative centers benefited disproportionately from central investment decisions. Industry was the force driving the spatial distribution of population into urban centers dispersed throughout Russia. By the late 1990s, in two-thirds of Russia's *oblasts*, the administrative centers accounted for a quarter of the *oblast*'s population. Many function like primate cities in other world regions, where investment, services, and labor are disproportionately concentrated in one city, creating uneven regional development.

This new territorial administrative system enabled central planners to realize Soviet economic priorities, especially rapid industrialization. *Oblast* centers became the locations for massive industrial investment and grew rapidly. Soon, historic industrial centers such as Moscow, Yaroslavl, and Kazan were joined by administrative/industrial centers in Siberia and the far east (e.g., Omsk, Novosibirsk, Krasnoyarsk, Irkutsk, and Vladivostok). Planners also used investments to develop a system of secondary industrial cities focused on heavy industry (e.g., the automotive industry in Togliatti, aluminum and related industrial production in Bratsk) or natural resource exploitation (e.g., nickel in Noril'sk, oil near Surgut). Although historically the location of Russian cities depended upon accessibility to river transportation routes, the location and growth of Soviet cities depended more on the concentration of industrial investments in selected regional centers. Thus a new system of large cities (i.e., cities of more than 50,000 people) developed in Russia. In a country where bigger was seen as better,

planners and politicians spoke glowingly of cities with more than 1 million inhabitants.

Soviet urban growth depended on transportation routes—connections with rail or water transportation that reflected the Soviet emphasis on industrial growth. In the 1970s, Soviet planners began constructing a second Siberian rail route, the Baykal-Amur Mainline (BAM), to increase the capacity of east–west movement already occurring along the Trans-Siberian Railroad. The BAM further facilitated new natural resource exploitation and the transportation of goods across Russia's vast expanse. These railroads provided lifelines to cities located thousands of miles from central Russia. In the far north, cities primarily depended on boats using the Northern Sea Route along the Arctic coastline or Siberian rivers. Even today, frozen rivers are used as winter roads until the ice breaks.

While planners directed investment resources to specific cities, they simultaneously pursued a contradictory policy: namely, limiting population growth in many of the same cities. Planners used formal control mechanisms such as the *propiska* (legal permission to live in a specific city) that were ineffective at limiting urban growth. Many individuals found legal ways around the system, such as marrying someone who had a *propiska* to live in the city or finding employment and having the employer secure a *propiska*. Ultimately, pressure for ever-greater production frequently translated into investments in established sites, instead of new sites, because this made economic sense. But additional investments created demand for increased labor. Attempts by central planners to reap the benefits of economies of scale reduced the effectiveness of city size limitations. This had the dual effect of increasing city sizes beyond formerly

Figure 6.7   Old and new apartment buildings, in close proximity, typify a typical Russian *micorayon*. Note the old five-story Khrushcheviki apartment building (center right) next to new high-rise construction. (Photo by Beth Mitchneck)

imposed growth boundaries and intensifying industrial production (and thus industrial pollution and waste) inside city boundaries.

Urban and Regional Planning

In addition to directing investment to particular cities, central planners influenced the internal spatial structure of Soviet cities. To create a new kind of city consistent with socialist ideals, planners adopted specific urban planning guiding principles including restricting urban growth in order not to exceed optimal city sizes; distributing consumer and cultural goods and services equitably to the population; minimizing journeys to work and providing public transportation for spatial mobility; and segregating urban land uses. Interestingly, some of these Soviet principles, such as creating urban growth boundaries and minimizing commuting, are not enforced in Russia today but are propounded in the West as "smart" growth.

The basic building block of Soviet cities was the *microrayon*. *Microrayons* were constructed near industry and other places of work to min-imize journeys to work. *Microrayons* housed 8,000–12,000 people in living areas designed as integrated units of high-rise apartment buildings, stores, and schools to provide consumers with cultural and educational services required by Soviet norms. Built using standardized plans irrespective of local environmental conditions, *microrayons* are numbingly similar whether in Novosibirsk, Vorkuta, or Moscow (fig. 6.7), and large tracts of identical or similar multistory apartment buildings still ring Russian cities. For example, similar construction materials and designs were used to build *microrayons* located in diverse physical geographic regions found across the former Soviet Union, such as in earthquake hazard zones (e.g., Alma-Ata in Kazakhstan); in cold, damp climates (e.g., Petropavlovsk-Kamchatsky); in flood hazard regions (e.g., St. Petersburg); or on the semi-arid steppe (e.g., Barnaul).

Microrayon locations were set by the so-called *General Plans,* which determined the location of *microrayons* within cities, as well as all other land uses. General plans were so detailed that a milk store could not be built legally on a

Figure 6.8   On-shore Russian-owned oil fields are found on the outskirts of the city of Okha on Sakhalin Island. Decades-long oil spills and seepages run into the Sea of Okhotsk, only 10 miles away. (Photo by Jessica Graybill)

site designated for a bread store. General plans were intended to complement the shorter-term, *five-year economic plans,* which determined what would be made, how it would be made, who would make it, who would receive the final product, and at what price.

Absent from Soviet planning principles were environmental impact concerns and environmental constraints. Planners, and the Soviet system in general, believed and practiced technological control over nature. This practice, combined with the zeal to reach economic goals, resulted in almost complete disregard for the ecology of Russia's cities. Teams of planners, geoengineers, and economic geographers choreographed large-scale development projects to modernize society, especially in large urban areas. For example, dams, hydroelectric power stations, and industrial complexes were constructed in and near cities. "Progress" was narrowly conceptualized as industrialization at all costs, and nature was society's tool to create the new socialist reality.

For example, near the city of Okha on Sakhalin Island, onshore oil deposits have been exploited since the early 1900s. Exploitation increased in the Soviet period, and the evidence of poor environmental standards for extraction remains today. On a road out of town, adjacent to local residents' summer homes (*dachas*) and with high-rise apartment buildings plainly visible, are numerous rusting and leaking oil pumps operating amongst pools of standing water mixed with leaked oil. Although signs are posted in this suburban oil field warning pedestrians of the toxins in the area, they are often illegible or are half-buried in oil muck (fig. 6.8). This mixture runs into local creeks, which in turn empty into the Sea of

Box 6.3   Russia's Street Children

New urban landscapes in Russia include retail operations, advertisements, traffic, and the homeless—especially homeless children. Official sources report up to 55,000 homeless children in Moscow alone in 2006, and up to 16,000 in St. Petersburg. These figures describe children without parents living on the streets in Russian cities. They are abandoned and runaway children; some work in slave-like conditions, whereas others engage in illegal activities such as child prostitution or drug trading. Russia's street children are part of the landscape across the country. They are present in the North Caucasus in North Ossetia and Chechnya and in the far east in Vladivostok. Many are teenagers but others are much younger.

These children work, take drugs, scavenge food wherever possible, and live in abandoned buildings and train and metro stations. Urban governments have meager funds to allocate for social services. For example, in 2005 in the North Caucasus, the North Ossetian government could allocate only 150,000 rubles (~$5,500) to run a homeless children's shelter in the republic's capital. Aiming to keep children off the streets and out of criminal activity, the shelter can hardly meet the children's needs. In Grozny, the capital of war-torn Chechnya, abandoned and orphaned children have nowhere to turn: as of 2004 there were no centers or shelters for street children. Even in Moscow, considered wealthier than other cities, only 1,600 beds in 2005 gave shelter to the entire homeless population (with homeless population estimates ranging from 30,000 to 1 million).

Why do so many children live on the streets of Russian cities? The Russian government claims that in the early 21st century, around 80% of street children have parents or guardians. Press reports and research suggest that children are running away from domestic situations that include extreme poverty, alcoholism, domestic violence, and neglect. Research also suggests that these social ills result from the post-Soviet economic restructuring and are experienced at the household level. Other causes include forced migration as a result of civil unrest in particular regions of Russia and a migration process in the 1990s that brought people to Russian cities from former republics, where they often failed to find employment or housing. Children are especially impacted by these forms of displacement, whether by choice or not; street children generally do not attend school, experience harmful health impacts (including the contraction of infectious diseases), and become targets of harmful illegal activities.

Okhotsk, where discharge from runoff pipes disrupts local ecologies in nearshore bays and coastlines. This environmental and human health hazard was—and remains—less important than the economic bottom line.

Examples like these abound in and around Russian cities and can be understood as examples of environmental and social injustice (box 6.3). Although many urban residents were and are aware of urban environmental issues, Soviet newspapers and scientific-engineering literature remained silent about the growing environmental problems across most of Russia's industry-driven cities until

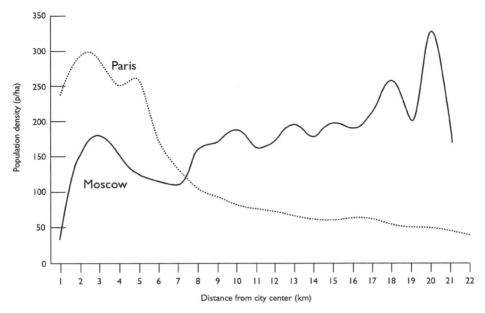

Figure 6.9   Comparative Density Profile in the Built-Up Areas of Moscow and Paris. *Source:* Beth Mitchneck and Ellen Hamilton.

the late Soviet period, when the extent of environmental degradation began to be publicized. Only in the late 1980s did people openly begin to express concern about environmental issues. That was only after nationwide reporting of air, water, and land pollution; environmental degradation with economic consequences (such as decreased fishing catches in lakes and rivers); and human health issues (e.g., asthma, kidney diseases, lung diseases). Many urban dwellers found a silver lining in the industrial decline of the 1990s—the spiraling decline of urban environments was temporarily disrupted until massive increases in automobile use caused air pollution to rebound. Disregard for impacts of economic development on ecology created certain investment practices that continue today.

The Soviet history of urban and regional planning has left an indelible mark on Russia's built and natural environments, precisely because types of buildings and industries were located without reference to market forces

and environmental conditions. In the command economy of Soviet cities, land was not bought and sold, but allocated roughly in accordance with the socialist ideology and planning principles outlined above. Compare, for instance, the population density of Paris and Moscow as it varies with distance from the city center (fig. 6.9). In Paris, market forces mean that valuable land near the city center is more densely populated than less valuable land on the city outskirts. In Moscow, just the opposite was true. The most densely populated parts of the city were on less valuable land far from the city center. Instead of building skyscrapers on valuable land in the city center, central planners built skyscrapers in the suburbs.

Soviet cities were also unique because the absence of a free market meant land was not recycled for other purposes, as would have been the case in market economies. As a result, the historic rings of development in Soviet cities remain densely populated and clearly visible today. Beginning in the 1930s, huge factories were erected outside tsarist-era city cores as part of the industrialization drive. In subsequent years, especially after the late 1950s, a near catastrophic housing shortage and renewed determination to improve people's living conditions began decades of construction of *microrayons* far from city centers.

Late Soviet Period: The Beginning of Change

Significant urban restructuring in the post-Soviet period was presaged in changes to the urban system that became evident earlier than the actual economic and political collapse. Starting in the 1980s, a pattern of "disappearing cities" signaled changes to the Russian urban system. Disappearing or shrinking towns in European Russia lost so many people that they no longer appeared on Soviet statistical accounts of urban places. Towns with declining populations are spatially distributed throughout Russia, with more than half in the industrial core regions around Moscow and St. Petersburg, and in the Urals. By the mid-1990s, however, Siberian cities accounted for a larger proportion of shrinking urban areas. This pattern began in the west and moved eastward, suggesting that the phenomenon was firmly rooted in manufacturing and industrial decline even before the collapse. Shrinking towns, combined with new migration patterns westward, have most likely contributed to the continued worsening situation of overburdened and decaying urban infrastructure, including housing and utilities, in many large Russian cities. In other words, despite natural decline (a greater number of deaths than births), many Russian cities are growing rapidly whereas others are shrinking (fig. 6.10).

Analysis of the functions of disappearing and shrinking towns opens a lens into the impact of restructuring on the urban system. Because of the boom–bust economies surrounding mineral and other resource exploitation, mining towns account for a large proportion of declining towns (roughly a quarter by 2000). Urban centers related to the MIC comprise another large proportion of declining cities. Previously, MIC cities received special attention from the central government, which meant better-than-average access to goods and services, as well as higher salaries for employees in these places. This special treatment does not continue today in most MICs.

An interesting counterpoint to the disappearance of many towns is the appearance of previously unacknowledged cities, known as *secret cities* or, in Soviet parlance, "closed administrative-territorial formations." Secret cities never appeared on maps, and some estimates place the number of secret cities around 40. Located throughout Russia, but with clusters in Murmansk Oblast and in the far east (related to naval operations), in the Urals, and in Moscow Oblast, employment was focused on highly classified military production including nuclear research and missile production (fig. 6.11).

Post-Soviet Russia: Reconfiguring the Urban System

Heavy industry was especially hard hit by the reintroduction of market forces and the reorientation of the economy away from defense. As Russia's borders opened, it was flooded with cheaper and better consumer goods, and demand for everything from locally produced steel to planes dried up. Deindustrialization ensued in many places. At the same time,

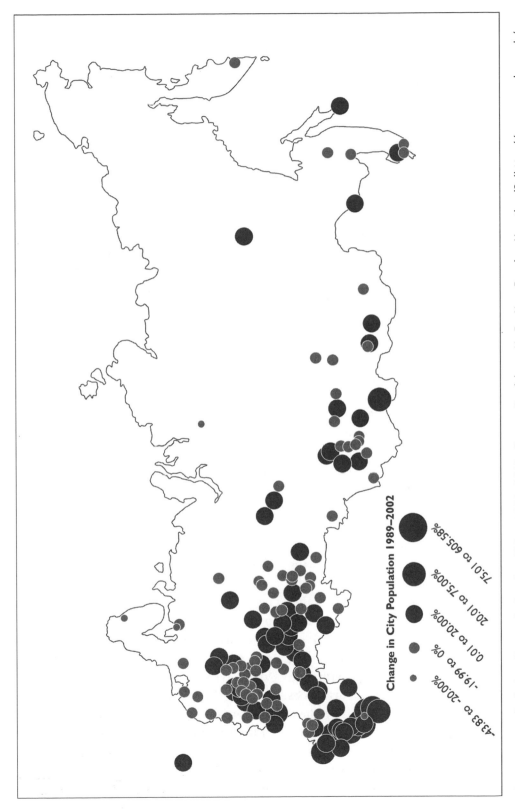

Figure 6.10 Population Change in Russian Cities, 1989–2002. *Source:* Bradshaw, M. J., New Russian Heartland? (http://www.geog.le.ac.uk/russianheartland/index.html), accessed 12/11/07.

Figure 6.11   A submarine in Kaliningrad, a former secret military city in the former Soviet Union, is now used as a tourist attraction. (Photo by Annina Ala-Outinen)

regions began scrambling for new investment capital to replace that which used to flow in from Moscow. Market forces introduced clear patterns of winners and losers and large differences among places.

The places with the highest rates of gross regional product today are found in just a few natural resource–rich regions in Siberia, the Far East, and in Moscow. For many cities in the older manufacturing regions of the Russian heartland and the industrialized regions along the Trans-Siberian Railroad, economic restructuring away from manufacturing to natural resource extraction and export means that these cities are struggling to cope with high unemployment rates and few opportunities for new development. It is precisely these deindustrializing cities that are losing population in the current period.

Cities in regions with growing economies and growing populations (like Moscow, Yakutsk, Yuzhno-Sakhalinsk, Nakhodka, and Kazan) have become attractive destinations for migrants from more depressed areas of the country. This contributes to reshaping the urban system. Indeed, it is not only migrants from across Russia but from across the former Soviet republics who are attracted to jobs associated with oil and gas development on Sakhalin Island. They are led in this task by expatriate bosses from Europe and North America, who actively reshape urban settings by introducing a formerly nonexistent global socioeconomic character to Russian cities. Cities in the Southern Federal Okrug, such as Krasnodar, Stavropol, Vladikavkaz, and Novorossiysk, are also growing, but mostly as a result of large influxes of migrants from conflict-ridden areas of the North Caucasus and the former Soviet republics. The level of foreign direct investment (FDI) in each of Russia's 89 administrative units (tab. 6.2) mimics the trend in

Table 6.2   Amount of Foreign Direct Investment (FDI) in Russia for All 89 Administrative Units

More than 600,000 US$	400,000–599,999 US$	200,000–399,999 US$	Less than 199,999 US$	No FDI
Chelyabinsk Oblast	Republic of Tatarstan	Archangelsk Oblast	Altai Krai	Aginsky Buryatsky Autonomous Okrug
City of Moscow	Sverdlovsk Oblast	Kostromskaya Oblast	Amur Oblast	Chukotka Autonomous Okrug
City of St. Petersburg		Krasnodar Krai	Astrakhan Oblast	Evenki Autonomous Okrug
Krasnoyarsk Krai		Perm Oblast	Belgorod Oblast	Koryak Autonomous Okrug
Lipetskaya Oblast		Rostov Oblast	Bryansk Oblast	Republic of Altai
Moscow Oblast		Vladimir Oblast	Chitinskaya Oblast	Republic of Chechnya
Omsk Oblast			Cmolensk Oblast	Republic of Dagestan
Republic of Sakha			Irkutsk Oblast	Republic of Ingushetia
Sakhalin Oblast			Ivanovskaya Oblast	Republic of Kabardino-Balkarsk
Samarskaya Oblast			Jewish Autonomous Oblast	Republic of Karachaevo-Kershessk
Tyumen Oblast			Kaluzhskaya Oblast	Republic of Karachaya-Cherkassia
Yamalo-Nenets Autonomous Okrug			Kamchatka Oblast	Republic of North Ossetia-Alania
Vologda Oblast			Kemerov Oblast	Republic of Tyva
			Khabarov Krai	Republic of Kalmykia
			Kirov Oblast	Taimur Autonomous Okrug
			Komi-Permyatskii Autonomous Republic	Ust-ordinskaya Buryatsky Autonomous Okrug
			Kurganskaya Oblast	
			Kursk Oblast	
			Leningrad Oblast	
			Magadan Oblast	
			Murmansk Oblast	
			Nenets Autonomous Okrug	
			Nizhnegorodskaya Oblast	
			Novgorod Oblast	
			Novosibirsk Oblast	
			Orenburg Oblast	
			Orlov Oblast	
			Penzenskaya Oblast	
			Primorskii Krai	
			Pskov Oblast	
			Republic of Adigea	
			Republic of Bashkortistan	
			Republic of Buryatia	
			Republic of Chuvashia	
			Republic of Karelia	
			Republic of Khakasia	
			Republic of Komi	
			Republic of Marii El	
			Republic of Mordovia	
			Republic of Udmurt	
			Ryazanskaya Oblast	
			Saratov Oblast	
			Stavropolskii Krai	
			Tambov Oblast	
			Tomsk Oblast	
			Tverskaya Oblast	
			Tyl'skaya Oblast	
			Ulyanovskaya Oblast	
			Volgograd Oblast	
			Voronezh Oblast	
			Yaroslav Oblast	

2004 data; Goskomstat of Russia; http://www.gks.ru/gis/map_invest_03.htm.

migration for work (e.g., Moscow, Sakhalin *oblasts*) or for political asylum (e.g., the southern regions).

POLITICAL CHANGE AND THE URBAN SYSTEM

Democratization and political decentralization rival marketization and capitalization as important influences over post-Soviet urban geographies. The first democratic elections took place in cities throughout Russia shortly before the end of the Soviet Union. For the first time, local politicians, at least in theory, became accountable to local populations instead of to higher-level government officials. This accountability has had important new implications for the spatial structure of cities, as urban geographies begin to reflect local economic needs instead of national needs.

One immediate result of newfound local autonomy is the popularity of renaming cities and streets: names associated with prominent Soviet leaders have been replaced with historic names of the tsarist past. For example, Leningrad reverted to St. Petersburg and Sverdlovsk (named after a local communist leader) reverted to Ekaterinburg (literally, "Catherine's City," after Tsar Catherine the Great). Similarly, streets were renamed: Moscow's Gorky Street, named after the Soviet writer, was renamed Tverskaya Street. Historic names were usually already well known, but the changes contributed to a feeling among Russians of reclaiming their cities and neighborhoods.

Urban governments also reclaimed their economies. In capitalist economies, urban budgets generally reflect political priorities. In healthy urban economies, budgets grow.

Russian cities were protected from the vagaries of fiscal self-management prevalent in capitalist economies because they did not manage their own budgets or accumulate budgetary resources until the late Soviet period. Urban budgets and the revenues that fed those budgets were simply provided to Russian cities. This meant that urban politicians neither directly set economic priorities nor directly influenced the health of the urban economy. Although individual Russian city governments managed some housing and most social services, they did not provide funding for these activities.

Virtually overnight, managing budgets and taxes, as well as economic change and social services, became priorities of urban politicians and important indicators of the rapid introduction of capitalism to Russian cities. Today, this change is reflected in the types of jobs many college students aspire to have: many are entering privatized, fee-based colleges and universities to obtain high-quality degrees in law, finance, and business management. In the Soviet era, engineering and the sciences were more attractive to bright young students.

Changing Urban Structure and Function

Notable changes to urban form include new kinds of infill within the city, suburbanization, and "slumification." Important changes to urban function include increased finance and retail commerce at multiple scales (fig. 6.12). These changes are governed by processes absent during most of the 20th century—market forces and the active participation of municipal and regional governments.

New infill appears in city cores as old factories on land surrounding historic city centers are increasingly torn down and the

Figure 6.12   New urban infill in older neighborhoods in Moscow indicates the rise of consumerism in Russian cities. McDonald's, complete with drive through, shares center stage with Megaphone and Hyundai. (Photo by Jessica Graybill)

land reused for other purposes, such as housing (apartment buildings) or retail. Existing buildings in poor condition but in good locations are purchased, upgraded, and converted into, for example, office space or up-scale, gated apartments (fig. 6.13). This is leading to gentrification in Moscow and some other Russian cities, as new capital moves in and displaces long-time residents from city cores.

Suburbanization is one of many visible changes in urban form resulting from the development of real estate markets in cities where they had been prohibited for most of the 20th century. Single-family housing has appeared seemingly overnight in what has become a new ring of housing developments referred to as cottages (*kottedgi*), in what should be called suburbs surrounding the older Soviet and new post-Soviet multifamily high rises.

"Slumification" of parts of Russian cities is a result of transition from a command to a market economy. Run-down high-rise apartment buildings far from the city center are located on nearly worthless and often polluted land near former industrial production sites. These high-rises, and sometimes entire *microrayons*, are deteriorating rapidly as better-off tenants move to superior locations, leaving only poorer residents behind in what will likely become vertical slums.

Figure 6.13   In cities across Russia, infill in urban areas is appearing as the demand for property near city centers increases. Here, a high-rise apartment is raised next to older apartment buildings in Yuzhno-Sakhalinsk. (Photo by Jessica Graybill)

Finance and banking (particularly international banking) is increasingly a feature of larger post-Soviet Russian cities. Like restructuring related to deindustrialization in North American and European cities, the economic function of Russian cities and the new labor market are more oriented toward services in general, and toward financial and retail services in particular. An international financial and banking sector marks an important change in Russian cities, especially those located near manufacturing or natural resources. For example, European and Japanese banks can be found in Yuzhno-Sakhalinsk today, which marks a change in the function of this city from a small regional capital to a globalizing city involved in oil and other natural resource exploitation. Other Russian cities actively seek foreign investment to restructure their cities through partnerships among government actors and local and international businesses.

Retail commerce, powered by market forces, has also visibly changed the economic geography of Russian cities. Previously, retail trade occurred in state-owned stores or in a limited number of farmers' markets. Now, the spatial structure of urban retail has been altered dramatically. Transportation hubs (subways, rail stations) are multi-scalar centers of retail trade where peddlers vend wares and where retail centers, such as malls, have been built (fig. 6.14). These retail sites are becoming more permanent and prominent, and prerevolutionary shopping centers have regained their functions. For example, Moscow's famous

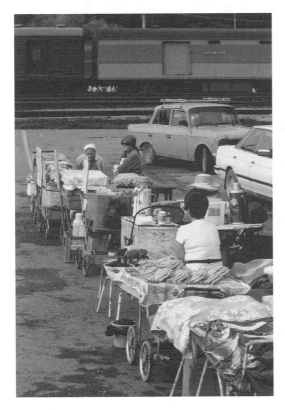

Figure 6.14   Any open space, especially if it is accessible to cars and trains, is fair game for street vendors. (Photo by Jessica Graybill)

Figure 6.15   The famous GUM department store on Red Square in Moscow was originally designed to showcase the new retail sector during the tsarist period. Now remodeled, it houses upscale foreign and domestic stores. (Photo by Beth Mitchneck)

GUM department store was remodeled as a high-end shopping mall (fig. 6.15). Cities like Moscow have also seen their urban periphery turned into new retail environments. Retail stores, such as IKEA, are opening outside of traditional retail centers, resulting in spatial extension of urban retail spaces.

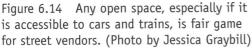

Sociocultural Change and the Urban System

Notable social transformations include changing labor and leisure structures. Transition from the Soviet to the post-Soviet era was difficult for those who were raised, trained, and already employed in the Soviet system, as it led to the disappearance of many jobs, the depletion of pension funds, and an unknown future.

Many turned to the countryside to survive (ruralization), but others (considered "victims" of economic transition) turned to alcohol, theft, and/or prostitution to survive (box 6.4). This has created social unrest, and because of Russia's slow response to providing social services to people in need a new and growing class of the very poor and the homeless exists today.

Although the *propiska* no longer exists, the current registration system exasperates people moving around the country for jobs. Nonpermanent residents working away from their hometowns must purchase temporary urban registration in a semi-legal system,

Box 6.4   Everyday Links between City and Country

Economic reform is occurring unevenly across post-Soviet Russia and has created vast differences among urban and rural places. Although some cities are clearly thriving in the transition to a market economy, 70 years of management under a command economic regime is making adjustment for many smaller urban and rural places difficult. In some cases, smaller urban and rural areas heavily depended on agriculture or urban subsidies in the Soviet era; without subsidization, these areas would not have been economically viable. In other cases, some urban and rural settlements were created explicitly for purposes of mass collectivization and industrialization. In the post-Soviet economy, residents have left for homelands, and as industry dries up, these cities become Soviet ghost towns scattered across Russia. The withdrawal of government support in all of these rural and urban hinterlands forces people to seek alternative ways to support themselves.

Although some out-migration has occurred from these regions, research indicates that many people stay because they depend on the informal social or strong kinship ties that they have forged in the hinterlands. Starting over in a new city is simply too difficult for many people, particularly for those originally from the hinterland, the elderly, the impoverished, and those who strongly believed in the Soviet system. Although rural areas across Russia are marked by poverty, declining living standards, and almost no integration into emerging capital markets, entrepreneurial activity is blossoming everywhere through barter-based and other informal economic networks. For those who stay behind, the foundation of the "new," traditional economy is products derived from activities like hunting, gathering, fishing, and domestic agricultural production.

For example, people have intensified agricultural crops and livestock numbers on household plots and at *dachas* (fig. 6.16). In some places, foresters report increased gathering of communal forest resources such as mushrooms, berries, or herbs. Although some products are consumed by families, they are often traded informally with neighbors or other village residents for other items, such as dairy products or clothing. Others drive into urban areas or sell products along the road for greater profit. In some cases, women have formed sales cooperatives for sharing the responsibility of selling gathered products in nearby cities. All of this activity is performed "off the books" and in addition to regular, paid jobs.

thus increasing their cost of living and jeopardizing their ability to succeed in Russia's new spatial economy.

There is a growing class with extra money to spend, resulting in increased consumerism and more availability of goods. A revived entertainment sector has also sparked a burgeoning service industry. However, although consumerism is increasing, goods, services, and entertainment remain expensive, and many people cannot afford a high quality of life in the new Russia.

Figure 6.16   Space around many Russian apartment buildings is devoted to agriculture during the short summer season. (Photo by Jessica Graybill)

Although traditional activities never ceased during the Soviet era, they are pursued in greater percentages today in rural regions and in nature areas (parks, forests) in or near urban areas. Many urbanites from smaller cities that are not part of strong, emerging capital markets in Russia have also turned to rural regions to cope with economic transition. For example, urbanites without access to affordable or fresh groceries are spending more time at their *dachas* or at rural relatives' houses to increase agricultural production for personal or familial consumption. The relationship is simple: the more tomatoes a family grows and processes collectively, the longer its members will all have fresh produce into the winter. Many urbanites increasingly hunt, fish, or forage in rural areas and transport these products back to the city, where they dry and store goods for personal use. In some cases, parents send preserved (dried, canned) foods to sons and daughters in other cities to supplement urban diets and reduce expenditures for the entire family, especially if the family was hit hard by economic transition. In this way, traditional activities are woven into everyday rural and urban lives across post-Soviet Russia.

Environmental Change and the Urban System

First raised in the late 1980s, environmental concerns are now growing across Russia. Ever-increasing publications relate the negative environmental legacy of Soviet urban development, suggesting the pub-lic's energized engagement with socio-environmental issues today. For example, one prominent issue plaguing urban areas is garbage. Larger amounts of waste in the post-Soviet era from imported packaged goods (Soviet goods were often wrapped only in paper and string) have not led

Figure 6.17   Increasing consumption and lagging public services are reflected in the garbage-strewn landscapes that surround many Russian apartment buildings. (Photo by Jessica Graybill)

to increased infrastructure to contain or remove garbage from urban centers. This results in garbage accumulating on streets (fig. 6.17), increasing environmentally hazardous conditions and socially contentious issues among citizens and city governments.

Remedying or eliminating urban environmental concerns and diseases, such as asthma, motor vehicle emissions, and chemical poisoning (such as lead) from contaminated water supplies, to name just a few, remain largely unaddressed in many cities. Urban environmental problems are largely understudied and misunderstood in the post-Soviet era. Many people feel that solving environmental woes is the government's responsibility and that they individually cannot respond because socioeconomic and political issues are currently more pressing (simply putting food on the table or obtaining rent money often constitute serious concerns).

On a positive note, however, federal environmental dialog since the mid-1990s includes the concept of sustainability. In creating new environmental policy directives, Russian policymakers are utilizing tsarist-era and Western ideas about living in harmony with the biosphere as a foundation for creating sustainable development. Indeed, some legislation from this period recognizes the need to achieve economic growth while balancing social and environmental goals and concerns. However, it remains to be seen how attainable these goals are in a market-driven Russia.

REPRESENTATIVE CITIES

Moscow: Russia's Past Meets Russia's Future

Perhaps no city captures Russia's long history as vividly as Moscow. Modern Moscow is a chaotic blend of brash and unfettered capitalism, seen in its casino lights and chic boutiques; monotonous housing estates from the Soviet period (where most residents live); new construction of glass skyscrapers and gated communities; and buildings renovated in the old Russian style. New Russian Orthodox churches join places of worship of many faiths (including other forms of Christianity and Islam) and are now part of the urban landscape.

In Moscow, Russia's past lives alongside its future. Founded over 850 years ago in the declining years of Kievan Rus, the city grew rapidly in importance until Peter the Great moved the capital to St. Petersburg. The 1917 Russian Revolution returned the seat of power to Moscow. On December 25, 1991, resignation of the last Soviet leader, Mikhail Gorbachev, once again brought Moscow into the international limelight and opened the city—its landscape and residents—to massive changes.

After the collapse of the Soviet Union, Moscow exploded with the signs of capitalism. Foreign investment flooded the city, and new foreign and Russian capital created business centers, real estate companies, and a new retail sector. Once empty avenues filled with cars—seemingly overnight. In the early 1990s, kiosks appeared everywhere stocked with an improbable mix of everything from candy bars to vodka, socks, and toys. Now, more permanent stores selling liquor, food, clothing, and toys, as well as every other possible consumer good, largely replace kiosks. Malls also have replaced hastily built and remodeled stores. Historically the political, economic, media, educational, and cultural center of the country, Moscow's new economy restructured and added to the city's existing functions, and it became the nation's banking and consumer capital (box 6.5).

Moscow is vastly richer than most other parts of Russia, partially as a result of inheriting immensely valuable real estate from the Soviet government and Communist Party. Using its control over most real estate along its borders, the city leveraged behind-the-scenes business deals with private sector investors. Acquiring office space often means establishing a business partnership directly or indirectly with the city. Some believe that the city's policymaking is often driven by organized crime agendas more than by citizen needs and desires.

The introduction of capitalism and economic explosion has resulted in a highly fractured city. Residents of the city experience life in vastly disparate ways. For the expatriate community, continuously growing as a result of foreign investment, Moscow is ranked as one of the most expensive cities in the world. Ratings vary, with some placing it as the most expensive city to live in and others raking it closer to the 40th most expensive. Expense is related to choices that expatriates make for housing, dining, and other forms of consumption. For the "New Russians," the city is a 24-hour shopping, dining, and business extravaganza. For the vast majority of Muscovites, however, life in the city is, as they say, "normal."

But what is normal in post-Soviet Moscow? Normal now includes choking traffic jams. An internet company, Yandex, studied traffic patterns and reported that from spring 2006 to spring 2007, drivers in Moscow spent an average of 11 hours a month standing still in traffic jams that on average would block 1,500 cars at a time. Always a multiethnic city, Moscow is now increasingly so because of a large, constant flow of labor migrants from other parts of Russia and former Soviet republics. "Normal" still means a highly cosmopolitan and

Box 6.5   Business Services in Moscow and the New Russian Yuppies

Olga Gritsai

In the 1990s, Moscow, as the hearth of reforms in Russia, has experienced dynamic structural transformations in both the economic and social spheres. One of the new and rapidly expanding sectors is business services: this sector's share in employment has grown from practically zero in 1990 to 8.5–10% in 2000 (still much smaller than in the largest Western cities but amazingly high for 10 years). By 2007 this figure rose to 15–16%. Such activities as banking, insurance, advertising, accountancy, corporate legal services, and management consultancies, along with a thriving real estate sector, became well established in the city economy. Big international companies operating in these sectors were among the first to register their offices in Moscow, followed by numerous Russian-owned companies, some of them quickly turning into quite successful competitors with the international giants.

Companies of this type created a specific job market, recruiting mostly young people with university diplomas, good knowledge of foreign languages, and sufficient computer skills. Given the relatively late start of language and computer training in Russia, it is clear why the age limit for the employees in new business services is very low: even those in command of such companies are in most cases not older that 40 or 45, and the general cohort of such employees is about 22–30 years old. Many of them start without any professional education or experience; they hail from disciplines as diverse as geology and journalism, and have to learn their new profession on the job. The same process is occurring in the service departments of the producing companies: the service departments' staffs are on average much younger than the production departments' staffs. The possibility of quickly obtaining a career with a high salary (comparable to Western salaries), prevents these young professionals from leaving Russia and looking for alternative jobs abroad. Additionally, another recent trend involves young Russians with Western diplomas returning to Russia to start their own businesses or to establish a career more quickly than they could in the West. The challenging atmosphere of a "new Klondike" seems to be often more attractive for young professionals than does a stable and comfortable Western environment.

These well-off, professionally educated, and culturally advanced young people have formed a particular social group, which is similar to the idea of the Western yuppie, but which combines pragmatism with the extravagancy and nonconformism of the BoBo (bohemian bourgeoisie) lifestyle. These individuals know the reward of a good education, an awareness often confirmed by their extra training abroad. Their monthly income is about $5,000–$7,000 higher than that of the average population; 70% of Muscovites still have incomes below $1,000 per month. The new Russian yuppies like comfort, are customers of fitness-clubs, prefer healthy food, and have nice cars and mobile telephones; at the same time, they are well informed about cultural events, they attend fashionable films and performances designed for an intellectually advanced audience, and they are among the most frequent Internet users, considering Internet to be their main source of information and means of communication. Their salaries are growing very quickly, but never quickly enough to keep pace with prices of the goods and services they desire. Moscow has for many years been one of the cities with the highest cost of living in the world, even competing with Tokyo for this distinction.

The quick growth of business services and their yuppie-like employees has been followed by the booming rise of a certain type of cultural industry: elite coffeehouses, trendy little restaurants with the functions of leisure clubs, fitness and bowling clubs, and so forth. Even in a city as large as Moscow, the world of yuppies seems to be rather small: very often, visitors of these clubs already know each other as colleagues, from their time spent jointly in university or from earlier visited clubs. The norm is "healthy" behavior: freshly pressed juices, alcohol-free cocktails, and private coaches. Exotic types of tea and coffee are more popular here than are strong drinks, beer, or non-alcoholic beverages (cola, tonic water, etc.). Many of these cafés and clubs have strong security, with controls at the entrance to protect their image; high prices are also used to filter outsiders. Material welfare, career advancement, and the freedom of self-realization are thus the main values of this new young group of Russians, making them quite distinct within the heterogeneous post-Soviet society.

Until recently, Russian yuppies seemed to be purely a Moscow phenomenon. Moscow still contains 25–30% of national employment in business services, and remains by far the largest location of corporate headquarters and the major national provider and consumer of Internet services. But things have begun to change in recent years. Contrasts between the prosperity of this group of young Muscovites and those of the same age outside the city are still large, but they are getting smaller. At the same time, a debate exists about polarization among the young Muscovites themselves: those who don't have the right education, intellect, or character to become yuppies have quite a chance to end up as "yuffies" (young urban failures): to get involved with drugs or other illegal activities and to slowly become marginalized. The problem is that there is very little in the middle between these two categories of youngsters.

The relative ease of making a career in private business also creates serious generational conflicts. It is indeed very difficult for many people, whose professional life occurred mostly in Soviet times, to accept that their children, who have zero experience and few skills, are able to earn salaries several times greater than those of their parents just after graduating from university—not to speak of how these new salaries compare to the tiny pensions received by the grandparents of this generation. Different values and priorities, rationalism instead of the traditionally praised Russian spirituality, a preference for the new, an appreciation for more technologically advanced sources of information, and an ease with the new market reality all enhance generational misunderstanding over and above the degree to which it would occur had Russia experienced an economically stable development trajectory.

Figure 6.18   In the post-Soviet economy, these street musicians perform for money on the streets of St. Petersburg, in the shadow of grand buildings from the tsarist and Soviet eras. (Photo by Stanley Brunn)

vibrant urban culture, but now one that also ranks as a world city.

St. Petersburg: Window on the West—Again?

Founded in 1703 by Peter the Great as Russia's "window on the West," St. Petersburg remains a city of ornate palaces and water-filled canals. Shots fired from the battleship *Aurora,* now docked across from the tsars' Winter Palace, signaled the start of the Russian Revolution in 1917. As victorious Soviet leaders concentrated economic and political resources to build a highly centralized and closed society in the new capital of Moscow, St. Petersburg, renamed Leningrad, faded quietly into its role as Russia's second city.

Leningrad continued growing, albeit not as quickly as Moscow, and the population doubled from 1917 to reach a high of about 5 million in 1989. Despite losing some population since the collapse of the Soviet Union, it remains Russia's second largest city. In the post-Soviet period, like other industrial Russian cities, its official population size declined to about 4.6 million in 2006. Home to many prestigious universities and research institutions, Leningrad depended on educational and research activities, defense-related industries, and the city's unique cultural legacy including the world renowned Hermitage Museum, which continues to attract visitors. Its dependence on the military–industrial complex necessitated significant restructuring in the post-Soviet period.

After 1991, the city's original name was restored and it moved to recapture and build on its distant past. Despite a deteriorating economic and financial situation caused by the near collapse of government support for defense, education, and culture, the newly elected city leadership began thinking strategically about St. Petersburg's future. In the mid-1990s, the city embarked on a strategic planning process, the first city in Russia to do so (fig. 6.18). Unlike top-down Soviet central planning, strategic planning is a participatory process, building on a partnership between local government, private businesses, and citizens to analyze a city's current situation and possible development scenarios. After extensive discussions with private businesses, residents, and local organizations in St. Petersburg, participants concluded the city's strengths lay in its highly educated population; its ranking as the largest-capacity port in Russia; and its favorable location, not far from Finland and the rest of Europe, with excellent access to major railroads and highways. To improve long-term development prospects, St. Petersburg is working to improve economic growth by creating a favorable business climate and by integrating into the world economy. To improve residents' quality of life, the city seeks to improve its natural environment and establish a more favorable social environment. For example, road congestion and air pollution has increased dramatically because per capita car ownership has more than doubled recently. It remains to be seen whether the government of St. Petersburg can improve living standards and promote long-term restructuring.

Recent evidence suggests that the city has been at least modestly successful at attracting investment and building upon its past economic and cultural strengths in the short term. It has attracted recent investment from Toyota and Hewlett-Packard. Unlike other cities that have not attempted to create a culture of participatory urban development, it is, however, beginning to experience public outcry over recent land use choices. The state-owned natural gas monopoly and wealthiest corporation, Gazprom, intends to build a new skyscraper in St. Petersburg. Because the city and its residents pride themselves on its low-rise city skyline built around the historic city

center, construction of a central skyscraper has created an international cause célèbre. UNESCO has even asked the city of St. Petersburg (on the list of World Heritage sites) to halt the project in order to study potential impact on the city's historical monuments. Yet the balance of power appears tilted toward private business, and the likelihood of a new St. Petersburg skyline is high.

Vladivostok: Russia Looks to its Eurasian Future?

From 1958 to 1991 Vladivostok was a closed city where even Soviet citizens needed permission to enter this home of the Russian Navy's Pacific Fleet. Before this, Vladivostok had been an international city. Valuable for its port facilities and proximity to Asian markets, the city drew a diverse international population, including Chinese, Koreans, Japanese, and Americans. Since 1991, these populations are back, as the city is now open to foreign tourists and businesses. Indeed, both the United States and Japan operate consulates in Vladivostok to aid citizens (and businesses) interested in the city and surrounding regions.

Founded in 1860, Vladivostok is the capital of Primorsky Krai and is the Russian far east's largest city, with nearly 600,000 residents. It is the largest Russian port on the Pacific Ocean and historically has been an important regional industrial center for shipping and fishing. Located 3,800 miles (6,430 km) from Moscow, it is the eastern terminus of the Trans-Siberian Railroad. The great distance to European Russia feeds the imagination of Vladivostok as a gateway to exotic, Asian Russia. Historically, it led Vladivostok residents to be self-reliant and to expect little from Moscow; indeed, the first Soviet leader to visit Vladivostok was Nikita Khrushchev in 1954. Now, citizens of Vladivostok look towards Asia for future economic growth. Also headquarters of the Far Eastern Division of the Russian Academy of Sciences, the city hosts 14 academic and research institutions. These factors have fueled hopes that Vladivostok could become an urban economic hub for a range of businesses. For example, entrepreneurs dream of Vladivostok-based regional eco-tourism, and port facilities are a strong asset in rebuilding a strong import–export city on the Pacific. Views of the bay from the hills around the city also provide incentive for restoration of the historic center and its tsarist-era buildings and monuments, many of which could be refurbished to rival those in St. Petersburg.

Unfortunately, Vladivostok has been plagued by two negative economic developments since 1991: (1) the rise of organized crime and (2) the legacy of environmental degradation. The rise of informal and mafia-driven economies has hindered the growth of legitimate, tax-paying businesses. The retail-oriented black market is largely controlled by illegal Chinese immigrants who have moved into the city. With the collapse of Soviet industry and subsequent deindustrialization, many people now purchase low-quality, unregulated Chinese goods as a result of Vladivostok's proximity to China. Increased organized crime in Vladivostok and Primorsky Krai since 1991 purportedly involves not only Russian mafia but numerous mafia-like groups from former Soviet republics in Central Asia. Many elected government officials work with, instead of against, organized crime. Illegal trade includes marine resources from China, cars from Japan, heroin from Central Asia, and timber exports from Russia to China and Korea.

In addition to economic difficulties, Vladivostok suffers from severe air, water, and soil pollution. Ecologists consider much of the city to be hazardously polluted by heavy metals and industrial (cadmium, mercury, arsenic) and agricultural (nitrates, phosphates) waste. Despite being located adjacent to the Pacific Ocean, local wind and offshore water circulation patterns in Amursky Bay do not remove pollutants from densely populated or industrial urban areas. As in many Soviet cities, urban housing and industrial sites are intermixed in the city; Vladivostok has over 50 intra-urban industrial sites. Unchecked, pollutants have built up over time, and their detrimental effects on human health are only slowly becoming recognized.

As an intellectual capital of the Russian far east, Vladivostok has much to offer post-Soviet Russia, despite the need for ecological and legal crackdowns on polluters and numerous illegal activities, respectively. The presence of a multitude of academic and research capital in this beautiful location could prove to be a boon to the city in the future, especially as foreign business maintains an interest in the city.

Yuzhno-Sakhalinsk: The International Power of Oil

Yuzhno-Sakhalinsk, located on Sakhalin Island in Russia's far east, is an oil boomtown fueled by multinational investment. This city, long a small urban hub for the military and natural resource exports (coal, oil, fish, timber), is ushering in the era of globalization in the Russian far east because of its proximity to offshore oil and gas reserves in the Sea of Okhotsk. The *oblast* is a leading destination for foreign direct investment (FDI), indicating the importance of natural resources and regional centers to Russia as a whole. Located 4,000 miles (6,500 km) from Moscow and only 110 miles (175 km) from Japan, Yuzhno-Sakhalinsk is sited on an tsarist-era settlement for exiled prisoners (Vladimirovka) that later became a Japanese village (Toyohara) during Japanese rule of southern Sakhalin Island (below the 50th parallel) from 1905–1945. After WWII, the USSR reclaimed the entire island, and Yuzhno-Sakhalinsk was created as the new *oblast* capital for Sakhalin and the Kuril Islands.

Yuzhno-Sakhalinsk embodies the multi-ethnic character of Soviet-era cities. Home to about 175,000 people, the urban population is comprised of ethnic Russians, Ukrainians, and other Slavs; ethnic Koreans; and native peoples of Sakhalin (Nivkh, Evenk). Koreans, the last "newcomers," were brought to Sakhalin during WWII to work the coal mines, and are today a distinct ethnic group (Sakhalin Koreans). Expatriates associated with the hydrocarbon industry have arrived since 1995, and it is common to find workers from Europe, North America, and Russia's neighboring states residing semi-permanently in city hotels. The city's multiethnic history is noted in the mélange of architectural styles in the city. The few remaining traditional Japanese structures stand next to tsarist-era frontier houses (turn-of-the-20th-century wooden multifamily dwellings with rudimentary utilities), Soviet-era five-story apartment buildings, post-Soviet suburban "cottages" (on the city's outskirts), and gleaming Western-style offices and houses occupied by expatriate executives. Previously a small urban center connected to the MIC, the large and increasing presence of foreigners in Yuzhno-Sakhalinsk is a big change for this formerly closed city. Many residents struggle to understand their rapidly changing place in the post-Soviet era.

Offshore hydrocarbon sites lie further north than Yuzhno-Sakhalinsk, but smaller settlements there lack the infrastructure and political capital necessary to accommodate international companies. Hence, as the *oblast* center, Yuzhno-Sakhalinsk has become the bustling urban hub for the hydrocarbon industry. New service industries associated with hydrocarbons are changing the labor market for the city, but not for the entire island. Current spatial patterns of economic growth mimic the Soviet urban settlement pattern where large urban centers were favored (box 6.6). The economic boom occurring in this city provides hope for future regional economic growth and is a refreshing change from the Soviet period when the government had to send people to work on Sakhalin using the *propiska* system. Today, it is a destination city both for younger generations from the Russian far east and for international migrants associated with the hydrocarbon industry, each of which seek promising jobs.

While Yuzhno-Sakhalinsk enjoys international investment and a relatively high standard of living, many residents wonder when they will see benefits from oil extraction promised to them by the regional government and multinational companies. Many fear that promises made in the mid-1990s to develop the island will remain unfulfilled. For example, infrastructure projects (transportation, education, etc.) promised in return for allowing hydrocarbon extraction have not actualized, and residents remain saddled with decrepit Soviet-era dwellings, transportation systems, and services. Gated and gleaming buildings for expatriate workers taunt neighboring buildings lacking decently operating heat, hot water, or electricity. This disparity raises questions about the strength of Yuzhno-Sakhalinsk as an emerging hub in Russia's globalizing economy, as well as the preparedness of urban and

---

Box 6.6   In the Shadow of Urban Growth

Sakhalin *oblast* today is a destination for multinational businesses because of offshore hydrocarbon extraction. This brings socioeconomic change in two places strongly associated with the offshore industry: the city of Yuzhno-Sakhalinsk and the town of Nogliki. Focusing on the relationship between a rural town (Nogliki) and a dominant city (Yuzhno-Sakhalinsk) shows how Soviet-era regional planning still dictates the growth (or decline) of a region's urban areas in the new market economy. It also indicates Russia's interest in developing natural resources over local places and people.

Yuzhno-Sakhalinsk, the regional headquarters for Sakhalin's multibillion dollar hydrocarbon industry, reaps most of the *oblast*'s economic benefits. Bureaucracy requires all expatriates working the offshore oil rigs near Nogliki to pass through Yuzhno-Sakhalinsk, where economic benefits include revenue from hotels, restaurants, and nightclubs, and social benefits include an increasingly cosmopolitan and diverse population.

Meanwhile, 350 miles (560 km) north, Nogliki is a desolate transit hub for laborers and oil products to and from offshore rigs. Nogliki's population (~10,000) includes people with Slavic heritages (93%), and Sakhalin's indigenous populations, Nivkh and Evenk (7%). An *urban-type settlement*, Nogliki is a large village that was created in the Soviet era to resettle and consolidate numerous scattered and smaller villages. In this way, Nogliki *rayon* (minor administrative unit) was urbanized, and labor and the distribution of goods and services were centrally managed.

Before 1991, Nogliki's industries included onshore oil extraction, logging, fishing, and caribou herding, all of which are now nearly defunct. To cope, many residents returned full-time to traditional activities, including hunting, gathering, small-scale agriculture, and fishing. In this process of ruralization, some people live year-round in summer *dachas* because they cannot afford Nogliki's cost of living in the new market economy (average monthly salaries are less than $200 a month). All goods are imported and cost around 50% more than in Yuzhno-Sakhalinsk. Grocery stores largely sell confections and alcohol, because staples like potatoes and fish don't sell: residents grow and catch their own food. In 2005, for example, 1 kg of salmon cost $15 but remained unpurchased because fishing in Nogliki's rivers and bays is unregulated.

---

regional governance to fight for even economic growth for all citizens in the post-Soviet era.

Noril'sk: The Legacy of Heavy Industry

Home to over 100,000 people, Noril'sk is the northernmost large city in the world. Temperatures in the city can reach −58°C, and snow cover lasts about 70% of the year.

This remote city was settled in the 1920s by gulag laborers (prisoners in the tsarist and Soviet penal systems of forced labor camps) who worked until the mid-1950s to construct many of the city's buildings, its mines, and its smelting facilities for nickel and other metal ores, most of which remain in operation today. Because of its location in the Russian far north, it is not surprising

Although infrastructure supporting the offshore industry could have been built in Nogliki, it was not considered a viable location because of its small size and limited urban infrastructure. Expatriate workers even bunk outside town limits in a gated, guarded camp, strangling Nogliki's ability to benefit from resource development by limiting investment in the town's infrastructure and service sectors. Foreigners only occasionally venture into town to visit the two or three restaurants, and then only for a few hours.

Initially, Nogliki was receptive to a multinational development path: residents saw it as their entry into the global market economy. However, despite its location in the path of multinational activity and despite company and government promises of local development, Nogliki is not thriving. Walking Nogliki's streets evokes an image of preindustrialized Russia: most buildings lack year-round water, electricity, and often even heat. Instead of thriving from multinational development, Nogliki is experiencing negative growth through ruralization. Realizing their town cannot grow because of the ways companies and the government have chosen to utilize Nogliki, residents blame legal contracts that favor profits for hydrocarbon companies and the federal government over local people and places.

However, Nogliki's residents are not tolerating negative development for the long term. Residents—particularly the indigenous population, whose industry and traditional livelihood (caribou herding) may be hardest hit—have utilized the freedom of speech afforded in the post-Soviet era to increasingly vocalize their discontent through global channels. Today, Nogliki is a hotbed of environmental and indigenous activism in the face of multinational resource development. Local and indigenous people document cultural and environmental degradation caused by on- and offshore hydrocarbon activity and broadcast this information through NGOs such as Sakhalin Environmental Watch (www.sakhalin.environment.ru) in Yuzhno-Sakhalinsk and abroad.

Nogliki exemplifies difficulties experienced in numerous smaller towns across Russia as the links among urban, rural, and industrial places change in the post-Soviet era. Understanding the growth of Yuzhno-Sakhalinsk and the decline of Nogliki raises questions about future urban and regional development, especially as Russia increasingly participates in the global economy.

to see native Evenk driving caribou-drawn sleighs through the city, a vivid juxtaposition with modern trams, cars, and buses. Noril'sk remains a closed city for most Russians and foreigners.

Noril'sk exemplifies the importance of natural resource extraction and industry to the Soviet Union, and now to Russia. Because of the priority placed on heavy industry in the Soviet era, Noril'sk gained enough citizens by 1939 to earn the status of an urban settlement, which marked the beginning of its industrial boom related to the nickel ore industry, a legacy lasting into the post-Soviet period. Once state owned but now in private hands, the smelting operations of Noril'sk Nickel remain a driving force for the continued existence of Noril'sk, as they are the primary employer in this city. Some out-migration has occurred since 1991: many people have left to join family members or find jobs in other parts of Russia. Others remain because of long-held social networks for everyday survival and the high wages from the ore industry (up to four times the national average).

Because the city did not exist prior to the Soviet era, Noril'sk is not graced with tsarist architecture or monuments: it is instead comprised of severely degraded Soviet-era concrete buildings in numerous high-rise *microrayons* that abruptly rise up from the vast zone of continuous permafrost (soil at or below the freezing point of water) in northern Siberia. As a result of the urban heat island, the permafrost has warmed up in the city, and the foundations of much urban infrastructure have been compromised. Much of this infrastructure is already in disrepair, which is one of the many issues that democratically elected local city governments must face in the post-Soviet period.

The industrial facilities for nickel smelting are located right in the city. This contributes to massive urban pollution problems that go largely unchecked by Noril'sk Nickel's corporate headquarters, located in Moscow (a remnant of command economic planning). Although Noril'sk's history as an "urban gulag" is legendary, the most notorious legacy of Noril'sk may be its reputation as the most polluted city in Russia today. Air, soil, and water pollution haunt the city, degrading both the environment and the health of all living inhabitants. One result of ore smelting is the emission of sulfur dioxide (SO_2), which causes the formation of acid rain (SO_2 combines with water to create and release sulfuric acid, H_2SO_4), which precipitates back on the city and releases contaminants (acid, heavy metals) into the soil and water supply. Some busi-

ness plans even propose mining Noril'sk's urban soils, because the proportion of metals in them is economically viable. Pollution not only contributes to the degradation of the built and natural urban environments; human illnesses (such as lung cancer, asthma, and sickness related to heavy metal contamination) are also common in this city. The forests and tundra that surround the city are mostly in decline today, which speaks to decades of neglect of both urban and regional environmental issues in Russia. It remains to be seen if newly developing environmental awareness among citizens can combine with democratic elections and market forces to help alleviate the dire urban environmental problems in Noril'sk.

Kazan: Volga Port in Tatarstan

Kazan, the capital of the Republic of Tatarstan, is the seventh largest city in Russia (1.1 million) and one of the largest outside of European Russia. Kazan is distinctive for many reasons, not least of which is the political struggle of the 1990s that resulted in the establishment of the republic as one of the leaders of the independence movement within the Russian Federation. Two recent events have drawn worldwide attention to this city along the Volga River. In 2000, UNESCO included the historical city center on its World Heritage List, which denotes places of universal value to the world community. And in 2005, the city celebrated its 1,000th anniversary.

While most cities in Russia are largely multiethnic, few have as large and powerful a non-Russian population as this city and republic. Tatars, whose origins are in the Central Asian steppes, make up the largest ethnic group in the republic: 48% of the population is Tatar whereas 43% is Russian. It is one of the few non-Russian political jurisdictions that actually have a plurality of the group for which it is named. Russian settlement and domination of the city, however, goes back to the 16th century when Ivan the Terrible invaded the region. Even today, despite a plurality of the Tatar population in the republic, the city has a slight majority of Russians (about 50% relative to about 42% Tatar). Other non-Russian populations from the Volga region also live in the city including the Chuvash, a Turkic group, and the Maris. Migration in the 1990s brought new ethnic groups to the city, namely those from the Caucasus and Central Asia.

The Tatar population is traditionally Islamic. Kazan's history as a prominent Muslim city extends back to the 14th century. Today, the city is home to a new school training Russians in the Islamic religion, the Islamic University. Since the early 1990s, at least 40 new mosques have been built in the city. The city government helped construct a new mosque on the grounds of the historic Kremlin. The political and social significance of both the site and the leading role of the city government should be recognized as a symbol of cultural as well as political independence from Russia. The city's cultural independence from Russia is also seen in the historic forms of architecture that make up the urban built environment. Buildings in the city combine many architectural styles, ranging from baroque to Moorish. Bas-reliefs created by traditional Tatar stone workers embellish buildings in the city, and minarets dot the skyline.

Kazan and the region have major economic significance to the Russian economy. The city is a major port on the Volga River, the main water route through European Russia.

The city and the region have been a transportation gateway for centuries. Currently, the European Union is helping to modernize its port facilities, and in 2005 it became one of only a few cities in Russia to receive a direct loan from the World Bank. The city's economy is also strongly tied to the production of transportation equipment. It has produced military transportation, including helicopters, and is home to KamAZ, still a gigantic automotive production firm.

PROSPECTS

Cities in Russia today are the products of tsarist, Soviet, and post-Soviet Russian societies, as well as of the many different ethnic groups and cultures that have inhabited the region for at least 1,000 years. The blending of this diverse set of cultures and histories results in cities with varied built and social landscapes. The natural environment, however, has always wielded an important influence over the location of urban settlements, irrespective of the time period or the dominant ethnic group. The harsh Siberian landscape originally posed barriers to Russian expansion and settlement. Like the construction of St. Petersburg (now heralded as a triumph although the city is located where many during the tsarist period thought it could not be built), widespread urban settlement of Siberia became a great accomplishment of Soviet central planners. This was in spite of environmental degradation wrought by settlement and the immense social and cultural costs of stranding of people in isolated and inhospitable places, not to mention the immeasurable financial implications. Cities in the post-Soviet period continue to struggle with the consequences of the harnessing of nature and the legacy of the Soviet era's internal spatial structure of cities.

City and federal governments are attempting to integrate cities as economically and politically disparate and distant as Krasnodar and Vladivostok. They must consider the implications of integration for internal Russian transportation and communications systems. Additionally, the integration of former Soviet cities into a larger geopolitical and economic framework is a critical issue for the 21st century. For example, should cities closer to Tokyo or Beijing than Moscow rely primarily upon trade within Russia for economic direction, or should they look to Asia for new markets and influence? What will happen to cities constructed within the Soviet system but now functioning under another? How will long-lived structures such as factories, housing, roads, school, and other buildings be adapted for new uses in a market economy? How (and by whom) should pollution in urban environments be addressed? How sustainable are cities in extreme environments, such as the Arctic and Siberia? How can cities quite distant from one another remain connected both economically and politically? Perhaps most importantly, what will happen to the people who live and work in Russian cities? What level and nature of integration into the European Union should the Russian government promote? How far down the path of destroying the Soviet housing system should Russian cities go? How best should Russian cities influence land-use change? Will the current increase in birth rates stem the overall population decline in Russia? What will national declining population mean for the regeneration of many Russian cities? Answers to these and many other questions confront the people of Russia today as they continue the process of reinventing their cities.

SUGGESTED READINGS

Axenov, Konstantin, Isolde Brade, and Evgenij Bondarchuk. 2006. *The Transformation of Urban Space in Post-Soviet Russia.* London, New York: Routledge. Focuses on the transition from socialism and communism to democracy and capitalism in urban areas of post-Soviet Russia and Eastern Europe.

Bater, James H. 1996. *Russia and the Post-Soviet Scene: A Geographical Perspective.* New York: John Wiley. Surveys the human geography of the former Soviet Union.

Chernetsky, Vitaly. 2007. *Mapping Postcommunist Cultures: Russia and Ukraine in the Context of Globalization.* Montreal: McGill-Queen's University Press. Focuses on post-Soviet cultural developments, puts them in a global context, and suggests that Russia and Ukraine form the basis of post-Soviet culture.

Feshbach, Murray. 1995. *Ecological Disaster: Cleaning Up the Hidden Legacy of the Soviet Regime: A Twentieth Century Fund Report.* New York: Twentieth Century Foundation. An early report on the underestimation of the former Soviet Union's health and environmental problems, with interesting coverage of satellite monitoring.

French, R. Antony. 1995. *Plans, Pragmatism and People: The Legacy of Soviet Planning for Today's Cities.* London: University College London Press. Examines the assumption that cities in the Soviet Union were the exemplification of Marxist social planning.

Hill, Fiona, and Clifford G. Gaddy. 2003. *The Siberian Curse: How Communist Planners Left Russia Out in the Cold.* Washington, D.C.: Brookings Institution Press. Traces the failed attempt to establish an industrial base in Siberia, and makes an argument for abandoning the eastern territories because of their economic instability.

Hemment, Julie. 2007. *Empowering Women in Russia: Activism, Aid, and NGOs.* Bloomington: Indiana University Press. Takes a look at Russian women's groups and the international foundations that supported them during the collapse of the Soviet Union in the 1990s.

Ioffe, Grigorii, and Tatyana Nefedova. 2000. *The Environs of Russian Cities.* Lewiston, NY: Edwin Mellen Press. Looks at the outlying areas of Russian cities, examines urban and rural areas, and presents case studies of Moscow and Yaroslavl through the 1990s.

Milner-Gulland, Robin, and Nikolai Dejevsky. 1998. *Cultural Atlas of Russia and the Former Soviet Union.* New York: Checkmark Books. Presents the historical culture of the former Soviet Union by analyzing geography, history, archaeology, anthropology, and the arts.

Turnock, David. 2001. *Eastern Europe and the Former Soviet Union: Environment and Society.* New York: Oxford University Press. Analyses the transition from centralized totalitarian government within the former Soviet Union and Eastern Europe.

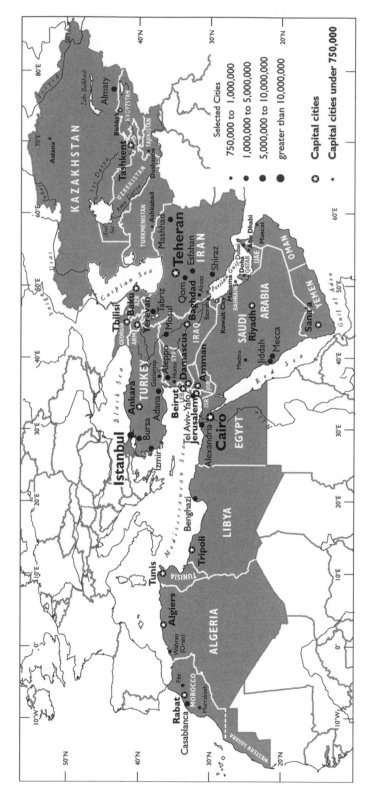

Figure 7.1 Major Cities of the Greater Middle East. *Source: UN World Urbanization Prospects, 2005 revision* [online].

7

Cities of the Greater Middle East

DONALD J. ZEIGLER AND DONA J. STEWART

KEY URBAN FACTS

Total Population	492 million
Percent Urban Population	58.7%
Total Urban Population	289 million
Most Urbanized Countries	Kuwait (98.3%)
	Bahrain (96.5%)
	Qatar (95.4%)
Least Urbanized Countries	Tajikistan (24.7%)
	Yemen (27.3%)
	Kyrgyzstan (35.8%)
Annual Urban Growth Rate	2.2%
Number of Megacities	1
Number of Cities of More Than 1 Million	37
Three Largest Cities	Cairo, Istanbul, Teheran
World Cities	Istanbul, Cairo, Jerusalem

KEY CHAPTER THEMES

1. Urban landscapes of the Greater Middle East have been shaped by the natural environment and by religion (particularly Islam, but also Judaism and Christianity).
2. The location of cities has been strongly influenced by the availability of water in the form of rivers, springs, and underground aquifers.
3. The world's first cities grew up in the Fertile Crescent, along the Nile, and on the Anatolian Plateau.
4. Traditional city cores are, or were, walled and dominated by a citadel, or *kasbah*.
5. Urban economic geography has traditionally been shaped by the commerce that coursed across the region, a result of its relative location at a tricontinental junction.

6. Some states have a primate city, some have two or more competing large cities, and a few have fully developed urban hierarchies.

7. The "urban triangle" that defines the region's core has a foothold on all three continents and in three different cultural realms (Arab, Turkic, Persian).

8. During the 20th century, oil and gas revenues have turned some of the least urbanized countries into some of the most urbanized.

9. The urban population geography of the oil-rich states has been transformed by the millions of "guest workers," particularly from South and Southeast Asia.

10. Major urban problems range from rapid population growth and unemployment to the preservation of heritage resources.

Urbanism as a way of life seems to have originated in the region we call the Middle East (fig. 7.1). Solidly anchored in this tricontinental junction are the roots of the Western city. Perhaps it is no accident that our word *urban* still carries the name of the world's first truly urban places, Ur and Uruk, in southern Mesopotamia. These early agglomerated settlements, dating from at least five millennia B.C., offered protection, security, and the ability to control resources (such as water) and trade. Ideas about urban development and planning originated here and spread as by-products of commerce and conquest.

Over the course of the 20th century, the "Middle East" as a regional appellation replaced the older "Near East." As a vernacular term, it has also expanded in geographical coverage. For the sake of brevity, the term "Middle East" is used in this chapter to refer to the "Greater Middle East," that crescent of territory stretching from Morocco, eastward across North Africa, through the lands of southwest Asia, to the steppes of Kazakhstan. This great sweep of territory is united by a basic core of similar geographical characteristics and shared history (fig. 7.2). First, in its physical attributes, the Middle East is predominantly arid, though river systems and oases mitigate the region's dryness. Second, in its cultural attributes, the Middle East is marked by the shared history experienced through successive Islamic empires and their interaction with the broader world. Third, in its relative location, the Middle East really is in the "middle"—it is in the center of the Eastern Hemisphere, a frontier between the civilizations of Europe, eastern Asia, and Africa. In short, cities here have been designed around access to water, God (or gods), and trade.

Dry and seasonally dry, arid and semi-arid, desert and steppe—these are descriptors of the Middle East's physical geography. Most of the region suffers a deficit of fresh water. Available water comes from winter showers, orographic precipitation, exotic streams, rivers, natural springs, and shallow aquifers. In arid areas, the location of water has historically determined the location of population centers and the growth of towns and cities. In turn, the dry environment presented a set of natural obstacles which these urban centers had to overcome: scorching sun, high daytime temperatures, desert winds, dusty air, and scarcity of water. The same dry environment—the desert—offered the earliest of cities a set of natural frontiers. The surrounding desert served as a buffer, providing protection from potential invaders.

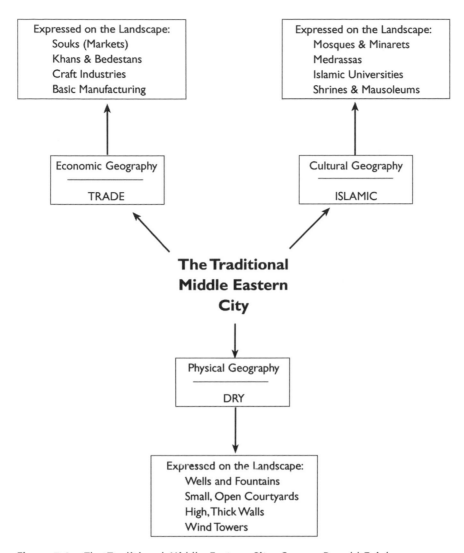

Figure 7.2   The Traditional Middle Eastern City. *Source:* Donald Zeigler.

Contemporary Middle Eastern cities also share a common element of cultural geography, that of religion. This region is the birthplace of the three largest monotheistic faiths: Judaism, Christianity, and Islam. All three have left their enduring stamp on the region, but it is Islam that is most widely associated with the Middle East, having begun here in the early 7th century. Within the region, cultural geography varies from place to place—Arab, Persian, Turk, Kurd—but the cultural matrix is webbed together by the historical and current impact of Islam and the religious, social, and political systems it created. Christians and Jews (along with some smaller groups like the Bahai, Druze, and Zoroastrians) are found living within the Islamic matrix, but they are the exception, not the rule. Only in a few select areas were the urban landscapes historically punctuated by anything but the minarets of mosques. In the Middle East, the city has always been a center of spiritual and intellectual life and a generator of new ideas about people's relationships with God and each other. Islam itself first developed in the urban centers of Mecca and Medina. The empires that evolved from those Islamic roots created the vast network of cities that dominate the region.

The relative location of the Middle East has given its cities a third set of common characteristics: they are centers of trade and commerce. Prior to the 15th-century discovery of water routes around Africa and around the world, trade between the great civilizations had to pass through the dry-land crescent separating Europe from eastern Asia and Sub-Saharan Africa. Trade among these three regions—by geographical necessity—passed through the Middle East. In fact, the configuration of land and water—the interpenetration of seas (e.g., the Red Sea), land bridges (e.g., Anatolia and Persia), and peninsulas (e.g., Arabia), suggested a multitude of routes through this dry-world barrier. Trade in food and fabrics, gold and copper, spices and perfumes, frankincense and myrrh, all helped build the cities of the Middle East. In fact, new ideas about how to create and expand wealth, perhaps even capitalism itself, were born in cities here. Their market places—called *bazaars* in the Persian language, *pazars* in Turkish, and *souks* in Arabic—are among the oldest in the world.

In other words, cities in the Middle East have evolved around water, the house of worship, and the marketplace. Until the late 20th century (with the genesis of oil economies), relative city size was, in fact, proportional to these factors—that is, larger cities evolved in direct proportion to the availability of fresh water, the abundance of "spiritual capital," and the bounty of trade. Powerful countries were, and are, built around powerful cities. As the concentration of political power in cities increased, it gave rise to a fourth essential element of the urban landscape, the palace. It was the symbol of secular power, the rival of the temple precinct. Today, the palace has evolved into the buildings of governmental administration.

Physical geography often commended sites for urban development: a hill, a natural spring or oasis, a small headland or peninsula, a harbor or river mouth, a confluence of streams, or a point able to command passage through a gap or across a river. It was a peninsula, for instance, that set the stage for the evolution of Istanbul, an oasis for Damascus, a spring for Tehran, a harbor for Beirut, a confluence of rivers for Khartoum, and a hilltop for Aleppo.

Site is only half the story, however. Site characteristics may be responsible for the founding of a city, but it is location relative to routes of commerce and seats of power that determines whether a settlement will grow and prosper or wither and die. Some cities have the potential to be trading hubs or imperial capitals; others do not. Furthermore, what is good in one age may be bad in another. Location matters. Baghdad replaced Damascus as the seat of the Islamic caliphate in 750 A.D. The opening of the Suez Canal drew trade away from the cities of the Fertile Crescent after 1869. Iskenderun (originally Alexandretta) on the Mediterranean was cut off from its natural Syrian hinterland in 1939 when the French transferred the territory to Turkey. During Lebanon's civil war (1975–1990) much of Beirut's economic activity, especially insurance and banking, relocated to Manama, Bahrain. All across the Middle East, "dead cities" and archaeological tells (hills created as one city was built on top of its predecessors) offer examples of how changing relative location can influence the geography of growth and decline.

THE ORIGINS OF THE MIDDLE EASTERN CITY

The Middle East was home to the world's first large, agglomerated settlements. They evolved as centers of production, worship, defense, and trade. They distinguished themselves from the countryside by offering the best life had to offer, at least for powerful elites and their clients. The oldest cities in the world, though most often classified as proto-urban, were born during the Neolithic period. They are all associated with the beginnings of agriculture. Their locations form a triangle with one vertex in Iraq, one in Palestine, and one in Turkey. In lower Mesopotamia (the "land between the rivers"), were the cities of Ur, Uruk, Eridu, Kish, and others. As truly urban places, they emerged in the 4th millennium B.C. They were the largest cities in the world until the rise of Babylon. Only archaeological tells remain, but these forerunners of the modern Middle Eastern city set off a chain reaction in urban innovation that continues to this day. Earlier than this, however, in Palestine, on the other side of the Fertile Crescent, ancient Jericho (now in the West Bank) boasted a wall and watchtower nine millennia before the Christian era. One has only to look at the natural endowments of Jericho's site to understand the impetus for prolific agriculture here. Deep within an arid rift valley, this "city of palms" is located next to a gushing spring and not far from the *wadi* (river bed), which brings runoff from the Judean Hills into the sun-drenched Jordan River valley.

On the Anatolian plateau, just to the north of the Fertile Crescent, stands the most recently discovered prototypical city, Çatal Höyük, which dates to about 6,500 B.C. It was located on a small river in the Konya Plain, today a rather desolate area of Turkey. It had an estimated 50,000 inhabitants, and was probably one of the largest and most sophisticated settlements in the world in its day. Why? Because of the successful domestication of wheat and other products. Just as its size proved the viability of largeness, its form proved to be a pacesetter in the development of urban landscapes. Çatal Höyük, Jericho, and Ur all illustrate the principle that civilization and urbanization evolve hand in hand.

The Iranian Plateau and the Mediterranean basin gave rise to some of the world's earliest empires. Each conquest opened a new chapter in urban history. Persian culture transformed Babylonian, Median, and Phrygian cities. Then, Greek culture, under Alexander and his successor generals, blended with various "Eastern" elements to create a new Hellenistic city. Later, Roman culture transformed Phoenician trading posts and gave rise to a new set of cities in northern Africa and southwest Asia, some built on their Hellenistic predecessors. Empires built by the Persians, Greeks, and Romans succeeded because they were successfully administered (sometimes brutally) and because they promoted trade, not just in goods but also in ideas. Innovations in urban form and function rolled across the region's urban landscapes, converging around the institutions of government, commerce, and religion. In the Roman city, for instance, forums, basilicas, coliseums, amphitheaters, public baths, and temples provided elements which linger in the landscapes of the Middle East today (fig. 7.3). El Djem, Tunisia, is no longer a major city, but it still

Figure 7.3   Volubilis, in Morocco, was one of the largest cities in the western Roman Empire. Today it is on the United Nations list of world heritage sites. (Photo by Jack Williams)

has its coliseum, second in size only to Rome's. Remnants of the Temple of Jupiter guard the western entrance to Damascus's grand *souk*. And, Istanbul, Turkey, still has its hippodrome, a racetrack for chariots, dating from 330 A.D., when Constantinople was built as a new capital for the aging Roman Empire.

The Roman Empire became officially Christian in the 4th century A.D. Thereafter, the followers of Jesus transformed the cultural landscape and social geography of the empire's cities. Its successor, the Byzantine Empire, became the guardian of Christianity in the eastern Mediterranean. Nevertheless, a new religion born on the Arabian Peninsula, Islam, was to conquer the Byzantine lands of southwest Asia and northern Africa. Between the 7th and 10th centuries, Islam created the unique urban landscape we know today as "the Islamic city." It was a city of mosques,

madrassas (religious schools), and universities, a city built on free thinking and scientific progress, a city of honest trade, tolerance, and justice. Its daily routines, seasonal rhythms, architectural appearance, and governing system were heavily influenced by Islam. The term Islamic city is often used to refer to the historic urban areas, originally constructed during the Islamic empires. It is characterized by the common elements of mosque, market, fort or palace, and city walls. The Ottoman city continued to be an Islamic city.

After World War I, when the Ottoman Empire was defeated, much of the Middle East came under the control of European powers. In European style, they added new sections onto the traditional city. Independence came to the region after World War II, and new independent governments built skyscrapers in the global style. Today, the "Middle Eastern" city often has an historic core composed of the original Islamic city, and new sectors, which often reflect European and global architectural influences. And yet the essence of the distinct Islamic matrix continues to characterize cities throughout the region.

Many countries of the Middle East have an urban tradition that transcends not just centuries but millennia: Iraq, Greater Syria, Turkey, Egypt, Iran, Uzbekistan. Yet some countries of the region entered the 20th century without an urban tradition at all. The emirates (principalities) of the Persian Gulf (known as the Arabian Gulf in Arab lands) knew nothing of city life—until recently (box 7.1). The Arab side of the Gulf was punctuated by small fishing and pearling ports. Arabia's urban population was almost entirely *hajj*-related (see below), with Mecca, Medina, and Jeddah surfacing at the top of the urban pyramid. The ancient cities of the frankincense trade, cities like Ubar, had been reclaimed by the desert, and the few large seaports, such as Aden and Musqat, served offshore interests more than their hinterlands. Today, whether a country's cities date back to antiquity or to the recent past, the Middle Eastern population tends to be decidedly urban, a response to declining viability of nomadism, rapidly growing numbers of people, restricted ranges of arable land, the rise of prosperous fossil fuel economies, increased educational opportunities, accessibility to international economic networks, and the political decisions of powerful elites.

CITIES AND URBAN REGIONS

The Middle East entered the 21st century as a majority-urban region. Today, over 60% of its population lives in cities. National statistics range widely, however. In some countries, more than 9 out of 10 inhabitants live in urban settings. The most urbanized are the small states of the Persian Gulf, the oil-rich/rain-poor country of Libya, and Israel. Lebanon is not far behind, at 87% urban. The most urban countries are all among the most economically developed in the region. The least urban countries are the least economically developed: Yemen and Tajikistan have fewer than 3 out of 10 inhabitants living in cities. Egypt and Syria, both with enviable agricultural resources, have large rural populations because the ability to make a living off the land holds people in the primary sector of the economy. Egypt's ratio of urban-to-rural, at 43%-to-57%, is one of the most stable in the region with very little change over the past three decades. In Central Asia, the rate of urbanization has been consistently low, and only Kazakhstan has a majority of its population living in cities. In the region, it is oil wealth that seems to have been the most effective stimulator of urban growth: Oman was 5% urban in 1980 but is 71% today; Saudi Arabia was then 24% and is 81% today; and Kuwait's urbanism increased from 56% to almost 100% over the same time period.

Why has dramatic urbanization characterized the Middle East over the last century? From a demographic perspective, two forces have been at work: natural increase and migration. As death rates have declined faster than birth rates since World War II, the population size of every country has soared. Some countries in this region (e.g., Syria, Iraq, Yemen, Palestine) continue to have among the highest birth rates in the world. In addition, migrants of two types have swollen the urban ranks: migrants from rural areas and, in oil-rich states and in Israel, migrants from abroad. For instance, one-quarter of Saudi Arabia's population and 80% of the UAE's

Box 7.1   Monitoring the Growth of a Desert City in the UAE

M. M. Yagoub

People have found Al Ain an attractive place to settle for thousands of years because of the availability of groundwater, its oases (for date farming), its low humidity, and its location at a transit point between inland areas and the Arabian Gulf. In just over 30 years Al Ain has gone from a desert oasis to a thriving modern city. Its population has increased from 51,000 in 1975 to an expected half a million by the year 2010. The city has achieved two international awards for development and landscaping; the first was from Spain in 1996 and the second was from the United States in 2000.

Figure 7.4   The Oasis of Al Ain in 1976. *Source:* M. M. Yagoub.

Figure 7.5   The Oasis of Al Ain in 2004. *Source:* M. M. Yagoub.

Those awards were due in part to the use of geographic tools in monitoring and planning the growth of the city: maps, color aerial photographs, satellite images, the Global Positioning System (GPS), and Geographical Information Systems (GIS). Change and development in the city is evident from a comparison of old maps, aerial photographs, and satellite images (fig. 7.4 and fig. 7.5). Since 1976, Al Ain has exhibited a tendency for major expansion in the directions of the west and southwest, in the direction of Abu Dhabi, the UAE's capital. Expansion has followed the road network, the water pipelines, and the power transmission lines that connect the two. Similar factors have led to the expansion of Al Ain to the north, toward Dubai. Expansion in both directions has been governed by the gravity model, the availability of utilities, and economic activities along roads. It has been shaped and limited by geographical constraints such as valleys, sand dunes, and mountains, and by legal constraints such as the boundary with the Sultanate of Oman, and domestic planning and institutional ordinances. Revenue from oil has been the main driver of this development.

In the absence of accurate socioeconomic data, remote sensing can be used to chart broad dimensions of change over time in socioeconomic indicators such as population, water consumption, electricity, and solid waste. The policy of the UAE has been to encourage farming and conservation of the environment while permitting urban development. In Al Ain, geospatial research has concluded that urban development is tied to *conservation* of agricultural areas (oases) and *reclamation* of the desert. The reasons for conservation of the oases are historical and social, and more recently have become associated with eco-tourism. Thus, while many (if not most) cities around the world expand at the expense of agriculture, the urban expansion of Al Ain has resulted in the expansion of agricultural land—a 77% increase between 1990 and 2000 according to satellite imagery.

Sources: Dona J. Stewart, "New Tricks with Old Maps: Urban Landscape Change, GIS, and Historic Preservation in the Less Developed World," *The Professional Geographer,* 53, no 3 (2001), 361–373; M. M. Yagoub, "Monitoring of Urban Growth of a Desert City through Remote Sensing: Al-Ain (UAE) between 1976 and 2000," *International Journal of Remote Sensing,* 25, no 6 (2004), 1063–1076.

population is foreign-born. Israel received a million Russian Jews between the mid-1980s and the end of the century. Israel has also received major immigrant streams from Ethiopia, Argentina, France, the United Kingdom, and the United States.

Rapid city growth in the Middle East is related to developments that have transformed life in urban settings faster than life in the countryside. Technology has created jobs in cities; governments have provided services in cities; and people have had greater access to health care and education in cities. Growth in the urban population may be related to political developments, as well. For instance, Amman, Jordan, a village of 2,000 people in 1950, has grown into a major regional metropolis. Much of that growth has been the result of refugees moving into Jordan from neighboring Palestine in the wake of wars between Arabs and Israelis. Today, the arrival of over 700,000 Iraqi refugees into Jordan, fleeing violence in

their own country, has caused the population of Amman to swell to beyond the 2 million mark. Refugee communities are also prominent in the cities of Syria and Lebanon.

The rapid growth of cities in the Middle East has created numerous environmental challenges. Not only does demand exceed the available water resources of many countries, but water quality is also suffering. In many places, sewage systems are inadequate or nonexistent, and waste and refuse are dumped into nearby canals or drainage ditches. Often these canals are used for bathing and for dish and clothes washing, and their water may also be used for drinking. Unregulated industrial activity, especially small-scale enterprises such as tanning add further pollutants to water sources. Moreover, the number of cars in Middle Eastern cities has increased dramatically with growth in population and prosperity. Not only do these cars clog ancient narrow streets, never designed to accommodate them,

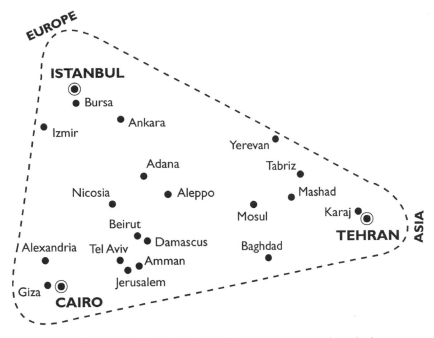

Figure 7.6   The Urban Triangle of the Middle East shows the relative locations of major cities, but without the base map underneath. *Source:* Donald Zeigler.

but they also contribute to air pollution. Car exhaust and industrial effluent, containing lead and other heavy minerals, pose health hazards to urban dwellers.

The core of the Middle East is defined by a decagon formed by five seas (Mediterranean Sea, Black Sea, Caspian Sea, Persian Gulf, Red Sea) and five land bridges (Anatolia, Caucasus, Iran, Arabia, Sinai). On the perimeter of this core lie 3 of the world's 20 most populous metropolises. They anchor an intercontinental, international, and intercultural urban triangle (fig. 7.6):

- Cairo, Egypt, on the continent of Africa, has 16 million people. It is the largest in the Arab realm.
- Istanbul, Turkey, on the continent of Europe, has 11 million people. It is the largest in the Turkic realm.
- Tehran, Iran, on the continent of Asia, has 8 million people. It is the largest in the Persian realm.

Yet in 1950, only one city in the entire Middle East, Cairo, had more than a million inhabitants. In 1900, there were no such cities. Today, there are 37 cities with populations over 1 million, including three in Egypt, five in Turkey, and six in Iran. Except for their historical centers, all are products of the late 20th century—they are new cities, not old. Virtually all of their growth has postdated World War II. Yet, the countries which anchor the Middle East's triangular urban core each have a less developed frontier side, too. Eastern Iran, eastern Turkey, and most of upper (southern) Egypt remind us that urbanization has not entirely transformed even the most urbanized countries in the region.

Beyond the Cairo–Istanbul–Tehran triangle and its immediate environs, there are important regional metropolises, all of which fall into the 1-million to 2-million population range. Only two exceed 2 million inhabitants: Casablanca, Morocco, and Tashkent, Uzbekistan. One anchors the far west, called Al-Maghreb by Arab geographers. The other anchors the far north, called Central Asia or, in its former incarnation, Turkestan.

Some states of the region are anchored by a single primate city (e.g., many Arab states on the Gulf and all of Central Asia); others have two rival urban cores, a condition which has the potential to set into motion strong centrifugal forces. Perhaps the best example of this is Syria. With about 2 million inhabitants each, Damascus and Aleppo are quiet rivals. Other countries with dual anchors and intercity rivalries include: Yemen (Sana'a and Aden), mostly as a result of its colonial history; Libya (Tripoli and Benghazi), as it was cobbled together by the Italians; Israel (Tel Aviv and Jerusalem), split by its secular and religious axes; and Kazakhstan (Almaty and Karaganda), with its Turkic and Slavic flanks. Iraq, on the other hand, has one clearly dominant city, Baghdad, but two smaller anchors, Mosul in the north and Basra in the south; they have such different cultural geographies that Iraq effectively is a country divided.

In between these two extremes are the states with complex urban hierarchies. Turkey and Iran are both punctuated by booming metropolises, regional centers, small towns, and villages. Morocco, likewise, is a country of cities large and small, many of which have assumed a highly specialized role in the Moroccan urban system. Morocco has a political capital, Rabat, but three other cities—Marrakesh, Fès, and Meknes—have historically served in that role. In addition, Morocco has an unofficial economic capital, Casablanca. Its former

diplomatic capital (as far as ambassadors were permitted to venture into the country), Tangier, now serves as a bridgehead to Europe. A city in the south, Ourzazate, has even surfaced as one of the movie-making capitals of the world, starring in films such as *Lawrence of Arabia, Star Wars,* and *Rules of Engagement.*

Not only have cities increased in population and territorial extent, but they have also begun to coalesce in a fashion reminiscent of Jean Gottmann's Megalopolis. In these urban mega-regions, life is at its most intense, a characteristic symbolized by the pace and volume of traffic along connecting thoroughfares. There are perhaps seven megalopolises developing on the 21st century map of the Middle East. The first four are rather well-defined linear regions. The most populous stretches from Cairo across the Nile to Giza and then to Alexandria. Now that the new superhighway has been completed across the desert, development is even more rapidly filling in this 100 mile (160 km) corridor. The second is the staple that holds together the continents of Europe and Asia. It is Turkey's Marmara megalopolis, anchored by Istanbul on the European side and Bursa, an old Silk Road city in Asia Minor (fig. 7.7). It virtually engulfs the entirety of the Sea of Marmara, whose ports attract industry and whose vistas attract residential and recreational developments. Third is coastal Morocco from Casablanca to Rabat, which lie only about 50 miles (80 km) apart. Fourth is the Israeli megalopolis, which begins in Haifa and Akko, stretches along the coast to Tel Aviv–Jaffa, and then to Jerusalem. Although punctuated by some Arab enclaves, this crescent is essentially a belt of intense Jewish settlement, tied together by highways and expanding residential development.

The next three megalopolises are best understood as nests of coalescing cities. The

Figure 7.7   Here in Bursa, a "young Turk" takes over the family kiosk while his father chats with some customers outside. (Photo by Donald Zeigler)

Mid-Mesopotamian megalopolis is anchored by Baghdad but stretches between the Tigris and the Euphrates Rivers. The Tehran–Karaj megalopolis stretches along the base of the Zagros Mountains. The only international megalopolis is the one which stretches from coastal Saudi Arabia, beginning with the oil-engorged cities of Dhahran (headquarters of Saudi Aramco, the world's largest oil company) and Dammam, and then across the four-lane causeway to Bahrain and its capital, Manama.

Capital Cities of the Middle East

In the Middle East today, there are almost 30 countries and hence almost 30 national capitals. Indeed the very concept of a capital city originates with the early states and empires that grew up in the river valleys of Egypt and Mesopotamia. Memphis, in Egypt, was one of the world's first real capitals. Its location served as a hinge between Lower Egypt (the delta) and Upper Egypt (the river valley). It was able to command the entire Nile from the Mediterranean to the first cataract (rapids). A later Egyptian capital, Thebes (today's small city of Luxor) served pharaonic Egypt, with only brief interruptions, for over 1,500 years, beginning in the 21st century B.C., thus giving it one of the longest runs in history. Its monumental architecture affirmed one of the rules of capital city development—nothing is too large, too beautiful, or too expensive for the head city of a proud and prosperous state. The power of the sovereign is expressed in powerful landscapes of control, where respect for and obedience to the ruler, or the law, is demanded by the symbolism of the built environment. Thebes is a case study in itself. It is still intimidating and inspiring. The feeling of grandeur, even today, is not unlike the 21st century's world capitals—Washington, London, Moscow, and others.

The Middle East may have the largest collection of historical capitals in the entire world. Some, such as Memphis, Carthage (Tunisia), and Persepolis (Iran), are well known; others are now but evocative ruins of the geopolitical past—Sardis, Susa, Ashur, Tuspa. The history of the Middle East is the history of major states and empires, amoeba-like in their evolution, and all anchored by capital cities. The 19th and 20th centuries, however, presented a major break with the past. These were eras of extraterritorial rule when the capital cities of the Middle East, the decision-making centers of the region, became Paris, London, Moscow, and Rome. Even earlier, Ottoman Istanbul became an extraterritorial ruler of the Arab lands of Southwest Asia and most of North Africa. With the collapse of the Ottoman Empire, the rule of Europe became even more widespread. Only a few states—Saudi Arabia, Oman, much of Yemen, modern Turkey, and, arguably Iran—avoided colonial domination or protectorate status.

With independence, which came to most states of the region after World War II, a new set of capitals was born. For some states, the choice was simple. Cairo was already serving as the national capital of Egypt. In Syria, Lebanon, and Jordan, the administrative centers that served French and British interests—Damascus, Beirut, and Amman, respectively—became the national capitals. Libya had to decide between two capitals, Tripoli and Benghazi, one in command of Libya's western coast and the other of Libya's east. Only with the creation of a highly centralized, unitary state, was Tripoli, the larger

of the two, designated as the sole capital. Nevertheless, regional tensions in Libya have inspired on-and-off plans to move the capital to a midway point along the coast, the small port city of Sirte, already an administrative center.

Turkey, born out of the Ottoman Empire after World War I, had an obvious choice of cities for its capital: Constantinople, now called Istanbul. It had served as head of an empire for 1,600 years under Romans, Byzantines, and Ottomans. In 1923, however, Atatürk, as one of his first acts as President, made a not-so-obvious choice: Ankara, a city of the interior. Why make such a dramatic change? To symbolize the death of an old state, the Ottoman Empire, and the birth of a new one, the Republic of Turkey, Ankara was chosen as capital. Turkey was not to be the Ottoman state with a new name: it was to be a new creation rooted in the civilizations of Anatolia, the plateau of Asia Minor. By choosing Ankara, a city of some antiquity, the modern state was able to emphasize its roots in a pre-Ottoman past (fig. 7.8). Except for the architecture of its mosques, Ankara bears almost no trace of the Ottoman Period.

Kazakhstan provides the most recent case study of a country which has chosen to relocate its capital. As a modern independent state, it began life in 1991 with Alma Ata, renamed Almaty, as its center of government. Alma Ata, the country's most populous city by far, had served as capital during the period of Soviet rule when Kazakhstan was a Union Republic (fig. 7.9). Within a few years, however, the President of Kazakhstan made known his intention to move the seat of government to Akmola, which was eventually renamed Astana, a word which means "capital" in the Kazakh language. Real and symbolic factors were at work in the decision. Almaty was not centrally located. To boot, it was

Figure 7.8   At the core of modern Ankara is the ancient citadel, where these women carry on traditional female roles. It was ancient Turkish traditions that commended Ankara as the post-Ottoman capital city of Turkey. (Photo by Donald Zeigler)

perilously close to the Chinese border. The choice of Astana solved both of these problems. Moreover, Astana is five meridians closer to Europe, and Kazakhstan has taken pride in calling itself a "Euro-Asian" nation, overlapping the continental boundary as it does. Yet, while flirting with the European connection, Kazakhstan draws its national identity from the steppes, the grasslands of Central Asia. Astana, the new capital, presides over those steppes, whereas the previous capital was in the mountainous foothills of Kazakhstan's east.

The urban geographer Jean Gottmann compares a capital city to a hinge, and the choice of Astana fits that analogy almost perfectly. First, the new capital serves as a hinge between the pre-Soviet past and the nation-building present. Second, it serves as a hinge (or at least it hopes to) between Asia and Europe. Third, it serves as a hinge between the

two sociocultural parts of the nation, the Russified north, inhabited mostly by transmigrant Slavs, and the Turkic south, inhabited by Kazakhs and their Uzbek brethren. By moving the capital city onto the Slavic frontier, Kazakhstan proclaimed its intention to maintain territorial integrity and to countenance no irredentist claims by Russia.

The Middle East also boasts a set of very specialized capitals that no other part of the world can equal: the "head cities" of the three great monotheistic faiths. Mecca, in Saudi Arabia, is the religious capital of the Islamic world, a pilgrimage destination for 2 million *hajjis* (pilgrims) annually. The flow of *hajjis* also makes Mecca the world's leading tourist city, but a destination reserved strictly for Muslims. Jeddah serves as the gateway to Mecca for those arriving by boat and by air. Those who make the *hajj* visit Islam's second holiest city as

Figure 7.9   Inner-city apartments with balconies are part of the residential landscape of Almaty, former capital of Kazakhstan. (Photo by Stanley Brunn)

well, Medinat al-Nabi, the "city of The Prophet," commonly called just "Medina." It was to this city that Mohammed fled in 622 A.D., marking the beginning of the Muslim calendar. For a short time under the first caliphs, Medina served as the capital of the expanding Islamic empire. The third holiest city to Muslims is Al-Quds ("the holy") in Palestine; it is known to the rest of the world as Jerusalem. These three cities are important to the entire Islamic world, but Shiah Islam has an additional set of holy cities, which are also pilgrimage sites: Najaf and Karbala in southern Iraq. The "capital" of Islam's predecessors, Judaism and Christianity, is also in the Middle East. The ancient walled city of Jerusalem is the holiest in the world to both Jews and Christians, and a focus of world pilgrimage for both. Medieval European T-in-O maps (with the top bar of the T representing the Mediterranean and above it Europe and the vertical bar separating Africa and Asia), in fact, showed Jerusalem to be at the center of the world, exactly where it remains today, but only in a religious sense.

Port Cities of the Middle East

Port cities are gateways to the world. Such is Egypt's major port of Alexandria, founded by Alexander the Great in 331 B.C. On a natural harbor created by an offshore island, Alexandria's hinterland comprises the most fertile and productive land in the Mediterranean basin, the delta and valley of the Nile River. Its earliest maritime links connected the port to the entire Hellenistic world, particularly the Greek Aegean. Alexandria hinged together Greek and Egyptian civilizations. The symbol of its commercial prosperity was its lighthouse, "the Pharos," one of the seven wonders of the ancient world. The symbol of its intellectual prowess, stimulated by the cultural encounter of Greece and Egypt, was the library of Alexandria, the greatest of antiquity. Neither has survived, but the lighthouse remains a symbol of port cities everywhere, and Egypt recently unveiled its magnificent new library, the Bibliotecha Alexandrina, to revive the city's standing in the intellectual world.

Just as some of the world's oldest capital cities are located in the Middle East, so are some of the world's oldest port cities: Tyre, Sidon, Acre, Jaffa, Ashquelon, and Gaza on the eastern Mediterranean coast, for instance. Older ports just cannot meet the needs of modern countries, however. If a port was mentioned in the Bible, it is almost surely inadequate for today's commerce. Acre has been superseded by nearby Haifa, and Jaffa by neighboring Tel Aviv. Beirut and Alexandria have built new ports beyond their natural harbors. Antioch (modern Antakya, Turkey), the premier city of the eastern Mediterranean in Roman times, is a port no more. Gaza, which is now challenged to become a modern port for an emergent Palestine, illustrates an important rule of port geography: every country (unless landlocked) must have a seaport of its own. Where good natural harbors are not available for port development, artificial harbors must be built. The configuration of international boundaries, virtually all products of extraterritorial decision-making, heavily influenced the port geography of the Middle East. Syria (historically the entire western fertile crescent), for instance, was cut off from its natural port cities, historic Antioch, Turkey, and modern Tripoli and Beirut, Lebanon, by European-drawn boundaries. The result has been a substantial investment in enlarging the small natural harbor at Tartous and building a large new port at Latakia.

Likewise, the impact of international boundaries on port geography is evident at the head of two arms of the sea: on the Persian Gulf where Iraq, Iran, and Kuwait converge, and on the Gulf of Aqaba where Jordan, Israel, Egypt, and Saudi Arabia converge. In both places one port, operating at economies of scale, would make more sense, but political boundaries dictate otherwise. Ditto, the UAE, the only federation in the Middle East. Here, there is lively competition among the seven emirates to capture a share of maritime trade and in-transit manufacturing. Consequently, a country of only 2 million people has 16 commercial seaports, the most important of which are in the emirate of Dubai.

In the Middle East, seaports are not the only port cities. Also important historically have been "ports" on the edge of the desert, cities that have dispatched caravans to distant places and opened their gates to merchant traders arriving from afar. The seas traversed by the caravan trade were desert seas—"seas of sand" (even though most are not sandy). Sijilmassa, in southern Morocco, now in ruins and only recently excavated, was one such desert port. It linked the Atlas oases with the Sahel—the southern "shore" of the Sahara—before coastal shipping proved more economical. Sijilmassa served the same function as a seaport, and so did its southern counterpart, Timbuktu. Likewise, Damascus grew up around an oasis on the edge of the Syrian Desert. It attracted caravans coming from Mesopotamia. In Central Asia, Samarkand, at the foot of the Tien Shan, was also such a desert port. Thus, on the edges of the Sahara, the Syrian Desert, and the Karakum, ports developed to act as hinges between civilizations.

Models of the Urban Landscape

At the heart of every traditional Islamic city was a fortress. It may be called the citadel, *al-qalat*, or, in the Maghreb, the *kasbah* (fig. 7.10). It usually covered only a few acres and occupied the most defensible site, often a hilltop. Typically surrounded by a wall, it might also have been protected by water. In the past, it would have served as the administrative

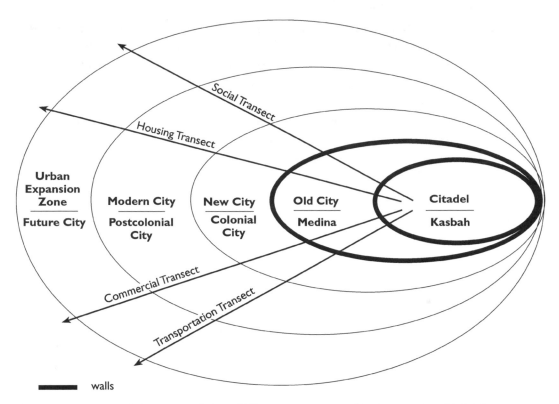

Figure 7.10   Internal Structure of the Middle Eastern Metropolis. *Source:* Donald Zeigler.

heart of the city, the site of the palace. Today, the citadel is most likely to be a preserve of history, valuable as a visual reminder of the past and important in building national identity, and part of the historic core within the modern city (fig. 7.11). Its landscape usually exudes a powerful spirit of place. It may or may not continue to be inhabited.

Surrounding the citadel is the old city itself. It, too, was usually walled, and its often-ornate gates gave access to the world beyond. In the Maghreb, the old Islamic city is called the *medina* (Arabic for "city"). It is the city of antiquity, at least as it has survived conquest, disasters, and well-meaning modernization attempts. For most people in the world, its landscape—compact, congested, cellular, and fortified—provides the stereotype for the

region's cities. Walls, along with their watchtowers, until the 20th century differentiated quite sharply between city and country. Outside the walls were olive groves, grazing lands, cemeteries, quarries, and periodic markets, not to mention potential enemies (fig. 7.12). At most, the *medinas* of modern Middle Eastern cities contain no more than 3% of the urban population, and residents of modern neighborhoods rarely patronize the old city cores.

Beginning with the colonial era (British, French, or Russian/Soviet), a new city typically developed outside the old city walls. In the Maghreb, it was called, in fact, *la nouvelle ville* ("the new city"). It was a city between two worlds, traditional and modern. The traditional elements of urban form, from mosques to bakeries to public baths, were incorporated

Figure 7.11   In the old part of the Middle Eastern city was the citadel, or old fort, as seen in this remnant in the United Arab Emirates. (Photo by Donald Zeigler)

Figure 7.12   In the classic *medina*, undesirable activities such as leather tanning were relegated to the margins of the city, as seen here in Fès, Morocco. (Photo by Donald Zeigler)

into the new city, but they were supplemented by modern amenities and architectural styles, including larger stores and hotels, wider boulevards and traffic circles, European-style churches, new government buildings, and corporate offices, all plastered with the language of the colonizers (fig. 7.13).

Gradually, the new city came to be enveloped by the modern, postcolonial city. Courtyard homes all but disappeared from the landscape, their place taken by apartment blocks, with high-income flats and single-family units becoming increasingly common. The postcolonial city became the zone of international hotels, corporate headquarters, and modern universities. It also became the zone of squatter settlements (which can invade even the inner zones if there is any unoccupied space) where recent in-migrants from villages find lodging while they work their way up the urban social pyramid. In some countries, such as Morocco, these squatter settlements remain poor, underserved by urban infrastructure, and socially marginalized. In other countries, such as Turkey, squatter settlements are quickly legitimized by the government, and the process of incumbent upgrading begins.

Beyond the modern city is the urban expansion zone. Here, small villages find

Figure 7.13   To ensure freshness, bread is baked where the people live. These young men are picking up bread at the bakery for delivery to stores and hotels in the Marrakesh *medina*. (Photo by Donald Zeigler)

themselves undergoing urbanization *in situ*. Here, also, may be new industrial estates, modest new housing tracts, or, in the case of Egypt and Saudi Arabia, new cities, built from scratch. For the richest countries, those able to afford automobiles and the gasoline to feed them, it can also be a zone of raging urban sprawl. Most often, the international airport is located there as well.

The Middle Eastern city today, therefore, can be seen as an interlocking set of zones, patterned in time: citadel, old city (Islamic), new city (European), modern city, and urban expansion zone. As one moves from the innermost zone to the outermost, changes in urban form and function are evident. What do transects through these zones reveal?

- The social axis: The old city is becoming increasingly marginalized by society, particularly as the well-to-do move out. The modern city is attracting the lion's share of new neighborhood investment and the best of social services. Even tourists typically stay in the modern city and depend on air-conditioned buses to drop them off at a city gate for a brief sojourn into the past.

- The housing axis: The old city (except in Turkey and Yemen) is a zone of traditional, two- or three-story courtyard houses. The modern city is a zone of mid-rise and high-rise apartments. In fact, the multistory apartment block is now the most typical component of the Middle Eastern city's residential landscape (and a reminder of how architecture has pulled away from the local environment and its indigenous roots).

Figure 7.14   The landscape of Amman, Jordan, shows the signs of global commercialization in the form of this bilingual advertisement for Subway. (Photo by Donald Zeigler)

- The commercial axis: The old city still displays fully functional *souks*, traditional industries, and small-scale, family-owned artisanal enterprises. The modern city displays its logo-laden landscape of chain stores, international (and national) franchises, and ever-increasing snippets of English (fig. 7.14).
- The transportation axis: The old city reveals narrow streets clogged with pedestrians, taxis, and even donkey carts. The new city reveals the proliferation of privately owned automobiles and the amenities, such gas stations and parking spaces, that they require.

These transects of Middle Eastern cities virtually recount the history of cities everywhere. Middle Eastern cities are the places where the 21st century B.C. meets the 21st century A.D.

It is not the periphery that defines the personality of a city, however. It is the center, the old city, the city of history. The preindustrial core also offers a glimpse of the prototypical

Islamic City, for Middle Eastern cities seemed to be held together by their mosques and minarets. Therefore, in the Islamic city, no one could live or work beyond earshot of a minaret. Without amplification as an aid to the human voice, this meant the network of mosques had to be very dense, indeed. In the Islamic city, the skyline is punctuated by minarets, occasionally joined by church spires in the Christian quarters. The so-called Friday mosques stand out as the city's architectural masterpieces. The religious landscape of the Middle Eastern city is typically supplemented by Koranic schools, traditional universities, shrines, and mausoleums.

Trade dominated the region long before Mohammed, himself a merchant, revealed a new religion, so it is little wonder that *souks* (markets) are another typical part of the traditional city landscape (fig. 7.15). Often, *souks* envelop the neighborhood mosques. Guided by the religious duty of *zakat* (alms), the surrounding businesses and residents help support the mosques and the social services

Figure 7.15   This *souk* in the old section of Casablanca is a distinctive feature of the *medina*. Note the Moorish arches. (Photo by Jack Williams)

they provide. The central *souks* usually evolved around the city's "grand mosque." These *souks* are specialized affairs: they feature shoes in one area, produce in another, and fast food (traditional style) available throughout. Merchants dealing in the same product compete with each other, and the concept of fixed prices does not exist. Shoppers know the techniques of hard bargaining and expect low prices. In the past, the *souks* were supplied by two institutions: (1) the city's artisans who made pottery, jewelry, carpets, and everything else, and (2) the city's *khans* (or caravanserais) which served as wholesale centers for goods coming in from distant lands (originally via camel caravans). The *khans* were essentially inns for merchant traders and their pack animals. In today's traditional city, however, mass produced goods are as common as locally produced products, and *khans* have been abandoned to other uses or turned into historical landmarks. In other realms of the traditional (albeit disappearing) city, bread tends to be purchased daily at the bakery itself, pub-

lic baths (*hammams*) are the social centers of neighborhoods (especially for women), coffee houses take the place of bars for men (no alcohol is permitted by the Koran), and private life takes place in very private places, such as the home (box 7.2).

In fact, the Islamic city is set up to assure privacy, particularly for women and families. Houses are not recognizable as discrete entities; they appear as doors (often brightly decorated) in thick earthen walls (whitewashed at most). Along a typically narrow street (often a dead end), doors are staggered and never give casual passers-by a view into the house; windows are well above eye-level; and second-story windows are enclosed by a wooden lattice so one can see out but not in. The lattice also wards off the sun and ushers in the breeze. The privacy of the house is carried into the street by a veil or simple head scarf. The traditional house is built around an open-air courtyard with covered, roomy bays on each side. Rarely does anyone but family make it deeper into the home. Courtyards

---

Box 7.2   Home Space in Tehran

Farhang Rouhani

Since 1979, the Islamic Republic of Iran's efforts to quell modernization along Western lines have imposed strict policies on Iranian citizens. In urban centers, most notably Tehran, these include the state policing of public spaces such as parks and commercial streets. What is particularly striking, however, is how these politics invade even the most private of spaces: the home.

Home spaces in Tehran were significantly rearranged over the course of the 20th century. The traditional home was divided into separate male (*birun,* outer, public) and female (*andarun,* inner, private) sections. A lack of street-facing windows accentuated the sense of privacy; indeed, internal courtyards served as the home's central focus. Modernization under the Pahlavi Shahs (1920s–1979) and the demands of rapid population growth ushered in western high-rise apartment-style living, without the physically gendered division of space, and more public street-facing windows. The importance placed on familial privacy, though, has been maintained in different ways, including the use of walls around complexes and buzzers to screen visitors.

On top of this urban transformation, the politics of satellite television viewing has brought the middle-class Tehran household to the forefront of Iranian state politics. The clerical government first instituted a ban on the sale, import, and use of satellite dishes in 1994 because of the proclaimed polluting effect of Western media products on Iranian society, particularly on its youth.

Under Iran's more liberal-democratic government, the late 1990s witnessed a relaxing of the ban, including the requiring a warrant for home searches. The current, more conservative-theocratic government, however, has recommended the policing of public and private morality. Although the ban on satellite dishes still exists, and periodic raids to confiscate them are made by the morality police, a majority of the population of Tehran has access to the air waves whether directly in their homes or through family and friends. Ultimately, police regulation and infiltration of people's homes has intensified fears in an already politically insecure society.

The practice of policing the home has led to dynamic conflicts in Iranian state and society over the role of privacy in a democracy, the importance of the home as a space of refuge, and the moral and social effects of the global media. It is within this context that *The Simpsons, American Idol,* and living room furniture are transformed into a realm of resistance.

---

tend to be small for the same reasons that streets tend to be narrow: to provide shade and to keep distances walkable. The middle of the courtyard is often anchored by a well for water or a fountain to humidify and cool the air. In houses of the Persian Gulf and Iran, wind towers were added for the same reason— they channel air downward creating a breeze. Along the edges of the courtyard, vines and arbors provided shade and produced fruit as a bonus. Mosques, *khans,* and palaces also included courtyards, making "cellular" one of the words most often used to describe the traditional Middle Eastern city. Supplementing courtyards are flat rooftops (used as a result of the lack of rain), often enclosed by low walls over which carpets are flung for cleaning. Rising from the rooftops are laundry lines, cisterns, antennas, satellite dishes, and solar water heaters. In the summer, roofs may be cluttered with mattress pads, for use at night, and ubiquitous plastic chairs.

The most coveted space in the preindustrial Islamic city was at the center, close to the seats of economic power and social interaction. Palaces and merchants' houses were central elements of the urban landscape, as were the central *souks*. Noxious enterprises like tanneries were relegated to the periphery. The residential population of cities, in the traditional city model, tended to be concentrated in "quarters": sections for Jews, for Europeans, for different Christian sects, different ethnic groups, and people of different villages or regional origins. In the past, many of these quarters had gates of their own. Residential space was highly segregated, yet it also mimicked the security and social cohesiveness of the village by providing a scale of life to which people were accustomed and a set of community institutions that people of like mind could control. Within each quarter lived both rich and poor.

As they have survived, the narrow streets of the residential and commercial quarters tend to be penetrable only by foot traffic and donkey carts. Still, this does not stop the occasional taxi or service vehicle from squeezing through. The cramped feeling is heightened by second and third stories jutting overhead, sometimes joining and creating tunnels. The largest streets lead into the city from gates in the walls, but a large public square dominating the center of town is a rarity (except in

Iran). A grid pattern manifests itself (sort of) in towns with a Roman or Byzantine heritage, and it is common for elements of the pre-Islamic landscape to have become part of the working city, as their historic value has usually gone unrecognized. Roman pavements may lie deep underneath the contemporary street, and what was a wide Byzantine thoroughfare may now be subdivided into three or four narrow, parallel alleys, each serving as a *souk* of its own. Periodically spaced along the most well-traversed routes, are richly decorated drinking fountains (or their remnants), often given to the public by wealthy merchants. Otherwise, water vendors (dressed like neon signs) wander around high-traffic areas selling drinks to the thirsty (fig. 7.16).

The preceding generalizations apply to the old cities of the Middle East, those that grew up at oasis sites and prospered because of trade. An entirely new set of cities has grown up on the 20th century's oil and natural gas fields. This style of city is best exemplified in Kuwait, Saudi Arabia, Bahrain, Qatar, and the UAE (though oil revenues have transformed cities in Iran, Iraq, Libya, and Algeria, as well). Urban landscapes from Kuwait to Dubai have been built on revenues from the world's largest oil fields. While lacking the historical depth of a city like Aleppo, they do offer a glimpse of what a modern Middle Eastern city can be. These are cities built on petro-dollars, largely since the 1960s. Generally, they consist of two zones patterned in time. First, in the center of each is a tiny core anchored by a fort and perhaps the remnants of a traditional wharf area or well-to-do neighborhood. Although small, these cores are the source of local identity, particularly in layout and architectural styles. Second, around each core is a postindustrial city of high-rise office buildings, shopping malls, gardens, golf courses,

Figure 7.16 Water is precious in the dry environments of most Middle Eastern cities. At these public water urns in Cairo, everyone drinks from the same cup. Note the political ads in the background. (Photo by Donald Zeigler)

apartment complexes, sprawling suburbs, and mosques. With oil wealth, the world's most creative architects are not out of range, and the cities they have built blend modern structures with traditional themes (box 7.3). One of the surprising elements of these new urban landscapes is how green they are. Turning itself into a Garden City, in fact, has been one of Dubai's urban planning objectives. Figuratively, oil is turned into water, and water into green space. Oil is also turned into new human geographies. Petro-economies have, by governmental design as well as economic magnetism, virtually eliminated nomadism as a way of life. The rural population has become urbanized. In addition, the faces of the oil-engorged "boom towns" have also changed. The economic magnetism of Kuwait, Dammam, Abu Dhabi, and others, draws unskilled workers from as far away as India, Pakistan, Sri Lanka, and the Philippines, along with skilled workers from Europe and the United States, as well as other parts of the Arab world.

What is missing from the landscapes of Arab cities on the Gulf is the industrial era. Manufacturing is limited to local craft industries and to manufacturing-in-transit at the free ports of the region, most notably those in the Emirate of Dubai (fig. 7.17). As banking and trading centers of the Middle East, however, some of these cities—Manama, Dubai, Abu Dhabi—have been thriving as increasingly important transactional nodes in the economic systems reshaping the region. The center of Arab World banking has shifted (in part) from Beirut to Manama, Bahrain, as a result of Lebanon's civil war. Doha, Qatar, is now the headquarters of Al Jazeera, the most popular satellite television channel in the Middle East. Since the 1990s, the port cities of the Persian Gulf have been the entrepôts supplying Central Asia with cars, electronics, and other high-end goods. Built on oil, the cities

Box 7.3   Cities of Spectacle: Abu Dhabi and Dubai

Dona Stewart

Renowned urban geographer David Harvey notes the role of spectacle on the urban landscape, in creating a city's identity and offering an experience for its inhabitants. The creation of spectacular urban landscapes is common in the postindustrial capitalist urban systems of North America and Europe, but it is less common in less economically developed countries.

In the Middle East, the oil rich United Arab Emirates is creating spectacular urban landscapes, designed to bring global attention, and investment, to the tiny nation. Costing billions of dollars and designed by architects of international renown, the skylines of Dubai and Abu Dhabi, the country's two largest cities, compete for the designation of most spectacular.

At present Dubai is completing the tallest skyscraper in the world. The Dubai Tower (Burj Dubai) will surpass the Sears Tower in number of floors and Taipei 101 and the Petronas Towers (Kuala Lumpur) in overall height. Though the final height of Burj Dubai has long been kept secret, it is expected to exceed 2,275 feet. The interior of the tower will be decorated by Giorgio Armani. The tower is part of a large-scale development that includes 30,000 homes, malls, and a human-made lake, at a cost of $20 billion.

While Dubai is the commercial hub of the UAE, Abu Dhabi is its capital, and has focused its attention on being the UAE's cultural center. Presently it is constructing a major cultural development on Saadiyat Island ("Island of Happiness") off its coast. It will contain branches of the Louvre museum, estimated to cost $1 billion, and will be the largest museum ever constructed by the Guggenheim Foundation. The Guggenheim collection will focus on modern and contemporary art. Abu Dhabi's cultural enterprises also include sport, such as Formula One racing and a golf tournament on the prestigious PGA tour.

of the Gulf are likely to continue thriving only if they diversify and lay the groundwork for post-petroleum economies.

With the growth of the global Internet, all cities in the Middle East are developing into *cyber cities*. The region's universities, manufacturing establishments, and traders are increasingly tied to constant flows of information that arrives by waves, wires, and photo-optic cables. Every computer terminal becomes its own harbor in the postindustrial landscape. The public is demanding frontage on these "harbors." Hence, internet cafés have appeared in cities all across the Middle East, with few exceptions. Internet cafés, born as a concept in 1984, numbered fewer than 100 worldwide by the early 1990s. Today, there are thousands throughout the Middle East alone. Turkey, Israel, and the emirates of the Persian Gulf lead the region, but Iran and Egypt are catching up. The UAE and Dubai have the highest Internet bandwidth of any countries in the region (followed by Egypt and Morocco). Kuwait is also developing into a

Figure 7.17   The Jebel Ali Export Processing Zone illustrates the effort to develop a more diverse economic base in the United Arab Emirates. (Photo courtesy UAE)

major cyber city, even as it lags in the development of a petrochemical industry.

REPRESENTATIVE CITIES

Cairo: Al-Qahirah, "The Victorious"

Al Qahirah means "victorious," and Cairo has emerged victorious as the most populous city in the Arab World, in the Middle East, and on the continent of Africa. The Arabic-language cinema and popular Arab music have made Cairo—along with Beirut, Lebanon—one of the cultural epicenters of the Arab universe. *Al-Ahram,* a Cairo daily newspaper, has the largest patronage in the Arab world, and its English edition circulates globally. As the headquarters of the League of Arab States, Cairo is also the head city of pan-Arab politics, a role facilitated not only by the city's size, but also by its relative location. Cairo is positioned between the western Arab world of North Africa, and the eastern Arab world of Asia.

Cairo, over a thousand years old, is a multilayered city; its buildings and neighborhoods reflect the impact of various historical periods. At its dense core lies the "Islamic" city. To the east of the Nile River this city began as a military encampment and grew to include a citadel, a mosque, and city walls. Today the walls are gone, torn down as the city's boundaries expanded. However, three of the original city gates remain to draw tourists, who mingle with the area's residents. In medieval times, Cairo was an epicenter of world trade; caravans brought luxuries and necessities to the city's famed markets. Today, tourists crowd the Khan al-Khalili to buy souvenirs, most often trinkets reflecting Egypt's pharaonic history, or sip tea in traditional coffee shops formerly frequented by Naguib Mahfouz, Egypt's Nobel laureate.

As dams tamed the Nile floods, in the 19th century, the city expanded onto its banks. At the same time, Europe was expanding its interests overseas, establishing colonies and political control over countries in Asia and Africa. In Cairo, new neighborhoods were constructed in European design. Houses were built in the style of Italianate villas. Parks were constructed. Indeed, a "new" downtown was created to mimic the design of Paris, and upper-class Egyptians enjoyed performances in the new opera house. In 1871, an opera premiered there that has become one of the world's most popular: *Aida* by Giuseppe Verdi.

Cairo's explosive population growth occurred in the era after World War II, when Egypt became an independent republic. Migrants from the rural areas flooded the capital in search of jobs and opportunities; they created enormous economic challenges for the young government. Massive high-density apartment blocks, with bleak architectural design and poor-quality construction, were built to accommodate the influx. At the same time the government became concerned about Cairo's massive size and its military vulnerability.

In an effort to stem the tide of urban expansion onto valuable farmland, the Egyptian government began to redirect growth into the desert. The result was, first, government-built, industry-based cities distant from Cairo. The 10th of Ramadan City, for instance, located on the way to the Suez Canal, was built to have an industrial base anchored by several thousand factories. Since the 1970s it has offered jobs, housing, and some services. The new towns, however, never met their target population goals and did little to relieve the population pressure on Cairo.

Since the 1990s, Cairo's landscape has increasingly reflected the impact of globalization. Chili's, TGIF, Hardee's and other fast-food chains with global reach are ubiquitous. Massive malls, office towers, and new hotels now line desirable locations along the Nile. As car ownership becomes more common, suburbanization is taking place. Suburban developments, with names like "Dreamland," boast large houses with lawns and clubhouses with pools and other sporting amenities that cater to the upper class.

As a megacity, Cairo is really a product of the 20th century. As it has expanded, however, it has engulfed dozens of predecessor settlements and unique historical landscapes (fig. 7.18). These visual reminders of the past, numbering in the hundreds, make Cairo a vast open-air museum. Their distribution most closely resembles the multiple nuclei model. Large tracts of 20th century blandness separate such historical nucleations as the following:

- The great pyramids (and sphinx) of Giza, on the west bank of the Nile, date back to the Old Kingdom, but have been encroached upon by an expanding city, deflating some of the excitement of first-time visitors who may be disappointed to find a Pizza Hut practically at the pyramids' base.
- Heliopolis (on the way to the airport) was one of the ancient world's cult centers, but only a single obelisk remains—now in the middle of an urban park.
- Babylon-in-Egypt, now known as Coptic Cairo (because of its Coptic Christian inhabitants), has a history associated with the world's most famous refugee family—Mary, Joseph, and Jesus. It is now engulfed by the modern suburb of Ma'adi.
- Cairo's Citadel was built by Saladin in the 12th century; it was transformed by the Mamluks and then the Ottomans.

Whether counting people or cars, the growth of Cairo has been meteoric. Today, the city's traffic snarls are of world renown. Not until the late 1980s was Cairo's long-anticipated metro rail system opened to help move the city's millions. It has since expanded to include a subway line tunneling under the Nile to the west bank.

Figure 7.18 The vast metropolis of Cairo sprawls to the horizon from the base of the old Citadel. (Photo by Jack Williams)

The new metro stations are conveniently sited, brilliantly lighted, and immaculately clean. The Metro links some outer suburbs (but not yet the satellite cities) with the center of the metropolis, and at least one car on every train is reserved for women. Trips that at one time took three hours by car, now can take as little as half an hour. As the city's circulation system continues to become more efficient, so will its economy.

Damascus and Aleppo: Fraternal Twins

The Arabs call them Sham and Halab. Outsiders know them as Damascus and Aleppo. With over 2 million people each, they are the most populous cities in Syria. Each one claims the same superlative: "the oldest continuously inhabited city on earth." It was Damascus that Mohammed deliberately decided never to visit because he wanted to enter Paradise only once. But it was Aleppo where Abraham (the father of monotheism) stopped to milk his cow on the journey south from Haran. Such stories tell more about the pride each city takes in its heritage than the cold facts of history. Like fraternal twins, their looks and personalities differ, but you can tell they are from the same family.

The location of each city is impressive enough to give credence to its storied history. To appreciate the site of Damascus, one need look no further than the mosaics of the Umayyad Mosque, built at a time when the city was the capital of the first Muslim empire, the only time in history when the entire Islamic world was politically united. In green and gold tiles, the mosaics portray a lush oasis where life was at its best. Thanks to the Barada River, Damascus is, in fact, one of the world's premier oasis cities. The Barada comes tumbling down the slopes of Mount Hermon. As its velocity diminishes, the channel splits into a handful of distributaries, and water sinks into the ground, forming an oasis on the edge of the Syrian Desert. Ancient Damascus, as if to avoid occupying precious agricultural land, lies to one side where growth has pushed it up the last fold in the mountains of Lebanon. Mountains to the west and desert to the east protected the ancient oasis city.

Damascus's site is dramatic when seen from the air; Aleppo's site is dramatic when seen at ground level. Rising from the surrounding plain is Aleppo's citadel, a fortified hilltop that identifies the original city. The north Syrian plain is a steppe (grassland) which stretches southward from the Anatolian plateau until it grades off into the Syrian Desert. In northern Syria, nature has set the stage for dry farming, and the Syrians have made it even more productive with irrigation. The region is a center of wheat, olive, almond, and pistachio production. Aleppo's potential as a breadbasket holds even more promise for the future, a promise affirmed by the United Nations when it located the International Center for Agricultural Research in Dry Areas here.

No matter how productive the oasis or how impregnable the hill, neither Damascus nor Aleppo would have occupied pivotal roles in Middle East history were they not situated at the crossroads of trade. The oldest trade routes followed the parabolic shape of the Fertile Crescent: from the Tigris and Euphrates Valleys, along the spring line at the base of the Anatolian Plateau, and south along the mountainous littoral of the eastern Mediterranean, thence on to Egypt and beyond. Between the two arms of the Fertile Crescent is the Syrian Desert. The desert provided a series of east–west shortcuts: the

northernmost shortcut focused on Aleppo, halfway between the Euphrates and the coast. A longer shortcut passed through the mid-desert oasis of Palmyra (today's Tadmour) and focused on Damascus. Both Aleppo and Damascus were also on the north–south axis of trade and thus became urban growth poles early in their history.

Damascus and Aleppo are modern cities today, but not as modern as they might be were it not for the protectionist, almost isolationist, stance of the Syrian government. Only in the early 1990s were strict rules of socialist planning and government ownership eased. The result was a mini-renaissance in economic activity in both cities, but too many restrictions remained in place, and the renaissance was short-lived. One positive result is that authentic Arab traditions, not the artificial niceties contrived for tourists, remain triumphant in both cities, and the global economy has yet to overtake either one. Each city still has a character of its own. One feels a greater reverence for the party line (the autocratic Baath Party) in Damascus. Aleppo, farther from the corridors of power, has a more freewheeling, freethinking air about it; nevertheless, more of its women are still fully veiled and its largest stores are no bigger than an American 7-Eleven. As Syria's capital city, Damascus is the almost-monopolistic gateway to the entire country. Aleppo, despite its comparable size, seems to yearn for a greater role in Syria and the world beyond.

Jerusalem: Clash of Religion and Politics

Jerusalem occupies neither an attractive site nor a strategic location. It is not central in a geographical sense, and it lies astride no major trade routes. It is a city that by all rights should have been bypassed by time. Instead,

Figure 7.19   The Dome of the Rock and the Western Wall are symbols of a religiously divided Jerusalem. (Photo by Donald Zeigler)

Jerusalem has become an epicenter of religious veneration and conflict. Three religions regard it as a holy city: Judaism, Christianity, and Islam. Muslims rank it behind only Mecca and Medina in importance. For them, it is the place from which Mohammed made his "night journey" to heaven to talk personally with God. To mark the place of his ascension, Muslims built the Dome of the Rock in 691 A.D. (fig. 7.19). It is one of the oldest Islamic structures in the world. To Jews, Jerusalem is the city of David's kingship and Solomon's Temple. The wall of the platform on which the Temple stood is all that remains; it is called the Western Wall and is the focal point of Jewish prayers. The Dome of the Rock may be located on the very site of Solomon's temple. To Christians, Jerusalem is the city where Jesus of Nazareth proved himself to be the

Messiah. Since Byzantine times, the Church of the Holy Sepulchre has sheltered the place of the crucifixion, entombment, and resurrection of Jesus (fig. 7.20). It is easily visible from the Temple Mount and the Dome of the Rock.

One always speaks of "going up" to Jerusalem. It began as a hill town at the very southern tip of the western fertile crescent, but it did not have a commanding position. The land enclosed by the "old city" walls is lower in elevation than the land to either the north or the east. The only feature of the physical environment that commended the site was a spring, now known as the Gihon. The Jebusite village at the site of the spring was destined for prominence, however, largely because its relative location made a difference 3,000 years ago. The village was conquered by the Hebrew king, David, who needed a centrally

Figure 7.20   A Greek Orthodox priest enters the courtyard of the Church of the Holy Sepulchre in Jerusalem. This church is the focal point of Christian history because it is built on the site of Jesus's crucifixion, entombment, and resurrection. (Photo by Donald Zeigler)

located capital between the northern and southern tribes of the Hebrew people. Jerusalem fit the bill. With the decision to move the Arc of the Covenant (containing Moses's tablets of stone) to Jerusalem, the city began to acquire the religious capital needed to sustain its spiritual centrality for three millennia. Jerusalem became the place where the God of Moses and Abraham permanently resided, and before the first Muslims prayed facing Mecca, they prayed facing Jerusalem. Religion endowed Jerusalem with elements of centrality that geography could not (fig. 7.21).

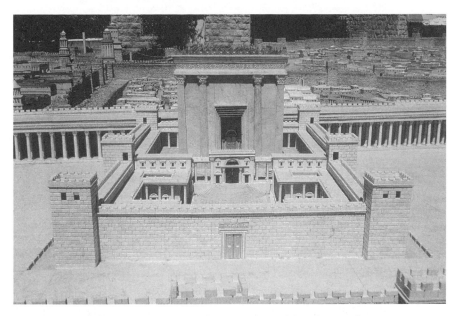

Figure 7.21   In present-day Jerusalem, one can visit a large, three-dimensional, open-air model of Jerusalem and see the Jewish Temple as it presumably looked at the time of King Herod. (Photo by Jack Williams)

The current walls of the old city of Jerusalem date to the Ottoman period. Within the walls, Jerusalem is divided into four so-called quarters: Muslim, Jewish, Christian, and Armenian. The mental map conjured up by such a description, however, belies the reality of the city's cultural geography. In fact, almost the entire old city has an Arab feel about it, save for the Jewish Quarter. Furthermore, the boundaries of the quarters no longer (and probably never did) define the cultural divisions of the city. Residential patterns and movement into and out of the four quarters challenge the idea that they are homogenous neighborhood groupings of like-minded souls. In the "old city," Muslims and Jews are the primary actors, Christians are diminishing in number, and Armenians are doing what they have done best for over 1,500 years: surviving as a culturally distinct Christian minority. Muslim Arabs are expanding into the Christian quarter, the

traditional niche of Christian Arabs. Jews are solidly in control of the Jewish quarter, but they are also acquiring property in the other three quarters, which they conspicuously mark with signs, synagogues, and Israeli flags (fig. 7.22). Jews moving into the old city are more likely to be extremely religious, and those leaving are more likely to be secular. Armenians, especially seminarians, flow through the Armenian quarter from all over the world, their identity bolstered since 1991 when Armenia reappeared on the map of sovereign states.

The "old city" is only one of two Jerusalems. The other is the sprawling modern metropolis. While the walled city is no larger than a college campus, metropolitan Jerusalem covers at least 50 square miles (130 sq km). Despite being governed as a single municipality, the metropolitan area is bisected by a cultural fault line. West Jerusalem is thoroughly Jewish and provides the site for

Figure 7.22   The Jewish Quarter of Jerusalem's old city has been entirely rebuilt since 1967. The Israeli flag was adopted when Israel became independent in 1948. (Photo by Donald Zeigler)

Israel's parliament, the Knesset. East Jerusalem is primarily Arab (it includes both Muslim and Christian Arabs)—a collection of Arab villages, one of which may someday become the capital of a Palestinian state. "Occupied" East Jerusalem, however, is not as homogeneous as West Jerusalem. In the east, Jewish settlements occupy a dozen hilltop sites, all of them new (post-1967), wealthy, and strategically positioned to maintain control of Greater Jerusalem for the Israelis. To the north, south, and east of Jerusalem, where border crossings are patrolled by Israeli soldiers, the Palestinian West Bank begins. The city's relative location between Israel proper and the West Bank gives it a frontier feel of lying along a tension-ridden international boundary with a more-developed country on one side and a less-developed country on the other.

The future of Jerusalem will be determined by the ability of the Israelis and the Palestinians to negotiate a peaceful resolution to their conflicting ambitions. In the meantime, repeated conflict between the Israelis and the Arabs has destroyed the infrastructure of many West Bank cities, such as Ramallah and Jenin. The construction of a separation barrier (also known as the separation wall or fence) by Israelis further complicates efforts to resolve the conflict. Fifty-six miles (90 km) of the barrier is in Jerusalem, much of it thrusting deep inside the pre-1967 border. The barrier separates Jerusalem from the West Bank. Although it was constructed to increase Israeli security, the barrier also restricts the ability of thousands of Palestinians to reach their jobs, fields, and medical services.

Istanbul: Bicontinental Hinge

It has existed for almost 27 centuries (since 657 B.C.), and for 16 of them as an imperial capital. Its original name was Byzantium, but it was rechristened the New Rome in 330 A.D. Almost immediately the people began calling it Constantinopolis, Emperor Constantine's city. Today, it appears on the map as Istanbul. It has been the dominant city of the eastern Mediterranean realm for more than a millennium, having surpassed a million inhabitants by 1000 A.D. Something about this location just begs for an urban place.

Istanbul's location makes it a hinge between continents. From its situation on the European side of the Bosporus, it is positioned to control overland trade between Europe and Asia and the shipping lanes between the Mediterranean and Black Seas. The huge empires that Istanbul commanded—Roman, Byzantine, Ottoman—also gave it the ability to control overland access to Arabia, the Indian Ocean, and eastern Asia. Until the round-Africa route was fully opened in the 16th century, Istanbul was able to call the shots in trade between north and south, east and west. As imperial capital of the Ottoman realm since 1453, it reached its peak in the 1500s when the emperor, Suleyman, commanded so much wealth that he was known to the world as "The Magnificent." His city was at that time larger in population than London, Paris, Vienna, or Cairo. During that century, however, the power of Constantinople began to wane. No longer did Ottoman subjects hold a monopoly on the ancient silk routes across Asia or on the fertile crescent caravan trade from the Eastern Mediterranean to the Persian Gulf. As technology enabled mastery of the sea, caravels replaced camels as the most reliable and economical modes of transport. Well before the end of the 19th century, the Ottoman Empire was the "sick man of Europe," and "Stamboul" was a city in decline. Modern Turkey was born out of the Ottoman Empire thanks chiefly to the secular nationalism inspired by Mustafa Kemal Atatürk (fig. 7.23).

The core of Istanbul, the historical city, occupies a peninsular site with deep water on three sides. Crowning the peninsula, and visually dominant from the sea, are seven hills, just like Rome. The peninsula is bordered on the south by the Sea of Marmara, on the east by the Bosporus, and on the north by the Golden Horn, the large, sheltered harbor that enabled the city to dominate the shipping trade. The Bosporus and its companion strait, the Dardanelles, enabled ocean-going vessels to penetrate central Eurasia. On the Black Sea's northern shore, the ancient Greeks implanted colonies. The fertile hinterlands of these colonies became a breadbasket, producing wheat for the Aegean core of the Hellenic world, wheat that went to market via the Bosporus. The first "world class" city to dominate these straits dates back to the Bronze Age. Its name was Troy, and it was located at the southern end of the Dardanelles. Troy was the Istanbul of its day.

In the 20th century, the Bosporus provided one of the Soviet Union's few outlets to the world ocean and was consequently a point of strategic significance during the Cold War. By controlling the strait at Istanbul, NATO could deprive Moscow of dominating one of the world's most strategic locations. Even now, the Bosporus continues to be important to Ukraine and the Russian Federation. It has also taken on a new strategic significance in the flow of crude oil from the landlocked Caspian Basin fields, much of which transits the Bosporus, already one of the world's busiest straits. At Istanbul, the Bosporus is at its narrowest, assuring full and busy roadsteads and shipping lanes, the ingredients of potential collisions, particularly given the swift currents that flow out of the Black Sea.

Figure 7.23   Istanbul is a city of thriving neighborhoods. Here men gather in the late afternoon under a bust of Atatürk, the revered father of modern Turkey. (Photo by Donald Zeigler)

Oil is not the only commodity important to Istanbul's economy, however. During most of the 20th century, Istanbul's European hinterland was all but severed by the Iron Curtain and the animosity of neighboring Greece. Now, however, Eastern European nations have opened their borders. The routes of commerce between Europe and Asia are once again funneling traffic across the Bosporus, and Turkey finds itself a candidate for European Union membership. The growth of trade is nowhere more powerfully symbolized than by the growing volume of truck traffic navigating the transcontinental Bosporus bridges, completed in 1974 and 1988. Now, a new rail line designed to carry passengers and freight under the Bosporus is in the offing, and Turkey is increasingly calling itself a European nation (box 7.4). At the same time, it is emerging as a gateway to Central Asia, where the Turkish people originated and where most of the languages spoken are Turkic in origin.

Fès and Marrakesh: Imperial Rivals

In Morocco it was Fès and Marrakesh that grew up as anchors of the country's urban system. Neither city functions as the capital today, but both have in the past. Nor is either located in the Rabat–Casablanca megalopolis, or even along the coast. Instead, Fès faces east towards Morocco's Arab Islamic heritage, and Marrakesh faces south towards the Atlas Mountains and Africa's desert oases beyond.

The seeds of Fès, and with it the seeds of the Moroccan state, were planted shortly after

Box 7.4 *Festival*

A native son of Istanbul is revolutionizing the world of popular Turkish music. Kenan Doğulu is currently Turkey's pop music icon. *Festival* is his latest album, released in 2006 (fig. 7.24). Although much of his music pursues nationalistic themes, he has also been able to ride the crest of globalization. He placed fourth in the 2007 Eurovision songfest, where he transcended the boundary between east and west by performing "Shake it up Şekerim"—in English. To hear what is shaking up Istanbul, plug into Kenan Doğulu's official website and learn some urban cultural geography: http://www.kenandogulu.com.tr/.

Figure 7.24   CDs are for sale all over Istanbul and the rest of Turkey.

"the Arab conquest," about 790 A.D. The Arabs arrived via the Taza Gap, the only natural corridor between the Maghreb and the rest of North Africa. An Arab village joined a Berber village on a tributary of the largest river in Morocco. This city, Fès al Bali, commanded passage through the Taza gap to the east. It was also located near well-watered and forested mountains to the north and south and had a rich agricultural hinterland to the west. As trade developed, the *souks* of Fès became the best in the Maghreb.

Marrakesh was born in the 11th century when the indigenous peoples of the Sahara established a trading post just north of the snow-capped High Atlas mountains. Their rulers were so successful in consolidating power and trade routes that the city soon became their capital. As a result, Marrakesh and Fès both claim to be the historical core of the Moroccan state, with Fès contributing its Arab and Andalusian culture (Arab culture transplanted from Spain) and Marrakesh contributing the culture of the African Sahara.

A comparative analysis of the cultural landscapes of Fès and Marrakesh illustrates their roles in building the national urban system. Like cities everywhere, the personality of each city is expressed most clearly in its center, within the walls of the old city, the *medina*. All Moroccan cities have their *medinas*, but the finest in the entire Maghreb, and arguably the best-preserved preindustrial city in the world, is Morocco's first imperial capital, Fès. The second finest *medina* may be in Marrakesh, the imperial capital of Morocco's south. So authentic are the landscapes of intramural Fès and Marrakesh that they were among the first to be placed on the United Nations' World Heritage List. Fès and Marrakesh have shaped the culture that is uniquely Moroccan. Common to the cultural landscape of both Fès and Marrakesh are the *souks*, or markets. They are the rabbit warrens of shops and craft merchants competing to provide not only the necessities but also the finer goods and higher-level services that mark the differences between urban and rural life.

Both Fès and Marrakesh served as focal points of commerce, political power, religious life, and public celebrations. But why have these ancient walled cores been able to stall the passage of time so well? Their survival is related to the survival of Morocco itself. More than most other places in the Middle East, Morocco held outside conquest at bay, turning back both the expanding European kingdoms to the north and the Ottoman Empire

to the east. Few Westerners even laid eyes on the interior of Morocco until the French established a protectorate in 1912. For an "infidel," penetrating Morocco was the equivalent of penetrating Tibet—one did it only under cover. Many of Morocco's *medinas*, therefore, survived intact. Fortunately, when the colonizing French did arrive, they chose not to modernize them, but to build new cities outside the old walls, thus saving medieval urban landscapes from disfiguring modernization.

The most well known symbols of Fès are the Kiraouan and Andalusian mosques. The first is among the most revered in the entire Muslim world. It stands not alone, but with its university, among the oldest in the world, and the tomb of the founder of Fès. The spiritual and intellectual life of Fès set the tone for the evolution of Moroccan culture. Like Fès, the most recognizable site in the Marrakesh *medina* is a mosque, the Koutoubia. It was built by a Berber dynasty that recentralized power in the south. The Koutoubia's minaret, its most conspicuous feature, arose as a statement of political power, as a mirror image of the mosque built in Córdoba, Spain, where Andalusian culture thrived. In Marrakesh commercial power blended with political power, whereas in Fès commercial and political power blended with the power of Islam. It was probably this religious anchor that kept the capital city function returning to Fès.

The physical settings of Fès and Marrakesh have influenced each city's urban landscape. The Fès *medina*, wedged into a narrow, V-shaped valley, epitomizes preindustrial urban crowding. Every square inch of space is accounted for. As a result of its more northerly location and higher altitude, Fès's climate is cooler and rainier. The Marrakesh *medina*, on the other hand, seems to epitomize the desert, which begins just to the south of the High Atlas. The spaciousness of the desert is reflected in the public square in the center of the Marrakesh *medina*. Such an expanse of open space in a Middle Eastern city is a rarity.

Tashkent: Anchor of Central Asia

With over 2 million people, Tashkent is Central Asia's largest city. Since independence from the Soviet Union in 1991, it has come to see itself as the region's anchor and gateway, and as a transcontinental bridge linking east and west. It is also the capital city of Uzbekistan, the most central state of Central Asia. Uzbekistan borders every other country in the region (but not Russia), giving it a pivotal geopolitical role in the 21st century's "great game" for influence over people, trade corridors, and resources (natural gas, gold, uranium, and cotton).

Almost every city of Central Asia originated as a trading post on the "silk roads." Tashkent is no exception. It was a port on the edge of the desert, a "stone town" on the northern route from Kashgar (now in China) to the Caspian Sea, and thence on to Europe. Its founding goes back at least 2,000 years to the place where the Syr Darya's tributaries back up to the water-laden Tien Shan (mountains). With such enviable access to the region's most precious resource, water, Tashkent offered opportunities for modern growth. The city is also situated near the mouth of the Fergana Valley, one of the choice spots for fruit and vegetable production in the region. It is also in a commanding position relative to the cotton fields snaking across the irrigated desert to the Aral Sea. These economic attractions, combined with the region's

gold resources, were the cause of Russia's interest in the area, which resulted in conquest. Tashkent was in the first khanate to be absorbed, in 1865, during a time when Europe had been cut off from American supplies of cotton by the Civil War.

During the Soviet period, Tashkent was selected to be the capital of the Uzbek SSR, replacing Samarkand in 1930. Before World War II its population was only half a million, but during the war, the Soviets mounted a massive effort and protectively located many strategic industrial operations beyond the Urals, thus swelling the city's population. In fact, Tashkent's most renowned product is still airplanes, and Seattle, Washington, home of Boeing Aircraft, is one of Tashkent's "sister cities." When the Soviet Union collapsed, the city was the country's fourth largest. It was also the most Soviet city in Central Asia thanks to two factors—communism's emphasis on centralized state planning and the forces of nature. Tashkent was almost completely destroyed by an earthquake in 1966. The Soviets seized upon the opportunity to refashion the landscape in a socialist mode: "a new Soviet city" for "a new Soviet man."

Tashkent's ancient core survives only in the four historic M's: market, mosque, *madrassa*, and mausoleum. Since independence, a fifth M has been added: a new museum, dedicated to the life of Tamerlane. Although Tashkent was not Tamerlane's capital, the city has seized upon Amir Tamur as the quintessential symbol of its independence and quest for respect. Like many states that cast off communist regimes, Uzbekistan has mined the archives for inspiration drawn from its pre-Soviet and pre-Russian past. The opening of the Tamerlane Museum symbolizes that transition. Tashkent was a regional city beholden to Moscow.

Today it is the capital city of an independent state seeking to play the same role in the modern world as did Tamerlane's empire when it stretched from the borders of Europe to the borders of China.

It is iconography rooted in Turkic culture that is now remaking the landscape of Tashkent (even though Tamerlane was probably Mongol, and his capital was Samarkand). Lenin and Marx are gone; heroes on horseback and other images of the steppes have taken their place. Government buildings fly flags that are Turkic blue, not Soviet red. New structures are conglomerates of steppe-colored brick, not piles of cinder blocks. One out of every five cars is a Daewoo, from Korea. Traditional domes and arches (bedecked with blue tiles) are replacing socialist perpendiculars. Mosques are being built again, after decades of antireligious propaganda. Uzbek, a Turkic tongue, has replaced Russian as the official state language (in 1989), and it is being written in the Roman alphabet, not Cyrillic, a fact of life easily read in the city's linguistic landscape.

Meanwhile, Tashkent still has a predominantly Soviet feel and appearance. About a third of the population is Slavic in origin and speaks Russian. Nine-story apartment blocks dominate residential neighborhoods. European-style parks and open space, a positive contribution of socialist planning, were incorporated into the landscape after the earthquake. Opera, ballet, and puppet theater still dominate the performing arts. The only subway system in Central Asia offers Tashkent the same efficient service and rich artistry as Moscow's metro. Flights to Moscow still far outnumber flights to any other destination. Finally, a layer of transnational landscape elements has appeared: Western products in the stores, logos of multinational corporations downtown, American fast-food chains, international hotels, copious commercial advertising, and the international tourist trade that has come to exploit the lure of Asia's "old silk road."

KEY PROBLEMS

Middle Eastern cities do many things well. First, they reflect the hospitality of their inhabitants, people who easily talk to visitors, are anxious to communicate despite linguistic barriers, and have time to spend in casual conversation on the street (fig. 7.25). Arabs, Turks, and Iranians are among the friendliest in the world, and their cities make you feel at home. Second, Middle Eastern cities, with few exceptions, are safe day and night. There are "eyes upon the street" all the time, whether you can see them or not; and family networks, undergirded by strict codes of conduct, hold family members accountable. Additionally, alcohol consumption among Muslims is prohibited, so drunkenness is uncommon. Third, the generations mix freely. Neither the old nor young are warehoused; parents are seen with children, teenagers use the same streets as the elderly, and young apprentices are common in the city's businesses. Households are often multigenerational. Fourth, homelessness, although it does exist, is less common than in Western cities. It is taken for granted that some people will not be able to live self-sufficient lives, so families compensate for personal inadequacies, and many social needs are taken care of by the Islamic emphasis on required almsgiving and charity. Fifth, almost every city takes pride in its food, whether served in sit-down restaurants or on the street. Middle Eastern cuisine helps to define both national

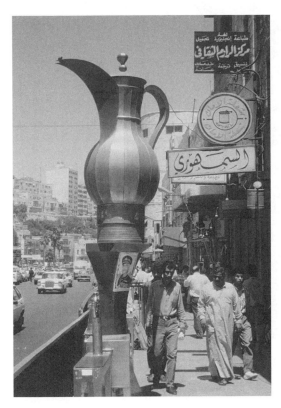

Figure 7.25 The coffee urn is a symbol of hospitality throughout the Arab world, as seen here in Jordan's capital, Amman. (Photo by Donald Zeigler)

world regions. These troubles include overly rapid population growth, unemployment and underemployment, pollution, transportation chaos (much of it caused by the impact of the automobile), and shantytowns or squatter settlements. In the case of the last element, unique names have been developed to describe them: *geçekondu* ("built overnight") in Turkey and *bidonvilles* (after the tin "oil cans," *bidon à pétrole*, used to build them) in the Maghreb and other former French colonial territories.

Three problems acutely felt in the Greater Middle East, however, are those of fresh water, cultural homogenization, and preserving the region's heritage.

Fresh Water

There is a shortage of water in the Middle East. As cities expand, they can accommodate growth only by developing water resources for new homes, businesses, and industries. Surface and groundwater resources are being utilized to the maximum throughout most of the region. Even the "fossil waters" of the Sahara are being used by the Libyans to supply their urban populations in the north, and the Arab states of the Persian/Arabian Gulf have all gone into desalination in a big way. Nevertheless, most cities do not use their water resources efficiently. What water they do have could go further if leaky pipes were repaired, if water-conserving technologies were used, and if irrigation systems could make do with less. Additionally, the water problem is not simply a problem of quantity; it is also a problem of quality. Virtually every city must concentrate on upgrading its water treatment operations so that tap water is safe to drink.

cultures and urban life. Furthermore, it is healthy food, not overly processed, and rarely fried. Sixth, cities are well served by a variety of transportation. Cars are not required; in the old cities, they may be a hindrance. City buses, taxis, service taxis (often 12-passenger vans), and fixed-rail lines (in a few cities) always make it possible to get around at very low cost. Besides, cities are compactly organized, so walking is always a possibility (fig. 7.26).

Urban life in the Middle East is not utopian, however. Cities have their problems, some seemingly intractable, just as in other

Figure 7.26 Walking is still the best way to cover short distances in most cities, and it is sometimes the most efficient way of delivering goods. Welcome to the streets of Istanbul. (Photo by Donald Zeigler)

Cultural Homogenization

The trend throughout the Middle East is toward more culturally homogenous populations, a concomitant of European-style nation building. Istanbul is more ethnically Turkish and more thoroughly Muslim than ever before in history, and Alexandria and Cairo more Arab. Slavs have left Tashkent by the thousands since independence from the Soviet Union. Many Israelis see Jerusalem as becoming ever more thoroughly Jewish. Religious minorities have been squeezed out of virtually all cities in Iraq and Iran. Europeans, seen as "the colonizers," have abandoned the cities of the Maghreb. The Jewish population of every Middle Eastern city outside of Israel has decreased substantially or disappeared since 1948. There seems to be a desire for "ethnic purity," and some see this as a problem of urban cultural geography.

Heritage

In all cities of the Middle East, modernization threatens heritage resources. New roads cut through walled cities, suburban expansion buries Roman villages, and property owners upgrade without considering historical preservation. In the architectural realm, urban expansion zones are looking more and more alike throughout the world. Meanwhile, the integrity of old urban landscapes is scarred by deterioration or unregulated incumbent upgrading. The new postwar landscape of central Beirut, for instance, has been rebuilt in an "international style," quite in contrast to Sana'a, the capital of Yemen, which has used United Nations aid to maintain the architectural unity of its historic core despite rapid population growth.

These problems, along with others too numerous to mention, are not unique to Middle Eastern cities. They are worldwide. As a majority of the world's population has become urban, the problems of cities are increasingly the problems of all humanity. Having invented the city in the 4th millennium B.C., the people of the Middle East are now challenged to see if they can perfect it in the 21st century A.D.

SUGGESTED READINGS

Abu Lughod, Janet L. 1971. *Cairo: 1001 Years of the City Victorious.* Princeton, NJ: Princeton University Press. A chronicle of Cairo from 969 to 1970 and a glimpse of how to make sense of any urban landscape.

Benvenisti, Meron. 1996. *City of Stone: The Hidden History of Jerusalem.* Berkeley: University of California Press. Offers a balanced view of Jerusalem's urban landscapes, boundaries, and demographics.

Bonine, Michael, ed. 1997. *Population, Poverty, and Politics in Middle East Cities.* Gainesville: University Press of Florida. Profiles of various cities and articles on political, historical, and gender-related themes.

Elsheshtawy, Yasser. 2004. *Planning Middle Eastern Cities: An Urban Kaleidoscope.* London and New York: Routledge. Presents urban planning in the context of globalization, with separate chapters on Cairo, Dubai, and Algiers.

Hitti, Philip K. 1973. *Capital Cities of Arab Islam.* Minneapolis: University of Minnesota Press. Thoughtful profiles of historical capitals: Mecca, Medina, Damascus, Baghdad, Cairo, and Cordova.

Hourani, Albert Habib, and Samuel Miklos Stern. 1970. *The Islamic City.* Philadelphia: University of Pennsylvania Press. Delves into the question of whether there is an "Islamic" city, with specific reference to Damascus, Samarra, and Baghdad.

Kheirabadi, Masoud. 2001. *Iranian Cities: Form and Development.* Syracuse, NY: Syracuse University Press. A thorough treatment of the spatial structure and physical form of Iranian cities.

Salamandra, Christa. 2004. *A New Old Damascus.* Bloomington: Indiana University Press. Presents a portrait of Damascus's cultural anthropology, with considerable attention focused on the problems of historical preservation.

Serageldim, Ismail, and Samir El-Sadek, eds. 1982. *The Arab City: Its Character and Islamic Cultural Heritage.* Riyadh, Saudi Arabia: Arab Urban Development Institute. Photographs, drawings, and readable text on city form and urban planning.

Wheatley, Paul. 2001. *The Places Where Men Pray Together.* Chicago: University of Chicago Press. Analyses of cities and urban systems in Islamic lands between the 7th and 10th centuries.

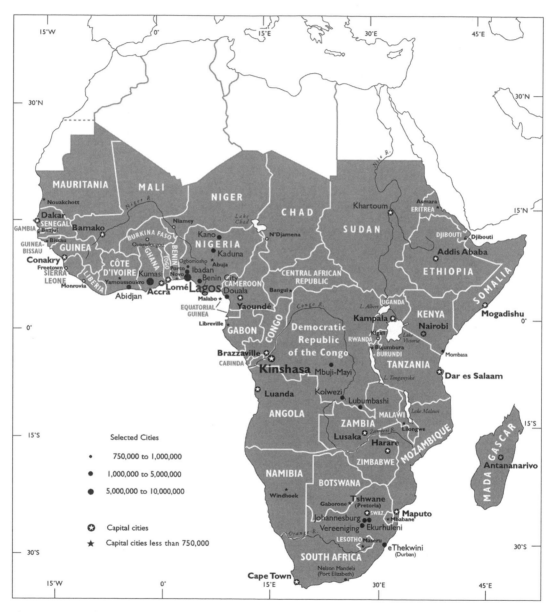

Figure 8.1 Major Cities of Sub-Saharan Africa. *Source:* UN *World Urbanization Prospects, 2005 revision* [online].

8

Cities of Sub-Saharan Africa
GARTH MYERS AND FRANCIS OWUSU

KEY URBAN FACTS

Total Population	751 million
Percent Urban Population	35.2%
Total Urban Population	264 million
Most Urbanized Countries	Djibouti (86.1%)
	Gabon (84.0%)
	Congo (60.2%)
Least Urbanized Countries	Burundi (10.0%)
	Uganda (12.6%)
	Ethiopia (16.0%)
Annual Urban Growth Rate	3.5%
Number of Megacities	1
Number of Cities of More Than 1 Million	36
Three Largest Cities	Lagos, Kinshasa, Khartoum
World Cities	Johannesburg

KEY CHAPTER THEMES

1. Sub-Saharan Africa (SSA) is among the least urbanized world regions, but it contains some of the world's most rapidly urbanizing countries.
2. A rich urban tradition preceded the arrival of colonialism in several parts of SSA.
3. Colonialism had profound impacts on urban development, particularly in the creation of what would become primate cities along the coast.

4. Rates of urban primacy are generally high across the region, and economic production and political power are concentrated in the primate cities.
5. Many, though not all, primate cities are also capital cities.
6. Many SSA cities have experienced major impacts from cultural globalization, such as changing patterns of consumption, but minimal impacts from economic globalization, in terms of production and investment.
7. Most SSA urban land-use patterns and economies are developing outside of formal regulations, but there is significant overlap between the "formal" and the "informal" sectors of the economy.
8. Many SSA cities are characterized by spatial and socioeconomic inequalities and by high rates of urban poverty.
9. Great cultural diversity and creativity help shape very dynamic urban life experiences for residents of SSA's cities.
10. SSA's interlocking urban environmental problems are magnified by shortcomings in management and oversight by both governments and the private sector.

Sub-Saharan Africa (SSA) has long been among the least urbanized world regions. But many countries south of the Sahara have been urbanizing rapidly since the 1960s (fig. 8.1). This rapid urban growth has come with limited opportunities for employment in the formal economy. African cities also suffer from a lack of effective governance, a lack of decent and affordable housing, failing infrastructure and basic urban services, and increasing inequalities. But negative views of contemporary cities are overly simplistic. African cities are also creative engines of cultural change and dynamic centers of political and associational life. Many accounts of cities in SSA miss the resourcefulness, inventiveness, and determination of millions of ordinary people who manage to negotiate the perils of everyday life to make something out of nothing.

Cities in Sub-Saharan Africa are diverse and heterogeneous. Scholars have not been able to come up with a single model of a generic "African city that fits all cases," though some attempts have been made

(fig. 8.2). Another general scheme was fashioned 25 years ago by Anthony O'Connor, but his effort led him toward not one but six possible types. O'Connor identified city morphologies that he classified as the indigenous city, the Islamic city, the European city, the colonial city, and the dual city, and offered examples from across the continent. His sixth category—what he termed the hybrid city—actually functions as a kind of catch-all for cities with multiple morphological characteristics. Over time, more cities in Africa seem to have become hybrid cities.

The paths to such African hybrid cities are complex and sometimes contradictory. While many cities came into existence as overseas extensions of European colonial powers seeking to establish beachheads on the African continent, their subsequent growth and development did not conform to a single pattern. City-building processes that took place under the dominance of European colonialism often left an indelible imprint on the original spatial layout, built

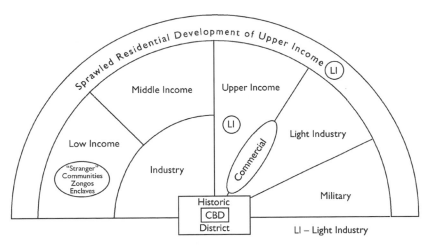

Figure 8.2   A Model of the Sub-Saharan African City. *Source:* Samuel Aryeetey-Attoh, "Urban Geography of Sub-Saharan Africa," in *Geography of Sub-Saharan Africa*, edited by Samuel Aryeetey-Attoh (Upper Saddle River, NJ: Prentice-Hall, 1997), 193. Reprinted with permission.

environment, and architectural styles of cities in Africa. Yet over time, these features have sometimes been modified beyond recognition. Thus, cities that were built specifically for Europeans (O'Connor's "European cities"), such as Cape Town or Nairobi, still have clear European influences, but these have been overwhelmed by African and even Asian influences. Colonial landscapes, too, have been dramatically transformed by what amounts to nearly 50 years of independence. Likewise, indigenous, Islamic, and dual cities have in nearly all cases witnessed the steady overlay and erasure of their original forms through colonial and postcolonial impacts.

In SSA cities, previous patterns of government dominance in urban centers have been replaced by patterns resulting from a greater reliance on private sector and/or nongovernmental institutions. Municipal authorities have not kept up with the demand for infrastructure, social services, or

access to resources. Many urban residents have looked outside the formal economy and conventional administrative channels to gain access to income, shelter, land, or social services (box 8.1).

The wide range of seemingly unsolvable problems has led some to conclude cities in Africa just "don't work." Others, like the urban scholar AbdouMaliq Simone, prefer to see them as "works in progress," driven forward by inventive ordinary people. In city after city, urban residents rely on their own ingenuity to stitch together their daily lives. SSA cities are often distressed places in need of good governance, management, infrastructure, greater popular participation in decision-making, sustainable livelihoods, and expanded socioeconomic opportunities. Yet, they are much more than a form of failed urbanism. To see SSA cities more complexly, we must appreciate the historical specificity and heterogeneous cultural vibrancy of different cities in Africa.

Box 8.1   Multiple Livelihood Strategies

The economic crisis that spread across Africa in the 1970s and 1980s and the structural adjustment programs that were introduced in the 1980s have caused major upheavals in the livelihood strategies of millions of people in African cities, including formal sector employees. For instance, although the introduction of cost-recovery measures has escalated the prices of critical urban services, the real salaries of formal sector employees, especially public sector employees have remained stagnant and in some cases have declined. Moreover, the limited job creation potential of the private sector in Africa, combined with employment freezes and retrenchment in the public sector, has reduced avenues for employment in the formal sector. At the same time, policies have led to increased poverty in urban areas. The combined effect of the economic reforms and the urbanization of poverty is that many formal sector employees, either by necessity or choice, have joined the informal sector in an effort to increase and diversify their income-earning opportunities.

Since the early 1990s, an increasing number of studies from selected African countries and cities have documented how people of various socioeconomic backgrounds and statuses seek additional income by engaging in multiple economic activities. Overall, this literature shows that participation in multiple activities is not limited to the urban poor, but it also includes other social classes such as the middle and professional classes that were previously assumed to be immune from the pressures of economic change and therefore did not need to diversify their livelihood options. Individuals and households across Africa have responded differently to these macroeconomic processes based on the nature of their employment, skills, access to resources, socioeconomic backgrounds, and places of residence. Individuals employed in the public or private sector as well as private entrepreneurs have all attempted to diversify their sources of income, although the motivations for doing so vary. Many formal sector employees supplement their incomes with part-time informal-sector jobs, such as cab driving or petty trading. Other members of their households may also supplement the family income by engaging in similar activities. For instance, many civil servants in Kampala engage in urban agriculture and poultry keeping, own taxis, or operate small kiosks, and about two-thirds of households in Accra engaged in at least two income generating activities. Such multiple livelihood strategies have become "the way of doing things" in many African cities, and as a result, the traditional distinction between the formal and informal sectors has become blurrier and more complex.

The proliferation of multiple livelihood strategies in SSA cities has significant implications for urban economic studies and urban planning in the region. First, it signifies the need to revise African city models to include urban cultivation as a legitimate urban activity. Urban agriculture poses a difficult challenge for planners and policy-makers because it is "a ubiquitous, complex and dynamic feature of the urban and socio-economic landscape in Africa." However, the practice cannot simply be wished away in African cities because of its widespread nature; rather, it should be seen within the broader context of the urban economy, urban management, and urban development. This would require documenting the benefits and disadvantages of urban agriculture and finding ways of creatively integrating the practice into the urban fabric. Second, one effect of participation in multiple economic activities is that the notion of the house or dwelling as a monofunctional (residential) unit is increasingly becoming out of sync with reality in many African cities. Many urban residents of different socioeconomic backgrounds have economic enterprises that are located in their homes—a space that conventional planning reserves for residential use only. Urban planners in the region need to introduce relevant changes in zoning regulations and housing design standards, because the multiple functions of the house in African cities and the proliferation of home-based enterprises do not appear to be stop-gap measures. Third, multiple livelihood strategies have also led to the emergence of nontraditional household living arrangements that challenge the conventional definition of households and the distinction between urban and rural residence. Historically, SSA households have used migration as a strategy for ensuring their survival, especially in southern Africa, but involvement in multiple livelihood strategies requires different and more creative living arrangements. To overcome the limitations of a particular local economy or to expand their options, some households adopt flexible arrangements that allow members to participate in multiple urban and/or rural economies. The final issue relates to the implications of the increased involvement of public-sector employees in multiple economic activities for public-sector efficiency. While participation in multiple economic activities by public-sector employees in the African context benefits those directly involved in the practice, the overall impact on society is often negative. As the involvement of civil servants in multiple income-generating activities becomes widespread, the moral authority of supervisors to reprimand moonlighting staff begins to be compromised, especially when the officials themselves are guilty of the same. Thus, the relationship between the proliferation of such practices among public-sector employees and efficiency of public institutions deserves serious scrutiny.

Source: Francis Owusu, "Conceptualizing Livelihood Strategies in African Cities," *Journal of Planning Education and Research* 26, no. 4 (2007), 450–463.

HISTORICAL GEOGRAPHY OF AFRICAN URBAN DEVELOPMENT

Simply because SSA is among the least urbanized world regions, outsiders assume that its cities must have been established recently. Because European colonialism was such a pervasive regional experience, it is also assumed that the urbanization of Africa ought to be attributed to colonialism. In fact, many SSA urban settlements were built long before the colonial era, and the relationships between formal colonialism and the urbanization process in Africa are more complicated than they first appear. Roughly speaking, we may divide contemporary African cities

Figure 8.3   An upscale home in Zanzibar is illustrative of socioeconomic inequality in Sub-Saharan Africa. (Photo by Assefa Mehretu)

into categories based on origin in (1) the ancient or medieval precolonial period, (2) the period of the trans-Atlantic slave trade and of European trade and exploration, (3) the period of formal colonial rule, and (4) the postcolonial period. However, it rapidly becomes difficult to differentiate cities using these categories. For instance, Zanzibar, Tanzania, an indigenous urban center with origins in the 1100s, was refashioned under the domination of outsiders from Portugal in the 1500s and from Oman in the 1690s; it then became caught up in the slave trade and in trade with Europe and the Americas in the 1700s and 1800s, then became a British colonial capital, and finally ended up as the symbolic heart of a postcolonial socialist revolution. Like so many hybrid cities of contemporary Africa, Zanzibar has elements of its fabric that belong to all four of the categories above (fig. 8.3). Rather than making sharp breaks between city types based on their origins, it is more helpful to simply lay out these different types of origin stories.

Ancient and Medieval Precolonial Urban Centers

Many urban centers that were prominent before 1500 A.D. are now ruins. Other cities of ancient and medieval times were bypassed by the new economic geographies that arose in Africa's relationships with Europe and the New World after 1500, which focused urban development along the coast.

There were at least five major centers of urban settlement before 1500, with the oldest being the ancient Upper Nile/Ethiopian centers of Meroë, Axum, and Adulis (fig. 8.4). The medieval Sahelian (or western Sudanese) cities of West Africa's great trading empires, such as Kumbi Saleh, Timbuktu, Gao, and Jenne, arose as desert ports on a network of caravan routes that crisscrossed the Sahara. They achieved significance in the medieval world as nodes of empires, trading entrepôts, and centers of learning. Timbuktu, Gao, and Jenne were widely regarded for their scholarship in medieval times, but they disappeared or stagnated after the 15th century. Timbuktu has about the same population as it had

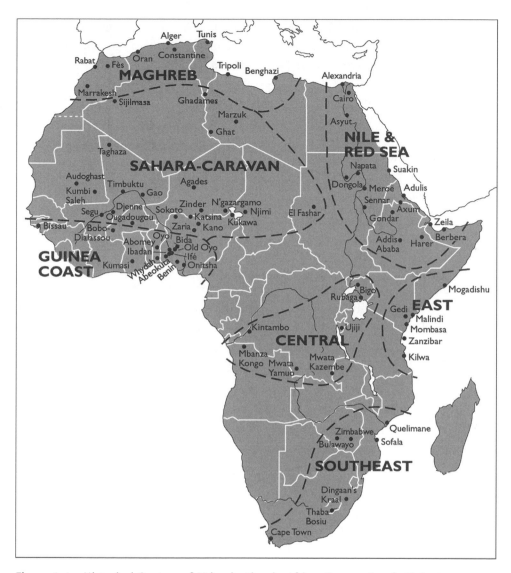

Figure 8.4   Historical Centers of Urbanization in Africa. *Source:* Assefa Mehretu.

700 years ago, and it is only now, in the early 21st century, attempting to restore its extraordinary libraries of medieval 13th and 14th century history and religion texts; Gao and Jenne, on the other hand, no longer exist. Other urban places of western Sudan survived the new, post-1500 world and developed into important contemporary settlements. For instance, because their 19th century rulers derived great strength from Islamic religious *jihad* movements, the Hausa cities of today's northern Nigeria and southern Niger, particularly Kano, emerged as important urban centers.

This post-1500 growth was even more common for many ancient and medieval cities of Nigeria, like Oyo, Ibadan, Benin in the Benin–Yoruba area of early urbanism. The Yoruba cities of southwestern Nigeria had developed metalwork artistry and skill unsurpassed in the first millennium world. Benin–Yoruba cities, and neighboring urban areas further to the west, were well positioned to capitalize on the new trade with Europeans after 1500.

Some of the trading city-states along the East African coast, including Mogadishu and Mombasa, also grew after 1500, but many coastal settlements, like the settlements of the southern interior (particularly in Zimbabwe) with whom they traded, largely disappeared. The ruins of the Great Zimbabwe in today's Zimbabwe still demonstrate the remarkable organizational and architectural features of the medieval empire whose central city was located there. The southern interior cities were connected by trade routes to those along the coast for many centuries before 1500.

Coastal trading centers on the Red Sea and Indian Ocean arose in ancient times, and an extensive trade linking the African interior from Zimbabwe north to Lake Victoria with the Arab and Persian peoples of Asia flourished for more than a thousand years. Beginning in the 9th century, the significance of the East African coast ratcheted upward with increased trade with the Arabian peninsula and the Persian Gulf area, based on the export of gold, ivory, and slaves from Africa in exchange for textiles, jewelry, and other commodities. East African coastal centers such as Kilwa, Malindi, and Mombasa derived their growth, character, and political organization from the encounters and exchanges between the African mainlanders who founded them and the small numbers of Arab, Persian, and even South Asian settlers who made perma-

nent homes there. Their rise is considered part of the medieval golden age of Swahili civilization. The greatest of these, Kilwa, now in ruins in southern Tanzania, had diplomatic exchanges with China in the 15th century.

Urban Development after 1500

Cities of the pre-1500 era were quite small, often with fewer than 50,000 residents. Europe's impact south of the Sahara changed the geographic pattern of African urbanization, beginning with the Portuguese in the 15th century. For about two and a half centuries, most contact between European traders and Africans occurred in coastal installations, from which Europeans gradually developed trade networks for various tropical commodities. The slave trade arguably contributed the most to coastal city development between about 1500 and 1870, but this impact was not an unambiguously positive one. During those years, more than 20 million Africans were forcibly relocated to the Americas or died en route; roughly an equal number died or were displaced within Africa. Nonetheless, it is remarkable how many of the major and secondary cities of coastal West and Central Africa in particular grew up in the midst of the trans-Atlantic slave trade.

The Portuguese established the first of these towns, St. Louis, in the 1440s at the mouth of the Senegal River, later creating centers at Bissau in today's Guinea-Bissau; Luanda and Benguela in Angola; and Lourenço Marques (now Maputo) and Mozambique in Mozambique. The Dutch, French, and British followed the Portuguese lead. The Dutch founded Cape Town in 1652 (fig. 8.5); the French and British established

Figure 8.5   In Cape Town, South Africa's crown jewel city, the harbor area has been redeveloped into this handsome tourist mecca. (Photo by Jack Williams)

West African coastal towns such as Conakry in Guinea and Calabar in Nigeria. Most towns were merely forts: the Dutch built Fort Ussher (now Accra) in 1650, and the British built Fort James on the Gambia in 1663.

During the 19th century, the trans-Atlantic slave trade declined, superseded by what was termed "legitimate trade" in African raw materials. In combination with competition between European firms and states as the century progressed, African urban areas that participated in this increasingly high-volume and high-value trade grew dramatically. Precolonial towns such as Ibadan in Nigeria witnessed considerable growth. The 19th century also saw the rise of new or rejuvenated cities in eastern and southern Africa. The city-state of Zanzibar grew into the "island metropolis of Eastern Africa" as the center of a mercantile empire whose tentacles stretched to the Congo. Khartoum emerged in the Sudan. A number of South Africa's major cities, including Port Elizabeth, Durban, Bloemfontein, East London, and Pretoria, were founded via European settlement (box 8.2).

During the period of European contact before formal colonialism in the 1880s, SSA's urban geography began to take form, but under constraints. First, most European contributions to settlement development were coastal, with minimal impacts in the interior. Second, many coastal settlements were intended as transshipment points for trade and lacked regular urban facilities, except those structures that served as European housing or as port and defense establishments. Third, there was a lack of diffusion of European technology and culture to the interior's indigenous urban centers.

Box 8.2   South Africa's New Names for New Cities

Symbolic renaming went along with the process of dismantling the geography of apartheid in South Africa. Two old provinces took on new names: the Orange Free State became simply Free State, distancing it from the Dutch ancestry of the white settlers that had established apartheid, and Natal became KwaZulu-Natal, an integration of the former British colony with the Zulu majority Bantustan. Some wholly new provinces were also assigned Africanized names. The former Cape Province was subdivided into the provinces of Western, Northern, and Eastern Cape, whereas the former Transvaal was reconfigured into Limpopo (for the river at its northern edge), Northwest, Mpumalanga (meaning Eastern), and Gauteng (SeSotho for "at the gold," home to Johannesburg).

New African names have been created for many of South Africa's cities and towns that once had names symbolizing apartheid or the colonial past. The approach often involved incorporating formerly whites-only cities and the nonwhite townships that surrounded them, retaining the old name (for example, Pretoria) for the area it used to apply to, but governing it as a part of a new Metropolitan Municipality (in this example, Tshwane, "Place of the Black Cow" in Tswana). South Africa now has six metropolitan municipalities, including Tshwane. Port Elizabeth was reconfigured as a constituent part of Nelson Mandela Municipality in honor of the multiracial democracy's inspiring first President (1994–1999). Durban is now a segment of eThekwini ("By the Bay" in Zulu), and East Rand is just a part of Ekurhuleni ("Place of Peace" in Tsonga). Johannesburg and Cape Town retain their names, albeit with many local nicknames taking their place in ordinary conversation or media (e.g., iGoli—"place of Gold" in Zulu—for Johannesburg).

Some urban place names have formally and informally been expunged. One dramatic example of this came just west of Johannesburg, in Sophiatown. The apartheid regime forcibly removed the multiracial and income-diverse cultural bastion of Sophiatown early in its reign, demolishing it in an effort to make a "black spot" into a middle-class white suburb like the neighborhoods around it. Apartheid's planners chose the Afrikaans name Triomf (Triumph) for the new white area when their courts gave them the right to remove the black spot. The new South Africa's board of geographical names promptly erased this example of arrogance and renamed the newly reintegrating settlement Sophiatown again. In keeping with the new openness and technical savvy of the multiracial rainbow nation, this board accepts applications for place name changes online on a continuous basis, in any of the eleven national languages.

Figure 8.6   The old CBD of Mombasa still evokes the ambiance of the colonial era in this tropical city near the equator. (Photo by Jack Williams)

African Urbanization in the Era of Formal Colonial Rule

The "European scramble for Africa" lasted from the 1880s through the 1914 outbreak of World War I. By that point, virtually the entire continent had fallen under European domination. Ethiopia and Liberia remained independent states, and South Africa became an independent, white-minority-ruled state in 1910, but the British, French, German, Italian, Portuguese, Belgian, and Spanish colonial powers controlled the rest of SSA. Urbanization followed suit, because social and physical aspects of urban development followed the social and political objectives of these European powers. Colonial regimes moved aggressively into the interior of their colonies, and urban settlements sprang up or expanded from existing towns along infrastructure lines (roads or railroads), near mines or large-scale plantation areas, and in regions requiring administrative

centers. Virtually all coastal ports and railheads from Dakar to Luanda became the capitals and/or primate cities of their respective countries, with external trade as their major function. In East Africa, where the resource hinterlands are far in the interior, towns such as Kampala, Nairobi, and Salisbury (Harare) were linked by railways to ports in or near each country, such as Mombasa in Kenya (fig. 8.6) and Beira in Mozambique. Other East African centers, such as Dar es Salaam (fig. 8.7) and Maputo, became important ports.

In South Africa, the pattern was somewhat different. Major European settlement in the interior predated the formal colonial era in most of SSA (1880s to 1960s), and major mining and agro-industrial towns were well established by 1900. In South Africa, as a result, there are now numerous urban centers in the interior served by a number of ports all around the southern tip of the continent. The railway pattern is much more intensive, with a high

Figure 8.7   Along this commercial street in present-day Dar es Salaam, one can buy a hot dog, a pool table, a school uniform, jewelry, chocolate, and seeds, according to shop signs. (Photo by Assefa Mehretu)

degree of connectivity between urban centers in the plateau hinterland as well as between the interior settlements and the port cities.

Under European colonialism, little real industrialization occurred in SSA. Colonial regimes prioritized the export of minerals, metals, or primary goods to Europe, so that industrial development was most intensive in places like the Zambian Copperbelt (in cities such as Ndola or Kitwe) and the neighboring mining province of Shaba (Katanga) in Congo. In many colonies, and in white-ruled South Africa, severe limits were placed on African residency in urban areas. To support the scale of trade that flowed between Africa and Europe and to control the colonies, larger administrations emerged, leading to an outsized service sector for the comparatively shrunken state of secondary-sector activities. Urban services were also generally quite warped by race and class (fig. 8.8).

As a result of the limited economic opportunities and restrictions on movement, many SSA urban centers remained relatively small until after World War II. The so-called second colonial occupation of the postwar era, when colonial regimes invested in African development largely in an effort to shape decolonization movements away from the influences of the Soviet Union, led to the growth of investment in many urban areas. Relaxation of migration and residency regulations with independence brought massive rural-to-urban migration in SSA.

There are differences among the respective colonial powers (particularly Britain, France, and Portugal) in terms of their urban legacies,

Figure 8.8   These colorful apartment houses dot the landscape of Cape Town's Bo-Kapap area. It is known as the "Cape Malay" district. (Photo by Brennan Kraxberger)

but there are also commonalities. British colonies, with substantial white settlement, developed more highly segregated urban residential patterns regulated by more rigid building rules and land-use laws than was the case for colonial cities of many French West African colonies, for instance. Cities with significant white populations in the colonial era tended to have larger investments from colonial states in infrastructure and from the private sector in industrial development. Yet exceptions to this pattern existed, and the distinctions between

Figure 8.9   A dramatic air photo of Lusaka, Zambia, today shows the formerly all-white township of Roma. *Source:* Garth Myers.

different colonial powers' strategies in urban areas are often overridden by the commonalities. In eastern and southern African cities one can still see some distinctly British features in architecture (many colonial government buildings still in use were designed by the British architect Herbert Baker and an army of his protégés) and in urbanism more generally (there are many small urban parks just adjacent

to CBDs that feature the same strict use rules on signs at their entrance that one sees in London or Hong Kong). Many of the neighborhoods formerly segregated by race are now just as segregated, but by class, as illustrated by the dramatic air photo from the late 1990s in Lusaka, Zambia (fig. 8.9). It shows what was, until 1964, the whites-only and separately governed township of Roma and the informal

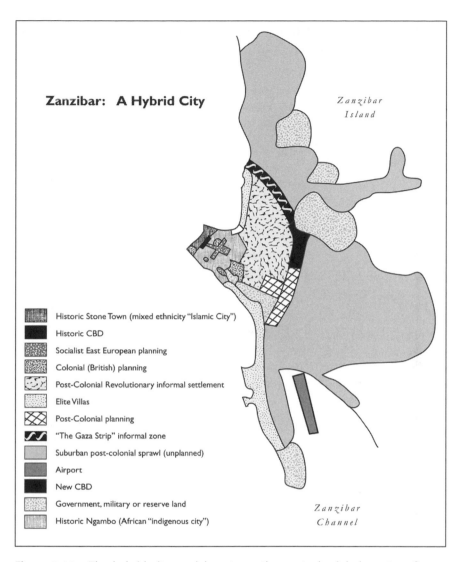

Zanzibar: A Hybrid City

Zanzibar Island

▦	Historic Stone Town (mixed ethnicity "Islamic City")
■	Historic CBD
▨	Socialist East European planning
▨	Colonial (British) planning
∿	Post-Colonial Revolutionary informal settlement
▨	Elite Villas
⊠	Post-Colonial planning
∿	"The Gaza Strip" informal zone
▨	Suburban post-colonial sprawl (unplanned)
▨	Airport
■	New CBD
▨	Government, military or reserve land
▦	Historic Ngambo (African "indigenous city")

Zanzibar Channel

Figure 8.10   The hybrid city model captures the postcolonial character of many African cities south of the Sahara. *Source:* Garth Myers.

settlement of Ng'ombe on its eastern edge. Today Roma is predominantly populated by the African professional class and political elite of Lusaka; their maids and gardeners—also African—still live in Ng'ombe. Distinctively French architectural and planning legacies also remain in former French colonies. But over time, cities all across the region are becoming more and more alike in their hybrid form and function as the postcolonial era brings unprecedented urban growth to SSA (fig. 8.10).

Postcolonial Urbanization

From the 1960s through the 1980s, SSA contained the world's most rapidly urbanizing countries. Eastern and southern Africa have led the world in urbanization rates for nearly half a century. Some countries had annual rates of urban population growth near or above 10% from 1960 to 1991. Even during the 1990s, when many observers noted a slowdown in African urbanization, several countries had estimated urban growth rates near or above 7%. In less than 50 years, some eastern and southern African countries have gone from being largely rural to predominantly urban.

The rapid growth of many cities has been somewhat distinct from what has been seen in other regions, particularly in wealthy European or North American settings. With some exceptions, the extraordinary story of urbanization in Sub-Saharan Africa has not accompanied a substantial economic transformation of society towards industry and manufacturing. In some countries, notably South Africa, industrial development occurred with the urban-ward trends. But in much of SSA, the ever-expanding numbers of urban residents have become increasingly dependent on what are termed informal activities—small-scale, low-technology manufacturing; petty wholesale trading; and informal service provision—for basic needs and daily life.

Current Urbanization Trends

Compared to the other regions, SSA still has one of the lowest levels of urbanization. According to the UN, only about 40% of the region's population lived in urban areas in 2005. There are, however, significant differences in levels of urbanization within the region. Coastal western Africa and southern Africa have the most developed urban hierarchies, and eastern Africa is the least urbanized (tab. 8.1).

Unlike regions of the world that play dominant roles in the globalization process, SSA lacks a dominant "world city." Although Johannesburg plays a regional role, most large SSA cities are centers of national economies. Despite its marginal position in the global economy, urbanization in the region has continued. The proportion of its population in urban areas was 15% in 1950; it then jumped to 25% in 1970 and is projected to exceed 53% by 2030. Thus, between 1950 and 1995, SSA's urban population increased by an average of 5% per annum—about twice the average population growth rate of the region. Since then however, the growth rate has slowed and is projected to be slightly below 3% by 2030. There are also significant variations in urban population growth rates among African countries (tab. 8.1).

The overall growth of urban population in SSA has slowed in recent years, and some public health experts are even predicting a decline in population (box 8.3). However, most major cities continue to grow for now. For instance, the population of the Lagos Metropolitan area is estimated to be over 11 million; Kinshasa-Brazzaville stands at 9.5 million, Johannesburg is at 7.4 million, and Abidjan is at 5.3 million. Between 1996 and 2006, Conakry doubled its population to 2 million, and Luanda nearly doubled its population from 2.2 million in 1995 to 4 million in 2007. Some secondary urban centers have also experienced growth since the 1960s as a result of deliberate government policies implemented to slow growth in national capitals.

Most of the largest cities in SSA are national capitals. Other urban centers tend to be much smaller, except when such cities house a major economic activity like a mine or a port. Development efforts and a host of functions, including administration, industry, commerce, and communications, have focused on

Table 8.1   Selected Urbanization Indicators for Sub-Saharan Africa

Urban Population as Percentage of Total Regional Population

Regions	1995	2007
Africa	34.6	39
Eastern Africa	21.9	23
Middle Africa	32.8	41
Southern Africa	49.7	57
Western Africa	36.3	44

Urban Population as Percentage of Total National Population

Five Most Urbanized Countries	1990	2007
Gabon	68	85
Mauritania	44	63
South Africa	49	60
Congo (DRC)	48	61
Botswana	42	59

Five Least Urbanized Countries	1990	2007
Malawi	12	18
Ethiopia	13	16
Niger	12	17
Uganda	11	13
Burundi	6	11

Average Annual Urban Growth Rate (%)

Countries with Fastest Urban Population Growth Rates	2005–2010	GNI/ capita (ppp) 2005
Burundi	6.8	640
Rwanda	6.5	1320
Eriteria	5.2	1010
Burkina Faso	5.1	1220
Congo, Dem. Rep.	4.9	720

Countries with Slowest Urban Population Growth Rates	2005–2010	
Swaziland	0.7	5190
Botswana	0.9	10,250
South Africa	1.0	12,120
Mauritius	1.1	12,450
Lesotho	1.1	3,410

capitals and megacities while ignoring the many smaller urban centers.

Many SSA cities derive their importance from their role during the colonial and/or postcolonial eras. An important postcolonial urban development phenomenon has been the creation of new planned cities. The first of such cities was the port of city of Tema, Ghana, built in the early 1960s in anticipation of the country's industrial development.

Box 8.3   HIV/AIDS and Urban Development in Sub-Saharan Africa

HIV/AIDS is a worldwide threat, but it is particularly concentrated in SSA's already weak and struggling nations. According to the 2006 Report on the Global AIDS Epidemic, a little more than one-tenth of the world's population lives in the region, but SSA is home to almost 64% of all people living with HIV—24.5 million. About 2 million of them are children younger than 15 years of age, and women comprise about 59% of adults living with HIV. The report also suggests that new HIV infections across the region peaked in the late 1990s, especially in Kenya, in Zimbabwe, and in urban areas of Burkina Faso. Southern Africa appears to be the global epicenter of the epidemic—almost one in three people infected with the disease globally live in this subregion. The hardest hit countries in 2005, in terms of percent of adults living with HIV, were (in descending order) Swaziland (34%), Lesotho (23%), Botswana (24%), Zimbabwe (20%), South Africa (19%), Zambia (17%), Namibia (17%), Mozambique (14%), and Malawi (14%). These countries are concentrated in the southern part of the continent, but most countries in SSA are affected to some degree. In many of these countries, the rate of infection among pregnant women is even higher.

Why such a disproportionate share in this already beleaguered part of the world? The reasons are many:

- Governments have been in denial, refusing to recognize the existence or severity of the threat.
- The health-care system, including the availability of effective drugs and blood-screening procedures, is woefully inadequate to the challenge.
- Widespread poverty and ignorance make it extremely difficult to educate people about the dangers and how to prevent infection.
- There are large numbers of people in high-risk groups (e.g., sex-industry workers, migrants, military personnel, truck drivers, drug users who share needles).
- Male-dominated societies put women at particularly high risk.

According to the South African Cities Network (SACN), rapid urbanization, often associated with the growth of informal settlements, appears to provide a favorable environment for the spread of diseases, including HIV/AIDS. Cities, by their very nature of concentrating

---

Other countries have since established new cities as their capitals: Dodoma in Tanzania, Lilongwe in Malawi, Yamoussoukro in Côte d'Ivoire, and Abuja in Nigeria. These new capitals were meant to give their nations a "fresh start" and to direct growth away from existing cities. However, considering that none of the new capitals have grown to more than even half a million inhabitants, one can say that these new cities have not had any significant influence on the growth of the already established cities.

Another characteristic of SSA urban centers is the importance of port cities. Apart

large numbers of people in small areas, increase the speed of transmission of HIV. Indeed, there appears to be a higher prevalence of HIV in urban areas compared to nonurban areas worldwide; in an international survey of countries with the highest HIV prevalence rates, UNAIDS found a strong trend towards higher HIV prevalence rates in urban areas compared to nonurban areas. The urban/nonurban differences in SSA are particularly significant in Botswana, Congo, Ethiopia, Lesotho, Mozambique, Namibia, Rwanda, Uganda, and Zambia. The only Sub-Saharan countries where HIV prevalence rates in nonurban areas were found to be higher than in urban areas were Liberia and the Democratic Republic of the Congo. The 2006 Report on the Global AIDS Epidemic estimates that HIV prevalence in urban areas is on average 1.7 times higher than in rural areas.

High HIV prevalence rates in cities threaten to make many other problems even worse. The disease mostly affects adults in their early productive years, thus directly impacting development of social capital and creating large numbers of orphans. This witches' brew makes it even harder for SSA nations to attract foreign investment and turn the tide economically. Some nations thus are caught in a downward spiral that eventually could result in depopulation, economic decline, and political collapse.

There are glimmers of hope, nonetheless, in various parts of SSA, where a wide variety of initiatives are making some progress. In Uganda, for example, the government supports awareness programs through the media and schools. South Africa was in complete denial for a number of years, but has finally faced the facts and begun to offer public education programs, too. A good example is a group in Cape Town called Wola Nani. This group airs radio announcements in the various languages of South Africa and provides counseling, home care, workshops, training for those living with someone infected with HIV, as well as providing community AIDS education and other activities.

From an urban development standpoint, the impact of HIV/AIDS may well mean that some cities in SSA will stop growing and even decline in population in coming years. Declining economies and political/social instability in cities might well discourage people from migrating to them, thus slowing or even reversing the current trend of increased urbanization. Thus, SSA may become the one region of the world in the 21st century to deviate significantly from the trends observable in cities of most other developing realms.

from landlocked countries in the region and those that have created new capitals, most countries have a port city as their capital. This is often a carryover from the colonial period when the main function of the capital city was to provide access to the mother country. In addition, SSA's role during the colonial era as the producer of natural resources led to urban development that was based on resource exploitation. Zambia provides a good example of urban centers that grew out of copper mining. For instance, Chingola grew up around the Nchanga copper mine; Kitwe is at the site of the Nkana mine, and Luanshya stems from the Roan Antelope copper mine. Another important feature of SSA's urban evolution is the increasing importance of tourism cities. Mombasa, the second largest city in Kenya and the center of the coastal tourism industry, attracts immigrants from the interior of Kenya because of employment opportunities in the tourist trade. Gorée Island, located just off the Dakar Peninsula, also attracts many tourists annually because of its Slave House. Similarly, Cape Coast and Elmina in Ghana attract many tourists who are interested in seeing the castles from which slaves were shipped to the New World.

REPRESENTATIVE CITIES

Kinshasa: The Invisible City

About 33% of the Democratic Republic of the Congo's (DRC) population lives in cities, with that percentage expected to top 50% by 2025. Kinshasa's population was estimated to be 9.5 million in 2007. This capital city contains more than 14% of the DRC's population. Instability and warfare (especially between 1996 and 2002) have hindered Kinshasa's economic development, despite having enhanced incentives for Congolese people to migrate city-ward. The city's rapid growth in the last half-century has outstripped its political and economic capacity to provide for its residents' needs.

For being Sub-Saharan Africa's second-largest city and one of the largest French-speaking cities in the world, Kinshasa has a relatively brief and notably turbulent history. The British-American explorer-agent for the Belgians, Henry Morton Stanley, built a new city adjacent to a set of preexisting settlements

in 1881, naming it Leopoldville to honor Leopold II, the Belgian king. A railway connection with the coastal port of Matadi soon made Leopoldville a key town for linking the vast interior of the basin with the world economy. In 1923, Leopoldville became the Belgian Congo's capital. Eventually, the Belgians extended the city's boundaries; at independence, this expanded entity was renamed Kinshasa.

Kinshasa had only about 30,000 residents in the 1880s, but this had risen to 400,000 by independence in 1960. As was the case in many cities in SSA, colonialism held the population down by enforcing restrictions on urban residence. At independence, the new government ended these controls, opening the doors for massive rural-to-urban migration. For much of the last half-century, the annual growth rate of Kinshasa's population has been above 10%.

Until 1945, most of the city's Africans lived not in Leopoldville itself, but in adjacent riverine settlements. After World War II, new neighborhoods arose, some planned for African workers by the colonial regime. These planned neighborhoods were nearly the only serious investments in African areas of the city made during the Belgian era. In fact, Leopold II's Congo Free State and the Belgian Congo that replaced it in 1908 are considered by many scholars to demonstrate the worst case for negative impacts of colonial rule, with extremely limited investments in human welfare and security in the colony's capital city. Thus, Kinshasa's infrastructure woes are not entirely the result of warped postcolonial politics—the colonial regime failed to provide urban services to African areas even when investing heavily in European areas of the city.

The governments that have ruled Kinshasa since 1960 and the private sector entities that have invested in the Congo's vast resources have not improved matters. Both government and the formal private sector failed to keep pace with Kinshasa's housing, infrastructure, and employment demands. Despite this, migration rates to Kinshasa continue to rise. Warfare, violence, hunger, insecurity, and the departure of industries from rural areas drive people to Kinshasa. Their perceptions do not match reality, however—some 60% of Kinshasa's work force is estimated to be unemployed, housing and sanitation conditions remain poor, and environmental health problems are rampant.

The most populous areas of Kinshasa are its far eastern and far western edges, and urban growth is mostly unregulated and uncontrolled. Post-independence efforts to provide public housing, credit facilities, and transport have been marred by gross corruption, mismanagement, and negligence, particularly under the notorious dictatorship of Mobutu Sese Seko, who ruled the DRC (which he renamed Zaire) with brutal inefficiency from 1965 to 1997. As a result, Kinshasa's residents do as much as they can informally, outside of the state's purview or the formal private sector. Therefore, much of what comprises Kinshasa in both physical and economic terms is undocumented, giving rise to discussion of it as an "Invisible City." Geographers Guillaume Iyenda and David Simon estimate that three-fourths of Kinshasa's houses are self-built by their owners, often in such close proximity to one another as to prohibit sufficient road construction. Roads, railroads, airports, port facilities, river transport, bridges, and public vehicles in Kinshasa have deteriorated steadily.

Industry in Kinshasa has been declining for 30 years or more. Rioting, looting, and urban violence in the 1990s and 2000s reduced the city's industrial capacity still further.

Kinshasa's manufacturing sector still produces soft drinks, beer, cigarettes, textiles, soap, matches, plastics, newsprint, and other lower-order goods, but in declining volume. The service sector completely dominates Kinshasa's economy, accounting for three-fourths of all urban activities (fig. 8.11). Yet the extraordinary degree of urban primacy that Kinshasa still maintains means that it continues to dominate the DRC's economy, accounting for between 19% and 33% of all establishments in each sector.

Despite the negativity that surrounds most descriptions of and scholarship about Kinshasa, this megacity is a thriving center of the arts, particularly for popular music. Kinshasa's musicians have produced chart-toppers and dance-hall favorites across Africa and Europe for decades, inventing new styles and pushing on through every new twist in the city's political and economic malaise. The 2006 democratic elections in the DRC appear to have marked a turning point toward peace and stability, and Kinshasa is—possibly, and arguably for the first time—poised to benefit from the DRC's tremendous and untapped base of natural resources. The country had been among the top five producers of industrial diamonds in the world, and these are still estimated to account for more than half of the DRC's export earnings, alongside extensive copper, cobalt, coffee, palm oil, and rubber exports. Such riches might provide for a rebirth of possibilities for Kinshasa.

Accra: An African Neoliberal City?

Ghana's level of urbanization in 2005 was 46%; it is projected to increase to over 58% in 2015. The two most important cities in the country are Accra, which lies along the coast, and Kumasi, which is situated in the interior.

Figure 8.11   Kinshasa workers waiting by the side of the road at an "artificial" taxi and bus stop. Note the poor road condition, the heavy air pollution in this large central African city, and the use of the median space for roadside gardens. (Photo by Daniel Mukena)

Accra, however, with an estimated 2007 population of 3.5 million, is the undisputed primate city of Ghana. Accra's dominance also manifests itself in the political, administrative, economic, and cultural spheres. The country's open economic policies and its relative political stability in a region characterized by instability have also elevated Accra's influence internationally. Accra has experienced a surge in business and industry, becoming a destination for many foreign visitors to West Africa. At the same time, a significant proportion of the city's residents have not benefited from the economic fortunes.

Accra began as a coastal fishing settlement of the Ga-Adanbge people in the late 16th century. Although there were other trade and political centers in the interior of the country at the time, there is no evidence that they were connected in any way to Accra. During the 17th century, a number of forts were established by Europeans in the area. The rise of Accra as an urban center began in 1877 when it replaced Cape Coast as the capital of the British Gold Coast colony. Unlike many capital cities such as Dakar that were selected because of preexisting economic advantages, the choice of Accra was influenced by the colonialists' desire to find a newer area that would protect Europeans from native-borne diseases. Accra's new status as the capital made it an attractive location for many merchants and investors, and by 1899, the city had been transformed into the busiest port on the Gold Coast with the largest number of warehouses. The colonial administration used legislation to limit the development of manufacturing in the city, so by independence in 1957, Accra had developed a reputation not as a factory city but a warehouse city. As the first city in Africa to become the capital of a new, independent nation after World War II, Accra also became an important political center for the independence struggle in all of Africa.

Post-independence governments in Ghana continued to promote the city's development by concentrating governmental functions and economic opportunities in the city and ignoring other important cities, such as Kumasi. As a result, Accra expanded as the administrative functions for the entire country expanded. In addition, the development of Tema port led to the abandonment of Accra harbor as a commercial port. However, like many cities in Ghana, Accra's growth slowed significantly in the 1970s and 1980s because of the economic crisis that engulfed the country.

The Ghanaian government accepted a World Bank–supported economic reform package in 1983 and agreed to pursue liberal economic policies, including the privatization of state-owned enterprises, deregulation of currency markets, promotion of the private sector and foreign direct investment, reduction in the public sector, and trade liberalization. These free-market policies are essential for understanding the contempo-

rary urban economy of Accra. They helped transform the state-controlled business environment in the country and encouraged development from the private sector. It became easier to import many commodities, including building materials, leading to rapid residential development in the city and an expansion in the number of motor vehicles that has cluttered Accra roads. In addition, the infrastructure-building program reshaped the urban landscape with projects focused on major road construction (new thoroughfares and flyovers), upgrading of Tema port and the international airport in Accra, and the creation of export processing zones to attract foreign investors. As the hub of Ghana's economic activities, Accra has also become the host to numerous national, regional, and multinational financial and business institutions that have flocked into the country. These activities have exceeded the ability of the old central business district to house them; as a result, many headquarters are now located around the outskirts of the city.

Yet not all residents in Accra have benefited from the free market policies, and their negative effects are widely visible on the city's landscape. Income levels of most residents, for instance, have not kept up with the rising cost of living. In the decade after the reforms, it is estimated that the number of households in poverty in Accra more than doubled, increasing to 23%. Lack of employment opportunities for the majority of residents has widened the gap between the rising small middle class and the poor majority. The unequal distribution of wealth can be seen in the proliferation of new housing developments on the city's outskirts, including gated communities, luxury apartment buildings, expensive urban shopping malls, and the increased securitization of architecture presumably for protection against crime. Although the crime rate in Accra is low (compared to other African cities such as Lagos), the growth of the private security industry shows residents' feelings of insecurity and points to the need to address this emerging problem. Poverty in the city can also be seen in the increasing number of street traders at busy intersections and in other hot spots. Many of the poor, including young children, make a living by hawking anything that they can find, especially the ubiquitous water in plastic bags. The effect of the liberalization policy has also been the flooding of the city with vehicles, which combined with lack of comprehensive transportation planning has created insurmountable traffic problems.

Ghana celebrated 50 years of independence on March 6, 2007, and has come to see itself as the birthplace of the region's independence movement. The country has boomed with many activities, and Accra has played an important role, not least as the nation's capital. It is hoped that the nationalistic overtones now pervasive throughout the country will translate into practical action to address the challenges facing the city's residents who have so far not benefited from liberalization.

Lagos: Sub-Saharan Megacity

Nigeria's population is more than 48% urban. Lagos, with 11 million inhabitants in 2005 and over 16 million projected for 2015, qualifies as SSA's most populous city and one of the world's megacities. The development of the petroleum industry in Nigeria has given a boost to urban development, especially in Lagos.

It is often said that Lagos owes its growth and dynamism to European influence. Yet it is also true that the city's development dynamic owes much to early African urban development. Lagos was established in the 17th century, when a group of Awari decided to cross over the lagoons and settle in a more secure setting on the island of Iddo. They later crossed over to Lagos Island in search of more farmland. In this manner, the three important parts of the city of Lagos were founded as fishing and farming villages by the indigenous population, well before major external influence in the 18th century.

Another important historical factor in the development of Lagos is its significance in the slave trade between 1786 and 1851, in which Africans, especially the Yoruba, played an important facilitating role. Lagos was not a slave market until 1760, but it soon became one of the most important West African ports in the slave trade. Lagos Island became an important center where slaves were barricaded as they awaited their export along with primary commodities, particularly foodstuffs and Yoruba cloth, which reached markets as distant as Brazil. Although in 1807 the British passed an act to abolish the slave trade, Lagos, because of its locational advantage, continued the trade until it was halted by the British invasion of the city in 1851. British bombardment of the city also caused a temporary decline in the city's population. With the cession of Lagos to Britain as a colony in 1861, the colonial era for Lagos had begun.

People continued to move into the "free colony," leaving behind slavery, war, and instability in the interior. Freed slaves also returned from Brazil as well as Sierra Leone and made their homes in Lagos. Toward the end of the 19th century, Britain intervened to stop internal hostilities and established a protectorate over the whole of Nigeria. A railway from Lagos, begun in 1895, reached north to Kano in 1912. As its effective hinterland now expanded to the interior of Nigeria, Lagos became even more important as a trade and administrative center. By 1901, the city had a population of more than 40,000 and, by this time, the future prominence of the "modern metropolis" was pretty much established.

Lagos has experienced spectacular population growth and spatial expansion in the past four decades. Its population grew at an estimated 14% per annum in the 1960s and early 1970s. This growth rate slowed down to an estimated 4.5% per annum in the late 1980s—a trend which has continued as the cost of living continues to rise and other problems continue to develop. Many of the city's current problems are rooted in its rapid growth. It has been called the "biggest disaster area that ever passed for a city." That may be overstating it, but Lagos has acute, sometimes incomprehensible, problems of congested traffic, inadequate sanitation, housing, social services, and urban decay.

Lagos is a primate city. The disparity in socioeconomic status between the elite and the mass of urbanites is very wide. That also means the city reflects two contradictory modes of living: one that is an extension of European style brought about by those who can afford the luxuries of a high level of technology and another that is an extension of the traditional mode of living, which has been distorted to fit an urban milieu. This curious amalgam, as it reflects itself in an African urban setting, loses the beauty, charm, and convenience of either of its parts and becomes a nuisance, as exemplified by the traffic congestion and slum dwellings of Lagos.

As a primate city, Lagos has the typical problems of rapid population growth and insufficient employment opportunities. The net effect of these problems is enormous. It depresses urban wages to almost marginal subsistence levels and adds to the pressure on urban amenities and housing. It also accentuates numerous other social problems, especially in the city's slums and peripheral residential communities. Lagos is a good example of an African primate city whose growth rate and attendant problems in distorted consumption patterns have created a stultifying effect that a weak and often disorganized city government is incapable of handling.

There are, however, some positive developments under way. Abuja, in the vicinity of the confluence between the Niger and Benue rivers, was designated as the new capital city of the country, and all government functions have steadily moved to that more central location. This has meant a major step toward decentralization, and it has reduced the concentration of functions in Lagos.

Lagos, even in the colonial period, had less than 5,000 expatriates. Hence, compared with Dakar, Nairobi, and Kinshasa, the character of the city and its spatial organization were considerably less European. The process that Lagos is undergoing, if there is any recognizable process at all, may throw light on the problems of indigenization of African primate cities that have been, and in most cases still are, exclaves of European economic systems, often as alien to their people as cities in Europe. Lagos is a *bona fide* African city and, as disorganized as it is, it may offer a lesson on the transition from a colonial to an indigenous urban environment.

Nairobi: Urban Legacies of Colonialism

East Africa has commonly been taken to be Sub-Saharan Africa's least urbanized region,

Figure 8.12   Regarded by many Africans as an artificial city, Nairobi nonetheless has risen in the century of its existence to be the key city of not only Kenya but East Africa as well. (Photo by Assefa Mehretu)

and until the 1980s, it was estimated that only 20% of Kenya's population lived in cities. That percentage has risen to 43% as of 2007; it is expected to hit 50% by 2015. Nairobi, the capital and primate city of Kenya, is currently estimated to have 2.9 million residents (fig. 8.12). It serves as a transport hub for much of East Africa, as a key site for international diplomacy, and as a headquarters site or conference location for many international organizations. Despite its short history, Nairobi has grown to become the economic engine of Kenya and the major industrial metropolis of the region. Nonetheless, it is a city with substantial rates of poverty, great disparities between rich and poor, and faltering urban services.

Nairobi is something of an accident of geography. Having been uninhabited forest and swampland as late as the 1890s, the site of Nairobi was by 1906 the home of the new capital of British East Africa (renamed Kenya

Colony in 1920). It became the headquarters of the Uganda Railway, conveniently positioned near the Nairobi River and the midpoint of the line. The site's drainage and health problems did not prevent colonial rulers from seeing the new railway headquarters as an ideally situated "forward capital" for the colony.

By 1906, the new city contained more than 13,000 people. By 1931, this population had grown to 45,000, nearly 60% of whom were Africans. Nairobi became the most important colonial capital in the region, as the seat of Britain's High Commission for East Africa (which included the colonies of Kenya, Uganda, Tanganyika, and Zanzibar). By 1948, the city had more than 100,000 people, and its growth continued steadily through to independence in 1963.

Nairobi's colonial legacy continues to haunt it. The first element of this legacy is its physical location. It might have been convenient as a site for railway administration and management, and its geographical centrality might have assisted the efficiency of colonial rule, but physically, colonial Nairobi was, as the early colonial administrator Eric Dutton once put it, "a slatternly creature, unfit to queen it over so lovely a country." Sanitation and urban services more generally lagged—and continue to do so—in part because much of the city lies in or near wetlands.

The second legacy scars Nairobi more heavily: the legacy of colonial segregation. Nairobi was built to be the capital of what its small population of European settlers claimed as a "white man's country." Although Africans were a majority in the city by 1922, most were not legally given rights of residency under colonial rule. When the colonial regime did begin to formally plan for African areas in Nairobi in the 1920s, these were consistently laid out in the lowest-lying, least desirable eastern areas of the urban zone. Whites invariably were situated in the higher-elevation areas west of Nairobi's downtown. Since the colonial regime also at times encouraged the immigration of Indians and Pakistanis to East Africa, Nairobi quickly developed a substantial Asian population that took up residence in the middle, literally and figuratively.

Under colonial rule, the Europeans—themselves divided between the administrative functionaries and an elite class of settlers—controlled the government, the resources, and the finances of Kenya despite the paltry percentage of the population they represented. More than half of the urbanized land of Nairobi in the 1960s still remained in white hands, even though whites composed less than 5% of the city population. The Asians of the colonial era were mostly shopkeepers and merchants, and a few were skilled artisans. Eventually, much of the land of the

eastern, African-dominated areas of the city came to be Asian owned. From the beginning, in Nairobi, Africans occupied the lowest ground and the lowest rungs of the economy. Most Africans lived in rented housing built by the city or their employers. The African residential zone of Eastlands, for example, was characterized by high turnover rates, high unemployment, and poor environmental conditions.

Although the tripartite racial geography of the city has faded somewhat in the 45 years since independence, Nairobi remains a heavily divided city, in class terms now as much or more than in racial terms. The western and northwestern suburbs remain low density elite—albeit increasingly multiracial—areas. Some African elites have moved into traditionally European and Asian neighborhoods, but they are a minority, in the upper echelons of political society. Upper Nairobi and the "Nairobi Hill" residential areas continue to be dominated by European single-unit and fashionable homes complete with servants' quarters. The well-to-do Asians inhabit Parklands, adjacent to the historically European sector. The poorer Asians live in Eastleigh. Some of the Asian population has moved to a second Asian quarter in Nairobi South. The CBD and middle-class or working-class zones predominate in Nairobi's geographical center, and most of the city east of downtown is dominated by informal squatter settlements. The mushrooming growth of the latter has been the major story of the post-independence landscape of Nairobi, and occasionally these squatter settlements interrupt the general geographical pattern.

Although both its growth rate and its economic health have declined in the past 20 years, Nairobi has become a major African metropolis. Its primate-city role for Kenya is

Figure 8.13   This modern office complex in Nairobi points to the city's role in building Africa's future as a command-and-control center for East Africa's economy. (Photo by Garth Myers)

augmented by its role as an international center for East Africa and even SSA more generally (fig. 8.13). Nairobi is a prime African example of a splintering urbanism, where one portion of the city is highly integrated with the world economy while another, larger portion is unintegrated, literally and figuratively. Compared to many SSA cities, Nairobi had a good record in industry in the 1950s and 1960s and an important financial services sector in the CBD. The average European, African elite, or Asian in the city lives in a comfortable home in Upper Nairobi or Parklands and works in the CBD or some other similar enclave. Many African residents are not integrated into the core functions of the city and find themselves locked out of the Nairobi economy that most Western visitors see—as exemplified by the development of gated communities for elites in the city. The informal economy provides the overwhelming majority of job opportunities and residences in Nairobi now.

The CBD of Nairobi represents one of the busiest spots on the continent. Its most prominent functions are commerce, retailing, tourism, banking, government, international institutions, and education. It gained unwanted international notoriety with the 1998 bombing of the U.S. embassy and an adjacent office building that caused 284 deaths, all but 10 being Kenyan. Despite this tragedy, the Nairobi CBD still provides SSA with arguably its most picturesque and captivating skyline of multistory buildings. Its double-lane streets, with their busy streetlights, full buses, massive congestion, gigantic billboards, neon signs, and automobiles from all over the world make Nairobi the ultramodern heartbeat of Kenya. The 2002 national elections that removed the Kenya African National Union party from power for the first time brought hope to many Nairobi residents that renewed government attention and reinvigorated foreign investments would reverse their city's steady decline, and though this reversal is not yet in evidence, Nairobi is reemerging as a lively and creative cultural center for Kenya and its surrounding region (box 8.4).

Box 8.4   Political Geography and Popular Music in Nairobi

Nairobi in the early 21st century is a highly cosmopolitan city with a great deal of racial and ethnic diversity. Yet its sociocultural map still reflects colonialism's racial division of space, albeit now much more a city divided by class than by race. The worlds of Asian, white, and African elites overlap, but they are largely disconnected from those of the African poor and working-class majority.

The divides of splintering urbanism extend into cultural life. Joyce Nyairo has shown how one of Nairobi's most famous nightclubs, Carnivore Simba Salon, segments its clientele by developing special nights that cater to followers of Indian bangra music, Kikuyu music, and Western pop. Meanwhile, on the other side of Nairobi, the new popular musical form of Kenyan rap has blossomed to play a significant role in the country's social and political life. The rap duo of Gidi Gidi Maji Maji, for example, provided Kenyans with what in effect became the soaring theme song of their country's transition out of authoritarian rule with their hit "Unbwogable" inventing a new word in the title, as a Luo–English mishmash meant to convey the unstoppable cause of democratization. Other rappers like Ndarlin P, Googs and Vinnie, and Deux Vultures are speaking for the underclass of the rapidly growing and changing metropolis. In Ndarlin P's remarkable song "4 in 1" the rapper plays four different characters (a *matatu* (minibus) driver, an Asian, and two rapper characters, one of whom is Ndarlin P himself) as they intersect in Nairobi's sprawling Eastlands. Nyairo shows how Ndarlin P maps onto his song the consistent pattern of deprivation Eastlands residents have faced, poking fun at elites, at government, and at himself in equal measure.

Nairobi's new music emphasizes the heterogeneous character of the city, even while it celebrates margins of the city into which few outsiders or local elites will go. As Nyairo puts it, through these new songs' lyrics "one captures the spatial and the social geography of these areas, and gains a better understanding of the people who inhabit these spaces, and of the pleasures and dreams that daily lubricate their existence." In such songs as "4 in 1," Nyairo argues, we hear a mimicking voice that "parallels Nairobi's own mimicry of global concepts of town planning and urban design. It is as if to say that Nairobi only pretends to be a modern enclave whereas in fact its character is derived more from the ethnic ingenuity that has collapsed all plans of a green city and made illegal densification and informal settlements the order of the city's development."

Source: Joyce Nyairo, "(Re)Configuring the City: The Mapping of Places and People in Contemporary Kenyan Popular Song Texts," in Martin Murray and Garth Myers, eds. *Cities in Contemporary Africa* (New York: Palgrave Macmillan, 2006), 71–94.

Dakar: Senegal's City of Contradictions

Senegal is about 51% urbanized and is thus among the most urbanized countries in SSA. With 2.5 million inhabitants, Dakar is a principal primate city in West Africa. The city is known for its beauty, modernity, charm, and style, as well as its agreeable climate, excellent location, and urban morphology. But, of course, this image applies to only part of Dakar—a city of phenomenal contradictions.

Dakar was founded in 1444, when Portuguese sailors made a small settlement on the tiny island of Gorée, located just off the Dakar Peninsula. In 1588, the Dutch also made the island of Gorée a resting point. Although the French came to the site in 1675, they did not move onto the mainland until 1857 and used Dakar as a refueling and coal bunkering point. A number of developments expanded Dakar's functions, leading it to be, in a short time, the most important colonial point on the west coast of Africa. In 1885, Dakar was linked to St. Louis, the old Portuguese port, by rail, giving it added importance as a trading center. Because of its situation and site advantages, Dakar soon became a focus for French colonial functions in the region. In 1898 Dakar became a naval base, and in 1904 it became the capital of the Federation of French West Africa. Dakar's location on the westernmost part of the continent made it the most strategic point for ships moving between Europe and southern Africa and from Africa to the New World. As capital of French West Africa until 1956, it served a hinterland stretching from Senegal in the west to the easternmost part of Francophone West Africa, which included Mali, Burkina Faso, and Niger.

After the French moved from the island of Gorée to the peninsula in 1857, there was some uneasiness about living in quarters surrounded by African villages. Although a policy of racial segregation was not officially pursued, the French settlers had always wanted to keep the two communities separate. However, only because of a natural calamity that befell the Africans could the French finally accelerate the establishment of their exclusive holdings. Progressive displacement of African dwellings was under way before the outbreak of a yellow fever epidemic in 1900, but the Europeans, invoking sanitation requirements, displaced the Africans at a greater rate afterwards, pushing them northward. Between 1900 and 1902, numerous African homesteads were burned down as a "sanitary measure" and the occupants were relocated after receiving compensation for their holdings. Another epidemic in 1914 again brought destruction of African homesteads in the south and more relocation of Africans to the north. On the eve of World War II, the French succeeded in almost completely dominating downtown Dakar, often called Le Plateau, concentrating the Africans in what became known as the African Medina, in the north central part of the peninsula. The problem of "cohabitation" as the French called it was at the root of the whole displacement campaign. Although the colonial authorities would never admit a policy of official segregation, many recommendations were made to openly enforce a system based on race. A commission charged with the study of Dakar in 1889 put forth a recommendation for separate residential quarters for European and African populations. In 1901, another report proposed relocating the Africans outside the confines of the city. A new plan, implemented in 1950–1951, gave further excuse to the colonial administrators to displace more Africans.

The present internal morphology of Dakar reflects this historical background. The city is composed of four main divisions. Although rigid, exclusive ethnic domains are no longer in evidence, Le Plateau still contains one of the most Westernized sectors in Africa. It compares easily with any European city, featuring high-rise buildings, expensive shops, exclusive restaurants, business offices, and many European residents. Characterized by its white-painted, tree-lined boulevards, Le Plateau is the most modern sector of the city, containing upper-class residential quarters, commercial and retail functions, and government offices and institutions. The African Medina, by contrast, reflects its background as a concentration of Africans into high-density housing projects and *bidonvilles* (squatter settlements). It is the popular area of the city, is still densely populated, and houses many markets and clubs. Its functions are primarily residential, but it also contains shops, markets, and cultural features. It contains the industrial laborers and those employed in the informal sector, both outside and inside the Medina. The population of the Medina, and the adjacent *bidonvilles* of Ouakem and Grand Yof, is uniformly poor and resides in poorly serviced parts of the city. Recent expansions of the city have also resulted in the development of a sector called Grand Dakar, which contains a variety of neighborhoods ranging from well-to-do through middle income to poor and includes a mixture of modern residential quarters, industries, and *bidonvilles*. There is also the Dakar industrial sector, which houses the bulk of the city's industrial activities.

Another important part of Dakar that deserves attention is Gorée Island. This island served for many centuries as one of the principal factories in the triangular trade between Africa, Europe, and the Americas. The popular Maison des Esclaves ("Slave House") built by the Dutch in 1776 serves as a poignant reminder of Gorée's role as the center of West African slave trade. The Slave House with its famous "Door of No Return" served as a place where Africans were brought to be loaded onto ships bound for the New World. The Slave House has been preserved in its original state and attracts thousands of tourists each year.

As with many African primate cities, Dakar faces the problem of rapid population growth. In 1914, the city had a total population of 18,000; by 1945 it had 132,000; and by 2007 it had about 2.5 million. Clearly most of the growth is attributable to rural–urban migration, which is characteristic of all Sub-Saharan primate cities. The rate of natural increase of the city's population has also been much higher than the national average on account of the better sanitation and medical services found there.

There is no doubt that Dakar is still an important center whose functions reach far beyond its national boundaries. Its ideal location still makes it a center of maritime as well as airline traffic. Many international organizations are located in Dakar on account of its situation and agreeable urban environment. Many international conferences and meetings are held there. Above all, it is one of the most favored vacation spots in West Africa for European tourists, especially those from the Mediterranean, who find a familiar climatic comfort in exotic surroundings.

The future of Dakar, nevertheless, depends on confronting two challenges. One is to stem the tide of rural–urban migration through a sound policy of regional and rural development, including development of satellite cities, and subsequent decentralization. The

Box 8.5   GIS and Cities of the New South Africa

The racist apartheid policies of South Africa's white minority regime from 1948 to 1994 built on the segregationist policies that preceded them. Both colonial urban policies and those of the independent white minority regime from 1910 to 1948 shared with apartheid the creation of a central role for geography in the establishment and maintenance of separate and unequal socioeconomic development, stratified by racial group. The highly regulated authoritarian apparatus of the apartheid regime increasingly depended on high technology—particularly in the form of weapons technology and police procedures—to enforce its order, particularly in South African cities.

Beginning in the early 1990s, though, new geographic technologies came into use in a very new and different way—in the cause of dismantling apartheid and reorganizing society along equitable multiracial lines. Geographic Information Systems (GIS) have been central to the recreation of South Africa as a rainbow nation, particularly within and around urban areas. This reorganization and the role of GIS within it have not been without contention, but the new South Africa does provide geographers with a vital example of the possibilities and limitations of GIS for the betterment of society.

The legal basis for the geography of separate development in South Africa took shape in the second half of the 20th century. With its Homelands Policy, the minority regime sought to legislate the displacement of the country's black majority to poor, marginalized rural homelands, termed *bantustans* in Afrikaans (fig. 8.14). Through the Group Areas Act, apartheid's architects sought to exclude blacks from residing in cities. Apartheid's urban system was built around the separation of cities, which were set aside as "white-by-night," from townships, which housed the black working classes (aside from domestic workers living in white homes) that made the cities function. Colored (mixed-race) and Asian groups also each had their areas. Townships were typically located at a distance from cities, with physical features, railways, and highways used as dividing lines. When preexisting black neighborhoods interrupted the racial map, the apartheid regime followed a program of forced removals for what it bluntly termed "black spots."

The dismantling of apartheid literally required South Africa to remake the internal maps of its human geography. Two of the country's four former provinces were subdivided into seven new ones (giving the country nine provinces). This was part of an effort to integrate government services for all races in a decentralized democracy, and it included the dissolution of Bantustan governments. Remaking South Africa's urban geography has been a much more complicated task. New boundaries needed to be created for every level of local government. The new government's 1998 Municipal Structures Act led to the establishment of a Municipal Demarcation Board (MDB) in 1999 to restructure the urban system from the bottom up using geographic information science.

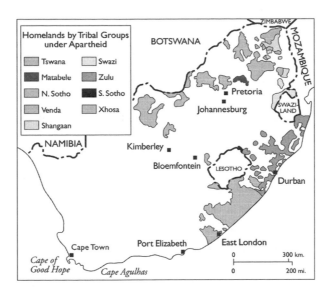

Figure 8.14   South African Homelands during Apartheid.
Source: Compiled from various sources.

   In keeping with the new era, the South African government sought to make the demarcation process as democratic and decentralized as efficient management would allow. Using the World Wide Web, the MDB and the Ministry for Provincial and Local Government produced more open access to spatial information than South Africa—or Sub-Saharan Africa—had ever seen before. The government seemed to genuinely want to use GIS data to provide for technocratic solutions to deeply entrenched problems. Although generally applauded for this effort and for making so much information available transparently, questions have been raised about the process in a number of cities. The criticism has been most notable in Johannesburg, where the formerly white-by-night city became integrated into the massive townships that surrounded it. When presented with a number of different GIS-derived internal boundary scenarios for the new Greater Johannesburg Metropolitan Council, the government apparently bowed to pressure from the ruling African National Congress elites to ignore what the geographers and GIS experts involved considered the most appropriate subdivisions for maximum equitability. Similarly, GIS applications have not prevented the skewing of policies such as that of the provision of free basic water away from the interests of the poorest of South Africa's urban poor. GIS itself will not solve South Africa's laundry list of urban problems, but it is clear to most observers that GIS has been a useful tool in apartheid's dismantling and its replacement with a multiracial democratic order. In cities, in particular, GIS has enhanced urban management and the efforts of the new black-majority regime to serve its urban constituents.

other, as is the case with African primate cities in general, is to bridge the gap between the city's ultramodern sectors and its *bidonvilles*, and make Dakar a true African city.

Johannesburg: A Multi-Centered City of Gold

South Africa has long been among the most urbanized countries in SSA. Some 58% of its population now lives in cities. With more than 3.3 million inhabitants, Johannesburg is the largest city in South Africa. Gauging its population is, however, both easier and more complicated than is the case in other parts of Africa. On the one hand, the relative wealth of the Republic of South Africa affords it the possibility of keeping more regular and reliable census figures than most SSA countries. On the other hand, the reorganization of municipal and local government in South Africa (box 8.5) and the presence of Johannesburg in the geographical center of Africa's greatest example of a polynodal (or multiple nuclei) conurbation make it complicated to decide where Johannesburg begins and ends. The major cities of Tshwane (formerly Pretoria) and Ekurhuleni (formerly East Rand), both of which have more than 2 million residents, are within the metropolitan area of Johannesburg, and other big cities adjoin it as well. Thus, the metropolitan conurbation is said to contain more than 7.5 million residents.

South Africa also has the most deeply developed urban hierarchy in SSA. The common issues surrounding primacy in African urban hierarchies are moot here. Johannesburg's population of 3.2 million in the 2001 census is nearly equaled by eThekwini (formerly Durban, 3 million), Cape Town (2.9 million), and Nelson Mandela (formerly Port Elizabeth, over 1 million), giving South Africa six municipalities (including Tshwane and Ekurhuleni) with more than 1 million residents. Six more cities have more than a half a million. This significantly dilutes any primacy Johannesburg might claim, although, when one considers the immediate proximity of Tshwane and Ekurhuleni it is still possible to recognize the greater Johannesburg area and Gauteng Province as the core of the South African economy. Johannesburg is, moreover, frequently the only SSA city to be considered a world city. It holds the largest mining and industrial center on the African continent. It is home to Africa's largest stock exchange, busiest airport, most diverse manufacturing sector, and ugliest urban racial history.

Johannesburg owes its establishment and phenomenal growth to the discovery of gold in 1886. The rush of settler communities from the south to share in the riches of the land caused the town's population to increase to 10,000 within a year of its birth. By 1895, hardly 10 years after its establishment, the city had about 100,000 people, half of whom were European. Johannesburg was the creation of the mining companies, which until recently probably had more to do with determining the spatial organization of the city than did civil authorities.

The City of Gold has the unfortunate distinction of having been at the heart of a notorious experiment in social engineering. This experiment was built around the notion of separate development for settlers and the indigenous African population. Johannesburg's separate development started with the assertion in 1886 that no native tribes could live within 70 miles (112 km) of the site of the new town. When the "native" problem first arose in 1903 and when it surfaced again in 1932, with the creation of the Native Economic Commission, the European settlers argued that Johannesburg had been built by the Europeans, for the Europeans, and belonged to them alone. They maintained that the "natives" were needed for unskilled labor and could come to the city to work but not to live, mainly because of their inability to handle European civilization. In this manner, the largest of the "European" cities in Africa came into being. Africans were denied permanence of dwelling while they worked in the city and were absolutely barred from living in the city, being restricted to guarded compounds or distinct townships during the tenure of their urban employment. The "pass law" (requiring all Africans to carry passes, or internal passports), begun in 1890, and the "compounding system" (restricting Africans to certain residential areas) contributed to severe urban structural problems with which Johannesburg still has to cope.

Johannesburg became Africa's largest manufacturing center and a principal center of culture and education. The prosperity of the city was derived from the labors of all the races, but was appropriated by the European minority, who enjoyed perhaps one of the highest living standards in the world. Today, the city is clean, with well-planned streets, skyscrapers, and extremely plush residential quarters. The downtown area is similar to that of any industrial city in Europe and North America, with high-rise development to house the offices of the numerous companies, trading firms, and government institutions. In the suburbs of Johannesburg, such as Sandton, are residential homes for well-to-do Europeans, whose architecture and amenities more than match those of their European and North American counterparts.

Separate development became a formal national policy, under the name *apartheid*, after the 1948 election of the white racist National Party into power in whites-only polls. The Nationalists' apartheid built on decades of gradual evolution and enforced unequal separation in an extremely geographical manner. Apartheid was a socially engineered, hegemonic tool to maintain a privileged status for the European settler population so that it could appropriate the vast amount of wealth that was being generated in the country. The impact of this policy was perhaps felt more in places like Johannesburg than anywhere else in the country. Apartheid's application was severely tested in the dynamic environment of Johannesburg, which was attracting a great number of Africans to supply the labor requirements of a rapidly growing industrial conurbation. The authors of apartheid followed a myopic vision by engineering an unsustainable institution of separate development for Africans in their native homelands, as they were later forced to tolerate settlements such as Soweto, growing by leaps and bounds in the shadows of Johannesburg (fig. 8.15). Apartheid was doomed to succumb to the social disorder its authors never anticipated. The 1976 race riot in Soweto was a watershed in the development of nonracist South Africa. The impatience of the world community with the brutal regime brought moral outrage from outside and increased violence from within. Under the weight of these two dynamics, and aided by a visionary leader, Nelson Mandela, South Africa emerged from its nightmare by the early 1990s, when apartheid came to a formal end, symbolized by Mandela's election as president in 1994.

The future of Johannesburg (and other South African cities) will lie in how the root causes of urban instability created by apartheid will be dismantled while the city's ability to

Figure 8.15   This is one of the famous shantytowns, or squatter settlements, near Johannesburg. It is part of Soweto (South Western Township). (Photo by Brennan Kraxberger)

continue as South Africa's most important industrial and business center is maintained. The challenges that Johannesburg faces are evident in its attempts to resolve its severe socioeconomic disparities. With the enforcement mechanisms of the apartheid influx control laws gone, making an orderly transition from a divided city into an integrated city has been a daunting task for policy makers and city planners. Johannesburg residents suffer from high rates of violent crime and continuing insecurity. Johannesburg is becoming a megalopolis, as a series of mining towns and industrial areas merge together. The previously marginalized townships such as Soweto and Alexandra are now firmly integrated into metropolitan life. With a nonracial central government at the helm and with ample human and physical resources for economic progress, all signs point to a more progressive trajectory for cities like Johannesburg. Success depends on whether people of all ethnic groups living in the city deal responsibly with the history of their relations and choose to build a diverse society in which everyone has a stake in the new South Africa's development.

URBAN CHALLENGES

Urban Environmental Issues

Because most SSA cities have experienced more limited industrialization processes than similarly sized cities of Europe, Asia, or the Americas, urban environmental problems are often thought to be of a smaller magnitude. Yet problems of solid waste

Figure 8.16   Erosion scars the suburban landscape on the outskirts of Zanzibar. (Photo by Garth Myers)

management, air and water pollution, toxic waste disposal, and environmental health are profound in much of urban SSA (fig. 8.16). In part because of the generally smaller formal industrial sector and smaller manufacturing-value-added base in urban Africa, revenues that accrue to urban local government are typically not sufficient to fund the broad array of urban services expected of city governments. This array includes environmental management services such as solid waste management, water and sanitation supply, and all forms of environmental monitoring and oversight.

As a consequence, services in SSA cities are often in very short supply. Solid waste services are one crucial example of the interlocking environmental problems that result. Many cities with more than a million inhabitants in the region report that only 3% to 45% of the residential solid waste produced actually makes it to a landfill; the majority remains in urban neighborhoods where it was generated. In an earlier era of smaller settlements, the burial or burning of such waste was not taken to be a major problem because its content was overwhelmingly organic and biodegradable. The increasing use of plastics and other inorganic materials, along with ordinary source items for toxic waste (such as batteries and household insecticides in aerosol canisters), and the staggering growth of unregulated settlements mean that the lack of proper solid waste management has become a severe crisis. Buried in congested neighborhoods, solid wastes can and do pollute the water supplies of untold millions of urban Africans. Pollutants sourced to uncontrolled landfills have been shown to enter into the fruits and vegetables urban farmers pluck from downstream gardens in Dar es Salaam, Lusaka, and elsewhere. Burned on the surface, the waste causes serious damage to the air quality of such neighborhoods. Left in ditches, the waste can inhibit proper drainage, leading to flooding and the increased presence of standing water that becomes breeding space for malarial mosquitoes. Mounds of waste left for months on the surfaces of African urban neighborhoods provide habitats for vermin that carry serious public health risks.

The interconnected water, sanitation, waste, air quality, and environmental health problems of African cities, though they may seem at first to pale in comparison to the infamous environmental crises of Southeast Asian or Central American megacities, may in fact be as bad or worse, proportionally. This is because the problems have great potential to magnify one another, in the absence of much regulation or amelioration. Even where significant industrial development is associated with African urbanization, such as in Nigeria's oil-rich Niger Delta, Zambia's Copperbelt, or South Africa's Gauteng Province (i.e., greater Johannesburg), colonialism, transnational capitalism, and repressive governments (or, in the latter case under apartheid, all three at once) make for a heady combination of roadblocks to environmental control. The levels of heavy-metal pollution downstream from the Copperbelt's largest copper smelter, for example, are mind-boggling, and yet even as the technology exists to prevent or significantly reduce the smelter's air and water pollution, successive colonial and postcolonial governments have for many decades shown reluctance to force environmental controls onto an industry that provides more than 90% of all of Zambia's export earnings.

Despite such limited or politically circumscribed capacity for urban environmental management, many African cities are witnessing substantial efforts to bring environmental crisis points under control. In line with the prevailing development models of the day, many cities are experimenting with private sector urban service provision, including in environment-related sectors. Dar es Salaam, as the pilot city for the United Nations Sustainable Cities Program, privatized solid waste management services and produced an increased rate of deposition from under 10% of residential waste to more than 40% in less than a decade. Other cities have privatized water supply and sometimes even sanitation services. Still more have attempted public–private partnerships where private sector companies have joined forces with governments to provide services. Not all of the new innovations have been private-sector driven, nor have they been automatically friendly to the environment. South Africa's post-apartheid regime has carried out a policy for free basic water provision, for instance, that has increased the supply of clean water for the poor, but many critics point to the strictures in that system as having caused poor urbanites to seek unclean water alternatives—a situation that exacerbated a cholera epidemic. In other cities, the driving forces for change in urban environmental management are found in grassroots community groups, such as Nairobi's Mathare Sports Club, whose local environmental planning and consciousness-raising earned it global attention at the World Summit on the Environment in Rio de Janeiro in 1992, which in turn improved the club's soccer match gate revenues. Regardless of the paths taken, though, it is clear that much more needs to change for African cities to gain control over the daunting array of environmental problems confronting them.

Primate Cities

Urban primacy continues to dominate the African scene (fig. 8.17). Indeed, one of the most significant factors in urban transformation in Africa in the post–World War II and post-independence period has been the dramatic growth of primate cities. Primate cities contain more than 25% of the total urban population in SSA. In small countries such as Lesotho, the Seychelles, and Djibouti, primate cities contain 100% of the urban population. However, urban primacy also characterizes large countries such as Angola and Mozambique. Generally, in countries where urbanization has had a relatively long history, the ratios are lower. But the degree of primacy will continue to be a significant factor in Africa's urban development for quite a long time.

In the 1960s, most primate cities in Africa accounted for about 10% of the urban population. By the year 2000, many cities, such as Kinshasa, Lusaka, Accra, Nairobi, Addis Ababa, Luanda, Dakar, and Harare, increased their share of their respective nations' urban populations to over 20%. Currently, many primate cities account for over 30% of the urban populations in their respective countries. It is also important to note that since the second half of the 1980s, some encouraging signs of deconcentration around primate cities have been observed, and the percent of urban populations residing in primate cities seems to be stabilizing. For instance, between 1990 and 2005, the share of the urban population in the primate city in several countries declined. The decreases in percent of urban population in the largest city were highest in Angola, Burkina Faso, and Guinea.

Although the dominance of primate cities in SSA has historical roots traceable to colonial administration policies, postcolonial governments have perpetuated this pattern by making these cities the centers of modern development. Primate cities in SSA tend to be capital cities and often have more influence than is warranted based on the magnitude of the populations living in them. They dominate the political, economic, infrastructural,

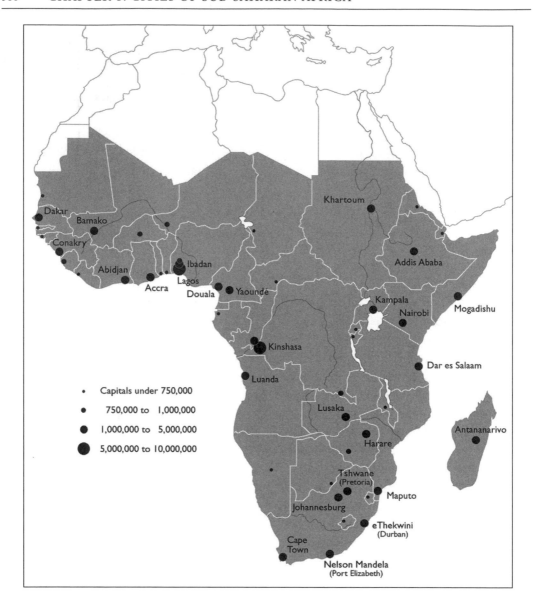

Figure 8.17   Principal Urban Centers of Sub-Saharan Africa. *Source:* Data from United Nations, *World Urbanization Prospects, 2001 Revision* (New York: UN Population Division, 2002), www.unpopulation.org.

and cultural scene of their countries. The strong influence they exercise also enables them to co-opt a good portion of national social and industrial investments. Concentration of power in these cities has produced large disparities in standards of living between those who live in them and the rest of the country. Primate cities also have some of the most serious urban problems in the region. These include mounting unemployment and the resultant increased crime and youth unemployment; severe housing problems, reflected in overcrowding and the spread of slums and squatter settlements; and immense pressure on urban infrastructure such as water, sewage, and transportation.

Rural-to-Urban Migration

A rapid increase in rural-to-urban migration has been a common feature of Sub-Saharan Africa. In the region, between 50% and 60% of urban growth comes from the migration of young adults seeking jobs and other livelihood opportunities in urban areas. This migration is one of the most crucial problems facing African governments. A massive flow of people into the few urban centers that became loci of power and investment, particularly in the period following decolonization of the continent, has strained the carrying capacity of most urban centers. This urban growth pattern far outstrips the capabilities of urban socioeconomic systems to generate needed employment opportunities, housing, and social services (fig. 8.18). As a consequence, the primate city has become, in most instances, a liability to the overall development process.

The paradoxical fact that rural–urban migration continues to grow in spite of rising unemployment in urban centers of LDCs has given rise to a migration theory based on rural–urban income differentials. This theory assumes that migration is "primarily an economic phenomenon" and that the potential migrant makes a calculated move in order to realize much higher "expected" earnings with varying probabilities. According to this theory, the wide differences between urban and rural wages, coupled with the fact that the long-run probability that a migrant could secure wage employment in the urban area explain the motives behind the increases in city-ward migration. Structural adjustment programs, which have been implemented

Figure 8.18   In Mombasa, Kenya's port city, hundreds of workers in this government-supported enterprise carve wooden handicrafts for tourist markets. These kinds of enterprises create badly needed jobs in today's African metropolises. (Photo by Jack Williams)

across the region, are meant to bridge this gap by increasing the prices of agricultural exports and instituting payment for previously free or subsidized services consumed mostly by urban dwellers.

Rural-to-urban migration in SSA can also be explained with reference to *push factors* that operate in rural areas and *pull factors* that attract migrants to urban areas. Push factors include deteriorating socioeconomic conditions in rural areas, including lack of access to agricultural land, which literally forces people to leave rural areas. Pull factors emphasize the attractions and socioeconomic opportunities available in urban areas. Economic opportunities in urban areas, as well as social, cultural, and psychological factors, including the desire to escape the social controls characteristic of rural areas, also attract people to cities.

Whether rural–urban migration in SSA is caused primarily by the difference in expected urban wages versus agricultural wages is an issue that is open to debate. It is important to note that more recent evidence seems to suggest that rural out-migration has not only abated in SSA, but that its counter-stream (i.e., urban out-migration) has progressed and even, in some cases, outnumbered the rural-to-urban flow of people. For instance, a number of major towns and cities in Ghana and Zambia experienced a negative migratory balance between the 1970s and 1980s. Zambian census data also indicated that the population of some urban areas decreased between 1990 and 2000. Similar patterns have been observed in the Francophone West Africa countries of Burkina Faso, Guinea, Côte d'Ivoire, Mali, Mauritania, Niger, and Senegal, where many secondary towns registered a negative net loss of residents between 1988 and 1992. In some of these countries, the net migration rates from rural areas were still negative; they were very close to zero, suggesting that rural-to-urban migration may not be as important as expected or that reverse movement has increased.

Because of its monopoly of economic opportunities and political power, the city in Sub-Saharan Africa has created a perception on the part of rural–urban migrants of certain and immediate opportunities for socioeconomic improvement, a perception that is rarely realized. The phenomenal growth of shantytowns and squatter settlements and the proliferation of informal employment in the cities of SSA are the result of this miscalculation.

SUGGESTED READINGS

Bryceson, Deborah Fahy, and Deborah Potts. 2006. *African Urban Economies: Viability, Vitality, or Vitiation?* London: Palgrave Macmillan. A wide range of scholars examine urban economic issues in mostly eastern and southern African cities.

Coquery-Vidrovitch, Catherine. 2005. *The History of African Cities South of the Sahara: From the Origins to Colonization.* Translated by Mary Baker. Princeton, NJ: Markus Wiener. Discusses the evolution of precolonial urban centers and how traditional African cities were influenced by Islam, the Atlantic slave trade, and colonization.

De Boeck, Filip, and Marie-Françoise Plissart. 2006. *Kinshasa: Tales of the Invisible City.* Antwerp: Ludion. Brings cutting-edge theory to bear on the despairing yet vibrant city that is now the second-largest in Sub-Saharan Africa—not for the faint of heart.

Enwezor, Okwei, Carlos Basualdo, Ute Meta Bauer, and Sarat Maharaj, eds. 2002. *Under Siege: Four African Cities—Freetown, Johannesburg, Kinshasa, Lagos.* Ostfildern-Ruit, Germany: Hatje Cantz. Famous architects, art critics, and urban scholars look at life in four very different African cities, breaking new ground along the way.

Hansen, Karen T., and Mariken Vaa, eds. 2004. *Reconsidering Informality: Perspectives from Urban Africa.* Uppsala, Sweden: Nordic Africa Institute. Contains insights from pioneering Nordic, European, and African experts.

Murray, Martin J., and Garth A. Myers, eds. 2006. *Cities in Contemporary Africa.* New York: Palgrave Macmillan. Includes chapters both on the largest cities (Lagos, Kinshasa, Johannesburg) and on those less frequently analyzed (Bulawayo, Kano, Luanda).

Myers, Garth A. 2005. *Disposable Cities: Garbage, Governance and Sustainable Development in*

Urban Africa. Aldershot, UK: Ashgate. Presents case studies of the solid waste management programs of the UN Sustainable Cities Program in Dar es Salaam, Lusaka, and Zanzibar.

Simone, AbdouMaliq. 2004. *For the City Yet to Come: Changing African Life in Four Cities.* Durham and London: Duke University Press. Combines policy-centered analysis with what is in effect story-telling about four different urban African experiences in Douala, Dakar, Johannesburg, and the African pilgrimage community in Saudi Arabia.

Simone, AbdouMaliq, and Abdelghani Abouhani. 2005. *Urban Africa: Changing Contours of Survival in the City.* London: Zed Books. A fine example of the interdisciplinary and multinational research efforts that the Council for the Development of Social Research in Africa (CODESRIA) has fostered.

Tostensen, Anne, Inge Tvedten, and Mariken Vaa, eds. 2001. *Associational Life in African Cities: Popular Responses to the Urban Crisis.* Uppsala, Sweden: Nordic Africa Institute. Tackles the burgeoning civil societies of African cities.

Figure 9.1 Major Cities of South Asia. *Source:* UN *World Urbanization Prospects, 2005 Revision* [online].

9

Cities of South Asia
GEORGE POMEROY AND ASHOK K. DUTT

KEY URBAN FACTS

Total Population	1.48 billion
Percent Urban Population	28.5%
Total Urban Population	422 million
Most Urbanized Countries	Pakistan (34.9%)
	India (28.7%)
	Bangladesh (25.1%)
Least Urbanized Countries	Bhutan (11.1%)
	Sri Lanka (15.1%)
	Nepal (15.8%)
Annual Urban Growth Rate	2.6%
Number of Megacities	5
Number of Cities of More Than 1 Million	62
Three Largest Cities	Mumbai, Delhi, Kolkata
World Cities	Mumbai

KEY CHAPTER THEMES

1. The duality of prosperity alongside poverty in the midst of a vibrant mosaic of language, ethnicity, and religion make cities in South Asia unique.
2. There are three basic types of South Asian cities: bazaar-based, colonial, and planned.
3. There have been five major influences on the development of cities: the Indus Valley civilization, the Aryan Hindus, the Dravidians, the Muslims, and the Europeans.
4. The current urban system most distinctly reflects the dominance of Presidency Towns during the colonial era.
5. The urban form of South Asian cities is reflected in two basic models: the colonial-based city model and the bazaar-based city model, with permutations of both.

Box 9.1   The Outsourcing Phenomenon

Have you done any of the following of late? Called to reserve a rental car? Telephoned technical support for help with your new computer? Spoken to someone via phone to straighten out a credit card issue?

If you have, then chances are very good that the person on the other end of the line was in India. If this was indeed the case, then you have had a personal encounter with "outsourcing." Outsourcing is a controversial concept and is more complex than most folks realize. As it evolves, outsourcing is transforming the way business is done across the globe. Finally, it is having a substantial and largely positive impact on the fortunes of more than a few Indian cities.

Outsourcing occurs anytime a firm takes activities done "in house" or "on site" and moves these activities to another location. Outsourcing first gained attention as U.S. auto makers began to subcontract the manufacturing of certain auto components to other firms in the United States. For example, Ford would contract with a smaller, independent firm (perhaps in a nearby city) for wheel assemblies.

Offshore outsourcing is when a firm takes activities and moves them overseas. This practice was first associated with manufacturing, as companies sought to limit labor costs by shifting to lower-wage locations. For example, companies such as Pendleton (famous for its flannel shirts made in the Oregon city of the same name) moved some of its production to Mexico after NAFTA was passed.

Although manufacturing job losses have occurred across the U.S. and Canadian economies for several decades, people have generally assumed that service activities, which comprise the bulk of all jobs in these two countries, were by nature "domestic." The rise of *business process outsourcing firms (BPOs)* shows that even service-sector employment can be outsourced. Business process outsourcing involves taking accounting functions, customer services, computer programming, and other activities outside and usually offshore.

6. India has a relatively well-balanced urban hierarchy; Pakistan has a dominant southern city and dominant northern one; all other countries are characterized by urban primacy.
7. Massive rural-to-urban migration in recent decades has led to exploding urban populations and has overwhelmed urban systems.
8. Civil wars and political instability have been major contributing factors to the destabilization of urban areas over the decades, most recently in Sri Lanka and Afghanistan.
9. Planned cities and new towns have played an important but subsidiary role in the region for a long time, with Islamabad (Pakistan) and Chandigarh (India) as notable recent examples.
10. Urban problems today reflect the region's limited integration into the modern global economy, a situation which began to change with India's economic reforms in the 1980s.

India is well placed to corner the market with respect to BPO opportunities. First, as a result of its relatively well-developed system of universities and technical colleges, it possesses a large supply of technically-qualified and well-educated personnel. Secondly, English language instruction, a legacy of British colonial rule, has fortuitously provided many of these very competent postsecondary graduates with the language skills needed to work in what has now become the international language of business. Third, the cost differential between hiring U.S. workers and hiring those in India may be has high as 10 to 1. This represents a potential cost savings that is hard for any firm to ignore. Finally, with the rise of modern information technologies (telephone, internet), distance has "collapsed": the cost of doing business over great distances has in many ways vanished.

BPOs may be found all over the Indian map and involve many well-known U.S.-based multinationals. Although Bengalūru (Bangalore) is perhaps the best known location of BPOs, other cities, including Mumbai, Pune, Hyderabad, and Chennai, are also prominent BPO centers. Just a small sampling of well-known firms with substantial investments and operations includes Accenture, Citibank, Dell, IBM, Infosys, Microsoft, Office Tiger, Verizon, and Wipro.

Careful observers are noticing several subtle trends in the outsourcing phenomenon. The first trend is that, increasingly, the BPOs are more Indian or more truly transnational, as opposed to being U.S.-based firms that are looking to cut costs; that is, the share of the entrepreneurial leadership that is Indian is increasing. The second observation is that outsourcing activities provide a medium for cultural diffusion. In an article subtitled "The Americanization of Chennai" ("Letters from India," *The New Yorker*, July 2004), Katherine Boo notes locals making payments in "American-style installments," "raising their kids by cell phone," and "educating working parents about American antidotes to guilt—roller coasters and Seven Dwarfs–like characters" at a theme park named M.G.M. Dizzee World.

In the cities of South Asia, a vibrant optimism and a newfound confidence abounds (fig. 9.1). Led by the 250 million strong Indian middle class, a rampant consumerism illustrates a giddy self-assurance and sense of hope. One merely needs to step into the bright, flashy, and glamorous automobile showrooms, where eager upper-middle income buyers may be seen purchasing not just a car, but in some cases a *fifth* family car and at prices of over $23,000—*more than 46 times* the average per capita income in India. This displayed affluence by the urban upper middle class only energizes the desire to acquire and consume into a frenzy across all social classes and in all parts of the city. What were once luxuries now seem necessities, and a burgeoning consumer class is engaged in status-conscious conspicuous consumption. This urban optimism is most evident on Indian city streets, where consumers aspire to drive vehicles that display their new wealth—Toyota Innovas for the wealthiest, Chevrolet Taveras for the generally better off, and Indian-made Marutis for those who can afford only the cheapest cars. The middle class, in particular, displays this penchant for consumer goods, and buyers are snapping up new purchases at fever pitch. Affluence, or at least the appearance of it, and consumption are the hallmarks of South Asian cities' incorporation into a global economy. With the rise of "call centers" and other outsourcing activities come the perception that globalization is enabling economic prosperity and upward mobility in cities like never before (box 9.1). In these cities, which for decades were characterized as dreadful and sometimes even hopeless places, there is now the popular sense that cities in South Asia are places where better lives are made. While not all fully or even partially agree with this assessment, the sense of excitement about what people can achieve in cities is unmistakable.

Nevertheless, there are tremendous urban challenges across all of South Asia. Urban poverty is as pervasive as the optimism of the moment. Mumbai (formerly Bombay), India, the city which best demonstrates the optimism noted above, also presents urban poverty at its most daunting. Within the city proper, 6.7 million slum dwellers comprise about 54% of the population. Across the wider Mumbai urban agglomeration these numbers swell further. Dharavi, with over 600,000 people (and perhaps as many as 1 million!) crowded into an area of 432 acres (216 hectares), or roughly under a full square mile, is Mumbai's largest slum and perhaps the best known (though, contrary to rumor, it is not the world's or even South Asia's largest). Pavement dwellers, those who have no shelter at all and sleep on sidewalks, doorsteps, and the like, number over 600,000. Across each of the

region's megacities the story is the same—tremendous numbers of people live in extreme poverty, with inadequate shelter, a lack of clean water, and filthy living conditions. Already racked with unemployment and underemployment, each swells with new migrants every day (fig. 9.2).

This duality of prosperity alongside poverty in the midst of the vibrant mosaic of language, ethnicity, and faith that characterizes South Asia is what makes cities in this region unique. Throughout South Asia, cities remain receptacles of hope and serve as powerful engines of social and economic change.

URBAN PATTERNS AT THE REGIONAL SCALE

South Asia is among the world's most populous regions; the magnitude of both present and future urban population is, therefore, distinctive. Already, there are over 450 million city dwellers across all sizes of cities, and this number will balloon to over 838 million by 2030. This means that cities will likely hold another 390 million or so people over the next two decades—more than the populations of Canada and Mexico combined! Most of the urban population is in India, Pakistan, and Bangladesh as these three countries currently rank as the world's second, sixth, and seventh most populous countries. Together, these three comprise 95% of South Asia's total population; three out of four live in India alone.

Although the number of people living in cities is large in terms of raw numbers, the overall level of urbanization is low. With its immense population, India, at 29% urban, largely determines the overall regional average, which is also 29%. Pakistan has just over one in three of its residents living in urban

Figure 9.2   As cities fill up with people, streets become more congested with not only cars, but bicycles and camels as well. (Photo by George Pomeroy)

areas; Bangladesh has just under one in four. The smaller countries of Afghanistan, Nepal, Sri Lanka, and tiny Bhutan each have smaller urban shares to match. Even by 2030, no country in South Asia is projected to have more than half its people living in cities. Although most of South Asia has seen steady urbanization, Afghanistan, Sri Lanka, and more recently Nepal have suffered civil conflict, revolt, or insurgency, making city growth and development more difficult and erratic.

Although cities of all sizes in South Asia have been growing, the five megacities have grown the most. Mumbai is already among the world's five largest urban agglomerations with over 18 million people. It is projected to grow to over 22 million over the next decade, at which time it will rank second to only Tokyo in population. Delhi and Kolkata (Calcutta), in India, also rank among the world's eight largest metropolitan areas. Dhaka, Bangladesh's capital, and Karachi, Pakistan,

are not far behind, ranking 11th and 13th, respectively. Each will have between 13 and 19 million people by 2015 and rank among the 12 largest urban agglomerations in the world. Altogether, over 60 cities in South Asia currently have metropolitan populations of over 1 million, with that number being projected to grow to 70 over the next decade. If one takes into consideration all cities of 100,000 or more in population, the number is over 400.

Within India, the largest six cities dominate the urban hierarchy. The megacities of Mumbai, Delhi, and Kolkata anchor points of a northern urban triangle. In the south, Chennai (formerly Madras), Bengalūru (formerly Bangalore), and Hyderabad form a second urban triangle. Together, these six cities make up a large chunk (21%) of India's urban population, an urban population that is being tied together by a great highway-building project known as the Golden Quadrilateral (box 9.2). Rather than true primacy, Pakistan's

Box 9.2   India's Golden Quadrilateral

The Golden Quadrilateral is a critical part of India's version of the U.S. Interstate Highway system, and it enables and symbolizes India's rapid development. This project is a component of the country's most ambitious plan to improve transportation infrastructure since independence. The Quadrilateral itself will run through 13 Indian states and connect the nation's four largest cities with 36,000 miles (58,000 km) of four- and six-lane highway. Construction is now largely complete (fig. 9.3). The overall scheme, termed the National Highways Development Plan (NHDP), is to widen and pave 40,000 miles (64,000 km) of highways over a 15-year period.

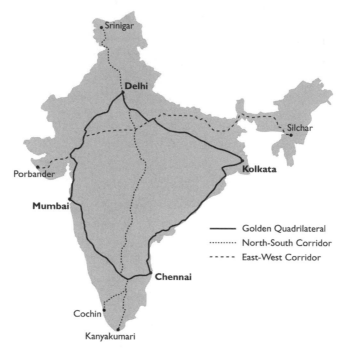

Figure 9.3   The Golden Quadrilateral of express highways is nearing completion. It links the anchor cities of India's urban hierarchy: Delhi, Mumbai, Kolkata, and Chennai.
Source: Compiled from various sources.

The parallels with the U.S. interstate system are difficult to ignore. Both were created in periods of sustained economic growth and optimism. Each constitutes national transportation infrastructure underwritten by the federal government. Even the total mileage is similar, as the U.S. system totals 46,000 miles (74,000 km).

With the Golden Quadrilateral as its linchpin, the revamped highway system is intended to facilitate interstate and regional trade and commerce, to reduce transportation costs, and to contribute to economic efficiency more generally. Truck transportation comprises 4% of the nation's GDP, and the potential for saving 40% on travel times translates into significant savings. "These micro gains make for macro benefit," noted a *New York Times* feature article as it profiled a milk seller who sliced his 90-minute commute time to market by a third, a child who took half as long to travel to school, and a truck driver who reduced his travel time by half.

The new highway system represents a reshaping of South Asian transportation in a manner that is rivaled only by the construction of the Grand Trunk Road and the railway network during previous centuries. Construction of the Grand Trunk Road was begun by an Afghan king during an intercession of the Mughal Dynasty. The road was then extended and upgraded during the remaining portion of the Mughal Dynasty, and later during British colonial rule. The railway network was constructed in the second half of the 19th century to facilitate movement of natural resources to colonial port cities. For example, cotton was taken from the hinterlands of Mumbai and then transported to Britain to be manufactured into cloth. Even as Mumbai and other port cities came to have their own textile mills, cotton continued to arrive via the rail network. What makes these mega-transportation projects even more impressive is that in the entire 50 years following India's independence in 1947, only 334 miles (537 km) of new four-lane road were built. Much of the transportation network still reflects the remnants of the Mughal and colonial past.

The construction of the Golden Quadrilateral is remarkable not only for its scale, but also for the process of its creation. Prior to the 1990s, there were limits on foreign investment in India. As trade liberalization and deregulation has occurred over the last two decades, the presence of foreign goods, services, and contractors has expanded dramatically. In constructing the Quadrilateral, 19 of the 35 component projects involve foreign contractors. For the highway system as a whole, construction companies from over 30 nations are involved.

Although many see highways as bringing urbanization, development, and prosperity to the country's urban and rural areas, their construction also reveals poverty, urban–rural income disparities, and obstacles to development. Because of the demand for bribes at check points (or "*check nackas*") and police posts, delays that should take one day often take nearly two. It is estimated that the bribes extracted are equivalent to the combined annual salaries of India's truck drivers. Petty extortion and *dacoity* (gang banditry) are worse in the northern half of the country and are especially notorious in Bihar, by many measures India's poorest state. "In Bihar, they'll cut off your neck and leave you six inches shorter" commented one truck driver (*New York Times*, December 4, 2005).

Construction often bifurcates neighborhoods and villages, exposing and revealing the poverty and desperation within. Along points of the highway, fresh concrete is sometimes scavenged by the poor before it can dry. For the poorest, the connection between the new roads and an improved daily life is a yawning chasm.

The Quadrilateral also inspires pride and nationalism. Reporters speak of a "wondrous journey along a world class highway" (*Times of India* [online], February 10, 2007). Others proclaim that "this highway will really change the face of India" and that "India is transforming" (*New York Times*, December 4, 2005). Perhaps most telling is a quote from B. C. Khanduri, India's Minister of Roads, made during an address to highway contractors: "You are not only making money, you are building a nation."

Figure 9.4   A picture of hope in this street scene from Lahore, Pakistan, in which a teacher uses the side of a boulevard as a makeshift outdoor classroom for his young charges, part of a broader UNICEF program to help the urban poor. (Photo courtesy of UNICEF—John Issac)

urban system is dominated by a pair of cities with a combined population of 18 million: Karachi dominates southern Pakistan, and Lahore, the smaller of the two, dominates the north (fig. 9.4).

Urban primacy characterizes the remaining countries of the region, especially the smaller ones. In Bangladesh, Dhaka is the center of gravity, as it is over three times the size of Chittagong, the second largest city. Kabul, Afghanistan, and Kathmandu, Nepal, are both national capitals and are over six times the size of their country's next largest city. Most extreme is Sri Lanka's capital of Colombo, which is over 11 times the size of the next largest city.

South Asian cities may be divided into three basic types: traditional cities, colonial cities, and planned cities. Traditional cities are those which were part of a thriving urban system prior to Western colonialism, whether as centers of trade and commerce, centers of administration, or religious pilgrimage destinations. Even today, after many centuries, these cities remain viable. Varanasi, for example, remains the leading pilgrimage center in South Asia. Because of its auspicious location on the Ganges, it is holy to both Jains and Hindus. It attracts millions of pilgrims each year.

For about 5,000 years, cities have been a part of the cultural landscape of South Asia, with the Indus–Ganges Valley system serving as one of the world's urban hearths. Many traditional cities, including Delhi, flourished with colonization. Western mercantile capitalist activities became commonplace and in some cases eventually dominated or overwhelmed traditional activities. Other cities stagnated as the colonial mercantile trade activities and networks bypassed them. Traditional cities could often be distinguished as being trade centers, such as Surat on India's west coast, or centers of religious pilgrimage, such as Varanasi, which is on the banks of the revered Ganges River.

Several of the region's largest cities, most notably Mumbai, Kolkata, Chennai, were the products of British colonialism. In the post-independence period, basically since 1947, various traditional and colonial cities have evolved further into commercial/industrial cities to serve the expanding economies and national development plans of the region.

South Asia's third basic urban type is the new planned city, of which there are two kinds: (1) political and administrative centers such as Islamabad, Pakistan, and Chandigarh, India, and (2) industrial centers for steel and other related heavy industrial activities, such as Durgapur, in the state of West Bengal, and Jamshedpur in Bihar, both in India. Islamabad was built in the 1960s to take the place of Karachi as Pakistan's capital city. With a location near the country's Northwest Frontier (the border with Afghanistan), Islamabad serves as a good example of a forward capital. Chandigarh was also built after independence as the new state capital of India's Punjab. When a new state was carved out of Punjab in the 1960s, Chandigarh found itself on the border and has since served as capital of both Punjab and newly formed Haryana.

A recent and remarkable change in the urban fabric of South Asia is occurring in India. With prosperity and growth has come the development of "urban corridors" broadly akin to Jean Gottmann's Megalopolis in the United States. Spurred by the construction of new express highways, city-regions are emerging along transportation corridors (box 9.2).

HISTORICAL PERSPECTIVES ON URBAN DEVELOPMENT

The cultural, linguistic, and religious diversity, and in turn the urban fabric, of South Asia are derived from five distinctive influences. Chronologically these are (1) the Indus Valley civilization, 3000 to 1500 B.C.; (2) the Aryan Hindus, since 1500 B.C.; (3) the Dravidians, since about 200 B.C.; (4) the Muslims, since the 8th century; and (5) the Europeans, since the 15th century.

Indus Valley Era

The Indus Valley is one of the "cradles of civilization" and is among the world's oldest urban hearths. The preeminent cities of the Indus Valley civilization, Mohenjo Daro and Harappa, located in what is now Pakistan, were established as planned communities as early as 3000 B.C. They flourished for about 1,500 years. As the largest urban centers of the region, they anchored an extensive settlement system that included at least three other large urban centers and perhaps over 900 smaller ones. First excavated in 1921, the ruins of Mohenjo Daro reveal a carefully constructed city reflective of a highly organized and complex society. No other city outside the Indus civilization possessed such an elaborate system of drainage and sanitation, signifying a

Figure 9.5   The *dhobi-wallahs,* or "washer-men," make their living washing clothes, here seen drying in the open air. (Photo by George Pomeroy)

generally high standard of living. This urban civilization came to an end around 1500 B.C., when the newly arrived Aryans—less civilized but more adept in warfare than the Indus people—overpowered the Indus civilization and turned the northern part of the South Asian realm into a mixture of pastoralism and sedentary agriculture. With the collapse of Mohenjo Daro, the realm entered a "Dark Age" lasting approximately a thousand years.

Aryan Hindu Impact

Eventually the demands of trade, commerce, administration, and fortification gave rise to the establishment of sizeable urban centers, particularly in the middle Ganges plains. Originating from a modest 5th century fort,

Pataliputra developed into the capital of a notable Indian empire, the Maurya (321–181 B.C.). Its location coincides with that of present-day Patna. Pataliputra possessed the urban forms of an Aryan city. It was organized to conform to the functional requirements of the capital of a Hindu kingdom, with residential patterns based on the function-based, four-caste social system and containing the requisite royal administrative features.

Although caste is not as important in determining contemporary residential patterns in cities as it was in Pataliputra, it is socially significant even today. Caste, the designation of social status by birth through the caste of one's parents, places a person into one of four broad groups: Brahmin, Kshatriya, Vaisya, and Sudra. Within the Sudra designation are

Figure 9.6   Low-caste Hindus wait to see a puppet show by proselytizing Muslims. (Photo by John Benhart Sr.)

those of very low caste and even those without caste or status. The people "without caste" are today more popularly referred to as Dalits. In the past, Dalits were often referred to as "Untouchables" because the touch or even the shadow cast by a member of this group was thought to "pollute" someone of higher caste. Traditionally each caste and its subcastes had certain designated occupations—for example, "washer-man" or *dhobi-wallah*" (fig. 9.5). Brahmins (priest caste) are at the top, followed by Kshatriyas (warrior caste), Vaisyas (commercial and agricultural caste), and Sudras (manual labor caste). Caste still plays a major role in society. Marriages are generally within caste, and there remain broad connections between caste status on one hand and income, quality of life, and social connections on the other. This remains true even after years of legal reforms such as a "reservation system" (similar to affirmative action in the United States) and broader social cam-

paigns led by people such as Mahatma Gandhi, spiritual leader of India's independence movement. Even today, urban land use patterns and socioeconomic structures somewhat reflect the caste system (fig. 9.6).

In ancient Pataliputra one could clearly see the spatial distribution of castes. Near the center and a little toward the east were the temple and residences of high-ranking Brahmins and ministers of the royal cabinet. Farther toward the east were the Kshatriyas, rich merchants, and expert artisans. To the south were government superintendents, prostitutes, musicians, and some other members of the Vaisya. To the west were the Sudras, including Untouchables, along with ordinary artisans and low-grade Vaisyas. Finally, to the north were artisans, Brahmins, and temples maintained for the titular deity of the city. A well-organized city government, a hierarchical street network, and an elaborate drainage system accompanied this functional distribution of population in Pataliputra.

Figure 9.7   The Taj Mahal has become the single most recognized icon of India. It was built in Agra as a tomb for Shah Jahan's wife and is now a UNESCO World Heritage Site. (Photo by George Pomeroy)

After the eclipse of the Maurya Empire in the 2nd century B.C., rulers of the Gupta Empire (320–467 A.D.) made it their capital, but the city lost its importance thereafter and was eventually buried under the sediments of the Ganges and Son rivers. Only small parts of the old city have recently been excavated. Other Hindu capitals that developed in both north and south India changed and modified the many urban forms used in Pataliputra.

Dravidian Temple Cities

In contrast to the subcontinent's north, Hindu kingdoms in south India had relative control for most of the historical period; distinctly Hindu forms of city development evolved uninterruptedly, minimizing Muslim influences. The rulers of south India constructed temples and water tanks as nuclei of habitation. Around the temples grew commercial bazaars and settlements of Brahmin priests and scholars. The ruler often built a palace near the temple, turning the temple-city into the capital of his kingdom; Madurai and Kancheepuram are examples, and both remain important pilgrimage centers today. The loftiness and grandeur of the temples imparted to the subjects a sense of protection by the Almighty. Thus, the kingdom was endowed with celestial favor, the king wielded power derived from Him, and a god-king concept was woven into the city design. Such city forms were also exported to Southeast Asia with further elaboration and modification; Angkor Wat (802–1432 A.D.) in Cambodia is one example.

Mentioned by Ptolemy, Madurai, the second capital of the south Indian Hindu kingdom of Pandyas, dates to about the beginning of the Christian era. The geographical advantage of the city was its site on the banks of the Vaigai River, which provided natural defense. Madurai and its cultural landscape were transformed in the 16th century,

Figure 9.8   The Red Fort, in Old Delhi, remains a potent feature of nationalism. (Photo by Jack Williams)

when it was turned into the capital of a Hindu Nayak dynasty. Though Madurai is now several times the size of the old walled city, with imprints from a brief Islamic period and a longer British dominance, its religious importance is nearly comparable to Varanasi in north India, which is the foremost Hindu pilgrimage center.

Muslim Impact

The first permanent Muslim occupation that significantly influenced the subcontinent began in the 11th century A.D. and resulted in the addition of many Middle Eastern and Central Asian Islamic qualities to the urban landscapes of South Asia. Shahjahanabad is a particularly good example of Muslim impact. The Moghul emperor Shah Jahan, who planned the Taj Mahal as a tomb for his wife in Agra (fig. 9.7), moved his capital from Agra to Delhi (about 125 mi [200 km] away) and started the construction of a new city, Shahjahanabad, on the right bank of the Yamuna River. The city was built near the sites of several previous capital cities and took nearly a decade to complete (1638–1648). In its architecture was a fusion of Islamic and Hindu influences. Though the royal palace and mosques, with their arched vaults and domes, adhered to Muslim styles, Hindu styles were found in combination. The Muslim rulers were most concerned with the magnificence of their royal residences and courts, the massiveness of their fortresses, and the typical Islamic loftiness in the design of their mosques. These features are represented most vividly in Shahjahanabad. Surrounded by brick walls without a moat, the city was completely fortified. Moreover, many settlements, including the extensive remains of the earlier city, were sprawled out in four different suburbs, all outside the walls.

Situated at the east end of the city was the Red Fort (fig. 9.8). Planned as a parallelogram with massive red sandstone walls and ditches on all sides except by the river, the fortress had an

Figure 9.9   To the left is a Muslim neighborhood and to the right a Hindu one in Old Delhi. (Photo by John Benhart Sr.)

almost foolproof defense. Inside were a magnificent court, the king's private palace, gardens, and a music pavilion. All were built either of red sandstone or white marble and displayed the exquisite designs of Moghul architecture. The Red Fort remains a central feature of Delhi today, often serving as platform and backdrop for many political proclamations and as a well-known tourist destination.

The two main thoroughfares, which connected the city with the fortress and the outside world, had shops of merchants along them. One, Chandni Chowk ("silver market"), ran straight westward from the Red Fort toward the Lahore Gate of the city. The Chandni Chowk was one of the great bazaars

of the Orient. The other thoroughfare, Khas Road, a shopping area of lesser importance, was built a little to the east of the Great Jama Mosque, largest and most famous of all the mosques in South Asia.

Shahjahanabad ceased to be the capital of India, more precisely north India, when British rule started in the 18th century, but it continued to be a functional city. Today, the area is known as "Old Delhi" and is part of the Delhi metropolis. Most of the city walls are gone, though all the basic structures of the Red Fort and Jama Mosque remain intact. Chandni Chowk continues to be a traditional, busy bazaar, where motorized vehicles have been prohibited. It is very densely populated with a mixture of Hindus and Muslims (fig. 9.9). Large parts of Old Delhi are gradually being transformed for commercial and small workshop uses.

Colonial Period

After Vasco de Gama discovered the oceanic route via the Cape of Good Hope and landed on the southwestern coast of India in 1498, the European powers of Portugal, Holland, France, and Britain were greatly interested in developing a firm trade connection with South Asia. Though initially all four powers obtained some kind of footing in India, the sagacious diplomacy and "divide-and-rule" policy of the British succeeded in ousting the other Europeans from most Indian soil. Eventually, the British established three significant centers of operation: Bombay, Madras, and Calcutta.

The British needed a firm footing in seaports for the convenience of trading and receiving military reinforcements from the parent country. Bombay, Madras, and Calcutta were the seaports. Hence, these three cities were designed as the headquarters for the three different Presidencies into which the British divided South Asia for administrative purposes. Consequently, the cities are referred to as the "Presidency Towns." In the 1990s they were renamed Mumbai, Chennai, and Kolkata, respectively, to reflect indigenous cultures and further downplay India's colonial heritage.

The Presidency Towns

When Mumbai, Chennai, Kolkata, and Colombo were established as Presidency Towns, their nuclei were forts. Outside these forts were the cities. Inside the cities, two different standards of living were set for two different classes of residents: Europeans and "natives" each had their own parts of the city. The rich were composed of absentee landowners from rural areas, moneylenders, businesspeople, and the newly English-educated elite and clerks. The poor comprised servants, manual laborers, street cleaners, and porters. The rich needed the services of the poor, and therefore the houses of the native rich in many instances stood by the houses of their poor, native service-providers.

As local industries grew in the 19th century, a new working class developed. In Kolkata, the industrial workers worked mainly for jute mills and local engineering factories; in Mumbai, for the expanding cotton and textile-related industries; and in Chennai, for tanning and cotton textiles. As these trades grew, the Presidency Towns turned from water to railways and roads for inland transportation. Train services began in South Asia in 1852. The Presidency Towns also developed huge hinterlands that catered to the needs of the colonial economy. The hinterlands supplied the raw materials to the three seaports for export to the United Kingdom; in return, the British sent consumer-type manufactured goods through the same ports. Thus, the Presidency Towns became the main focus of the colonial mercantile system.

Accompanying the new technology were new forms of architecture, particularly the expanding use of the Western Gothic and Victorian styles (fig. 9.10). Public buildings of the Presidency Towns, such as railroad terminals, post offices, the governor's house, high courts, central and provincial secretariats, museums, and educational institutions, were built in these designs. One of the best examples of the use of these architectural

Figure 9.10   The "Gateway of India," a distinctive symbol of India's largest city, was built in 1911 on Mumbai's harbor to commemorate the landing of King George V. (Photo by George Pomeroy)

styles in combination with some Indian forms is the Victoria Memorial Building (built 1906–1921) in Kolkata. The building was done in white marble with European designs, and the architects originally intended it to surpass the Taj Mahal in massive grandeur.

MODELS OF URBAN STRUCTURE

Early on in the study of South Asian cities, some theorists would mechanically try to apply Western models, such as Burgess's Concentric Zone Theory, irrespective of their applicability. No comprehensive model explaining the growth patterns of indigenous cities' structures has been offered, though three basic models have been proposed to explain the distinctive form of

South Asian cities: the bazaar-based city model, the colonial-based city model, and the planned city model. The basic characteristics of the three types of cities have been summarized in a matrix (tab. 9.1). Whichever model is used, however, it is important to note that two principal influential forces—colonial and traditional—have combined to create the existing forms of South Asian cities.

The Colonial-Based City Model

South Asia's colonial city patterns parallel those found in other world regions, but the Indian subcontinent presents a specific and hybrid model, being neither Western nor Indian, nor the same as in other world regions. The need to perform colonial functions demanded a particular form of city growth

Table 9.1 Topological Characteristics of South Asian Cities

	Land Value	Population Density Gradient	Physical Aspect	Land Use Composition of the City Center	Historical Roots	Mixture of Three Forms
Bazaar City	Highest at the center; declines as one moves to the periphery	Highest at the center and declining inversely as one moves to the periphery	Narrow streets, commercial establishments at the center occupying the road; front, back, and second-/third-floor residential; generally congested and dirty	Retail and wholesale business mainly, with limited recreation and combined with high-density residential	May have origins from ancient medieval, or recent times and accordingly may have imprints from Dravidian, Hindu, Muslim or Western forms at the periphery	When a bazaar city was implanted with colonial aspects, gardenlike, semiplanned "civil lines" were added; similar addition of planned neighborhoods may also be at the periphery after independence
Colonial City	Highest at the center; generally declines as one moves to the periphery, but relatively higher in the European town compared to the "native" town	Center with minimum density, with highest densities around the CBD, creating a "carter effect" at the center; thereafter declines as one moves to the periphery	Wide streets at the center and the European town, with garden like, affluent appearance; the "native" town characterized by narrow, sinuous, streets and generally shabby condition	Offices, banks, main post office, transport headquarters, government buildings with large open space, hotels, retail and recreational activities and residential use	Origins no earlier than 16th century; Victorian, neo-Gothic, and other Western forms widely prevalent; native forms also implanted	Parts of colonial city—particularly adjacent to the CBD and some specific locations in the "native" town—evolving characteristics of the bazaar center; planned neighborhoods added, particularly adjacent to the periphery of the European town after independence
Planned City	May vary according to predetermined values for different locations	May vary at different locations of the city, but the initial plan is for low density	Organized and generally pleasing appearance	Combination of retail, office, and recreation in a systematic fashion	May have origins in any historical period, but over time bazaar aspects will begin to dominate the center if restrictions are not strictly adhered to	Planned towns with addition of "civil lines" at the periphery and bazaar central forms evolving at one or many locations

Source: A. K. Dutt and R. Amin, "Towards a Typology of South Asian Cities," *National Geographic Journal of India* 32 (1995): 30–39.

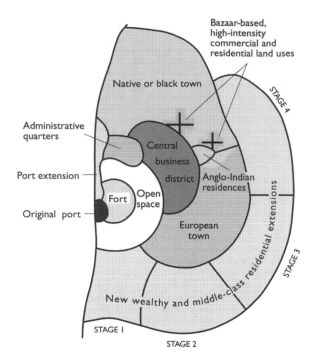

Figure 9.11   A Model of the Colonial-Based City in South Asia. *Source:* Ashok Dutt.

relevant to the subcontinent, which produced the following characteristics (fig. 9.11):

1. The need for trade and military reinforcements required a waterfront location accessible to oceangoing ships because the colonial power operated from Europe. A minimal port facility was a prerequisite and was the starting point of the city. Thus, coastal locations became the main attractions of the colonial city site.

2. A walled fort was constructed adjacent to the port with fortifications, white soldiers' and officers' barracks, a small church, and educational institutions. Sometimes inside the fort, factories processed agricultural raw materials to be shipped to the mother country. Thus, the fort became not only a military outpost but also the nucleus of the colonial exchange.

3. Beyond the fort and the open area, a "native town" or town for the native peoples eventually developed, characterized by overcrowding, unsanitary conditions, and unplanned settlements. It serviced the fort and the colonial administration, as the central business district (CBD) and further administrative activities developed near the fort and the native town.

4. A Western-style CBD grew adjacent to the fort and native town, with a high concentration of mercantile office functions, retail trade, and low-density residential areas. The administrative quarters consisted of the governor's (or viceroy's) house, the main government office, the high court, and the general post office. Also in the CBD were Western-style hotels, churches, banks, and museums, as well as occasional statues of British

Figure 9.12 One of the first buildings constructed (1889) in Allahabad University is typical of British colonial structures, with a melding of Gothic and Indian architectural styles. (Photo by Ashok Dutt)

monarchs, viceroys, and other dignitaries at important road intersections, reminiscent of royal eternity (fig. 9.12).

5. The European town grew in a different direction from the native town. It had spacious bungalows, elegant apartment houses, planned streets with trees on both sides, and a generally European look. It featured clubs for afternoon and evening get-togethers, European indoor and outdoor recreation facilities; churches of different denominations; and garden-like graveyards.

6. Between the fort and the European town (or at some appropriate nearby location), an extensive open space (*maidan*) was reserved for military parades and Western recreation facilities such as race and golf courses, and soccer and cricket fields. The racecourse opened on Saturday afternoons, when the whites and a few moneyed native people frequented the track to gamble.

7. When a domestic water supply, electric connections, and sewage links were available or technically possible, the European town residents utilized them fully, whereas their use was quite limited in the native towns.

8. At an intermediate location between black towns and white towns developed the colonies of Anglo-Indians. They were the offspring of mixed marriages (European and Indian), and they were Christians. Never were they fully accepted by either the native or the European communities.

9. Starting from the late 19th century, the colonial city became so large that new living space was necessary, especially for the native elite and rich people. Extensions to the city were made by reclaiming the lowland and/or developing in a semiplanned manner the existing nonurban areas.

10. From the very inception of such colonial cities, population density was very low at the center, which housed Europeans, whereas a much larger group of "natives" lived outside the colonial center. When the European center was gradually replaced by a Western-style CBD during the second half of the 19th century, there was a further decline in the population of the center, giving rise to a density gradient with a "crater effect" at the center. Though such a density crater is typical of large Western cities, it existed in colonial-based cities of the developing countries right from their inception.

As the colonial system became deeply entrenched in the Indian subcontinent, and an extensive railway network was made operational, waterfront locations accessible to oceangoing ships were no longer a prerequisite for a colonial headquarters. Kolkata, Mumbai, Chennai, and Colombo were not the only suitable locations on the subcontinent for high levels of administration. Hence, in 1911, the capital of British India was moved to the inland city of Delhi, which was not a seaport. Thus, a new inland colonial city was implanted by the side of an historic city, Old Delhi, and designated New Delhi.

Three other lesser (but numerous) colonial urban forms (cantonment, railway colony, and hill station) were also introduced to the subcontinent to serve very specific purposes.

Cantonments

Cantonments (from the French word *canton*, meaning "district") were military encampments, some 114 in all by the mid-19th century, which housed a quarter of a million soldiers

(both European and native). Strict segregation by class and ethnicity was practiced in these camps.

Railway Colonies

These surrounded a railroad station or a regional headquarters for railway operation and administration, also with strict segregation in their design. Often situated near urban centers, they eventually formed part of the greater urban area. These colonies were innumerable; wherever the railroad went, railway colonies followed.

Hill Stations

Hill stations, at altitudes between 3,500 and 8,000 feet, served as resort towns for Europeans to escape hot summers on the plains and spend time in the midst of a more exclusive European community. By the time of independence, there were 80 such stations, such as Simla and Darjeeling (fig. 9.13). The Europeans transplanted all the class distinctions and characteristics of the lowland cities to these smaller urban centers in the hills and mountains.

The Bazaar-Based City Model

The traditional bazaar city is widespread in South Asia and has certain features that date back to precolonial times. Ordinarily, these cities grew with a trade function originating from agricultural exchange, temple location, existence as a transport node, or the presence of various administrative activities (fig. 9.14). Usually, at the main crossroads a business concentration occurs where commodity sales dominate. In north India such an intersection is known as a Chowk, around which develops

Figure 9.13   Simla serves as the companion hill station for Delhi and remains a popular destination today. Sited at 7,500 feet, the elevation provides relief from the heat at lower elevations. (Photo by Ashok Dutt)

the houses of the rich. Most merchants live either on the upper floor or in back of their shops. Often the same house is used as a warehouse.

The bazaar, or the city center, consists of an amalgam of land uses that cater to the central-place functions of the city. The commercial land use, dominating the center, consists of both retail and wholesale activities. Because the greatest portion of family income is spent acquiring the basic necessities of life—food, clothing, and shelter—most streets are related to the retail sale of foodstuffs and clothes. Perishable goods, such as vegetables, meat, and fish—which are bought fresh daily because many homes lack refrigeration facilities—are sold in specific areas of the bazaar. These areas often lack enclosing walls and instead have a common roof. In the process of bazaar evolution, functional separation of retail businesses

occurs: textile shops stay together, attracting tailors; grain shops cluster with each other near the perishable goods market; and pawnshops are adjacent to jewelry shops. Sidewalk vendors are present almost everywhere in the bazaar.

Wholesale business establishments also form part of the bazaar landscape (fig. 9.15). Situated near an accessible location, they tend to separate according to the commodities they deal in, such as vegetables, grains, and cloth, depending on the size of city the bazaar serves. Traditionally, public or nonprofit inns provide modest overnight accommodation in the bazaar for a nominal fee. However, as a result of Western impact, some kinds of hotel accommodation are now available in the medium-sized and large cities. Prostitutes or dancing girls, once a source of evening entertainment in the bazaar, have been supplanted

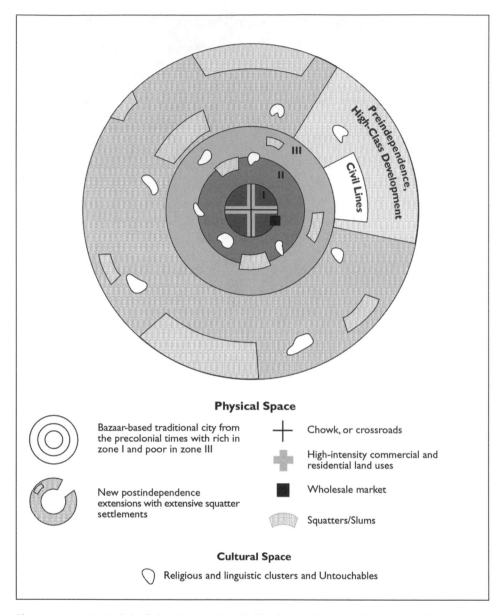

Physical Space

Bazaar-based traditional city from the precolonial times with rich in zone I and poor in zone III

Chowk, or crossroads

High-intensity commercial and residential land uses

New postindependence extensions with extensive squatter settlements

Wholesale market

Squatters/Slums

Cultural Space

Religious and linguistic clusters and Untouchables

Figure 9.14   A Model of the Bazaar-Based City in South Asia. *Source:* Ashok Dutt.

by cinemas that in turn have declined as a result of the prevalence of television, VCRs, and DVD players. Traditionally, the shops selling country-made liquor were never located in the bazaars, probably because drinking alcohol in public places was considered ill-mannered by both Hindu and Muslim soci-eties. Only in recent years have Western bars and liquor stores started to appear in city centers. Whereas at one time the only doctors were practitioners of indigenous medicines, now the practitioners of modern Western medicine join them near the main streets of the bazaar. Barbers who used to work outdoors

Figure 9.15　A produce vendor in Chennai typifies the bazaar-based city. (Photo by George Pomeroy)

now have regular shops like those in Western countries, but many still operate on the sidewalks. Their establishments are, however, scattered all over the bazaar. Long distance private telephone centers along with Internet access enterprises have become commonplace in city centers.

Thus, the inner core of the city develops an increased concentration of trade, commerce, and wealthy people. Beyond this inner core, in a second zone, rich people live in conjunction with poorer servants, but not in the same structure. The rich need the services of the poor as domestic servants, cleaners, shop assistants, and porters. The residences of the poor surround this second zone in a third area, where the demand for land is less and its price is low. Beyond the third zone, Civil Lines were established during British colonial rule. Here, particularly after independence, the native upper and middle classes settled in neighborhoods, and squatter settlements developed alongside. In the bazaar-based city,

one sees elements of the inverse concentric zone model.

As the city grows, ethnic, religious, linguistic, and caste neighborhoods come to be formed in specific areas. Their location varies in accord with the time of settlement and the availability of developable land. The "Untouchables" always occupy the periphery of the city, although sometimes other housing develops later beyond their neighborhoods. In Hindu-dominated areas of India, Muslims always form separate neighborhoods. Similarly, Hindu minorities in Srinagar and Dhaka, for instance, live in enclaves of the old city. Often people who have migrated from other linguistic areas form specific neighborhoods of their own.

Planned Cities

Though there were several planned historic cities on the subcontinent (Mohenjo Daro and Pataliputra, for instance), they did not survive. There were, however, others that were planned during precolonial, colonial, and independence periods that not only survived but also formed nuclei for major urban developments. Jaipur is an example from precolonial times, and Jamshedpur from the British Colonial period. Jaipur, India's 12th largest city with an estimated 2.3 million people, was founded as a planned city in 1727 by the Maharajah of Jaipur. A hierarchy of streets divided it into sectors and neighborhoods. Though the planned city covered only 3 square miles (5 sq km) and is now surrounded by a built-up area of about 22 square miles (35 sq km), the original identity of the 18th century planning has been retained.

Jamshedpur is a similar case; it was planned as a company town for the first steel mill on the subcontinent by a Mumbai-based industrial family, the Tatas. Jamshedpur is about 150 miles (90 km) southeast of Kolkata. The raw materials used for steel-making—iron ore, coal, and limestone—are found nearby. The city underwent four different plans during colonial times and one during the independence period. In 1943, the Koenigsberger plan (named after a German Jew who took Indian citizenship) remodeled Jamshedpur on the basis of the neighborhood unit concept, a novel idea and probably the first of its kind in South Asia. Fortunately, Koenigsberger's innovative experiment proved successful, and not only for one city: now almost all the new industrial and administrative cities of the subcontinent incorporate this idea in their planning.

In 2001, the city of Jamshedpur itself had about 1.1 million residents and a wider metropolitan population of well over 1.24 million (estimated as of 2005). Metropolitan growth has spread much beyond its original planned area. Thus, true to the characteristics of the planned-city model, Jaipur, Jamshedpur, and other such cities each have a planned central core that has undergone modifications over time and is surrounded by unplanned traditional developments and semi-planned post-independence extensions.

Mixtures of Colonial and Bazaar Models

The functional demands created by activities in colonial, bazaar-type, and planned cities generated interaction among city types. British administrative requirements in the traditional cities resulted in the establishment of Civil Lines, generally on the urban periphery. Each Civil Line was composed of a courthouse, a treasury, a jail, a hospital, a public library, police facilities, club houses, and residential quarters for high administrative and judicial officials. The streets of the Civil Lines were well planned, paved, and had trees planted on both sides. In the provincial capitals, a governor's house, a secretariat, and extensive residences for different levels of government employees were also constructed. In the native states of the subcontinent, where an indirect colonial rule was operational, a British regent with his staff resided at the state capital within a Civil Station, which looked like a colonial appendage attached to the bazaar or planned city.

During the 20th century, both before and after independence, when the local rich needed to build houses of their own, several governmental, semi-governmental, cooperative, and private agencies planned developments surrounding the traditional city. Consequently, many traditional cities developed new extensions on their peripheries. For the most part, however, colonial cities never grew as conceived by their colonial masters. Traditional factors played an unavoidable role in altering colonial forms. The traditional bazaar, inherent to the indigenous cityscape, always interacted with other city forms. The bazaar thrived side by side with the CBD. As a result, to correctly model classic colonial cities, such as Kolkata, Mumbai, Chennai and Colombo, it is essential to consider the impact traditional bazaars had on them. All colonial cities bear imprints from bazaar forms, just as bazaar cities were impacted by colonial functional demands. Planned cities, too, as they expanded, often added colonial and bazaar city forms, and sometimes the two latter city types created new planned entities as their expanded appendages.

REPRESENTATIVE CITIES

Mumbai: India's Cultural and Economic Capital

Mumbai is India's largest urban agglomeration and the nation's most cosmopolitan city. Two dimensions have been critical in its rise to preeminence, one commercial and one cultural. The skyscrapers in the Nariman Point area are the heart of the city's—and nation's—corporate and financial sectors and signify the city's role as the single most important command-and-control point in the national economy. The two largest stock exchanges of Mumbai handle an overwhelming majority of the country's stock transactions and figure among the world's largest in volume and value. In terms of trade, 40% of the country's foreign trade is conducted through the city. The city has emerged as the nation's cultural capital

through its prolific film industry, which is among the world's largest: films produced in "Bollywood" are eagerly consumed not only by the viewing public in India, but also in Bangladesh, the Middle East, and Africa (box 9.3).

In 1672, Mumbai became the capital of all British possessions on the west coast of India. The 17th-century British possession of the seven islands, which now form the oldest part of this city, initiated the construction of the fort. Beyond the fort grew a filthy "native town," where sanitary conditions were miserably poor and drainage was a serious problem. The "European town" grew around the fortress on higher ground, and protective walls were erected around it. The native or Black town was separated from the European town by an Esplanade, which was kept free of permanent houses. A main spur to Mumbai's development occurred when Britain's supply of raw cotton temporarily diminished in the 1860s during the U.S. Civil War. India became an important supplier of cotton, most of which moved through Mumbai. This resulted in an accumulation of huge reserves of capital by Mumbai-based businessmen, and the city became the main cotton textile center of the realm. In 1853, the opening of railways eventually connected Mumbai with a hinterland covering almost all of west India. Mumbai further prospered with the opening of the Suez Canal in 1869, which enhanced the city's trade advantage by further cutting the distance to Europe. This closer proximity helped earn the city its nickname: "Gateway to India."

When the fort area developed into a Western-style CBD, the British, followed by rich Indians, moved to Malabar Hill, Cumballah Hill, and Mahalakshmi on the southwestern

Box 9.3   "Bollywood"

What city produces more motion pictures than any other? While Hollywood may come to mind first, it is actually "Bollywood" that provides the correct answer. Each year, the Mumbai movie industry churns out over 1,000 films, surpassing the number produced in any other country. "Bollywood," with its stars, studios, and magnetism, is almost synonymous with the city itself. With its thriving film industry and financial markets, Mumbai in a sense serves as both the Los Angeles and the New York of India, adding to the magnetism of the city and bolstering its ranking among the great urban centers of the world.

Most Bollywood films are in Hindi, though anyone viewing a typical Bollywood film for the first time will likely figure out the plot. Characterized by generous quantities of glitz and glamour, at least a half dozen songs, and nearly as many dance sequences, the stories are usually quite simple and crammed with clichés. Many are love stories—a handsome young man meets a sweet, beautiful woman and falls in love; they are separated; and then, later, they are haphazardly brought together again and live happily ever after. Though much is implied that is not shown on the screen, the movies are actually rather clean, with kissing being as risqué as it gets. Also, good wins out over evil almost without exception. A closer analysis reveals that most of the films are based on a distinctive style with a mix of nine critical elements—love, hate, sorrow, disgust, joy, compassion, pity, pride, and courage—as dictated in the ancient Naya Shastra ("science of theater").

"Bollywood," of course, is a combination of Bombay, Mumbai's old name, and Hollywood. Its acceptance is affirmed by its inclusion in the *Oxford English Dictionary*, with the earliest citation dating from 1976.

portion of the island. These remain exclusive neighborhoods today. In the 1940s, the rich settled in another attractive area of the island, Marine Drive (now renamed), which lay along the Back Bay. Because of the ever-increasing demand for commercial and residential land in the fort area and the lack of land on the narrow peninsula and the island city, dozens of skyscrapers have been erected since the 1970s at Nariman Point, generating a skyline resembling a miniature Manhattan. The most recent phenomenon in Mumbai's commercial land use is the partial shifting of office- and finance-related activities to the newly built high-rise buildings of Nariman Point, though the old fort area is still considered the main core of the CBD. Mumbai is an expensive city to conduct business in and ranks 6th in the world with respect to office occupancy costs. The poor, the middle class, and a few native businessmen settled mostly at the center and in the northern part of the island. At present, the Western-colonial influence created by European settlements can be observed in the southern part of the city proper (fig. 9.16). The more traditional influences have remained observable in the north. Most recently, the northern part of Greater Mumbai has seen the development of semi-planned housing suburbs and industrial

Figure 9.16   The Mumbai Municipal Corporation Office, in front of the Victoria Terminus in the old colonial center of town, mixes Western design and European Gothic to create one of Mumbai's landmark buildings. (Photo by Ashok Dutt)

parks. Unsanitary slums, built of flimsy materials and serving as habitats of the poverty-ridden, continue to mushroom all over the city.

As a state capital and the largest metropolis in South Asia, Mumbai has also become the largest port of the entire subcontinent; not only does it handle the largest share of foreign trade, but it also collects 60% of India's duty revenues. Though employment in cotton textiles manufacturing remains important, other sectors including general engineering, silk, chemicals, dyeing and bleaching, and information technology (IT) are now emerging as important employment sources. Total industrial employment has declined, and the service sector is increasingly prominent. Still, the Mumbai Metropolitan Region accounts for a disproportionately large share of India's industrial employment and fixed capital, and the Mumbai–Pune corridor is India's second most important center of employment for IT.

Mumbai attracts an enormous number of migrants from the western and central parts of India, thus giving it a religious and linguistic diversity that surpasses all other cities in South Asia. Yet Mumbai does share some religious characteristics with other South Asian cities. For example, its Muslim population declined between 1941 and 1951 as a result of the partitioning of British India into India and Pakistan in 1947, an action which prompted mass exoduses of Hindus from East Pakistan (now Bangladesh), Hindus and Sikhs from West Pakistan (now Pakistan), and Muslims from India. Hindus are thus the most dominant group in Mumbai today, constituting 69% of the city's population, followed by Muslims (14%); Sikhs (7%); and a mix of Christians, Jains, and Buddhists (less than 10% each). Two minority religious groups play a socioeconomic role far beyond their numbers. First, the Zoroastrians, or Parsis as they are called in Mumbai, are a very significant minority group. Even though their numbers in Mumbai are small, more Parsis live here than anywhere else across the globe. Also significant are the Jains, mainly migrant businessmen from nearby Gujarat State, who were drawn by Mumbai's increasing commercial attraction. The number of Buddhists has increased as a result of the mass conversion of local Untouchables during the Neo-Buddhist movement launched in Maharastra in the 1950s. In terms of linguistic characteristics, no other metropolis of the subcontinent is quite like Mumbai. The regional language, Marathi, is spoken by less than half the population. Mumbai is a linguistic microcosm of India itself.

Bengalūru and Hyderabad: India's Economic Frontier

When asked to identify economic success stories in South Asia, two cities immediately spring to mind: Bangalore (renamed Bengalūru in 2006) and Hyderabad. Globalization is the vehicle that both cities have ridden to prosperity, as each has become a center for IT development and business process outsourcing. The success of each is built upon the country's supply of capable, technically-skilled, and English-proficient (but underemployed) college graduates, combined with the forces of technology and globalization that have reduced distances and, hence, costs. Other elements distinctive to these two cities are the presence of an entrepreneurial spirit, government flexibility, and critical investments in infrastructure. Both cities also serve as state capitals.

Bengalūru's association with IT dates to the arrival of Texas Instruments in the mid-1980s. Even before that, however, the city had become a center of India's aerospace and defense manufacturing industries. By the late 1990s, so many multinational firms had established operations here that the city had been christened "India's Silicon Valley," an appropriate nickname because it accounts for over one-third of the nation's software exports. The city's concomitant wealth and affluence has

given it a reputation for being rather cosmopolitan and trendy.

Hyderabad's emergence as an IT center came in part through the visionary efforts of the state's chief minister during the late 1990s. He pulled out all the stops to provide incentives and infrastructure for high-technology-related development. Today, the city prides itself as being referred to as "Cyberabad" (box 9.4). It hosts a Genome Valley and a Nanotechnology Park, outgrowths of the city's leading role in the nation's pharmaceutical industry. Microsoft's largest development center outside Redmond, Washington, is located here, as are many other multinational firms.

Delhi: Those Who Control Delhi Control India

Delhi, the seat of India's capital, combines a deep-rooted historical heritage with colonial and modern forms. Historical records confirm that 18 different capital sites in the Delhi area have been chosen over the past 3,000 years; 17 sites have actually been identified. Fifteen different names have been given to the various capital sites, but in spite of the many efforts by the rulers to change it, the name Delhi, derived from one of the earliest capital sites named Dilli, has remained the name of the city.

The attraction for Delhi as the capital site was rooted in South Asia's physiography, and the locations of advanced civilization centers and migration/invasion routes. Delhi occupies a relatively flat drainage divide between the two most productive agricultural areas of the realm, the Indus and Ganges plains, where the most notable centers of civilization and power developed in the past. North of these plains, and of Delhi, lie the difficult-to-cross Himalayas; in the southwest lies the

---

Box 9.4 "High Speed" Hyderabad versus "Low Speed" Patna

Several years ago, South Asianist Graham Chapman observed that India could be broadly and geographically divided into the "Low Speed India" and the "High Speed India." Low Speed India, with about half the population, includes large parts of the northern half of the country. It is characterized by low levels of economic growth, lower levels of urbanization, and greater poverty. Low Speed India seems mired in stagnation. In contrast, High Speed India includes the southern Indian states and is characterized by increasing wealth, prosperity, and relative urban growth.

In a passage from *In Spite of the Gods,* Edward Luce captures the distinctions of what Alex Perry in *Time* (February 2004, 16) calls the "Sub-Continental Divide" of India. Luce describes Patna, the prototypical Low Speed Indian city, in comparison to Hyderabad, the classic High Speed city:

> I was in Patna, the capital of Bihar in India's north to observe an important state assembly election that would choose the next government of India's third largest state. I had just come from the buzzing city of Hyderabad in the southern state of Andhra Pradesh, which is a magnet for much of India's software investment. The contrast between the two cities could not be greater. In Hyderabad there are as many five-star hotels as you would find in any Western city. Most of them offer seamless "wifi" service you can connect to the Internet from anywhere in the building. At Patna's best hotel the crackle on the internal phone system was so noisy you could not communicate with the receptionist. "Hello, hello, is this a long-distance call?" No, I am calling from room 212. "Hello, hello? Do you have a reservation?" Naturally, Internet access was unthinkable. Likewise, although often clogged with traffic, Hyderabad's roads are paved and smooth. Meanwhile in Patna, a city of three million people, there is not a single functioning traffic light. Such is the reigning inertia; the city has not even changed the colonial names of its streets. (Edward Luce, *In Spite of the Gods: The Strange Rise of Modern India.* [New York: Doubleday, 2007], 115.)

---

inhospitable Thar (Rajasthan) Desert. After following the strategic Khyber Pass and entering the vast Indus plains of Punjab, the continent's migrants and invaders from the northwest frontiers of South Asia were impelled to control Delhi to ensure a firm hold over the North Indian Plains. The control of Delhi was so vital to the rule of north India that a popular saying arose: "He who controls Delhi, controls India." Moreover, Delhi's location gave it access to the year-round waterborne traffic of the northern part of South Asia.

Most of the historical sites of Delhi were located between the Delhi ridge (on which the 19th century British cantonment was located) and the Yamuna River, but the extensive developments that occurred after India's independence caused expansion of the city across the ridge and on the east bank of

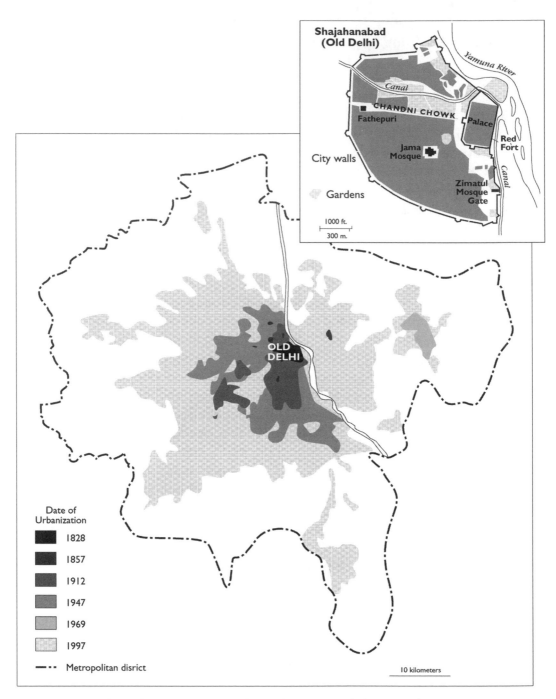

Figure 9.17   Delhi and Shajahanabad (Old Delhi). *Source:* Ashok Dutt and George Pomeroy.

Figure 9.18   Piped water is a luxury in most South Asian cities. Most people use public wells such as this one near the beach in Chennai for bathing and washing clothes. (Photo by Jack Williams)

the river. Old Delhi (the former Shahjahanabad) is a traditional bazaar-type Indian city, with the Chandni Chowk as its main commercial center (fig. 9.17). Here, sanitation used to be a major problem, but since independence the area has been fully served by underground sewers and piped water (fig. 9.18). Rich merchants and ordinary working people live close to each other. West of the Yamuna, connected by bridges with the main city, are a post-independence semi-planned area and squatter developments, where one-third of Delhi's population lives—some in unhealthy slums with very little or no basic facilities of water, sewer, electricity, or paved roads.

New Delhi, situated south of Old Delhi, is a majestic colonial creation that emerged as a new city after the capital of British India was moved from Kolkata. The capital was temporarily moved to Delhi's Civil Lines and Cantonment in 1911 before being installed in New Delhi (1931). New Delhi was planned by a British architect, Edwin Lutyens, in a geometric form that combined hexagons, circles, triangles, rectangles, and straight lines (fig. 9.19). Spacious roads, a magnificent viceroy's residence (now the President's Palace), a circular council chamber (which is now Parliament House), imposing secretariat buildings, a Western-style shopping center (Connaught Place) with a large open space in the middle, officers' residences in huge compounds, and a garden-like atmosphere formed the main elements of New Delhi. The new capital was separated from the congested, unsanitary, and generally poor conditions of Old Delhi by an open space. To British eyes, the congestion was so pathetic that in 1937 a Delhi Improvement Trust was formed to tackle Old Delhi's problems.

The main economic base of New Delhi is government services. After India's independence, an increasing demand for housing was created by new government employees, which

Figure 9.19   This spacious road illustrates the harsh imperial geometry stamped upon Delhi by Edwin Lutyens. The domed building in the distance is Rashtrapat Bhavan, the President's residence. (Photo by John Benhart Sr.)

led to large-scale public housing developments around earlier settlements of New Delhi. The most noticeable feature of such developments was the segregation of larger neighborhoods according to the rank of the government employees and foreign residents. Class rather than caste determined the new neighborhood composition. Delhi has expanded in a planned manner as the Delhi Development Authority (DDA) has worked to coordinate the land development process with an innovative revolving funding scheme. The dark side of this strategy is that the lower and middle classes are left without affordable housing options (fig. 9.20). That one in five Delhi residents lives in a slum blurs any gains registered.

Delhi's problems are so intense it is numbered among the five worst cities in the world with respect air pollution. Motor vehicles are the leading source of air pollution, followed by industrial activities. Steps taken to ameliorate the problems over the last decade include the banning of leaded gasoline, the conversion to compressed natural gas (CNG) buses, the mandating of the use of low-sulfur diesel fuel, and the implementation of other tighter emission restrictions. With these steps, pollution levels have stabilized.

Kolkata: Premier Presidency Town

The popular image of Kolkata to foreign commentators over time has evoked a number of nicknames, including geographer Rhoads Murphey's "City in a Swamp," Dominique LaPierre's "City of Joy," Rudyard Kipling's "Cholera Capital of the World," and our own

Figure 9.20 The use of makeshift materials, as seen here in Delhi, is an indicator of slum housing. (Photo by John Benhart Sr.)

"City of Pavement Dwellers." As the administrative capital for much of the colonial period, and as an important commercial center even before then, Kolkata set the tone for urban imagery in South Asia.

"City in a Swamp" appropriately describes the city even today. Sited on the levees sloping east and west from the riverbank, the 40-mile (65-km) long metropolitan district is for the most part less than 22 feet above sea level (fig. 9.21). Problems associated with this flood-prone elevation are further aggravated by the monsoon, which brings most of the city's annual rainfall of 64 inches between June and September, coinciding with the river's highest level. Waterlogged soils and extensive flooding substantially impact a majority of slum dwellers. Despite these physical disadvantages, the city's location on the river Hugli (a tributary of the Ganges) provided the advantages that were critical to its future growth. Its location 60 miles (100 km) upriver from the Bay of Bengal allowed access to 19th-century ocean vessels, provided a populous hinterland with rich mineral and agricultural resources, and provided access to the Ganges plain via waterborne transport on perennial river systems. These advantages, coupled with the later development of extensive rail and road connections, combined to spur growth and development. Finally, the establishment of the trading post and military garrison by the British in 1756 provided the mechanism through which trade was conducted.

Spatial growth of the city, and the business district in particular, centered on the original fort and continued from that point even after the fort's relocation several years later. A European component grew in the south end, and a native town in the north. The native town included a wealthier, middle-class component that resided at the northern edge of the CBD. This area, the Barabazar, is reminiscent of traditional bazaars. It remains the most desirable residential area today,

Figure 9.21   In Mumbai and many South Asian cities, drainage is often poor. Here a stagnant creek, strewn with garbage and sewage, runs alongside slums and middle-class apartments. (Photo by Ashok Dutt)

especially for wealthy Marwari and Gujarati merchants who migrated from western India and are now a bulwark of the business community. With such commercial activities, particularly commodity sales, high residential and commercial densities, and an incumbent population of wealthier residents, Barabazar presents many characteristics of a traditional bazaar center. Immediately to the south is the Western-style CBD, mainly an office, administrative, and commercial district with a low density of residents.

As the city grew, its northern part reflected more traditional characteristics, whereas the southern section developed more of a European look. In between is the CBD, including the Chauringee, the main activity center of the metropolis. With the formation of the Kolkata Improvement Trust in 1911, new areas were reclaimed in the southern and eastern portions of the city to be inhabited mostly by wealthy Bengalis, the native inhabitants of the state.

Kolkata is a leading port in India and the capital of the state of West Bengal. The Kolkata (Calcutta) Metropolitan District (CMD), of which the city of Kolkata is part, has an area of 500 square miles (1,300 sq km) and a population of well over 14 million. The colonial characteristics of Kolkata city, however, were restricted to its own municipal jurisdiction. The CMD expanded along both banks of the Hugli River in a linear and continuous pattern for about 50 miles (80 km). The CMD consists of about 500 local governing bodies, of which the City of Kolkata is the largest, with 40 square miles (90 sq km) and 4.6 million inhabitants (an estimate based on the 2001 Census). Away from Kolkata, the local centers of the CMD, including Kolkata's twin city, Howrah, are typically characterized by traditional, bazaar-based land uses and are devoid of any imprint of a Western-style CBD.

The situation of the city was advantageous in forming an industrial nucleus. In the 19th century, its seaport facilitated the importation of wholesale machinery for the jute industry, the most significant industrial activity of the metropolis. Raw jute was produced in the nearby fields of the Ganges delta. From then until today, the jute industry has grown as a chain of mills stretching along the banks of the Hugli River, turning the metropolis into the largest concentration of jute mills in the world.

Because of its role as British colonial capital (1757–1911) and because of the introduction of western education from the early part of the 19th century, the city was regarded as a pacesetter in terms of education and politics. As a pioneer center of education it was often viewed as possessing an elitist heritage. The large number of Kolkata University graduates (who migrated to different parts of India) and their active and patriotic political activities helped generate the common saying that "What Bengal [meaning Kolkata] thinks today, India thinks tomorrow." After independence, with the strong attraction of Delhi, the national capital of independent India, Kolkata's leadership role significantly diminished.

Today, the CMD is highly industrialized. Post-independence manufacturing activities were initially hurt by the partition of the subcontinent, which severed the jute mills of the city from their supply areas, contributing to the city's relative industrial decline. Today, it is the engineering industry that is an important component of the local economy. It is concentrated mainly on the right bank of the Hugli in Howrah. Other important industries are paper, pharmaceuticals, and synthetic fabrics. Information technology firms and related employment are growing, but Bengalūru and the Mumbai–Pune corridor remain ahead of Kolkata. Commercially, the city now ranks second to Mumbai. It has headquarters of native business firms, banks, and international corporations.

In spite of recent stagnations in Kolkata's economy, the city attracts migrants from many different parts of northeastern India. Many Hindu refugees arrived from the former East Pakistan (now Bangladesh) when partition occurred. Their arrival boosted the proportion of those speaking Bengali, who now account for two-thirds of the city's population. Another one-fifth speak Hindi, and one in ten speaks Urdu. The majority of slum dwellers, however, speak Hindi, reflecting their non-Bengali origins. Partition also altered the religious composition of the city: Hindus came to constitute 83% of the population, with most of the remaining percentage being Muslim.

Karachi: Port and Former Capital

Situated by the western edge of the Indus River delta and with approximately 13 million people, Karachi is Pakistan's largest city and former capital. It is highly industrialized and relies upon cotton textiles, steel, and engineering for its industrial core. It remains by far the nation's leading port. It is also an important center for educational and medical facilities.

Despite its status as the country's leading vibrant and cosmopolitan center of finance and trade, it has gained a notorious international reputation for its lawlessness. One-dimensional characterizations of the city in the international press underscore this reputation and obscure the city's full nature:

One block down and just around the corner from the U.S. Consulate, which was shaken by a car bomb, stands the restaurant where *Wall Street Journal* reporter Daniel Pearl disappeared. Three blocks farther along is the Sheraton Hotel, where another car bomb killed 11 French engineers. From there it's just a hundred yards to the bridge where a man with an AK-47 shot dead four Houston oil company auditors on their way to work. And this would be Karachi's very best neighborhood. (*Source:* Karl Vick, "In a Dangerous City of Dreams, Survival Rules: Karachi's Lawless Streets Attract Mix of Militants," *Washington Post,* June 24, 2002.)

When one examines the city's history and geographic setting, Karachi's rapid industrial growth is not surprising. It provides the city its economic, social, and cultural prominence, but it also plays a role in its reputation as a very dangerous place. These are indeed parallel elements in Karachi's development.

The city's job opportunities have long provided an urban "pull" not only for Pakistanis, but also for large numbers of Muslim refugees leaving India, especially in the period immediately following partition. Thus, the city has a relatively small percentage of natives. In the 1960s only 16% of Karachi's citizens were native born, whereas 18% were in-migrants from different parts of Pakistan, and 66% were Indian Muslim refugee immigrants from the late 1940s.

While the city has become more homogenous in terms of religion as a result of the in-migration and the effects of the 1947 partition, it has also become more linguistically and ethnically diverse and less politically stable. The partition led to the departure of all but a few thousand Sindhi Hindus; simultaneously, Urdu-speaking Muslim immigrants came in large numbers from the north and central parts of India. After the 1947 partition, Urdu became Pakistan's national language, providing an additional impetus for its becoming the majority language of Karachi's citizens. Even before partition, however, there were flows of Gujarati Muslim refugees from India into the city. Thus, apart from English (a lingua franca of the elite), three languages are prevalent in the city: Urdu, Sindhi, and Gujarati. A considerable influx of Pushtu-speaking Pathans from the Northwest Frontier Province (NWFP) and from Afghanistan occurred in the 1980s, and these migrants often clashed with the Urdu-speaking migrants from India. Only a few Afghan refugees returned to Afghanistan after the Soviet pullback in the late 1980s. With increased violence, a number of warring groups have materialized. The combination of linguistic, religious, and ethnic differences, exacerbated by ineffective and corrupt law enforcement, a bureaucratic judicial system, and the availability of arms supplied by the United States during the Afghan War in the 1980s has contributed to an alarming level of violence. This violence has escalated since the 1980s and continues today. Crime, along with declining employment opportunities and crumbling infrastructure, has led to urban discontent and near anarchy.

The center of Karachi still represents a true bazaar model: it features high population density, high intensity of commercial and small-scale industrial activity, and a relatively higher concentration of rich people. Toward the east from the center of the city were the planned cantonment quarters that originated during the British occupation dating back to 1839. During much of colonial times, Karachi remained confined to a land-use pattern that placed the docks in the southwest, the bazaar in the center, and the

Civil Lines and military establishments in the east and toward the north, after Karachi became the capital of the new Province of Sind. After independence, new suburban residential developments occurred surrounding the eastern two-thirds of the colonial city, and planned industrial estates were built mainly toward the northern and western fringes. Thus, the trends of colonial expansion continued, with the native rich settling toward the east, adjacent to the former Civil Lines and cantonment.

Dhaka: Capital, Port, and Primate City

Modern Dhaka, Bangladesh's largest urban center and capital, is a city of mosquitoes and cycle-rickshaws. Its streets are jammed with vehicles, each attempting to overtake the others. The contrast between rich and poor is glaring (box 9.5). Dhaka's noise pollution is deafening. It is generated from horns, sirens, and the loudspeakers of restaurants and mosques, the latter of which broadcast prayers five times a day, along with the festivities of an occasional wedding party. The city's numerous cinemas show "Bollywood" films, generally filled with overtones of sex and violence. Though the observance of *purdah* (seclusion of women) by both urban-dwelling women (since the 1950s) and rural women (at present) has declined, women still keep a low public profile.

Situated in the center of the country, Dhaka is sited on the left bank of a tributary of the Meghna–Ganges system. Founded in the 7th century A.D., the city was subsequently governed by Hindu Sena kings (from the 9th century) and by Muslim rulers (1203–1764), for which it served as an intermittent regional capital and

attained great commercial importance. Toward the end of the 17th century, the city had over 1 million inhabitants and stretched 12 miles (19 km) in length and 8 miles (13 km) in breadth. The European traders, largely Portuguese, Dutch, English, and French, started coming to Dhaka after 1616. The loss of regional capital status in 1706, however, precipitated a decline that continued well into the colonial period. Kolkata's status as a colonial capital and trade center eclipsed Dhaka's sphere of economic and political influence.

The early 20th century and the city's status as a temporary regional capital brought about important changes, resulting in a resurgence of growth that took the population from 104,000 in 1901 to 239,000 in 1941. Partition in 1947 prompted large-scale immigration of Muslims from India and stimulated industrial growth from an almost non-existent base. Spearheading the industrial growth was jute processing, which had then come to take place in Bangladesh because of the new international boundary that provided an effective barrier to the jute mills of Kolkata. Subsequently, Dhaka's Urdu speakers swelled in numbers. As least as significant in spurring growth and development after partition was Dhaka's reclaimed role as regional capital of East Pakistan. Later, Dhaka became the national capital of Bangladesh, which separated from West Pakistan (now Pakistan) and became independent in 1971. The resultant multifarious administrative–commercial activities provided the necessary pull factors to trigger the most rapid growth in Dhaka's history. Today, with its metropolitan population of approximately 11 million, the city ranks as the fifth largest in South Asia (see fig. 9.1).

Box 9.5   Micro-Credit Comes to Main Street

Few things better validate a "good idea" than a prize, and no prize is bigger than the Nobel Peace Prize. So when Bangladeshi Mohammed Yunus and the Grameen Bank which he founded were awarded the Nobel Peace Prize in 2006, it was in recognition of tremendous accomplishments. He and the bank pioneered the innovative idea of micro-credit. Once thought to be useful only in rural areas, this poverty-alleviation strategy is now successfully making its appearance in cities.

Although the idea of micro-loans has been around for over a century, the current model was firmly established by Yunus and his bank. Yunus's first loan—$27 to 42 families for making bamboo furniture—was made in 1976, shortly after Bangladesh suffered a terrible series of natural disasters. Since then, his bank has made 97% of its loans to women, has established over 2,000 branches, and has a loan recovery rate of over 95%! Today, the model may be found across the developing world.

Micro-credit, or micro-lending, is the idea of making very small loans to people who, lacking collateral, regular employment, or credit history, cannot get credit from standard financial institutions such as banks. Upon receiving a micro-loan, these borrowers invest the money in their own informal or formal sector small business. The business savvy that they may already possess, combined with the credit, allows many of these entrepreneurs to flourish. These individuals really are "bankable"; they simply did not possess the formal qualifications needed to obtain loans through standard financial channels. One reason micro-credit is seen as a success is that the rate of repayment is very high.

Micro-credit institutions are distinctive, too. The initial funds loaned by these "banks" may originate in grants and loans from aid organizations, but they often consist in part of pooled funds generated from the local poor. To ensure repayment, small informal support groups of borrowers, bank representatives, and others are required to attend weekly or bi-weekly meetings.

There are many advantages to micro-credit. The foremost of these is that it builds wealth so that the borrowers can exit extreme poverty. It helps those most who have had the least access to traditional financing—women, minority populations, and the poor. In South Asia, this includes those of lower caste, especially widowed women of lower caste. Dignity is enhanced, too, as the borrowers are not simply receiving aid as a handout. Instead, they can rightfully see their success as their own creation instead of as someone else's. One must also consider the total societal wealth created, which provides a critical element on the path to economic development. Finally, the socioeconomic status of the poor and other socially excluded groups is enhanced.

Micro-credit is seeing success in the cities of South Asia and beyond. In Bangladesh, for example, the Shakti Foundation for Disadvantaged Women is using the Grameen Bank model in Chittagong and Dhaka. In Dhaka, one-third of the 105,000 borrowers have now crossed the national poverty line. As South Asian cities swell and urban underemployment persists, it is clear that the micro-credit model will be of increasing relevance in urban settings.

The long history of Dhaka has left an obvious imprint on the city's structure and landscape. The legacies of successive Hindu, Muslim, and British rulers are present in various buildings and place names. With over 90% of the city's population Muslim, mosques are so numerous in Dhaka that some refer to it as the "City of Mosques." Hindus are the most important minority group (about 8%); the rest are Christians and Buddhists. Linguistically, Dhaka is very homogenous, as over 95% of the population speaks Bengali, the native language. During the period when Bangladesh and Pakistan were united (1947–1971), a substantial number of Urdu-speaking Muslims who came from either north India or West Pakistan were in the city; but since the creation of Bangladesh, the majority of them have been forced to depart. It was during 190 years of British rule that a more active Muslim culture was superimposed over an indigenous Hindu base in the city. The conspicuous products of Muslim construction combined with Western styles and urban expansion led to diversity in the Dhaka landscape.

Kathmandu, Colombo, and Kabul: Cities on the Edge

Colombo, Kabul, and Kathmandu are the premier cities and national capitals of Sri Lanka, Afghanistan, and Nepal, respectively. Officially, however, the capital of Sri Lanka has moved to Sri Jayawadenepura, located within the Colombo metropolitan area. As the former capital, the city of Colombo itself continues to be the seat of administration and decision-making. The three cities are greatly different in size: Kabul has a population of 3 million; Colombo, 652,000; and Kathmandu, 825,000.

Kabul is the oldest, so long-standing that it was even referred to in the RigVeda, a 3,500 year old Hindu scripture, and mentioned by Ptolemy in the 2nd century A.D. Kabul's strategic position by the side of the Kabul River and at the western entrance of the famous Khyber Pass—through which came the Hindu Aryans and other migrants and invaders to India—gave the city great political and trading significance. Sited at an elevation of 5,900 feet, it has served as a regional or national capital for numerous regimes over the centuries, most notably for the Moghul Empire (1504–1526) and, after 1776, for an independent Afghanistan. Later attempts by both the Russians and the British to subjugate the country and its capital failed. After 1880, modern buildings and gardens were constructed, but these have not diminished the identity of the old bazaar city.

The city has suffered greatly since the 1970s as a result of internal and international conflicts. The overthrow of the king in 1974 initiated a series of events that included the establishment of a Soviet-backed Marxist government (1978), the establishment of a weak puppet state (1989), a period of warlord-dominated chaos (1992), and the establishment of the Taliban regime (1996). Under the socially repressive Taliban, Afghanistan served as a haven for those responsible for the World Trade Center attacks of September 11, 2001. Retaliation by the United States led to intense and destructive bombing of Kabul, as well as Kandahar and other cities. In the wake of almost continuous strife, it remains to be seen if the interim government and its successor will be able to rebuild the city and provide a stable socioeconomic setting. The new post-Taliban regime seems determined to establish stability and democracy, but it remains only nominally in control of the country beyond the vicinity of Kabul.

Kathmandu, in a valley of the same name, lies in the mid-mountain region of the Himalayas, at an elevation of about 4,400 feet. Because of its physically sheltered valley location, it remained free from invasion from the plains of India. Kathmandu occupies a central position in Nepal and is the most important commercial, business, and administrative center of the country. The Gurkha ethnic group, after conquering Nepal, made Kathmandu its capital in 1768. Reconstruction efforts after the devastating 1934 earthquake and post–World War I developments added more buildings, but the older section of the city has retained its bazaar-style characteristics. Though the overwhelming majority of Kathmandu residents are Hindus, there are also some Buddhists. The city serves as the seat of government for the world's only Hindu Kingdom. Autocratic rule by the king and sporadic violence by Maoist guerillas makes the situation unstable. Nonetheless, the city remains a major center of South Asian tourism and is a launching ground for treks into the Himalaya Mountains.

Situated on the west coast of the pearl-shaped island of Sri Lanka, Colombo has functioned as an important port city since at least the 5th century. Nonetheless, it was Western contact, beginning with the Portuguese settlement in 1517, which really initiated the growth of Colombo as the key port for Sri Lanka (then known as Ceylon to the West). The Dutch occupied the port in 1656, but the British replaced them in 1796 and turned the city of Colombo into their main administrative, military, and trading center in Sri Lanka. After independence in 1948, Colombo became the national capital. It continues to be Sri Lanka's most important city in terms of business, administration, education, and culture. It is a colonial-based city. The CBD-like center with high-level government offices situated within the former fort area of the colonial times lies by the side of the old section of the city, Pettah ("the town outside the fort" in the Tamil language). Pettah represents the characteristics of the Bazaar-city enclave. Cinnamon Gardens, the former cinnamon-growing area of the Dutch period, has been turned into a high-class, low-density residential quarter. The city has expanded significantly since independence and has industries that mainly process the raw materials that are exported through the port of Colombo. In order to diversify the national economy through industrialization, an export-oriented Free Trade Zone has been established near the port of Colombo.

The impacts of the prolonged Tamil insurgency have been detrimental to the development and growth of Colombo, as well as that of most other urban centers throughout Sri Lanka. With the conflict dragging on for two decades now, industrial activities and critical infrastructure investments are becoming even more spatially uneven. Transportation across the island has been split in two, as the north and east have become war zones. Finally, the cost of rehabilitation and reconstruction are substantial.

URBAN CHALLENGES

Today's urban optimism poorly masks the enormity of the challenges in South Asian cities. Poverty, particularly in the form of inadequate housing and lack of public services such as clean water and sewers, is pervasive across the urban landscape. Add in a lack of employment opportunities compounded by environmental degradation, and the situation becomes especially challenging.

The push factors associated with the rural economy, coupled with accentuated rates of natural increase in urban areas, has augmented urban populations, particularly in large cities. This has happened without a reciprocal increase in manufacturing-sector employment, resulting in large-scale unemployment. Moreover, most rural migrants are unskilled and are therefore incapable of gaining employment in modern industries. They are forced to swell the ranks of the informal sector, working, for example, as low-paid porters, rickshaw pullers, domestic servants, and construction workers. Even a large number of educated youth find it difficult to obtain suitable employment.

Housing shortages emanating from large-scale in-migration and a relatively lower rate of new residential construction plague all the cities of South Asia. The demand for housing leads people to live in small units and in unsanitary environments. Many people who cannot afford to rent or buy homes (legally or illegally) turn into pavement dwellers. Estimates of the number of pavement dwellers vary widely. For Mumbai alone, the estimates vary from 250,000 to 2 million. In most places, pavement dwellers are essentially concentrated in the central areas of the city and are irregularly employed in low-skill occupations that pay the least. In Kolkata, about one-half of the city's pavement dwellers are employed in transport. They are predominantly men, aged 18 to 57 years, although nearly one-third are

children, most of whom add to the family income by working as child laborers or by begging and scavenging.

Slums, or *bustees,* have developed in almost all the major cities of South Asia. The name *bustee* is used in Kolkata and Dhaka, whereas *jhunggi* is used in Delhi, and *chawl* in Mumbai. The *bustee* has been defined by the Indian government's Slum Areas (improvement and clearance) Act of 1954 as a predominantly residential area where dwellings (by reason of dilapidation; overcrowding; faulty arrangement; and lack of ventilation, light, or sanitary facilities—or any combination of these factors) are detrimental to safety, health, and morality. The slums mainly consist of temporary or semi-permanent huts with minimal sanitary and water supply facilities and are usually located in unhealthy waterlogged areas. They develop ubiquitously in the metropolises, though there is always a greater concentration of large slum areas away from the central business area. They begin with temporary settlements, which are sometimes started by landlords, but are more often initiated by squatters who illegally establish settlements on public lands, along the sides of railroad lines or canals, on unclaimed swamp-like lands, in public parks, and on any other vacant land available. In Mumbai it is estimated that nearly 60% of the population lives in slums; this proportion is representative of most large cities in South Asia.

In the past, such unsanitary conditions combined with environmental factors left some cities especially prone to diseases such as cholera. Notoriety from this phenomenon at one time led Kipling to describe Kolkata as the "cholera capital of the world." Similarly, most lowlands in Mumbai, which flood during the monsoon season, are inhabited by slum

Figure 9.22   This housing project is soon to be completed in Chennai. Such housing is often poorly located with respect to slum dwellers' employment opportunities. (Photo by George Pomeroy)

dwellers, giving rise to some of the world's most unsanitary living conditions.

In India, slum upgrading policies for the nation as a whole have seen several shifts, and the last 50 years can be divided into three policy stages, with each making a slow transition into the next. Through the 1950s, slum-upgrading policies consisted of slum "clearance"—that is, the bulldozing of slums—a policy wholly unrealistic in solving housing supply problems, even when housing projects were built to compensate for those units cleared (fig. 9.22). A "transitional stage" in the 1960s was followed by "improvement" in combination with "sanitary environment" in the 1970s. These policies are reflected in the metropolitan plans of Indian cities and in India's five-year national development plans. In spite of the various policy approaches, slums remain, and they continue to be places of little hope, low incomes, and a generally poor quality of life.

SUGGESTED READINGS

Das, Gucharan. 2002. *India Unbound: The Social and Economic Revolution from Independence to the Global Information Age.* New York: Anchor. A well-received book that provides insight into India's rapid development.

Chapman, Graham P. 2003. *The Politics of South Asia: From Early Empires to the Nuclear Age,* 2d ed. Aldershot, UK: Ashgate. General in scope, but offers a very useful introduction to South Asian history, culture, and development.

Chapman, Graham P., Ashok K. Dutt, and Robert W. Bradnock. 1999. *Urban Growth and Development in Asia: Making the Cities,* 2 volumes. Aldershot, UK: Ashgate. This set of volumes contains a number of chapters devoted to cities, urbanization, development, and planning in South Asia.

Luce, Edward. 2007. *In Spite of the Gods: The Strange Rise of Modern India.* New York: Doubleday. A newspaper correspondent's perspective on India's rapid economic development.

Khilnani, Sunil. 2003. *The Idea of India,* 2d ed. New York: Penguin. A very readable treatment of modern India and the formative role that cities play in the development process.

King, Anthony D. 1976. *Colonial Urban Development: Culture, Social Power, and Environment.* London: Routledge and Kegan Paul. A comprehensive analysis of colonial urban forms of New Delhi, the hill station of Simla, and cantonment towns.

Nair, Janaki. 2005. *The Promise of the Metropolis: Bangalore's Twentieth Century.* New York: Oxford University Press. A timely, well-written, informed, and empirically rich case study of the South Asian city most closely associated with globalization.

Noble, Allen G., and Ashok K. Dutt, eds. 1977. *Indian Urbanization and Planning: Vehicles of Modernization.* New Delhi: Tata McGraw-Hill. A classic work containing more than 20 chapters contributed by leading geographers and planners.

Ramachandran, R. 1989. *Urbanization and Urban Systems in India.* New Delhi: Oxford University Press. A straightforward and comprehensive treatment of urban India.

Turner, Roy, ed. 1962. *India's Urban Future.* Berkeley and Los Angeles: University of California Press. Of particular interest in this classic collection of articles is the contribution by John E. Brush, "The Morphology of Indian Cities."

Figure 10.1 Major Cities of Southeast Asia. *Source:* UN *World Urbanization Prospects, 2005 revision* [online].

10

Cities of Southeast Asia

JAMES TYNER

KEY URBAN FACTS

Total Population	556 million
Percent Urban Population	43.8%
Total Urban Population	244 million
Most Urbanized Countries	Singapore (100%)
	Brunei (73.5%)
	Malaysia (67.3%)
Least Urbanized Countries	Cambodia (19.7%)
	Laos (20.6%)
	Vietnam (26.4%)
Annual Urban Growth Rate	3.0%
Number of Megacities	2
Number of Cities of More Than 1 Million	16
Three Largest Cities	Jakarta, Manila, Bangkok
World Cities	Singapore

KEY CHAPTER THEMES

1. Urban landscapes of Southeast Asia have been shaped by Chinese, Indian, Malay, and international influences, especially colonialism and more recently globalization.
2. All of the world's major religions are represented in the landscapes of Southeast Asia's cities.
3. All of the major cities of the region have experienced rapid population growth since independence.
4. Primate cities (notably Jakarta, Manila, and Bangkok) dominate the region, but the key urban center of Southeast Asia is the city-state of Singapore.
5. Foreign influences, especially through foreign direct investment, play a critical role today.
6. Land reclamation is increasingly used in port areas to provide space for urban expansion.

7. Land-use patterns in the cities are very similar throughout the region.
8. Many cities are restructuring their economies to become IT ("information technology") cities.
9. Some of the world's largest cargo ports—notably Singapore—are located in this region.
10. Transnational cities, which reach across international boundaries in their influence, are becoming more important.

Towering glass-encased skyscrapers, flashing Coca-Cola signs, McDonald's restaurants—the increasingly universal symbols of central cities around the world—are very evident in the cities of Southeast Asia, especially the larger ones, giving these cities a deceiving sense of familiarity. Closer examination, however, reveals many subtle, and sometimes not-so-subtle, differences. Southeast Asia as a whole is a cornucopia of cultures, with hundreds of different languages and many distinct religions. Nestled between two dominant cultural hearths, China and India, and exhibiting a storied colonial past, Southeast Asia is a blend of indigenous and foreign elements. This diversity, not surprisingly, has been and continues to be inscribed on the region's urban landscape, from the lotus-blossom-shaped stupas of Buddhist temples in Bangkok, to the brightly colored Hindu temples in Singapore, and from the golden-domed Muslim mosques of Kuala Lumpur to the Roman Catholic cathedrals of Manila and Ho Chi Minh City.

Yet for many travelers to the region, the extent of Southeast Asia's urban regions comes as a surprise. The typical image of the region is agrarian: thatched huts perched atop stilts and brilliant green rice paddies with water buffalo. The reality is very different. Flying over Manila, Bangkok, or Ho Chi Minh City is like flying over Los Angeles, New York, or Tokyo. The landscape reveals not a dense green three-tiered canopied jungle but instead a dense concrete jungle of apartment complexes, shopping malls, financial districts, and amusement parks.

Southeast Asia's major cities provide focal points; they serve as centers of political and cultural activity and centers of commercial circulation and exchange (fig. 10.1). Some, such as the "postsocialist" cities of Ho Chi Minh City, Hanoi, and Phnom Penh, are undergoing phenomenal political and economic changes; others, such as Rangoon, remain aloof from broader global trends. The cities of Southeast are also sites of vast inequality between the rich and the poor as well as the healthy and the malnourished. In Bangkok, Manila, and Jakarta, Toyota Land-Cruisers and Louis Vuitton designer stores are as much a part of the urban landscape as are shanty-towns and raw sewage.

Beyond the limits of Southeast Asia's primate cities are a host of medium, or intermediate, cities. Many, such as the Philippines' Cebu and Thailand's Chiang Mai and Chiang Rai, are fast becoming important regional urban centers in their own right. And still other, predominantly rural areas, such as the Central Highlands of Vietnam, are sites of contestation and conflict resulting from indigenous land-use practices and national urban policies.

The urban and urbanizing areas of Southeast Asia are more than just containers of people and commodities. They are agents in their own right and, in the coming years,

Figure 10.2   The Central Market in downtown Phnom Penh was built in 1937 in art deco style. It is the soul of the city, a place where you can purchase just about anything. (Photo by James Tyner)

will continue to influence and be influenced by local, national, and global affairs.

URBAN PATTERNS AT THE REGIONAL SCALE

Downtown Phnom Penh, the capital of Cambodia, is dominated by its mustard-colored Central Market (fig. 10.2). Built in the Art Deco style of the 1930s, the market is cruciform in design, with four halls radiating out from a central, cavernous dome. Inside, hundreds of venders ply their wares. Care to buy hand-woven silks or a traditional Khmer scarf (known as a *krama*)? Perhaps you're in the mood for some fresh vegetables or pork? No matter your taste, whatever you seek can probably be found at Phnom Penh's Central Market. And if not, it is but a short motorbike to visit Phnom Penh's Russian Market. On the surface, the two markets are very much alike. Many of the same fruits, vegetables, and souvenirs, for example, may be found in them. However, the sweeping arches and vaulted ceilings of the Central Market give way to the Russian Market's dimly-lit and claustrophobic feel. The Russian Market is a rabbits-den of activity, as shoppers jostle elbow-to-elbow with merchants and tourists. Inside, the air is stifling and sweltering, the mix of too many people and too many cooking pots bubbling stews of fish and vegetables.

Stepping inside any of Southeast Asia's historic (and even many of the region's new) markets is like Alice stepping into Wonderland. Whether you find yourself wandering the stuffy aisle-ways of Binh Tay Market in Ho Chi

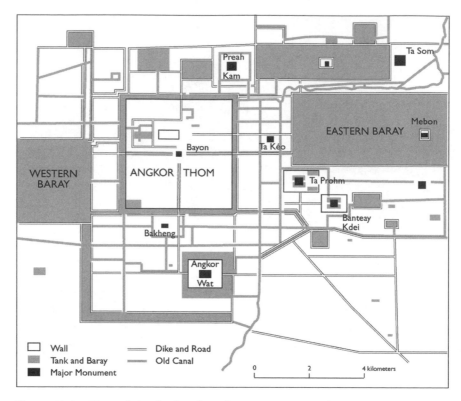

Figure 10.3   Plan of the Angkor Complex, ca. 1200 A.D. *Source:* T. G. McGee, *The Southeast Asian City* (New York: Praeger, 1967), 38.

Minh City, window-shopping in Bangkok's upscale River City shopping complex, or sipping an iced-coffee while shopping along Orchard Road in Singapore, you are guaranteed to be dazzled with new sights, sounds, and smells. The intoxicating aroma of sandalwood incense combines with fresh fruits, vegetables, and spices to provide an aromatic bouquet that is found nowhere else. And unlike the sedate, antiseptic shopping malls of North America (which are, incidentally, increasingly popping up in Southeast Asia), the labyrinthine markets of Cambodia, Thailand, Vietnam, and elsewhere seem to embody much of the region's urban geography.

As a whole, Southeast Asia remains one of the least-urbanized regions of the world. Only four countries—Singapore, Brunei, Malaysia, and the Philippines—are more than 50% urban. Other states are considerably more rural in character: Cambodia, Laos, Burma, and Vietnam, for example, are all less than 30% urbanized. However, recent years have seen massive growth. Many countries have registered startling urban population growth rates in excess of 3% per year, with some countries (Cambodia and Laos) experiencing more than 6%.

Such urban growth is not new to Southeast Asia (fig. 10.3). Before the Portuguese ever arrived in Malacca or the Spanish landed in the Philippines, Southeast Asia was home to some of the world's most impressive cities: Angkor in Cambodia, Ayutthaya in

Figure 10.4   Angkor Wat, built between 1113 and 1150 by Suryavarman II, is one of hundreds of *wats* spread throughout Cambodia. Because it symbolizes the golden age of Cambodian history, its image can also be found on the nation's flag. (Photo by James Tyner)

Siam (now Thailand), and Luang Prabang in Laos. Their names continue to evoke rich histories of commerce and conquest, for it was through Southeast Asia that the fabled spice trade coursed. And it was through Southeast Asia that ships laden with goods from China, India, and beyond sailed. Then and now, the cities of Southeast Asia were centers of economic, religious, and cultural exchange.

Historically, one or two urban areas would dominate the region. The Kingdom of Angkor, for example, exerted its influence between the 9th and 14th centuries over much of present-day Cambodia, Laos, and Thailand (fig. 10.4). Centered on the city-state of Malacca, the Srivijayan Empire ruled much of insular Southeast Asia from the late 14th century to the early 16th century. And today, most countries in Southeast Asia continue to exhibit phenomenally high levels of urban

primacy. In Thailand, the capital city of Bangkok stands as second to none. Not to be outdone, both Jakarta and Manila exert their dominance over Indonesia and the Philippines, respectively.

But Southeast Asia's urban patterns of the 21st century reveal many remarkable differences from previous eras. Whereas many earlier cities were densely populated and compact, the cities of Southeast Asia today are densely populated and sprawling. Rapid urban growth is occurring on the peripheries of many major cities: Manila, Bangkok, Phnom Penh, Jakarta, Ho Chi Minh City. This growth, some planned, some not, has led to conflicts over land use, has threatened once-prime agricultural lands, and has spurred attendant economic problems of land-speculation and landlessness.

In light of persistent problems of overurbanization—traffic congestion, pollution, unemployment—local government

Figure 10.5   In Pleiku, Vietnam, a woman makes a living by selling fresh fruits and vegetables—as proudly displayed as in an American supermarket—to shoppers in the early morning hours. (Photo by James Tyner)

officials throughout Southeast Asia have initiated regional economic development projects. Often these projects are multipurpose in scope, promoting economic growth and development in more peripheral regions (i.e., northeast Thailand) and lessening the burdens of primate cities. Still other governments have relocated entire cities for unknown reasons. The always secretive leaders of Burma, for example, have recently relocated its capital from Rangoon (Yangon) to the interior, semi-rural town of Pyinmana. The few western journalists who have been fortunate enough to visit the new Burmese capital—named Naypyidaw ("Seat of Kings")—write of expansive residential areas, reminiscent of any suburban development found in North America, and impressive office buildings. But no one lives there! Streets are empty; most Burmese are denied access to the new city.

Other changes are more visible, more transnational in scope. As government officials grapple with their country's own comparative advantages and disadvantages, they look for solutions beyond their political borders. Coincident with their greater integration into the global economy, many urban areas are becoming transnational. Singapore, for example, is at the heart of a major economic growth triangle that also includes Indonesia and Malaysia. Similar urban-economic megalopolises include parts of Malaysia, Thailand, the Philippines, and Indonesia. Other developments include the transnational linkage of countries via transportation routes, such as a major international highway that, when completed, will integrate northeastern Thailand, Laos, and central Vietnam.

Similar to Phnom Penh's Central, the cities of Southeast Asia reflect the past and the future; they are centers of intense commercial activity and cultural exchange (fig. 10.5). And although they share many commonalities, they—like Phnom Penh's Central and Russian Markets—exhibit remarkable differences.

HISTORICAL PERSPECTIVES ON URBAN DEVELOPMENT

Precolonial Patterns of Urbanization

Southeast Asia is characterized by more coastline than perhaps any other major world region, and much of this coast is accessible to sea traffic. Indeed, Neptune's vast domain in Southeast Asia is approximately four times the combined land area of the 11 countries that compose the region. It is understandable, therefore, that maritime influences have contributed significantly to the Southeast Asian urbanization process.

The region, but most especially mainland Southeast Asia, also contains many fertile river valleys. These include the Mekong, Chao Praya, Irrawaddy, and Red Rivers, along with their tributaries. Consequently, densely populated settlements emerged in these areas. Bangkok, Phnom Penh, Hanoi, and Ho Chi Minh City all continue to reflect the importance of these highways of water.

Southeast Asia's physical geography—its complex environment of river systems and coastlines—contributed to the region's importance as a crucial crossroads of commerce between China, India, and beyond. And it was this factor that precipitated the urbanization process of Southeast Asia. Although it is commonplace to speak of the global economy as beginning in the 16th century, it is important to recognize that international trade existed long before European states like England and Spain began colonizing the Americas, Africa, and Asia. Indeed, long-distance trade existed between China and India, and linked these areas with places as far afield as Africa, as far back as the early centuries of the first millennium A.D. The importance of long-distance trade in the eastern Indian Ocean and South China Sea regions, in fact, led to the appearance of a series of cities and towns along the coast of the Malay Peninsula and on the islands of Sumatra and Java. In time, Southeast Asia would be home to some of the largest urban centers in the world. Indeed, prior to the era of European colonialism (from the early 16th to the mid-20th century) Southeast Asia was one of the world's most urbanized regions. As late as the 15th century, for example, the city of Angkor (in present-day Cambodia) had a population in excess of 180,000; Paris, in contrast, had a population of only 125,000.

Southeast Asia's geographical location made it a natural crossroads and meeting point for world trade, migration, and cultural exchange. A century before the Christian era began, seafarers, merchants, and priests traversed the region, contributing to the urbanization process. In turn, the nascent towns and cities of Southeast Asia became centers of learning through the diffusion of new religious, cultural, political, and economic ideas. Most Southeast Asian societies (with the exception of Vietnam and the Philippines) were influenced primarily by India, and this is most pronounced in religious and administrative systems. The process of "Indianization," however, was not marked by a mass influx of population, such as the movement of Europeans into North America. Neither was this a process of replacing indigenous Southeast Asian culture with Indian elements. Rather, the influence of India on Southeast Asia represented a more gradual and uneven process of exposure and adaptation. China provided the other major cultural impetus, although this impact was greatest in Vietnam and through tributary arrangements with various maritime Southeast Asian kingdoms bordering the South China Sea.

Two principal urban forms emerged in precolonial Southeast Asia: the *sacred city* and the *market city.* Although both types of cities performed religious as well as economic functions, the two exhibited many differences. First, sacred cities were often more populous; wealth was gained from appropriating agricultural surpluses and labor from the rural hinterland. Market cities, in contrast, were supported through the conduct of long-distance maritime trade. Through the market cities passed the riches of Asia, including pearls, silks, tin, porcelain, and spices. Second, sacred cities were sprawling administrative, military, and cultural centers, whereas market cities were mostly centers of economic activity. In physical layout, sacred cities were planned and developed to mirror symbolic links between human societies on earth and the forces of heaven. Monumental stone or brick temples commonly occupied the city center. Market cities, in contrast, tended to occupy more restricted coastal locations and thus had more limited hinterlands. These cities were more compact in their spatial layout, with much activity being associated with the port areas. Lastly, compared to sacred cities, market cities were ethnically more diverse, populated by traders, merchants, and other travelers from all parts of the earth.

The earliest city to emerge in Southeast Asia was apparently Oc Eo, located along the lower reaches of the Mekong Delta, in present-day Vietnam. Flourishing between the 1st and 5th centuries A.D., Oc Eo was an important center for the exchange of cargo, ideas, and innovations. It served as an important city for both Chinese and Indian traders, as well as for other seafarers as far away as Africa, the Mediterranean, and the Middle East.

After the decline of Oc Eo, Srivijaya emerged as an important maritime empire, flourishing between the 7th and 14th centuries. It depended on international maritime trade and on China's sponsorship through a tributary system, which meant paying tribute (goods and money) to the Chinese emperor in exchange for independence. Located on the straits of Malacca on the island of Sumatra, Srivijaya controlled many important sea-lanes, including the Sunda Strait. Evidence suggests that the Srivijayan Kingdom had numerous capitals, one of which was Palembang, located on the southern end of Sumatra. Palembang provided an excellent, sheltered harbor and served as an important Buddhist pilgrimage site. To this day, Palembang remains an important port city and marketplace in Indonesia.

Another example of a market city is Malacca (fig. 10.6). Founded around 1400 on the western side of the Malay Peninsula, Malacca was a counterpart to Palembang and emerged as an important entrepôt and key node in the spice trade. Although Malacca never had a permanent population of more than a few thousand people, it was an extremely vibrant city, inhabited by many foreigners as well as indigenous Malays. Malacca has been nominated to become a UNESCO World Heritage Site. Other important market cities located throughout Southeast Asia included Ternate, Makasar, Bantam, and Aceh.

Sacred cities often occupied more inland locations. One of the earliest was Borobudur, situated on the island of Java. It is at Borobudur that the world's largest Buddhist temple is located. Built between 778 and 856 A.D., the 10-level Borobudur corresponds to the divisions within the Mahayana Buddhist universe and is one of the great cultural treasures of Southeast Asia. A UN-sponsored program rebuilt the complex several decades ago to preserve the site for future generations.

Arguably, the best known and most famous of all inland sacred cities is Angkor.

Figure 10.6   Malacca is one of the oldest towns in Southeast Asia and has changed hands many times as successive rulers and colonial powers came and went. Today, it is an important commercial and tourist city in Malaysia. (Photo courtesy Malacca government)

Centered at the northern end of the Tonle Sap basin, the Angkorian Empire, at its peak, included present-day Cambodia and parts of Laos, Thailand, and Vietnam. The Angkor Kingdom was founded in 802 A.D. and by the 12th century contained a population of several hundred thousand. According to some historians, it may even have exceeded 1 million. The temples at Angkor—there are more than 70 recognized sites—were designed to mirror the complex Hindu and, later, Buddhist cosmologies.

By the 16th century many of the once-prosperous inland sacred cities were in decline. In part, internal factions, economic collapse, and foreign intervention hastened the collapse of Angkor and other empires. Coastal market cities, however, continued to thrive on maritime trade. For the region as a whole, the coming years of European colonial dominance would irrevocably alter the course of urbanization in Southeast Asia.

Urbanization in Colonial Southeast Asia

Nutmeg and cloves, cinnamon and sandalwood: these were the prized commodities that drove the world's economy for hundreds of years. And these were the goods that spurred European colonial activity in Southeast Asia. Five hundred years of colonial and postcolonial influence dramatically affected cities in Southeast Asia. Compared to other world regions, Southeast Asia was relatively urbanized by the time of European colonialism. By the 16th century, there were at least six trade-dependent cities that had populations of more than 100,000: Malacca, Thang-long (Vietnam), Ayutthaya (Siam, present-day Thailand), Aceh (Sumatra), and Bantam and Mataram (both on Java). Another half-dozen cities had at least 50,000 inhabitants. Spatially, the urban system of Southeast Asia was characterized by a predominance of strategic coastal locations that served an extensive international maritime trading system. Only the Philippines, because of its more peripheral location vis-à-vis the major sea-lanes, lacked an urban tradition. But even there, by the early 16th century, the seeds of urbanization had been planted. The Sultanate of Brunei had extended its authority into the Philippine archipelago and with this came the spread of Islam.

In 1511, however, a Portuguese fleet captured the port city of Malacca, thus ushering in nearly 500 years of European colonialism. The Portuguese came primarily to gain access to and control of the lucrative spice trade. They were soon followed by the Spanish (1521), the British (1579), the Dutch (1595), and the French (mid-17th century). Other colonial activities, such as religious conversion, were present but less important at this time.

Colonial practices in the early years of European colonialism in Southeast Asia were similar to those exercised in Africa and the Americas. Europeans captured or built garrisons in coastal cities, established treaties with local rulers, and thus brought about a transformation of the urbanization process in Southeast Asia. Many former empires and kingdoms, as well as cities, suffered tremendous population declines. Malacca, for example, once the premier entrepôt on the strait that shares its name, declined in size and importance after its capture by the Portuguese. From a peak of over 100,000 inhabitants, its size dwindled to 30,000 inhabitants in a very short time. The history of Malacca, and of many of cities of the region, reveals a dynamic of ebb and flow in the urbanization process.

During the first three centuries of colonialism, European influence was most pronounced in two regions: in Manila (the Philippines) under the Spanish and in Jakarta (Indonesia) under the Dutch. The first permanent Spanish settlement, Santisimo Nombre de Jesus (Holy Name of Jesus), was established in 1565 on the Philippine island of Cebu. Five years later the Spanish occupied a site on the northern island of Luzon, situated on the Pasig River and proximate to Manila Bay. Two existing fishing villages known as Maynilad (from which the present city takes its name) and Tondo were occupied and expanded. Apart from accessibility, defense was often an important consideration in early city planning. In the Philippines, for example, the Spanish had to contend with European rivals, namely the Dutch and Portuguese, as well as Chinese pirates. Consequently, construction began on a fortified structure known as the Intramuros (walled city) in 1576. In time, Manila would become the commercial hub of the Philippines and a key node in the Spanish galleon trade that stretched from India to Mexico.

The early European presence was also pronounced on the island of Java in Indonesia. The Dutch East India Company during the 17th century established a few permanent settlements, one of which, Batavia, would become the largest city in the region. It is now known as Jakarta. From its inception Batavia exhibited numerous situational advantages. Geographically, it was located near both the Sunda Strait and the Strait of Malacca, thus allowing easy access to maritime trade. The first Dutch building, a combination warehouse and residence, was built in 1611, and by 1619 a plan was laid out for the city. Much of early Batavia was modeled after the cities of Holland; canals were dug,

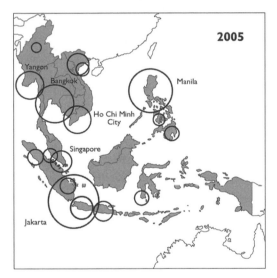

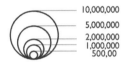

Figure 10.7   Urban Growth in Southeast Asia, 1900–2005. *Source:* compiled by the author from various sources.

and the narrow, multistoried style of Dutch residences was also copied. However, the architecture found in Europe was not functional in hot, humid locations such as Java, so building styles were altered to better fit the tropical environment. Batavia soon eclipsed Bantam as the preeminent city of Java and served as the key node of the Netherlands' Southeast Asian empire.

Many of the great cities of Southeast Asia today trace their roots to European colonialism (fig. 10.7). Singapore (from the Malay words *singa,* lion, and *pura,* city), for example, began as a small trading post located on an island south of the Malay peninsula, at the southern entrance to the Strait of Malacca. The town was known as Temasek (Sea Town) before 1819, when Sir Stamford Raffles of the

Figure 10.8   Fast food—or "good food fast"—is widely available on the streets of Southeast Asian cities. Here, early morning breakfast is served in Ho Chi Minh City (Saigon). (Photo by James Tyner)

British East India Company signed an agreement with the Sultan of Johor allowing the British to establish a trading post at the site. Benefiting from its strategic location and deep natural harbor, the incipient Singapore began to attract a large number of immigrants, merchants, and traders. As a British colony, Singapore emerged as one of the paramount trading cities of the world—a role it has maintained to this day.

Saigon (now Ho Chi Minh City), which became the capital of French Indochina, likewise began as a small settlement, one that included a citadel and fortress, surrounded by a Vietnamese village (fig. 10.8). Saigon's location in the Mekong delta region—one of the world's great rice granaries—provided the city an important function as agricultural collection, processing, and distribution center. The French, also, were intent on refashioning

their colonial capital as a microcosm of French civilization. In 1880 the French erected Notre Dame Cathedral in the heart of Saigon. Stones were imported. The beginning of the next decade saw the completion of Saigon's French-built Central Post Office. This latter structure, complete with an iron and glass ceiling, was designed by Gustave Eiffel.

Bangkok, the current capital of Thailand, was never colonized by the European powers, yet it still reflects considerable Western influence. Bangkok proper is a relatively new city; it was not founded until 1782. Prior to this date, the capital of Siam, as Thailand was then known, was located at Thon Buri along the Chao Phraya River. Beginning in the 1780s, however, construction began on an easily defensible but swampy site located opposite Thon Buri, on the east bank of the Chao Phraya. Later, during the reigns of King

Mongkut and his son King Chulalongkorn (1851–1910, collectively), major public works were initiated, often with Western advice and assistance. This is particularly evident in the expansion of rail and road networks, port facilities, and telegraph services.

The most significant impact of colonialism was the establishment of urban nodes, such as Bangkok, Manila, Batavia, Saigon, and Rangoon, that would grow into primate cities. Geographically, these cities were located at sites that provided access to seas or rivers. These locations afforded the European colonizers easy access, so that their ships could export primary products from the region and import secondary products from Europe and elsewhere. Such a dependence on maritime trade, and the subsequent concentration of political and economic functions in these selected cities, contributed to the decline of other, more inland cities. In this manner, the urban system of Southeast Asia was turned inside out, as development was encouraged on the coast and suppressed inland.

The primate cities also provided multiple functions. Thus, political, commercial, financial, and even religious activities were concentrated in these urban areas. Saigon, for example, was an administrative and manufacturing center, as well as the dominant trading port of Indochina. Primate cities also became exceptionally large. Stemming from the increased concentration of economic and political functions, these cities served as magnets for both internal and international migration. Moreover, their populations were characteristically diverse. In many colonies, the colonizers encouraged contract labor. The British, for example, actively encouraged the importation of labor from China and the Indian subcontinent (fig. 10.9). By the 19th century, immigration facilitated the establishment of Chinese communities in cities such as Singapore, Manila, and Bangkok, and an Indian community in Singapore. As a result, segregated foreign quarters and Chinatowns emerged, for example, Cholon in Saigon and Binondo in Manila. It was not uncommon for these segregated areas to arise through European force and prejudice. In Manila, for example, the Spanish government issued a series of decrees that required, with few exceptions, all Chinese, Japanese, and even Filipinos to leave the Intramuros section of Manila before the closing of the city gates at nightfall. Additionally, Spanish authorities enacted regulations enforcing ethnic segregation and commercial activity.

Apart from the establishment of primate cities, a second impact European colonialism had on Southeast Asian cities was the establishment or transformation of smaller cities. This included the establishment of mining towns, such as Ipoh in Malaysia, or regional administrative centers such as Medan on the island of Sumatra and Georgetown on the Malay Peninsula. Also notable was the emergence of upland resort centers or hill stations. To escape the oppressive heat and humidity of the lowlands, colonial powers would erect cities high in the mountainous regions. Bandung, for example, a small city located in a deep mountain valley on the island of Java, was established by the Dutch. The cool climate of Bandung served as a welcome relief from the tropical climate and also facilitated the cultivation of coffee (still known as "Java" worldwide), cinchona (for quinine), and tea. Other examples of hill stations include Dalat, a French-built city located 4,800 feet above sea level in the Central Highlands of Vietnam; Baguio City, a mountain resort atop a 4,900-foot plateau in the Philippines, developed by the Americans in the early 20th century; and the Cameron Highlands of peninsular Malaysia.

Figure 10.9   The overseas Chinese are a pervasive presence in Southeast Asia, especially in cities. This Chinese temple is in Georgetown, Penang, one of the original Straits Settlements that began British colonial rule in Malaya, and which brought the Chinese here. (Photo by Jack Williams)

Lastly, European colonialism significantly affected the development of regional transportation and urban systems within Southeast Asia. Along the Malay Peninsula, for example, the British-built railways ran from the Perak tin-mining areas to the coast and were later expanded along a north–south axis to provide access to the ports and tin-smelting facilities in Penang and Singapore. Consequently, the major urban areas along the western coast of the Malay Peninsula—Kuala Lumpur, Ipoh, Seremban, and Singapore—formed an interconnected urban system that remains evident today. Similar patterns are also visible in Indonesia, where road and rail networks reflect access between sites of resource extraction (plantations and mines) and ports. To a lesser extent a similar colonial-derived infrastructure remains in the Philippines and the former French Indochina. Colonial powers also exploited river systems (such as the Irrawaddy in Burma, now Myanmar) for internal transportation systems, to exert political and economic control, to link administration functions, and to provide access to sites of resource extraction.

Recent Urbanization Trends in Southeast Asia

In 1940 no city in Southeast Asia registered a population of more than a million; by 1950, just two cities had surpassed this mark. In 2000, however, 13 cities exceeded the 1 million threshold. Three megacities—Jakarta (13.7 million), Manila (11.8 million), and Bangkok (10.3 million)—have also emerged. These massive urban agglomerations contain a disproportionate share of the region's urban population and stand as exemplary primate cities. Bangkok, for example, contains more than 54% of Thailand's urban population, while Manila accounts for nearly a third of the Philippines' urban population. Such growth is indicative of the pattern of urbanization that has characterized Southeast Asia throughout the 20th century.

Recent urban growth in Southeast Asia is the result of three basic demographic processes. First, urban areas in Southeast Asia have increased in population resulting from the excess of births over deaths. In general, this natural increase accounts for about one-half of urban population growth in Southeast Asian countries. It is important to remember, however, that although overall natural increase may contribute to *urban growth,* it may not contribute significantly to *urbanization,* that is, the increasing proportion of people living in urban areas relative to rural areas.

Second, cities in Southeast Asia have increased through a net redistribution of people from rural to urban areas though migration. Studies reflect that, overall, rural-to-urban migration has resulted from larger regional and global economic transformations, and subsequently has played a major role in both rapid urbanization and urban growth in Southeast Asia over the past two decades. Internal migration is extremely important to urban growth in Thailand, for example. In 1990, the Thai census recorded more than 1.5 million rural-to-urban migrants, although there were more than twice as many rural-to-rural migrants. Currently, approximately one out of every seven urban residents in Thailand is classified as a recent migrant. In Malaysia, economic growth is concentrated in Kuala Lumpur and in Johor Bahru, the city closest to Singapore; these cities have attracted sizeable numbers of migrants in recent years. The Central Highlands of Vietnam have also experienced rapid urban growth through both government-sponsored and spontaneous migration. At the beginning of the 20th century, for example, the four provinces that compose the Central Highlands—Kontum,

Gia Lai, Dak Lak, and Lam Dong—had a combined population of approximately 240,000; today, the region exceeds 4 million residents. The majority of these inhabitants, approximately 75% of the total, are lowland migrants, their children, or refugees. Unfortunately, such remarkable urban growth has resulted in an escalation of land conflicts and political violence (box 10.1).

Third, immigration has contributed to the growth of urban areas in Southeast Asia. This occurs because, in general, overseas migrants tend to move to urban areas as opposed to rural areas. Singapore and, to a lesser extent, Kuala Lumpur, are two of the major immigrant receivers in Southeast Asia. That said, many governments (including Singapore's) often try to prevent immigrants from settling permanently. Overall, however, urban growth in Southeast Asia via international migration remains a relatively insignificant component. Emigration also is inscribed on the urban landscape (box 10.2).

A final component of urban *change* must be introduced: "reclassification." As a result of bureaucratic decisions, urban populations may change simply through administrative acts. In Malaysia, for example, the number of people needed for an area to be classified as urban changed from 1,000 to 10,000 in 1970. Such statistical changes reflect the changing perception of urbanization for many governments.

Within Southeast Asia over the past two decades, the combined components of migration and reclassification have accounted for the largest portion of urban growth (tab. 10.1). There has also been considerable variation among countries. Urban growth in Burma, the Philippines, and Vietnam, for example, has occurred primarily through natural increase, whereas natural increase has assumed a lesser role in Cambodia,

Box 10.1   Conflict in the Central Highlands

Between the plains of eastern Cambodia, the Annamite mountains of northern Vietnam, and the coastal lowlands of southern and central Vietnam lie the Central Highlands of Vietnam. Although not as daunting as the Himalayas of South Asia or the Alps of Europe, the Central Highlands—with peak elevations over 5,000 feet—are impressive nonetheless. Dense, jungle-covered forests give way to dazzling rice paddies; rain-fed waterfalls cascade down to white-capped rushing rivers. Clusters of stilt-houses occupy cool valley bottoms.

The Central Highlands are home to approximately 1 million indigenous people. Known generically by the French term *Montagnard*, meaning "mountain dwellers," these people actually hail from 54 officially recognized groups, with the Jarai, Rhade, Bahnar, and Koho being among the most numerous. For centuries these people have lived in the region, practicing swidden agriculture and fishing. By custom and tradition, agricultural lands were defined by family use rights. Collective lands, such as streams, grazing pastures, and drinking water sources, were managed by village elders. Owing to a French colonial presence, an estimated 230,000 to 400,000 highlanders are followers of evangelical Protestantism.

History, however, has not been kind to the indigenous peoples of the Central Highlands. During the long Indochina War (known as the Vietnam War in the United States), many areas of the Central Highlands were targeted for aerial bombing raids; the use of chemical defoliants were also widespread (fig. 10.10). Additionally, both the United States and the North Vietnamese enlisted indigenous peoples to serve as scouts, spies, and soldiers. After the war, the victorious Democratic Republic of Vietnam continued to view the Central Highlands as an area of potential ethnic and religious strife.

Vietnamese urban policies, however, have fueled rising tensions in the region. Supposedly in response to increasing population densities and urban development in the lowlands of northern and southern Vietnam, many ethnic Vietnamese—known as *Kinh*—have been resettled into the Central Highlands. These government-sponsored migrations have been accompanied by sizable flows of spontaneous migrants. State agencies maintain that resettlement contributes to the overall economic development of the country. However, these resettlements carry political and economic undertones. Land is at the heart of these conflicts.

As the Kinh continue to move into the Central Highlands, traditional lands used by the highlanders are being converted to sprawling coffee and rubber plantations. In fact,

Thailand, Malaysia, and Indonesia. The importance of internal migration to the urbanization process of Cambodia, of course, is a consequence of the forced displacement of urban-based people during the murderous Khmer Rouge regime (box 10.3).

The growth of the Republic of Singapore, at 100% urban already, consists mostly of natural increase.

Aggregate numbers such as these mask significant social and economic changes that are occurring. Internal migration in Southeast

Figure 10.10   Pleiku, in the Central Highlands of Vietnam, was important during the Vietnam War. It has been the focus of considerable in-migration from northern Vietnam, and the surrounding area has been beset by conflict between the Vietnamese and the Montagnards. (Photo by James Tyner)

Vietnam has emerged as the world's second largest exporter of coffee. The economic bene-fits of this trend, however, have not been felt by the indigenous peoples. Indeed, a lack of land security, an escalation in the state confiscation of land, and consequent rising levels of landlessness have led to considerable unrest among the highlanders. The indigenous peoples, likewise, charge that they have been neglected by the government in terms of edu-cation and employment opportunities. In light of rising protests, the Vietnamese govern-ment has responded aggressively. Many highlander organizers have been arrested and detained; reports circulate of torture and other forms of reprisals.

Here, on the slopes and in the valleys of the Central Highlands, the conversion of pris-tine agricultural lands to row upon row of coffee plantings provides a tangible reminder that the confluence of religious freedom, ethnic autonomy, economic development, and urban growth does not occur without struggle.

Asia, for example, is increasingly dominated by female migrants, a process that mirrors that occurring elsewhere in the world, such as in China. In Thailand, for example, the share of female migrants increased from 53% of all Bangkok-bound migrants in the 1970s to more than 62% in the 1980s. The increased feminization of internal migration in Thailand is related to structural changes occurring in both rural and urban areas. The majority of these women—most of whom are in their early twenties—originate in northeastern

Box 10.2   A Geography of Everyday Life

Mong Bora is a twelve-year-old boy. He lives in a stilt-house with his mother, father, and four sisters. The village in which he lives lies approximately one hour north of Phnom Penh. During the rainy season, much of the area is inundated with water: hence the necessity to live in houses perched on stilts. In the surrounding vicinity of Bora's village are acres of rice fields and fish ponds. Bora's diet is typical of many Khmers: a staple of rice and fish, coupled with fresh fruits and vegetables. Bora is particularly fond of ripe mangoes, watermelon, and papayas.

Increasingly, Bora's village is being encroached upon by urban sprawl from Phnom Penh. This is considered both a blessing and a curse. On one hand, villagers are concerned about maintaining their way of life. On the other hand, they also recognize that urban growth may translate into better economic opportunities. Many residents of Phnom Penh, for example, visit the area for Sunday picnics, seeking a respite from the chaotic hustle-and-bustle of the capital city. And many villagers are able to supplement their incomes from these weekly picnickers. Villagers, like Bora's mother, sell bottled water or lotus-blossom seeds as snacks. Others rent "cabanas" or tent-awnings, under which the visitors can escape the intense heat.

Bora's house sits near the base of two hills, the larger of which is called Phnom Reach Throp, or "hill of the royal treasury." In part, it is because of this hill that people—locals and international travelers alike—come to the area. Between 1618 and 1866 Cambodia's capital was located on this site. Known as Udong (meaning "victorious"), the former capital once dominated the landscape. Today, however, little remains of Udong's former glory. The passage of time and especially the effects of war and genocide have devastated much of Udong's former architectural greatness. Several stupas remain at the site, as does a colossal Buddha figure. Blown up the by Khmer Rouge, the Buddha and many of the *stupas* are actively being restored.

On any given morning Bora travels by foot 1.25 miles (2 km) to the other side of Phnom Reach Throp to attend school. Among his favorite classes is English. He also enjoys learning about Cambodia's ancient history and geography. It is Bora's dream that these subjects will help him in his chosen career: when Bora is not attending school, or playing soccer with his friends, he is informally working as a "tour guide" for the many visitors who travel to Udong. Walking step-in-step with tourists, both local and international, Bora happily details the specifics of the former capital: how many stairs from one stupa to the next, the height of the Buddha, the dates of former kings' reigns. Through these activities, Bora gets to practice English—and earn some extra money to help his family.

Perhaps, if your future travels include the ancient site of Udong, you may be approached by a youthful man by the name of Bora who will offer to guide your tour. Be sure to accept, for Udong is the young man's home.

Table 10.1   Components of Urban Growth in Southeast Asia (percentage of urban growth)

	1980–1985		1990–1995		2000–2005	
	Natural Increase	*Migration and Reclassification*	*Natural Increase*	*Migration and Reclassification*	*Natural Increase*	*Migration and Reclassification*
Southeast Asia	49.1	50.9	44.9	55.1	41.7	58.3
Cambodia	70.9	29.1	49.5	50.5	30.6	69.4
Indonesia	35.2	64.8	37.0	63.0	36.7	63.3
Laos	43.8	56.2	44.7	55.3	43.8	56.2
Malaysia	22.0	78.0	38.0	62.0	40.0	60.0
Myanmar	110.0	–10.0	63.2	36.8	44.5	55.5
Philippines	66.0	34.0	62.4	37.6	57.0	43.0
Singapore	100.1	–0.1	100.1	–0.1	98.9	1.1
Thailand	39.6	60.4	31.4	68.6	31.2	68.8
Vietnam	71.7	28.3	50.5	49.5	38.1	61.9

Source: Graeme Hugo, "Demographic and Social Patterns," in *Southeast Asia: Diversity and Development,* edited by Thomas R. Leinbach and Richard Ulack, 74–109 (Upper Saddle River, NJ: Prentice Hall, 2000), table 4.17.

Thailand, one of the most impoverished regions in the country. Faced with minimal prospects in the rural areas, these women are increasingly moving to Bangkok to obtain employment in factory work, the service sector, or the informal sector. A certain number of these migrants find employment in the sex sector and end up working in brothels, massage parlors, or strip clubs. Likewise, internal migration to Jakarta, Manila, and Phnom Penh has also become more feminized in response to the structural transformations occurring in these cities.

Not all internal migration is permanent. Indeed, many cities in Southeast Asia, but especially Bangkok and Ho Chi Minh City, are impacted by daily or seasonal circular migration. Three factors are readily identifiable. First, circulation is highly compatible with work participation in the urban informal sector. Migrant laborers are able to circulate between rural villages and urban sites depending on the season. Circulation thus offers a flexible solution to the seasonality of labor demands; laborers are able to work on the nearby farms during the peak agricultural period, and during downtimes, they can shift to participation in the informal economies of cities. Second, circular migration diversifies families' income-generating activities. Depending on the relative economic strength of urban and rural areas, workers may alternate their activities accordingly. Third, circular migration has, with advances in transportation systems, become a more viable option. Improvements in mass transportation systems, such as paved roads and mass-transit bus lines, have permitted people to move with greater ease, thus contributing to the growth of suburban residential areas. The spectacular urban growth to the south and west of Ho Chi Minh City is indicative of this process.

Globalization, Urbanization, and the Middle Class

The most significant development in the world economy during the past few decades has been the increased globalization of economic activities. The transnational operations

Box 10.3   Devastated by Genocide

On April 17, 1975, the Khmer Rouge—the Communist Party of Kampuchea (CPK)—marched through the hot and dusty streets of Cambodia's capital city, Phnom Penh. Their arrival marked the beginning of a four-year period of unimaginable horrors, a genocide that would claim nearly 3 million people, or approximately one-third of Cambodia's total population.

The Khmer Rouge, led by a mysterious figure who called himself Pol Pot, sought to transform Cambodia into a communist utopia. The revolution of the Khmer Rouge was envisioned to be complete. A massive program of social and spatial engineering was set in motion, designed to eradicate all previous social, political, and economic relations.

Flush with victory following years of civil war, the Khmer Rouge began to immediately evacuate Phnom Penh and other major cities throughout Cambodia. Cities, according to the ideologues of the Khmer Rouge, were viewed as bastions of immorality, vice, and corruption. These were also, according to the Khmer Rouge, sites of foreign dominance. Phnom Penh, for example, contained a sizeable minority population of Vietnamese-Khmer and Chinese-Khmer people. The Khmer Rouge also viewed cities as home to those people who resisted, or opposed, its revolution: members of the monarchy, foreigners, and merchants. A forcible evacuation was deemed the most efficient means to demobilize any potential opposition and to ensure security for the newly imposed government. Lastly, the depopulation of urban areas would provide a surplus of labor that could be exploited on the agricultural communes and collectives that were initiated under the Khmer Rouge.

In 1979 the Khmer Rouge was defeated by invading Vietnamese forces. Decades of painful rebuilding ensued. This resurgence, however, has come with a price. Following the genocide, thousands of survivors have moved back into the cities, especially Phnom Penh. Many of these refugees had nothing. They established shantytowns; many of these make-shift encampments, located along the muddy banks of the Bassac, Mekong, and Tonle rivers that converge at the capital, have lasted for nearly three decades. But now the government is attempting to rebuild and to redevelop the city. As a result, local governments have been evicting residents of the shantytowns. In their place are new luxury housing projects, but the vast majority of Phnom Penh's residents will never be able to afford these new homes and apartments. Other lands, formerly occupied by those less well-off, are being cleared for rapidly proliferating five-star hotels in hopes of capitalizing on rising flows of international tourism.

The future of Cambodia, as well as its cities, is unclear. Decades of civil war, genocide, occupation, and now urban land-use conflicts have taken a toll on the Khmer people. One thing is certain: the cities of Cambodia, particularly Phnom Penh, will remain sites of struggle.

of multinational firms have given rise to a new international division of labor, one that has witnessed a shifting of manufacturing sectors from developed to developing economies, and the emergence of new corporate headquarter activities, producer services, and research/ development sites. Final assembly and testing of audio-video equipment are located in Singapore and Penang, Malaysia; assembly and packaging, low-skilled and labor-intensive in

Bangkok, Jakarta, and Manila; and marketing and sales functions and mid- to high-end manufacturing in Singapore. In Southeast Asia, these far-reaching changes are evidenced by the spectacular growth of assembly plants in Phnom Penh as well as the emergence of Cyberjaya, Malaysia's high-technology city (the "Silicon Valley of the East") that forms the hub of that country's Multimedia Supercorridor.

Shifts in the structure of Southeast Asia's economies have led to remarkable societal and occupational changes. Declines in agricultural workers are matched by increases in the number of workers employed in the service and manufacturing centers. Consequently, the increasing portion of clerical, sales, and service workers, in particular, has translated into redefined social categories. One change that is especially salient is the emergence of a new middle class. And given that many of the economic transformations have occurred disproportionately within the urban areas of Southeast Asia, it should come as no surprise that the emergent middle class in Southeast Asia is likewise urban-based.

The rise of Southeast Asia's new urban middle class has drastically altered the urban landscape. Demographically, Southeast Asia's middle class tends to have small families; economically, it tends to have high and rising levels of consumption and to spend money on nonessential items, such as luxury cars. Many members of this emergent class express "Western" middle-class fantasies to materially project their newfound social status. In terms of housing, Southeast Asia's middle class demands more space and more privacy (hence leading to demand for western-style housing in the form of detached and semi-detached single-family dwellings). Having the ability to purchase an automobile, middle class individuals are able and willing to commute longer distances to work, thus fueling the sprawl of cities into traditional agricultural hinterlands. Others prefer to live closer to the traditional downtown districts, fueling the proliferation of condominiums and apartment complexes. The emergence of the middle class, and its growing spending power, is likewise reflected in the mushrooming of shopping malls and country clubs, and the proliferation of leisure activities and nightclubs. It is seen in the growth of gourmet restaurants, coffee bars (Starbucks franchises are becoming all-too pervasive), theaters, galleries, and boutiques.

Cities in Southeast Asia have historically been segregated. During the colonial years, British, French, Spanish, and American authorities often restricted residential and commercial activities by ethnic classification in their respective colonies. The Spanish, for example, disallowed Filipinos from living in Intramuros Manila; the French restricted Vietnamese settlements in Saigon. Today, segregated areas remain, but these often reflect class differences as much as anything. This segregation is epitomized by the rise of gated communities. The desire among the new middle class for gated communities results from demands for privacy, security, and prestige. New land developments are gated, often with armed guards. Many of these housing schemes provide tennis courts, golf courses, exclusive clubs, and spacious houses; some even provide heliports for their residents.

The growth of Southeast Asia's middle class is a major contributor to the sprawl of cities. A key prerequisite for the construction of gated communities, for example, is land. In Jakarta, Ho Chi Minh City, and Manila, local governments have allowed the spread of new middle-class enclaves on their peripheries and the conversion of old land-uses for middle class condominiums in the cities. Many

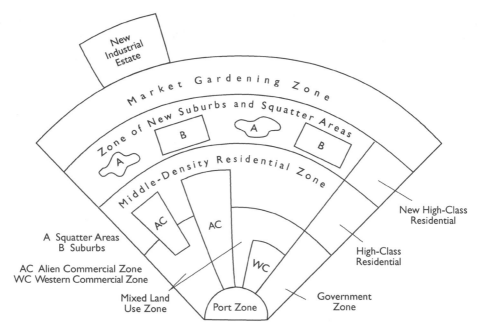

Figure 10.11   A Generalized Model of Major Land Use in the Large Southeast Asian City. *Source:* T. G. McGee, *The Southeast Asian City* (New York: Praeger, 1967), 128.

lower-cost housing units in Phnom Penh, for example, have been razed in order to erect higher-cost apartments and condominiums for the middle class. Such changes have resulted in conflict.

Often, these new middle-class enclaves sit side by side with ever-rising numbers of the urban poor, who continue to migrate toward cities in search of jobs. Displaced by land scarcity and the mechanization of agriculture, these rural-to-urban migrants must compete with the wealthy, and now the middle class, for limited resources in the cities. The poor provide their own housing, usually make-shift houses of corrugated tin, cardboard, or plywood. Often, these structures sit discordantly next to the golf courses and gated communities of the better off. The urban landscape of Southeast Asia thus reflects the social and economic transformations of a region enmeshed in much broader changes; the growing disparity

between the "haves" and the "have-nots" is all too apparent.

MODELS OF URBAN STRUCTURE

For more than three decades, thinking about Southeast Asian urbanization has developed out of T. G. McGee's model of city structure (fig. 10.11). Building on a long tradition of urban modeling in North America, McGee's model presumed, first, that no clear zoning characterizes land use in the large cities of Southeast Asia. Instead, he proposed that only two zones of land use remained relatively constant: the port district and, on the periphery of the city, a zone of intensive market gardening. In between were areas of mixed economic activity and land use, along with other areas of dominant land use, characterized, for example, by the spines of high-class residential areas or by clusters of squatter settlements.

As cities in Southeast Asia have experienced rapid urban growth, in part associated with more intense integration into the global economy, our understanding of these places has changed considerably. Although remnants of McGee's initial model are still visible (e.g., a central port zone and mixed land-use patterns), some aspects of Southeast Asian cities have been radically transformed. Urban scholars now speak of *extended metropolitan regions* (EMRs). This distinctive form of Asian urbanization has its origins in the way in which Asian cities (not just limited to Southeast Asia) have been incorporated into the global economy. The colonial-influenced primate cities are increasingly penetrating their surrounding hinterlands, urbanizing the countryside and drawing rural populations deeper and deeper into the urban economy. In certain respects, EMRs are similar to metropolitan regions in the United States. However, EMRs in Southeast Asia differ from their North American counterparts in that the former exhibit a greater population density in both the urban cores and the surrounding rural periphery.

EMRs may be differentiated into three basic forms. The first is the *expanding city-state.* Singapore provides the only example. In recent decades, Singapore has extended its political and economic influence into the territory of its neighbors, Indonesia and Malaysia. A second type is the *low-density* EMR, exemplified by Kuala Lumpur. These EMRs have been able to maintain relatively low population densities through the successful development of satellite cities that fringe the dominant urban area. In other words, low-density EMRs reflect controlled and managed growth, as opposed to the more

rapid and unplanned growth of other cities. Ho Chi Minh City likewise reflects aspects of a low-density EMR. The third and most prevalent type is the *high-density* EMR. This form, epitomized by the massive cities of Jakarta, Manila, and Bangkok, exhibits a chaotic spillover of urban economic functions into the rural hinterland, with an accompanying conversion of agricultural land to residential and industrial development.

Related to EMRs is a new urban form, identified by McGee as *desakota.* The term itself is derived from the Indonesian words for village (*desa*) and town (*kota*) and is meant to capture the process whereby urbanization overtakes its surrounding hinterland. A number of elements have been associated with *desakota*. First, these cities exhibit considerable diversity in their land use. Characteristically, a *desakota* region encompasses cities with mixed residential and industrial land uses, as well as a densely populated wet-rice agricultural area. Within *desakota,* moreover, there is significant interaction between village and town. This is made possible by an integrated transportation system that permits high levels of population mobility. Indeed, the increased daily commuting patterns seen in Bangkok testify to this increased circulation within *desakota*. Second, these regions also are strongly integrated into the global economy. Foreign investment is generally important in these areas, as multinational corporations tap into large and readily available labor surpluses. Lastly, it is the *process* of formation of the *desakota* that is perhaps more important than the resulting pattern itself, because surrounding rural areas become urbanized without the transfer of population that occurs in, say, rural-to-urban migration. Moreover, it is the process of urban change that captures the broader political, economic, and social transformation that typifies Southeast Asian cities within a globalized world.

But is the process of *desakota* unique to Southeast Asia? Many urbanists remain unconvinced. Some writers contend that the high-density EMR is largely synonymous with the *desakota,* while others are convinced that the *desakota* is not unique at all and is simply another variant of urban sprawl. Still other scholars contend that Southeast Asian cities, despite new nomenclature, are not that distinctive; these authors suggest a series of alternating phases of convergence and divergence from, especially, Western European cities. These writers contend that from traditional, precolonial forms, during the peak period of colonization from about 1880 to the 1930s, there was considerable convergence between Southeast Asian and Western European cities. This convergence was manifested in the urban landscape, as reflected in architectural styles and land-use patterns. By the late 19th century, for example, most large Southeast Asian cities had distinct central business districts that were dominated by European firms; ethnic residential segregation was also prevalent. Singapore perhaps best exemplified the European colonial city. Other cities, of course, were remade by the European powers. These include Rangoon (occupied by the British in 1834) and Saigon (occupied by the French in 1859). Even Bangkok, which avoided colonization by the European powers, was still influenced by both the British and the French.

The years spanning the 1940s through the 1970s constituted a period of divergence. These decades witnessed considerable rural-to-urban migration, a proliferation of informal-sector employment, and an expansion of squatter settlements. These were the years of decolonization, and cities in Southeast Asia reflected an increased nationalism and symbolic transformation of their urban landscapes. In Manila, for example, Dewey Boulevard, named after George Dewey, the American admiral who defeated the Spanish at Manila Bay in 1898, was renamed Roxas Boulevard, after Manuel Roxas, the first president of the independent Philippines. In Jakarta, President Sukarno ushered in a period of massive monument building to provide his capital city with new, highly visible symbols that would reflect his nationalist ideologies. One such construction was the National Monument, or *Monas,* a towering 429-foot marble obelisk with a bronze and gold top designed to resemble an eternal flame.

Lastly, the 1980s and 1990s reveal convergence again with Western cities. These transformed cities are increasingly becoming characterized by a rise of private transportation, increased consumption and the corresponding emergence of consumer landscapes (e.g., shopping malls, entertainment centers), a privatization of space (e.g., a proliferation of gated, and often armed, residential communities), and a decline in urban planning. These decades likewise witnessed the emergence of massive plaza malls throughout Manila, Bangkok, Jakarta, and Kuala Lumpur.

Apart from urban growth associated with primate cities, Southeast Asia is also experiencing a rise in "transnational urban areas." Similar to urban changes occurring in East Asia, cities in Southeast Asia are increasingly extending their scope across national boundaries. Variously known as *regional economic zones, borderless cities, growth triangles,* and *urban corridors,* these urban forms consist of social, political, and economic linkages between two or more states. These are usually government-created economic regions that represent a new organization of space across political jurisdictions. Within Southeast Asia, the three countries of

Singapore, Indonesia, and Malaysia best illustrate the concept of transnational urban areas. In 1989 Singapore announced the formation of a growth triangle integrating Singapore, Indonesia's Riau Archipelago, and the Malaysian state of Johor. Known by the acronym of Sijori (from the combination of Singapore, Johore, and Riau), the arrangement combines Singapore's capital, technology, and managerial talents with land and labor provided by Johor and the Riaus. Linkages have been expanding within the Sijori growth triangle, including sizeable flows of goods, information, and people. Examples include the development of Batam Island's international telephone system, which is routed through Singapore, as well as a possible extension of the Singapore subway system into Johor.

In 1993 an agreement was reached between Indonesia, Malaysia, and Thailand for a Medan–Penang–Songkhla growth triangle. This would incorporate the four northern states of Malaysia, two provinces in northern Sumatra, and five provinces in southern Thailand. Elsewhere a proposed growth triangle includes southern Mindanao (the Philippines), northern Sulawesi (Indonesia), and Sabah (Malaysia). Many of these zones are informal arrangements, and they are often defined in name only. In other words, few of these mega-urban corridors have any official recognition by the countries involved. They do, however, reflect both materially and symbolically the increased integration of Southeast Asia into regional and global economies.

REPRESENTATIVE CITIES

Singapore: World City of Southeast Asia

There is truly no other city in the world quite like Singapore (fig. 10.12). Its striking modernity, Disneyland-like cleanliness, and extreme orderliness seem unreal, especially if one has just arrived from the sprawling, chaotic and noisome cities of Bangkok, Jakarta, or Manila. To some, Singapore is a model of efficiency, a mosaic of well-manicured lawns, efficient transportation, and planned development. To others, Singapore represents a draconian police state masquerading as utopia. The reality, of course, lies somewhere in between and depends on one's personal tastes and values.

Singapore is unique within Southeast Asia, and in the world, in that it is both a city and a sovereign state. And it is small. At just 246 square miles (640 sq km), it is one-fifth the area of Rhode Island. But despite its size, Singapore is also very prosperous. In per capita income, the city-state is second only to Japan in all of Asia. In part, Singapore's economic success has been tied to its geography. Both historically and currently, the city has benefited from its strategic location and superb natural harbor. Furthermore, effective government policies and dynamic leadership have propelled Singapore into its role as Southeast Asia's leading port and industrial center, as well as a leading banking and commercial center. Indeed, Singapore ranks along with Tokyo and Hong Kong as one of Asia's three key urban centers in today's global economic system.

Singapore's economy is based on a strong manufacturing sector (initially processing raw materials such as rubber, but more recently electronics and electrical products), oil refining, financial and business services, and tourism. The economic success of Singapore has translated into a very favorable quality of life. Singapore registers the region's lowest infant mortality rate and the lowest rate of population increase, in addition to the highest

Figure 10.12   Singapore's ultramodern skyline towers over remnants of the British colonial era, a vivid reminder of how far this unique city-state has come. (Photo by Jack Williams)

per capita income. This quality of life is facilitated through subsidized medical care and compulsory retirement programs.

Singapore is a truly cosmopolitan world city. The affluence of Singapore is vividly seen along the city-state's major shopping and tourist corridor, Orchard Road. In the 1830s this area was home to fruit orchards, nutmeg plantations, and pepper farms. Now, the mangoes, nutmeg, and peppers are gone, replaced by jeweled necklaces, designer clothes, and perfumes. Orchard Road currently extends 1.5 miles (2.4 km) and is lined with major shopping centers, upscale boutiques, luxury hotels, and entertainment centers such as the Raffles Village (built around the carefully restored classic Raffles Hotel, one of the great hotels of the past).

True to its place at the center of Southeast Asia, the urban landscape of Singapore reflects its rich ethnic heritage (fig. 10.13).

Approximately 75% of Singapore's population is ethnic Chinese; Malays and Indians constitute 15% and 7% of the population, respectively. Consequently, Singapore has four official languages: English, Mandarin Chinese, Malay, and Tamil, a language of southern India. The immigrant history of Singapore, moreover, is well preserved in the city-state's architecture (fig. 10.14). The Chinatown area of Singapore, for example, located at the mouth of the Singapore River, began in 1821, when the first junkload of Chinese immigrants arrived from Xiamen, in Fujian province. In 1842 these Chinese immigrants completed the Thian Hock Keng Temple and dedicated it to Ma-Chu-Po (Matsu), the goddess of the sea. Nearby is Nagore Durgha Shrine, built by Muslim immigrants from south India, and further down the road is the Al-Abrar Mosque, also known as Indian Mosque, which was built between 1850 and

Figure 10.13   Arab Street in Singapore is a quaint reminder of the multicultural environment that lies beneath the city-state's Chinese majority population. (Photo by Richard Ulack)

Figure 10.14   This gaudy Indian temple in Singapore is one of the best-known cultural landmarks of the city and a center of the Hindu minority population. (Photo by James Tyner)

1855. Because of land reclamation projects, the ultramodern skyscrapers of Singapore's financial district now eclipse Chinatown's oceanfront view.

Given the large number of historical temples and monuments, urban preservation is important in Singapore, although this has not always been the case. During the 1960s and 1970s, for example, many older buildings were demolished to make room for a more modern infrastructure. However, a movement to preserve Singapore's urban history was initiated, for reasons of both national prestige and tourism. Today, many areas, such as the

waterfronts along Collyer Quay and Boat Quay, have been renovated (fig. 10.15).

Singapore is also instructive for its public housing programs. Beginning in the 1960s, the Singaporean government, primarily through the efforts of the Housing Development Board (HDB), moved to ensure adequate housing for its population. The result was the establishment of numerous new towns and housing estates. The Queenstown housing estate, for example, located in the central region of Singapore, was one of the earliest estates developed by the HDB. Tao Payoh New Town and Ang Mo Kio New

Figure 10.15   Sir Stamford Raffles, founder of Singapore, stands along Collyer Quay with restored houses on the opposite bank as reminders of Singapore's colorful past. (Photo by Jack Williams)

Town, both located within the Northeastern Region, were initiated in 1965 and 1973, respectively. A more recent development is Woodlands New Town, located on the northern coast of Singapore. These new towns are designed to be self-sufficient communities of many thousands of residents. Ang Mo Kio, for example, registered a 1990 population of 223,000, occupying more than 54,000 housing units. As such, new towns also exhibit a mix of land uses. In Ang Mo Kio, for instance, one-third of the land is devoted to residential use; one-third is either undeveloped, or is water or open space; one-sixth is commercial/industrial/institutional; and the remaining sixth is mostly roads and infrastructure. By 2000, nearly 90% of Singaporeans lived in one of the high-density housing estates built by the HDB. Moreover, in recognition of Singapore's ethnic diversity, the government has mandated ethnic-based occupancy rates

to offset the emergence of hyper-segregated enclaves.

New towns perform functions beyond housing. In particular, these areas are thought to contribute to an overall employment/housing balance, enhance environmental conservation, and contribute to economic growth. The Woodlands Planning Area, for example, is envisioned to serve as a regional hub and gateway between Singapore and Malaysia.

Despite these successes, urbanization in Singapore remains, and will continue to remain, hindered by two physical obstacles. First, Singapore cannot readily—or cheaply—expand its area because it occupies only a small island. In response, the Singaporean government has utilized land reclamation schemes and has also been working to expand its economic growth beyond its own political boundaries into neighboring Malaysia and Indonesia. In this manner, the government hopes to exploit the comparative advantages of Singapore and neighboring countries. A second, and perhaps more immediate, obstacle confronting Singapore is that of water. Water is a serious problem because the island contains no significant rivers or lakes to collect freshwater and so must rely on reservoirs and stormwater collection ponds to provide freshwater for its nearly 4 million residents. Most water is supplied by Malaysia. In response to its limited water resources, Singapore has pursued to twofold strategy. First, it has initiated a series of conservation measures, including the installation of water-saving devices, water-recycling programs, and water-consumption taxes. Second, Singapore has pursued other means of obtaining water, such as the installation of desalinization plants and the construction of more reservoirs, and it has explored the possibility of acquiring water from Indonesia.

Kuala Lumpur: Twin Towers and Cyberspace

The skyline of Kuala Lumpur is one of the most recognizable sights in all of Southeast Asia. Whereas Paris has its Eiffel Tower and Shanghai its futuristic TV tower, Kuala Lumpur has the 88-story Petronas Twin Towers. Standing like a giant double-barreled beehive, the Petronas Towers dominate the capital city of Malaysia (fig. 10.16). They are Kuala Lumpur's signature landscape feature and are symbolic of the lofty goals set by the Malaysian government.

Kuala Lumpur is a relatively young city. It was founded in 1857 by Chinese tin miners at the swampy confluence of the Klang and Gombak rivers. In fact, the name "Kuala Lumpur" translates as "muddy confluence." The settlement grew rapidly and, by 1880, had become the capital of the state of Selangor on the Malay Peninsula. A railroad connected the

site with the coast in 1895, and in 1896 Kuala Lumpur became the capital of the Federated Malay States.

Despite its growing political importance, Kuala Lumpur throughout much of the early 20th century was still overshadowed in population by other cities along the Malay Peninsula, including Georgetown to the north and Singapore to the south. Although it was designated capital of the Federated States of Malaysia in 1963, Kuala Lumpur trailed both Singapore and Georgetown as a preeminent commercial center on the peninsula. In 1972, however, Kuala Lumpur gained city status and was declared a Federal Territory (similar to Washington's District of Columbia).

Kuala Lumpur experienced tremendous population growth throughout the late 20th century. Currently the population is approximately 2 million. However, unlike Bangkok and Manila, Kuala Lumpur has made a more concerted effort to manage urban growth. Planned satellite cities, for example, were designed to relieve the urban congestion of the capital. In the 1950s, the satellite city of Petaling Jaya was established; it is now home to more than 500,000 residents and is a major industrial center. Nearby, the satellite town of Shah Alam, initially planned to be half residential and half industrial, was built in the 1970s. Although shantytowns are visible in parts of Kuala Lumpur, as a whole the city exhibits a sedate orderliness more reminiscent of Singapore than of other Southeast Asian cities.

The economy of Kuala Lumpur, once dominated by tin mining, is now an exceptionally diverse mix of manufacturing and service activities. Many of these industries are clustered within the Klang Valley conurbation, an urbanized corridor stretching from Kuala Lumpur westward through Petaling Jaya and Shah Alam to the port city of Klang. Also,

Figure 10.16   When Kuala Lumpur's Petronas Towers opened in 1999, they became the world's tallest, a title they held until 2004. (Photo by Richard Ulack)

indicative of the information economies emerging in Southeast Asia, Kuala Lumpur is a key anchor in Malaysia's "Multimedia Supercorridor" (MSC). Planned to be a setting for multimedia and information-technology companies, the MSC is seen as the catalyst in propelling Malaysia's economy into the global information age. When fully complete, the MSC will consist of more than 240 square miles (625 sq km) of research, development, manufacturing, and distribution services. In related developments, two new cities are being constructed to the south of Kuala Lumpur: Putrajaya, which will become the administrative capital of Malaysia, and Cyberjaya, billed as an "intelligent city," complete with a state-of-the-art, integrated infrastructure that will attract multimedia and information-technology companies.

Jakarta: Megacity of Indonesia

Most visitors to Indonesia arrive first in Jakarta, a sprawling metropolis situated on

Figure 10.17   The sprawl of Jakarta is visible in this bird's-eye view that simultaneously shows the old (the largest mosque in Southeast Asia) and the new (a line of the rapid-transit system designed to bring order to the city's traffic chaos). (Photo by Jack Williams)

the north coast of Java. At two and a half times the size of Singapore, Jakarta is the largest city in population and land area in Southeast Asia (fig. 10.17). From its origins as a small port town called Sunda Kelapa, the Special Capital Region of Jakarta (Daerah Khusus Ibukota, or DKI Jakarta) has experienced phenomenal growth over the past five decades. From fewer than 2 million in 1950, Jakarta's population had swollen to more than 9 million by 1990 and had reached more than 13 million by 2000. As with many primate cities in Southeast Asia, urban growth has sprawled into the hinterland. In recognition of this sprawl, in the mid-1970s officials began to refer to the entire region as Jabotabek, an acronym derived from the combination of Jakarta and the adjacent districts of Bogor, Tangerang, and Bekasi.

When the entire Jabotabek region is considered, the population of the Jakarta metropolitan area includes a mind-boggling 20 million people. Similar to other major cities in the region, Jakarta's population is also impacted by *seasonal* and daily commuting. Hundreds of thousands of workers, the majority of whom live in new residential communities in the Jabotabek region, commute daily to Jakarta.

Jakarta remains Indonesia's largest and most important metropolitan area. It is the national capital and the principal administrative and commercial center of the archipelago. The city also plays a vital role in Indonesia's international and domestic trade and receives a disproportionate share of foreign direct investment. This investment, focused primarily on manufacturing but also on construction and service sectors, produces a multiplier effect for Jakarta's economy. It also accounts for a rapid rise in the middle class, with a corresponding impact on the urban landscape. In some respects, though, Jakarta has undergone a period of deindustrialization similar to that of other cities in the world, such as London. Thus, although the city remains an important manufacturing center, economic growth has been accounted for largely by increases in both tertiary and quaternary sectors (especially financial services, communications, and transportation).

Economic and social changes have also contributed to changing land-use patterns. The central core of Jakarta has experienced significant changes over the past decade, such as a conversion from residential to higher-intensity commercial and office land use, as well as the emergence of luxury high-rise apartments. In the Jabotabek region, the development of new towns (e.g., Lippo City, Cikarang New Town, and Pondok Gede New Town) and corresponding large-scale residential subdivisions has also transformed previously agricultural land into urban spaces. Indeed, upwards of 80,000 new housing units are added each year to the Jabotabek region. Other changes include the emergence of larger industrial estates as well as leisure-related land uses (e.g., golf courses).

Jakarta also reflects the urban woes characteristic of primate cities, including a lack of adequate public housing, traffic congestion, air and water pollution, sewage disposal, and problems associated with the provision of health services, education, and utilities (fig. 10.18). Because of the megacity's sheer size, not to mention the heightened political, social, and economic instability of Indonesia, Jakarta's problems are magnified to dangerous levels.

Manila: Primate City of the Philippines

Unlike walking the regimented, disciplined streets of Singapore and Kuala Lumpur, traveling within Manila is an experience unto itself. Indeed, with the possible exception of Bangkok, no other city in Southeast Asia is as famous—or infamous—as Manila for its traffic. Throughout the day, and frequently well into the night, traffic grinds slowly through the rabbit-den of highways and alleyways that constitute Manila's overburdened road network. Diesel-spewing *jeepneys,* rickety buses, and luxury sport-utility vehicles all compete in bumper-car-like fashion (fig. 10.19). Turn lanes and stoplights are largely ignored. Yet beyond the chaos and congestion that puts the freeways of Los Angeles to shame, Manila exhibits its own charm and appeal. Indeed, much of Manila's charm stems precisely from its outwardly confusing appearance.

Politically, socially, economically, and in terms of total population, Manila far surpasses all other cities in the Philippines. Indeed, with the exception of Thailand, no other major country in the region has a higher primacy rate than does the Philippines. Currently, Manila is approximately nine times as large as the Philippines' second-largest metropolitan area, Cebu. And similar to Jakarta's Jabotabek, the Manila Metropolitan Area (MMA) is composed of many different political units. In 1975, the MMA was formed through the integration of the four preexisting, politically separate cities of Manila, Quezon City, Kaloocan, and Pasay, plus 13 municipalities.

The Metropolitan Manila region, reminiscent of Harris and Ullman's multiple nuclei model, is a polynucleated area with many distinct personalities. Binondo, for example, located next to the Pasig River, was originally

Figure 10.18   Only a minority of Jakarta's residents have access to piped water, so water vendors such as this wend their way through the streets selling this precious commodity. (Photo by Jack Williams)

a Christian Chinese commercial district during the Spanish colonial period and to this day remains the heart of Manila's Chinatown. Nearby is Tondo, today an impoverished, densely populated district of rental blocks; prior to the arrival of the Spanish, it was a collection of Muslim villages. To the south, abutting Manila Bay, is Ermita. Once a small fishing village, the area developed into a prime tourist destination, packed with bars, nightclubs, strip shows, and massage parlors. In recent years, however, these establishments were closed down in Ermita and have since relocated to other areas of Manila. As a final example, Makati, originally a small market village, is now Manila's major financial center, occupied by banks and multinational and national corporations. Makati also contains some of Manila's most expensive housing subdivisions, sprawling box-like shopping centers, and five-star hotels.

Within the greater Manila Metropolitan region is Quezon City. Named after Manuel

Quezon, who served as president of the Commonwealth of the Philippines (1934–1946), Quezon City was the Philippines' national capital from 1948 to 1976. Now it is home to many important government buildings, medical centers, and universities, including the main campuses of the University of the Philippines and Ateneo de Manila University. Quezon City also consists of upscale gated residential communities patrolled by armed guards. These estates, home to middle- and upper-class residents, are equipped with luxurious air-conditioned homes, tennis and basketball courts, golf courses, and swimming pools. However, reflective of Manila's complex land usage, as well as the highly polarized nature of Philippine society, just outside of these gated communities are numerous squatter settlements.

Characteristic of large cities in Southeast Asia, Manila exhibits increasing consumer spaces. In recent years large shopping malls have been built, catering to a rising middle

Figure 10.19   Unique to Manila, the jeepney is a form of urban transport that got started after World War II using old U.S. jeeps. Decked out with frills and gaudy decoration, the jeepneys play an important role and have become a symbol of Manila. (Photo by Jack Williams)

class. For many visitors, these malls are remarkably similar to those found in the United States and Europe. Major department stores anchor the malls, while in between are dozens of specialty stores, food courts, and entertainment venues (fig. 10.20). The SM Megamall, for example, in addition to its numerous stores and restaurants, contains an ice-skating rink, bowling lanes, a twelve-screen cinema, and an arcade room.

Similar to both Jakarta and Bangkok, the increased concentration of foreign direct investment into the Philippines has translated into rapid changes in the economy of Manila, as well as to changes in land use. During the 1990s, the greater Metro Manila region and surrounding provinces experienced remarkable industrial and manufacturing growth. This expansion, however, occurred at the expense of Manila's rural and agrarian hinterland. Metro Manila is, in fact, located toward the center of the Philippines'

major rice-producing region, and continued urban sprawl is rapidly encroaching on these agricultural areas.

Urban poverty and landlessness continue to be major problems in Manila. The extent of these problems, however, remains a contested issue. Estimates of the number of poor vary widely, ranging from 1.6 million to more than 4.5 million. What is certain, however, is that landownership in Manila is decidedly uneven, with the majority of its population being landless. High urban land values mean that the majority of residents are unable to obtain legal housing, a situation exacerbated by continued high rates of in-migration. Their recourse is to resort to illegal housing and to settle in urban fringe areas, such as along railroad tracks and in vacant lots. Residents of squatter settlements are subject to deplorable health conditions and pollution problems. Squatters have inadequate access to toilet and plumbing facilities and often must purchase

Figure 10.20 The informal economy thrives in the cities of Southeast Asia, as exemplified by this vendor selling corn on the cob in the streets of Manila. (Photo by Richard Ulack)

fresh water from itinerant water vendors. Historically, squatter settlements have been demolished and their residents evicted. More recently, the Philippine government has attempted to provide low-cost housing for its urban poor.

Aside from poverty, Manila faces other serious problems. Accessibility to water, for example, looms large. Manila is also confronted with serious air and water pollution problems, as well as an inadequate sewerage system. Indeed, during the rainy season many streets throughout Manila, such as those in the port district and in Tondo, become impassable because of flooding.

Bangkok: The Los Angeles of the Tropics

Bangkok, at 34 times the size of Thailand's second-largest city, Nakhon Ratchasima, is the textbook example of an urban primate city. While only one-fifth of the country is urbanized, fully two-thirds of this urban population is concentrated in the Bangkok Metropolitan Region (BMR). Currently, the core of Bangkok has a population of about 6 million; when the entire BMR is considered, the region's population is more than 10 million. Furthermore, like the ocean's tides, Bangkok's population ebbs and flows, both daily and seasonally. An estimated 1 million people commute daily into Bangkok, and hundreds of thousands of other workers seasonally circulate throughout the city in search of temporary jobs in the informal sector. This seasonal migration is particularly acute in the hot, dry months of February and March, a slack agricultural period.

The official name of Bangkok is Krung Thep, which translates as "The City of Angels" (the same meaning as Los Angeles), and in many respects, notably with regard to traffic, pollution, and urban sprawl, Bangkok might be considered the Los Angeles of Southeast Asia, and Los Angeles might be considered the Bangkok of the United States of America.

Currently, Bangkok remains poised to become an international communications and financial center, as well as a major transportation hub in Asia. Initially, much of Bangkok's growth was tied to massive amounts of investment brought about by the United States' involvement in the Vietnam War. During the 1960s, in particular, Bangkok served as a major military supply base. In subsequent decades, it continued to attract large sums of foreign investment. Between 1979 and 1990, nearly 70% of all foreign investment projects in Thailand were concentrated in the BMR. Economically, Bangkok has capitalized on its reserves of cheap labor, favorable tax incentives, and (until recently) political stability.

Similar to Jakarta and Manila, Bangkok is a multinucleated city. And while the "old city" remains the principal administrative and religious core of Bangkok, considerable expansion has occurred into the surrounding districts of Pratunam, Raja Prasong, Siam Square, Silom, and Suriwong. Bangkok has also experienced a rapid conversion of land use, with many residential areas in the city being converted to commercial use, and many former small shop-houses being transformed into high-rise office buildings and large shopping complexes.

Radiating outward in a concentric pattern, urban growth surrounding Bangkok has largely been haphazard and unplanned. Until 1992, Bangkok did not have an official city plan. And even now, former prime rice-producing and fish-farming areas are being converted to industrial uses and capital-intensive enterprises.

The over-urbanization of Bangkok has resulted in serious environmental problems. Air and water quality have deteriorated in recent years, and the disposal of solid waste is an ongoing problem. Also, Bangkok is sinking. As a result of the overdrawing of well water, the city suffers from land subsidence, as its elevation drops at a rate of about 4 inches per year. Indeed, some areas have subsided by more than three feet since the 1950s. Global warming should be firmly on the minds of Bangkok's urban planners!

Bangkok is also plagued by severe transportation problems. The number of motor vehicles (excluding the ubiquitous motorcycles) increased from 243,000 in 1972 to more than a million in 1990; concurrently, only about 50 miles (80 km) of primary roads were added. As a result, the average speed on most roads in Bangkok is less than 6 miles (10 km) per hour (fig. 10.21). Numerous proposals and strategies have been advanced to rectify traffic congestion, including increased road capacity measures, improvements in public mass-transit systems, improvements in the traffic control system, and strategies to control the volume of traffic (e.g., staggered employment hours to reduce peak commuting traffic). The government is also encouraging the growth of satellite cities as a means of promoting regional economic growth and relieving the congestion of Bangkok.

Phnom Penh, Ho Chi Minh City, Hanoi: Socialist Cities in Transition

In the early morning, the dusty streets of Phnom Penh are alive with swarms of noisy motorbikes that surge like schools of fish. Luxury cars and sport utility vehicles compete for limited space with the motorbikes. Plodding along the roadsides, in a vain attempt to escape the mechanized frenzy of Phnom Penh's traffic, are converted tractors with wooden trailers that ferry scores of young women—all dressed in identical green-and-white uniforms—to the foreign-owned assembly plants that ring the periphery of the city. Such is Phnom Penh in the 21st century: a frantic, disorderly city that is rebuilding after decades of tumultuous revolutions and genocide. The experience (and landscape) of Phnom Penh, combined with those of Ho Chi Minh City and Hanoi, provide vivid proof that urbanization is intimately associated with broader social movements, including revolutions.

Socialist cities in Southeast Asia have experienced, and reflect, a different pattern of urbanization than is the case with capitalist-based

Figure 10.21   Bangkok, where private automobile ownership is widespread, has some of the worst traffic jams in the world despite the construction of urban expressways. (Photo courtesy Bangkok government)

cities. The urbanization process in Southeast Asia's socialist countries (i.e., Burma, Cambodia, Laos, Vietnam) has been analyzed in a three-stage model. The first stage consists of a process of deurbanization, whereby major cities were depopulated. For example, as the Khmer Rouge assumed control of Cambodia in 1975, the socialist government undertook a forced evacuation of the capital city, Phnom Penh. Prior to this time, the population of Phnom Penh had swollen in size from around 700,000 in 1970 to approximately 2.5 million by 1975. This population increase resulted mostly from an inflow of refugees from the countryside escaping war. In 1975, however, the Khmer Rouge forcibly emptied Phnom Penh and other cities and villages throughout Cambodia. This process of deurbanization was but one act of the Khmer Rouge's genocidal reign that took the lives of nearly 3 million people (box 10.3).

Today, Phnom Penh still bears the scars of its genocidal past, although these are slowly being repaired. The streets of Phnom Penh, unpaved and pockmarked with potholes in 2001, now shimmer darkly with fresh asphalt. Where once stood hollowed-out buildings, destroyed by war and neglect, now stand freshly-painted apartment buildings and shopping complexes. Phnom Penh is indeed rebuilding, though not without difficulties, and this urban growth reflects a new orientation toward the global economy. For example, along the major road linking Phnom Penh and Cambodia's Pochentong International Airport, multinational corporations have established a visible presence in the form of assembly plants and factories. In Phnom Penh itself, many streets are lined with English-language schools and other centers of advanced learning.

In Vietnam, a similar, though less brutal, process of deurbanization occurred. The population of Saigon (now Ho Chi Minh City), like that of Phnom Penh, had also increased dramatically through in-migration and refugee flows. By 1975, Saigon had an estimated 4.5 million people. Following the victory of the

Figure 10.22   The Communist Party still holds power in Vietnam, but the skyline of Ho Chi Minh City is responding to capitalist forces. The city is expanding vertically, and the new is displacing the old. (Photo by James Tyner)

communist Democratic Republic of Vietnam, the new government planned to move as many as 1.5 million people out of Saigon; ultimately, however, only about 1 million people were relocated. The process of deurbanization in these socialist countries was often accompanied by a refashioning of the cities. Initially, Western-style establishments and customs were replaced with a Spartan milieu. Cities were drab and monotonous, composed of row upon row of uniform, box-like buildings. Conforming to socialist ideology, the new governments attempted to eliminate the private sector; shops, restaurants, hotels, and services were generally run by government enterprises or cooperatives. Consequently, cities were typically devoid of the mass advertising and consumer spectacles that are commonplace in capitalist cities. The new governments fostered symbolic changes as well. The renaming of Saigon to honor Ho Chi Minh, who led the fight against the French and established communism in Vietnam, provides the clearest illustration. Another visible difference between socialist and capitalist cities was the traffic. In Hanoi, the streets were practically empty of motor vehicles, save for an occasional Soviet-era limousine and a few battered and decrepit buses. Instead, bicycles thronged the streets, especially during peak hours, when residents cycled to and from work and school. In short, the newly formed socialist governments attempted to wipe clean, so to speak, the slate of capitalist-based urbanization.

Following this initial stage, socialist governments entered into a second, bureaucratic

Figure 10.23   As a result of reforms known as *doi moi*, initiated in 1986, Vietnam at first tolerated and then encouraged private enterprise, as evidenced by these shops and vendors in Ho Chi Minh City. (Photo by Jack Williams)

stage wherein longer-term strategies of socialist urbanization were implemented. Especially in Vietnam, the socialist government developed spatial strategies to ameliorate the problems of large cities, including the provision of adequate food, employment, and housing. Policies were enacted to restrict population mobility, thereby affording relief to the infrastructure of large urban areas, such as Ho Chi Minh City and Da Nang (fig. 10.22).

Socialist reform constitutes the third stage of the model. Although economic reforms were first introduced in Vietnam in 1979, it was not until 1986, with the initiation of *doi moi* (renovation), the slogan for the government's new development strategy, that substantial improvement occurred. *Doi moi* entails the gradual introduction of capitalist elements, including private ownership, foreign investment, and market competition. In short, Vietnam remains politically committed to socialism, but economically the country is exhibiting a shift toward capitalism and a greater level of integration into the global economy (fig. 10.23).

Spatially, economic reforms have focused predominantly on the southern region of Vietnam, and especially Ho Chi Minh City, because of that city's much longer tradition with free-market economics and linkages with the outside world. By analogy, Hanoi is Vietnam's Beijing and Ho Chi Minh City is the country's Shanghai. Approximately 80% of all foreign investment flowing into Vietnam is directed toward the south. Investments in tourism, assembly, and manufacturing are concentrated in the larger urban areas. Not surprisingly, therefore, regional disparities of foreign investment and economic reforms have transformed urban areas. Indeed, the cities of Hanoi and Ho Chi Minh provide

---

Box 10.4   HIV/AIDS in Southeast Asia

HIV, the virus that causes AIDS, currently infects 40 million people worldwide. As of 2003, an estimated 31 million people had already died of the disease. More than 3 million people continue to die each year, or about 8,200 every day. As of 2006 an estimated 7.2 million people were living with HIV/AIDS in Southeast Asia, the highest number of cases in the world outside of Africa. In Thailand alone there are over 580,000 HIV/AIDS cases, with an adult prevalence rate of 1.4. Statistics for other countries are equally grim: Burma has 360,000 cases; Cambodia, 130,000; Laos, 3,700; and Vietnam, 260,000.

HIV/AIDS is spread via many pathways. It can be transmitted through both heterosexual and homosexual intercourse and through the sharing of tainted needles (i.e., while injecting drugs such as heroin). HIV/AIDS may be transmitted from mothers to children in utero and during birth and breastfeeding. HIV/AIDS can also be passed on through transfusions with infected blood.

Within Southeast Asia, key social, economic, and political factors have contributed to the spread of HIV/AIDS. A major contributing factor is the mobility of migrant workers, both internally and internationally. In Southeast Asia, all countries are engaged in size-able and complex transnational migratory flows as sending and/or receiving nations. Over 1 million workers from both Burma and Laos, for example, find employment in Thailand. Thousands of migrants leave Cambodia to work in Thailand and Malaysia, and thousands of other workers leave China and Vietnam to work in Laos and Cambodia. Millions of other workers, from the Philippines, Indonesia, and Thailand, find employment throughout Europe and North America.

---

stark contrasts to the evolution of cities in socialist Southeast Asia. Although both retain remnants of their colonial histories, Hanoi—the political capital of Vietnam—remains the more sedate, regimented, and subdued of the two, while Ho Chi Minh City is a bustling metropolis, an urban forest of hotels, restaurants, bars, nightclubs, and discotheques. Ho Chi Minh City (still called Saigon by many residents) has returned to its prewar capitalist character, with luxury hotels—Hyatt, Ramada, and Hilton—competing side by side with government-run hotels. Hanoi, conversely, contains many symbols of Vietnamese nationalism, such as

the Ho Chi Minh Mausoleum and the Ho Chi Minh Museum. By the end of the 1990s, however, Hanoi was beginning to show the effects of increased globalization and was beginning to take on some of the color and dynamism of its rival to the south. Tourism, with thousands of global visitors interested in seeing the heart of the Democratic Republic of Vietnam, is leading the change.

URBAN CHALLENGES

Cities in Southeast Asia are not immune to serious problems. Challenges run the gamut,

These networks of migrant labor frequently intersect with other transnational networks, namely the trafficking of sex workers. Throughout Southeast Asia, Europe, and beyond, many women (and men) are forced or coerced into sex work. Some work in brothels, catering to migrant workers. In 2002, a survey revealed that 28% of all HIV-infected Filipinos were returning overseas contract workers. When these migrant laborers and sex workers return to their home villages, they may carry the disease with them.

Another form of population mobility includes regional and international tourism: in many countries of Southeast Asia, including the Philippines and Thailand, sex tourism is big business. As a result, the heterosexual and homosexual transmission of HIV/AIDS has increased precipitously with the continuance of sex tours.

The diffusion of HIV/AIDS is also associated with the prevalence of drug use. Southeast Asia is a key node in the global distribution of heroin and the sharing of infected needles has been identified as a crucial factor in the rise of HIV/AIDS in the region.

It is not uncommon for these various pathways to come together in the major cities, such as Manila, Bangkok, Chiang Mai (Thailand), and Phnom Penh. Consequently, as people continue to circulate, the cities of Southeast Asia serve as "infection pumps"—centers of HIV/AIDS diffusion. It is for this reason that the governments of Vietnam, Cambodia, and Thailand have concentrated many of their prevention strategies in cities. Such efforts include educational campaigns, provision of blood screening test-kits, and the distribution of condoms and clean needles. Tragically, however, the diffusion of HIV/AIDS will be slowed only if many other contingent problems of Southeast Asia—civil strife, repression, censorship, political corruption, government neglect, and poverty—are addressed. As such, the cities of Southeast Asia will remain battlegrounds in the war on AIDS.

from health issues (box 10.4) to environmental concerns. Arguably, though, the inability of urban residents to obtain adequate employment and housing looms among the most serious. Many inhabitants of these cities remain mired in poverty. As of the early 1990s, for example, more than 30% of Metro Manila's population lived below the poverty line, as did nearly 30% of Indonesia's urban population. Indeed, the figure for Indonesia escalated sharply in 2000–2001, as the country struggled with instabilities of all kinds. Rampant poverty, moreover, contributes to other serious problems, including political unrest and terrorist activity.

In part, conditions of poverty exist and persist because the urban economies are unable to satisfy the needs of a rising labor force brought about through natural increase and rural-to-urban migration. As a case in point, during the 1980s Jakarta's population grew at an annual rate of 3.8%, whereas urban employment grew at only 2.8%. One obvious solution is the promotion of labor-intensive industrialization. In Malaysia, for example, small-scale business operations have been encouraged. These have been assisted through credit management schemes and other forms of assistance. Thailand, likewise, has pursued income-generating projects and the decentralization of industries and employment based on urban centers in outlying regions. The Thai government has also proposed to expand highway and communication links between urban areas in the BMR and has emphasized different roles for urban centers throughout the country. The government, finally, also plans to broaden urban planning practices to include region-serving development functions, such as agroprocessing services, regional marketing, and communications functions, and to formulate a regional network or cluster strategy of urban and regional development. Not all regional growth programs, of course, are successful. The Philippines, for example, initiated a regional policy scheme in 1973 to help lessen the overurbanization of Manila. Included in this policy was a proposed ban on locating new manufacturing plants within 30 miles (50 km) of Manila. This policy, however, resulted in an intensification of urban growth around the fringes of Manila, thereby adding to the congestion of the city.

Even without the problem of continued population growth, the generation of employment is neither easy nor free of political pitfalls. Many of the labor-intensive industries established in Southeast Asia have been extremely exploitative. As especially exemplified in the export processing zones controlled by multinational corporations, these jobs are low paid, are often of a temporary nature, and lack health and safety benefits. Employment opportunities are also gender selective, as factory managers prefer to hire female workers.

Another option is for governments to obtain overseas employment for their citizens. Since the 1970s many governments in Southeast Asia, but mainly the Philippines, Thailand, and Indonesia, have initiated overseas employment programs. Evidence is mixed as to the effectiveness of these programs. For example, the Philippines are currently the world's largest exporter of government-sponsored temporary labor migrants. Annually, more than 800,000 Filipinos are deployed to more than 190 countries and territories. This number, however, is offset by the estimated 750,000 new entrants to the Philippines' labor market each year. Thus, unless other alternatives are pursued, overseas employment will remain a stopgap program.

Conditions of unemployment and underemployment are reflected in inadequate housing. For example, in the 1990s in Manila, approximately 40% of the urban population was estimated to be living in squatter settlements, with another 45% of the population living in slum conditions. In Bangkok, 23% of the population was estimated to be living in slum and squatter settlements; in both Kuala Lumpur and Jakarta, squatters constituted approximately 25% of the population.

The rise of squatter settlements and slum areas is explained by factors other than population increase. Escalating land prices, compounded by real estate speculation, for example, exacerbate the problem of housing. So too does the creation of artificial land scarcity. In Metro Manila, for example, large tracts of land, even within the central business district of Makati, remain vacant. And lastly, the demolition of low-cost housing units, and their replacement by more affluent condominiums and gated communities, results in the rise of squatter settlements.

Sadly, many governments continue to view eviction and demolition as the most effective means of confronting squatter settlements. In the Philippines, for example, more than 100,000 people were evicted from Manila each year between 1986 and 1992. Not surprisingly, a policy of relocating squatters to sites 20 to 50 miles (30–80 km) outside the city and placing them in high-density residential apartments proved ineffective. Only Singapore has achieved substantial results in the provision of public housing. Other cities, especially Manila, Bangkok, and Phnom Penh, trail woefully behind. While many of these governments have agencies charged with developing public housing, most lack the required economic resources and political resolve to be effective.

Many Southeast Asian governments also are unable to provide adequate services, such as clean water, sewerage, and other utilities. Only about 7% of Burma's urban population, for example, has access to piped water. In Jakarta, only a quarter of the population has solid waste collection; in the remainder of the city, it is collected by scavengers. One effective strategy has been Indonesia's Kampung Improvement Program (KIP). This program is a far-reaching initiative that concentrates primarily on the improvement of infrastructure and public facilities. Specific projects include footpaths, secondary roads, drainage ditches, schools, communal bathing and shower facilities, and health clinics. Since its inception, the KIP has been expanded to more than 200 cities throughout Indonesia and has benefited more than 3.5 million people.

Air pollution poses serious health hazards to residents and visitors alike in Southeast Asian cities. Jakarta, for example, exceeds the health standards for ambient levels of airborne particulate matter on more than 170 days of the year. Moreover, topographic features may augment pollution problems. The surrounding hills of the Klang Valley around Kuala Lumpur and the mountains ringing Manila, for example, confine pollutants and thus exacerbate air quality problems.

Water pollution, likewise, remains a major obstacle to quality of life in Southeast Asian cities. Many rivers, including the Pasig in Manila, the Chao Phraya in Bangkok, and the Ciliwung in Jakarta, are considered biological hazards. The canals and waterways in Bangkok, especially, are highly polluted from a combination of industrial and household discharge. Only 2% of the city's population is connected to Bangkok's limited sewerage system. Consequently, most solid waste is discharged into waterways. Compounding the problem is the fact that more than 15% of the garbage disposed of daily is left uncollected.

An additional problem is traffic congestion. The traffic problems of Bangkok and Manila were discussed previously. In Jakarta, likewise, private car ownership has outpaced road construction. Similar problems are being felt in Ho Chi Minh City, which is currently home to more than 2.5 million motorbikes, and, increasingly, in Phnom Penh. Some governments, including those of Malaysia and Indonesia, have utilized toll roads to reduce traffic congestion. Other efforts concentrate on the development of mass-transit systems, such as the construction of light-rail transit systems in both Manila and Kuala Lumpur. These projects, however, are extremely expensive, and many have been temporarily halted. To this day, half-completed overpasses and bridges in Bangkok and incomplete rail systems in Manila stand as silent reminders of continued underdevelopment.

AN EYE TO THE FUTURE

Like Gregor Samsa in Franz Kafka's novella *The Metamorphosis,* the cities of Southeast Asia have awoken from unsettled dreams to find themselves changed into something potentially monstrous: agglomerations of sky-scrapers and street vendors, palatial residential neighborhoods and impoverished squatter settlements, overburdened utilities and under-developed transit systems.

What does the future hold for the cities of Southeast Asia? Three themes come to mind. First, continued population pressures and environmental degradation will most likely accelerate rural-to-urban migration, thereby exacerbating overurbanization problems. Consequently, the cities of Southeast Asia will continue to expand geographically. How this development occurs, however, and how governments respond or manage this growth, will greatly affect the livability of these cities. Will growth continue unabated, in an unplanned, haphazard manner, or will decentralization strategies and growth-diversion measures effect desired changes? In economically poor countries and in those saddled with massive foreign debts, fiscal capacity, management, and political motivation may hinder these attempts.

A second theme is that these cities will continue to be incorporated into the global economy. This holds especially true for the socialist cities of Phnom Penh, Ho Chi Minh City, and Hanoi. Consequently, manifestations of globalization processes at the local scale will become more apparent. For example, the mushrooming of McDonald's, Starbucks, and Kentucky Fried Chicken franchises will continue. But underneath these superficial changes lie deeper structural transformations resulting from the infusion of foreign capital. Just as political revolutions had impacts on urban areas in the socialist countries, social changes, such as the emergence of a new urban middle class, are likely to stem from and reflect back on urban transformations.

Part and parcel of increased globalization is the continued mobility of workers throughout the region. Whether they are in the form of internal movements or international migrations, the resultant population changes will further test the social and political stability of the cities and countries of Southeast Asia. Recent events in the Central Highland of Vietnam should serve as a warning. Likewise, the ethnic diversity of some cities, such as Singapore and Kuala Lumpur, will continue to influence urban planning efforts.

Southeast Asia, because of its strategic location and longstanding ties to the global economy, is destined to grow ever more important in world affairs. The cities of Southeast Asia will continue to transform, and be transformed, by broader global changes.

SUGGESTED READINGS

Askew, Marc. 1994. *Interpreting Bangkok: The Urban Question in Thai Studies*. Bangkok: Chulalongkorn University. A look at various facets of Thailand's primate capital.

Berner, Erhard. 1997. *Defending a Place in the City: Localities and the Struggle for Urban Land in Metro Manila*. Quezon City, Philippines: Ateneo de Manila University Press. An examination of the complex issues of land rights and squatting in overburdened Manila.

Bishop, Ryan, John Phillips, and Wei Wei Yeo. 2003. *Postcolonial Urbanism: Southeast Asian Cities and Global Processes*. New York: Routledge. A collection of essays that explore topics such as sexuality, architecture, cinema, and terrorism within the context of global urbanism.

Dale, Ole Johan. 1999. *Urban Planning in Singapore: The Transformation of a City*. Oxford: Oxford University Press. A study of the process of urban planning in Singapore from its early growth on the banks of the Singapore River to the present.

Evers, Hans-Dieter and Rüdiger Korff. 2000. *Southeast Asian Urbanism: The Meaning and Power of Social Space.* Singapore: Institute of Southeast Asian Studies. Examines a variety of topics related to the urbanization process, such as the cultural creativity found in slum areas.

Ginsburg, Norton, Bruce Koppel, and Terry McGee, eds. 1991. *The Extended Metropolis: Settlement Transition in Asia.* Honolulu: University of Hawaii Press. A variety of authors look at various aspects of some of the key cities of Asia.

Logan, William S. 2000. *Hanoi: Biography of a City.* Seattle: University of Washington Press. An exploration of Hanoi's built environment and how the shape of the city reflects changing political, cultural, and economic conditions.

McGee, Terry. 1967. *The Southeast Asian City: A Social Geography of the Primate Cities of Southeast Asia.* New York: Praeger. An urban geography classic.

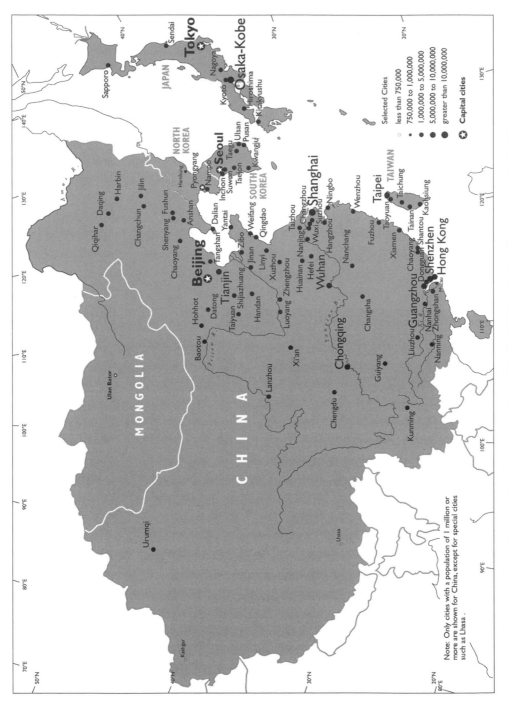

Figure 11.1 Major Cities of East Asia. *Source:* Data from UN, *World Urbanization Prospects: 2005 Revision,* http://esa.un.org/unup/.

11

Cities of East Asia
JACK F. WILLIAMS AND KAM WING CHAN

KEY URBAN FACTS

Total Population	1.54 billion
Percent Urban Population	44.5%
China	40.4%
Remainder	69.9%
Total Urban Population	678 million
China	532 million
Remainder	146 million
Most Urbanized Country	South Korea (80.8%)
Least Urbanized Country	China (40.4%)
Annual Urban Growth Rate	2.4%
China	2.7%
Remainder	0.9%
Number of Megacities	4
Number of Cities of More Than 1 Million	105
China	84*
Remainder	25
Three Largest Cities	Tokyo, Shanghai, Osaka–Kobe
World Cities	Tokyo, Osaka, Beijing, Shanghai, Hong Kong, Seoul
Global City	Tokyo

   * See box 11.2.

KEY CHAPTER THEMES

1. China is one of the original centers of urban development in history and has some of the oldest continuously occupied cities in the world.

2. Colonialism had a less important role in urban development in East Asia in comparison with other realms of the world, even though many large Chinese cities were treaty ports under colonialism and Hong Kong and Macau were entirely creations of colonialism, which formally ended in this region on the eve of the 21st century.

3. Japan, South Korea, Hong Kong/Macau, and Taiwan are already highly urbanized and deeply involved in the global economy, a status reflected in cities that are already in a "post-industrial" phase, with predominantly service-based economies and major high-tech sectors.

4. China has been following in the footsteps of the rest of the region since the late 1970s and is now one of the most rapidly urbanizing countries in the world and a major player in the global economy.

5. China is unique in being the country with the largest total population and in still being primarily rural in its population distribution, yet it has the largest urban population and the greatest number of million-plus cities of any country in the world.

6. Some of the world's most important world cities are in East Asia, especially Tokyo and Hong Kong, with cities such as Shanghai, Beijing, Seoul, and Taipei in the second tier. The larger cities especially reflect the wealth of the region.

7. North Korea is the lone holdout in East Asia in clinging to a rigid, isolationist, socialist system in its cities and economic development, in contrast with China and Mongolia, which are leaving that era to history.

8. Urban development in the region was heavily influenced by the Cold War, which lingers on in the Korean peninsula, and by the ongoing dispute between Taiwan and mainland China.

9. Most major cities of the region show evidence of the concentric zone and multinucleic models of urban land use.

10. Most cities of East Asia have experienced the usual urban problems: environmental pollution, income polarization, and, especially in China, migration, both internal and international.

East Asia exudes power and success. Nowhere is this more evident than in its great cities, such as Tokyo, Beijing, Shanghai, Seoul, Hong Kong, and Taipei (fig. 11.1). Emerging in the past half century to rival the old power centers of the world—North America and Europe—East Asia's cities have been the command centers for the prodigious economic advances of much of this region. These are also among the largest cities in the world; indeed, Tokyo has been widely recognized as the world's largest metropolis for the last three decades. Compared with the often-struggling urban agglomerations found in poorer realms of the world, East Asia's cities have been relatively more successful in coping with rapid growth and large size. Wealth does make a difference.

The region is still sharply split between China, which is rapidly urbanizing but still only about 43% urban, and the rest of the region, which is already around 71% urban. This dichotomy is reflected in many ways, including the character of the cities and the processes, past and present, that have shaped them. One can get some sense of the relative strengths and weaknesses of East Asia's cities from various international rankings that are done from time to time. In the economic arena, a recent scholarly analysis of 314 cities in the world placed three Asian cities among the world's top 6 "international cities"; 2 of them are in East Asia (Hong Kong and Tokyo).[1]

In "quality of living" (QOL) rankings, especially those produced for use by Western expatriates, however, Asian cities tend to fare less well. For example, in the 2007 Mercer QOL survey (www.mercerhr.com), 18 of the top 30 cities were in Western Europe; the rest were in Australia/New Zealand and North America. No Asian cities were in the top 30. Tokyo came out first in East Asia and ranked 35th internationally, followed (in order) by Yokohama, Kobe, Osaka, and Nagoya (38th, 40th, 42nd, and 54th internationally, respectively). Hong Kong came in 70th, Taipei 83rd, Seoul 87th, Shanghai 100th, and Beijing 116th, internationally. In other words, Japanese cities tend to lead the pack in East Asia from a quality-of-living perspective; those in China tend to rank last (ignoring the aberration of North Korea), reflecting that country's ongoing struggle to come to terms with the consequences of the past and of recent rapid economic growth.

THE EVOLUTION OF CITIES

The Traditional or Preindustrial City

East Asia, especially China, is one of the original centers of urbanism in world history. Many cities here can trace their origins directly back two millennia or more. One can see interesting parallels with the earliest cities in other culture realms, with their focus on ceremonial and administrative centers planned in highly formal style to symbolize the beliefs and traditions of the cultures involved.

In its idealized form, the traditional city reflected the ancient Chinese conception of the universe and the role of the emperor as intermediary between heaven and earth. This idealized conception was most apparent in the national capitals, but many elements of this conception (grid layout, highly formalized design, a surrounding wall with strategically placed gates, etc.) could be seen in lesser cities at lower administrative levels. The Tang Dynasty (618–906 A.D.) capital of Changan (present-day Xi'an) was one of the best expressions of the classic Chinese capital city. Inevitably, the demands of modern urban development have necessitated, in the eyes of planners at least, the tearing down of most city walls, and thus the removal of a colorful legacy of the past. The sites of the old walls commonly become the routes of new, broad boulevards. One of the few cities whose original wall has been retained almost in its entirety is Xi'an, because of its historic role.

Of all the historic, traditional cities, none is more famous than Beijing (Peking), the present national capital. Although a city had existed on

[1] This refers to "Class A" cities in Yefang Huang, Yee Leung, and Jianfa Shen, "Cities and Globalization: An International Cities Perspective," *Urban Geography,* 28, no. 3 (2007), 209–231. The study is based on data about the distribution of global producer service firms.

the site for centuries, Beijing became significant when it was rebuilt in 1260 by Kublai Khan as his winter capital. It was this Beijing that Marco Polo saw. The city was destroyed with the fall of the Mongols and the establishment of the Ming dynasty in 1368. Nanjing served as national capital briefly after that, but in 1421 the capital was moved back to the rebuilt city (now named Beijing, or "Northern Capital," for the first time), where it has remained with few interruptions since. The Ming capital was composed of four parts: the Imperial Palace (or Forbidden City), the imperial city, the inner city, and the outer city, arranged like a set of nested boxes. It is the former Forbidden City that can still be partially seen within the walls of what is today called the Palace Museum.

The Chinese City as Model: Japan and Korea

Changan was the national capital at a time when Japan was a newly emerging civilization adopting and adapting many features from China, including city planning. As a result, the Japanese capital cities of the period were modeled after Changan. Indeed, the city as a distinct form first appeared in Japan at this time, beginning with the completion of Keijokyo (now called Nara) in 710. Although Nara today is a rather small prefectural capital, it once represented the grandeur of the Nara period (710–784). Keiankyo (modern-day Kyoto) was to survive as the best example of early Japanese city planning. Serving as national capital from 794 to 1868, when the capital was formally shifted to Edo (now Tokyo), Kyoto still exhibits the original rectangular form, grid pattern, and other features copied from Changan. However, modern urban/industrial growth has greatly increased the size of the city and obscured much of its original form. Moreover, the

Chinese city morphology, with its rigid symmetry and formalized symbolism, was alien to the Japanese culture. Even the shortage of level land in Japan tended to work against the full expression of the Chinese model.

Korea also experienced the importation of Chinese city planning concepts. The Chinese city model was most evident in the national capital of Seoul, which became the premier city of Korea in 1394. The city has never really lost its dominance since. Early maps of Seoul reveal the imprint of Chinese city forms. Those forms were not completely achieved, however, in part because of the rugged landscape around Seoul, which was located in a confining basin just north of the lower Han River. Succeeding centuries of development and rebuilding, especially in the 20th century during the Japanese occupation (1910–1945) and after the Korean War (1950–1953), obliterated most of the original form and architecture of the historic city. A modern commercial and industrial city, one of the largest in the world, has arisen on the ashes of the old city (reinforcing the popular name for Seoul, the "Phoenix City," after the mythological bird that symbolizes immortality). A few relics of the past, such as some of the palaces and a few of the main gates, stand today as a result of restoration efforts.

Colonial Cities

The colonial impact on East Asia was relatively less intrusive than what occurred in Southeast and South Asia, but it was notable nonetheless.

First Footholds: The Portuguese and the Dutch

The Portuguese and the Dutch were the first European colonists to arrive in East Asia; the

Portuguese were much more important in their impact in this region, because the Dutch largely confined themselves to Southeast Asia. Seeking trade and opportunities to spread Christianity, the Portuguese made some degree of penetration into southern Japan via the port of Nagasaki in the later 16th century. Their greatest influence was actually indirect, however, through the introduction of firearms and military technology into Japan. This led to the development of stronger private armies among the *daimyo* (feudal rulers) of Japan, which in turn led to the building of large castles in the center of each *daimyo's* domain. These castles, modeled after fortresses in medieval Europe, were commonly located on strategic high points, surrounded by the *daimyo's* retainers and the commercial town. These centers eventually served as the nuclei for many of the cities of modern Japan.

The Portuguese also tried to penetrate China. Reaching Guangzhou (Canton) in 1517, they attempted to establish themselves there for trade but were forced by the Chinese authorities to accept the small peninsula of Macau, near the mouth of the Pearl River, south of Guangzhou. Chinese authorities walled off the peninsula, and rent was paid for the territory until the Portuguese declared it independent from China in 1849. With only 10 square miles (26 km²) of land (land reclamation in recent years has added a little to the total), Macau remained the only Portuguese toehold in East Asia, especially after the eclipse of their operations in southern Japan in the 17th century. Macau was most important as a trading center and a haven for refugees. The establishment of Hong Kong in the 19th century on the opposite side of the Pearl River estuary signaled the beginning of Macau's slow decline, from which it has never fully recovered.

Figure 11.2   Gambling is a pillar of Macau's economy. The Casino Lisboa (photo taken in 1999) was the flagship gambling house for a long time, until the Venetian Casino, the world's largest, opened in 2007. Macau's gambling revenues are reportedly now larger than those of Las Vegas. (Photo by Kam Wing Chan)

In the post-1950 era, Macau survived largely on tourism (a sort of seedy reminder of what Hong Kong looked like before being Manhattanized) and gambling (a downscale Asian version of Las Vegas, gangsters and all). In the 1990s, Macau attempted some modest industrialization, as it integrated economically with the Zhuhai Special Economic Zone just across the border, and sought to become a regional air hub by constructing an international airport (still underutilized) on reclaimed land (fig. 11.2). Since reversion to the People's Republic of China (PRC) in 1999, the emphasis has been on gambling and tourism, with the addition of investments by Nevada gambling interests and construction of a number of new, gaudy casinos around the reconstructed harborfront that are starting to pull in large numbers of gamblers, especially the *nouveau riche* from a booming China. Right next to the emerging casino quarter lies the historic heart of old Macau that has been restored to its picturesque colonial-era glory and turned into a pedestrian-only area for the tourism business.

The Treaty Ports of China

It was the other Western colonial powers, arriving in the 18th and 19th centuries, that had the greatest impact on the growth of cities in modern China. Most important were the British and Americans, but the French, Germans, Belgians, Russians, and others were also involved, as were the Japanese, who joined the action toward the close of the 19th century.

It all began officially with the Treaty of Nanjing in 1842, which ceded to Britain the island of Hong Kong and the right to reside in five ports—Guangzhou, Xiamen (Amoy), Fuzhou, Ningbo, and Shanghai. Further refinements of this treaty in succeeding years gave to the other powers the same rights as the British (the "Open Door" policy). A second set of wars and treaties (1856–1860) led to the opening of further ports. By 1911, approximately 90 Chinese cities—along the entire coast, up the Chang Jiang (Yangtze River) valley, in North China, and in Manchuria—with a third of a million foreign residents, were opened as treaty ports or open ports (fig. 11.3).

The treaty ports introduced a dynamic new order into traditional Chinese society. The Westerners were there to make money, but they also had the right of extraterritoriality, which guaranteed them protection by Western legal procedures. Gradually, taxation, police forces, and other features of municipal government were developed by the colonial countries controlling the treaty ports. China's sovereignty thus was supplanted in cities in the concession areas, leased in perpetuity by the foreigners for modest rents paid to the Chinese government.

Shanghai

The most important treaty port was Shanghai ("On the Sea"), which had existed as a small settlement for two millennia. By the 18th century, the city was a medium-sized county seat with a population of about 200,000 and was built in traditional city style, with a wall. Deposition of silt by the Chang Jiang over the centuries, however, had made Shanghai no longer a port directly fronting the sea. The town was now located about 15 miles (24 km) up the Huangpu River, a minor tributary of the Chang Jiang.

Western control of Shanghai began with the British concession in 1846 and expanded over the years to cover most of the city. In 1863, the British and American areas were joined to form the Shanghai International Settlement, which by the heyday of the 1920s contained some 60,000 foreigners, the largest concentration in China. Shanghai, as well as the other treaty ports, served as magnets for wealthy Chinese entrepreneurs and for millions of impoverished peasants seeking a haven in a disintegrating China. The wealthy Chinese invested in manufacturing and other aspects of the commercial economy; the peasants provided abundant cheap labor. By the end of its first century under Western control,

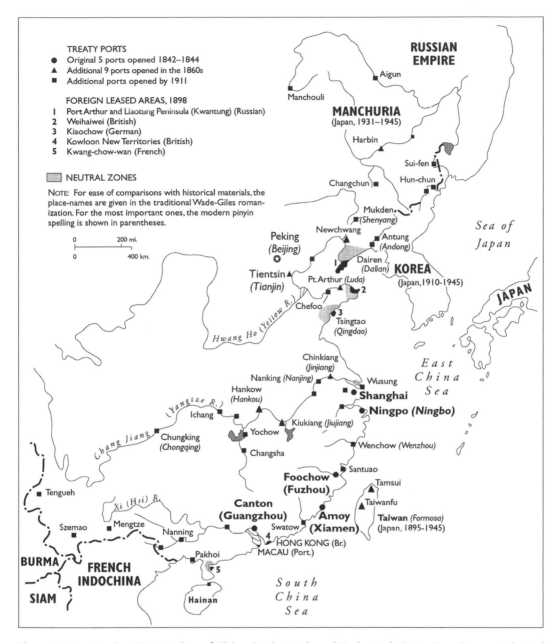

Figure 11.3   Foreign Penetration of China in the 19th and Early 20th Centuries. *Source:* Adapted from J. Fairbank et al., *East Asia: Tradition and Transformation* (Boston: Houghton Mifflin, 1973), 577.

just before World War II, Shanghai handled half of China's foreign trade and had half the country's mechanized factories. The city's population of 4 million made it one of the largest cities in the world; it was more than twice the size of its nearest rivals, Beijing and Tianjin.

Shanghai profited from a natural locational advantage near the mouth of the Chang Jiang delta for handling the trade of the largest and most populous river basin in China. During the 20th century, Shanghai's manufacturing was able to compete successfully with that of other centers emerging in China, despite the absence of local supplies of raw materials, because of the ease and cheapness of water transport. This was achieved also in spite of occupying a relatively poor site—an area of deep silt deposits, a high water table, poor natural drainage, an insufficient water supply, poor foundations for modern buildings of any great height, and a harbor on a narrow river that required regular dredging for oceangoing ships. Shanghai thus became one of the best examples in the world of how a superb relative location can trump a poor physical site to create a great city.

There was a colonial impact on other Chinese cities, too, of course. Particularly significant was the Japanese impact. In Manchuria (Northeast China), which the Japanese took over in the 1930s, many of the major cities were modernized and developed along Western lines—a style which the Japanese had adopted in the development of their own cities after 1868. The Japanese also introduced the beginnings of the industrial base that was to make Manchuria the most important industrial region in China up to that time. Industry was concentrated in a string of major cities, particularly Harbin, Changchun, and Shenyang, connected by the railway network that the Japanese built. As with Shanghai, in these cities there arose a new Western-type commercial/industrial city alongside the traditional Chinese city, which was eventually engulfed and left behind as a remnant of the past.

The Japanese Impact

The Japanese also greatly influenced the urban landscape in their two other colonies in East Asia. During their rule of Taiwan (1895–1945) and Korea (1910–1945), the Japanese introduced essentially the same Western-style urban planning practices, filtered through Japanese eyes, that they later brought to Manchuria's cities. Taipei (renamed Taihoku) was made the colonial capital of Taiwan and transformed from an obscure Chinese provincial capital into a relatively modern city of about 250,000. The city wall was razed, roads and infrastructure were improved, and many colonial government buildings were constructed. The most prominent was the former governor's palace, with its tall, red-brick tower, which still stands in the heart of old Taipei and is now used as the Presidential Office and executive branch headquarters for Taiwan's democratic government. Like Taipei, Seoul was also transformed to serve the needs of Japanese colonial rule on the Korean peninsula. In Seoul's case, however, this meant deliberately tearing down traditional palaces and other structures and replacing them with Japanese colonial buildings as part of a brutal effort to stamp out Korean resistance to Japanese rule.

Hong Kong

Hong Kong ("Fragrant Harbor") differed from other treaty ports in that there was little pretense of Chinese sovereignty there (though the PRC government insisted after 1949 that Hong Kong was part of China). Hong Kong was ceded to Britain at the same time Shanghai was opened up in the early 1840s. Hong Kong became second only to Shanghai as the most important entrepôt on the China coast during the following century of colonialism.

The reason for the importance of Hong Kong is not difficult to see. In 1842, the city was established with the acquisition of Hong

Kong Island, a sparsely populated rocky island some 70 miles (113 km) downstream from Guangzhou (Canton). The Kowloon peninsula across the harbor was obtained in a separate treaty in 1858. Then, in 1898, the New Territories—an expanse of islands and land on the large peninsula north of Kowloon—were leased from China for 99 years (hence, reversion to China took place in 1997), creating a total area of about 400 square miles (1,040 km²) for the entire colony. The site factor that so strongly favored its growth was its inclusion of one of the world's great natural harbors (Victoria Harbor), between Hong Kong Island and Kowloon. Indeed, the advantages of the harbor outweighed the site disadvantages—limited level land for urban expansion, an inadequate water supply, and insufficient farmland nearby to feed the population. The city's location at the mouth of southern China's major drainage basin gave Hong Kong a large hinterland, which greatly expanded when the north–south railway from Beijing was pushed through to Guangzhou in the 1920s. Thus, for about a century, Shanghai and Hong Kong, two great colonial creations, largely dominated China's foreign trade and links with the outside world.

Japan: The Asian Exception

Following the development classic capitals of Nara and Kyoto around the 8th century, other cities, principally the centers of feudal clans, were established in Japan. Most of these were transitory, but a sizeable number survived into the modern era. One of the best-preserved historic towns today is Kanazawa, on the Sea of Japan in the Hokuriku region. The city was left behind by Japan's modernization after 1868 and escaped the devastation of World War II because it had no industrial

or military importance. Historic preservation since the 1960s has retained much of the lovely 19th century architecture and character of the old city, a rare exception to the urban development patterns found throughout most of Asia.

Japan is referred to as the "Asian exception" because it had only a minor colonial experience internally. Indeed, Japan was itself a major colonial power in Asia. Hence, the urban history of Japan involved an evolution almost directly from the premodern, or traditional, city to the modern commercial/industrial city. Japan did have treaty ports and extraterritoriality imposed on it by the Treaty of 1858 with the United States, which led to foreigners residing in Japan as they did in China. However, this colonial phase was short-lived. Japan was able to change its system and reestablish its territorial integrity by emulating rather than resisting the West. Extraterritoriality came formally to an end in 1899, as Japan emerged an equal partner among the Western imperial powers. The relatively benign impact of the Western colonial presence in Japan can still be seen in a few places, nonetheless, such as the former colonial residential area in Kobe.

Gradual political unification during the Tokugawa period (1603–1868) led to the establishment of a permanent network of cities in Japan. The castle town served as the chief catalyst for urban growth. One of the most important of these new castle towns to emerge at this time was Osaka. In 1583, a grand castle was built that served as the nucleus for the city to come. Various policies stimulated the growth of Osaka and other cities, including prohibitions on foreign trade after the mid-1630s, the destruction of minor feudal castles, and prohibitions on building more than one castle per province. These

Figure 11.4   The beautifully restored castle of Hikone, in Shiga Prefecture, central Honshu, is a classic example of an old castle town from Japan's feudal past. (Photo by Jack Williams)

policies had the effect of consolidating settlements and encouraging civilians to migrate to the more important castle communities.

The new castle towns, such as Osaka, were ideally located (fig. 11.4). Because of their economic and administrative functions, they generally were located on level land near important landscape features that gave the castle towns an advantage for future urban growth. Thus, Osaka emerged as the principal business, financial, and manufacturing center in Tokugawa Japan. The cities of that period were tied together by a network of highways that stimulated trade and city growth. The most famous of these early roads was the Tokaido Highway, running from Osaka eastward through Nagoya (which emerged as another major commercial and textile manufacturing center) to the most important city of this period and after—Edo (Tokyo).

Among the major cities of Asia, Tokyo was a relative latecomer. It was founded in the 15th century, when a minor feudal lord built a rudimentary castle on a bluff near the sea, about where the Imperial Palace stands today. The site was a good one, however, for a major city—it had a natural harbor, hills that could easily be fortified, and plenty of room on the Kanto Plain behind for expansion. Tokyo really got its start, though, a century later, when Ieyasu, the Tokugawa ruler at that time, decided to make Edo his capital. Part of Tokyo still bears the imprint of the grand design that Ieyasu and his descendants laid out. They planned the Imperial enclosure, a vast area of palaces, parks, and moats in the very heart of the city. Much of the land on which central Tokyo stands today was reclaimed from the bay, a method of urban expansion that was to typify Japanese city building from then on, reflecting the shortage of level land and the need for good port facilities. By the early 17th century, Edo already had a population of 150,000, surrounding the most magnificent castle in Japan. By the 18th century, the

Figure 11.5   This dramatic entranceway to the train station in Osaka reveals the modernity of Japan and the sophistication of its transportation system. Yet Osaka still struggles to compete with Tokyo for economic growth and influence in contemporary Japan. (Photo by Kam Wing Chan)

population was well over 1 million, making Edo one of the largest cities in the world.

Edo's growth was based initially on its role as a political center, tied to the other cities by an expanding network of roads. An early dichotomy was established between Osaka, as the business center, and Tokyo, as the cultural and political center, that lingers even today in the rivalry between the two (fig. 11.5). With the restoration of Emperor Meiji in 1868, Japan's modern era began. The emperor's court was moved from Kyoto to Edo, which was renamed Tokyo ("Eastern Capital") to signify its additional role as national political capital. This transfer of political functions, combined with the great industrialization and modernization program that was undertaken from the 1870s on, gave Tokyo a boost that launched it on its astounding 20th-century growth trajectory.

INTERNAL STRUCTURE OF EAST ASIAN CITIES

It is not easy to generalize about the internal structure of cities in East Asia. This is partly because of the basic division between socialist and nonsocialist urban systems that characterized the region for so long. It also is because of the imperfect fit of Western urban models to even the nonsocialist cities of the region. In most of East Asia, and now increasingly also in reformist China, the forces that have produced and continue to shape cities are much the same as in the Western world, but with modifying local conditions peculiar to each country and society. These forces include (1) rapid industrialization focused in cities, combined with increasing inequalities between urban and rural residents, leading to high rates of rural-to-urban migration, rates which have now tapered off in the more developed economies (Japan, South Korea, Taiwan), but which are escalating in China (and Mongolia); (2) private ownership of property and dominance of private investment decisions affecting land use; (3) varying degrees of government involvement in zoning and urban planning, some of it successful but a great deal of it ineffective; (4) high standards of living and consumption and increasing reliance on the private automobile (or motorcycle) for transportation, in spite of often very good public transport systems; and (5) a relatively high degree of racial (ethnic) homogeneity, but sometimes significant socioeconomic class stratification. These and other factors have had varying degrees of impact on the growth of cities and on how space is used in cities, and hence on the types and severity of problems. Western urban models of the internal structure of cities, discussed elsewhere in this book, do not entirely fit the cities of East Asia. Nonetheless, elements of each model can often be found, as noted in various places in this chapter.

REPRESENTATIVE CITIES

With the exception of (British) Hong Kong and (Portuguese) Macau, the colonial era in East Asia ended with the defeat of Japan in 1945. The emergence of communist governments in the late 1940s in China and North Korea, joining the already communist government of Mongolia (established in the 1920s),

split the region into two distinctly different paths of urban (and national) development: the path of the socialist cities of China, North Korea, and Mongolia versus that of the nonsocialist (free-market) cities of Japan, South Korea, Taiwan, Hong Kong, and Macau. This became the basic classification of cities of the region until the late 1970s at least. It also reflected the alignment of the Cold War era in this part of the world. In the late 1970s, China entered the post-Mao or Reform Era, in which free-market forces increasingly began to drive the economy and determine the path of urban development. Only North Korea remains basically wedded to a rigid socialist path, one of the last holdouts in the world as the great experiment with communism as an alternative path of national development came to a grinding halt.

One can also classify the major cities of the region on the basis of function and size. From this perspective, several cities illustrate distinctive types: megalopolises or superconurbations (Tokyo); recently decolonized cities (Hong Kong); primate cities (Seoul); regional centers (Taipei); and formerly socialist cities undergoing transformation (Beijing and Shanghai).

Tokyo and the Tokaido Megalopolis: Unipolar Concentration

Japan illustrates especially well the phenomenon of superconurbations or megalopolises. A distinctive feature of Japan's urban pattern is the concentration of its major cities into a relatively small portion of an already small country. In spite of more than a century of industrialization, Japan did not pass the 50% urban figure until after World War II. Between 1950 and 1970, the percentage of people living in cities with a population of 50,000 or more

Figure 11.6 The A-Bomb Dome, officially the Hiroshima Peace Memorial, is now on the list of World Heritage Sites. It survived the nuclear explosion that ravaged the city on August 6, 1945, and now stands as a symbol of the need to eliminate nuclear weapons. (Photo by George Pomeroy)

rose from 33% to 64%, while the total urban population reached 72%, a figure comparable to that of the United States in the same year. In other words, Japan went through a process in 25 years that took many decades in the United States. Since 1970, the proportion of the population that is urban has continued to increase, but more slowly, reaching 78% by the late 1990s (and projected to reach 85% by 2025). As the urban population grew dramatically, so did the number and size of cities. Small towns and villages (those with fewer than 10,000 people) declined sharply in numbers and population, whereas medium and large cities grew rapidly, all the outcome of Japan's phenomenal economic growth after the war.

Almost all major cities are found in the core region. (The one significant exception is Sapporo, the regional center of the northern island of Hokkaido.) This region consists of a narrow band that begins with the urban node of the tri-cities of Fukuoka, Kitakyushu, and Shimonoseki at the western end of the Great Inland Sea, which separates the major islands of Japan and stretches eastward along both shores of Honshu and Shikoku to the Tokyo region. In between, especially along the southern coast of Honshu, are strings of industrial cities, such as Hiroshima, which grew to importance in the last century (fig. 11.6).

Within this core is an inner core, containing more than 44% of Japan's total population of 126 million, known as the Tokaido Megalopolis (named after the Tokugawa-era road through this area) and consisting of three urban/industrial nodes: (1) Keihin (Tokyo–Yokohama), with more than 30 million people; (2) Hanshin (Osaka–Kobe–Kyoto), with more than 16 million; and (3) Chukyo (Nagoya), at nearly 9 million. There really are two distinct parts of Japan, in fact, in a classic core–periphery imbalance—the "developed" capital region centered on Tokyo, and the

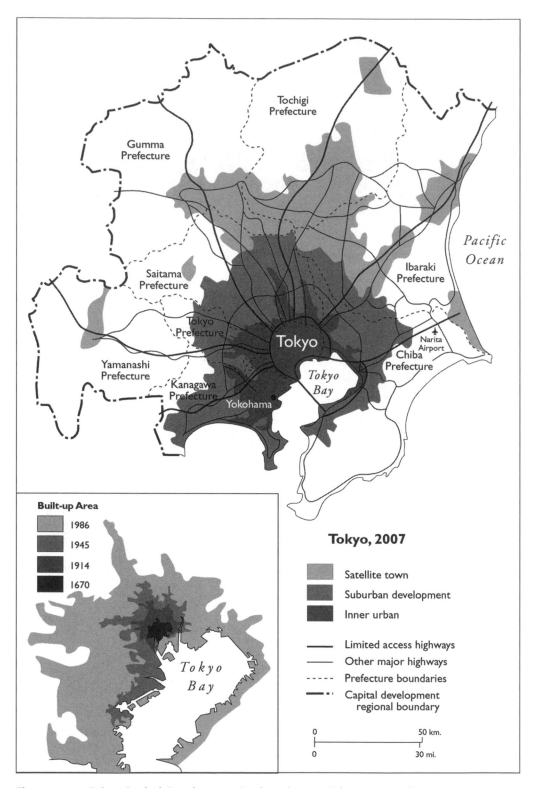

Figure 11.7 Tokyo Capital Development Region. *Source:* Tokyo Metropolitan Government.

Figure 11.8   This Landsat image of the Tokyo Bay region illustrates the sprawl of Greater Tokyo, which completely surrounds the bay along a largely human-made coastline. The Tokyo Bay Aqua Line, a combination bridge-tunnel connecting Tokyo City (upper left) with Chiba Prefecture (lower right), is faintly visible (the white streak in the middle is the entrance to the tunnel). (Landsat image)

"underdeveloped" regions (in a relative sense) elsewhere in Japan (fig. 11.7). Rapid growth from the late 1950s through the early 1970s saw a shift from rural areas to big cities. Since then, migration and growth have been increasingly toward Tokyo at the expense of the rest of the country, including Tokyo's long-standing rival, Osaka, a phenomenon dubbed *unipolar concentration* (i.e., urban primacy). Tokyo continues to expand, draining people and capital investment from the other regions, many of which are stagnating. The Osaka region (also known by the premodern name of Kansai) has not seen

---

Box 11.1 Tokyo Consumers

As a marketplace, Tokyo has distinctive attributes that distinguish it from other Japanese cities. First, the sheer size and the average level of household income: on both counts, Tokyo definitely holds the edge, and year by year since the 1970s, the margin in Tokyo's favor has widened. Second, Tokyo has for more than a century combined East and West, past and present, with a style and verve that has sharpened the sophistication of consumers.

Beyond that, Tokyo's consumers are unusually willing to push the boundaries of fashion, to expand the range of wants by seizing on a product, and to initiate the buzz that starts a trend or launches a new fad. For clothing, accessories, and electronic consumer products, Tokyo is the mecca for shoppers looking for the latest fashions and technologies and, by the same token, for producers waiting to try out their latest offerings. Harajuku, Shibuya, and Aoyama are where Tokyo's young and well-heeled consumers congregate, sample the newest fashions in clothing and accessories, and pass judgment. For instance, Shibuya station, where six different train lines meet, caters to 2.2 million passengers per day and has more than 900 retail stores within the train station itself, with close to 600 restaurants and bars just outside the train station.

Ten percent of all electronics sales and a rising volume of sales of video games and software in Japan occur in Akihabara, which has come to be known as "Electric Town." The strength of this district lies in its wide product offerings, ranging from the newest finished product to the smallest parts imaginable, such as transistors and even vacuum tubes. Until 1995, more than 50% of all personal computers sold in Japan were through Akihabara. This sprawling electronics bazaar is where a vast array of products and components jostle for attention and where the pioneering shoppers—the ones who are willing to experiment with new products and to pay premium prices—play a decisive role. Producers need these intensively competitive and demanding markets, which give them rapid and valuable feedback. Akihabara, for example, is a vital part of the innovation system for electronic products, such as digital cameras and now video games, which are the lifeblood of the Japanese electronics industry.

Source: Shahid Yusuf and Kaoru Nabeshime, *Post-Industrial East Asia Cities* (Stanford University Press and World Bank, 2006), 37–38.

---

much growth of new industries to replace its former smokestack industries, such as steel and shipbuilding, and Osaka businesses continue to relocate to Tokyo. This combination encourages out-migration and depresses personal consumption. Nagoya has fared somewhat better than Osaka by managing to maintain employment and central-city vitality. For people eager to be in the mainstream of modern Japan, living in or near Tokyo is essential.

Tokyo truly is a primate city; its dominance within Japan is awesome (box 11.1). Tokyo's roughly one-quarter share of Japan's total

Figure 11.9   The Ginza is the swankiest and most expensive shopping area in Tokyo. Major department stores and hundreds of boutiques compete for attention and the contents of shoppers' wallets in this affluent Japanese society, the richest in Asia. (Photo by Jack Williams)

population is concentrated in barely 4% of the nation's land area. The city's population density is 16 times that of the country. Whatever quantitative measures one uses, Tokyo has a disproportionate share, whether of workers, factories, headquarters of major corporations and financial institutions, institutions of higher education, industrial production, exports, or college students. As the national capital, Tokyo has all the major governmental functions. All 47 prefectural governments have branch offices in Tokyo, in order to maintain effective liaison with the national government. One observer likened the situation to that of the Tokugawa era of the 18th century, when the provincial feudal lords were required to maintain a second household in what was then Edo (as hostages, in effect), as a means of maintaining the power of the Tokugawa Shogunate. The obeisance to Tokyo remains, albeit in a new form.

Tokyo City itself has increased in population only slightly, while the 23 central city wards have actually declined. By contrast, the three key surrounding prefectures (Saitama, Chiba, Kanagawa) gained significantly, evidence of the sprawl into satellite towns and cities. Because land has become so scarce and expensive in Tokyo, virtually the entire perimeter of Tokyo Bay now consists of reclaimed land (fig. 11.8).

Western influences played some role in the prewar development of Tokyo. However, the devastation of the 1923 earthquake and

Box 11.2   Defining the Chinese City

Mainland China has probably the most complicated and confusing system of urban and city definitions in the world owing to its *hukou* system (see box 11.3), which often excludes migrants without local *hukou* in the local population counts of the city, and to its way of designating urban areas, as explained below. This complexity is compounded by the rapidity of change in the country. A Chinese city or municipality (*shi*) is a political-administrative unit, usually covering an area much larger than the urban (i.e., urbanized) area as we know it. Many large Chinese cities today have urbanized cores (high-density built-up areas), surrounded by numerous towns and large stretches of rural (predominantly agricultural) land. These cities are so large in area that they are aptly called "regions," and in some case, "provinces"—in fact, four of them are officially provincial-status "cities." The most extreme example is Chongqing, which has an administrative area of 31,800 square miles (82,300 km^2) (about the size of the entire country of Austria), and a population of 30.5 million in 2000. This figure cannot be taken as the population of the "metropolitan area" or "urban agglomeration," however, as it is often mistakenly labeled by the less informed. The same situation also applies to Beijing, Shanghai, and many other large cities.

For studying city development, we need to delimit a city with a meaningful geographical boundary. Almost all cities of any size contain a continuous built-up area (urban core), and many also have nearby residential or industrial suburbs. In addition, many cities, especially in developed countries, have an extensive daily commuting zone closely related functionally to the urban core. However, the current geographical extent of the administrative boundaries of larger Chinese cities goes far beyond this familiar pattern by including rural counties, some with dense farming populations.

Three common population indicators of four of the largest cities in China (based on official census and survey data) are shown in the accompanying table and diagram (fig. 11.10). Among these "city population" indicators, C, which tabulates the population in the urbanized areas of all the districts of the city, is the closest to the concept of "urban

the urgent need for quick rebuilding precluded widespread adoption of Western urban planning ideas. World War II bombing had the same effect. In spite of ambitious plans drawn up immediately after the war, few were implemented. The result was a tendency for the city to grow haphazardly in a manner that resulted in congestion, a disorganized city layout, and the lack of a clear central business district (CBD). In many ways, Tokyo came to resemble Los Angeles, except with a higher population density (and vastly superior public transport). Growth has been concentrated around key subcenters, such as Shinjuku (now the city government headquarters) and Shibuya, and along the key transport arteries (rail and expressway) radiating outward from the old historic core of the Imperial Palace (Chiyoda District) (fig. 11.9). Hence, the city has a distinct

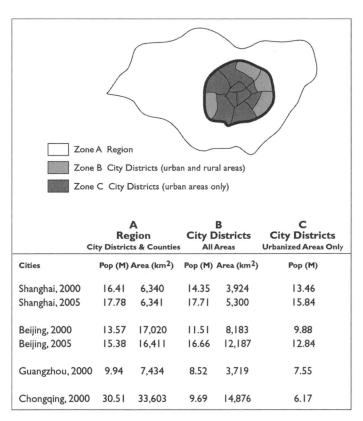

Zone A	Region
Zone B	City Districts (urban and rural areas)
Zone C	City Districts (urban areas only)

Cities	A Region City Districts & Counties		B City Districts All Areas		C City Districts Urbanized Areas Only
	Pop (M)	Area (km²)	Pop (M)	Area (km²)	Pop (M)
Shanghai, 2000	16.41	6,340	14.35	3,924	13.46
Shanghai, 2005	17.78	6,341	17.71	5,300	15.84
Beijing, 2000	13.57	17,020	11.51	8,183	9.88
Beijing, 2005	15.38	16,411	16.66	12,187	12.84
Guangzhou, 2000	9.94	7,434	8.52	3,719	7.55
Chongqing, 2000	30.51	33,603	9.69	14,876	6.17

Figure 11.10   Conceptual Diagram of the Components of a Large City in China. (Kam Wing Chan)

agglomerations" used by the United Nations though it is still "overbounded" because it includes population in some urbanized areas which do not have much labor market linkage with the core city.

concentric ring pattern intermixed with elements of the multinucleic model. The city also has elements of the American-style "doughnut" model, because of spiraling land costs in the 1980s and desertion by middle-class people seeking affordable suburban housing. They commute to the central city to work in the daytime, but return to the suburbs in the evening. Unlike in U.S. cities, however, there are no serious racial/socioeconomic class differences fueling this residential pattern, except for those relating to the minority *burakumin* (untouchables, a social legacy of Japan's feudal past that stubbornly lingers on), and the Korean minority, who tend to live in their own ghettoes.

Japan's "bubble" economy burst starting in the early 1990s, when both residential and commercial land prices peaked at 200–300% of what they were in the early 1980s. Land prices slid precipitously downward, returning to early 1980s levels or lower by the early 2000s. The bottom of the real estate bust appears to have been reached, at least for Tokyo.

Beijing: The Less Forbidden City

Beijing, the great "Northern Capital" for centuries, was a horizontal, compact city of magnificent architecture and artistic treasures of China's past grandeur when the "New China" began in 1949, although the magnificence of the old city had suffered greatly from general neglect during the century of foreign intrusion, civil war, and "revolutionary reconstruction" since the 1840s. Centered on the former Forbidden City (Imperial Palace), Beijing was renowned for its sophisticated culture and refined society. The beautiful Beijing dialect (Mandarin) became the national spoken language (*putonghua*) after the collapse of the dynasty in 1911. The city's only real function was as political and cultural center of a vast nation. There was little industry and a small population.

In 1949 the city was chosen as the national capital of the new communist government (Nanjing was the national capital during the republican era, from the late 1920s to 1949). During the 50 years after 1949, Beijing expanded from 1.7 million people in 24 square miles (62 km^2) to a metropolis with an administrative area of about 6,500 square miles (16,800 km^2). This huge Beijing administrative region housed 15.4 million people in 2005. It includes 16 city districts and 2 counties, but some of the districts and counties are only partly urban. Nor is this large area a "metropolitan area" as it is often mistakenly conceived (box 11.2). Only 12.8 million in this area are considered "urban." The population growth occurred as a result of the

physical expansion of the administrative area, natural population growth, and net migration. During the 1960s and 1970s, migration to the city was strictly regulated. Indeed, because of its prime importance as the restored national capital, migration to Beijing was the most strictly controlled among all China's cities. Only the well-educated and those needed for the jobs created by the central government could move to Beijing; for the rest, it remained the "forbidden city."

Functionally, Beijing was also transformed into a *producer* city, as it became one of China's key industrial centers, while retaining its ongoing function as center of government, culture, and education. Other functions such as commerce and services were greatly curtailed in the command-type economy geared to central planning and five-year plans, much like those of the then Soviet Union. Beijing became even more strongly the power center of China, analogous to Moscow.

The changes inflicted on Beijing's urban landscape were enormous in the Maoist era (1949–1976), especially during the Cultural Revolution (1966–1976). Although objectives, policies, and urban plans for Beijing fluctuated during the Maoist era, the end result was the transformation of Beijing into a vast, gray city of arrow-straight, wide boulevards and huge Stalinist-style state buildings, punctuated by seemingly endless rows of drab apartment blocks for the working class, with an emphasis on uniformity, minimal frills, and lowest possible construction costs. The city lacked a human scale and was deliberately designed to emphasize the power of the state (i.e., the Party). The charm of traditional middle-class courtyard houses in *hutong*, or narrow alleys, in the old city was totally lost in the need to subdivide the housing space for

Figure 11.11 Traditional, single-family courtyard houses in a *hutong*, or alley, of old Beijing. Many of these houses today hold several families. These houses are disappearing rapidly to make room for high-rise apartments and offices. (Photo by Kam Wing Chan)

multiple families, but often without the necessary updates and maintenance (fig. 11.11). A huge area in front of the Tiananmen (Gate of Heavenly Peace) entrance to the Palace Museum was cleared of structures, greatly expanding the existing square. As the largest open square of any city in the world, Tiananmen became the staging ground for vast spectacles, parades, and rallies organized by the government. Mao and other party leaders would orchestrate the scene from on top of the gate like a latter-day imperial court (this area is now open to tourists). Not surprisingly, after Mao died in 1976 his body was embalmed and put in a crystal display case inside a huge mausoleum on the south end of Tiananmen Square, exactly along the north–south axis running through the Palace

Museum. The parallel with the display of Lenin's body in Red Square in Moscow was intentional, as was the attempt to link Mao with the imperial tradition and the role of Beijing as the center of China. Though the square was designed and used mostly by those in power, it also became the staging ground of mass protests organized by students, intellectuals, and workers, from the famous May Fourth Movement in 1919 to the failed pro-democracy movement in 1989, which a shocked world watched on television (fig. 11.12).

The greatest sacrilege, in the eyes of some critics, was the tearing down of Beijing's city walls, with only the one around the former Forbidden City having been spared. The sites of the walls became ring roads designed ostensibly to ease traffic flow. Only a few

Figure 11.12   The Monument of People's Heroes in Tiananmen Square in Beijing looms behind a parading group of PLA soldiers on a chilly morning in December 1989, shortly after the infamous crackdown of the student-led democracy movement that convulsed through China. The square is in the heart of Beijing and is symbolic of so much that is socialist China. (Photo by Kam Wing Chan)

crumbling city gates were kept as relics of another era. A subway system lies under the Second Ring Road. Removal of the walls totally shattered the original form of Beijing and forever altered its architectural character.

To be fair, the government was faced with enormous problems, especially in providing housing and meeting basic human needs. Historic preservation tends to take a backseat to more urgent practical needs in almost every country. Moreover, the government kept the Forbidden City (plus some other national treasures, such as the magnificent Temple of Heaven and the fascinating Summer Palace in northwest Beijing) and worked toward restoration of its former grandeur, transforming the huge enclosure into the Palace Museum (Gu Gong)—a

collection of former palaces, temples, and other structures, many housing collections of art from the imperial ("feudal") past. The motive was largely political, but the net result was indeed historic preservation. The Palace Museum remains one of the world's top cultural treasures (fig. 11.13).

China's large cities in the Maoist era were both production (manufacturing) centers and administrative nodes of an economic planning system that focused on national, regional, and local self-reliance. The functions of business and commerce were weak. Most cities tried to build relatively comprehensive industrial structures, resulting in much less division of labor and exchanges than would be found in a market economy. The periurban (adjacent rural) areas controlled by the municipalities

Figure 11.13   The opening of a Starbucks right in the heart of the Palace Museum became a symbol of globalization and China's opening to the outside world. Critics, however, considered the coffee shop at that location a symbol of voracious American capitalism trampling over Chinese culture. The store was closed, replaced by a Chinese-owned teahouse in 2007. Currently, there are over 250 Starbucks franchises in China, the best market outside the United States. (Photo by Kam Wing Chan)

provided food, mainly vegetables, for the cities. Some satellite towns accommodated the spillover of industries. Without a land market, many self-contained work-unit neighborhoods dominated the landscape of large cities, which expanded in concentric zones. Beijing was no exception (fig. 11.14).

The new policies in the late 1970s were meant to cover some of the aforementioned weaknesses and to transform Chinese cities through a series of market reforms. Those reforms have brought rising affluence, especially in the eastern coastal provinces and cities, reflected in the urban consumption boom of the 1980s and after. In Beijing, this has resulted in thousands of new stores and restaurants. Beijing now has major commercial/financial districts, such as Xidan, a busy shopping area with modern architecture and expensive shops, and Wangfujing, an old retail strip that received a major facelift in 1999.

Growing per capita income also fueled a housing boom in the 1990s. With a real estate market beginning to function, a greater demand for floor space has intensified use of urban land. Greater separation of workplace and housing has become increasingly feasible for a portion of the labor force. In the late 1980s, suburbanization began on a noticeable scale. Foreign investment now focuses not only on export processing but also on retail, insurance, finance, and producer services which increased the functional differentiation of city centers and suburbs linked by highways.

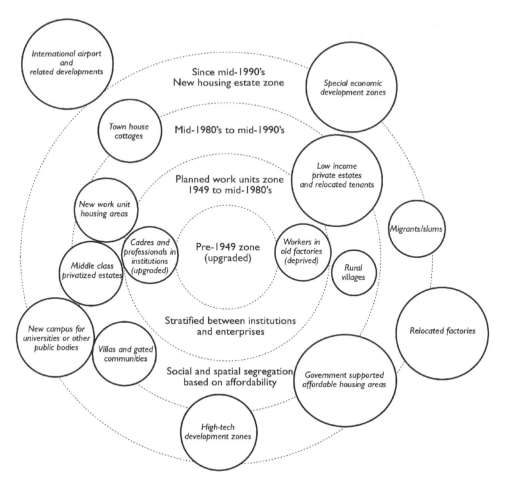

Figure 11.14   Model of the City in the People's Republic of China. *Source:* Adapted from Wang Ya-ping, *Urban Poverty, Housing and Social Change in China* (New York: Routledge, 2004), 44.

To attract industry, Beijing's government has established more than a dozen development zones, mostly in the urban fringe. For example, Zhongguancun, set up in the Haidian District close to China's top universities in the northwest part of the city, is China's "Silicon Valley." Beijing's growth is increasingly linked to the southeast with Tianjin, an international port city with provincial-level status, and to the east with Tangshan, a major center of heavy industry and coal mining, to form one of China's emerging conurbations. This process of outward expansion will intensify along with China's integration with the world, especially as it is now a member of the World Trade Organization (WTO). Beijing, as the home of many major multinational firms, will continue to be a major player in the globalization of the Chinese economy.

The rise in personal income also paralleled a noticeable increase in income disparities and social differentiation. In the outskirts north of Beijing, expensive, detached, Western-style bungalow houses have begun to appear, catering to expatriates and the new rich. At the same

---

Box 11.3   Cities with Invisible Walls

The development strategy pursued by China during the Maoist era (1949–1976) was based on strictly controlling rural-to-urban migration. The major means for doing this was the *hukou* (household registration) system, set up in 1958. Under this system, all citizens were classified as either urban or rural residents. Urban residents had state-guaranteed food grains, jobs, housing, and access to an array of subsidized welfare and social services (known as the *iron rice bowl* system). Rural residents had very few of those and had to rely on themselves or their collectives. These obvious disparities generated strong incentives for rural residents to migrate to urban areas. However, for the great majority of the rural population, the option of migrating to the cities was not available. The government used strong administrative measures to stem migration to the cities. By law, anyone seeking to move to a place different from where his or her household was registered had to get approval from the *hukou* authorities (typically the public security bureau), but approval was rarely granted. In essence, the *hukou* system functioned as an internal passport system, similar to the *propiska* system used in the former Soviet Union and the *ho khau* system in Vietnam. Although old city walls in China had largely been demolished by the late 1950s, the power of this newly erected migration barrier has been likened to "invisible" city walls.

Since the late 1970s, development of markets and the demand for cheap labor for sweatshop productions for the global market have led to easing of some migratory controls. Rural migrants are now allowed to work in cities in low-end jobs shunned by urban residents, but they are not eligible for basic urban social services and education programs. It is estimated that in 2005 about 150 million people were in this category (the so-called floating population, i.e., migrant workers), most of whom are in the cities. This two-tier system of urban citizenship and the unequal treatment of the migrant population have drawn much concern from inside and outside China.

---

time, with the relaxation in migration controls since the mid-1980s, Beijing now has a large migrant ("floating") population of about 4–5 million. These mostly rural migrants fill many low-level jobs shunned by the locals. However, these migrants are not given legal residency status (*hukou*) in the city and are often denied access to many urban services (box 11.3). Most come from the countryside and are poor. Several migrant communities have sprung up in Beijing's outskirts, such as "Zhejiang Village" (fig. 11.15) and "Xinjiang

Village." Living conditions in these migrant villages provide a stark contrast with those of wealthier neighborhoods. In the inner city, laid-off workers from bankrupt state enterprises are gradually forming Beijing's new urban poor.

In the early 1980s, the government became serious about planning for the aesthetics of Beijing's future, trying to bring air and water pollution under some control, and giving the city a more human feel. The 1990 Asian Games provided the stimulus for much beautification

Figure 11.15   Lunchtime in the "Zhejiang Village" on the outskirts of Beijing, a major garment wholesaling center run by migrants from Zhejiang Province in east China. (Photo by Kam Wing Chan)

effort and for improvements in urban infrastructure, such as extending several major expressways across the city and connecting the central city with the airport. Another round of even larger-scale construction was carried out as Beijing prepared to host the Olympic Summer Games in 2008. Many residents hoped the Olympics would transform Beijing into a truly world-class city. But there were also concerns that this massive reconstruction could have a negative impact on the poor, as old houses were torn down and farmers' land expropriated to make way for the well-to-do and for showcases to the outside world. The 2008 Olympic Games definitely put the spotlight on Beijing (and China as a whole).

Shanghai: China's Future?

Shanghai is considered by many to be China's most interesting and vibrant city. This is because of its unique colonial heritage and because in many ways it is the "New York of China"—the center of change and new frontiers in social and economic behavior. Shanghai still is the largest and perhaps the most cosmopolitan city in China (along with perhaps Guangzhou) and has one of the highest standards of living.

Of all China's cities, Shanghai also offers a good example of the past Chinese socialist city, because of its special role within socialist China in both urban planning and national economic development. Shanghai city itself is part of the Shanghai administrative region, comprising 14 city districts and 1 county covering a huge area of 2,400 square miles (6,300 sq km) with a combined total population of over 17.8 million (in 2005) and an urban population of 15.8 million in this region (fig. 11.16).

Shanghai came the closest to a true "producer" city in the socialist era. Prior to the

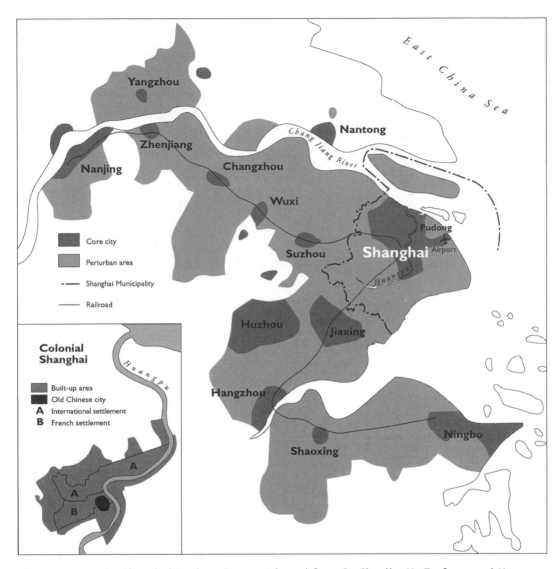

Figure 11.16   The Shanghai Region. *Source:* Adapted from Gu Chaolin, Yu Taofang, and Kam Wing Chan, "Extended Metropolitan Regions: New Feature of Chinese Metropolitan Development in the Age of Globalization," *Planner* 18, no. 3 (2000): 16–20.

reform era, revenues for the Chinese government relied heavily on taxes on state-owned enterprises (SOEs); Shanghai, being the prime center of SOEs, was a major generator of government revenues. This revenue cash cow was heavily favored by the central government and was therefore protected. Not only was competition limited for industry, but prices of manufactured goods were often set high in Shanghai's favor. Between 1953 and 1978, the economic growth of Shanghai averaged about 9% per year, far above the national average. In 1978, this region accounted for 8% of China's GDP and 18% of its exports.

Figure 11.17   Since the early 1990s, Shanghai's new CBD has arisen across the river in Pudong, centered on the futuristic TV observation tower around which modern high-rise buildings have sprung up. Pudong and Shanghai are depicted by the government to be the "Head of the Dragon" in development of the Chang Jiang Valley and the rest of China. (Photo by Jack Williams)

As with many cities in the Maoist era (with the exception of Beijing), little was reinvested in Shanghai in terms of new construction and upgrading of facilities. The downtown area, particularly around the Bund, or riverfront district, where the major Western colonial settlers built trading houses, banks, consulates, and hotels, had the look of a 1930s Hollywood movie set. In 1933 the Park Hotel was built on Nanjing Road, a major commercial artery. That hotel remained the city's tallest building for 49 years, until 1982, when high rises were again constructed. It was the relative neglect of many cities, including Shanghai, that contributed to the impression that the Maoist government was "anti-urban," although the reality was far more complex.

With the reopening of China in the late 1970s, under the "New Open Door" policy, foreigners again returned to China, particularly the coastal zone in Guangdong in the south, this time at the invitation of the Chinese. Although Shanghai was designated as one of the 14 "open cities" (for foreign investment) in 1984, Guangdong was really the initial region developed in cooperation with foreign (including Hong Kong) capital. Thus, in the 1980s Shanghai lagged behind Guangdong in attracting foreign capital and in economic growth; its share of the nation's exports declined sharply, to only 7% in 1990 (compared to 20% for Guangdong). The portion of national GDP accounted for by Shanghai also slipped to only 4%. The city's turning point came in 1990 in the aftermath of the 1989 Tiananmen catastrophe, as the government struggled to regain foreign investors' confidence. China decided in April 1990 to open up Pudong ("East of the Pu," i.e., the Huangpu River, which bisects Shanghai), an essentially farming region on the east side of the old city core (fig. 11.17).

Figure 11.18   In this corner of the People's Park, Shanghai, Saturday morning is time for the "marriage market," when parents help their adult children, most of whom live overseas, look for prospective spouses. (Photo by Kam Wing Chan)

The new development plan established a package of preferential policies, very similar to those in China's five export-oriented special economic zones (SEZs), to woo foreign capital. These policies included lower taxes, lease rights on land, and retention of revenues. The Pudong plan emphasized high-tech industries and financial services rather than simply export processing. Pudong was also supposed to be the answer to choking congestion in the old city center and the catalyst for the renaissance of Shanghai as a whole (fig. 11.18). Foreign investors were encouraged to get in on the ground floor of what is touted as one of China's most ambitious undertakings. Among the foreign investors, Taiwanese businesses have been some of the most important in Pudong. Shanghai is now home to several thousand Taiwanese companies, with an estimated 200,000–300,000 Taiwanese residing nearby. A "Little Taipei" has emerged in the Zhangjiang High-Tech Park in Pudong.

With the full backing of the central government, Shanghai improved its infrastructure and throughout the 1990s greatly strengthened its role as China's prime economic and financial center (figs. 11.19 and 11.20). The Shanghai Stock Exchange opened in December 1990 and was designated to become the financial hub of a more powerful future China. The skyline of Pudong is intentionally

Figures 11.19 and 11.20   These two photos dramatically illustrate the transformation of Shanghai since the end of the Maoist era. In the mid-1970s, Nanjing Road, a key commercial artery of old Shanghai's International Settlement, slumbered in socialist stagnation. By the end of the 1990s, much of Nanjing Road had been turned into a glittering, throbbing pedestrian mall devoted to high mass consumption and the free-market economy. (Photos by Jack Williams)

futuristic, with flickering neon-lit glass-and-steel skyscrapers, including a TV observation tower that has become an icon for Pudong and the New China. It is quite a contrast to the neo-classical Bund on the other side of the river. Today many of the world's big corporations have set up offices or plants in Shanghai. One survey in the late 1990s even showed that Shanghai had outdistanced Beijing among China's top university graduates as the most popular city in China in which to make a career.

In the bigger scheme, Shanghai is part of a larger, dynamic, and sprawling Chang Jiang delta region composed of a dozen closely linked cities and surrounding counties. This region, stretching from Hangzhou and Ningbo in the southeast to Suzhou and Nanjing in the northwest, contains about 70–80 million people, including many millions of migrants. Wuxi, Suzhou, and Changzhou, and newer county-level cities, such as Kunshan, Jiangyin, Zhangjiagang, and Xiaoshan, are major industrial cities in the urban system. Shanghai definitely has reacquired some of its prerevolutionary glamour (box 11.4). Shops and architecture in some sections have a very cosmopolitan feel and again there is a sizeable expatriate community. The government hopes that Shanghai will become the "Head of the Dragon"—an economic powerhouse that will stimulate development of the whole Chang Jiang valley (the "body" of the dragon) and the whole nation. Critics, however, point to a host of problems: serious interjurisdictional rivalries among local governments, inadequate port facilities, unwise location of

Figure 11.20

the new international airport in Pudong, overheated real estate development, serious traffic congestion, and severe pollution. Perhaps most important, Shanghai still lacks a well-established legal system that can truly protect citizens' rights and rein in officials from abuses of their powers. These are criticisms that could be directed at all of China today, for that matter.

Hong Kong: Business as Usual after 1997?

At the stroke of midnight on June 30, 1997, Hong Kong was officially handed over to China and became the Hong Kong Special Administrative Region (HKSAR). This was an extraordinary historic event, marking the end of the colonial era in Asia and the rise of China's power. Hong Kong was one of the last two colonial enclaves left in all of Asia by the late 20th century. The other colony, Macau, likewise was returned to China by Portugal in December 1999 and became the Macau SAR. Hence, as China entered the new century, its humiliating experience with foreign colonialism finally ended after almost 160 years.

The 1997 event committed China to guarantee Hong Kong 50 years of complete

---

Box 11.4   Shanghai Impressions

Kam Wing Chan (December 17, 2005)

Shanghai is enchanting, though quite cold (2°C). This morning I woke up in a warm big bed in the classy Park Hotel to seven windows of glistening modern and ultra-modern skyscrapers with a rising sun behind. What a different Shanghai from what I knew nine years ago!

It was also intense. I arrived quite late last night and missed my dinner. After checking into the hotel, I decided to get some food. In a nearby basement food court, I easily found my favorite beef noodle soup and dainty Shanghai wontons. This was a type of food court I had never seen before—with only chain restaurants. The McD's, Burger King, Pizza Hut, and Yonghe (a noodle chain from Taiwan) all were fighting fiercely face-to-face for a share of the pie in a tiny basement in this global city. Behind all this (figuratively) and me (literally), there were a bunch of 6–7 year olds (where are they from?) running around. On closer look, they were snapping and gobbling up unfinished noodles and food left on the tables. One even approached me for the beef in the soup while I was still working on it! They were obviously hungry, but they also seemed to enjoy themselves doing this, almost like playing a game. They ran and giggled—is that happy or sad?

When I got out of the food court, I realized that I was already on China's busiest pedestrianized shopping street, Nanjing Road. Even though it was already close to 10 p.m., this place was still full of people; many shops were still open. I decided to take a walk and get a feel for the town. There were many slim women, even in their winter coats, scarves, hats, and boots (they must be in vogue), quite chic, of course. I took some pictures of a few illuminated old Western, mostly neoclassical buildings, but soon found myself caught in a struggle, having to continuously fight off solicitations by different kinds of strangers—three flirting women "wanting to make friends," four rather persistent "tour guides," and three beggars in a span of only 20 minutes. What a busy place! With so many years of China experience, I thought I could mingle in a Chinese street crowd; apparently, I couldn't. I think I had the right color, black, for my jacket, but I looked (I was?) a bit older than the average crowd on this street—I had left my Kangol hat in the hotel room. Or perhaps any unattached man strolling alone on a Friday night is an obvious target.

---

autonomy in its internal affairs and capitalist system. China would have control only over Hong Kong's defense and foreign relations. Since 1997, Hong Kong has been under the model known as "one country, two systems." The latter refers to the "socialist" system in the PRC (even though it has deviated from many "socialist" norms) and the full capitalist system in Hong Kong. In the years before the handover, the biggest concern was what would happen after 1997. Indeed, in the decade preceding the transition, these concerns triggered an exodus of about half a million Hong Kongers, mostly wealthy professionals, to Canada (especially Vancouver and Toronto), Australia, and the United States. Other observers believed that the inherent assets of Hong Kong, which had fueled its extraordinary economic rise, would see Hong Kong through the stresses of political transfer. So far, the optimists seem generally vindicated, at least on the economic front.

Back in 1949, when Shanghai and the rest of China fell to the communists, few thought that Hong Kong could long survive under British rule. The UN embargo on China during the Korean War effectively cut off most of Hong Kong's entrepôt trade with China. The population soared from half a million in 1946 to more than 2 million by 1950, with refugees fleeing the raging civil war and communist takeover in China. Huge squatter settlements appeared, and the economy was in shambles. The British, in collaboration with Chinese entrepreneurs, including many wealthy industrialists who had fled Shanghai and other parts of China, began to turn Hong Kong's economy around. They did it by developing products, "Made in Hong Kong," for export. It was a spectacularly successful transformation, with investment pouring in from Japan, the United States, Europe, and the overseas Chinese. Cheap, hardworking labor was available. Site limitations were overcome by massive landfill projects, and freshwater and food were purchased from adjacent Guangdong Province.

During the Cold War period of the 1950s and 1960s, Hong Kong commanded a unique geopolitical position. One of the paradoxes of Hong Kong was that China continued to permit this arch symbol of unrepentant Western capitalism and colonialism to exist and thrive on what was rightly Chinese territory. The Chinese did this partly because Hong Kong made lots of money for them,

too—several billion dollars a year in foreign exchange earned from the PRC's exports to Hong Kong and from investments in banking and commerce. Moreover, a struggling, isolationist, socialist China saw practical advantage in keeping the door open a crack to the outside world, and also in not being responsible for solving Hong Kong's then staggering problems. Banker's Row in Central District came to symbolize the financial powerhouse that Hong Kong had become, with the Bank of China, the Hong Kong Shanghai Banking Corporation (HSBC), and the Chartered Bank of Great Britain lined up side by side. The first two are regarded today as among the most important architectural structures of the 20th century and in some ways are symbols of Hong Kong's emergence as a true world city.

One of the top tourist meccas in the world, Hong Kong is, by any standards, a stunning sight, whether one is arriving for the first time or the hundredth (fig. 11.21). The skyline is spectacular, especially at night, with its glittering, ultramodern high-rise buildings packed side by side along the shoreline and up the hillsides. There is so much money to be made in Hong Kong that every inch of space is extremely valuable and must be used to maximum advantage. The authorities have used remarkable ingenuity in designing the road system and other features of the built environment, especially on crowded Hong Kong Island. Kowloon, on the mainland side, has relatively more land, but even there the intricacy of the urban design is impressive. After the international airport moved to Chek Lap Kok on the north shore of Lantau Island in 1997 (now widely regarded as one of the finest airports in the world), building height limitations in Kowloon were ended. The Kowloon side is now taking on the Manhattan-like

Figure 11.21   This view of Hong Kong Island, taken from Kowloon across the harbor, dramatically conveys the modernity and wealth of modern Hong Kong. The Central Plaza building towers over the wave-like profile of the Convention Center, where the handover to China took place in 1997. (Photo by Kam Wing Chan)

profile of Hong Kong Island. There seems no limit to the construction boom and demand for new buildings and other structures. Hong Kong remains incredibly dynamic.

Less eye-catching to the average tourist, but themselves impressive social accomplishments, are Hong Kong's public housing and new town programs. The two were begun simultaneously in the 1950s as measures to cope with the large influx of refugees from China. The programs gradually expanded into some of the world's largest. Today, about half of Hong Kong's population of 7 million lives in public housing. Indeed, because of much lower rents, public housing has been a major mechanism for decentralizing the population outside of the main urban area. Reclamation has been a main strategy for creating new land for the city. Many of the large new towns, such

as Shatin and Tuen Mun, were built almost totally from scratch.

Until the late 1980s, the economy that had fueled the creation of this machine—with the goal of making money, as much and as fast as possible—was heavily based on consumer goods manufacturing and exports, especially textiles, electronics, and toys. The top markets became the United States, Europe, and Japan. But with China's opening in the late 1970s, integration with China escalated rapidly. Hong Kong quickly took advantage of the cheap land and labor in the Pearl River Delta and has steadily outsourced its manufacturing to the delta (whereas company headquarters remain in Hong Kong). Currently, well over 100,000 Hong Kong–invested enterprises operate in the delta region and employ several million workers. In economic terms, the delta and

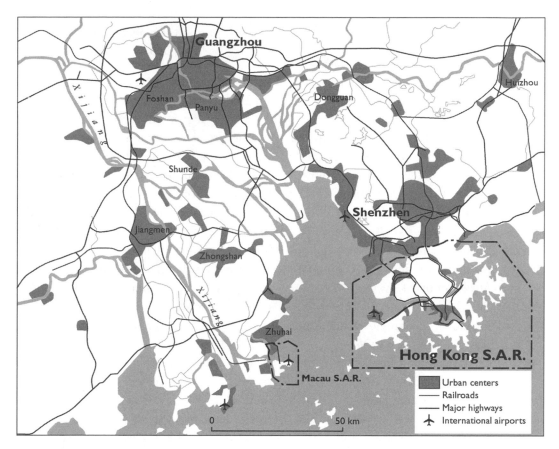

Figure 11.22   Hong Kong and the Pearl River Delta. *Source:* Adapted from various sources.

Hong Kong now form a highly integrated region, one of the world's major global export centers, with Hong Kong serving as the "shop front" and the delta as the "factory" (fig. 11.22).

Hong Kong is the banking and investment center for China's trade, as well as the regional headquarters for many international corporations. In the rapid opening of China, Hong Kong has played a crucial role as the intermediary between China and the world, including serving as middleman for Taiwan's huge economic dealings with the PRC. Tourism remains vital, with the bulk of tourists now coming from the PRC, for whom Hong Kong is often their first taste of the Western capitalist world.

Immediately after handover, the Asian financial crisis of 1997–1998 pushed Hong Kong into a recession that continued past the 9/11 events. A series of mishaps further undermined people's confidence in the new SAR government. Rising economic competition, including from other Chinese cities (especially Shanghai, Shenzhen, and Guangzhou) made many wonder if Hong Kong could maintain its strength and standard of living. It has since pulled out of that recession, but a host of serious problems continue:

1. There is a widespread perception that Hong Kong lacks strong local political leaders in the current SAR structure, and

this weakness has shown in several administrative and policy blunders in such incidents as the public health scare brought on by the bird flu and SARS, and the issues of right of abode and freedom of the press.

2. Environmental problems, especially air and water pollution, have significantly worsened since 2000. The government fears loss of foreign investment, vital to the economy.

3. Guangdong and its cities grow ever stronger, and there is fear of their siphoning off the port and other functions currently dominated by the SAR. Hong Kong still has to define its niche in the evolving global economy of which China is a huge and growing part.

4. The new towns have lost some of their vitality because of changes in the economy. Originally patterned after the British "garden city" concept, as self-contained centers where people lived and worked without need to go to the central city each day, the new towns increasingly have reverted to nothing more than well-planned bedroom suburbs, with workers sometimes having to make long commutes to jobs. Once-thriving factories in the new towns are now largely used as warehouses.

5. Maintaining a balance in relations with mainland China has been a very delicate issue. Many people (inside and outside of Hong Kong) have concerns over the SAR's political and legal autonomy and there are also rising concerns among native Hong Kongers about the inevitable cultural integration of Hong Kong into the PRC.

Whatever happens, Hong Kong's future is irrevocably tied to that of China.

Taipei: A Regional Center in Search of a Region

Although regional centers are found throughout East Asia, a particularly good example is the city of Taipei, which has been emerging from its provincial cocoon in recent years and acquiring some of the aura of a world-class city, following in the footsteps of Hong Kong. There is some ambiguity about how to classify Taipei, because after 1950 it became the "temporary" capital of the Republic of China (ROC) government-in-exile and, as such, experienced phenomenal growth beyond what it might have undergone if it had remained solely the provincial capital of an island province of China. For certain, if the communists had succeeded in capturing Taiwan in 1950, as they had hoped, Taipei would be a vastly different place today, probably something akin to present-day Xiamen (Amoy) across the Taiwan Strait. Instead, Taipei skyrocketed from the modest Japanese colonial capital city of a quarter million in 1945 to the present metropolis of more than 6 million that completely fills the Taipei basin and spills northeast to the port of Keelung, northwest to the coastal town of Tanshui (now a high-rise suburban satellite), and southwest toward Taoyuan and the international airport (fig. 11.23). Functionally, the city shifted gears from being a colonial administrative and commercial center to becoming the control center for one of the most dynamic economies in the postwar world.

When the Republic of China government retreated to Taiwan in 1950, the provincial capital was shifted to a new town built expressly for this purpose in central Taiwan, not far from Taichung. Taipei was theoretically concerned with "national" affairs and hence had all the national government offices re-created there

Figure 11.23   The Taipei Metropolitan Region, with 6 million people, is one of Asia's largest. This relief map was generated from Taiwan DEM data. *Source:* Bor-Wen Tsai, National Taiwan University, October 2007.

(transplanted with administrators and legislators from Nanjing). The provincial capital dealt with agriculture and similar island (local) affairs. This artificial dichotomy, designed to preserve the fiction that the ROC government was the legal government of all of China, held until the early 1990s, when the government finally publicly admitted it had no jurisdiction over the mainland. The impact on Taipei over the decades was great, resulting in a large bureaucracy and the construction of national capital-level buildings in the city. Huge tracts of land formerly occupied by the Japanese were taken over by the government after 1945, and the single-party authoritarian political system under the Kuomintang (KMT) allowed the government to develop the city in whatever way it desired, largely free of open public debate. This even included renaming many streets in Taipei after well-known mainland cities and places, to ease the homesickness of exiled mainlanders. After President Chiang Kai-shek died in 1975, a huge piece of military land in central Taipei was transformed into a gigantic memorial to Chiang, one of the largest public structures in Taiwan. In 2007 the Taiwanese government (under the DPP) attempted to rename the CKS Memorial Hall as the "National Taiwan Democracy Memorial Hall" as part of an ongoing effort to reduce the memories of the KMT era in Taiwan. The renaming ran into legal difficulties and intense political wrangling, however. In the interim, the site is simply known as "Memorial Hall." Two huge concert halls, also built in the classic palace architectural style, were added to the immense grounds of the memorial in the 1980s to signify Taipei's coming of age as a world-class city and a center of sophisticated culture.

Taipei has come to assume many primate-city functions, although statistically it is only twice the size of Kaohsiung, the main heavy industrial center in the south. No longer touted as the "national" capital, with the gradual dissolution of the provincial government in central Taiwan in the 1990s, Taipei remains overwhelmingly the center of international trade and investment and includes a large expatriate community. Culture, entertainment, and tourism are all focused on Taipei. Japanese especially like to visit Taiwan, because of its colonial heritage; the city's culture has a distinctly Japanese flavor to it (some people regard the Japanese food in Taipei as even better than that in Japan). The metropolitan region also is one of the island's key industrial areas; most of the manufacturing is now concentrated in a number of satellite cities, to the west and south of the capital. The old port of Keelung, once the key link with Japan, serves as the port outlet for the Taipei Northern Industrial Region. As with Seoul, most of the city's huge population increase over five decades was the result of in-migration from the densely populated countryside, a migration that in recent years has been primarily toward the suburban satellite cities. By 2005, the Northern Industrial Region had a total population of 9.5 million (out of Taiwan's nearly 23 million people), of which Taipei Municipality accounted for 2.6 million, and the surrounding satellite cities 3.9 million, or 6.5 million total for the urban agglomeration. The city has been growing toward the margins. Eastern Taipei ("New Taipei"), focused symbolically around the World Trade Center, has seen astounding growth, with hundreds of new high-rise luxury apartment buildings and office towers. Taipei in 2004 also became the site (temporarily) of the world's tallest building, with the opening of the 101-story Taipei 101. Large-scale suburbanization has also taken place, as affluent yuppies have moved to the northern suburbs, to high-class residential neighborhoods in Tienmu and Neihu, or southward toward Hsintien. Taipei, to some extent, reflects elements of the concentric zone model and the multinucleic model. In some respects, Taipei looks like Seoul on a smaller scale, with modern buildings; broad, tree-lined boulevards; and a high standard of living. Substantial cleanup and improvements came with the 1990s as the political system was democratized, the environment became an important concern, and urban development became an open topic for public input. An excellent mass rapid transit system helps to ease the transportation crush, composed of hordes of motorcycles and increasing numbers of private automobiles. As with cities around the world, parking is a monumental problem for all drivers.

Seoul: The "Phoenix" of Primate Cities

Seoul exhibits urban primacy in an especially acute form. It is home to 10 million people, more than 25% of South Korea's total population of 47 million, putting it in the ranks of the world's megacities (one of four such cities in East Asia). More than 40% of the country's population lives within the greater Seoul metropolitan region. In 1950, Seoul had barely more than 1 million people, just slightly more than second-ranked Pusan (Busan), the main port on the southeast coast. By 2005, Pusan had about 4 million people.

As the national capital, Seoul has a large tertiary sector devoted to the national government and the large military forces that South Korea must maintain. In addition, there is a large expatriate community, composed mostly of U.S. military forces and civilians (mostly business people and diplomatic personnel). Seoul is the political, cultural, educational, and economic heart of modern South Korea, the nerve center for the powerful state that South Korea has become. Although Seoul does not rank with Tokyo or New York as a true global city, it is moving in that direction, and it certainly has become much more cosmopolitan in the past 10 years, with the democratization and globalization of South Korea as well as Taiwan. In some ways, the new international airport, one of the world's finest, which recently opened at Inchon, west of Seoul, symbolizes the full coming of age of Seoul as a major player in the global economy.

The rise of Seoul to become one of the largest cities in the world is surprising, if only from a locational viewpoint. The city's site, midway along the west coast plain of the Korean peninsula, where most people live, was originally a logical place for the national capital of a unified Korea. However, since the division of the peninsula in the late 1940s and the bitter stalemate between North and South Korea since 1953, Seoul's location just 20 miles (32 km) from the demilitarized zone (DMZ) makes the city highly vulnerable. Suggestions for moving the capital functions to a more southerly and theoretically more defensible site have regularly met with indifference or outright opposition. Most Koreans believe that national reunification is inevitable, and when that happens, Seoul would then resume its historic role as national capital, revered by all Koreans for what it symbolizes.

The city was nearly leveled during the savage seesaw fighting in the Korean War, when the North occupied the city twice. Growth since the 1960s has been primarily the result of massive rural-to-urban migration, encouraged by Korea's transformation into an

Figure 11.24   Seoul constructed an impressive subway system for the Olympic Games in 1988. Each station is different in its architecture and artistic decoration. This is the handsome Kangnam station. (Photo courtesy Seoul city government)

urban/industrial society. The economic takeoff started in the 1960s, as the South embarked on an export-oriented industrialization strategy, much of it concentrated in the Seoul area. Urbanization thus accelerated, and the South passed the 50% urban mark in 1977. Seoul has spilled over into other areas, including south of the Han River, and has completely filled the basin of the river; it now covers an area equal to the island of Singapore. The southerly expansion was made possible by increasing the number of bridges across the Han from the original 2 to more than 20.

Seoul has its own grandness and beauty, such as in the layout of new districts or restored monuments. But parts remain terribly congested and shabby, especially some residential areas built on steep hillsides, the result of spontaneous rather than planned urbanization. Seoul could be said to have come of age when it host-ed the Olympic Summer Games in 1988, which gave authorities the rationale to spend billions of dollars to beautify the city and upgrade its infrastructure. In addition to a huge Olympics complex (used also for the Asia Games and other events), an extensive subway system was completed (fig. 11.24). The downtown CBD is a typical conglomeration of high-rise luxury hotels and office buildings, interspersed with relics of Korea's past. Newer high-rise residential/commercial districts, such as Kangnam south of the Han River, now contribute to a multinucleic pattern of development. Just south of the downtown and the prominent Mt. Namsan (whose observation tower still affords the best overall view of central Seoul) is Itaewon District, long the center for U.S. military personnel, a honky-tonk reminder of an era of the past and of the uneasy fit of American pop culture with Korean values.

URBAN PROBLEMS AND THEIR SOLUTIONS

The relatively clear-cut dichotomy between the socialist path of China, North Korea, and Mongolia and the nonsocialist path of the rest of East Asia that characterized the region through the 1970s is no longer valid. China has been abandoning orthodox socialism, for all practical purposes, since the late 1970s, though one-party rule remains. North Korea occasionally hints that it might be tempted to do so also, but then slips back into its Stalinist suspicion of the outside world (box 11.5). Mongolia, like Russia, abandoned not only a socialist system but also single-party rule and is now struggling to join the world, too. The colonial era is now completely over in the region. As a result of all these changes, urban problems and solutions take on new guises and, except for in North Korea, are becoming increasingly similar across the region.

The Chinese Way

To appreciate what China has attempted and accomplished in the reform era, one needs to briefly review urban development policies before then.

The Maoist Era (1949–1976): Anti-urban?

By nationalizing the economy, taking control of all the means of production, and adopting a planned, or command, type of economy, China's government after 1949 thought it had the solution to the country's immense problems. Events proved it wrong. The overwhelming emphasis on industrial growth; the suppression of personal consumption (the "nonproductive" side of cities); the guaranteeing of the needs of urban dwellers through the *iron rice bowl* welfare system to the relative neglect of rural areas; the enforcement of strict controls over internal migration within the country through the *hukou* (household registration) system; and strict monitoring of peoples' lives in the cities through neighborhood committees all in combination with other policies produced an artificial, unworkable urban and national system that was clearly failing by the mid-1970s, when Mao died. The system had to change.

The Reform Era (1978–): Opening China

Starting in the late 1970s, China's leaders began to make significant changes in policy across the board, abandoning or severely diluting some of the key policies of the Maoist era, including some of those in urban development. Two major exceptions were the Communist Party's retention of a rigid, one-party, authoritarian political system and the heavy control of the economy by the state.

The major policy change was in the *kaifang* ("opening") policy, or what might be dubbed the "New Open Door" policy (a voluntary opening this time, in marked contrast to the forced "Open Door" of the colonial era in the 19th century). China was opened to foreigners for investment, trade, tourism, technical assistance, and other contacts. The policy of self-reliance was set aside. Rapid growth in links with the outside world had a profound impact, but especially on cities and urban development in the coastal zone, which was earmarked for preferential treatment. The establishment of export processing zones with concessionary tax policies to attract foreign investment included the designation of four special economic zones (SEZs) (Shenzhen, Zhuhai, Xiamen, and Shantou) in Guangdong and Fujian in 1979 and of 14 "coastal open

Box 11.5   The Isolation of Peripheral Cities

Isolation can be a huge handicap for cities, but isolation is a relative concept in that it can arise from either physical or human geography. Four cities in East Asia—Pyongyang, Ulan Bator, Urumqi, Lhasa—play important roles in their respective regions, yet really are isolated—peripheral geographically and in terms of their linkages with the rest of the world.

Pyongyang is perhaps the biggest anomaly of the four. The government of North Korea rules this austere, reclusive nation of some 22 million from the capital city of Pyongyang. With an estimated 3.5 million in its metropolitan region, Pyongyang is three times larger, in classic primacy fashion, than the next two largest cities, Nampo and Hamhung. This is hardly a surprise, given the centrally planned, Stalinist system that continues to hang on, long after the Soviet Union, Maoist China, and communist Mongolia saw the light. Leveled to the ground during the Korean War (1950–1953), Pyongyang was totally rebuilt in the true socialist city model, with broad boulevards and massive government buildings, a superficially modern showcase of socialist dogma, but a city that gets terrible reviews from the few foreigners who have managed to visit. Pyongyang is little more than a grandiose monument to the whims of North Korea's autocratic rulers. The city may be geographically sited in the heart of East Asia, but it might as well be in the middle of Siberia.

By contrast, Mongolia's capital city of Ulan Bator (Ulaanbataar), although much smaller at about 800,000 people, is the center of a country now doing everything possible to integrate with the outside world. The main problems are Mongolia's tiny population (2.9 million), sprawling land area, and geographical isolation. Ulan Bator is also a primate city, many times larger than number two city, Darkhan (about 71,000). As Mongolia sheds its socialist past and democratizes, the country is rapidly urbanizing and trying to find alternatives to the processing of animal products for its small economy. Tourism is growing, but industry is never likely to be significant here. It will be difficult to overcome the country's geographical limitations; hence, Ulan Bator will likely remain largely a minor regional center.

Urumqi is also a regional (but not a national) capital, for the Xinjiang Autonomous Region in China. An ancient city, Urumqi has become a booming metropolis of over 2 million, with a largely Han Chinese population, as the center of China's administration and development of Xinjiang. As such, Urumqi in recent decades has increasingly taken on the character and physical appearance of a Chinese city, very similar to those found throughout the eastern, more populous part of the country. Although geographically the most isolated of these four peripheral cities, Urumqi is actually very much in touch with the outside world, largely because of China's prodigious economic growth in recent decades. The city is the focal point of large-scale tourism, industrialization, and development of the region's oil and other resources. Urumqi is also the center of efforts by the Chinese government to contain separatist tendencies among Xinjiang's largely Muslim population (especially among the Uigur). Hence, the city's geopolitical importance may well exceed its economic role.

Lhasa, the capital city of Tibet, is similar in many ways to Urumqi, although much smaller (under 300,000 in the urban area). If not for Chinese rule, Lhasa would be even more geographically isolated as one of the world's highest cities (nearly 12,000 ft in elevation). Also an ancient city and the center of Tibet's unique Buddhist culture under the Dalai Lama (now in exile in India), Lhasa was thrust into the modern world with China's takeover in the 1950s and became the focal point of China's efforts to contain Tibetan separatism, drawing much international attention in the process (fig. 11.25). Like Urumqi, Lhasa is rapidly becoming essentially a Chinese city, with the Han Chinese population steadily increasing and Chinese urban forms displacing much that was traditional and Tibetan. Also a primate city, Lhasa is several times larger than second-place Shigatse (at 80,000). Without Xinjiang's natural resources, and with a smaller population, Tibet remains one of China's poorest regions, and Lhasa's economy is largely dependent on tourism and services, subsidized by the Beijing government in its determination to ensure that peripheral regions (and their key cities) like Xinjiang and Tibet remain firmly within the PRC. One powerful demonstration of this effort was the opening in 2006 of the first railway linking Tibet with the rest of China (via Qinghai province to the north). Tibetan nationalists view the railway as one more tentacle of Beijing's grip. Beijing, in turn, sees the railway as an essential tool to further bring Tibet into the modern world and irrevocably into the PRC.

Figure 11.25   The Tibetan capital of Lhasa is dominated by the Potala Palace, now a World Heritage Site but no longer the home of Tibet's traditional ruler, the Dalai Lama. (Photo by George Pomeroy)

In sum, these four cities, in their historical as well as recent development, illustrate that isolation can be imposed by nature or by government, and that overcoming isolation is no easy task.

Figure 11.26   Modern high-rise buildings in Shanghai serve as a backdrop for banners advertising the appearance of a Russian ballet troupe, while a sign for Maxim's Restaurant (a popular restaurant chain in East Asia) pokes up in the foreground—dramatic symbols all of China's globalization and modernization. (Photo by Kam Wing Chan)

cities" in 1984. At the end of the 1980s, Hainan Island became both a new province and the fifth SEZ, while Shanghai's Pudong district joined the category of "open" zones. By the mid-1990s, practically the entire coastal region was one large open zone. One of the most notable consequences was the creation of the new city of Shenzhen, just across the border from Hong Kong. A small village at the border-crossing point became, within one decade, a city of several million, with a large proportion of migrants (without the local *hukou* status). Today its population is over 10 million, much larger than its neighbor,

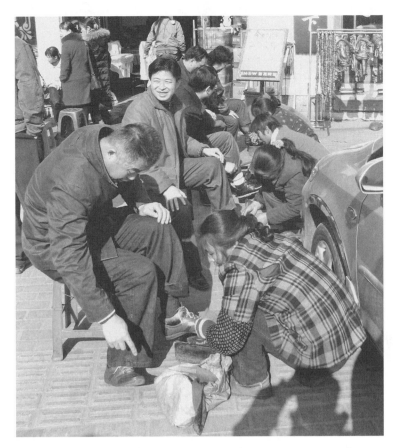

Figure 11.27   Migrant workers shine shoes on a street in Wuhan, a city in central China. Migrant workers are found in all of China's major cities, performing all manner of jobs in a desperate search for employment and income, symptomatic of China's severe need for job creation in the economy. (Photo by Kam Wing Chan)

Hong Kong. Shenzhen today makes a striking sight when viewed from one of the vantage points in Hong Kong's New Territories. Most of the land along the Hong Kong side is undeveloped farmland or nature preserves, while immediately on the other side rises a sprawling Manhattan-like urban landscape.

The negative side of China's New Open Door era has been to increase imbalances between rural and urban areas, between provinces and different regions, and between socioeconomic classes. There is nothing remotely egalitarian about China anymore, within the city or in the countryside. This was

the result of a deliberate policy by the Chinese government, which followed Deng Xiaoping's famous dictum, "To get rich is glorious." In addition, the government has relaxed controls in many areas. With decollectivization and the return to private smallholdings (under the Household Responsibility System), agriculture showed significant increases in labor productivity, with greatly improved living standards in the countryside. At the same time, though, many rural workers became unneeded, putting pressure on the government to relax restrictions on internal migration. Out of this has emerged the "floating

---

Box 11.6   Environmental Hazards

The cities of East Asia face environmental hazards from two fronts—problems caused by humans and those caused by nature. Human environmental problems are the result of the region's huge population and economic success. Rapid urbanization and industrialization inevitably lead to increased concentrations of humans in crowded urban settings consuming ever-increasing quantities of goods and services. The result is escalating strains on air, water, and land resources, and thus on the overall quality of life, even as the material standards of living rise. One can see this paradox around the world, of course.

Within East Asia, thus, development success spread in the post–World War II era from Japan, where it all started in the 1950s, through the "Little Tigers" of South Korea, Taiwan, and Hong Kong/Macau in the 1960s and 1970s, and finally on into China in the 1980s and 1990s. That tidal wave of success, however, brought with it like a cancer some of the world's worst environmental pollution. The expanding cities became centers of extreme air and water pollution. Rural areas became debased by the careless disposal of toxic wastes by industry and by the mountains of garbage created by urban dwellers. Increasing population pressure put enormous strains on precious land, causing dangerous deforestation, improper use of slopelands, wasting of land on frivolous activities such as golf courses, suburban sprawl that gobbled up valuable farmland, and pollution of coastal fishing areas by urban and industrial sewage. The abuses went on and on. The presence of high mass-consumption societies in densely populated areas makes for a lethal combination, especially in the face of numerous natural hazards. Much of maritime East Asia lies in a highly active earthquake zone, and the urban centers and economies in much of the region are vulnerable. This maritime realm also lies within the typhoon belt of Asia, so that the destructive winds and torrential rains and flooding associated with typhoons periodically wreak havoc, especially on the region's urban areas.

---

population" of migrant workers, estimated at 150 million, who provide plentiful low-cost labor and help make Chinese industry competitive in international markets. The migrants fill many jobs shunned by urban workers, but under the current *hukou* policy these migrants do not have the same citizens' rights and social benefits. This two-tier system of urban citizenship and unequal treatment of the migrant population have become major concerns and the source of many problems in the cities.

There has also been an exponential growth in the number of people living in towns (distinguished from cities) over the past 30 years, because of the government's relaxation of controls over entry into the economy by non-state-owned enterprises. This has led to a burgeoning of rural enterprises (Township-Village Enterprises, or TVEs) and of small-scale entrepreneurs going into business for themselves, especially in the 1980s and early 1990s. These activities absorbed more than 100 million rural laborers from the countryside, who can now fairly easily gain permission to move to a town in many provinces, as long as they have a job and

China is currently the most vulnerable state in the region. The sheer enormity of its land mass and population, combined with its breathtaking economic growth, has made its environmental impact gargantuan in scope and severity. Water, for example, is in critically short supply in most of the north and west, and the country is struggling to meet its huge demands for potable water in coming decades, made worse by terrible pollution of available water in rivers, lakes, and underground aquifers. The air in China's cities is among the worst in the world, just as the country is in the midst of massive industrialization and whole-hearted adoption of automobiles. Meeting the country's vast energy needs in the coming decades will put huge strains on China's own energy resources as well as those of the rest of the world.

Japan was the first to take notice of the environmental cost of development, starting in the 1960s and 1970s. Thanks to its abundant wealth and a growing environmental consciousness, it has started to make significant progress back to an environmentally responsible, "green" country. With about a 20-year lag, the "Little Tigers" have followed in Japan's footsteps. Taiwan has made the most progress, followed by South Korea. Hong Kong is just beginning its efforts, made more difficult by its proximity to China. Indeed, the rest of East Asia cannot avoid being impacted by China's bad environment, especially from air pollution that drifts eastward over the region. Air pollution truly is not confined by national boundaries. Likewise, China's growing contribution to greenhouse gases means that the rest of East Asia (not to mention the rest of the world) is hostage to China's eventual success (or failure) in gaining control of its environmental impact.

If global warming does result in significant sea level rises, then East Asia is doomed, because so much of its modern economy and a good share of its population are concentrated in low-lying port cities that will be drowned. The other environmental problems facing cities will become moot issues in the event of such a worldwide calamity.

a place to live. The government hopes to divert some of the rural population to small towns.

The new focus on markets and private enterprise in cities, alongside the state-owned economy, has created a demand for advertising and the need to spruce up store-fronts and display windows. Urban life appears increasingly similar to that of the rest of East Asia and has unquestionably improved for most residents, because it offers greater variety and quality of goods and services, in contrast to the stifling conformity and drabness of the Maoist years. In fact, some sections of many large cities today have the look of wealthier cities like Hong Kong or Taipei (fig. 11.26). One of the costs, however, is that economic polarization and social polarization seem to be on the increase. There is an expanding class of urban poor in China, consisting of migrants and laid-off state-owned enterprise (SOE) workers. Unemployment is likely to worsen in the face of continued population growth and difficulties in creating jobs fast enough to absorb the surplus population (fig. 11.27).

Impacting virtually everyone, rich or poor, is the critical state of the environment. Reputedly, a majority of the 10 most polluted major cities in the world are found in China today (box 11.6).

Other Paths in East Asia

As with big cities around the world, the industrial cities of East Asia are experiencing profound problems of overcrowding, pollution, traffic congestion, crime, and shortages of affordable housing and other services. Yet most people in the cities of East Asia are relatively well off, with the obvious exception of many migrant workers. This has been a region of extraordinary economic growth and advancement in recent decades, such that residents of these cities have standards of living among the highest in the world. They dress smartly, are well fed, and have considerable disposable income. Westernization (or, more properly now, globalization) is very evident in its impact in terms of popular culture and lifestyles. Retail stores of all types provide every conceivable consumer good for affluent residents. At night, the cities glitter with eye-popping displays of neon, nowhere more dazzling than in Japan.

Expensive land is a major constraint to the development of these cities. Increasingly, thus, the major cities are following in the footsteps of most other large cities with high-rise syndrome. There is even a growing competition among the cities of the region to see which can build the tallest skyscraper, as if having the tallest building somehow conveys status and superiority. Shanghai, Hong Kong, Taipei, Seoul, and others are involved in this one-upmanship. Even Japan's cities, long characterized by relatively low skylines (because of earthquake hazards), have succumbed to the trend toward high-rise construction, such as in the cluster of 50-plus-story buildings centered around the city government complex in Tokyo's Shinjuku District, or the new high-rise profile in the port of Yokohama. Japanese cities, and now increasingly other cities in the region, also make maximum use of underground space, with enormous, complex underground malls interconnected by subway systems.

Movement outward from the central city (suburbanization) is the only other alternative to going upward or downward. New communities have sprung up, including bedroom towns where people, for less money, can obtain better housing with cleaner air and less noise, even though doing so often means long commutes to work. Fortunately, most of the large cities have developed relatively good public transport systems. Nonetheless, the automobile culture is spreading rapidly, with the private automobile purchased as much for status as for convenience in getting around. The automobile culture first took hold in Japan in the 1960s, but other countries have followed suit and even China is now firmly on the private automobile bandwagon and just replaced Japan as the world's second largest market for automobiles.

Closing the Gap: Decentralization in Japan

The Japanese have been struggling for several decades to decentralize their urban system and reduce the relative dominance of Tokyo, by and large without success. The task really has two dimensions: improving living conditions in Tokyo and physically decentralizing

Figure 11.28   Chiba Port already handles the largest volume of freight among Japan's port cities and also illustrates the widespread practice of creating artificial land for urban expansion in Japan's post–World War II growth. (Photo courtesy Chiba government)

the urban system. Within the Tokyo area, the solution to overcrowding and the still high cost of land lies in finding new land, such as through continued landfill projects to expand the shoreline and make greater use of Tokyo Bay, as well as moving further outward toward less-developed areas in the Tokyo region. A prime example of the latter is the Tokyo Bay Aqua Line, an expressway across the middle of Tokyo Bay connecting Tokyo (in the north and west) with Chiba Prefecture and designed to enhance development along the eastern and southern shore. The hope is that Chiba Prefecture, occupying the whole peninsula opposite Tokyo City,

will be the new high-growth area for the Tokyo region, anchored around three new core cities—a high-tech Kazusa Akademia Park, Makuhari New City, and Narita Airport (fig. 11.28).

An alternative supported by many is to decentralize. How to decentralize is a tough question over which there is anything but consensus. Over the decades, Japan has had a succession of National Development Plans, all of which have addressed in some way the need for more balanced regional development. Proposals for relocating the national capital out of Tokyo have gone nowhere. Various kinds of subcenter ideas have been tried;

however, none have been substantially successful in reducing the drawing power of Tokyo. Neither has the decline of regions such as the Kansai been stopped, in spite of efforts such as the opening of the new Kansai International Airport on an artificial island off the coast of Osaka in 1990, in an effort to give Tokyo's Narita some competition. In 2001 the government launched a major effort at revitalization of the Kansai, with limited results so far.

Nonetheless, the dream persists. If Japan had not suffered serious economic stagnation over the past decade or more, the prospects for real change would be better today. Now, fearing that Tokyo might be supplanted as Asia's premier business center by some other city, such as Hong Kong or Singapore, the government has stepped up efforts to revitalize the capital. In sum, the inability of Japan—with its enormous wealth and relative social homogeneity—to solve this regional imbalance problem does not suggest a high probability of success for solving the same problem in other countries.

Seoul: The Problems of Primacy

Somewhat like its larger cousin, Tokyo, Seoul suffers from the typical problems of urban primacy. There is crushing traffic congestion, made worse by a growing middle class determined to have the status symbol of a private car in a society where status means almost everything. There is smothering air pollution caused by too many motor vehicles, by the burning of charcoal and coal, by the presence of thousands of factories, and by a basin topography that traps pollutants beneath temperature inversions, as occurs in Los Angeles or Mexico City. There is a severe shortage of affordable housing; with land

so scarce and expensive, the small Korean homes cluster together like bees on the steep, rocky hillsides. Elsewhere, especially south of the Han River, huge apartment complexes march to the horizon in a monotonous precision of layout. Property values soared in the 1980s as redevelopment contributed to large-scale real estate speculation, a problem common in East Asia (and now raging in China). The property bubble burst in the early 1990s with a gradual decline in prices, spurred further by the Asian financial crisis of 1997–1998. That crisis hit South Korea hard and actually contributed to a decrease in Seoul's total population from its peak of 12 million in 1999 to the present roughly 10 million. The economy has since recovered much of its vigor.

Seoul would probably be even larger and more congested than it is today if the government had not adopted a policy of promoting urban/industrial growth elsewhere in the country. In spite of the attraction of Seoul to would-be migrants, considerable urban growth has occurred in secondary and tertiary cities, including Pusan, Ulsan, Taejon (Daejon), and Kwangju (Gwangju). The government also has attempted to decentralize the Seoul metropolitan region by constructing new towns, such as Guri, Banweol, and Sungnam. These have had limited impact, however. As in Japan's case, South Korea has debated the merits of moving the national capital out of Seoul for some time. President Roh Moo Hyun, elected in 2002, made balanced regional development and relocation of the capital a top priority, and plans were formulated to build a new capital city at Gongju, about 100 miles (160 km) south of Seoul. Construction was to start in 2007 and be completed by 2030. However, the prospects for a full-scale relocation are as dim as they are for Tokyo, and for many of the same reasons (money, politics, history, culture). Indeed, South Korea's high court ruled the relocation unconstitutional. The debate continues.

Taipei: Toward Balanced
Regional Development

Taipei has made dramatic progress in recent years in solving some of its urban problems. Completion of a mass rapid transit system and stepped-up enforcement of traffic rules have brought order to what was once one of the worst cities in Asia for traffic chaos. Pollution (especially air pollution) has been drastically cut through various programs. While housing is still expensive, it is becoming relatively more affordable. Overall, the city is cleaner and is decidedly a better place in which to live or raise a family. Although many people have moved to the suburbs, a large residential population still lives within the central city, so that the "doughnut" model does not fit Taipei. The multiple nuclei model is perhaps more applicable.

In part to solve the problems of overcrowded Taipei, the national government embarked on an island-wide regional planning program in the early 1970s. The end result was a development plan that divided the island into four planning regions, each focused around a key city. The Northern Region, centered on Taipei, has about 40% of the island's total population. Through a variety of policies, including rural industrialization, massive investment in infrastructure, and programs to enhance the quality of life and economic base of other cities and towns, Taiwan has managed to slow the growth of Taipei (never as severe as the dominance of Tokyo or Seoul in their countries)

and to diffuse some of the urbanization. Taiwan, for instance, has developed its own sleek version of Japan's "bullet" train; it started operation in late 2006 and has cut the travel time between Taipei and Kaohsiung to about 90 minutes. The rivalry between Taipei and Kaohsiung is often fierce. Historically, these two cities have been controlled by the two main competing parties, the KMT and the DPP, which have their power base in the North and the South, respectively. The current central government policy under the DPP is aimed at lowering the relative proportion of population and economic activity in the Northern Region and spreading it more evenly among the other three regions. The Central Region (around Taichung) has actually seen the most rapid growth in recent years. There is even a fledgling movement afoot to shift the island's capital functions from Taipei to Kaohsiung for the same reasons promoted in Japan and South Korea. Like those two states, the prospects for change in Taiwan are equally remote.

PROSPECTS

Urban dwellers in many poorer cities around the world must look with some envy at the more prosperous cities of East Asia. To citizens of the region, however, and especially to urban planners, the overall problem of most cities of East Asia is how far short the cities still fall from expectations. As leading Japanese observers put it:

- "Japan's foremost urban centers lack anything resembling the character and depth of their European counterparts. Instead, they seem to be forever under construction."

- "There is huge potential demand for urban redevelopment."
- "Japanese city planning shows little vision regarding a living environment."

These may be excessively harsh criticisms from idealistic planners (perhaps biased because of their Western training). Much the same could be said of the rest of the region. The continuous demolition and construction that leaves little history and character are the price of rapid growth and economic success. But it is fair to say that cities of East Asia are also in many respects ingenious designs by generations of people trying to create hospitable urban habitats in the relatively unfavorable environment of high population pressure and scarce land.

So where do these countries and cities go from here? East Asia is unquestionably going to be a region of continuing high economic growth, with strong continued urbanization, especially in China. There are vast amounts of capital in the region for urban development. Marshalling that capital to maximize the quality of urban life is the challenge facing all of these states. East Asia is in the forefront of the information technology and transportation revolutions, which are rapidly diminishing the importance of distance and national boundaries. Transnational urban linkages within the region and between the region and the rest of the world, especially Southeast Asia and North America, are going to become stronger. The cities of East Asia are destined to play leading roles in world affairs in the 21st century, belonging as they do to one of the three power centers of the global economy. The top player of all may well be China with its great cities superseding those of Japan, which dominated the region in the 20th century. There are many who predict the 21st century will be the "Chinese century."

SUGGESTED READINGS

Brandt, Loren, and Thomas G. Rawski, eds. 2008. *China's Great Economic Transformation.* Cambridge and New York: Cambridge University Press. A comprehensive examination of various aspects of the Chinese economy, including the spatial dimensions of China's development.

Chan, Kam Wing. 1994. *Cities with Invisible Walls: Reinterpreting Urbanization in Post-1949 China.* Hong Kong: Oxford University Press. An examination of the major features of socialist urbanization in China, especially the industrialization strategy and the need for a migration control system.

Golany, Gideon S., Keisuke Hanaki, and Osamu Koide, eds. 1998. *Japanese Urban Environment.* New York: Pergamon. An attempt to explain the success of Japanese urban design and planning, based primarily on Japanese scholarship.

Karan, Pradyumna P., and Krtistin Stapleton, eds. 1997. *The Japanese City.* Lexington: University Press of Kentucky. A readable review of various aspects of urban development, historical and contemporary.

Kim, Won Bae, Mike Douglass, Sang-Chuel Choe, and Kong Chong Ho, eds. 1997. *Culture and the City in East Asia.* New York: Clarendon Press. A collection of chapters, most by geographers and urban planners, on the history and transformation of East Asian cities, including Hong Kong and Taipei.

Lo, Fu-chen, and Peter J. Marcotullio, eds. 2001. *Globalization and the Sustainability of Cities in the Asia/Pacific Region.* Tokyo: United Nations University Press. Chapters devoted to individual cities in Asia (including Tokyo, Seoul, Taipei, Hong Kong, Shanghai) as well as broader regional themes. Very useful.

Sorensen, Andre. 2002. *The Making of Urban Japan: Cities and Planning from Edo to the Twenty-First Century.* London, New York: Routledge. An examination of Japan's urban development from earliest times to the present.

Wu, Fulong, JiangXu, and Anthony Gar-On Yeh. 2007. *Urban Development in Post-Reform China: State, Market, and Space.* London, New York: Routledge. A detailed look at various aspects of urban planning and development in China by leading authorities in the field.

Yusuf, Shahid, and Kaoru Nabeshime. 2006. *Post-Industrial East Asia Cities.* Stanford: Stanford University Press and World Bank. A book on technologies and innovations in several major cities in East Asia as they move away from manufacturing.

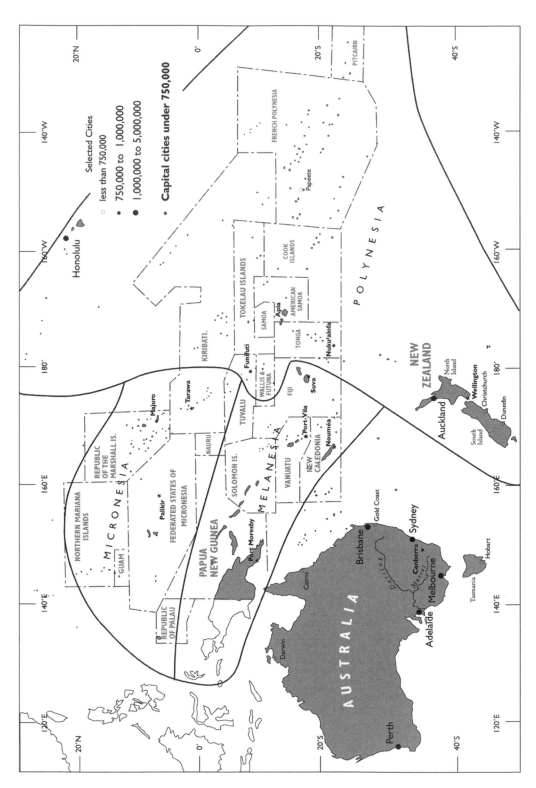

Figure 12.1 Major Cities of Australia and the Pacific Islands. *Source*: UN *World Urbanization Prospects, 2005 revision* [online].

12

Cities of Australia and the Pacific Islands
ROBYN DOWLING AND PAULINE MCGUIRK

KEY URBAN FACTS*

Total Population	33 million
Percent Urban Population	70.8%
Australia and New Zealand	87.9%
Total Urban Population	23 million
Most Urbanized Countries	Nauru (100%)
	Northern Mariana Islands (94.5%)
	Guam (U.S.) (94.0%)
Least Urbanized Countries	Papua New Guinea (13.4%)
	Solomon Islands (17.0%)
	Micronesia (22.3%)
Annual Urban Growth Rate	1.26%
Australia and New Zealand	1.16%
Number of Megacities	0
Number of Cities of More Than 1 Million	6
Three Largest Cities	Sydney, Melbourne, Brisbane
World Cities	Sydney

* Excluding Hawaii

KEY CHAPTER THEMES

1. Cities in this region may be understood as forming two groups—those of Australia and Aotearoa/New Zealand and those of the Pacific Islands—each with distinct characteristics.
2. All countries in this region are dominated by primate cities, but in the case of Australia, the primate cities are the capitals of states in a federal union.
3. Australia and Aotearoa/New Zealand exhibit many of the urban characteristics of other developed countries, such as the United States.

4. The urban character of Pacific Island cities is similar to that of less developed countries, though they are smaller and have considerably lower rates of population growth.

5. Sydney is by far the most globally linked city and the key economic center in this vast realm, though the global economic, cultural, and social connections of all cities have increased dramatically.

6. Many of the cities in the region were established as colonial or national capitals, and urban patterns and character are tied to this political influence.

7. In Australia, a popularly documented "sea change" phenomenon is drawing people away from the big cities toward small coastal towns.

8. Suburbanization and gentrification remain key residential forces in Australian and Aotearoa/New Zealand cities, and globalization is a central driver of urban economies.

9. A multicultural population is increasingly the norm in most cities in the region, especially in Australia and Aotearoa/New Zealand.

10. Awareness of the environmental impacts of urbanization is rising, with attempts to adapt planning frameworks and everyday life to sustainable outcomes.

11. Environmental vulnerability, especially to the direct and indirect consequences of climate change, is a key issue confronting the cities in the Pacific Islands.

The Pacific region is a constellation of islands of varying sizes (fig. 12.1). Australia (the island continent) and Aotearoa/New Zealand (now carrying both Maori and Pakeha, or settler, names) dominate the region geographically and economically. However, many smaller islands are to be found in the vase realms of the Pacific Ocean known as Melanesia, Micronesia, and Polynesia. Socially, politically, economically, and biophysically, this is a diverse region with diverse cities.

In this part of the world, it is easiest to understand cities as forming two main groups: those of Australia and Aotearoa/New Zealand, and those of the Pacific Islands. The former have cities with characteristics of more developed countries: they are large (in regional rather than global terms) and industrialized, generally have high level of affluence, and are connected in global flows of people, money, information, and services. There are two key urban characteristics shared by both these na-

tions. First, they are urban. Currently, over 85% of Australians and 70% of Aotearoa/New Zealanders live in urban areas. Second, they are, and long have been, nations of urban primacy: their urban pattern is dominated by a small number of large cities. Approximately one-quarter of all Aotearoa/New Zealanders live in just one city—Auckland—and Australia's two largest cities—Melbourne and Sydney—are home to more than 38% of the nation's population (tab. 12.1).

The islands within Micronesia, Polynesia, and Melanesia have starkly different urban characteristics. They have highly nonurban populations. Although reliable statistics are difficult to obtain, it is estimated that 35% of the population lives in urban areas, with a projected increase to over 50% by 2025. There are 35 towns and cities with a population greater than 5,000. Two-thirds of the southwest Pacific realm's urban dwellers are found in Papua New Guinea (PNG) and Fiji, the most

Table 12.1   Australia and Aotearoa/New Zealand: Changes in Distribution of National Population

Nation/Cities	Percentage of National Population, 1981	Percentage of National Population, 2006
Australia		
Sydney	21.8	20.7
Melbourne	18.6	18.1
Brisbane	7.2	8.9
Perth	6.2	7.3
Adelaide	6.3	5.6
Hobart	1.1	1.0
Darwin	0.4	0.5
Canberra	1.6	1.6
Aotearoa/New Zealand		
Auckland	26.1	29.2
Christchurch	10.1	8.7
Wellington	10.8	9.6
Dunedin	3.6	2.7

Sources: New Zealand Official Yearbook, 88th ed.; Year Book Australia; New Zealand Census of Population and Dwellings 2006; Australian Census of Population and Housing 2006.

populous nations in the region (tab. 12.2). The region's largest cities—Suva (Fiji), Noumea (New Caledonia), and Port Moresby (PNG)—are tiny by world standards. Negligible population growth is occurring in these cities, where economic opportunities remain limited. These are far from urban nations: prestige and status are still very much tied to the land and the rural, rather than to cities and the urban.

HISTORICAL FOUNDATIONS OF URBANISM

Australia, Aotearoa/New Zealand, and the Pacific Islands have indigenous peoples with long histories of settlement—up to 40,000 years in the case of Australian Aboriginals. The Maoris,

Aotearoa/New Zealand's indigenous inhabitants, settled there about 800 years ago. Cities in this part of the world are, however, very young. Urban settlement began with the arrival of numerous colonizers in the 18th and 19th centuries. Australia became a penal colony of the British in 1788, with the arrival of convicts to Sydney and Port Arthur (near Hobart, Tasmania) and later to Brisbane. The continued arrival of convicts to these coastal towns and the establishment of additional settlements like Melbourne and Adelaide, for purposes of colonial administration, commerce, and trade, cemented metropolitan primacy. The political independence of each of the British colonies (later to become states) also meant that the capital cities operated independently of each other throughout the 19th century, providing services to their rural hinterlands, acting as ports for the import and export of commodities to and from Europe, and functioning as centers of colonial administration. Indeed, competition between the capitals further worked to bolster primacy. With each capital focused on ensuring continued economic growth, backed by political force, within its respective territory, the establishment of alternative, prosperous, and comparable urban centers was made more difficult.

Two major events of the mid- to late 19th century did not challenge metropolitan primacy but instead were part of a snowball effect that further enhanced the size, functions, and importance of Australia's six colonial capitals. Railroads were focused on the capitals, facilitating more efficient connections between the cities and their hinterlands. Industrialization similarly occurred within, rather than beyond, these coastal centers of colonial administration, though there were to be later exceptions like Wollongong and Newcastle in New South Wales, and Whyalla in South Australia. By the

Table 12.2   Population of Pacific Island Cities

Island Nation/ Cities	Population	Percentage of National Population
Fiji	864,700	
Suva	199,455	23.1
Nadi	53,783	6.2
Lautoka	49,331	5.7
Kiribati	90,300	
Bairiki	44,429	49.2
Taburao	3,822	4.2
Bonriki	3,711	4.1
Marshall Islands	54,600	
Rita	21,019	38.5
Ebeye	9,824	18.0
Laura	2,675	4.9
Vanuatu	213,900	
Vila	35,901	16.8
Luganville	13,397	6.3
Norsup	2,998	1.4
Tonga	102,800	
Nukualofa	23,611	23.0
Mua	4,869	4.7
Naiafa	4,320	4.2
Solomon Islands	460,100	
Honiara	56,298	12.2
Gizo	6,154	1.3
Auki	4,336	0.9
Samoa	180,900	
Apia	39,800	22.0
Vaitele	5,300	2.9
Faleasiu	3,300	1.8
Papua New Guinea	5,261,200	
Port Moresby	283,733	5.4
Lae	76,255	1.4
Arawa	40,266	0.8

Source: Country Watch 2004, *Country Review: Asia Pacific.* http://countrywatch.ecnext.com/coms2/browse_CR_ASIA

end of the 19th century, Australia had a total population of a little less than 4 million. Sydney and Melbourne each had populations of approximately half a million; Adelaide, Brisbane, and Perth had more than 100,000 each; and Hobart remained small at 35,000. Thus, colonialism was responsible for this uniquely Australian urban primacy and settlement pattern in at least two ways. The sites of European settlements (either convict or free), with their coastal locations and trading functions, formed the foundations of the colony and its growth. Second, the functions of colonial administration and competition among the capitals fueled the growth of existing rather than new urban centers.

The first half of the 20th century saw urban Australia grow in the spatial pattern established by British colonialism. A manufacturing boom that began in the 1920s reinforced the primacy of the capital cities. This era also saw the beginning of the systemic suburbanization of Australian cities. The establishment of middle-class suburbs in attractive surroundings away from the central city was facilitated by the development of public transport lines radiating out from the city center, as well as by the activities of land developers and house builders. With the absence of inner-city slums of the scale of those in Britain, the social differentiation of Australian cities took on a sectoral or wedge-like pattern, related to transport links and to features of the natural landscape.

The turn of the 20th century did see one challenge to the existing capital cities with the planning of the new city of Canberra. The federation of Australia's colonial territories in 1901 was designed to both create and unite a nation. The colonial capitals became capitals of states in the newly formed Commonwealth of Australia, and a new national capital—Canberra—was established between the two cities that dominated the national urban hierarchy—Melbourne and Sydney. Canberra's location between these two urban leaders was a compromise. The Australian Parliament did not formally relocate to Canberra until 1927, and the city remains comparatively small, with fewer than

Figure 12.2 Canberra's distinctive but controversial Parliament House is difficult to appreciate from the outside because much of the structure is underground. The inside is breathtaking, filled with beautiful art and materials native to Australia. (Photo by Jack Williams)

400,000 inhabitants (fig. 12.2). The dominating characteristic of the city is the prominent role played by formal urban planning. A master plan developed by an American—Walter Burley Griffin—guided its development as a "garden city" built around a large lake, with a central focus on a "parliamentary triangle" and satellite suburbs with town centers of their own. Canberra's expansion was slow—only 16,000 people lived there in 1947—and its early economy was reliant on public service and diplomatic functions. Today, its economy is supplemented by a large student population which attends the relatively large number of public and private institutions of higher learning, including the Australian National University, now located there.

In Aotearoa/New Zealand, European settlement and modern urbanization began in 1840 with the signing of the Treaty of Waitangi between the British and the Maoris. Unlike the convict bases of Australia's settlements, free

setters in Aotearoa/New Zealand were encouraged to migrate and invest, with the resultant economy being largely dependent on pastoral activities like sheep and cattle grazing. Unlike Australia, urban primacy was not a 19th century phenomenon here, because of the originally more dispersed settlement pattern and more diverse reasons for urban settlement. For example, early towns like Wellington and Christchurch were established by trading and/or religious interests, Auckland's natural harbor made it an ideal port (fig. 12.3), and gold rushes underpinned the growth of Dunedin. Thus by 1911, Auckland had a population of 100,000, Christchurch 80,000, Wellington 70,000, and Dunedin 65,000. Over half of the non-Maori population lived in urban areas. In contrast, throughout the 19th century and the first half of the 20th century, Maori settlement was predominantly rural.

Like Australia and Aotearoa/New Zealand, Oceania has a long-established indigenous

Figure 12.3 A city built on an isthmus and connected to a rich hinterland, Auckland now hosts many activities found in major world cities, including the famous Sky Tower and casino that dominates the skyline. (Photo by Richard Le Heron)

population, and also similarly it was the colonial context that underpinned the development of an urban system in this region. Oceania was one of the last regions of the world to be colonized, with British, French, American, and Dutch powers establishing presences in countries like Fiji, Samoa, Tonga, and Vanuatu at various points during the 19th century. Towns first developed as trading ports, usually close to existing villages, good harbors, and viable anchorages. These towns grew slowly, and some, like Levuka in Fiji, declined over time because of relative inaccessibility. They were never large: in 1911 Suva had a population of only 6,000 people, about 5% of Fiji's population.

The first half of the 20th century saw a diversification of urban functions and sporadic urban growth. Although widespread industrialization did not occur, the processing of agricultural commodities like sugar, and the extraction of resources through mining, saw a diversified economic base and growth in the cities of Fiji and New Guinea. Indeed, these mining towns were nearly as large as the colonial capital of Port Moresby. In Micronesia, intense Japanese colonialism saw cities like Koror, on the island of Palau, grow substantially; other administrative capitals grew slowly. By the middle of the 20th century, urbanization remained limited.

CONTEMPORARY URBAN PATTERNS AND PROCESSES

The contemporary urban system of Australia, Aotearoa/New Zealand, and the Pacific Islands is based upon the patterns established in previous decades. Economic, social, and political influences across the region have consolidated urban primacy. Processes producing urbanization, the overall urban pattern of the region,

Table 12.3   Range of Incompatibilities between Customary Land Tenure and Urban Development

Incompatibility	*Manifestation*
• Conflict with commercial desire for certain, privatized title	• Disincentive to invest in land and development
• Demands for compensation by traditional landowners	• Disruption of infrastructure provision (e.g., roads, water) as a result of costs of compensation demands
	• Violent urban conflict
• Limits on land available to house urban residents	• Squatter settlements
	• Lack of land for government-provided affordable housing
	• Rising rentals (e.g., Nuku'alofa)

and the characteristics of cities within it are far from uniform. For cities of the Pacific Islands, tourism, political independence and instabilities, migration, and environmental hazards play significant roles. In Australia and Aotearoa/New Zealand, in contrast, industrialization followed by deindustrialization, globalization, international immigration, urban governance, and simultaneous rural population and depopulation are the primary urban influences.

The Pacific Islands

The historical pattern of urban primacy in a largely nonurban region remains a hallmark of the Pacific's urban geography (tab. 12.2). By 1960, only Suva and Noumea had populations greater than 25,000, and even today the cities of this region remain small. Political independence from colonial powers began in the 1970s. Only a few territories, such as French Caledonia, where Noumea is located, remain in colonial hands. Independence had a number of significant impacts on the region's urban system. Colonial administration was no longer the primary purpose of the largest cities in the region, but processes associated with independence cemented the primacy of these towns. In some, like Port Moresby, independence fostered urban growth because of

new investment in urban housing and services. Across the region accelerated urban growth followed independence because, for example, of the removal of negative perceptions of urban living and the establishment of some countries as tax havens (e.g., Port Vila in Vanuatu). Independence also required bureaucracies in national capitals and encouraged education and urban living in general.

Land and land tenure systems are a defining characteristic of Pacific cities. In Melanesia, Polynesia, and Micronesia, customary land tenures pose significant challenges for urban growth, housing, and infrastructure provision, as well as for improving the quality of urban life. In Port Moresby, for example, one-third of the city's total area is held by traditional owners. Land is seen as a communal resource, an attachment that is often incompatible with urbanization and urban life (tab. 12.3). A number of possible solutions to the limitations customary land tenure places on capitalist urban growth have been proposed. These include proposals to lease customary allotments and the ability to use land to generate income through means other than compensation. Such proposals have been severely hindered by the limited capacity of urban governance across the islands.

Connected to issues of land tenure are the general housing characteristics of the urban

Box 12.1   Urbanization and Human Security

Existing insecurities (e.g., income inequalities, environmental degradation, lack of services, etc.) are catalysts in the process of urbanization (fig. 12.4). Rural to urban population movements, however, give rise to vulnerabilities within urban places, including pollution, exposure to hazardous substances, resource scarcities and inequalities. Vulnerability is defined as having biophysical and social components. Biophysical vulnerability refers to the potential for loss from environmental threats. . . . Social vulnerability refers to the social and institutional capacity that defines both the susceptibility and

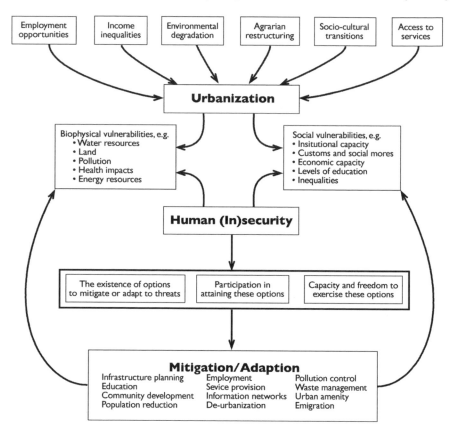

Figure 12.4 People in urban settings are typically subjected to increased biophysical and sociocultural threats to their security. *Source:* Redrafted from Chris Cocklin and Meg Keen, "Urbanization in the Pacific," *Environmental Conservation*, 27 (2000), 395.

Pacific. Palatial houses exist, but they are often built by expatriates. Formal housing of the type commonly found in Australian and Aotearoa/New Zealand cities exists as well. Far more common, however, are informal settlements. The great demand for housing, in the context of substantial urban poverty and limited employment opportunities, means that informal housing is common. Public housing is available, though waiting lists are extremely lengthy.

the ability to cope with environmental threats. . . . [I]t is the interaction of social and biophysical vulnerability that contributes to the vulnerability of specific places. At the center of the figure is the definition of human security, especially in the context of urbanization. The definition suggests that the state of human security will be determined by environmental threats, referred to in the figure as biophysical vulnerabilities, which in an urban setting would include scarcities of basic resources, such as water, land and energy, and degradation of environmental quality. These threats have potential to undermine human security in myriad ways, but include most notably their implications for human health and physical well being, economic welfare, nutrition levels, and access to adequate housing.

Source: Chris Cocklin and Meg Keen, "Urbanization in the Pacific: Environmental Change, Vulnerability and Human Security," *Environmental Conservation* 27, no. 4 (2000), 392–403.

Finally, the present and future of the cities of the island Pacific cannot be understood without reference to environmental contexts and threats (box 12.1). Urban settlement has involved degradation of islands' fragile coastal environments. The waste and water requirements of growing urban populations threaten to overwhelm already stressed ecosystems. Urban water is typically sourced from freshwater lenses, and if these are overpumped, saltwater contamination can occur and render the water unsuitable for human use. Because of the geology of the islands, waste disposal also affects the environment. Other forms of water supply contamination can occur (e.g., by chemicals, sewerage), which in turn affects human health. The most important environmental issue for these cities in the 21st century is climate change, especially global warming. These largely low-lying islands are at risk of inundation because of sea level rise. For example, in Tonga a rise in sea level of 1 meter would affect 9,000 people and involve the loss of 4 square miles (10 sq km) of urban land. Climate change is also believed to involve increased storm activity, accelerated coastal erosion, saltwater intrusion into reserves of freshwater, and increased landward reach of storm waves. Each of these

events has the potential to dismantle city infrastructure and urban livelihoods. These problems are further exacerbated by social vulnerabilities, especially limited institutional capacities for urban planning.

The global economic context is crucial to urban economies in the Pacific. Many nations like Fiji have turned to tourism for economic survival, with urban consequences. Global commodities and mining, as well as the presence of wealthy expatriates, underpin the urban hierarchy of Papua New Guinea (PNG). And finally, global migration, and in particular outmigration, can relieve some of the social, economic, and environmental pressures in cities. In Tonga especially, migration to Aotearoa/New Zealand, Australia, and the United States operates as an urban "safety valve," allowing Tongans to realize economic opportunities overseas rather than in overcrowded and economically limited urban areas. This safety valve has also become part of new, informal, urban economic activities.

In sum, cities of the island Pacific are places of vulnerability and opportunity. In a largely nonurban context, in which effective urban planning and coordination is nonexistent at worst and problematic at best, urban living is still sought as a chance for a better quality of

Figure 12.5 As Australia's second-largest city and a major industrial center, Melbourne prides itself on being more traditional than exuberant Sydney, its long-standing rival. (Photo courtesy Australian government)

life. Though officially derided, life in informal settlements remains attractive.

Australia

The dominance of state capital cities remains the defining characteristic of Australia's urban system. The primary drivers of urban development in the 20th century—industrialization, migration, and, more recently, globalization—have only reinforced the importance of the state capitals and fueled their population growth. Between 1947 and 1971, the population of Australia's five largest cities doubled, and growth has continued since then. Historically, Sydney (capital of New South Wales) and Melbourne (capital of Victoria) have been the island continent's largest and most economically dominant cities. Australia's manufacturing growth after World War II was centered in Melbourne, which,

until recently, housed the majority of Australian corporate headquarters (fig. 12.5). Other state capitals served their rural and resource-based hinterlands, with smaller and less diversified economic bases. In the immediate postwar period, Adelaide was somewhat of an exception, as the center of Australia's car industry.

Aboriginal Australians are much less likely to be urbanized than the broader Australian population. They are also more likely to live in small towns rather than large cities. Indeed, a little over 1% of Sydney's population and 1.7% of Perth's population is indigenous. Indigenous movement to the capital cities is often temporary and linked to kinship and friendship ties with rural areas. Aboriginal people have tended to dwell on the fringes of cities, often in substandard housing. For indigenous Australians, places of residence within the city are related to the provision of public housing

Table 12.4   Recent Migrant Arrivals to Australia, 2001 and 2006

City	Migrants Arriving 2001	Cities' Share of All People Migrating to Australia in 2001 (%)	Migrants Arriving 2006	Cities' Share of All People Migrating to Australia in 2006 (%)
Sydney	37,764	35.4	29,550	26.3
Melbourne	24,831	23.3	26,364	23.5
Brisbane	11,577	10.9	12,110	10.8
Adelaide	3,995	3.7	7,156	6.4
Perth	10,216	9.6	12,751	11.3
Hobart	410	0.4	644	0.5
Darwin	396	0.4	576	0.5
Canberra	1,601	1.5	1,753	1.6
Total	106,602		112,371	

Source: Australian Bureau of Statistics *Census of Population and Housing 2006* (www.censusdata.abs.gov.au).

and also to a strong sense of identification with place. One area of large indigenous urban settlement is "The Block," in Sydney's inner-city Redfern, where housing and other cultural services are concentrated.

The past 25 years have seen some shifts in the distribution of economic and population growth across Australia's large cities. Two factors have underpinned these slight alterations in the urban system. The first is the influx of people into Australian cities through international migration and its uneven distribution (tab. 12.4). For the past 20 years, more than 100,000 people annually have migrated to Australia from around the world, most of them to the capital cities, particularly Sydney, Brisbane, and Perth (fig. 12.6). Cities that have not received substantial numbers of migrants,

Figure 12.6 Although the immigrant stream to Australia has taken an Asian turn, the United Kingdom still supplies a major share of newcomers, including a young migrant from England who joins a newfound Australian friend near Kings Park in Perth. (Photo by Donald Zeigler)

Box 12.2   The Geography of Everyday Life in Suburban Sydney

Australia is a suburban nation. Despite increasing urban consolidation and gentrification, more than 72% of Sydney's population lives in detached housing, and 33% in areas more than 9 miles (15 km) from the city center. Suburban Sydney, unlike North American suburbs, is heterogeneous. Sydney's greatest concentration of migrants is found in its suburbs, and hence pockets of affluence and poverty neighbor one another. What is everyday life like in this differentiated world city?

Suburban Sydney residents live in houses of varying age and design. New houses are more likely to be large—27% of houses have four or more bedrooms, a double garage, formal and informal living areas, separate rooms for each child, perhaps a game/media room, and a backyard that may just be able to accommodate a cricket pitch. Family members—both adults and children—typically know their immediate neighborhood and participate in local sporting and recreational activities. The family shops locally, sometimes at a small corner shop or on a main street, but more likely at a supermarket in a large shopping mall. Here, not only can they pick up their weekly provisions, but they can also eat a meal and see a movie.

Daily travel patterns are increasingly complex spatially and socially. One adult (more likely male) will commute to the CBD for his job in the finance or business sector or to another suburb for manufacturing employment. The other (typically female) is likely to work in her own or a nearby suburb, most likely in retailing or in a similar service-sector job in banking, hospitality, or education. The limited availability of public transport in certain parts of suburban Sydney, and the generally poor of cross-suburban travel service options mean that these journeys to work are most likely to be undertaken by car. For parents of young children, the importance of the car is even more pronounced, as they drop children at school/childcare on their way to work and take them to social and sporting activities on the way home (fig. 12.7). For these suburbanites, the time and cost of car travel is becoming an increasing burden with no relief in sight.

---

like Adelaide and Hobart, have declined in relative terms. The second factor is globalization, or more specifically changing urban functions, as the Australian economy became increasingly tied to, and driven by, global flows of commodities and money and increasingly reliant on globally networked business services. Globalization has seen Sydney rise in prominence and prosperity and become Australia's only world city. The headquarters of Australian-based businesses, and the regional offices of multinationals, are now more likely to be in Sydney than in Melbourne. The relative growth of Brisbane and its surrounding region during the same period can be attributed to internal migration (principally from Sydney), the rise of a tourist-based economy, growing economic ties between Brisbane and the Asia-Pacific region, and Queensland government incentives for business to relocate to Australia's sunbelt.

Australia's capital cities are highly suburbanized and geographically expansive by international standards (box 12.2). Historically,

The Car as a Management Tool

Figure 12.7 New roles for women, and new problems, have emerged in Australian cities over the past three decades. (Courtesy of Robyn Dowling)

the predominant housing preference is for a detached house, producing sprawling suburban conurbations (fig. 12.8) such as that between Brisbane and the Gold Coast, 35 miles (60 km) away. The continued proliferation of suburban housing is currently under some threat. The high energy demands of suburban life—use of the private car and the heating, cooling, and water use levels of large houses—are increasingly questioned. Limited availability of land and the high costs of servicing the social and physical infrastructure needs of new suburbs have led to policies of urban consolidation across the nation (box 12.3). Mixed-use residential and commercial developments on former industrial land are increasing, and in some years the construction of new apartments outstrips that of detached houses. Equally important is a cultural and economic reevaluation of living in Australia's inner cities. Australian inner cities are vibrant, cosmopolitan spaces, with a wealth of retail, social, and recreational opportunities, and they are highly accessible by public transport.

Box 12.3   Using GIS to Analyze Urban Consolidation

Since the late 1980s, urban consolidation—increasing the density of dwellings or population (or both)—has been a central part of Sydney's official planning policy, aimed to minimize fringe development, improve infrastructure efficiency, limit car dependence, reduce pollution, and provide greater housing choice. Despite the potential environmental benefits, many communities in traditionally low-density Sydney have reacted negatively to consolidation, particularly where higher densities have been seen as insensitive to neighborhoods' urban character and landscape. However, adapting consolidation policies to balance ecological needs with community concerns requires detailed spatial information and analysis of the location, intensity, spread, and characteristics of higher density residential development. In 2003, researchers Holloway and Bunker at the University of Western Sydney used GIS to provide this analysis. For the period since 1981, they combined census information on population and housing stock, data on the dynamics of building approvals, and local government information on development applications for different types of dwellings to analyze the impact of urban consolidation and to assess outcomes over time on the built form of three specific local government areas (LGAs) in south and southwestern Sydney: Campbelltown, Sutherland, and Hurstville.

Their examination of the general distribution of higher-density dwellings showed the intensification of consolidation in established higher-density areas such as central and south Sydney; in the inner west, inner north, and eastern suburbs; and on linear concentrations along the major transport routes (particularly rail lines). More importantly, they could show the diffusion of higher-density housing forms through the middle suburbs as local authorities implement policy changes allowing dual occupancy and multiple small-lot developments. But the researchers also wished to understand how each LGA's context produced

The internal structure of Australian cities has changed over the past three decades. Based on an analysis of social and economic characteristics, metropolitan localities may be divided into seven types of places (fig. 12.9): three advantaged and four disadvantaged. In *new economy* localities are found people employed in new global industries, along with many educated professionals. *Gentrifying* localities are found across Australia's inner cities, and are home to those with ties to the global economy but have a sizeable proportion of low-income residents as well. *Middle-class suburbia* houses many educated professionals, though with a low density of connections to the global economy. *Working-class battler* communities house tradespeople, often homeowners, whereas *battling family communities* have above average levels of single-parent and nonfamily households. In *old economy* localities, primarily in suburban areas and especially in Adelaide, the decline of manufacturing has seen concentrations of unemployment. Finally, *periurban* localities on

different contributions to Sydney's consolidation, reflecting the LGAs' different histories and the differential effect of state and local policies. The older suburb of Hurstville in Sydney's south was shown to have been consolidated through major in-fill redevelopment and renewal of the ageing built environment, especially through the development of flats and units along rail and transport routes. High-rise apartment towers increasingly replaced the more traditional one-story bungalows or three-story flats that had characterized the neighborhood. The more recent development of neighboring Sutherland was reflected in the dominance of greenfield, low-density, separate-housing developments until the early 1990s when development pressure brought a steep increase in higher-density forms of residential development, especially in established town centers, along rail routes, and on the coastal fringe of the LGA. In contrast, Campbelltown's location on the city's southwestern fringe meant it was still dominated by Greenfield, low-density development with little high-density development, although a scattering of medium-density development has occurred on sites set aside in local planning policies for this purpose.

Applying GIS may not directly change community concerns in Sydney about urban consolidation, but it has armed planners with a fine-grained, integrated description and analysis of how market forces and planning policies of consolidation have combined to deliver dwelling stock in various patterns over the last two decades and to compare the characteristics of urban consolidation achieved in the distinctive circumstances of each LGA. These sorts of understandings have been important in producing recent adaptations to Sydney's consolidation policies in light of detailed knowledge of different housing submarkets, the supply of suitable sites, and the changing character of a neighborhood's built landscapes and social geography.

Source: Darren Holloway and Raymond Bunker, "Using GIS as an Aid to Understanding Urban Consolidation," *Australian Geographer*, 41 (2003), 44–57.

the fringe of the capitals attract low-income people seeking cheaper housing or housing for retirement.

While state capitals have, on average, been growing, small towns in rural and regional Australia have exhibited divergent patterns. Many rural towns, traditionally operating as service centers for the surrounding farms, have experienced population declines. Decreasing farm incomes, the closure of many public and commercial services such as banks, and limited employment and education op-portunities for young people have encouraged migration out of these towns and into larger regional centers or, more commonly, capital cities. A counter trend of growth in Australia's coastal towns is also evident. The 21st century boom in resource prices has meant that towns in coastal Australia have grown rapidly, instigating severe housing shortages and consequent escalations in housing prices. The "sea change" phenomenon, in which city dwellers swap a hectic city lifestyle, transportation congestion, and high housing costs for a slower

Figure 12.8 Sydney is known as a city of suburbs and single family homes such as this one. (Courtesy of Robyn Dowling)

pace of life and cheaper housing in coastal towns is also important. Initially confined to older people, principally retirees and those nearing retirement, sea changes are now undertaken by young professionals who able to run businesses outside the major cities, as well as by less affluent families seeking cheaper home ownership. Towns like Byron Bay, Coffs Harbour, and Port Macquarie in New South Wales; Barwon Heads in Victoria; and Denmark in West Australia are commonly identified sea-change locations. "Tree change" is a more recent but similar phenomenon in which urban dwellers move to greener locations like rural Tasmania, inland New South Wales (e.g., Orange, Mudgee), or Victoria (e.g., Daylesford).

Aotearoa/New Zealand

After World War II, the growth trajectories of the cities in Aotearoa/New Zealand largely paralleled those of Australia. The four largest cities of Auckland, Wellington, Christchurch, and Dunedin continued to grow, as did the primacy of Auckland (see tab. 12.1). A number of processes underpinned this pattern. Market reforms since the 1980s have strengthened global economic, cultural, and social ties, which in turn have transformed large cities. Second, immigrants, initially from the Pacific Islands but also more recently from China and India, have flowed into the large cities, especially Auckland and Christchurch. The third factor is the internal shift in economic activity. Although a general process of deindustrialization in Aotearoa/New Zealand occurred in the late 20th century, employment losses in manufacturing were more severe in Wellington, Christchurch, and Dunedin, and some manufacturing relocated to Auckland. Finally, entrepreneurial urban governance processes were deployed to make cities more attractive and to stem population decline. In Wellington, for example, the waterfront was redeveloped using both public-

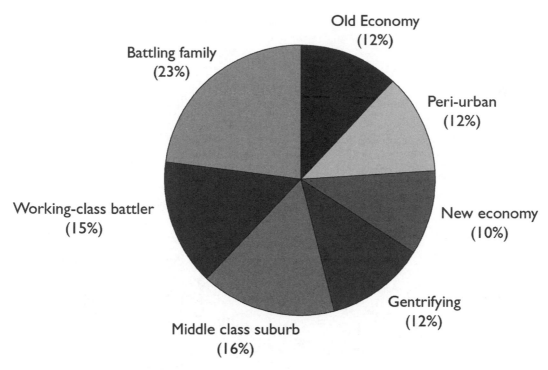

Figure 12.9 Locality Types in Australia's Large Cities. Changes over the past three decades have produced new types of urban localities in Australia. *Source:* Compiled by authors from statistics in Scott Baum, Kevin O'Conner, and Robert Stimson, *Faultlines Exposed* (Melbourne: Monash University ePress, 2005).

and private-sector investment. The aim was for the city to become an international conference venue, and the government also located the new Te Papa National Museum there.

Aotearoa/New Zealand cities are low density, though suburban living is no longer the only residential option. High- and medium-rise apartments are becoming more common across the urban landscape. The proportion of Maoris living in urban Aotearoa/New Zealand is now almost on par with that of the non-Maori population, because of the loss of Maori land and consequent rural-to-urban migration. Maoris face significant disadvantages in the cities, with high rates of unem-

ployment and lower levels of home ownership and education. Increasing ethnic diversity is also an important characteristic.

REPRESENTATIVE CITIES

Sydney: Australia's World City

From the earliest days of European colonization to the 1980s, Sydney and Melbourne have jostled for national dominance of Australia's emergent urban system. Since then, Australia's increasing global integration and the deregulation of its financial system have seen Sydney emerge as an international finance market,

Figure 12.10 Completed in 1932, the Sydney Harbor Bridge opened up the North Shore of the harbor. Tourists, tethered by lifelines, have been climbing the arch since 1998. (Photo by Donald Zeigler)

attract a growing concentration of corporate headquarters and becoming not only the nation's dominant city but Oceania's highest value-generating economy and a dominant world city. With a population currently just over 4 million and tipped to reach 5 million by 2025, Sydney is the most populous and most prosperous city in Australia. The city is home to some of Australia's most widely recognized iconic landmarks: the Harbour Bridge (fig. 12.10), the Opera House (fig. 12.11), and Bondi Beach. More revealingly, it demonstrates some of the defining characteristics of contemporary Australian urban life: suburbia, urban-based prosperity arising from an ad-

vanced service economy, multiculturalism, and environmental threat.

Sydney entered the 20th century as the primate city and highest-order service center in the state of New South Wales (fig. 12.12). By 1911, just 123 years after European settlement began, it had a population of 652,000 and was already a city of suburbs. Substantive population growth had coincided with the development of a radial suburban railway system so all but the lowest-income residents had settled in expanding residential suburbs away from the dense rows of terraced houses of the inner city. The completion of the Harbour Bridge in 1932, connecting the harbor's North Shore to

Figure 12.11 A newly-designated UNESCO World Heritage site, the Sydney Opera House has become the symbol of the island continent. (Photo by Donald Zeigler)

the central business district (CBD), enabled further development of high-amenity suburbs to the city's north. Sydney's post–World War II "long boom" brought unprecedented economic and population growth and set in motion the formative settlement patterns that have shaped the contemporary city. Between 1947 and 1971, population expanded by 65% to reach 2.8 million; it grew to 4.1 million by 2006. The vast majority of growth has been accommodated in expansive suburban developments, including large scale public housing estates built mainly across the city's western suburbs. Despite planned expansions of public transport networks, the rate of urban expansion and rising levels of car ownership meant that the city quickly assumed the car-oriented form of autosuburbia, connected by networks of freeways rather than by public transport corridors. Speculative developers' and housing consumers' preferences for low-density, detached dwellings meant that the city assumed a sprawled metropolitan form, poorly served by the existing rail network radiating from the CBD (fig. 12.13). Twenty years of urban consolidation policy has contained the extent of sprawl, but strong population growth (50,000 per year since the late 1990s) has meant that fringe expansion has continued. Sydney's employment, retailing, and services have been decentralizing since at least the 1970s. The development of regional centers of commercial activity, such as Ryde, North Sydney, Parramatta, Penrith, and Liverpool, has given the city an increasingly polycentric form. Indeed, the most recent metropolitan planning strategy (2005) labels Sydney "the city of cities."

Figure 12.12 In 1916, Sydney's government decided to locate the Taronga Zoo right on Sydney Harbor. As a result, many long-necked ungulates have a better view of the city's skyline than do human bipeds. (Photo by Donald Zeigler)

Despite Sydney's predominantly low-rise suburban form, the city center is characterized by high-rise office towers, global tourist landscapes, and lately residential towers tightly grouped on the edges of one of the world's most spectacular natural harbors (fig. 12.14). Since the late 1960s significant waves of international property investment—in commercial office and hotel developments—have transformed the CBD's built environment, as has the transformation of Sydney's economic base to one dominated by increasingly globally connected financial and other advanced services. Sydney has become one of the most significant financial centers in the Asia-Pacific realm, making up 40% of Australia's telecommunications market. By 2001, finance, insurance, property, and business services made up 21% of Sydney's employment. A measure of Sydney's economic dominance is that this constitutes more than 35% of the entire national workforce in these sectors. Although such employment is found in

regional centers across the metropolis, it is particularly concentrated in and around the city center where many of the estimated 600 multinational companies that run their Asia Pacific operations from Sydney are clustered, along with the headquarters of approximately 200 of Australasia's top companies. The economy of the city center now generates 30% of the value of metropolitan Sydney's economic output and contains 28% of all metropolitan employment, with high concentrations in the highly paid professional and managerial occupations.

Concentrated in Sydney's city center are high-paid, advanced-services workers, as increasingly globalized connections have driven long-standing processes of gentrification, the recent resurgence of high-rise luxury residential dwellings, and the multiplication of globalized consumer spaces. Inner suburbs of 19th-century housing have been revitalized. New up-market residential locales have been built on high-density, previously used land on

Figure 12.13 Australia is a land of open space, a fact of geography reflected in its sprawling suburbs. (Photo by Rowland Atkinson)

the edges of the CBD (fig. 12.15) and in a host of high-rise high-density towers throughout the CBD. These developments have meant that the resident population of Sydney's inner city has increased by 40% since 1996. The development of a range of globalized consumer spaces, catering both to global tourists and inner-city residents, have also transformed the city center and have tended to be politically contentious, not least because many have been state managed. In the 1980s the New South Wales government redeveloped Darling

Figure 12.14 Sydney's skyline, typical of a world city, dominates Sydney Harbor. (Photo by Richard Lever)

Figure 12.15 Jackson's Landing is being developed on the former site of a sugar refinery in Pyrmont, an inner suburb of Sydney. (Photo by Rowland Atkinson)

Harbour container terminal as an international conference, festival, shopping, and entertainment precinct. In the 1990s, special legislation was passed to enable redevelopment of heritage wharves at Walsh Bay as an exclusive residential, commercial office and restaurant precinct. The current state government proposal for a major urban renewal scheme for Redfern-Waterloo just south of the CBD is likely to be similarly contentious as growing demand for "world city" spaces clashes with the needs of socially disadvantaged populations whose inner-city location is now under threat. A special purpose Redfern-Waterloo Authority (RWA) has been formed to oversee redevelopment of vast tracts of publicly owned land into residential, commercial, and consumer spaces suited to Sydney's trajectory as a dominant world city. Controversially, much of the public land to be redeveloped is currently occupied by public housing. More controversially still, the area targeted for redevelopment contains The Block, an aboriginal-owned site, a renowned center of Sydney's aboriginal community, and a symbolic locus of urban aboriginal identity. The RWA has been granted exceptional powers as the sole planning authority for the area, exempt from heritage protection legislation. Political clashes between government plans and community demands seem inevitable.

Sydney's world city status is also reflected in the fact that between 1996 and 2001, 40% of all migrants to Australia settled in this city. This both deepened and diversified the long-established multicultural nature of Sydney's population (box 12.4). The 2006 census showed that 1.63 million of Sydney's population of 4.12 million were born overseas, with a further 1.7 million being second generation (i.e., the children of migrants). The United Kingdom (174,404), China (109,142), and Aotearoa/New Zealand (81,065) have been the dominant source countries, though there are also substan-

Box 12.4 Multiculturalism and Local Government in Australia

Cities in Australia have long been immigrant cities. After World War II, labor migration to Australia was dominated by people from the United Kingdom, Ireland, and southern Europe. The 1980s and 1990s saw a shift in source countries toward Southeast Asia, and more recently toward Africa and the Middle East. Hence, cities like Sydney are characterized by considerable cultural diversity. It is largely within urban neighborhoods that "everyday multiculturalism," the ordinary living of cultural diversity, occurs. Sometimes, this engenders conflict, as seen in the following excerpt from an article by a religious affairs reporter for the *Sydney Morning Herald*.

A Muslim centre built in the heart of Sydney's Bible Belt is facing fresh opposition—over its plans to host midnight prayers. But plans to extend the Annangrove prayer centre's hours and permit it to open late at night on three holy days have attracted four objections—well short of the thousands of complaints that almost blocked its construction four years ago. . . . The trustees [of the Imam Hasan Centre] want permission to open the doors until midnight three times a year, an increase in capacity from 120 to 150 people and a 45-minute extension in operating hours to permit cleaning and the occasional committee hearing. "Can you tell me any church that has any time restriction or limit on numbers?" said Abbas Aly, one of the centre's trustees. . . . "If you ring up our neighbours they'll tell you they hardly notice us here. It's hardly used midweek and most of our programs are on a Saturday."

The [Baulkham Hills] council originally refused to approve the centre when more than 900 local residents claimed its existence threatened the ambience and character of the semi-rural suburb, in Sydney's north-west. Mr. Aly appealed to the Land and Environment Court, which reversed the decision on the grounds that the local objections were not based on facts. Once construction started, the site was vandalised, sprayed with racist graffiti and smeared with animal offal. Pigs' heads were impaled on wooden stakes. Mr. Aly said tensions between local people and the centre had long since dissipated, except for the occasional persistent critic, especially as it had become clear that the centre looked more like a community centre than a mosque. "We've had quite a positive response to our latest development application from neighbours, compared to the 8500 complaints to our construction. We get quite a number of people who have come in to apologise. I asked them did they see the plans, they said, 'No, we just believed what we were told,' and I take my hat off to them for coming in and making their peace." The Mayor of Baulkham Hills, Tony Hay, said four complaints had been lodged against the variation in consent orders, mainly expressing concern that creeping changes were undermining the intent of the original Land and Environment Court proceedings. No decision had been taken yet. . . . (Linda Morris, "Midnight Prayers Raise Objections," Sydney Morning Herald, September 10, 2007.)

tial numbers of residents who were born in Vietnam (62,143), Lebanon (54,502), India (52,974), the Philippines (52,088), Italy (44,562), Hong Kong (36,866), Korea (32,124), and Greece (32,022). Historically, particular migrant groups—especially those of non-English-speaking backgrounds—have tended to settle initially in particular Sydney suburbs: Greeks in Marrickville and Italians in Leichardt in the 1950s and 1960s, Vietnamese in Cabramatta in the 1970s and 1980s, Lebanese in Auburn in the 1990s. However, recent research has shown that Sydney's settlement is characterized more by multiethnic suburbs than by ethnic minority concentrations, and by the intermixing of different ethnic minority groups both with each other and with the host society rather than by ethnic segregation. Over time, spatial and social assimilation of migrants into a predominantly multicultural city has been the dominant pathway.

Whether growing evidence of social polarization in Sydney will produce more entrenched sociospatial segregation along lines of class and ethnicity is a concern both to Sydney's planners and its citizens. In a trend common to many global cities, Sydney's median dwelling price rose by 100% between 1996 and 2003, such that housing stress (i.e., paying more than 30% of household income for housing) now affects nearly 170,000 households across the city. As the median house price has crept up, lower income groups, including recent migrants, have been increasingly confined either to rental housing or to less-accessible suburbs removed from employment opportunities and services. It remains to be seen whether Sydney's social divides, traditionally nowhere near as pronounced as in U.S. cities, are set to become increasingly stark.

Nonetheless, Sydney remains renowned for its quality of life. It habitually enjoys a top-five position in international benchmarking exercises assessing physical and cultural lifestyle assets. However, the city's beautiful natural environment, open spaces, and national parks belie the environmental challenges generated by Sydney's car-dependent nature and population pressure, especially regarding air quality and water supply. Car ownership is ubiquitous, and 70% of trips are taken by private motor vehicle. Sydney's sprawling form, with a density that is 2.5 times less than London, has meant that car travel is increasing at about 15% per year. Consequently, air quality suffers as a result of photochemical smog-producing ozone at levels that, although improving, still regularly exceed the four-hour standard for ozone concentration an average of 21 days a year. In addition, despite falling rates of water use per capita, Sydney's population growth is challenging the adequacy of the city's water supply (box 12.5). In 2002, Sydney's water consumption was at 106% of the amount that can be sustainably drawn from the drainage basin. Continuing urban development poses a significant threat to Sydney's water quality.

Perth: Isolated Millionaire

With a population of 1.5 million, Perth may be the world's most isolated large city (fig. 12.17). Located on Australia's west coast, Perth was established in 1829 along the banks of the Swan River. The city was laid out according to the grid pattern commonly associated with colonial planning. As the colonial capital of Western Australia until 1901 (when the states were united as a Commonwealth),

Perth grew slowly for its first 100 years. Throughout its history Perth served both a rural and a mining hinterland, as much of Australia's key mineral resources were located in Western Australia—gold and bauxite, for example. It is mining and other global connections that have shaped the city over the past 50 years. The mining boom of the 1960s and 1970s, coupled with immigration (primarily from the United Kingdom but also from parts of southeast Asia), instigated an acceleration of the city's economic and population growth. The location of offices of mining companies and associated services saw tall buildings emerge on the city skyline. The 1980s were characterized by a spirit embraced by both government and business. A consumption and leisure-based economy emerged, aided by the city's hosting of the 1987 America's Cup Challenge and by the presence of a substantial number of entrepreneurs and developers. Throughout the 1990s, the Perth economy continued to thrive, through its mining and tourism base, again boosted by substantial immigration.

Now capital of the state of Western Australia, Perth today is far removed from its colonial beginnings. Not only does it have a modern skyscraper-dominated skyline, but the entrepreneurial governance of the 1980s and 1990s involved substantial redevelopment of older parts of the city as tourist and leisure spaces. The redevelopment of the old Swan Brewery site in inner Perth is one example of these processes. In the late 1980s, the State Government's development corporation proposed to redevelop the site, which was once home to the factory making Perth's famous beer. It now hosts a myriad of leisure activities including theatres, dining, and office space, as well as car parking. Across Australian cities such redevelopment plans are invariably contested, and conflict at the old Swan Brewery is representative of indigenous struggles to claim space within urban Australia. In this particular case, Aboriginal protesters drew attention to the symbolic significance the site held for them; they wanted the brewery buildings demolished and the land returned to parkland. Their point was made in a variety of ways, including an eleven-month period in which they camped on the site. The protests were unsuccessful, with the government authority going ahead with the redevelopment and incorporating elements of Aboriginal culture into the design. On another level, however, the protest was successful for the ways it brought an Aboriginal presence into the urban world.

Perth, like other Australian cities, is a sprawling city. Population growth has spawned metropolitan growth, initially to the east and more recently southward toward the municipality of Mandurah. For much of the 20th century it was presumed that the private car would adequately cater to the transportation needs of this growing population. More recently, however, the necessity of public transportation has increasingly been recognized. A new, profitable, and well-patronized suburban railway line to east Perth was opened. Perth is also home to a wide variety of other sustainable transport initiatives. Foremost here are "TravelSmart" programs, run by employers, schools, universities, or workplaces. These programs encourage individuals to consider non-car travel, and sometimes provide incentives to do so. Like Auckland's "walking school buses," they have been successful in reducing private automobile travel in Perth and in raising awareness of the city's precarious environmental future.

Box 12.5   Heat, Fire, and Flood

Nature and culture—geographical location, environmental conditions, and human practices—combine to ensure that the cities of Oceania face a daunting array of environmental hazards including bushfires, drought, and the impacts of climate change.

When the yearly Australian bushfire season crosses paths with urban development the impacts can be devastating. There have been eight major bushfire events—mainly caused by human agency—in the Sydney region since the late 1950s. They have resulted in extensive losses of property, wildlife, and human life. In the catastrophic Sydney fires of 1993–1994, 800 fires resulted in four deaths and the loss of 206 homes. 800,000 hectares were burnt, including most of Sydney's historic Royal National Park. Fires reached within 6 miles (10 km) of the CBD, and 25,000 people were evacuated as smoke shrouded the city and black tidemarks of ash were washed up on Sydney's famous beaches. The historic drought conditions afflicting all of eastern Australia since 2001 have heightened the severity of individual fire events, producing "unstoppable" fire conditions.

January 18, 2003, saw Australia's capital city, Canberra, engulfed by fires that had been triggered by lightning strikes in drought-affected vegetation areas and had burned around the city for several days previously. High temperatures and strong winds took the fires out of control as they reached the urban limits. As the city set alight, more than 500 homes were destroyed and four people killed; many more were afflicted by smoke inhalation and fire-related illnesses. At the margins of Australia's cities, as residents seek to live close to high quality natural environments at the edge of the bush, the interface of fire-prone ecosystems and urban development continues to expand, meaning that bush-fire hazard will be an ongoing feature of Australian urban life (fig. 12.16).

Many further forms of environmental hazard arise from climate change. By 1999 Australia was the world's worst per capita emitter of climate-change-inducing greenhouse gases, with about half of those emissions attributable to urban activities including coal-based energy generation. Despite research suggesting that carbon dioxide emissions could be significantly reduced through economically feasible technological advances, shifts to renewable energy, and subsidized promotion of energy efficiency practices, the political will to secure this transformation is currently lacking. As long as this continues to be the case, both Australian

Auckland: Economic Hub of New Zealand

Although not the nation's capital, Auckland has dominated Aotearoa/New Zealand's urban system since overtaking Dunedin and Christchurch as Aotearoa/New Zealand's largest city in the late 19th century. Like Sydney, it developed on an aesthetically and economically advantageous harbor and is similarly renowned for its natural beauty. Historically, it too served a rich agricultural and forested hinterland. The deregulation of the Aotearoa/New Zealand economy in the mid 1980s paved the way for the transformation of

Figure 12.16 Cricketers in Cessnock carry on regardless of huge bushfires, October 19, 2002. *Source: Sydney Morning Herald*, picture by Darren Pateman.

cities and those of neighboring Pacific Island nations will continue to live with the threat of the escalating hazards of climate change. For the Pacific Island nations, the most devastating of these is sea level change, already disrupting tourism and local livelihoods, and pushing islanders to migrate. Australian cities are liable to become increasingly vulnerable to flooding related to intensive storms and sea level change: a particular concern to a nation in which the population is intensely concentrated in coastal cities. Simultaneously, rising temperatures will bring intensified photochemical smog, water shortages, and rising numbers of days with very high temperatures. In a peculiar circularity, this will limit the number of days in which controlled burns to reduce the fuel load of bushland on the urban margins are possible, and the product of this will be intensified risk of severe bushfires.

Auckland. It is Aotearoa/New Zealand's largest, most prosperous and economically active city. In 1993 it hosted more than a third of the nation's employment in manufacturing, transport, communication, and business services. It increasingly occupies a strategic position in the national economy because it is a place of importance in the global economy. It is the location of multinationals, international financial transactions, and global property investments and is a hub for international tourists. Global rather than local connections are also important in explaining a number of other facets of urban life in Aotearoa/New Zealand.

Figure 12.17 Perth sits in splendid isolation on the southwest coast of Australia, the primate city for a vast, underpopulated region. (Photo courtesy Australian government)

The 1980s saw the transformation of Auckland's residential and commercial landscapes. High-rise residential towers (like the famous Sky Tower, the tallest building in the Southern Hemisphere) were built around the city's CBD, often financed in foreign currencies, designed by architects outside Aotearoa/New Zealand, and managed by global property conglomerates. High-rise residential living has become increasingly popular. The building of medium-density housing has added to the city's density. Sometimes modeled on "new urbanist" ideas imported directly from the United States, these new suburbs modify the conventional suburban way of life with smaller houses, a gridded street pattern, and sometimes communal open space. Though not gated communities in the strictest sense, the role of these new suburbs in fostering social exclusion is an ongoing issue. In fact, the

same issue often arises as inner-city neighborhoods undergo gentrification (box 12.6)

Lifestyle television programs and home-focused magazines are hugely popular and foster expenditures on household items and renovation projects. Suburban backyards may be getting smaller, but they still serve the important purpose of providing a place for children to play, vegetables to be domestically cultivated, and aesthetic and economic aspirations to be fulfilled. Some new groups of migrants do aspire to and fulfill these suburban ideals, such as residence in a detached house. Migration has also transformed suburban landscapes. Suburbs such as Sandringham, with new places of worship and retail landscapes, were the destination of many migrants from Asia in the 1990s.

The sustainability of a large, dynamic city like Auckland is attracting increasing scholarly

Box 12.6   Gentrification and Ponsonby Road, Auckland

Whether the claim that gentrification is now a global phenomenon is valid or not, this urbanization process has certainly reshaped the inner suburbs of many of Australia and New Zealand/Aotearoa's cities. The process has witnessed middle-class renovation and resettlement of formerly working-class housing in inner-city neighborhoods in all the major metropolitan centers, as well as in regional cities such as Newcastle and Wollongong in New South Wales. Gentrification is not merely a residential phenomenon but one involving the refashioning of local shopping streets, leisure and recreation facilities, and neighborhood services, as residents' aesthetics, ethos, and consumption patterns combine to mold local streetscapes. These impacts are evident on King Street in Sydney's Newtown, Brunswick Street in Melbourne's Fitzroy's, Boundary Road in Brisbane's West End, Darby Street in Newcastle's Cooks Hill, and Ponsonby Road in Auckland's Ponsonby.

The suburb of Ponsonby is located less than a mile west of Auckland's CBD. After World War II, many of Ponsonby's more prosperous residents relocated to the expanding outer suburbs and were replaced by lower-income Pacific Island and Maori migrants. However, waves of gentrification commenced in the 1970s, as diverse groups of young, well-educated Pakeha (white New Zealanders of European descent) were attracted to the area by its cheap property, low rents, and social and ethnic diversity. Ironically, that diversity can be threatened by the very process of gentrification. In Ponsonby's case, gentrification overlapped with an Auckland-wide housing boom and property-price inflation in the 1990s; the result has been significant displacement of lower-income, less-educated inhabitants, driven out by rising rents and spiraling house prices. Ponsonby's population has, proportionately, become distinctly "whiter" and higher income. Nonetheless, despite price inflation, the area has maintained a relatively young population and a significant proportion of rental housing.

Certainly, diversity is characteristic of the dramatic transformation of the consumption spaces and public culture of Ponsonby Road (http://www.ponsonbyroad.co.nz/ponsonbyroad/). Gentrification has combined with changes in licensing laws to see the birth of a thriving agglomeration of over 90 cafés, restaurants, and bars, interspersed with specialty stores, greengrocers, butchers, and newsagents. Mark Latham's research has shown how the plethora of cafés and bars—often flamboyantly and expensively styled and open to the street—depart from the more traditional, enclosed spaces of pubs and the culture of hard-drinking masculinity they accommodate more readily than other forms of sociality. As a result, gentrification has seen Ponsonby Road develop a range of more ambiguous spaces for consumption and sociability that are welcoming to women, that are gay-friendly, and that are less confined to traditional norms of gendered identity. In this particular site of gentrification, working-class displacement and middle-class colonization have been accompanied by the development of a diverse public culture that, although definitely accessible (most easily to those with disposable income), is open to diverse expressions of identity and diverse ways of inhabiting the city.

Source: Alan Latham, "Urbanity, Lifestyle and Making Sense of the New Urban Cultural Economy," *Urban Studies*, 40 (2003), 1699–1724.

and policy attention. Contradictions between reliance on the private motor vehicle and a strong environmental consciousness have seen the widespread adoption of "walking school buses" in Auckland. Rather than children being driven individually to school, they are dropped at locations along a designated route and walk to school with other children and parents to supervise. Walking school buses now operate in many Auckland suburbs, typically in middle-class neighborhoods. They have been credited with removing cars from the road, reducing air pollution, reducing obesity, and enhancing community. Official urban policies of sustainability have already influenced the building of medium-density housing and of housing with a small ecological footprint. A more widespread implementation of urban sustainability in Auckland has also recently been discussed.

Port Moresby and Suva: Representative Capitals of the Island Pacific

Port Moresby and Suva are the largest cities, and also the political capitals, of their respective nations of Papua New Guinea (PNG) and Fiji. They have parallel histories, urban patterns, and contemporary influences. Although their current political instabilities may be unique, their other characteristics are broadly representative of large cities in the island Pacific.

Neither PNG nor Fiji has a prosperous economy. They have weak manufacturing sectors, are reliant on an agricultural sector that is beset with inefficiencies, and are at the mercy of low global prices for their commodities. Hence, Suva and Port Moresby have similarly fragile economic bases. Although population has been steadily growing in both cities, employment opportunities have not. Conse-

quently, unemployment is high, with one estimate putting unemployment in Port Moresby at around 60% in 2003. These fragile economic circumstances underpin the most salient characteristics of both these cities: a large informal sector, including informal settlements, and political problems and unrest (fig. 12.18).

Informal, squatter-like settlements are common in these cities. Port Moresby has at least 84 agglomerations of substandard, poorly serviced housing, in which urban poverty is concentrated; Suva has just a little less. Basic urban infrastructure—water, sewerage, electricity, garbage collection—is either lacking or is minimally provided in such settlements. Problems are exacerbated by a lack of formal employment opportunities. Urban poverty is rising, as exemplified by the increasing number of street children. Informal employment, particularly prostitution, has arisen to counter the lack of formal-sector employment opportunities.

Policy responses to urban poverty and marginalization in Suva and Port Moresby have been small and problematic. The underfunding of basic infrastructure has contributed to the problem. There is widespread opposition to the urban poor and to street prostitution. The governments' responses to prostitution, street children, and informal settlement have been largely negative. In PNG, problem settlements have been bulldozed rather than adequately resourced. More generally, these cities have been sites of social unrest. External interventions, such as an Australian military presence in Fiji in 2003, have sometimes followed. Such political unrest has also had implications for the internal structures of these cities. In Port Moresby, for example, security concerns have seen European and other expatriates withdraw

Figure 12.18 Outdoor markets, such as this one in Suva, the capital of Fiji, are a staple of life in the scattered towns of the Pacific Islands. (Photo by Richard Ulack)

further into barricaded residential estates on the hillsides of the city.

Gold Coast and Honolulu: Tourism Urbanization

Australian sociologist Patrick Mullin has used the term "tourism urbanization" to describe a scenario of tourism-sustained urban growth, where (1) urban development is based primarily on tourist consumption of goods and services for pleasure, and (2) urban form is shaped by the city's function as a leisure space. Both the Gold Coast on Australia's Queensland coast and Honolulu in the U.S. state of Hawaii can be understood in these terms.

Gold Coast, Queensland, Australia

On Australia's Gold Coast—25 miles (40 km) south of Queensland's capital city, Brisbane—white settlement began in the 1840s with log-ging and agricultural development. By the 1870s wealthy Brisbane residents were already discovering the area as a leisure destination, known simply as the South Coast. The development of a rail connection from Brisbane in the 1930s saw the area's appeal broaden and some minor beach resorts emerge. But it was not until the boom of the 1950s that the area took on the name "Gold Coast" and began its development as Australia's highest intensity high-rise tourist destination. Through many cycles of boom and bust from the 1950s to the 1990s, intense real estate investment in tourist accommodation, retail, restaurants, and entertainment ventures along this 35-mile (56-km) strip of spectacular surfing beaches, transformed the Gold Coast into the most intensely developed coastal tourist strip in Australia and a key international tourist destination (fig. 12.19).

By the 1980s, the area—especially Surfers Paradise at the heart of the Gold Coast—had

Figure 12.19 Like some futuristic vision, high rises on the Gold Coast soar above the beaches that draw tourists by the millions to Queensland's coast. (Photo by Jack Williams)

gained a dubious reputation as a place of relaxed social norms, brashly opulent neon-lit landscapes, and get-rich-quick real estate deals. Nonetheless, the 1980s and 1990s saw it mature as a tourist destination. Large-scale foreign direct investment in real estate, especially from Japanese interests in the 1980s and more recently from the Middle East, brought significant diversification to the array of tourist products and consumption landscapes in Surfers Paradise and its hinterland. The area developed a series of integrated tourist resorts such as the Marina Mirage and the golf-themed Sanctuary Cove; large-scale retail malls such as Pacific fair, Conrad Jupiters casino; multiple golf courses; and 17 theme parks, including Movieworld, Sea World, Dream World, and Wet 'n' Wild Waterworld.

The Gold Coast (incorporated as a city since 1959) has had a rapidly expanding resident population, reaching 480,000 in 2006. Its more than 13,000 accommodation rooms in hotels and serviced apartments accommodate an additional 3.5 million domestic visitors and

800,000 international visitors annually, primarily from Asian countries and Aotearoa/New Zealand. Day trippers also add to the local population. But the Gold Coast today is underlain by more than a consumption-driven tourist economy. It is also one of the most rapidly developing cities in Australia, characterized by sustained rapid annual population growth rates of around 2%. Its growth is largely migrant driven as lifestyle attractions have drawn in-migrants from across Australia. In the 1980s and 1990s, many were housed in low-density canal-estates built behind the high-rise coastal strip. More recently, as the Gold Coast has expanded, more conventional forms of suburbia have developed, including a major new-town development in Robina in the city's southwest. As this has occurred, the initial dominance of retirees amongst in-migrants—which prompted one author to label the city "God's waiting room"—has subsided such that the largest in-migrant group is now those between 20 and 29 years old. The city's population is expected to reach nearly 700,000 by 2021, but the Gold Coast is also blending into the extended urban region of southeast Queensland (SEQ), a conurbation which stretches 125 miles (200 km) from Noosa southward through Brisbane and the Gold Coast to Tweed in northern New South Wales. SEQ's population reached 2.78 million in 2006, representing more than two-thirds of Queensland's population. The population of SEQ is projected to reach 4 million by 2026, an average growth of around 60,000 each year.

As the Gold Coast blends into this urban region, its economy is diversifying. Tourism-related industries have tended to support lower-skilled occupations and low-paid and/or casual employment, prone to seasonal fluctuation. Now, the state-supported Pacific Innovation Corridor initiative aims to promote the region's high-tech, biotech, computing, and multimedia industries that will integrate the region into a globalized knowledge economy and improve rail and road connections to Brisbane. Nonetheless, Gold Coast is still one of the lowest-income cities in Australia and has higher levels of socioeconomic disadvantage than other Australian cities, in part a product of its occupational structure. The tourism-dominated economy is reflected in lower-skilled occupations, low rates of higher education, high rates of low-paid casual employment, and high rates of unemployment. As the conurbation expands, challenges emerge: managing disadvantage, enabling economic diversification, building roads and transit systems, developing sustainable communities, and balancing environmental protection against development.

Honolulu, Hawaii, United States

Honolulu's tourism urbanization has occurred in the midst of relative geographic isolation, 2,400 miles (3,900 km) from the continental United States and 3,850 miles (6,200 km) from Japan. Yet annexation by the United States in 1898 and U.S. statehood in 1959 have meant that Honolulu's development has been sustained by its links to the U.S. economy and particularly by flows of American tourists to the Hawaiian Islands. Honolulu's size and economic development make it an anomaly among the diverse and generally much smaller urban economies of the Pacific islands. The city is located in the southeast corner of Oahu, the most populous of Hawaii's eight main islands, on which reside 73% of Hawaii's 1.2 million people. It is Hawaii's capital and the state's largest city. The 377,000 residents of Honolulu's concentrated urban settlement make up 42% of Oahu's population and 31% of Hawaii's total population.

Historically, Honolulu developed as a whaling port and refueling stop for trans-Pacific trade in the mid-19th century. It traded in sandalwood, whale oil, and fur, and later in sugar and pineapples. As a business and trading hub for the Hawaiian Islands, it is the main seaport for the region (and it includes an economically important foreign trade zone), though the long shipping distances to export markets have limited its development. A series of U.S. military defense bases also provide important revenue flows. However, since achieving statehood, tourism has been the dominant industry. Oahu's renowned surfing beaches, rugged volcanic landscapes, and lush tropical vegetation have seen Honolulu develop as a major tourist destination, particularly for American and Japanese visitors, assisted by Honolulu International Airport's role as the main Pacific airline hub for international travel to the South Pacific, Australia, and Aotearoa/New Zealand.

Honolulu's tourist economy is overwhelmingly focused along the world famous Waikiki

Beach where, in 2005, a concentration of 66 hotels, rental apartments, and time-shares offered nearly 38,000 tourist accommodation rooms. A dense mixture of hotels, nightlife, and tourist shops, including Ala Moana—the world's largest open-air shopping center—stretch along Waikiki, capped on its eastern end by the volcanic Diamond Head and to the east (or landward) by the exclusive residential neighborhoods of Wai'alae and Kahala.

The dominance of tourist development has meant that Honolulu's employment structure offers predominantly lower-skilled, seasonal, casual, and low-paying employment opportunities. Moreover, the economy is highly vulnerable to fluctuations in the global tourism industry. The immediate post-9/11 downturn in international travel, for instance, saw airlines cut back on flights to Honolulu. Waikiki's hotel rooms lay empty despite major discounting, and staff lay-offs drove many into unemployment. Recovery from this major economic disruption has taken several years. Low-paid employment, tourism's inflationary impact on housing costs, and high food and fuel prices endemic to remote Pacific economies mean that half of Honolulu's residents say they cannot adequately cover their expenses. One-eighth of the population lives below the poverty line.

Hawaii's remote location and limited economic opportunities create a scenario in which turning economic diversification away from tourism urbanization is challenging. The state government offers direct financial incentives to promote capital investment in new industrial development, particularly targeting technology-related companies. It is looking to build on existing research capabilities of the University of Hawaii and synergies with the defense industries to pursue economic development in information and communication technologies, biotechnology, and space sciences. For the present time, tourism continues to attract greater foreign investment and it remains to be seen whether Honolulu can move beyond its dependence on a combination of tourism and government employment and realize its ambitions to diversify.

TRENDS AND CHALLENGES

Many of the cities in Australia and the Pacific are cradled by fragile ecosystems and are extremely vulnerable to the multifaceted impacts of climate change. Australian cities are further challenged by the impacts of long-term drought on urban water supplies. Some cities (e.g., Perth and Sydney) have, or are constructing, desalination plants to convert seawater to drinking water. This may be a solution to water supply, but it has other environmental impacts because of the voluminous energy demands of the desalination process. In addition, the geographic expansion of urbanized areas involves cutting down trees and increases energy use. The imperative in all cities has thus become reduced energy consumption alongside increased use of renewable energy resources.

Urban governance provides many challenges across the region. The challenge is the establishment of effective urban governments able to meet environmental and security needs (fig. 12.20). Governance processes that contribute to social cohesion are also key. In Australia and Aotearoa/New Zealand, urban governance is now characterized by a variant of neoliberalism in which market processes and solutions underpin policy. Waterfront redevelopments in many cities are classic outcomes of neoliberal policies. The extent to which such governance is equitable

Figure 12.20 One of the challenges of urban governance in Australia is maintaining safe streets. Signs like this one in Sydney have been increasing rapidly as people everywhere become more security conscious. (Photo by Donald Zeigler)

remains questionable, and ways to produce more "just" cities within such a framework are still being sought. Equitable outcomes for indigenous peoples of these cities are especially important.

Finally, the provision of adequate, appropriate, and affordable housing is a pressing issue for all cities in the region. In Sydney particularly, where house-price escalation has been intense, affordability has now reached historic lows. In 2006, 183,000 low-income households and a further 42,000 moderate-income households were spending at least 30% of gross household income on housing. Personal insolvencies involving home repossessions increased by up to 70% in some parts of the city between 2005 and 2006. The impacts of the affordability crisis include the displacement of younger people and lower-paid workers from high-cost urban areas, labor market shortages, and growing debt burdens in households with mortgages.

SUGGESTED READINGS

Badcock, Blair, and Andrew Beer. 2000. *Home Truths*. Melbourne: University of Melbourne Press. An overview of housing in Australia.

Baum, Scott, Robert Stimson, and Kevin O'Connor. 2005. *Fault Lines Exposed: Advantage and Disadvantage across Australia's Settlement System*. Clayton, Victoria: Monash University ePress. Uses quantitative analysis to identify categories of places that are differentially advantaged and disadvantaged by processes of global change.

Connell, John, and John P. Lea. 2002. *Urbanisation in the Island Pacific*, 3d ed. London: Routledge. An overview of urbanization in 11 independent island states.

Economic and Social Commission for Asia and the Pacific. 2004. *Experiences and Challenges in Urban Management Issues in Pacific Island Countries*. United Nations Economic and Social Council. Available at http://www.unescap.org/60/E/PIDC8_1E.pdf Outlines a Pacific urban agenda that would provide a framework for urban development and management.

Forster, Clive. 2004. *Australian Cities: Continuity and Change*. South Melbourne: Oxford University Press. Explores the urban experience across the Pacific Islands, including the role of cities in national development and as centers of globalization.

Jacobs, Jane M. 1996. *Edge of Empire: Postcolonialism and the City*. London and New York: Routledge. An analysis of how the connections built by globalization and the postcolonial world shape and reshape the composition of cities.

Le Heron, Richard, and Eric Pawson. 1996. *Changing Places: New Zealand in the Nineties*. Auckland: Longman Paul. Provides an overview of the transforming geography of New Zealand, including its cities and regions, in the context of globalization.

McGillick, Paul. 2005. *Sydney, Australia: The Making of a Global City*. Singapore: Periplus. A photographically illustrated history of Sydney's built environment.

McManus, Phil. 2005. *Vortex Cities to Sustainable Cities: Australia's Urban Challenge*. Sydney: University of New South Wales Press. Examines the histories and planning decisions that have contributed to the unsustainability of Australian cities.

O'Connor, Kevin, Robert Stimson, and Maurice Daly. 2001. *Australia's Changing Economic Geography: A Society Dividing*. Melbourne: Oxford University Press. Provides an overview of the impacts of economic and social change, including globalization, on spatial patterns of economic performance across Australia.

13

Cities of the Future

STANLEY D. BRUNN, RINA GHOSE, AND MARK GRAHAM

KEY URBAN FACTS

Largest in Population	Tokyo (35.7), Delhi (28.4), Jakarta (28.3),
(in millions: 2007–20 projections)	Mumbai (25.7), New York (21.8), Seoul (21.7)
Urban Areas Adding Most Residents	Delhi (9.8), Jakarta (9.0), Shenzhen (7.0),
(in millions: 2007–20 projections)	Mumbai (6.3), Shanghai (4.8)
Fastest Annual Growth Rates (%)	Kabul (5.5), Surat (4.8), Lagos (4.4), Dar es
(2007–20 projections)	Salaam (4.7), Las Vegas (4.5), Kinshasa (4.2)
Slowest Annual Growth Rates (%)	Budapest (–0.19), Rome (–0.16), Milan (–0.16),
(2007–20 projections)	Naples (–0.13), Daegu (–0.13),
	St. Petersburg (–0.13)
Sharpest Declines	Milan (100), St. Petersburg (100),
(in thousands: 2007–20 projections)	Budapest (50), Rome (50), Naples (50)

KEY CHAPTER THEMES

1. Two established urban trends will continue: slow and no growth and graying populations in much of the developed world and rapid growth of youthful cohorts in much of the developing world.
2. Regional and global migrations will continue, with marked Asianization occurring in Australia, Europe, and North and South America.
3. Increased cultural homogenization will characterize cities in the Arab, Chinese, Japanese, and Indian worlds, and increased cultural diversity will characterize cities in Europe, Australia, the United States, and Canada.
4. The cultural, social, and economic faces of globalization will result in both core and peripheral urban locations having similar built environments, while making difficult the preservation and conservation of indigenous cultures and practices.

5. The future of cities may be glimpsed today by examining data on airline connections, quality of life, cost of living, stock exchanges, sister-city relationships, and universities with missions to serve international and global regions.

6. Time-space convergence, attributed to improved information and communications technologies, is providing increased flexibility in the location of key banking, health, and education institutions and in the empowerment of traditionally marginalized populations.

7. Flash points of potential ethnic and cultural conflict, including anti-globalization and anti-Western worldviews, and "gaps" between rich and poor countries are likely in some cities of the periphery: the Caribbean and U.S.–Mexico borderlands, the Mediterranean, and Southeast Asia.

8. Regional and global environmental problems, including global warming, pollution, solid waste, and water quality and availability, are certain to be center stage in planning the futures of cities.

9. Human security issues are destined to be major problems facing cities heavily dependent on imported energy, food, and water and on skilled and semiskilled immigrants from the developing world.

10. Commitments to solve 21st-century global urban problems will call for the growth and export of knowledge economies and new cohorts of internationally trained, experienced, and well-traveled professionals, along with creative grassroots empowerment initiatives.

We have approached cities from historical and contemporary perspectives in the previous chapters. Now it is time to think about the future. One prediction that has been borne out in the first decade of this century is that the majority of the world's residents would soon be living in urban regions. That milestone was reached sometime in 2007. That transition from majority-rural to majority-urban was significant on a global scale, but less so in more developed regions where more than half of the residents have been living in cities for a half century or more. The United States, for example, reached the urban-majority mark in 1920; the developing world will reach this mark well before 2020. What does the future hold for such a world and its people? Will present trends continue, or will there be a sea change in the very nature of urban life? Will cities in More Developed Countries (MDCs) continue to stabilize in population and even-

tually decline, while those in Less Developed Countries (LDCs) experience continued high population growth? What will be the consequences of divergent development paths on urban economies, communication and transportation, and human organizations? These questions intrigue urban geographers as we examine the early 21st century.

URBAN POPULATIONS: WINNERS AND LOSERS

The United Nations periodically publishes reports on urban futures, with particular emphasis on numbers, housing, food, health, and environmental quality. A 2006 UN publication provides data on the projected populations of major world regions such as Southern Europe and Central Africa, and on countries within them. But this report does not provide

Table 13.1   Projected Populations of Largest Agglomerations in 2050

Based on population increases from 2010–2015 and projected for 2050

Rank	City	Population (millions)	Rank	City	Population (millions)
1	Dhaka	48	25	Chittagong	14
2	Delhi	41	26	Chongqing	14
3	Mumbai	38	27	Manila	14
4	Karachi	32	28	Hyderabad	13
5	Jakarta	32	29	Kabul	13
6	Tokyo	28	30	Lima	13
7	Kolkata	26	31	Chennai	13
8	Mexico City	26	32	Rio de Janeiro	13
9	São Paulo	26	33	Surat	13
10	Kinshasa	25	34	Addis Ababa	12
11	Lagos	21	35	Abidjan	12
12	New York	21	36	Ahmedabad	12
13	Lahore	18	37	Luanda	12
14	Shanghai	18	38	Pune	12
15	Los Angeles	17	39	Tehran	12
16	Bangkok	16	40	Baghdad	11
17	Beijing	16	41	Cairo	11
18	Buenos Aires	16	42	Guatemala City	11
19	Istanbul	16	43	Ho Chi Minh City	11
20	Bangalore	15	44	Hong Kong	11
21	Riyadh	15	45	Jiddah	11
22	Tianjin	15	46	Osaka	11
23	Wuhan	15	47	Seoul	11
24	Bogotá	14	48	Yangon	11

Source: 2010–2015 data available in United Nations, *World Urbanization Prospects*, 2001 Revision, table A12 (www.unorganization.org).

any projections for individual cities within the next decade or two. In the appendix of this book are UN data on the projections for urban growth rates for urban agglomerations in 2015. Another useful data source is *Demographia*. This 2007 publication provides data on populations for 209 of the world's largest urban areas, their growth rates, and their projected population sizes in 2020. These data are used below.

Projecting population increases, as well as decreases, is fraught with some danger as estimated rates may change with social, political, and environmental conditions. For example, a civil war could rapidly increase the population of a capital city, a pandemic could result

in smaller projected population increases, or an influx of new residents (legal and illegal) could result in numbers currently unforeseen. Long-term economic declines might be attributed to factory closures and less-than-anticipated production from farms and mines.

According to *Demographia* there are likely to be major changes in population sizes, growth rates, and rankings of cities on all continents. The largest urban areas will continue to add people. The 10 largest urban areas in 2007 had 203 million residents and were expected to have nearly 225 million 13 years later (tab. 13.1). Fifteen urban areas are projected to add more than 3 million residents each between 2007 and 2020. These additions range from nearly 9.8 million for Delhi to 3.1 million for Surat, both in India. What is significant about these 15 cities is their location: 14 are in developing world regions. Asia alone is home to 12 of them: India has Delhi, Mumbai, Surat, and Kolkata; China has Shenzhen, Shanghai, Beijing, and Dongguan. Kinshasa (adding 5.7 million) is the only such city not located in Asia.

The fastest-growing cities are in East, South, and Southeast Asia, and in Sub-Saharan Africa. Thirty-three urban areas are projected to increase more than 3% by 2020. The most rapid increases are expected to be seen in Kabul, Surat, Dar es Salaam, Lagos, Kinshasa, Chittagong, and Luanda, all with increases above 4%.

Although rapid urban growth is predicted in regions of the developing world (save Central and South America), slow growth and even no growth are anticipated for much of the developed world, that is, Europe, the United States, Canada, Japan, and Australia. Modest declines are predicted for 11 older industrial cities, most of which are in Europe, including London, Manchester, Rome, and Milan, as well as Kyiv (formerly Kiev) and St. Petersburg (formerly Leningrad). Growth rates of less than 1% are predicted for another 53 urban areas including New York, Seoul, Osaka–Kyoto–Kobe, Paris, Rio de Janeiro, Hong Kong, Boston, Singapore, Rotterdam–Hague, Cape Town, Havana, Warsaw, and a few old industrial cities in China, including Harbin, Jinan, and Xian.

A third feature is the change in the rankings of urban areas over the 13 year period 2007–2020. Not surprisingly, old industrial cities in Europe will increase slowly or decline in population and will therefore move down in rank. They will be replaced by faster growing cities in the developing world. Italian,

German, British, Polish, and Japanese cities are among the major cities expected to drop in rank. These include Osaka (from rank 10 to rank 15), London (from 26 to 38), Rome (from 114 to 152), Manchester (from 148 to 189), Sapporo (from 159 to 183), and Rotterdam–Hague (from 164 to 193). Some traditionally large U.S. cities are also expected to drop, including San Francisco–San Jose (from 48 to 62), Detroit (from 69 to 85), and Boston (from 59 to 71). Sub-Saharan Africa and South Asia are the regions with the most cities expected to advance in rank. Those expected to experience truly dramatic increases include Dongguan (from 43 to 29), Surat (from 75 to 50), Luanda (from 101 to 70), Dakar (from 120 to 102), and Addis Ababa (from 106 to 82). The large U.S. city expected to advance the most is Las Vegas, which is predicted to move from rank 173 in 2007 to 129 in 2015.

In 1950, urban residents numbered approximately 750 million worldwide. By 2000 the figure was 2.8 billion, and by 2050 it is expected to be 6.5 billion (fig. 13.1). In 1950, Africa and Southwest Asia had 6% of all urban residents, whereas Europe had 32%, and Asia about 30%. Between 1950 and 2000, Africa more than doubled its city residents, while Asia's urban population grew by 40%. In 2000, Europe's share of the world's urban population had declined to about 15%, and North America's to only 8.5%. By 2050, more than one in four urban residents will be living in African and Middle Eastern cities and one in two will be living in Asian cities. Europe and Latin America will have almost the same number of city residents. U.S. and Canadian urbanites will almost equal the number living in urban West Africa. In aggregate, there are currently more rural than urban residents in LDCs, but this pattern will be reversed by about 2020 (fig. 13.2). Cities of the developing

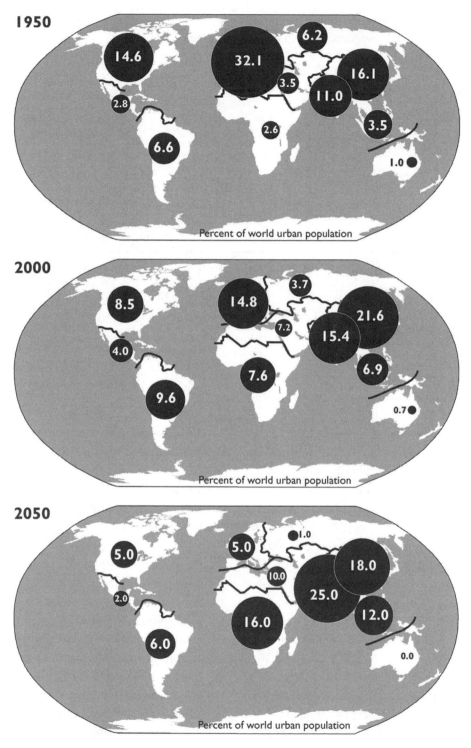

Figure 13.1 Urban Populations: 1950, 2000, and 2050. *Source:* Data from United Nations, *World Urbanization Prospects, 2001 Revision* (New York: United Nations Population Division, 2002), www.unpopulation.org. Projections for 2050 by authors.

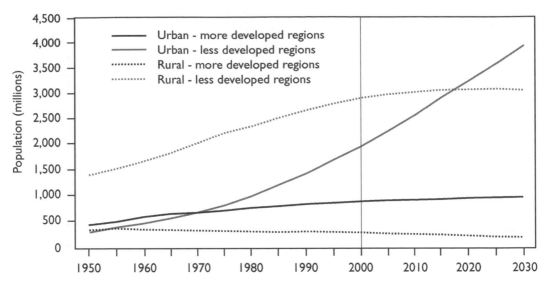

Figure 13.2 Urban and Rural Populations in MDCs and LDCs, 1950–2030. *Source:* United Nations, *World Urbanization Prospects, 2001 Revision* (New York: United Nations Population Division, 2002), www.unpopulation.org.

world, and especially Asia, are accounting for an increasingly larger share of the world's urban population (box 13.1).

The world's largest cities by 2050 will be largely in the LDCs, especially countries in Asia (fig. 13.3). Significant questions emerge about the implications of these changes for human and natural resource bases and the future of humanity. Tokyo (27 million) is expected to remain the world's largest agglomeration, but it will be followed by cities in the LDCs: Dhaka and Mumbai (each about 23 million), São Paulo (21 million), and Delhi (20 million). The UN lists 524 urban agglomerations with 750,000 inhabitants or more in 2000 (see the appendix for a complete list). Their combined population was 1.2 billion, or 40% of all urban dwellers. More than 40% of these agglomerations were in China (119), India (50), and the United States (46). Altogether, in 2000 the top nine countries had 303 agglomerations exceeding 750,000, or 57% of the world's urban dwellers.

TEN HUMAN GEOGRAPHIES OF THE EARLY 21ST CENTURY

Economic, social, and political futures in any region are affected by local cultures and events as well as external regional and global actions and institutions. These futures are likely to surface first in large cities; they are not listed in any order of magnitude.

1. *An urbanizing world.* Urbanization will continue to concentrate growing populations on comparably less land. Urban agglomerations will grow bigger, and urban institutions will increasingly dominate even rural areas. Interactions and associations are likely to be increasingly between cities near and distant rather than between cities and rural trade areas.

2. *Urban connectedness, anomie, and placelessness.* Faster transportation and information and communication technologies may lead people to lose their

Box 13.1   A Global Urban Village

How has the composition of the world's urban population changed during the past half century? One way to answer this question in a meaningful way is to consider, using UN data, the 30 largest agglomerations in 1950, 1975, 2000, and 2015, and then reduce the huge numbers into a "global urban village" of only 100 people. The largest number of residents in our village in 1950 would be from New York (10 residents), but then Tokyo would have the most residents in the other years (9, then 8, then 7). Both cities would be losing citizens in each year, such that by 2015, New York would have only 4 residents and Tokyo only 7.

Not unexpected from what we have seen described elsewhere in this chapter are declines in numbers from European and U.S. cities and increases from cities in LDC regions. Europe and the United States would account for half of all villagers in 1950, but for only 13 combined by 2015. Manchester, Birmingham, Rhine–Ruhr, and Boston would have lost representation. In 1950, 19 villagers would have come from East Asia, and 30 in 1975, but only 29 in 2015. The largest number of newcomers would be from South and Southeast Asia, growing from 6 in 1950 (all these from South Asia) to 36 from 10 different cities in these two regions in 2015. The lion's share of these additions would hail from Dhaka, Mumbai, and Delhi which would contribute 5, 5, and 4 residents, respectively, in 2015.

There would be no Russian residents in this village after 1975 (4 would come from Moscow and 2 from St. Petersburg in this year) and there would be none any year from Oceania. Sub-Saharan Africa would have none in 1950, but 6 residents (from Lagos and Kinshasa) in 2015. Cairo would have 1 resident in 1950 and by 1975 it would be joined by Tehran as the only cities contributing residents from the Middle East; these two cities would have 6 residents combined in 2015. Mexico City would be the sole representative of Central America; there would be 2 from this agglomeration in 1950 and 5 in each succeeding year. South American cities would always be represented, initially by Buenos Aires and Rio de Janeiro, but later by São Paulo, Lima, and Bogotá. By 2015, there would be 15 residents in our village from these 5 cities, with most hailing from São Paulo. What is clear from the cities of origin of residents in our "global village" is that the number from MDC regions would decrease and the number from LDC regions would increase. Whereas in 1950 there would be 61 villagers from 18 different cities in North America, Europe, and Russia, in 2015 there would be only 13 citizens from just 4 cities in those regions. By contrast, the numbers from LDC regions would increase, from 12 cities and 39 residents of our village population of 100 in 1950 to 26 cities and 87 residents by 2015. (Note: Japan is included in the East Asia region. If counted with the MDC regions, the numbers would change somewhat.)

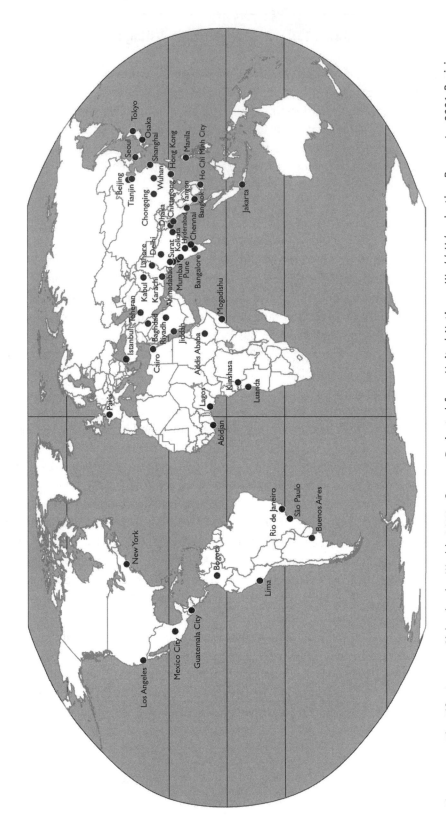

Figure 13.3 The Fifty Largest Cities in the World, 2050. *Source:* Projected from United Nations, *World Urbanization Prospects, 2001 Revision* (New York: United Nations Population Division, 2002), www.unpopulation.org.

Figure 13.4 Wireless fidelity, commonly known as wi-fi, is a local area network that has been used since 1997 to turn cities, even small ones, into Internet hubs. Here in West Palm Beach, surfers depend on waves, not wires, to keep them connected. (Photo by Donald Zeigler)

sense of place. The result could be anomie—alienation and social instability. Cell phones, fax machines, the Internet, and wireless communications will diminish the significance of place (fig. 13.4).

3. *Meshings of the local and global in daily life.* Scale meshings will be evident in transactions and interactions—where one works; with whom one works; and the destinations of goods and services produced, including luxury crops, telecommunications equipment, digitized health records, and components in a global product (computer or motor vehicle). Although some urban residents will interact predominantly at very local scales, others will interact at extraregional and global levels.

4. *Asianization of Europeanized worlds.* An ongoing contemporary global process is the impact of Asian diasporas on traditionally Europeanized worlds (fig. 13.5). Although non-Asian cultural groups are also involved in worldwide migration, Asians are having a significant visible impact, as large numbers of skilled and unskilled, legal and illegal residents enter into gateway cities of urban Europe, North America, and Oceania (fig. 13.6). These new cultures add new layers of food, music, entertainment, and intellectual diversity to city life.

5. *Increased regional and global awareness.* The diffusion of information and communication technologies (ICTs) and instant global reporting of major crises will increasingly transcend cultural, national, and political

Figure 13.5 The first generation of Vietnamese immigrants to Australia came after 1975 when South Vietnam fell, beginning a chain of Vietnamese migration to a Europeanized world, in this case Brisbane. Can you identify the two flags? (Photo by Donald Zeigler)

will be of increased significance in globally competitive and creative cities.

7. *Contested legal structures.* Increased volumes and densities of transborder urban networks and circulations will raise questions about the effectiveness of traditional city and state governments in daily life, including individual versus group rights and the legal structures affecting temporary and permanent residents. Additional fuzzy issues will include the rights of those without property and statehood, legal status of NGO international employees, and the ownership of natural resources and cultural properties.

8. *Redefining norms and abnorms.* Urban cultural and political clashes (subtle and violent) are likely to continue to emerge among groups: those calling for tolerance and diversity in work, living, lifestyle, and social spaces versus those seeking to retain traditional norms based on religious and rural values or outdated modes of authority. Extremists may have a profound impact on future urban life.

9. *Continued technological breakthroughs and limits.* Now that we have faster transportation and nearly instant communications (at least in MDCs), will there be constraints on the adoption and dissemination of new technologies because of adverse social impacts on a culture, high fixed costs, or government security? Will the technology "gaps" between haves and have-nots begin to narrow? What are the impacts of those cultures experiencing "leapfrog innovations," for example, experiencing the wireless and digital worlds without fixed landlines or solar energy without fossil fuel dependency?

10. *Veneers of homogeneity amidst diversity.* The "McDonaldization of the world,"

boundaries and raise awareness of planetary concerns. International boundaries will further diminish with globalization. Examples include the free flow of goods, services, labor, and capital throughout the European Union, the importance of global and regional environmental treaties, and global pressure to assure basic human rights of women, children, the elderly, the disabled, and cultural minorities.

6. *Competitive K-economies.* "K" is for knowledge. It symbolizes the transition from hardware to brainware and the importance of images and symbols in product consumption. These brain economies

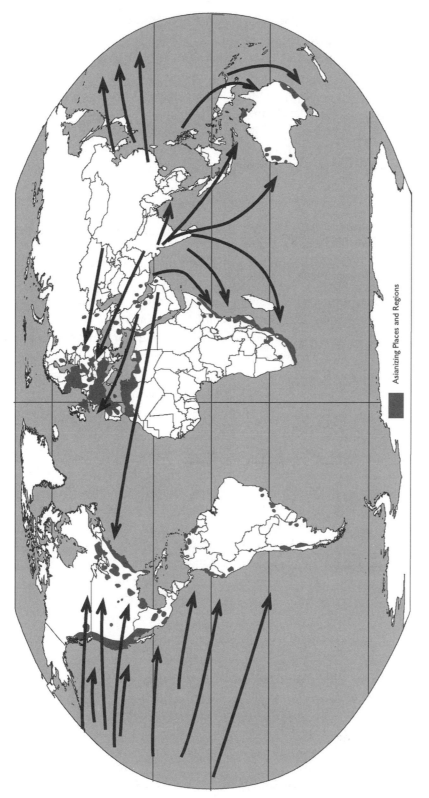

Figure 13.6 The Asianization of Europeanized Worlds. *Source:* Stanley Brunn.

or the creation of a Western globalized consumer world dominated by major Western food, music, fashion, and entertainment, will reflect a certain visible sameness in many urban landscapes. But beneath and alongside these landscapes and icons of Western and American hegemony in LDCs will be the rich historical and cultural mosaics of enduring regional cultures.

We next posit some distinguishing features of future cities and city life. Much of this thinking comes from professional social scientists, planners, and engineers in the MDCs, who design new architectures and technologies, plan urban infrastructures, collaborate with governments and universities, and serve as consultants with LDCs. They also learn applications to improve life in MDCs.

GLOBALIZATION AND URBAN LINKAGES

Urban form has always been, in part, shaped by communication and transportation systems and structures. Canals, tram lines, subways, and expressways have all significantly altered not the physical distance but instead the time it takes to travel between any two connected places. The time that it takes to move people, goods, and information within or between cities (i.e., distance in time-space) affords places distinct advantages and disadvantages. The contemporary and future linkages between and among urban places can be illustrated using a number of different programs and initiatives that promote greater regional awareness, understanding, and activities. Examples of linkages exist at the international and corporate levels, others at the scale of organizations

and groups, and still others at local levels (box 13.2). Local and global worlds are becoming increasingly fluid and fused with top-down and bottom-up initiatives linking places people work to places their consumer goods come from to places they spend leisure time and money. We illustrate these networks and linkages using several different examples, realizing, of course, that many more examples exist in cities and between cities.

Globalization and Anti-Globalization

Globalization is, and will likely continue to be, one of the most frequently repeated themes of the 21st century. The idea that cities are becoming economically, culturally, and politically more global or connected is grounds for hope, desire, fear, and despair. Globalization can lead to shared advances in science and technology, economic growth, and the exchange of philosophic, political, and artistic ideas between people and places that were once disconnected. However, increased connections can also result in economic and political exploitation and the destruction of cultural exchange (fig. 13.7).

Globalization is not something that spreads across the surface of the globe like fog rolling over a chain of hills. Rather it is evident only in specific times and places. In other words, if we take the example of any city experiencing transformations because of global connections that city is not necessarily spatially proximate to the sources of those transformations or spatially proximate to other cities experiencing similar transformations. A useful way to conceptualize cities is through the concept of a wormhole. Geographer Eric Sheppard used it to imagine how connections between cities are specific and contingent while ignoring in-between places.

Box 13.2   Globalization and World Cities

Peter Taylor

Although there is a large body of literature on "world" or "global" cities, little evidence has been gathered on what actually makes such cities so important: their connections with other cities across the world. Thus, if world cities are indeed the crossroads of globalization, then we need to consider seriously how we measure intercity relations. It was just such thinking that led to the setting up of the Globalization and World Cities (GaWC) Study Group and Network at Loughborough University, United Kingdom, as a virtual center for world cities research. GaWC currently carries out three strands of research:

- Comparative City Connectivity Studies: These focus on relations between chosen cities as they respond to particular events. In one study, Singapore, New York, and London were compared in the way in which their service sectors responded to the 1997 Asian financial crisis. In another study, relations between London and Frankfurt were studied in the wake of the launch of the euro currency. The generic finding of this work is that city competitive processes are generally much less important than are cooperative processes carried out through office networks within the private sector.
- Elite Labor Migrations between Cities: Moving skilled labor around to different world cities is found to be a key globalization strategy for financial firms wanting to embed their businesses into the world-city network. For instance, London firms regularly send staff to Paris, Amsterdam, and Frankfurt to provide "seamless" service across European cities. The prime finding of this research is that a transnational space of flows is produced as a necessary prerequisite for firms accumulating financial knowledge.
- Global Network Connectivity of Cities: A world city network is an amalgam of the office networks of financial and business service firms. This network has three levels: a network level of cities in the world economy, a nodal level of cities as global service centers, and a subnodal level of global service firms that are the prime creators of the world city network. This specification directs a data collection that enables the global network connectivities of world cities to be calculated. These results are based on a uniquely large set of data for the year 2000 covering 100 firms in 316 cities across the world.

GaWC research goes beyond world city formation to study world city network formation. The focus has been on this complex process within economic globalization. For a full global urban analysis, further research is required within other important strands of globalization. The Study Group's website is www.lboro.ac.uk/gawc.

Figure 13.7 McDonald's has become the symbol of globalization around the world, but anti-globalization forces envision a future without the "golden arches." (Photo by Donald Zeigler)

A widely repeated idea is that the absence of globalization is responsible for global inequities. In other words, cities that remain disconnected from global processes and flows of trade are unlikely to have high living standards. Such ideas are usually based on nonliberal economic theories that rely on "the logic of the marketplace." By allowing the global market to regulate society instead of being regulated by society, it is argued that market forces will render residents of poor cities better off by effectively governing and creating wealth for all participants.

The counterpoint of this argument is the idea that ever-increasing globalization and integration of cities will only exacerbate global inequalities. Within the globalized economy, capital and jobs can now be moved rapidly from place to place, but the actual populations of cities remain rooted. The effects of globalizing processes have led some scholars to refer to "a race to the bottom," in which people have to accept increasingly lower wages and bene-fits in order to perform the same jobs. These concerns have fueled a massive global movement of protest and highlight inequalities caused and intensified by globalization, including anti-globalization demonstrations at the World Trade Organization's conferences in Seattle (fig. 13.8).

Airline Connections

One of the most important ways that globalization can be measured is through the movement of people and cargo by air. However, the most globalized airports are not always located in cities that most people would associate with a high degree of global connectivity. Of the world's three largest cargo airports in 2006, only one might be expected to have a significant amount of traffic. Surprisingly, Memphis, Tennessee, tops the list, with more cargo landing or taking off from its runways than any other city on the globe, mostly because FedEx's primary hub is there. Memphis

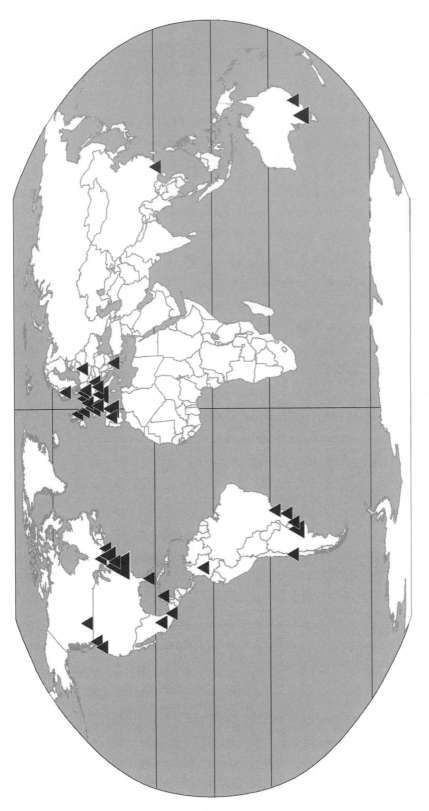

Figure 13.8 Sites of Recent Major Anti-Globalization Protests. *Source:* Mark Graham.

is followed closely by Hong Kong. Anchorage is in third place, serving as the crossroads between North America and Asia. The next five largest cargo airports are in Seoul, Tokyo, Shanghai, Paris, and Frankfurt.

When passenger flows between cities are considered, we get a more familiar picture of cities that are the most networked into the global economy. Europe and particularly North America dominate the rankings. While some highly ranked cities have high connectivity because they serve as major airline hubs (e.g., Atlanta as a hub for Delta Airlines), others including London or New York are highly connected as a result of their central position in global economic and tourist flows. In regards to international passenger traffic, European and Asian cities dominate the list: London's Heathrow ranked first and Gatwick seventh in passenger traffic. Atlanta, Chicago, Tokyo, and Los Angeles are all in leaders in busiest passenger traffic; Paris, Amsterdam, Frankfurt, and Hong Kong are leaders in international traffic. New York, London, Los Angeles, Washington, Chicago, and Frankfurt are leaders in the number of destinations served. The absence of North American cities from the top 10 in some ways reflects the fact that there are relatively few nation-states (and thus international flights) in North America.

Quality and Cost of Living

Many individuals, corporations, organizations, and governments are interested in quality of life measures. These parameters not only measure one's standing vis-à-vis other cities but can also be used to promote a city's climate for investment, international conferences, and sporting events and to attract specific groups, including artists, scientists, wealthy retirees, and tourists. The Mercer Consulting group ranked over 350 cities in 2007 using 39 quality-of-living criteria for each city; these included measures of its personal health and safety, its economy and physical environment, transportation and communications, public services, and its overall political climate. Not surprisingly, the top cities were in high income European countries, plus similar cities in Canada, Australia, and New Zealand. The top cities were Zurich, Geneva, Vancouver, Vienna, and Auckland. The highest U.S. cities were Honolulu, which ranked 27th, and San Francisco, which ranked 29th. The cities with the lowest rankings were Baghdad (not a surprise), followed by the African cities of Brazzaville, Bangui, and Khartoum. Some cities improved their ranking over the previous year: Vienna moved from number 4 to 3 (it was one of two cities tied for a number 3 ranking in 2007), and Washington, D.C., improved its ranking from number 44 to 41. Some lost their rankings; Oslo moved from 26 to 31, and Madrid from 42 to 45. By contrast, the cities with the lowest rankings have major transportation, pollution, health, and housing problems.

Examining cost of living also reveals vast differences. In 2007 Moscow ranked at the top followed by London, Seoul, Tokyo, Hong Kong, Copenhagen, and Geneva. Those ranked 45–50 in order were Abu Dhabi and Berlin (tied at 45), Dusseldorf, Taipei, Prague, and Algiers. In the developing world, Beijing and Shanghai ranked 20th and 24th, respectively, while Douala ranked 24th and Almaty ranked 30th.

Stock Exchanges

The investment market watches closely the movements of money in major currencies around the world each day. These flows are monitored not only by private and public banks, but also by key investors, including companies and corporations. The stock exchanges are assuming a greater role in national, international, and transborder investments for a wide variety of projects, including airports; highways; pipelines; landlines and Internet communication systems; new mining, forestry, and agribusiness projects; and urban health and antipollution projects. *Stock Exchanges World* in July 2007 listed 93 stock exchanges. Not surprising, most were in Europe (33 in 25 countries), Asia (20), the United States (12), and Canada (9). There were also 20 listed in South America, 6 in Central America, 4 in the Caribbean, 5 in the Middle East, 3 in Sub-Saharan Africa, 2 in Australia, and 1 in New Zealand. The Asian list includes 5 in Japan; 2 each in Hong Kong, India, Indonesia, Pakistan, Singapore, and Sri Lanka; and one each in China, Malaysia, Taiwan, and Thailand. In Europe, most were in the United Kingdom (5), France (4), and Spain (3).

Sister Cities

During the past 50 years, the Sister Cities program has promoted a wide variety of economic, cultural, social, and political programs between large and small cities on all continents (fig. 13.9). This program encourages local grassroots groups as well as organizations and governmental bodies to explore ways to learn about each other's heritage, culture, and citizens. Many also have similar names and economies. Sister Cities International holds annual conferences, publishes newsletters (print and online) and travel guides, and assists other groups to explore sister-city relationships. In 2007 there were 1,749 international communities in 134 countries. European cities have 35% of all such relationships. Japan has the most relationships with 228 communities and 239 partnerships. The United States has 122 communities with 388 partnerships. Chicago and Oakland have 25 relationships each. There is a wide variety of sister-city relationships. Cairo has 25 relationships with cities in Asia, North America, Europe, and the Greater Middle East. The sister cities of Lexington, Kentucky, are other major horse capitals in France, Ireland, and Japan. Shanghai has 29 sisters scattered on all continents. Dubai, São Paulo, Rotterdam, and Seoul also have sister cities in widely scattered places. Tokyo and Auckland's sisters are mostly in Asia, Tel Aviv's are mostly in Europe, and Karachi's are mostly in the Muslim world. Visits of public officials, industrialists, teachers, students, athletes, and children represent examples of these local-to-local global networks.

Regional Universities

Universities provide another setting for the mixing of cultures. Some, in fact, have a distinct mission to promote transborder and international awareness. One example is the University of the West Indies (UWI) whose main campus is in Mona, Jamaica, a suburb of Kingston, with satellite campuses in Barbados and Trinidad. It serves the students of the Commonwealth Caribbean, basically the Anglophone islands, with specialized training in agriculture, planning, health care, cross-cultural education, and telecommunications. The diverse faculty, likewise, come with degrees from universities in various countries in Europe, Canada, the United States, and the wider Caribbean region. Another example is the University of the South Pacific in Laucala, a suburb of Suva, Fiji, with campuses in 10 other Pacific island states. It offers many distance-learning courses to island residents in Micronesia and Melanesia. The American University of Central Asia in Bishkek, Kyrgyzstan, is another example

Figure 13.9 "Town twinning," or the creation of sister-city relationships, became a popular trend in the 20th century. Roanoke, Virginia, for instance, is twinned with seven cities on four continents. (Photo by Donald Zeigler)

of an institution with a transnational student body, in this case from all five post-Soviet Central Asian states. During the years of the Soviet Union, the leading international university, drawing from the world's Marxist and communist countries, was Patrice Lumumba University in Moscow, named after the Soviet-backed Marxist leader in the Congo. It employed faculty and had students from countries in Africa, Central America, South America, and Cuba, as well as the Middle East and China. They were trained in Marxist economics, communist ideology, and Soviet politics. The university, currently named the People's Friendship University of Russia, has over 13,000 students (mostly Russian) who today study capitalism. The United Nations University in Tokyo, with its 13 Research and Training Centers, is a UN think tank and community of scholars studying security, peace, and development issues. In the planning stages is a new university that would serve the European Union. Its location remains under discussion, but it is expected to offer de-grees in economics, and various health, policy, science, and engineering fields. These regional universities are unique in their missions in that they bring together students and faculties from different cultures, economies, and political systems and encourage the region's present and future leaders to think beyond their traditional national borders. Other major national universities also have many international students. These include Oxford, Massachusetts Institute of Technology, the University of California Berkeley, the National Autonomous University of Mexico, La Sorbonne, and the University of Sydney.

TYPOLOGIES OF URBAN SYSTEMS

Future cities and city systems will have some features similar to those of today, but also some new features. Realizing that many cities may exhibit more than one form, we suggest some snapshots of future urban systems (fig. 13.10).

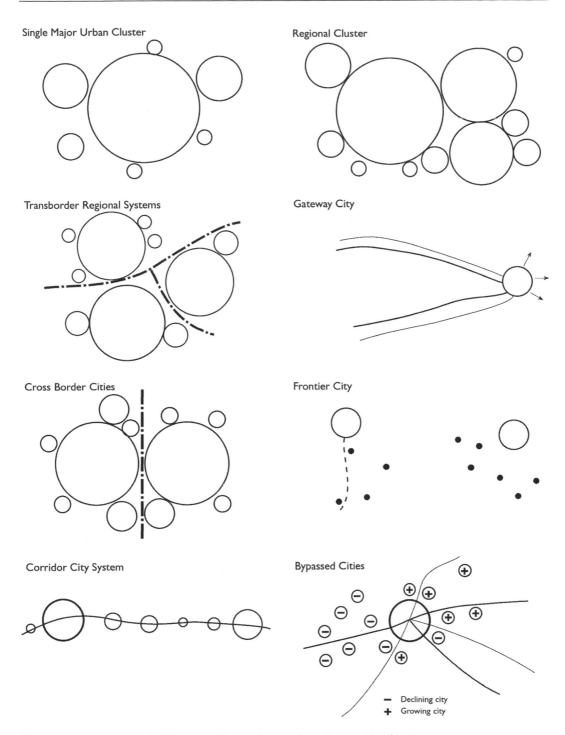

Figure 13.10 Systems of Cities: Existing and Emerging. *Source:* Stanley Brunn.

- *Single major urban clusters that will increase in numbers, density, and territory.* Frequently these are LDC primate cities. Examples include Addis Ababa, Nairobi, Mogadishu, Manila, Ho Chi Minh City, Tegucigalpa, and Lima.
- *Regional clusters of small and large cities within the same state that will grow and gradually coalesce.* Examples include southeast Brazil, southeast Korea, the Ganges River, the lower Nile, southwest Nigeria, southeast Australia, and many parts of the United States (fig. 13.11).
- *Transborder regional systems that cross several international boundaries.* Examples include El Paso–Ciudad Juarez, Detroit–Windsor, the Tashkent–Osh corridor, and the Malay Peninsula.
- *New international gateway cities with access to new water and land frontiers that will present opportunities for investors and workers.* Examples are cities in South America's "Southern Cone," Amazonia, and Northeast Asia.
- *Cross-border cities that will continue to experience either symmetrical or asymmetrical growth.* Examples include Brazzaville and Kinshasa, Buenos Aires and Montevideo, San Diego and Tijuana, Seattle and Vancouver, Vladivostok near the Russian/Chinese border, and Yanji near the Chinese/Korean border.
- *Frontier cities that will emerge with development of new natural (mineral) or human resources (tourism, retirement, etc.) or that will serve as hubs for new transportation and communication networks.* Examples are cities in Brazil's circumference highway, Dunedin for the Antarctic, Darwin for Southeast Asia, Kashgar and Urumqi for Central Asia, Lhasa in Tibet, Ushuaia and Punta Arenas in southern South America, and Magadan on the Sea of Okhotsk in northeast Siberia.
- *Corridor city systems—cities spaced unevenly along railroads, highways, and rivers.* These "beads on a string" will experience asymmetrical growth. Examples include the Trans-Siberian railroad, the Trans-Amazonia highway, the highway between Istanbul and Ankara, cities on the revitalized Old Silk Road, the proposed Trans-African highways from Dakar to Mombasa and Cairo to Cape Town, the Brazilian "megalopolis" (Recife to Porto Alegre), and the cities on India's new Golden Quadrilateral.
- *Bypassed cities that will experience economic declines, out-migrations of youth, aging populations, and dated infrastructures (bridges, highways, railroads).* Examples include many old mining and heavy-industrial centers in Eastern Europe, Siberia, the Canadian Maritimes, and Appalachia.
- *Isolated cities located at the termini of transportation and communication networks, which are often located in inaccessible and hostile physical environments.* Examples include the single-resource cities in Siberia and capitals in the Sahara, highland Andes and Central America, the eastern Caribbean, and the Pacific Islands.
- *Ephemeral cities that have fluctuating populations with seasonal employment.*

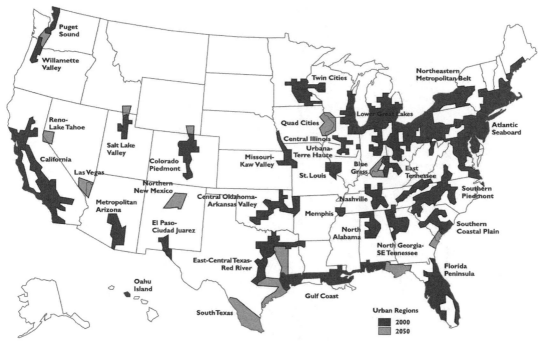

Figure 13.11 U.S. Urban Regions in 2050. *Source:* Stanley Brunn.

These include specialized university, military-defense, tourism, and entertainment cities.

- *Historic preservation cities that celebrate their pasts and use their heritage to generate income from tourism, retirees, and investments in historic preservation.* Examples include Williamsburg (Virginia), Vienna, the Rivera, Timbuktou (Mali), and Fès.

- *Fun cities that are centers of hedonistic activities and have economies that thrive on the pursuit of entertainment and leisure.* Examples include Orlando with Disney World; Las Vegas, Reno, Monaco, and Macau for casino gambling; Dubai in the Middle East; and cities with major theme parks, regular sports events, or exotic and quasilegal forms of entertainment.

- *World cities that anchor dense commercial and cultural networks and play leading roles in regional finance, investment, tourism, arts, and culture.*

- *Global cities—Tokyo, London, and New York—that are recognized for their pinnacle ranking in international business networks.*

- *Worldwide urban systems, or Ecumenopoli— a concept developed by Constantinos Doxiadis, the originator of the term ekistics (the science of human settlements)—that link major populated areas on major transportation and communication corridors (fig. 13.12). Such intercontinental cities are not beyond the realm of possibility.*

Figure 13.12 Ecumenopolis: The Global City. *Source:* Adapted from C. A. Doxiadis, "Man's Movements and His Settlements," *Ekistics* 29, no. 174 (1970), 318.

SPACE-TIME TRANSFORMATIONS

Urban form has always been, in part, shaped by communications and transportation systems and structures. Canals, rail lines, subways, and expressways significantly altered not only physical distance but also the time required to travel between connected places. The time required to move people, goods, and information within or between cities (i.e., distance in time-space) affords places both advantages and disadvantages. Much of the dispersal that has taken place in many metropolitan areas can in large part be attributed to the shrinking of time-space through transportation technologies. Outlying areas have rapidly converged in space-time with other areas in the same metropolitan region.

The Internet and cyberspace have now brought about an entirely new time-space dynamic. Communications allow for a rapid convergence of space-time between all places connected to IT networks. In theory, when discussing the movement of information, all places linked into the Internet have a time-space distance of zero from one another. All connected districts and cities are in the same cyberspace and any competitive advantages of earlier eras are supposedly diminished by a reduction in the amount of time required to conduct social practices. This idea is not to suggest that shrinking time-space can render physical distance meaningless for cities in the future. As long as the world continues to consist of more than bits and bytes, physical distance will exert powerful effects on cities. However, the reorganization (or shrinking) of time-space brought about by new technologies will undoubtedly cause fundamental changes to our metropolitan environments and societies as well as having impacts on individual travel (box 13.3). The following sections outline some of those implications.

DIGITAL TECHNOLOGY AND THE CITY

Alongside the real (or "ground truth") city, a new city is emerging in MDCs. This digital city is where digital technologies, especially geographical information systems (GIS), are used to plan, build, and manage the urban environment. Since the early 1970s, GIS has become routine in urban planning tasks in North America, Western Europe, Japan, and Australia. These systems are also penetrating the cities of some LDCs, particularly India, China, South Africa, Senegal, Ghana, Brazil, and Mexico. GIS is the science and technology that integrates vast databases with georeferenced data (exact latitudinal/longitudinal coordinates) to prepare maps, satellite images, and aerial photographs. These data allow researchers and planners to perform a range of statistical and spatial analyses, including modeling, visualization, and simulation in order to design, plan, and manage urban environments and to propose future scenarios. GIS can easily be linked to the Global Positioning System (GPS) to ensure highly accurate spatial analysis. Also, mobile and hand-held GPS units integrated into GIS programs can be taken to remote areas to conduct real-time analysis. A common use of GIS in urban planning in MDCs is facilitating citizen participation.

Another digital technology that is vital to urban economic growth and governance is Internet access. Many cities are being restructured as wired cities in order to compete for a vast array of high-technology digital transfers

Box 13.3   Global Travel at Zero Cost

Mark Graham

In a single 12-month period, I flew 77,334 miles (over 43,000 km), or about three times the circumference of the planet at the equator, for a cost of almost nothing. This zero-cost mobility was achieved by acquiring airline tickets in two ways: through frequent flyer miles and through coding errors in online booking engines. Most of the methods I have used to earn frequent flier miles are free, for example, applying for credit cards, opening bank accounts, and filling out surveys. Other methods came with some monetary cost and have been as unusual as purchasing 120 pounds of Swiss cheese branded with stickers that could be redeemed for miles.

Frequent flyer miles can be redeemed for free flights within defined regions, irrespective of distance traveled. For example, a ticket from Boston to Reykjavik (4,826 actual miles or 2,540 km) costs the same (50,000 frequent flier miles or 30,000 km) as a ticket from Los Angeles to Istanbul (13,740 miles or 8,380 km). I designed my routings to maximize the number of places that I could visit free. For example, when I wanted to travel to Japan (for which I redeemed 60,000 frequent flyer miles), I instead booked a ticket to Phnom Penh, Cambodia, with stopovers in Seoul, Taipei, Bangkok, and, of course, Tokyo and Osaka (fig. 13.13). It was irrelevant that Cambodia is nowhere near Japan. All that mattered was that Cambodia and Japan are in the same frequent flyer award region.

The second method I used to travel is even less grounded in conventional geographies of cost-distance. The major online travel agents have developed highly automated booking systems which can accept orders, process payments, and issue tickets without any human interaction. Such systems are highly efficient, but are occasionally prone to mistakes. I have been able to book about half of the approximately 6 mistake fares I hear about each year. In one instance, I was able to book business class tickets from North America to Europe for $28 each instead of $2,800 (a decimal point placement error). In another case I reserved a beach villa in Thailand for 400 Ugandan Shillings (about $0.22) a night instead of USD $400 a night (a currency conversion error).

that link businesses and households. San Francisco, Seattle, San Diego, San Jose, Los Angeles, New York, Washington, D.C., Chicago, Boston, and Miami are among the top U.S. cities in Internet penetration. The Internet is being utilized not only for luring capital and businesses, but also for security purposes. For example, web cameras monitor London's streets and its financial district. Internet penetration in LDCs is also significant and is a deliberate strategy to attract economic investment from MDCs. Delhi, Mumbai, and Bangalore are all wired cities in India's globalized economy.

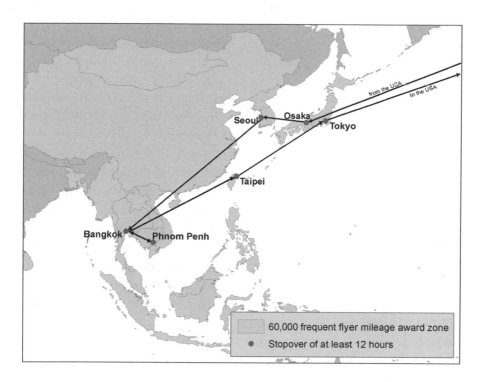

Figure 13.13 One ticket purchased with 60,000 frequent flyer miles permitted travel to all 6 cities shown on this map by scheduling flights with stopovers. *Source:* Mark Graham.

In all of these cases, neither absolute nor relative cost-distance played an important part in determining where I traveled. Although cost, distance, and time were largely irrelevant, my movements were still heavily influenced by specific understandings of geography. It is the rules and spatial logic within frequent flyer programs that have enabled my movement to far off places and constrained how I moved to those places. Pricing errors similarly re-define nearness by drastically altering conventional relationships between cost and distance. Geography is thus more complicated than it seems, and lines on a map are not always good indicators of how far away places really are.

Examples of countries making heavy investments in national and urban digital economies are Singapore, Estonia, Slovenia, the Gulf States (as part of their post-petroleum economic planning), Hong Kong, Ireland, Jamaica, and Trinidad. Digital cities invest in computer hardware and software design and support large and small companies performing various digital tasks, as do many intergovernmental organizations (IGOs), NGOs, and governmental institutions. These include libraries, courts, hospitals, and employment and environmental offices. Digital cities contain multiple cyber land uses and cyberinstitutions, including

- Cyber-cafés (a worldwide phenomenon)
- Cyber-music (downloadable in infinite varieties from the Web)
- Cyber-photography (posted and distributed via the Internet)
- Cyber-education (available no matter how close one is to a school or library)
- Cyber-healing (links a person's vital signs with a distant doctor)
- Cyber-conferencing (with full visualization among participants)
- Cyber-tourism (where virtual reality tries to substitute for reality itself)

Physical Networks of Cyberspace

In the past, cities thrived or atrophied based on their relative positionality within global flows of trade. Most large urban agglomerations still owe their prosperity to transportation facilities, including important roads, canals, and airports. Although positionality will be no less important for cities of the future, prosperity will increasingly rely on an alternate structure. Cables and satellite dishes grounded in specific physical places are the prerequisites for time-space compression. Such networks, as well as the social, economic, and political opportunities for people in cities to access such networks, are currently very unevenly distributed across the globe. Broadband and fiber optic cables are heavily concentrated in (and link) East Asia, Europe, and North America. Heavily wired cities include Seoul, London, and Boston; they are much more likely to experience change brought about by time-space compression than cities lacking high network connectivity, such as Pyongyang or Kinshasa.

Inclusion and Exclusion

Certain cities are thus more included in global networks than others. However, physical connections do not ensure that a majority of a city's inhabitants will benefit from globalized networks. Large groups in a highly connected city, as measured by bandwith, can remain disconnected. Unfamiliarity with world languages that dominate the Internet, such as Chinese, Spanish, and especially English, can render network connections lacking in meaning and value. Similarly, various cultural and political restrictions can exclude people, based on gender, ethnicity, or religion, from regular Internet use. For instance, in certain cities it is considered highly inappropriate for women to spend time in male-dominated Internet cafés. Finally, economic barriers may be the most powerful exclusionary force. Both the means (a computer and a mobile device) and the cost of access (hourly or monthly fees) can be prohibitively expensive for many residents even in the most connected cities. Questions of inclusion and exclusion are becoming ever more important for cities, because unequal access to distant information and communications will likely cause other increasing urban inequalities.

Hybrid Spaces

What all this means is that the scale of space-time transformations for cities is never the metropolitan level, but instead always at the individual or group level. The city becomes a very different place for different residents. Individuals exist in a hybrid cyber–physical space, which some geographers have dubbed a "DigiPlace," whereas others remain rooted in the physically proximate present. For example, imagine how two different people commuting to work on a San Francisco cable car could have vastly different experiences of, and with, the same city. The first person does not own a cell phone, laptop, or PDA and is restricted to direct sensory experiences arising from the proximate urban landscape: conver-

Figure 13.14 The camera phone was invented in the 1990s and has since come to dominate the market. Here in Athens, images of a parade are shared with far-away friends. (Photo by Donald Zeigler)

sation between other passengers, the view from a window, advertisements, a newspaper, etc. In contrast, the second person possesses a multifunctional mobile phone (fig. 13.14). She spends the commute time immersed in both the physical- and cyber-spheres she is passing through. She is, furthermore, able to interact with true DigiPlaces in her cities, places that she can experience both physically and in cyberspace. These DigiPlaces can be restaurant reviews, localized chat rooms and forums, maps and satellite images, search engine rankings, and countless others.

Hybrid spaces significantly alter the meaning and significance of many elements in urban environments. To return to the previous example, when looking for a restaurant, our first person might ask a friend, be swayed by an advertisement, or see a restaurant on a main street. Our second person might also see a physical advertisement for a restaurant, but be put off by mediocre online reviews. Prominence of a restaurant in the listings of a local search engine (Google Maps or Yahoo maps) would more likely determine which establishment is ultimately chosen. As DigiPlaces expand and become more commonly used, we will see far-reaching changes in the fabric of cities. Cities will exist as not only bricks and mortar, but also as constantly changing drapes of electronic information. The digital and the material will thus become increasingly blended and blurred in daily urban life.

Transcending the Fog of Distance

Space-time transformations afforded by new information and communication technologies alter the meaning of distance for intra- and intercity relationships. Distance has previously always been a powerful social force. It had the power to obscure detailed knowledge about (and hinder rich communication with) distant places, thus leading geographers to talk about the "fog of distance." People were more likely to interact with those in their own neighborhood than with those in other districts or cities. Such localized interactions and spaces of knowledge gave rise to myriad traditions, dialects, fashions, cuisines, philosophies, and musical styles. The combination of fast, inexpensive transportation and cyberspace access now allows people to "cut through" the fog of distance in a variety of ways. Cheap transportation had profound effects on making urban economies highly dependent on non-local products and allowing large cultural exchanges to take place through mass tourism. These developments over the centuries occurred gradually in tandem with incremental advancements in transportation technologies. However, revolutionary changes in the ways in which distance affects urban life are now materializing with the diffusion of various Internet applications. As noted above, a number of online tools allow individuals and groups to gain local knowledge about distant regions and cities. Mapping tools such as Mapquest or Google Earth offer standardized visions of faraway places. We can proceed from looking at street level pictures of Manhattan to satellite images of Baghdad's layout in a few clicks. User-generated websites such as Wikitravel, Wiki-Chains, and MySpace offer alternate means through which to transcend the fog of distance by allowing us to virtually experience other places through detailed, localized descriptions of people, places, and landscapes.

Although technology will never fully eliminate the significance of distance, it will likely render it increasingly opaque. As cyberspace brings about fundamentally altered space-time relationships, "distance" will take on new meanings and will feed back into the ways in which urban culture is generated and reproduced.

Urban Change

Space-time transformations will undoubtedly have a profound effect on the new urban form of cities around the globe. Some areas may ex-

perience further suburbanization as office workers choose to telecommute. Cities with large concentrations of office jobs may then see workers living hundreds of kilometers away as they only need to connect a day or two every week. Many jobs can be performed from anywhere and are becoming entirely unrooted from any attachment to specific cities. These developments could result in large in-migrations to cities such as Rome, Las Vegas, or Phuket, Thailand. The altering of space-time relationships through communications technologies is also the impetus behind large migrations of whole company divisions to cities with low labor and production costs, thus changing the employment possibilities of these places. This multiplying practice of moving certain types of jobs, such as back office work and call centers, to cities with low costs suggests that a certain kind of "geographical unrootedness" is defining urban employment. At the same time, cities may start to develop strong specializations in certain functions that can best be performed electronically. Manila might become a center for digitizing architectural drawings and Bangalore a hub for call centers.

Empowerment through GIS

Usage of geographic information systems has become popular with citizen-based grassroots organizations because GIS enables them to be informed—and powerful—participants in community planning efforts. "Public Participation GIS" (PPGIS) is a critical arena for GIS researchers. It directly addresses the issues of providing equitable access to spatial data and GIS technology to marginalized groups, which have traditionally been deprived of access to GIS owing to its technical complexity and high cost. Through intermediary institutes, such as universities, governmental agencies, and NGOs, free access to data and GIS is being provided.

Key PPGIS applications include natural resource management and conservation efforts, community-based planning and neighborhood revitalization in urban areas, and activism organized at local, national, global, and multiscalar levels. In such efforts, local, qualitative knowledge is integrated with quantifiable public data sets, and mental maps and sketch maps are integrated with official digital maps, aerial photographs, and satellite images. These practices have been used in a number of projects among indigenous societies in the non-Western world where local knowledge and cultural practices are preserved through oral histories, songs, dances, and alternative representations of the world. One Kenyan project integrates traditional Maasai songs, dances, sketch maps, and mental maps with digital video recordings, photography, and satellite imagery. The project aims to draw on the environmental knowledge and pastoralist practices of the Maasai to inform community conservation and development initiatives and ecosystem management policies.

In the context of neighborhood revitalization in the Western world, community organizers use public data sets through GIS to inform and legitimate local knowledge to obtain action and formulate strategies, monitor neighborhood conditions and predict changes, prepare for organizational tasks and funding recruitment efforts, generate new information based on their own experiential knowledge to enhance service-delivery tasks, and explore spatial relations to challenge or reshape urban policy. GIS analysis has enabled these community organizers to fight blighted housing conditions by tracking down absentee landlords through property records, to fight crime issues through crime hot spot

analyses, to analyze land use data to track vacant and boarded up houses, to track data on sanitation issues and garbage removal, to combine mortgage-lending data with demographic data to address discriminatory investments, and to use various indicator data to generate sophisticated multiscalar maps to measure a community's changing well-being.

PPGIS activities have been aided by the emergence of the Internet mapping sites such as Google Earth, in which high-resolution satellite images of places across the world can be accessed in minutes for free by anyone. The power of Google mapping is evident in the case of the Surui people of southern Brazil, whose Chief Almir Surui approached Google for high resolution satellite imagery to monitor illegal loggers and miners on the tribe's 600,000 acre reserve. While high-tech mapping has already been used to track illegal activity and to record knowledge, this will be the first time an Amazon tribe will share its own vision of its territory with the rest of the world via Google Earth. In the western world, various government agencies provide easy access to public databases through Internet GIS sites. One site, COMPASS, enables citizens of Milwaukee to access, view, query, and map detailed property data, health data, crime data, community asset data, and demographic data at no cost. Such Internet GIS sites are particularly useful for resource-poor organizations that have difficulties in creating and maintaining in-house GIS.

URBAN ENVIRONMENTAL PROBLEMS

A major source identifying the scale and scope of urban environmental problems and challenges is the Worldwatch Institute's *State of the World* report (tab. 13.2). Some salient facts drawn from the 2007 report include the following:

Table 13.2 Environmental Problems and Initiatives in Selected World Cities

CITY	Urban Farming	Natural Disasters	Mass Transit	Water	Slums and Squatters	Renewable Energy	Health and Sanitation	Grassroots Empowerment	Green City	Global Warming	Urban Violence	Waste and Garbage	Air Pollution
Accra	■			■			■	■					
Bangkok			■										
Beijing	■			■	■	■			■				■
Boston	■				■			■		■			
Buenos Aires				■					■				
Cairo												■	■
Copenhagen	■		■						■				
Chicago									■				
Delhi			■		■								
Dhaka		■					■						■
Hanoi							■						
Houston										■			
Jakarta			■	■			■	■	■			■	
Karachi			■	■	■		■				■		■
Kolkata					■							■	■
Lagos	■												
Los Angeles										■			■
London			■		■							■	
Melbourne				■		■			■				■
Mexico City	■		■		■			■					■
Mumbai		■		■	■			■	■		■		
Nairobi								■					
New Orleans								■	■	■			
New York	■			■				■					■

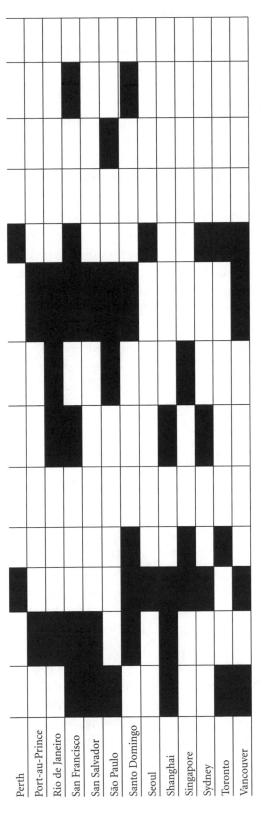

Perth
Port-au-Prince
Rio de Janeiro
San Francisco
San Salvador
São Paulo
Santo Domingo
Seoul
Shanghai
Singapore
Sydney
Toronto
Vancouver

Degree of importance noted in shadings: Dark: an existing problem, White: not reported.
Source: Worldwatch Institute. *State of the World 2007: Our Urban Future.* (Washington, DC, 2007).

- Nearly 850 million people are hungry, and 15% of the estimated 1.6 billion people who lack electricity and other modern energy services live in the world's cities.
- The UN Millennium Project estimates that improving the lives of 100 million slum dwellers will cost $830 billion over the next 17 years.
- According to the International Labor Organization, 184 million people on the planet do not have jobs; this figure would approximate 1 billion if underemployment were considered.
- The per capita footprint of high income countries is eight times that of the low income countries.
- An assessment of 116 cities by the World Health Organization (WHO) in 2000 estimated that only 43% of urban dwellers had access to piped water.
- Of the 292 large river systems in North America, Europe, and Russia, 42% are strongly affected by impoundments and diversions putting at risk humans, and plant and animal species.
- In 1970 there were 200 million cars in the world; by 2006 the number was 800 million, and that number will again double by 2030.
- The WHO estimates that each year about 1.2 billion people are killed as a result of road accidents and perhaps as many as 50 million are injured.
- The majority of the world's CO_2 emissions are traced to cities, even though they cover only 0.4% of the earth's surface.

Some problems that still merit attention at local, regional, and global scales are discussed below. These range from food production,
 sanitation and waste issues, natural disasters, and mass transit initiatives to health and diseases, slums and poverty, and global warming.

Natural Disasters and Global Warming

Natural disasters remain major problems affecting the planet's largest cities. These include flooding, hurricanes, tsunamis, and earthquakes. The Worldwatch report noted that the growing number of natural and other disasters is resulting in more loss of life each decade. In the past 25 years, 98% of the people injured in natural disasters lived in the 112 countries classified as low or middle income by the World Bank. These countries accounted for 90% of lives lost to natural disasters. Earthquakes alone affect more people in the developing than the developed world. The same is true for the melting of sea ice, which results from global warming. The U.S. Geological Survey estimated that the economic losses from natural disasters in the 1990s could have been reduced by $280 billion if just $40 billion had been invested in preventive measures. Less than 3% of LDC residents have insurance compared to about 30% in the richer parts of world. The poor suffer losses of housing, crops, livestock, and housing goods.

There are many examples of large and small cities that are vulnerable to multiple natural disasters. Flooding affects Melbourne, New Orleans, Dhaka, Port-au-Prince, Mumbai, and Delhi. Earthquakes affect San Francisco, Shanghai, Tehran, Jakarta, and Tokyo. Tsunamis affect coastal cities in the western and eastern Pacific. For some residents, early warning systems save lives. Cities have to consider when and how to rebuild their destroyed and damaged infrastructures, allow residents to return to their homes, and implement enforceable security systems.

Global warming will also affect major cities of coastal North America, Europe, and Asia.

Comparing a map of the world's largest and fastest growing cities with one showing shallow continental shelves reveals that many prosperous U.S. cities from Boston to Miami to Houston will be affected by a 6 foot (2 m) rise in sea level. Cities in northern and northwest Europe are also vulnerable, as are cities at the mouth of the Ganges, on the Malay Peninsula, in insular and mainland Southeast Asia, in eastern China, and in Japan.

Health Care and Diseases

This category includes a city's sanitation system; the quality of its drinking water; and programs to stem air, water, and land surface pollution, as well as the spread of diseases by human contact, livestock, and foods consumed. One could also include inadequate disposal of urban waste and trash, which affect the spread of diseases and the overall quality of urban life. Populations of all ages, in increasing numbers, are crossing international boundaries for work, pleasure, or study, thus increasing the likelihood of local epidemics reaching pandemic proportions. Hardly a year goes by without the reported outbreak of some new disease or the contamination of an urban water supply. Some cities alert their residents about high and dangerous levels of pollution. Air pollution kills an estimated 800,000 people annually; China has 16 of the 20 most polluted cities.

European, North American, Australian, and Japanese cities implement programs designed to protect the quality of living, working, and leisure environments, whether they be indoors or outdoors. For many LDC cities, health issues are often considered of secondary importance in a country's or region's economic development goals. Polluted air from automobiles or from industries is a fact of daily life just as much as polluted drinking water and

piles of garbage that can appear anywhere. Ecological problems abound including the outbreak of diseases, insufficient health vaccinations, and sporadic public safety warnings.

Slums and Poverty

For much of the developing world, the rising number of people living in substandard housing is a fact of daily life. Neighborhoods frequently lack electricity, running water, and sufficient food and energy sources. Many factors contribute to poverty, including employment in the informal sector, lack of effective urban networking to find jobs, low wages of multiple-member households, low rates of literacy, and lack of job skills. The UN Development Programme estimated that there are more than 800 million people on the planet who are urban farmers, most of whom live in China and India. About 200 million provide food primarily for the market, but a great majority raise food for themselves. Growing food, the report states, is not a hobby for most people on the planet. The urban poor are also those who have to carry water to their residences (equivalent to eight suitcases a day); they experience irregular and unexpected losses of water and electricity (if available), lack readily available and safe fuel sources to heat food and for their homes, use various outdoor facilities for toilets, and live in constant fear of eviction, loss of income and employment, injury from work or reckless drivers, and random violence brought on by criminal gangs or police.

Empowerment and Greening

In large and small LDC and MDC cities, there are grassroots efforts working to improve the quality of the urban physical and human environments. Many LDC initiatives stem from disenfranchised and previously powerless groups that see government officials and agencies as being insensitive to their demands for improved living. Their concerns include the provision of safe water sources; the installation of lights for safe streets; the provision of places where children can play (green spaces); safe transportation to places of employment (even central markets); recycling systems for waste products and the organizing of neighborhood trash collection; the promotion of urban farming along roadsides and hillsides; the organizing of neighborhood music, arts, and sporting programs for youth; and the development of microcredit initiatives, especially for women. In the rich world there are organizations that promote green city development by planting trees, installing bicycle lanes, placing mass transit proposals on public ballots, closing streets to vehicle use, encouraging and subsidizing renewable energy sources, and advocating effective recycling programs. Many projects are also on the agenda of Sister Cities. Examples of grassroots empowerment are legion. They include the Grameen Bank in Bangladesh, which provides microcredit to poor women; the Pakistani NGO Oranji Pilot Program, which works for better sanitation programs in poor neighborhoods; the Villa Maria del Triunfo in Lima, which supports urban farming; the National Slum Dwellers Federation in Mumbai; the Metro Cebu urban forestry initiative in the Philippines, a music program for Rio's favela youth; and Slum/Shack Dwellers International, which works with groups in Brazil, Kenya, Sri Lanka, Swaziland, and elsewhere. In the developed world there are many examples of local groups in Miami, Philadelphia, Seattle, Toronto, Perth, Amsterdam, and elsewhere that work with local and state governments and the private sector on various green efforts.

Sustainable Cities

These are cities with commitments to conservation, recycling, and sustainable economies, and with environmental ethics, that is, the idea that societies should make wise use of resources for future generations to develop an ethic of recycling and reuse. They are also committed to issues of social justice, gender equality, livable wages, affordable housing, and ready access for all members of society to education and health care. Integrating elements of ecology, economy, community, and social cohesion are thus the lynchpins of sustainable city development. Typical physical characteristics of sustainable cities include compact forms of residential development; mixed land use; use of mass transit along with widespread use of pedestrian and bicycle paths; heavy use of wind and solar energy; protection of natural hydrologic systems; protection of wetlands, woodlands, natural open space, and habitats; use of natural fertilizers and integrated pest management systems; use of natural means of sewage treatment; reduction of waste; and recovery, reuse, and recycling of waste materials. These cities encourage strong citizen participation as well as coalitions with businesses (box 13.4).

The UN's Sustainable Cities Programme (SCP) operates in scores of cities, mostly capitals. Among the countries involved are China, Chile, Egypt, Ghana, India, Kenya, Korea, Malawi, Mozambique, Nigeria, the Philippines, Poland, Russia, Senegal, Sri Lanka, Tanzania, Tunisia, and Zambia. Preparatory activities are under way in Bahrain, Cameroon, Iran, Kenya, Lesotho, Rwanda, South Africa, and Vietnam. Similar projects undertaken by the International Centre for Sustainable Cities are ongoing in Thailand, Indonesia, Poland, Turkey, Canada, the Philippines, and China. Locally, there are more than 40 partnering cities in 26 countries applying planning and management practices.

This program aims at developing local capacities for environmental planning and management (EPM), as poorly managed urbanization creates serious environmental and social problems. At the municipality level, development issues generally include water resources and water supply management; environmental health risks; solid and liquid waste management/on-site sanitation; air pollution and urban transport; drainage and flooding; industrial risks; informal-sector activities; land-use management in the context of open space/urban agriculture; tourism and coastal area resource management; and mining.

SCP identifies and organizes key stakeholders to identify critical issues, which are then addressed through plans and are implemented through public–private partnerships. These efforts lead in many ways to city-wide initiatives with supporting technical and financial investments and assistance to address the needs of the poor:

- Nationally, by supporting national partners (currently in nine countries) to implement these practices at the national level and to incorporate them into national policies on environment and poverty and into legal frameworks
- Regionally, by promoting exchanges of ideas, knowledge, experience, and technologies through networks of support and conferences among developing countries
- Globally, by integrating the strengths of the two agencies to develop technical

expertise, build awareness, and formulate policies that support sustainable urbanization across the world

The projects aimed at developing sustainable cities should be designed to generate outputs, including

- Development planning information (i.e., an environmental profile and a GIS-based environmental management information system)
- A strategic-development planning framework for the municipality
- Priority-investment packages and technical-assistance projects
- Capacity-development programs
- Stakeholder-based review mechanisms for evaluating the impact of interventions, documenting learning experiences, and sharing lessons learned

Human Security

Human security issues are emerging as important topics for those in the social and policy sciences. They are also important for those studying urban worlds, as security concerns affect the daily lives of individuals and the places in which they reside, work, and play; they also affect governmental and nongovernmental agencies at local and regional levels. Human security concerns include more than simply dealing with terrorism in its many dimensions, installing alarm systems in homes, purchasing antitheft car insurance, or dealing with preferences for gated communities. Transnational terrorism and biological and environmental terrorism are considered high-priority problems for state and multistate decision makers. Many public officials

Box 13.4   Inadequate Urban Services: Municipal Solid Waste in Lagos, Nigeria

Akin L. Mabogunje and Stanley Okafor

A defining feature of Nigerian cities is the inadequacy of urban infrastructure and services. Roads, transport services, energy supply, water supply, health care, and waste disposal services, among others, are all inadequate. These inadequacies are clearly visible in Lagos, Nigeria's largest metropolis with a population of some 14 million inhabitants and a population growth rate of 8%. It is Nigeria's economic capital, with the largest seaports, the busiest international airport, and the largest concentration of manufacturing industries and financial institutions in the country.

The generation of municipal solid waste has been on the increase in Nigeria over the past three decades or so, due largely to rising population, urbanization, and industrialization. The composition of municipal solid waste has also changed during the same period. In the early 1970s, prior to the oil boom, 55% of urban solid waste consisted of food and paper, with plastics making up 1% or less. With higher income brought about by the oil boom, the share of non-biodegradable materials has increased. Data for selected representative zones obtained from Lagos State Waste Management Authority (LAWMA) show that the percentage composition of urban waste in 2002 was as follows: leaves, 5.1%; food remnants, 8.4%; paper, 16.0%; rags, 9%; plastics and polythene, 20%; tins and metals, 15%; bottles and glasses, 13%; and ash, dust, and stones, 12%.

Rising population, urbanization, and industrialization are not the only factors responsible for the production of urban waste in Nigerian cities. Another factor is the continual expansion of the informal sector in Nigerian cities, which is the result of several developments. These include not only the usual rural–urban migration that exceeds the growth of urban jobs, but also, more recently, globalization and economic reform policies that have led to the loss of some manufacturing industries and the retrenchment of workers, as well as the down-sizing, or "right-sizing," of the labor force in both the public and private sectors of the economy. Most of the workers who lose their jobs enter the urban informal sector, and, along with other informal sector operators, set up some of the ubiquitous small-scale roadside and other enterprises, many of which generate significant quantities of waste.

Lagos generates about 9,800 tons of waste per day, out of which LAWMA collects about 7,000 tons per day. This leaves a shortfall of 2,800 tons per day to litter the streets of the

must insure that dangerous individuals, goods, and substances do not enter their country's airports and ports or cross their borders. They are ever vigilant in monitoring for contaminated products, whether foods, beverages, or other materials, that might en-

ter their country and endanger their food supplies, livestock, public water systems, and unique natural environments that attract tourists. The security industry will remain one of the "growth industries" for much of this century, with much evidence already in

metropolis. Two of the nine zones in the city—Mushin and Somolu—account for about 34% of the waste generated. These zones are among the predominantly low-income zones in Lagos. The government of Lagos State adopts a number of strategies to address the problem of urban waste. One way the state government tries to keep the city clean is through the institution of the monthly environmental sanitation day. This is usually the last Saturday of the month, from 7 a.m. to 10 a.m., during which time movement is prohibited except for people on essential services. This exercise is designed to enable people to stay home and clean their surroundings; it generates substantial amounts of waste that are dumped into designated sites where bins are provided. These bins are fabricated from local materials.

Another strategy is the waste-to-wealth program, which converts waste to bio-organic or compost fertilizer, and in the process creates employment opportunities and delivers a healthy and clean environment. The fertilizer that is produced is sold to local farmers, who have attested to its efficacy. There is a waste-to-wealth project site at Odogungan in Ikorodu Local Government Area, and there are plans to establish similar projects in other parts of the state. These projects are implemented through public–private partnerships and are in the spirit of the extant neoliberal economic reforms. A final strategy is night sweeping in some parts of the metropolis. Busy daytime traffic and commercial activities impede clean-up and waste collection during the day. In fact, these activities exacerbate the notorious traffic jams in Lagos.

Since the waste-to-wealth projects cannot, for now, handle all of the waste generated in Lagos, some is trucked to three landfill sites for final disposal. The sites are Olushosun (42 hectares), Abule Egba (10 hectares), and Solous (7 hectares). Olushosun receives about 65% of the total. In order to check the indiscriminate dumping of waste on the streets of the city, LAWMA procured many large and small bins and placed them in different parts of the city. However, the bins often overflow with urban waste, especially after the monthly sanitation exercises, because of irregular and infrequent refuse collection, and the paucity of trucks and other equipment. Between 1987 and 1991, Lagos State government, with World Bank assistance, procured 400 trucks and plants. But by May 2005, when the new management of LAWMA took charge, only two functional trucks were left. Most of the trucks broke down because of lack of spare parts and funds. However, within six months, the new management rehabilitated some of the trucks and increased the number of functional trucks to 50. Even this number is grossly inadequate for a city the size of Lagos. Right now, LAWMA has fewer than 100 trucks, but it needs at least 400 trucks for effective waste management. The problem of waste disposal in Lagos metropolis is therefore far from being resolved.

airports, train stations, and harbors, and at border crossings.

Many residents of rich-world cities see security as dealing mainly with personal security purchases (e.g., residential alarm systems, theft-proof windows and doors), policing, and law enforcement. In the developing world, security assumes some different faces: it is also a function of such daily concerns as having sufficient food, safe housing, lighted streets, and safe drinking water. Security also includes programs to prepare women and men for respectable jobs; to stop the spread of sexually transmitted diseases; to empower grassroots groups for representation in neighborhood and city government; to receive basic medical care including vaccinations for communicable diseases; to protect women and children from domestic violence; to prevent the spread of violence brought on by gangs, paramilitary forces, and urban police; and to reduce and eliminate the trafficking of drugs and deadly weapons. Some of these issues are of major concern to girls, women, and children, others to new or old racial, religious, and ethnic minorities, and still others to political and ecological refugees who cross borders seeking a safe place to live, work, worship, and play.

WHAT IF ? TWELVE SCENARIOS

One way to consider the severity of regional problems is to consider scenarios, that is, series of "what if" events. When considering urban or regional futures, some events might easily be predicted, such as growing energy demands associated with population increases. But there also likely will be unanticipated events, such as the social impacts of inexpensive cures for HIV/AIDS, more women leading political parties, major environmental crises (the politics of water shortages), and the rise of maverick city mayors. Regardless of whether predicted or unexpected scenarios occur, their impact usually transcends the administrative limits of any city. Below, we identify 12 scenarios to stimulate our thinking.

The Natural Environment

1. From the monsoons of South Asia to the earthquakes of California, major natural disasters will bring more death and de-struction to coastal urban areas around the world.

2. Global climate change will threaten coastal cities; anomalous new weather patterns will destroy crop and livestock economies, urban food supplies, and mega-engineering projects (river diversions, gigantic hydropower dams, and the "concretization" of rapidly growing cities), and will result in the widespread environmental destruction of the earth's biota and the loss of prime agricultural land.

3. Unknown and deadly human, plant, and animal diseases and viruses will be carried by humans traveling to various destinations for holidays, pilgrimages, sporting events, and military campaigns or will be spread by unknowingly consuming tainted foods and drinks.

4. Cities will face unexpected disruptions and collapses in their energy supplies, as a result of unusual weather, overloaded power sources, malfunctioning satellite systems, accidents at antiquated nuclear power facilities, or the spread of "deadly" computer viruses.

The Social and Cultural Environment

5. Surprise military, biological, computer, and environmental terrorism will be directed against major cities by international, domestic, or local renegade groups that are regionally and globally networked and have multiple "home bases." They will threaten major political, military, and corporate headquarters (banking, media, medical, data processing); transportation and communication networks; high-rise office buildings; sites of major sporting events; water supplies; research centers; and cherished religious sites and national monuments.

6. Large-scale refugee populations will flee across political borders in Africa and Asia in search of food, employment, safety, and freedom. Regions where rich cities border the poor world include North Africa/Southern Europe, Southeast Asia/Australia, and U.S./Mexico.

7. Civil unrest and violence will be accompanied by massive breakdowns in law and order because of the influx of large numbers of new rural migrants moving to primate cities, high unemployment among immigrants, sharp increases in food prices, and confrontations between the wealthy few and the many living in despair.

8. Social and economic gaps will continue to surface between the landless and propertied, the educated elite and illiterate, the favored few and marginalized masses, and those who are and are not "wired." Cultural clashes will emerge because of differences in religious values (traditional vs. secular views), conflicts between patriarchal and cosmopolitan worldviews, ethical issues related to medical breakthroughs (organ transplants, genetic counseling, and euthanasia), changing gender roles, and unwholesome values depicted in Western media.

9. The number and percentage of elders will continue to increase in MDCs and this group will eventually become an important cohort in many LDC cities.

The Economic Environment

10. The financial collapse of entire cities and metropolitan regions in older industrialized parts of Europe, North America, Russia, and East Asia will occur because new capital and skilled labor are moving to prosperous city regions, and because national governments fail to bail out troubled cities.

11. Investment capital will be directed away from traditional centers of investment (Europe, North America, and East Asia, especially Japan) and to selected "low risk" primate cities and small states in Africa, Asia, the Caribbean, and the Pacific.

The Political Environment

12. New and influential actors, including professional entertainment stars, bankers, rich exploration executives, high-flying jet-setters, and "stateless nomads," will appear on the political scene of MDC and LDC cities and use their power to affect elections and support changes in property and banking regulations.

SOLVING URBAN PROBLEMS

All problems have solutions. Below we suggest some, many of which will require huge financial investments, local empowerment, civic leadership, and bold, creative thinking to implement at national and global scales.

Investment in New Infrastructure

Investments can be made to construct new transportation and telecommunications corridors linking cities not currently integrated, such as macroreginal and continental systems in the Andes and Amazon, West to East Africa, and across Central Asia into northeast Asia.

LDCs Investing in MDCs

Emerging rich, well-endowed, and powerful LDCs, including China, India, Brazil, Mexico,

Kazakhstan, Saudi Arabia, Iran, and South Africa, could use revenues from natural resource extraction to assist marginalized cities in Europe and elsewhere with loans and credit for economic restructuring.

Subsidizing Investment in Frontier Areas

Governments could provide subsidies and tax havens for corporations, universities, individuals, and charity groups willing to commit themselves to long-term residence in marginal, worn out, and frontier regions. These might be gated communities, smart cities, or eco-cooperatives.

Empowerment of Women

Change will occur when and where there are strong commitments to eradicating illiteracy, HIV/AIDS, and child labor; to reducing violence in the home and the workplace; to investing in local grassroots efforts; and to supporting investments in local politics.

Living with Alternative Structures

Rather than uniform policies of rigid conformity, there could be groups and communities exploring alternative models of policing, participation, and administration. Whereas some groups may choose very traditional and local forms of government and group participation, others may exhibit high degrees of nonconformity and totalitarianism.

Mafias and Clans

Criminal and business-oriented "mafias" or clans could administer and even finance bankrupt cities in parts of North America, Europe, and Russia, and even new cities in Asia

and Africa by assisting in solving local and regional environmental, health care, educational, and security concerns. Island states and gated communities might serve as examples.

Corporate Ownership of Cities

Cities could be bought and sold on international financial markets like food, energy supplies, and industrial products, and administered by transnational corporations rather than by traditional political parties or the state.

Triage Planning Strategies

Government officials in rich and poor countries might divide cities and urban regions into three groups: those that (a) have healthy economies and societies, (b) might respond to short-term infusions of skilled labor and capital, and (c) face dismal futures and should be left to fend for themselves.

Greater Voice

Two new groups could call for increased participation and representation in urban governance: the new Latin, African, and Asian diaspora communities in MDCs and the dispossessed, poor, and recent rural migrants in LDC cities.

Transborder Governing Systems

New forms of coordinated city government and planning could emerge in rich and poor world cities that straddle international boundaries and are already linked by thousands of daily commuters; they could merge for mass transportation, solid waste, health care, and public safety programs.

A World Urban Cabinet

An organization of the world's largest cities could operate either separately or alongside the United Nations to address problems facing MDCs and LDCs, including transborder pollution, water and sanitation, and transportation and communication systems

Environmental Awareness

To alleviate loss of human life and destruction from natural and technological disasters, there could be increased investments in disaster preparedness, post-disaster delivery systems, and effective reconstruction planning, perhaps with the assistance of PPGIS.

Transnational "Urban Response Teams"

These teams, drawing on talent from around the world, could assist communities facing major power outages, disease outbreaks, destruction of water systems, massive refugee populations, major industrial and transportation accidents, prolonged social conflicts, and collapses of governance and security.

Measuring the Ecological Footprint

Sustained efforts could be made to accurately measure and map the impacts or "footprints" of environmental destruction on neighborhoods, communities, cities, and city systems.

LOOKING AHEAD

Numerous questions arise when contemplating cities at 2050, 2100, and beyond. Given faster and cheaper transportation, will humans always have a need for cities? Although diversity has long been a distinguishing feature of the urban fabric, might new forms of identity and social separation emerge that are based on new loyalty units such as sports and lifestyles, more than on cultural traditions, ethnicity, and class? Might transurban loyalties replace those that are territorially based? Could global information and communication technologies be used as vehicles to generate feelings of belonging to a place rather than placelessness?

What will be the impacts of wireless communications on privacy and city culture? Will new behavioral norms evolve based on hypermobility? Do new technologies promote gender, class, and cross-cultural equity? Will voiceless and visual Internet worlds inhibit or resolve pressing urban problems? Will fluidity in time more than space define the urban resident of the mid-21st century? What happens to the mosaic of the world's languages if international commerce is increasingly conducted in American English or if Chinese becomes the second major language of global commerce? What are the impacts of single-child households on urban population with growing numbers of elders? What are the long-term impacts of increased rates of HIV/AIDS on rural and urban residents in Africa and Asia or of the rapid global diffusion of unforeseen pandemics associated with greater commercial travel and new foods?

Will rural ways of life disappear? Will "wilderness" rather than rural become the antithesis of urban (box 13.5)? Will rural areas become "future museums" and fantasy places for the urban world to visit, the places where die-hard traditionalists, a society's rejects, and those with nonacceptable lifestyles live? Will the production of food (long associated with supporting rural livelihoods and city food supplies) be

---

Box 13.5   Rural Futures in an Urban World

Christopher Bryant

We live an increasingly urban world, but are we destined to be completely urbanized? Does the rural world of our distant ancestors have a future?

Rural areas have traditionally provided resources and commodities to support cities: food, fuel, water, and raw materials (and sometimes space) for industrial development. The role of rural areas near major urban centers, however, has become less significant—especially in developed countries—as world trade in food has reduced our reliance on locally produced foodstuffs. As a result of major advances in transportation technologies during the 20th century, cities have been able to supply their food needs from around the world. However, the food-supply function is still important for rural areas near cities in most developing countries. And even in developed countries, there is usually a premium placed on "farmers market" food.

The post–World War II era has seen the development of the regional city. It has resulted partly from the widespread diffusion of the automobile and, in Europe, from public transportation systems. The regional city's evolution is partly related to the search by some urbanites for a more peaceful, quasi-rural living environment in which to bring up their families while maintaining ties to employment opportunities in urban areas. Major changes in urban settlement systems occurred—at the macro scale, the increasing metropolization of society, but at the meso-scale, a decentralizing phenomenon within metropolitan regions.

Rural areas in expanding regional city systems took on more and more important roles in providing leisure and recreational opportunities, perhaps in the form of "near urban parks" and other facilities catering to the "needs" of the mobile urbanites. Furthermore, although it has become common to think of areas with second homes as lying within an hour's drive (and often much farther) from main urban areas, it is not uncommon to see second-home areas located very close to the large cities!

Increasing rural–urban linkages in metropolitan regions have spawned an interest in the multi-functionality of rural space—food production and water supplies, of course, but also landscape amenities, leisure and recreational uses, ecological sustainability, and conservation of natural and cultural heritage. Should we think of preserving some farm areas simply

---

replaced by chemical and pharmaceutical factories and signal the end of agrarian life?

How will cities be affected by major catastrophes such as September 11, 2001 (box 13.6)? Will people choose to work in different environments? Will urbanites become more supportive of each other? Will skyscrapers, places of high density, and the neighborhoods of new immigrants become new urban landscapes of fear? Will the perception of increased domestic and international terrorism change lifestyles, modes of transportation,

because of the cultural and historical assets embedded in their landscapes? This is a debatable issue, as most farmers are not keen on becoming museum pieces! However, finding ways of maintaining historical and cultural assets (e.g., the long-lot field system in Quebec, the hedgerow patterns in England and France) and bio-physical assets (e.g., environmentally sensitive areas) in many metropolitan zones, while still permitting and encouraging farming, has taken on much greater importance. It can even be observed in some developing countries (e.g., Morocco). This interest covers both urban fringe areas and more remote rural areas. Urban populations and their governing authorities are widely promoting "quality" agricultural produce, often organic, as an alternative to total dependence on large-scale, industrialized farming ventures. Western European countries, such as France and Italy, have been in the vanguard of supporting the "branding" of local agricultural produce to help rural areas establish niche markets and therefore contribute to their own economic survival as well as the conservation of historical, cultural, and natural assets embedded in their landscapes. Likewise, tourism can refocus on "authenticity" and personal contact through rural and "green" tourism.

Many rural areas will be able to hold their own because the consumer market is still a force to reckon with, certainly in developed countries. How else can we explain the rise of organically produced foodstuffs, Community Supported Agriculture, and the like? Likewise, new migration patterns such as counterurbanization and neo-ruralite development are directed toward finding peaceful living environments, cheaper housing, and a better quality of life.

Consider also the impact of other powerful forces on the relationship between urban and rural. Climate change might lead to a reconcentration of population and economic activities. On the other hand, the dominance of economic activities that do not depend upon proximity between production and consumption (particularly those in the high-level service sector) may feed rural and small town growth. Telecommunication technologies are diminishing the differences between rural and urban (functionally) and extending the reach of metropolitan core areas. Simultaneously, newcomers to rural communities, often retirees, support diversification of the local economic base. When there are newcomers to rural areas, there is no simple way of characterizing them. They come to rural areas for many different reasons: to seek a quieter life, to seek closeness to nature, to maintain access to city services but live in a rural environment, to live more cheaply, or to escape from something—or someone!

and discretionary spending? Will fantasy and exotic tourism be casualties of the leisure economy?

What new places and types of living might emerge? Some futurists foresee huge residential ocean liners or floating cities that circle the globe or ply major tourist rivers and the coastlines of wealthy megacities. Still others suggest using the "oil platform" model to build huge permanent or temporary residences anywhere. Others envision the world's wealthy becoming peripatetic global nomads

---

Box 13.6   Cities in a Post–9/11 World

Geographers, urban planners, architects, and engineers are among those considering the short- and long-term impacts of the events of September 11, 2001, in New York and Washington on cities around the world. Peter Marcuse, a professor in urban planning in the Graduate School of Architecture, Planning, and Preservation at Columbia University in New York City, wrote an essay a week after the 9/11 events that called attention to a number of pertinent issues. These included the impacts of the terrorist attacks on high-density cities, how personal travel (commuting) might be affected, whether employment patterns of high- and low-wage service employees might shrink, and whether the benefits of agglomeration, long crucial for downtown development and economic strength, might shift with new priorities and political considerations. He went on to suggest that perhaps global companies would shy away from huge cities such as New York and choose to locate in more outlying areas. The impact of the destruction of the World Trade Center was already being felt in other cities with what he called "trophy skyscrapers," including Frankfurt and Kuala Lumpur. His final comments were directed at security issues that "threaten the core of social and political life" of those living and working in cities. Public spaces, Marcuse added, will become less public and likely subject to more surveillance, while increased funding for police and law enforcement is expected, even though this will reduce the civil liberties of citizens. By contrast, controlled spaces such as malls will become more popular. In conclusion, Marcuse reflected on what the events of September 11 may mean to those in the academy who have devoted their careers to studying cities and the effects of globalization. He wrote, "Whatever we have thought and said and written up till now has been subjected to a major shock from 'outside the system' (although inside it in a terrible way), and will need significant reassessment."

In late 2001, a task force of the Association of American Geographers, composed of leading scholars with interests in urban technology and GIS, explored ways to collect and map data to aid in delivering vital services during and following emergencies, to rebuild infrastructures, and to support homeland security initiatives.

Source: Peter Marcuse, "All Cities Will Change," urbgeog@listserv.arizona.edu, September 17, 2001.

---

with multiple "international homes." Might terratexture (underground) spaces become more popular? These alternative settings might be used to house the wealthy, the elites, and the powerful, but also the undesirable and unwanted.

Will the world's future political agendas be dominated by cities rather than nation-states, and/or by large urban agglomerations in the present LDCs rather than the MDCs? Will the rich MDCs and their large cities be able and willing to adjust to "A South World"? Will the world's development "divide" be increasingly urban–rural rather than North–South? What will China's urban future look like as the population becomes more urban, globally aware, and wealthy? Will China, India, and Indonesia form the "Global Growth Triangle" of the late 21st century? Will the ethnic diversity of Sub-Saharan African cities make them cauldrons for conflict or models for cooperation?

Will urban homogeneity also contribute to conflict, a feature of some agglomerations in Africa and Asia? Can cities of 10, 20, or 30 million be governed? Could the future megacity be composed of 50 rival "city governments," each competing for the best talent and most financial resources? Will territory cease to be the basis for administration and be replaced by loyalties to transnational corporations, new diasporas, and regional sports? Where can one look for solutions for megacities faced with vast contrasts in income, formal and informal economies, and religious and ethnic diversity? What can MDC cities learn from LDC cities and vice-versa? How applicable are Western urban growth, economic development, transportation, and community planning models to African, Latin American, and Asian cities?

How prepared are global megacities and small cities for natural and technological disasters? What top-down strategies and grassroots (bottom-up) efforts in LDCs could be successful in preventing losses of life and the destruction of homes and urban infrastructures? How can GIS and PPGIS initiatives be incorporated into community and regional preparedness and responses?

Will urban and national governments, as well as non-governmental and intergovernmental lending organizations, be able and willing to consider food availability, quality health care, water and sanitation networks, and protection of the vulnerable (poor, disabled, children, women, and elderly) as being important in defining human security as thwarting domestic and international terrorism and the proliferation of dangerous weapons? What kinds of grassroots efforts by women, gangs, sports teams, artists, and religious groups, have been successful in stemming the tide of hatred, fear, and terrorism?

It is not difficult to envision future human settlements that include preindustrial remnants existing alongside postmodern cities, safe cities alongside unsafe cities, and smart (wired) cities alongside bypassed (little-wired) cities (fig. 13.15). There may even be governable and ungovernable places, innovative and laggard cities in the same region.

Although pessimism about the future of cities might be justified, based on the problems detailed in previous chapters, to succumb to this view is to give up hope. Humanity survives on hope, including hope for the future of cities. It is important to remember that contemporary cities continue to resonate with the very qualities that characterized the first cities in history. For thousands of years, humans have chosen to live in concentrated settlements of varying sizes. Cities will always be

- Tapestries of rich cultural diversity (religious, ethnic, lifestyle, etc.)
- Places where new identities transcend traditional social-class, local, and regional identities
- Places of innovation in culture, economics, identities, and governments that may "leapfrog" some earlier forms of urban development
- Loci of opportunities to improve the quality of life for all ages and residents
- Nexuses of integrated communication and information technologies that transcend existing social, political, and cultural identities and boundaries (fig. 13.16)

World Time Regions

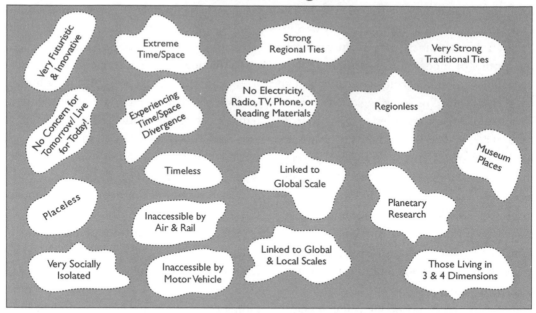

Examples of Cultural Time Regions in the 2000s

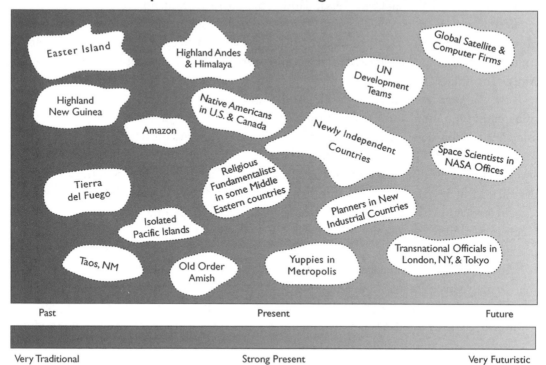

Figure 13.15 World Time Regions. *Source:* Stanley Brunn, "Human Rights and Welfare in the Electronic State," in *Information Tectonics*, ed. Mark I. Wilson and Kenneth E. Corey (New York: Wiley, 2000), 60. Reprinted with permission.

Figure 13.16 The Asianization of Atlanta is evident in the commercial landscapes of the suburbs. (Photo by George Pomeroy)

There never has been and never will be a single city anywhere in which all residents are happy, content, and peaceful. Utopia is unattainable. But among the new and old inhabitants there can be conscious efforts to improve the human condition and to recognize that cities can bring out the best of human qualities. International collaboration and opportunities to attain these goals offer many opportunities for current and future generations of citizens on the planet.

SUGGESTED READINGS

Castells, Manuel. 2001. *The Internet Galaxy: Reflections on the Internet, Business, and Society*. New York: Oxford University Press. One of the leading scholars on Internet culture and commerce examines how the Internet is affecting urban planning as well as society.

Craig, William J., Trevor H. Harris, and Daniel Wiener. eds. 2002. *Community Participation and Geographic Information Systems*. London: Taylor and Francis. Includes numerous examples of community groups using GIS for empowerment and for gaining voice in public policy.

Dodge, Martin, and Rob Kitchen. 2000. *Mapping Cyberspace*. New York: Routledge. This team of human geographers/cartographers explores, with many innovative graphics, cyberspace at all scales.

Graham, Stephen, ed. 2004. *The Cybercities Reader*. London: Routledge. A splendid collection of short and lengthy essays on the built environment, work and living, technologies and politics.

Hall, Peter G. 1988. *Cities of Tomorrow. An Intellectual History of City Planning in the Twentieth Century*. Oxford, England: Blackwell. A history of the ideology and practice of urban planning, regarded by some as the successor to Lewis Mumford's *The City in History*.

Kotkin, Joel. 2000. *The New Geography: How the Digital Revolution Is Reshaping the American Landscape*. New York: Random House. Explores how the digital revolution is changing the way we live and work, and also the role of cities.

Leinbach, Thomas R., and Stanley D. Brunn, eds. 2001. *The Worlds of e-Commerce: Economic, Geographical and Social Dimensions*. New York: Wiley. Discusses developments in banking and finance, retailing, job searches, government regulations, and international development.

Ruchelman, Leonard I. 2006. *Cities in the Third Wave: The Technological Transformation of Urban America*, 2d ed. Lanham, MD: Rowman and Littlefield. Considers the impact of new space-adjusting computer technologies on cities and emerging city types.

Urban Land Institute. 2002. *ULI on the Future: Cities Post 9/11*. Washington, DC: ULI. Five articles on issues facing American cities, including security, immigration reform, corporate (re)location, housing, and civic leadership.

Worldwatch Institute. 2007. *State of the World 2007*. Washington, DC: Worldwatch Institute. The single most valuable reference on problems facing urban humankind; contains many valuable tables, footnotes, and references.

Zook, Matthew. 2005. *The Geography of the Internet Industry: Venture Capital, Dot-Coms, and Local Knowledge*. Malden, MA: Blackwell. Explores the history of global Internet networks and their impacts on contemporary economic and social geographies.

Zook, Matthew, and Mark Graham. 2007. "From Cyberspace to DigiPlace: Visibility in an Age of Information and Mobility." In Harvey J. Miller, ed., *Societies and Cities in the Age of Instant Access*. London: Springer, 231–244. Introduces "DigiPlace" as a way of conceptualizing movement through hybrid spaces comprised of physical and virtual elements.

SUGGESTED WEBSITES

Center for Sustainable Urban Development
www.earth.columbia.edu/csud
Projects and research papers on sustainable development around the world.

Demographia World Urban Areas: Population Projections 2007 and 2015 (World Agglomerations)
www.demographia.com also
demographia2@earthlink.net
A very useful source on urban population numbers, land area, change, and rankings.

Mega-Cities Project
www.megacitiesproject.org
Identifies both challenges and plans to address problems in the world's mega-cities.

Mercer Cost of Living Survey
www.mercer.com/costofliving
City ranking based on cost of housing, transport, food, clothing, entertainment.

Places OnLine (Association of American Geographers)
http://www.placesonline.org/
A map-based portal to websites from around the world.

Sister Cities International
www.sister-cities.org
Includes a global sister city directory.

UN Sustainable Cities Programme
www.unhabitat.org/caategories.a:catid=540
An excellent source of data on the urban environment.

Urban Age: A Worldwide Investigation into the Future of Cities
www.urban-age.net
Aim is to shape the thinking and practice of sustainable urban development.

Wikitravel
www.wikitravel.org/en
An evolving "free, complete, up-to-date and reliable worldwide travel guide."

Appendix: Populations of Urban Agglomerations with 750,000 Inhabitants or More in 2005, by Country: 1950, 1975, 2000, and 2015 (projected)

Country/Agglomeration	Population (thousands)			
	1950	*1975*	*2000*	*2015*
UNITED STATES AND CANADA				
CANADA				
Calgary	132	457	953	1,193
Edmonton	163	543	947	1,118
Montréal	1,343	2,791	3,471	3,897
Ottawa-Gatineau	282	676	1,079	1,262
Toronto	1,068	2,770	4,747	5,938
Vancouver	556	1,150	2,040	2,389
UNITED STATES OF AMERICA				
Atlanta	513	1,386	3,542	4,864
Austin	137	320	913	1,271
Baltimore	1,168	1,650	2,083	2,410
Boston	2,551	3,233	4,049	4,751
Bridgeport-Stamford	415	703	894	1,103
Buffalo	899	1,041	977	1,091
Charlotte	142	315	769	1,093
Chicago	4,999	7,160	8,333	9,469
Cincinnati	881	1,216	1,508	1,755
Cleveland	1,392	1,848	1,789	2,019
Columbus, Ohio	441	813	1,138	1,370
Dallas–Fort Worth	866	2,234	4,172	5,121
Dayton	350	637	706	837
Denver-Aurora	505	1,198	1,998	2,489
Detroit	2,769	3,885	3,909	4,342
Hartford	425	700	853	984
Honolulu	250	511	720	850
Houston	709	2,030	3,849	4,767
Indianapolis	505	829	1,228	1,554
Jacksonville, Florida	246	564	886	1,069
Kansas City	703	1,079	1,365	1,576
Las Vegas	35	325	1,335	2,001
Los Angeles–Long Beach–Santa Ana	4,046	8,926	11,814	13,095
Louisville	476	751	866	1,023
Memphis	409	720	976	1,167
Miami	622	2,590	4,946	5,940
Milwaukee	836	1,228	1,311	1,488

Country/Agglomeration	Population (thousands)			
	1950	*1975*	*2000*	*2015*
Minneapolis–St. Paul	996	1,748	2,397	2,795
Nashville-Davidson	261	484	755	954
New Orleans	664	1,021	1,009	1,096
New York–Newark	12,338	15,880	17,846	19,876
Oklahoma City	278	573	748	850
Orlando	75	427	1,165	1,461
Philadelphia	3,128	4,467	5,160	5,806
Phoenix-Mesa	221	1,117	2,934	3,822
Pittsburgh	1,539	1,827	1,755	1,962
Portland	516	925	1,595	2,025
Providence	703	963	1,178	1,374
Richmond	260	558	822	987
Riverside–San Bernardino	139	645	1,516	1,882
Sacramento	216	714	1,402	1,731
Salt Lake City	230	573	890	1,042
San Antonio	454	859	1,333	1,585
San Diego	440	1,442	2,683	3,110
San Francisco–Oakland	1,855	2,590	3,236	3,666
San Jose	182	1,103	1,543	1,789
Seattle	795	1,663	2,727	3,289
St. Louis	1,407	1,865	2,081	2,346
Tampa–St. Petersburg	300	1,094	2,072	2,481
Tucson	77	368	724	893
Virginia Beach	391	996	1,397	1,598
Washington, D.C.	1,298	2,626	3,949	4,613

MIDDLE AMERICA AND THE CARIBBEAN

COSTA RICA				
San José	148	440	1,032	1,506
CUBA				
La Habana (Havana)	1,147	1,827	2,187	2,151
DOMINICAN REPUBLIC				
Santo Domingo	219	1,016	1,834	2,449
EL SALVADOR				
San Salvador	194	596	1,353	1,807
GUATEMALA				
Ciudad de Guatemala (Guatemala City)	428	715	908	1,269
HAITI				
Port-au-Prince	133	575	1,766	2,785
HONDURAS				
Tegucigalpa	73	292	793	1,230
MEXICO				
Acapulco de Juárez	29	232	726	864
Aguascalientes	94	233	736	1,059
Ciudad de México (Mexico City)	2,883	10,690	18,066	21,568
Ciudad Juárez	123	474	1,239	2,008
Culiacán	49	230	750	931
Guadalajara	403	1,850	3,697	4,456
León de los Aldamas	123	589	1,293	1,785

Country/Agglomeration	Population (thousands)			
	1950	*1975*	*2000*	*2015*
Mérida	143	351	849	1,097
Mexicali	66	302	771	1,015
Monterrey	356	1,589	3,267	4,140
Puebla	227	858	1,888	1,861
Querétaro	49	159	798	1,185
San Luis Potosí	132	378	857	1,103
Tijuana	60	355	1,297	2,194
Toluca de Lerdo	54	309	1,420	1,770
Torreón	189	556	1,012	1,200
Tuxtla Gutierrez	28	95	539	1,209
NICARAGUA				
Managua	110	443	1,021	1,461
PANAMA				
Panamá (Panama City)	171	528	1,072	1,527
PUERTO RICO				
San Juan	451	1,069	2,237	2,791

SOUTH AMERICA

Country/Agglomeration	*1950*	*1975*	*2000*	*2015*
ARGENTINA				
Buenos Aires	5,098	8,745	11,847	13,396
Córdoba	429	905	1,348	1,552
Mendoza	248	537	838	956
Rosario	554	883	1,152	1,280
San Miguel de Tucumán	224	424	722	868
BOLIVIA				
La Paz	319	703	1,390	1,864
Santa Cruz	42	234	1,054	1,724
BRAZIL				
Baixada Santista	246	770	1,468	1,940
Belém	242	706	1,748	2,524
Belo Horizonte	412	1,906	4,659	6,354
Brasília	36	827	2,746	4,282
Campinas	152	773	2,264	3,239
Cuiabá	27	162	686	923
Curitiba	158	922	2,494	3,581
Florianópolis	68	221	734	1,262
Fortaleza	264	1,136	2,875	3,850
Goiânia	53	527	1,608	2,372
Grande São Luís	120	342	876	1,192
Grande Vitória	85	493	1,398	1,974
João Pessoa	117	362	827	1,087
Maceió	123	342	952	1,391
Manaus	90	411	1,392	2,059
Natal	108	367	910	1,253
Norte/Nordeste Catarinense	64	278	815	1,146
Pôrto Alegre	488	1,727	3,505	4,342
Recife	661	1,867	3,230	4,070
Rio de Janeiro	2,950	7,557	10,803	12,770
Salvador	403	1,341	2,968	3,950
São Paulo	2,334	9,614	17,099	20,535
Teresina	54	276	789	1,029

Country/Agglomeration	Population (thousands)			
	1950	*1975*	*2000*	*2015*
CHILE				
Santiago	1,322	3,138	5,326	6,191
COLOMBIA				
Barranquilla	294	832	1,658	2,191
Bucaramanga	110	410	921	1,201
Cali	231	1,052	2,237	2,963
Cartagena	107	334	829	1,152
Cucuta	70	265	760	1,012
Medellín	376	1,541	2,814	3,522
Santa Fé de Bogotá	676	3,061	6,964	8,932
ECUADOR				
Guayaquil	258	890	2,077	2,975
Quito	206	628	1,357	1,839
PARAGUAY				
Asunción	223	551	1,457	2,606
PERU				
Arequipa	128	348	724	994
Lima	973	3,651	6,811	8,026
URUGUAY				
Montevideo	1,140	1,178	1,285	1,277
VENEZUELA				
Barquisimeto	127	475	923	1,243
Caracas	676	2,342	2,864	3,144
Maracaibo	260	825	1,901	2,911
Maracay	89	432	1,015	1,463
Valencia	108	519	1,893	3,499
EUROPE				
AUSTRIA				
Wien (Vienna)	1,787	2,002	2,158	2,379
BELGIUM				
Bruxelles-Brussel	806	940	964	1,062
BULGARIA				
Sofiya (Sofia)	522	960	1,164	1,059
CZECH REPUBLIC				
Praha (Prague)	934	1,125	1,181	1,186
DENMARK				
København (Copenhagen)	1,216	1,381	1,079	1,098
FINLAND				
Helsinki	366	582	1,019	1,135
FRANCE				
Bordeaux	306	614	763	822
Lille	723	936	1,007	1,063
Lyon	564	1,173	1,362	1,446
Marseille-Aix-en-Provence	624	1,185	1,357	1,421
Nice-Cannes	367	699	894	946
Paris	5,424	8,630	9,692	9,858
Toulouse	275	527	778	868

Country/Agglomeration	Population (thousands)			
	1950	*1975*	*2000*	*2015*
GERMANY				
Berlin	3,338	3,227	3,392	3,389
Hamburg	1,602	1,731	1,715	1,755
Köln (Cologne)	656	975	966	961
München (Munich)	827	1,260	1,211	1,303
GREECE				
Athínai (Athens)	1,783	2,738	3,179	3,251
Thessaloniki	292	617	797	841
HUNGARY				
Budapest	1,618	2,005	1,787	1,655
IRELAND				
Dublin	626	833	989	1,186
ITALY				
Milano (Milan)	1,883	3,133	2,985	2,937
Napoli (Naples)	1,498	2,096	2,232	2,252
Palermo	594	783	855	862
Roma (Rome)	1,884	3,300	3,385	3,330
Torino (Turin)	1,011	1,838	1,694	1,642
NETHERLANDS				
Amsterdam	855	989	1,126	1,201
Rotterdam	741	1,032	1,092	1,143
NORWAY				
Oslo	468	644	774	842
POLAND				
Kraków (Cracow)	339	644	756	767
Lódz	608	796	799	764
Warszawa (Warsaw)	768	1,444	1,666	1,687
PORTUGAL				
Lisboa (Lisbon)	1,304	2,103	2,672	3,005
Porto	730	1,008	1,254	1,443
ROMANIA				
Bucuresti (Bucharest)	652	1,338	2,009	1,942
SERBIA				
Beograd (Belgrade)	411	873	1,128	1,100
SPAIN				
Barcelona	1,809	3,679	4,548	5,057
Madrid	1,700	3,890	5,162	6,086
Valencia	506	695	790	813
SWEDEN				
Göteborg	352	691	793	867
Stockholm	741	1,359	1,652	1,760
SWITZERLAND				
Zürich (Zurich)	494	713	1,074	1,200
UNITED KINGDOM				
Birmingham	2,229	2,365	2,285	2,279
Glasgow	1,755	1,601	1,171	1,162
Liverpool	1,382	1,018	818	816
London	8,361	7,546	8,225	8,618

Country/Agglomeration	Population (thousands)			
	1950	*1975*	*2000*	*2015*
Manchester	2,422	2,370	2,243	2,223
Newcastle upon Tyne	909	838	880	887
West Yorkshire	1,692	1,618	1,495	1,534

RUSSIA

BELARUS

Minsk	284	1,120	1,694	1,903

RUSSIAN FEDERATION

Chelyabinsk	573	966	1,088	1,055
Kazan	514	942	1,103	1,111
Krasnoyarsk	290	734	911	912
Moskva (Moscow)	5,356	7,623	10,103	11,022
Nizhniy Novgorod	796	1,273	1,331	1,264
Novosibirsk	719	1,250	1,426	1,424
Omsk	444	933	1,136	1,129
Perm	498	937	1,014	967
Rostov-na-Donu (Rostov-on-Don)	484	874	1,061	1,093
Samara	658	1,146	1,173	1,121
Sankt Peterburg (Saint Petersburg)	2,903	4,325	5,214	5,375
Saratov	473	816	878	861
Ufa	418	887	1,049	1,027
Volgograd	461	884	1,010	1,019
Voronezh	332	732	854	834
Yekaterinburg	628	1,135	1,303	1,268

UKRAINE

Dnipropetrovs'k	536	981	1,077	998
Donets'k	585	963	1,026	960
Kharkiv	758	1,353	1,484	1,390
Kyiv (Kiev)	815	1,926	2,606	2,757
Odesa	532	982	1,037	985
Zaporizhzhya	315	730	822	775

GREATER MIDDLE EAST

ALGERIA

El Djazaïr (Algiers)	516	1,507	2,754	3,924
Wahran (Oran)	269	466	706	944

ARMENIA

Yerevan	341	911	1,111	1,102

AZERBAIJAN

Baku	897	1,429	1,803	1,977

EGYPT

Al-Iskandariyah (Alexandria)	1,037	2,241	3,506	4,518
Al-Qahirah (Cairo)	2,494	6,450	10,391	13,138

GEORGIA

Tbilisi	612	992	1,100	1,021

IRAN (ISLAMIC REPUBLIC OF)

Ahvaz	85	313	871	1,152
Esfahan	184	767	1,381	1,836
Karaj	10	124	1,063	1,483
Kermanshah	97	274	750	994

Country/Agglomeration	Population (thousands)			
	1950	*1975*	*2000*	*2015*
Mashhad	173	685	1,990	2,515
Qom	78	227	888	1,261
Shiraz	128	418	1,124	1,456
Tabriz	235	662	1,274	1,651
Tehran	1,041	4,273	6,979	8,432
IRAQ				
Al-Basrah (Basra)	116	350	759	1,028
Al-Mawsil (Mosul)	145	397	1,056	1,565
Baghdad	579	2,814	5,200	7,242
Irbil (Erbil)	30	191	773	1,195
ISRAEL				
Hefa (Haifa)	204	350	888	1,104
Tel Aviv-Yafo (Tel Aviv-Jaffa)	418	1,206	2,752	3,453
JORDAN				
Amman	90	500	1,132	1,615
KAZAKHSTAN				
Almaty	354	860	1,137	1,183
KUWAIT				
Al Kuwayt (Kuwait City)	81	688	1,549	2,341
KYRGYZSTAN				
Bishkek	150	485	766	902
LEBANON				
Bayrut (Beirut)	322	1,500	1,487	2,055
LIBYAN ARAB JAMAHIRIYA				
Banghazi	53	306	945	1,399
Tarabulus (Tripoli)	106	611	1,877	2,533
MOROCCO				
Dar-el-Beida (Casablanca)	625	1,793	3,043	3,570
Fès	165	433	870	1,184
Marrakech	209	367	755	1,032
Rabat	145	641	1,507	1,991
SAUDI ARABIA				
Ad-Dammam	20	136	639	1,025
Al-Madinah (Medina)	51	208	795	1,251
Ar-Riyadh (Riyadh)	111	710	3,567	5,438
Jiddah	119	594	2,509	3,612
Makkah (Mecca)	148	383	1,168	1,661
SYRIAN ARAB REPUBLIC				
Dimashq (Damascus)	367	1,122	2,035	2,872
Halab (Aleppo)	319	879	2,212	3,185
Hims (Homs)	101	312	806	1,183
TURKEY				
Adana	138	471	1,123	1,471
Ankara	281	1,709	3,179	4,191
Bursa	148	345	1,180	1,718
Gaziantep	104	299	844	1,202
Istanbul	967	3,600	8,744	11,211
Izmir	224	1,046	2,216	2,929
Konya	97	247	734	1,061

Country/Agglomeration	Population (thousands)			
	1950	*1975*	*2000*	*2015*
UNITED ARAB EMIRATES				
Dubayy (Dubai)	20	167	938	1,688
UZBEKISTAN				
Tashkent	755	1,612	2,137	2,460
YEMEN				
Sana'a'	46	141	1,365	2,931
SUB-SAHARAN AFRICA				
ANGOLA				
Luanda	138	665	2,322	3,904
BURKINA FASO				
Ouagadougou	35	168	771	1,489
CAMEROON				
Douala	95	433	1,432	2,350
Yaoundé	32	292	1,192	1,995
CHAD				
N'Djaména	25	231	707	1,374
CONGO				
Brazzaville	83	329	986	1,653
CONGO (DEMOCRATIC REPUBLIC OF)				
Kinshasa	202	1,479	5,942	9,304
Kolwezi	31	146	1,047	1,998
Lubumbashi	96	396	971	1,856
Mbuji-Mayi	70	337	843	1,616
CÔTE D'IVOIRE				
Abidjan	65	966	3,055	4,525
ETHIOPIA				
Addis Ababa	392	926	2,494	4,078
GHANA				
Accra	177	738	1,674	2,666
Kumasi	99	397	1,187	2,095
GUINEA				
Conakry	31	566	1,222	2,001
KENYA				
Mombasa	94	298	686	1,181
Nairobi	137	677	2,233	4,001
LIBERIA				
Monrovia	15	226	776	1,357
MADAGASCAR				
Antananarivo	177	454	1,361	2,182
MALI				
Bamako	89	363	1,110	2,117
MOZAMBIQUE				
Maputo	92	456	1,095	1,872
NIGER				
Niamey	24	192	680	1,308

Country/Agglomeration	Population (thousands)			
	1950	*1975*	*2000*	*2015*
NIGERIA				
Benin City	46	210	937	1,394
Ibadan	427	960	2,195	3,152
Kaduna	28	299	1,220	1,812
Kano	107	609	2,658	3,920
Lagos	288	1,890	8,422	16,141
Maiduguri	44	244	758	1,129
Ogbomosho	115	432	818	1,268
Port Harcourt	58	300	863	1,284
Zaria	41	272	752	1,121
RWANDA				
Kigali	20	90	497	1,544
SENEGAL				
Dakar	217	782	1,862	2,819
SIERRA LEONE				
Freetown	92	284	698	1,098
SOMALIA				
Muqdisho (Mogadishu)	69	445	1,189	1,855
SOUTH AFRICA				
Cape Town	618	1,339	2,715	3,401
Durban	484	1,019	2,370	2,876
Ekurhuleni (East Rand)	546	997	2,326	3,212
Johannesburg	900	1,547	2,732	3,674
Port Elizabeth	192	531	958	1,070
Pretoria	275	624	1,084	1,439
Vereeniging	117	372	897	1,150
SUDAN				
Al-Khartum (Khartoum)	183	886	3,949	6,022
TANZANIA (UNITED REPUBLIC OF)				
Dar es Salaam	84	572	2,116	3,831
TOGO				
Lomé	33	257	1,053	1,969
UGANDA				
Kampala	95	398	1,097	2,054
ZAMBIA				
Lusaka	31	385	1,073	1,564
ZIMBABWE				
Harare	143	532	1,379	1,788

SOUTH ASIA

AFGHANISTAN				
Kabul	171	674	1,963	4,666
BANGLADESH				
Chittagong	290	969	3,271	5,707
Dhaka	417	2,173	10,159	16,842
Khulna	45	498	1,264	2,048
Rajshahi	39	150	668	1,062

Country/Agglomeration	Population (thousands)			
	1950	*1975*	*2000*	*2015*
INDIA				
Agra	369	681	1,293	1,892
Ahmadabad	855	2,050	4,427	6,298
Aligarh	139	280	653	963
Allahabad	327	568	1,035	1,420
Amritsar	340	520	990	1,444
Asansol	93	289	1,065	1,584
Aurangabad	65	218	868	1,336
Bangalore	746	2,111	5,567	7,939
Bareilly	207	374	722	966
Bhopal	100	491	1,426	2,045
Bhubaneswar	16	144	637	1,020
Chandigarh	40	301	791	1,170
Chennai (Madras)	1,491	3,609	6,353	8,280
Coimbatore	279	810	1,420	2,005
Delhi	1,369	4,426	12,441	18,604
Dhanbad	71	525	1,046	1,477
Durg-Bhilainagar	20	330	905	1,305
Faridabad	22	153	1,018	1,685
Ghaziabad	42	181	928	1,634
Guwahati (Gauhati)	43	252	797	1,174
Gwalior	237	465	855	1,156
Hubli-Dharwad	192	437	776	1,054
Hyderabad	1,096	2,086	5,445	7,420
Indore	302	663	1,597	2,413
Jabalpur	251	621	1,100	1,519
Jaipur	294	778	2,259	3,470
Jalandhar	166	340	694	1,023
Jamshedpur	214	538	1,081	1,542
Jodhpur	177	388	842	1,181
Kanpur	688	1,420	2,641	3,718
Kochi (Cochin)	163	532	1,340	1,785
Kolkata (Calcutta)	4,513	7,888	13,058	16,980
Kota	64	266	692	986
Kozhikode (Calicut)	156	412	875	1,119
Lucknow	489	892	2,221	3,180
Ludhiana	151	479	1,368	1,954
Madurai	361	790	1,187	1,514
Meerut	228	432	1,143	1,662
Mumbai (Bombay)	2,857	7,082	16,086	21,869
Mysore	237	404	776	1,049
Nagpur	473	1,075	2,089	2,885
Nashik	149	330	1,117	1,769
Patna	277	642	1,658	2,578
Pune (Poona)	581	1,345	3,655	5,524
Raipur	88	255	680	1,053
Rajkot	126	356	974	1,513
Ranchi	103	342	844	1,247
Salem	197	458	736	1,039
Solapur	272	445	853	1,263
Srinagar	248	494	954	1,353
Surat	234	642	2,699	4,623
Thiruvananthapuram	182	454	885	1,118
Tiruchirappalli	287	522	837	1,123
Vadodara	207	571	1,465	2,077

Country/Agglomeration	Population (thousands)			
	1950	*1975*	*2000*	*2015*
Varanasi (Benares)	349	680	1,199	1,589
Vijayawada	155	419	999	1,341
Visakhapatnam	105	452	1,309	1,804
NEPAL				
Kathmandu	104	180	644	1,280
PAKISTAN				
Faisalabad	168	907	2,140	3,326
Gujranwala	118	427	1,224	1,937
Hyderabad	232	667	1,221	1,864
Karachi	1,047	3,989	10,020	15,155
Lahore	836	2,399	5,448	8,271
Multan	186	599	1,263	1,944
Peshawar	153	347	1,066	1,669
Rawalpindi	233	670	1,520	2,371
SOUTHEAST ASIA				
CAMBODIA				
Phnum Pénh (Phnom Penh)	364	397	1,160	2,057
INDONESIA				
Bandung	511	1,493	3,448	5,338
Bogor	64	406	683	1,064
Jakarta	1,452	4,813	11,065	16,822
Malang	316	413	807	1,273
Medan	284	1,031	1,931	2,981
Palembang	277	597	1,442	2,270
Pekalongan	50	214	713	1,167
Semarang	371	660	832	1,273
Surabaya	679	1,471	2,536	3,883
Surakarta	275	478	649	1,008
Tegal	30	266	774	1,233
Ujung Pandang	162	502	1,074	1,688
MALAYSIA				
Kuala Lumpur	208	645	1,306	1,696
MYANMAR				
Mandalay	167	442	809	1,192
Rangoon	1,302	2,151	3,634	5,184
PHILIPPINES				
Cebu	178	415	721	1,006
Davao	124	488	1,152	1,680
Manila	1,544	4,999	9,950	12,917
SINGAPORE				
Singapore	1,022	2,263	4,017	4,815
THAILAND				
Krung Thep (Bangkok)	1,360	3,842	6,332	7,439
VIETNAM				
Ha Noi	280	1,884	3,752	5,320
Hai Phong	167	968	1,704	2,411
Thanh Pho Ho Chi Minh (Ho Chi Minh City)	1,213	2,808	4,621	6,436

Country/Agglomeration	Population (thousands)			
	1950	*1975*	*2000*	*2015*

EAST ASIA

CHINA (PEOPLE'S REPUBLIC OF)

Country/Agglomeration	*1950*	*1975*	*2000*	*2015*
Anshan, Liaoning	479	1,082	1,552	1,864
Anshun	191	331	763	992
Anyang	108	360	763	1,057
Baoding	179	401	890	1,356
Baotou	530	918	1,655	2,473
Beijing	4,331	6,034	9,782	12,850
Bengbu	233	461	805	1,045
Benxi	414	713	979	1,144
Changchun	765	1,558	2,730	3,765
Changde	293	700	1,341	1,700
Changsha, Hunan	623	942	2,091	3,169
Changzhou, Jiangsu	111	360	1,068	1,623
Chengdu	768	1,911	3,919	4,637
Chifeng	133	343	1,148	1,490
Chongqing	1,680	2,439	6,037	7,258
Dalian	678	1,396	2,858	3,664
Dandong	236	449	776	1,021
Daqing	264	605	1,366	2,067
Datong, Shanxi	618	877	1,518	2,285
Dongguan, Guangdong	379	904	3,770	5,370
Foshan	94	224	754	1,156
Fushun, Liaoning	634	1,082	1,433	1,653
Fuyu, Jilin	682	836	1,025	1,244
Fuzhou, Fujian	492	1,012	2,096	3,172
Guangzhou, Guangdong	1,491	2,673	7,388	10,420
Guilin	152	343	795	1,210
Guiyang	675	1,140	2,929	4,446
Haerbin	1,012	2,288	3,444	4,392
Handan	378	769	1,321	1,992
Hangzhou	638	1,097	2,411	3,656
Hefei	256	637	1,637	2,481
Hengyang	167	410	873	1,211
Heze	381	780	1,277	1,519
Hohhot	318	617	1,389	2,107
Huai'an	829	997	1,198	1,441
Huaibei	207	375	733	1,121
Huainan	498	875	1,353	1,664
Hunjiang	553	653	772	925
Huzhou	678	879	1,141	1,417
Jiamusi	220	437	853	1,230
Jiaozuo	206	404	742	1,019
Jiaxing	448	613	877	1,160
Jilin	396	867	1,928	2,918
Jinan, Shandong	598	1,236	2,625	3,184
Jining, Shandong	258	448	1,044	1,397
Jinxi, Liaoning	226	583	1,908	2,988
Jinzhou	326	530	858	1,118
Jixi, Heilongjiang	177	556	908	1,106
Kaifeng	349	536	793	1,015
Kunming	641	1,223	2,594	3,406
Langfang	57	135	711	957
Lanzhou	348	1,042	2,071	3,117

Country/Agglomeration	Population (thousands)			
	1950	*1975*	*2000*	*2015*
Leshan	604	863	1,118	1,308
Lianyungang	116	303	682	968
Liaoyang	109	329	725	922
Linfen	99	236	719	994
Linyi, Shandong	411	1,013	1,932	2,387
Liuan	861	1,157	1,553	1,948
Liupanshui	405	633	989	1,494
Liuzhou	139	427	1,201	1,829
Luoyang	387	797	1,481	2,031
Luzhou	89	232	1,208	1,878
Mianyang, Sichuan	479	699	1,152	1,689
Mudanjiang	209	464	1,004	1,522
Nanchang	343	896	1,822	2,913
Nanchong	109	189	1,712	2,649
Nanjing, Jiangsu	973	1,938	3,477	4,151
Nanning	167	602	1,743	2,641
Nantong	185	331	759	1,160
Nanyang, Henan	75	205	1,512	2,371
Neijiang	137	239	1,388	1,670
Ningbo	470	819	1,551	2,345
Pingdingshan, Henan	157	373	904	921
Pingxiang, Jiangxi	166	359	775	1,178
Qingdao	894	1,106	2,698	3,248
Qinhuangdao	148	324	805	1,229
Qiqihaer	721	1,090	1,535	1,877
Quanzhou	219	358	1,158	1,788
Shanghai	6,066	7,326	13,243	17,225
Shangqiu	58	143	1,349	2,140
Shantou	322	606	1,255	1,980
Shenyang	2,091	3,697	4,599	5,377
Shenzhen	174	301	6,069	8,958
Shijiazhuang	335	828	1,947	2,943
Suining, Sichuan	763	1,044	1,352	1,621
Suzhou, Anhui	61	150	1,509	2,396
Suzhou, Jiangsu	457	619	1,326	2,014
Taian, Shandong	829	1,157	1,534	1,858
Taiyuan, Shanxi	629	1,519	2,521	3,434
Tangshan, Hebei	640	1,161	1,703	2,176
Tianjin	2,374	4,870	6,722	8,119
Tianmen	1,073	1,314	1,609	1,946
Tianshui	165	522	1,143	1,405
Tongliao	110	283	790	1,036
Ürümqi (Wulumqi)	253	715	1,730	2,621
Weifang	183	472	1,372	1,822
Wenzhou	255	437	1,845	2,862
Wuhan	1,311	2,666	6,662	8,204
Wuhu, Anhui	211	386	692	969
Wuxi, Jiangsu	572	730	1,410	2,135
Xiamen	208	419	1,977	3,066
Xi'an, Shaanxi	708	1,715	3,725	4,559
Xiangfan, Hubei	104	248	855	1,310
Xiantao	1,000	1,213	1,470	1,772
Xianyang, Shaanxi	103	353	946	1,355
Xingyi, Guizhou	282	449	715	965
Xining	257	480	849	1,284

Country/Agglomeration	Population (thousands)			
	1950	*1975*	*2000*	*2015*
Xinxiang	240	432	770	1,081
Xinyang	94	183	1,195	1,882
Xinyu	234	425	772	1,096
Xuanzhou	586	694	823	987
Xuzhou	341	667	1,648	2,566
Yancheng, Jiangsu	145	313	677	1,029
Yantai	190	329	1,684	2,578
Yibin	81	192	805	1,058
Yichang	108	279	704	1,073
Yichun, Heilongjiang	554	741	816	849
Yichun, Jiangxi	335	664	917	1,127
Yinchuan	100	274	795	1,214
Yingkou	122	320	694	942
Yiyang, Hunan	397	734	1,223	1,572
Yongzhou	835	903	976	1,128
Yuci	88	210	660	1,042
Yueyang	673	903	918	880
Yulin, Guangxi	194	420	909	1,379
Zaozhuang	282	896	1,990	2,458
Zhangjiakou	304	521	897	1,248
Zhanjiang	406	734	1,340	1,905
Zhaotong	133	316	724	948
Zhengzhou	521	1,227	2,472	2,989
Zhenjiang, Jiangsu	86	255	688	1,047
Zhuhai	44	104	809	1,254
Zhuzhou	127	302	868	1,322
Zibo	1,453	2,032	2,806	3,517
Zigong	564	795	1,049	1,260
Zunyi	198	304	679	1,041
CHINA (REPUBLIC OF)				
Kaohsiung	255	986	1,469	1,744
Taichung	194	537	930	1,281
Taipei	604	2,023	2,640	2,863
CHINA, HONG KONG SAR				
Hong Kong	1,682	3,943	6,637	7,764
JAPAN				
Fukuoka-Kitakyushu	954	1,853	2,716	2,834
Hiroshima	503	1,774	2,044	2,045
Kyoto	1,002	1,622	1,806	1,805
Nagoya	992	2,293	3,122	3,202
Osaka-Kobe	4,147	9,844	11,165	11,309
Sapporo	754	1,751	2,508	2,539
Sendai	538	1,566	2,184	2,240
Tokyo	11,275	26,615	34,450	35,494
KOREA (DEMOCRATIC PEOPLE'S REPUBLIC OF)				
Hamhung	169	518	769	864
N'ampo	52	215	1,016	1,182
P'yongyang	516	1,348	3,194	3,531
Kinshasa	202	1,479	5,042	9,304
Kolwezi	31	146	1,047	1,998
Lubumbashi	96	396	971	1,856
Mbuji-Mayi	70	337	843	1,616

Country/Agglomeration	Population (thousands)			
	1950	*1975*	*2000*	*2015*
KOREA (REPUBLIC OF)				
Goyang	39	122	744	1,210
Ich'on	258	791	2,464	2,712
Kwangju	174	601	1,346	1,499
Pusan	948	2,418	3,673	3,534
Seongnam	54	268	911	994
Soul (Seoul)	1,021	6,808	9,917	9,545
Suwon	74	220	932	1,248
Taegu	355	1,297	2,478	2,551
Taejon	131	501	1,362	1,516
Ulsan	29	246	1,011	1,097
MONGOLIA				
Ulaanbaatar	70	356	764	999

AUSTRALIA AND THE PACIFIC ISLANDS

Country/Agglomeration	*1950*	*1975*	*2000*	*2015*
AUSTRALIA				
Adelaide	429	881	1,102	1,230
Brisbane	442	928	1,624	1,946
Melbourne	1,332	2,561	3,433	3,933
Perth	311	770	1,373	1,627
Sydney	1,690	2,960	4,078	4,701
NEW ZEALAND				
Auckland	319	729	1,063	1,240

Source: Population Division of the Department of Economic and Social Affairs of the United Nations Secretariat, *World Population Prospects: The 2004 Revision and World Urbanization Prospects: The 2005 Revision*, http://esa.un.org/unup, Thursday, September 13, 2007.

Cover Photo Credits

Clockwise from top left:

These colorful apartment houses dot the landscape of Cape Town's Bo-Kapap area. It is known as the "Cape Malay" district. (Photo by Brennan Kraxberger)

View of Charlotte Amalie, St. Thomas, from the tram station. (Photo courtesy of United States Virgin Islands Department of Tourism.)

A produce vendor in Chennai typifies the bazaar-based city. (Photo by George Pomeroy)

The Taj Mahal has become the single most recognized icon of India. It was built in Agra as a tomb for Shah Jahan's wife and is now a UNESCO World Heritage Site. (Photo by George Pomeroy)

The Coliseum in Rome. (Photo by Linda McCarthy.)

A panoramic view of Monterrey illustrates the process of metropolitanization and shows the distinctive physical feature of this Northern city: the Cerro de la Silla. (Photo by Google-Earth)

Modern Panama City, with its many ultra-modern skyscrapers, is a vision of economic growth. (Photo by Jorge González)

Venice, Italy. (Photo by Lisa Benton-Short)

A Greek Orthodox priest enters the courtyard of the Church of the Holy Sepulchre in Jerusalem. This church is the focal point of Christian history because it is built on the site of Jesus' crucifixion, entombment, and resurrection. (Photo by Donald Zeigler)

Graffiti and protesters amid the water wars in Cochabamba, Bolivia. (Photo by Tom Perrault)

The Houses of Parliament dominate the City of Westminster. The Clock Tower (often called Big Ben) and the London Underground (the subway) are landmarks that symbolize London to the world. (Photo by Donald Zeigler)

Most Guatemalan indigenous women still wear a traditional blouse called the huipil. This ornate garment is woven on traditional looms and then hand-embroidered. Villages and towns have their own unique design, which is particularly useful at periodic and regional markets, so both vendors and buyers can readily identify the community of the seller, which in turn means that certain goods and produce might be available there. (Photo by Matthew Taylor)

Oblique aerial view of row housing in Toronto, Canada. (Photo by John Rennie Short)

Geographical Index

Index to Subjects

About the Editors and Contributors

Adrián Guillermo Aguilar is director of the Institute of Geography at the National Autonomous University of Mexico, where he has served as head of the social geography department. He has been Tinker Visiting Professor at The University of Texas, Austin. His research on intermediate-sized cities, metropolitan development, and urban systems has been supported by IDDRC-Canada and CONACYT-Mexico. He received a PhD at the University of London.

Lisa Benton-Short is associate professor of geography at George Washington University. She teaches courses on cities and globalization, urban planning, and urban environmental issues. An urban geographer, she has research interests in environmental issues in cities, parks and public spaces, and monuments and memorials. She is also interested in globalization, urbanization, and migration.

Stanley D. Brunn is professor of geography at the University of Kentucky. He has taught classes on world cities, future worlds, political geography, and geographies of communication and cyberspace. He has also taught in a dozen European and Central Asian countries. His recent research focuses on the images of places, creative cartographies, disciplinary histories, humane geographies, the impacts of 9-11, Wal-Mart, and the impacts of megaengineering projects.

Kam Wing Chan is professor of geography at the University of Washington. He is the author of *Cities with Invisible Walls: Reinterpreting Urbanization in Post-1949 China* (1994) and some 50 articles and book chapters on China's urbanization, migration, urban labor market, the household registration system, and urban finance. He has served as consultant for the UN, the Asian Development Bank, the World Bank, the International Labor Organization, and McKinsey & Co. on various policy issues related to urban development and migration in China.

Robyn Dowling is an urban cultural geographer at Macquarie University in Sydney, Australia. Her primary research interests are in cultures of everyday urban life, focusing on gender, home, and suburbs. She publishes widely on issues such as home ownership, suburban gender identities, and cultures of transport. She recently coauthored the book *Home* with Alison Blunt. Her current research explores the contours of privatization and privatism in Sydney's residential life.

Ashok K. Dutt is professor emeritus of geography, planning, and urban studies at the University of Akron in Ohio. His research focuses on religion, language, development, crime, and medical geographies of Indian cities. He has authored, coauthored, edited, or coedited 23 books, and authored or coauthored more than 80 journal articles and 60 book chapters.

Irma Escamilla earned her bachelor's and master's degrees in geography at the National Autonomous University of Mexico. She is currently a doctoral student there as well as full-time researcher in the department of social geography within the Institute of Geography. She has conducted research in urban, regional, human, and population geography, and the history of geographic thought.

Rina Ghose is associate professor of geography at the University of Wisconsin–Milwaukee. Her teaching interests include urban geography, GIS, world regional geography, and South Asia. Her research focuses on public participation GIS, the role of GIS in planning, neoliberalism and collaborative urban governance, and urban and rural gentrification.

Brian J. Godfrey is professor of geography at Vassar College. He specializes in historical and urban geography with particular focus on cities of the Americas, especially those of Brazil and the Amazon Basin. His recent scholarship addresses global cities, sustainable development, and historic preservation. He has conducted research in both the United States and Latin America, including extensive fieldwork in Brazil. His most recent books include *Cidades da Floresta* and *Rainforest Cities* (both coauthored with John Browder). He is currently writing a book on the heritage-based redevelopment of Brazil's historic cities.

Mark Graham is a PhD candidate in geography at the University of Kentucky in Lexington. His research interests center on the economic, social, and spatial effects of technology. Recent publications have appeared in *Environment and Planning B, Geoforum,* and *Geography Compass.* His current work, funded by the National Science Foundation, focuses on the promises and the perils of the Internet as a tool of economic development in the Thai silk industry.

Jessica K. Graybill, with a PhD in geography and urban ecology, is an assistant professor of geography at Colgate University. Her interdisciplinary pedagogy and research is in environmental geography, urban geography, and ecologies of the city. In Russia, her research interests have carried her from Moscow to the Russian Far East, and in the United States, from the Pacific Northwest to upstate New York.

Maureen Hays-Mitchell is associate professor of geography at Colgate University. Her teaching and scholarly interests include international development, political geography, feminist thought, and spatial justice. She has conducted grassroots fieldwork in Andean America on the urban informal economy and on micro-enterprise development. Her current scholarship involves the role of grassroots women's organizations in post-conflict reconciliation and reconstruction in several Latin American countries.

Boian Koulov until recently taught at George Washington University. He is currently a senior research associate at the Bulgarian Academy of Sciences. Political, environmental, and economic geography are his major interests. His current research projects include the policy implications of European integration in the Black Sea region.

Linda McCarthy is associate professor of geography at the University of Wisconsin–Milwaukee. She holds an undergraduate degree from University College, Dublin, and graduate degrees from the University of Minnesota. Her teaching interests include Europe, urban geography, and globalization. Her research focuses on comparative urban and regional development, government competition and cooperation for private investment, and brownfield redevelopment.

Pauline McGuirk is professor of human geography and director of the Centre for Urban and Regional Studies at the University of Newcastle, New South Wales, Australia. Her research focuses on the politics, development, and governance of metropolitan cities, but she has also published widely on aspects of urban development, city politics, planning, urban identity, and place marketing. Pauline is currently investigating new forms of governance and residential housing in Sydney.

Beth A. Mitchneck is associate dean for academic affairs at the University of Arizona, where she also serves as associate professor of geography and regional development. Her teaching interests include economic geography, regional development, research design, and the geography of the former Soviet states. Her current research focuses on local governance, economic development, and internal migration in Russia.

Garth Myers is director of the Kansas African Studies Center, and associate professor of geography and African/African-American studies at the University of Kansas. He is author of *Verandahs of Power* and *Disposable Cities* and coeditor of a third book (*Cities in Contemporary Africa*) on African cities. He has published more than three dozen articles and book chapters on African urban development, and he regularly teaches a variety of courses on African geography.

Francis Owusu is an associate professor in the department of community and regional planning at Iowa State University. Dr. Owusu is originally from Ghana and has conducted research in several African countries. He has published extensively on urban livelihood strategies, development policy, and public sector reforms. He edited a special issue of *Geojournal* on the theme "Opportunities and Challenges for Development in Africa." He has taught several geography courses, including geography of Africa.

George Pomeroy is associate professor of geography–earth science at Shippensburg University of Pennsylvania. He teaches land-use planning, environmental planning, and courses related to both South and East Asia, including a field studies course in China. His research focuses on garden cities/new town planning, and on building capacity for local government planning activities.

Joseph L. Scarpaci is professor of geography at Virginia Tech. He recently published *Plazas and Barrios* (2005) and *Havana: Two Faces of the Antillean Metropolis* (2002, with Roberto Segre and Mario Coyula). His forthcoming book, *Cuban Landscapes*, is coauthored with Armando Portela

John Rennie Short is professor of geography and public policy at the University of Maryland–Baltimore County. He has also taught in Europe, the UK, and Australia. He teaches urban geography and public policy courses. He has published thirty books and numerous articles and is recognized as an international authority on the study of cities. His current research interests include the history of cartography, Australian Aboriginal art, maps and culture, and urban trends in Northeast cities.

Dona J. Stewart is the director of the Middle East Institute and associate professor of geosciences at Georgia State University. Her research focuses on economic and political issues in the Middle East, and particularly the political economy of urbanization. She is the author of *Good Neighbourly Relations: Jordan, Israel and the 1994–2004 Peace Process* (2007) and

The Middle East Today: Political, Geographical and Cultural Perspectives.

James Tyner is professor of geography at Kent State University, where he teaches East and Southeast Asia, political geography, and other specialized courses on social, population, and urban geography. His current research focuses on political violence in Southeast Asia and international population movements. He is author of numerous books and articles, including *The Philippines: Mobilities, Identities and Globalization.*

Jack F. Williams is professor emeritus at Michigan State University, having done his academic training in geography and Chinese studies at the University of Washington and the University of Hawaii. He specializes in China/Taiwan and East Asia, with a focus on urban and regional development and environmental issues. He was coeditor of the previous three editions of this text.

Donald J. Zeigler is professor of geography at Old Dominion University–Virginia Beach. He teaches courses on the Middle East and political and cultural geography. He has held fellowships in Morocco, Syria, and Jordan. His current research focuses on Middle Eastern cities, maps in society, and the connections between geography and history in the Mediterranean world.

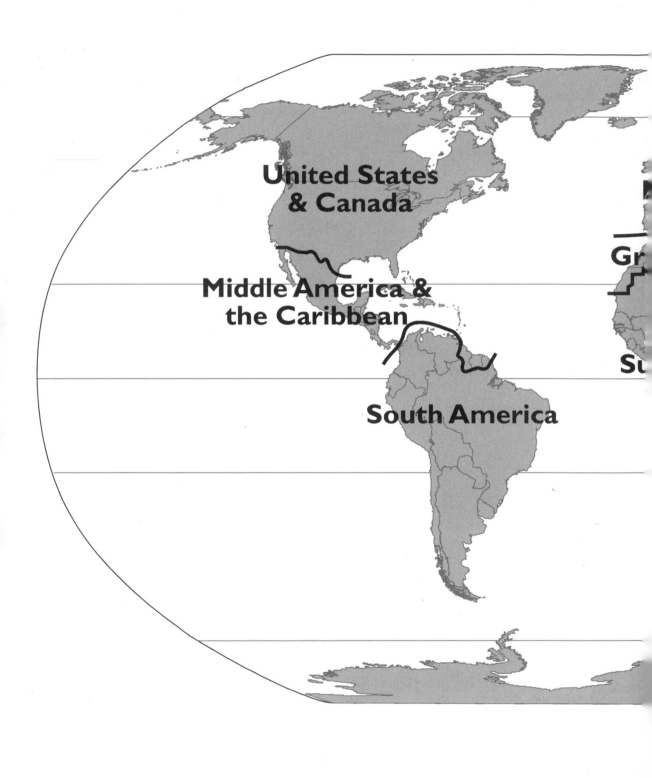

United States
& Canada

Middle America &
the Caribbean

South America

Gr

Su